12/98

MIDLOTHIAN PUBLIC LIBRARY

3 1614 00078 8498

P9-CBP-844

MIDLOTHIAN
PUBLIC LIBRARY

Midlothian
Public Library

14701 S. Kenton Ave.
Midlothian, IL 60445

DEMCO

859 *U.S. Senate Hearings*

915 *Still More About the Comics*
917 Selected Bibliography
920 Notes on the Contributors

927 *Appendices*
929 A: Code of the Comics Magazine Association of America
930 B: Reuben Award Winners
931 C: Directory of Newspaper Syndicates
932 D: Directory of Comic Book Publishers

933 *Indices*
935 A: Proper Name Index
955 B: Title Index
983 C: Media Index
991 D: Contributors Index
1001 E: Geographical Index
1011 F: Illustration Index
1021 G: Subject Index

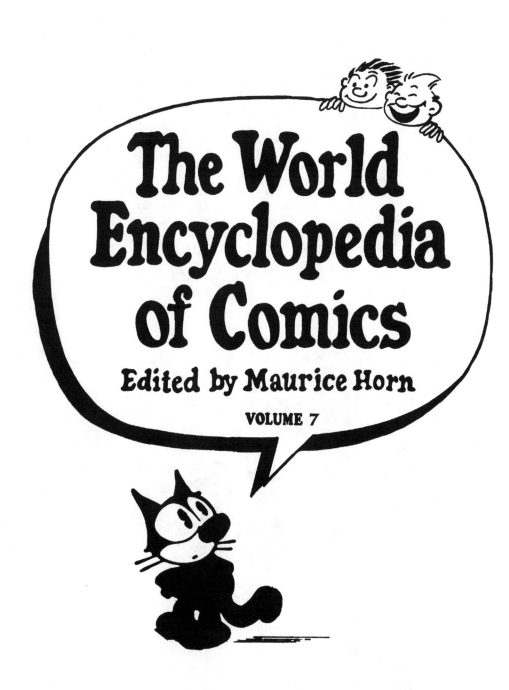

The World Encyclopedia of Comics

Edited by Maurice Horn

VOLUME 7

BOOK COVER ART CREDITS

Mr. Natural art by Robert Crumb © Robert Crumb; reprinted with permission; all rights reserved. *Brenda Starr* art by Dale Messick © Tribune Media Services, Inc.; reprinted with permission; all rights reserved. *Krazy Kat* and *Ignatz* art by George Herrimann © King Features Syndicate; reprinted with permission; all rights reserved. *Peanuts* art by Charles Schulz © United Features Syndicate Inc.; reprinted with permission; all rights reserved. *Archie* and *Veronica* art by Dan DeCarlo © Archie Comics; reprinted with permission; all rights reserved. *Spider-Man* art by John Romita © Marvel Comics; reprinted with permission; all rights reserved. *Superman* © DC Comics; reprinted with permission; all rights reserved. *Weird Science #9, The Grey Cloud of Death* art by Wallace Wood © William M. Gaines, Agent, Inc.; reprinted with permission; all rights reserved. *The Dreamer* art by Will Eisner © Will Eisner; reprinted with permission; all rights reserved. *Calvin and Hobbes* art by Bill Watterson © Watterson/distributed by Universal Press Syndicate; reprinted with permission; all rights reserved. *Fantastic Four* art by Jack Kirby © Marvel Comics; reprinted with permission; all rights reserved. *Haunt of Fear #14, A Little Stranger* art by Graham Ingles © William M. Gaines, Agent, Inc.; reprinted with permission; all rights reserved. *Blondie* art by Chic Young © King Features Syndicate; reprinted with permission; all rights reserved. *Mutts* art by Patrick McDonnell © King Features Syndicate; reprinted with permission; all rights reserved. *Flash Gordon* art by Alex Raymond © King Features Syndicate; reprinted with permission; all rights reserved. *Tarzan* art by Burne Hogarth © Edgar Rice Burroughs, Inc.; reprinted with permission; all rights reserved. *Maus* art by Art Spiegelman © Art Spiegelman; reprinted with permission; all rights reserved. *Hey Look* art by Harvey Kurtzman © Harvey Kurtzman; reprinted with permission; all rights reserved. *Popeye* art by Bud Sagendorf © King Features Syndicate; reprinted with permission; all rights reserved. *Weird Fantasy #14, The Cosmic Ray Bomb Explosion* art by Al Feldstein © William M. Gaines, Agent, Inc.; reprinted with permission; all rights reserved. *Captain America* art by James Steranko © Marvel Comics; reprinted with permission; all rights reserved.

THE CONTRIBUTORS

Manuel Auad (M.A.), *The Philippines*
Bill Blackbeard (B.B.), *U.S.*
Gianni Bono (G.B.), *Italy*
Joe Brancatelli (J.B.), *U.S.*
MaryBeth Calhoun (M.B.C.), *U.S.*
Javier Coma (J.C.), *Spain*
Bill Crouch (B.C.), *U.S.*
Giulio Cesare Cuccolini (G.C.C.), *Italy*
Mark Evanier (M.E.), *U.S.*
Wolfgang Fuchs (W.F.), *Germany*
Luis Gasca (L.G.), *Spain*
Robert Gerson (R.G.), *U.S.*
Denis Gifford (D.G.), *Great Britain*
Paul Gravett (P.G.), *Great Britain*
Peter Harris (P.H.), *Canada*
Hongying Liu-Lengyel (H.Y.L.L.), *China*
Maurice Horn (M.H.), *France/U.S.*
Pierre L. Horn (P.L.H.), *U.S.*
Slobodan Ivkov (S.I.), *Yugoslavia (Serbia)*
Bill Janocha (B.J.), *U.S.*
Orvy Jundis (O.J.), *The Philippines*
Hisao Kato (H.K.), *Japan*
John A. Lent (J.A.L.), *Asia*
Richard Marschall (R.M.), *U.S.*
Alvaro de Moya (A.M.), *Brazil*
Kalmán Rubovszky (K.R.), *Hungary/Poland*
Ervin Rustemagić (E.R.), *Yugoslavia*
John Ryan (J.R.), *Australia*
Matthew A. Thorn (M.A.T.), *Japan*
Dennis Wepman (D.W.), *U.S.*

The World Encyclopedia of Comics

Edited by Maurice Horn

VOLUME 7

MIDLOTHIAN PUBLIC LIBRARY
14701 S. KENTON AVE.
MIDLOTHIAN, IL 60445

Chelsea House Publishers
Philadelphia

Acknowledgments

The editors of *The World Encyclopedia of Comics* wish to extend their sincere thanks to the following persons: Bill Anderson, Jerry Bails, Larry Brill, Mary Beth Calhoun, Frank Clark, Bill Crouch, Leonard Darvin, Tony Dispoto, Jacques Glénat-Guttin, Ron Goulart, George Henderson, Pierre Horn, Pierre Huet, S. M. "Jerry" Iger, Jessie Kahles Straut, Rolf Kauka, Heikki Kaukoranta, Roland Kohlsaat, Maria-M. Lamm, Mort Leav, Vane Lindesay, Ernie McGee, Jacques Marcovitch, Victor Margolin, Doug Murray, Pascal Nadon, Harry Neigher, Walter Neugebauer, Syd Nicholls, Tom Peoples, Rainer Schwarz, Silvano Scotto, Luciano Secchi, David Smith, Manfred Soder, Jim Steranko, Ernesto Traverso, Miguel Urrutía, Jim Vadeboncoeur, Jr., Wendell Washer, Peter Wiechmann, Mrs. John Wheeler and Joe Willicombe.

We would also like to thank the following collectors who donated reproductions of art from their collections: Wendy Gaines Bucci, Mike Burkey, Tony Christopher, Russ Cochran, Robert Gerson, Roger Hill, Bill Leach, Eric Sack, and Jim Steranko.

Special thanks also to Michel Mandry, Bernard Trout, José Maria Conget of Instituto Cervantes in New York, Four-Color Images Gallery, Frederik Schodt, David Astor, Alain Beyrand, Manuel Halffter, Dominique Petitfaux, Annie Baron-Carvais, Janice Silverman.

Our appreciation also to the following organizations: Associated Newspapers Ltd., Bastei Verlag, Bulls Pressedienst, Comics Magazine Association of America, Editions Dupuis, ERB Inc., Field Newspaper Syndicate, Globi Verlag, The Herald and Weekly Times Ltd., Kauka Comic Akademie, King Features Syndicate, Marvel Comics Group, San Francisco Academy of Comic Art, Strip Art Features, Walt Disney Archives and Walt Disney Productions.

Finally, we wish to thank Don Manza for his photographic work.

Chelsea House Publishers
1974 Sproul Road, Suite 400
P.O. Box 914
Broomall PA 19008-0914

Copyright 1999 Chelsea House Publishers. All rights reserved. Printed and bound in the United States of America.

Typeset by Alexander Graphics, Indianapolis IN

Library of Congress Cataloging-in-Publication Data

The world encyclopedia of comics / edited by Maurice Horn.
    p. cm.
    Includes bibliographical references and index.
    ISBN 0-7910-4854-3 (set). — ISBN 0-7910-4857-8 (v. 1). — ISBN 0-7910-4858-6 (v. 2). — ISBN 0-7910-4859-4 (v. 3). — ISBN 0-7910-4860-8 (v. 4). — ISBN 0-7910-4861-6 (v. 5). — ISBN 0-7910-4862-4 (v. 6). — ISBN 0-7910-4863-2 (v. 7)
    1. Comic books, strips, etc.—Dictionaries. I. Horn, Maurice.
PN6710.W6   1998
741.5'03—dc21

97-50448
CIP

U.S. Senate Hearings

**Official Facsimile
Excerpts from the Record
U.S. Senate Subcommittee
of the Committee on the Judiciary
to Investigate Juvenile Delinquency**

April 21, 22, and June 4, 1954
New York, New York

U.S. SENATE HEARINGS

Hearings before the Subcommittee to Investigate Juvenile Delinquency of the Committee on the Judiciary United States Senate, Eighty-Third Congress, Second Session, pursuant to S.190

Investigation of Juvenile Delinquency in the United States
April 21, 22, and June 4, 1954

United States Government Printing Office
Washington 1954

Judiciary Committee

William Langer, North Dakota, *chairman*
Alexander Wiley, Wisconsin
William E. Jenner, Indiana
Arthur V. Watkins, Utah
Robert C. Hendrickson, New Jersey
Everett McKinley Dirksen, Illinois
Herman Welkes, Idaho
John Marshall Butler, Maryland
Pat McCarran, Nevada
Harley M. Kilgore, West Virginia
James O. Eastland, Mississippi
Estes Kefauver, Tennessee
Olin D. Johnston, South Carolina
Thomas C. Hennings, Jr., Missouri
John L. McClellan, Arkansas

JUVENILE DELINQUENCY
(Comic Books)

_____

WEDNESDAY, APRIL 21, 1954

UNITED STATES SENATE,
SUBCOMMITTEE OF THE COMMITTEE ON
THE JUDICIARY, TO INVESTIGATE JUVENILE DELINQUENCY,
New York, N. Y.

The subcommittee met at 10 a.m., pursuant to call, in room 110, United States Courthouse, New York, N. Y., Senator Robert C. Hendrickson (chairman of the subcommittee), presiding.

Present: Senators Hendrickson, Kefauver, and Hennings.

Also present: Herbert J. Hannoch, chief counsel; Herbert Wilson Beaser, associate chief counsel; and Richard Clendenen, executive director.

The CHAIRMAN. This meeting of the Senate Subcomittee on Juvenile Delinquency will now be in order.

Today and tomorrow the United States Senate Subcommittee Investigating Juvenile Delinquency, of which I am the chairman, is going into the problem of horror and crime comic books. By comic books, we mean pamphlets illustrating stories depicting crimes or dealing with horror and sadism. We shall not be talking about the comic strips that appear daily in most of our newspapers.

And we shall be limiting our investigation to those comic books dealing with crime and horror. Thus, while there are more than a billion comic books sold in the United States each year, our subcommittee's interest lies in only a fraction of this publishing field.

Authorities agree that the majority of comic books are as harmless as soda pop. But hundreds of thousands of horror and crime comic books are peddled to our young people of impressionable age.

You will learn during the course of these hearings that we shall also not be speaking of all crime comic books. Some of the types of crime and horror comic books with which we are concerned have been brought into the hearing room for your attention.

I wish to state emphatically that freedom of the press is not at issue in this investigation. The members of this Senate subcomittee—Senator Kefauver, Senator Hennings, and Senator Langer—as well as myself as chairman, are fully aware of the long, hard, bitter fight that has been waged to achieve and preserve the freedom of the press, as well as the other freedoms in our Bill of Rights which we cherish in America.

We are not a subcommittee of blue-nosed censors. We have no preconceived notions as to the possible need for new legislation. We want to find out what damage, if any, is being done to our children's minds by certain types of publications which contain a substantial degree of sadism, crime, and horror. This, and only this, is the task at hand.

Since last November the subcommittee has been holding many public hearings into the various facets of the whole problem of juvenile delinquency. The volume of delinquency among our young has been quite correctly called the shame of America. If the rising tide of juvenile delinquency continues, by 1960 more than one and a half million American youngsters from 10 through 17 years of age, will be in trouble with the law each year.

Our subcommittee is seeking honestly and earnestly to determine why so many young Americans are unable to adjust themselves into the lawful pattern of American society. We are examining the reason why more and more of our youngsters steal automobiles, turn to vandalism, commit holdups, or become narcotic addicts.

The increase in craven crime committed by young Americans is rising at a frightening pace. We know that the great mass of our American children are not lawbreakers. Even the majority of those who get into trouble with our laws are not criminal by nature.

Nevertheless, more and more of our children are committing serious crimes. Our subcommittee is working diligently to seek out ways and means to check the trend and reverse the youth crime pattern.

We are perfectly aware that there is no simple solution to the complex problem of juvenile delinquency. We know, too, that what makes the problem so complex is its great variety of causes and contributing factors. Our work is to study all these causes and contributing factors and to determine what action might be taken.

It would be wrong to assume that crime and horror comic books are the major cause of juvenile delinquency. It would be just as erroneous to state categorically that they have no effect whatsoever in aggravating the problem. We are here to determine what effect on the whole problem of causation crime and horror comic books do have.

From the mail received by the subcommittee, we are aware that thousands of American parents are greatly concerned about the possible detrimental influence certain types of crime and horror comic books have upon their children.

We firmly believe that the public has a right to the best knowledge regarding this matter. The public has the right to know who is producing this material and to know how the industry functions.

Our work during this investigation will be to determine the possible delinquency producing effect upon children of certain types of crime and horror comic books, and whether or not there are certain offshoots growing out of the industry.

This phase of our investigation is but the first of several into questionable, or, should I say, disturbing phases of the mass media fields.

At a later date, the subcommittee will be attempting to determine what negative effects, if any, upon children, are exerted by other types of publications, by the radio, the television, and the movies. This is not to say that juvenile delinquency is wholly or even substantially the result of certain programs and subject matters presented by the mass media. But there can be no question that the media plays a significant role in the total problem.

I will now ask the assistant counsel to call the first witness.

Senator KEFAUVER. Mr. Chairman, before we call the first witness, I just want to compliment the chairman upon a very excellent statement of the purposes of this subcommittee and of this hearing here.

I would like to reemphasize that I feel that congressional hearings must be related to something that the Federal Government has jurisdiction of. This subcommittee is looking into the violations of various Federal laws, such as the Dyer Act, Mann Act, violations of the interstate commerce, and in connection with the subject matter under investigation we, of course, do have a postal statute which prohibits the mailing or using the mails for the distribution and dissemination of indecent and scurrilous literature which will be part of the subject matter of this hearing.

The CHAIRMAN. That is correct, Senator.

Senator KEFAUVER. I think it is also important to point out that Mr. J. Edgar Hoover's report of yesterday shows that whereas the increase in population last year was 5 percent, crime had gone up 20 percent and the particularly large increase was in connection with burglary and stealing of automobiles.

The interesting point is that a large part of the burglaries was committed by juveniles. Also juveniles, according to the FBI report, comprise 53.6 percent of those arrested for stealing automobiles.

As the chairman said, we do not have all the answers, but I think that it is important to look into the various matters which Mr. Hoover and other experts do bring out in connection with the increase in juvenile delinquency; and certainly as to horror and crime comics, not the good kind as the chairman said, but the various small part, most all the witnesses do have something to say about these.

We are not going into this hearing with the idea of condemning anybody or censoring the press or impairing the freedom of the press and bringing out in relation to a Federal statute something so that all of these experts on juvenile delinquency are talking about.

That is my understanding.

The CHAIRMAN. The Senator from Tennessee is entirely correct and the Chair wishes to congratulate and commend the Senator for his contribution.

Now, will counsel call the first witness?

Mr. BEASER. Mr. Richard Clendenen.

The CHAIRMAN. Do you solemnly swear that the testimony you will give before this subcommittee of the Senate Committee on the Judiciary, will be the truth, the whole truth, and nothing but the truth, so help you God?

Mr. CLENDENEN. I do.

The CHAIRMAN. The Chair with pleasure announces the presence of the distinguished Senator from Missouri, Senator Hennings.

TESTIMONY OF RICHARD CLENDENEN, EXECUTIVE DIRECTOR, UNITED STATES SENATE SUBCOMMITTEE TO INVESTIGATE JUVENILE DELINQUENCY

Mr. BEASER. For the record will you state your name, your address, and your present occupation?

Mr. CLENDENEN. My name is Richard Clendenen, 1445 Ogden Street NW., Washington, D.C.

I am executive director of the Senate Subcommittee to Investigate Juvenile Delinquency.

Mr. BEASER. Mr. Clendenen, will you outline briefly your education and experience in the field of juvenile delinquency?

The CHAIRMAN. Before Mr. Clendenen answers that question, I would like to say that the Senate Subcommittee on Juvenile Delinquency feels that we have a very able staff director.

Mr. CLENDENEN. Thank you.

Prior to coming to my present position I had worked in the United States Children's Bureau for a period of 7 years, and held there the position of Chief of the Juvenile Delinquency Branch.

Prior to that time I had served in administrative capacities in institutions for emotionally disturbed children and delinquent children and also have had experience as a probation officer in a juvenile court.

Mr. BEASER. You are a trained social worker?

Mr. CLENDENEN. I am.

Mr. BEASER. Speaking on behalf of the staff, have you conducted an investigation into the comic-book industry?

Mr. CLENDENEN. Yes sir, we have. Our investigation into the comic-book industry has been almost exclusively limited to those comics which themselves center about horror and crime.

The particular type of comics to which I refer present both pictures and stories which relate to almost all types of crime and in many instances those crimes are committed through extremely cruel, sadistic, and punitive kinds of acts.

Now, in connection with that question, I should like to make it perfectly clear that our investigation has not been concerned with other types of comics, many of which all authorities seem to agree represent not only harmless, but many times educational entertainment.

I should also add that even within that type of comic books known as the horror crime comics, there are gradations within this group, too. That is, some are much more sadistic, much more lurid, than others in the same class or category.

Now, although our investigations have been limited to this particular segment of the comic-book industry, we should not give the impression that this is a small portion of the comic-book industry.

According to estimates which were provided us by the Audit Bureau of Circulations and the Controlled Circulation Audits, the two firms that publish circulation figures, there were about 422 different kinds of comic or comic-book titles on the newsstands in March 1954.

About one-fourth were of the crime and horror variety.

Now, as far as all comic books are concerned, although exact figures are lacking, most authorities agree that there are probably somewhere between 75 million and 100 million comic books sold in this country each month.

If one-quarter of these are of the crime variety of comics, this means that there are some 20 million comic books, crime comic books placed on the newsstands of this country each month.

Mr. BEASER. When you say crime and horror comics could you be more specific in describing what you are talking about?

Mr. CLENDENEN. Well, we have prepared a certain number of slides which show pictures taken from comic books of the type to which we have addressed ourselves.

Now, I would like, for the purpose of illustration, to relate very briefly in summary fashion 6 stories, together with pictures illustrating these 6 stories which will give you a sampling of the type of comic books that we are talking about here.

Now, in presenting these I would like to say that while it is not a random sampling actually it is a deliberate sampling in trying to present the various types of stories and pictures that appear.

These are not typical, rather they are quite typical of the stories and pictures which appear in this type of publication. The first such crime comic is entitled "Black Magic."

This is a picture showing the cover or title page of this comic. Now, one story in this comic is entitled "Sanctuary," and the cover shots relate to this particular story.

You will note that this shot shows certain inhabitants of this sanctuary which is really a sort of sanitarium for freaks where freaks can be isolated from other persons in society.

You will note 1 man in the picture has 2 heads and 4 arms, another body extends only to the bottom of his rib. But the greatest horror of all the freaks in the sanctuary is the attractive looking girl in the center of the picture who disguises her grotesque body in a suit of foam rubber.

The final picture shows a young doctor in the sanitarium as he sees the girl he loves without her disguise.

The story closes as the doctor fires bullet after bullet into the girl's misshapen body.

Now, that is an example of a comic of the horror variety.

The next slide, the second story, is the cover shot of a comic entitled "Fight Against Crime."

One story in this particular issue is entitled "Stick in the Mud." This is a story of a very sadistic schoolteacher who is cruel to all of the children in her classroom with only one exception. The one exception is the son of a well-to-do man who has lost his wife. Through her attentions to the son the teacher woos and weds the father.

The following picture shows the schoolteacher as she stabs her husband to death in order to inherit his money. She then disguises her crime by dragging his body into a bullpen where his corpse is mangled and gored.

The small son, suspecting his stepmother, runs away so that she will chase him into the woods where a bed of quicksand is located.

Our last picture shows the stepmother sinking into the quicksand and crying for help. The small son gets the stepmother to confess that she murdered his father by pretending he will go for help if she does so.

After her confession he refuses to go for help and stays to watch his stepmother die in the quicksand.

The next comic is entitled "Mysterious Adventures." This particular issue of which this is a cover shot contains a total of 6 stories in which 11 people die violent deaths.

One story, I think, in this particular issue, has to do with a confirmed alcoholic who spends all his wife can earn on alcohol.

As a result their small son is severely neglected. On the day the small son is to start in the first grade in school the mother asks his father to escort him to the school. Instead the father goes to his favorite bootlegger and the son goes to school by himself. En route he is struck and killed by an automobile.

Informed of the accident, she returns to find her husband gloating over his new supply of liquor.

This next picture shows the mother killing her alcoholic spouse with an ax. She then cuts up his body into small pieces and disposes of it by placing the various pieces in the bottle of liquor her husband had purchased.

If you will look at the picture in the lower right-hand panel, you will see an ear in one bottle, an eye in another, and a finger in another, and so forth.

Senator HENNINGS. I wonder if Mr. Clendenen has any figures on the relative circulation or sale of this character of things as against the more innocuous kind of comics? To what extent, in other words, do these appeal to the children to a greater or less degree than the kind we are all more or less familiar with, the harmless comic strips?

Mr. CLENDENEN. Well, about one-fourth of the total comic-book titles, that is the different comic books are of the crime and horror variety.

Now, perhaps not all of those are as rough as some of these that are shown.

On the other hand, this does constitute a not insubstantial segment of the comic-book industry.

Mr. BEASER. It is about 20 million a month, Senator Kefauver suggests.

Mr. CLENDENEN. That is right; 20 million a month of the crime and horror variety.

The CHAIRMAN. The Senator from Tennessee.

Senator KEFAUVER. Do I understand, Mr. Chairman, the 20 million per month is the number sold or placed on sale? How do you get that figure, Mr. Clendenen?

Mr. CLENDENEN. That is a circulation figure which refers to sales.

The CHAIRMAN. Distribution and sales?

Mr. CLENDENEN. Yes, sir.

Senator KEFAUVER. Is that from the industry itself?

Mr. CLENDENEN. No sir; those figures, Senator, are from Audit Bureau of Circulations and the Controlled Circulation Audits.

The two organizations are companies that collect and issue data on circulation of various kinds of magazines.

Senator KEFAUVER. Thank you, Mr. Clendenen.

The CHAIRMAN. Does the Senator from Missouri have any more questions?

Senator HENNINGS. I just wanted to ask Mr. Clendenen another question and I do not want to break into his fine presentation of this—The Yellow Kid was the first comic strip, was it not?

Mr. CLENDENEN. Yes, sir.

Senator HENNINGS. Then we went into the Happy Hooligan and Katzenjammers and the ones we used to think were funny as youngsters.

At any rate, the funnies we knew were really funny, there were things in them that were calculated at least to amuse. The daily papers throughout the country nowadays carry more and more of the so-called serials, whether they deal with crime or whether they deal with romance or whether they deal with one thing or another, they are more stories now and less of the old comic-strip variety.

Have you any material on that transition and any observations to make as to why obviously that must appeal to the public, or they would not run these syndicated strips in the papers as they do.

What is your view of that, Mr. Clendenen? Why has public taste changed apparently? Are we advancing or progressing in that sort of thing, or is it the obverse?

Mr. CLENDENEN. There really, of course, are not research base data on which an answer to your question could be founded. I am not sure whether the public taste has changed or not.

Certainly the comic-book industry which was born in and of itself during the depression years of the thirties, the latter thirties, represented perhaps rather than reflected any change in the taste of the public, represents a new idea, that is, to put the comics up in book form of this kind.

Just exactly why you have had a transition from the type of comics—and now I refer to comic strips, which appeared in an earlier day and on which each separate day represented a separate episode and were funny to the serious type of strip—I don't have any idea and no opinion on it.

I am not at all sure I said, and if I failed to say, I would like to say, that our investigation has not pertained at all to the comic strips appearing in the daily newspapers but rather the comic books.

Senator HENNINGS. Thank you.

Mr. CLENDENEN. The next slide, the next comic that we would like to present to you is entitled "Crime Must Pay the Penalty." This particular comic has 4 stories in which 27 people meet a violent death. One story in this particular issue called "Frisco Mary" concerns an attractive and glamorous young woman who gains control of a California underworld gang. Under her leadership the gang embarks on a series of holdups marked for their ruthlessness and violence.

Our next picture shows Mary emptying her submachine gun into the body of an already wounded police officer after the officer had created an alarm and thereby reduced the gang's take in a bank holdup to a mere $25,000.

Now, in all fairness it should be added that Mary finally dies in the gas chamber following a violent and lucrative criminal career.

Now, this is strictly of the crime variety.

The next comic book is entitled "Strange Tales" and has five stories in which 13 people die violently. The story actually begins with a man dying on the operating table because the attending doctor is so absorbed in his own troubles that he pays no attention whatsoever to his patient.

It develops that this is the story of a promising young surgeon who begins to operate on wounded criminals to gain the money demanded by his spendthrift wife.

After he has ruined his professional career by becoming associated with the underworld, the criminal comes to get help for his girl friend who has been shot by the police. When the girl is placed upon the operating table the doctor discovers that the criminal's girl friend is none other than his own wife.

This picture shows the doctor, first of all, as he recognizes his wife, and as he commits suicide by plunging a scalpel into his own chest.

His wife also dies on the operating table for lack of medical attention.

The next comic, The Haunt of Fear, has 4 stories in which 8 people die violently. One story entitled "Head-Room" has to do with a spinster who operates a cheap waterfront hotel. The renter of one room is a man she would like to marry.

To win his favor she reduces his rent by letting his room, during daytime hours, to an ugly and vicious appearing man. This shot shows her renting the room to that individual.

Meanwhile there are daily reports that a murderer is loose in the city who cuts off and carries away his victim's heads.

The hotelkeeper suspects the vicious appearing daytime roomer and searches his room where she discovers six heads hanging on hooks in the closet.

She is discovered there by her favorite roomer who is returning to the hotel for the night.

It develops that he is the murderer and the next picture shows the hotelkeeper's head being added to the closet collection.

From a psychological point of view, however, there is another story in this same issue which is really even more perturbing. This is the story of an orphan boy who is placed from an orphanage to live with nice-appearing foster parents.

The foster parents give excellent care and pay particular attention to his physical health, insisting that he eat nourishing food in abundance.

A month later the boy discovers the reason for their solicitude when they sneak into his room late at night and announce they are vampires about to drink his rich red blood.

It might be said that right triumphs in the end, however, since the boy turns into a werewolf and kills and eats his foster parents.

The final story is one entitled "Shock Suspense Stories." It contains 4 stories in which 6 persons die violently.

One particular story in this issue is called "Orphan." This is the story of a small golden-haired girl named Lucy, of perhaps 8 or 10 years of age, and the story is told in her own words.

Lucy hates both her parents. Her father is an alcoholic who beats her when drunk.

Her mother, who never wanted Lucy, has a secret boy friend. The only bright spot in Lucy's life is her Aunt Kate, with whom she would like to live.

Lucy's chance to alter the situation comes when the father entering the front gate to the home meets his wife who is running away with the other man. Snatching a gun from the night table, Lucy shoots her father from the window.

She then runs out into the yard and presses the gun into the hands of her mother who has fainted and lies unconscious on the ground.

Then through Lucy's perjured testimony at the following trial, both the mother and her boy friend are convicted of murdering the father and are electrocuted.

This picture shows, first, "Mommie" and then "Stevie" as they die in the electric chair.

The latter two pictures show Lucy's joyous contentment that it has all worked out as she had planned and she is now free to live with her Aunt Kate.

The last two comic books I mentioned are published by the Entertaining Comic group and I mention it because the publisher of Entertaining Comic group will be appearing here later this morning.

Now, that completes the illustration of the type of comics to which we are addressing ourselves.

Mr. BEASER. Just one point, Mr. Clendenen. In talking about the child who is placed in a foster home, turned into a werewolf, you said that psychologically that was disturbing. Why do you say that?

Mr. CLENDENEN. Let me refer back to the time that I was operating an institution for emotionally disturbed children. Any child who is not able to live, continue to live, with his own family and who is disturbed and goes into an institution and then later is facing foster-home placement has a great many fears both conscious and unconscious regarding the future. That is, he is very much afraid, very fearful about going out and living with the family.

He has met them, to be sure, but he does not know them and he is a very insecure individual to begin with. This is the type of material that I myself would feel would greatly increase a youngster's feeling of insecurity, anxiety, and panic regarding placement in a foster-family home.

Mr. BEASER. Mr. Clendenen, you produced a number of comic books with different titles. Are they all, each one of them, produced by a different company?

Mr. CLENDENEN. No, they are not. The organization of the publishers in the comic-book industry is really a very complex type of organization.

I would like to refer here to the Atlas Publishing Co., or Atlas publishing group as an example. Atlas represents one of the major publishers in the comic-book field and, incidentally, there will be a representative of the Atlas Co. appearing also at these hearings. The Atlas Co. is owned by a man-and-wife team, Mr. and Mrs. Martin Goodman.

Now, the Atlas Publishing Co. publishes between 49 and 50 different comic titles. However, this number of comic titles, the 45 or 50 comic titles, are produced through no less than some 25 different corporations.

The Atlas organization also includes still another corporation through which it distributes its own publications. This particular exhibit shows 20 of the different groups of crime and weird comics they produce through 15 corporations.

Now, although several of the other publishers who are in the business of publishing comic books are smaller, the patterns of organization are essentially the same.

In other words, many times they organize themselves in forms of 2, 3, 4 or more different corporations. The end result of this type of corporation is that while there are many corporations involved in the publishing of comic books, the entire industry really rests in the hands of relatively few individuals.

Mr. BEASER. When you say they organize into different companies, do they organize into companies that produce nothing but comic books or do they produce other types of literature?

Mr. CLENDENEN. No, they also produce other types of literature. Many of them produce different kinds of magazines in addition to producing comics.

Now, not only may a particular organization be engaged in producing comics, both comic and magazines, but many times they will produce both comics and magazines through one individual corporation within the group.

In this exhibit, for example, this particular comic, which is produced once again by Atlas—and we are using Atlas merely as an example—these particular publications are not only both produced by the Atlas, but they are produced by a single corporation within the Atlas group.

Mr. BEASER. You say Atlas group. That is a trade-mark?

Mr. CLENDENEN. Yes, all their publications carry the Atlas trademark.

Mr. BEASER. In the course of your investigation has your staff had occasion to review scientific studies which have been made on the effect of crime and horror comics upon children and the relationship to juvenile delinquency?

Mr. CLENDENEN. Yes, we have. That is, we have reviewed virtually all of the surveys and studies that have been made; that is, we have reviewed all that we have been able to find.

I might say that it probably is not too surprising that the expert opinions and findings of these studies are not wholly unanimous. That is, there is certain diversity of opinion regarding the effects of these materials on youngsters even among these individuals whom we might properly qualify as experts.

Now, in this connection, I would like to submit to the subcommittee a few items here which relate to this matter of effects of these materials upon youngsters. One of these is a survey that was made at our request by the Library of Congress which summarizes all of the studies that they could locate having to do with the effects of crime comics upon the behavior of youngsters.

The CHAIRMAN. Is it your desire that this material be put in the record, or made a part of the subcommittee's files?

Mr. CLENDENEN. The latter, I believe.

The CHAIRMAN. I think that would be preferable.

Mr. CLENDENEN. I also would like to submit a letter which we received from Dr. Robert Felix, Director of the Institute of Mental Health, to whom we submitted samples of these materials and this is his reply to us indicating his feelings on the effects of these materials.

The CHAIRMAN. Without objection, that will be made a part of the record. Let that be exhibit No. 1.

* * * * * * * *

We just do not know. We are trying to learn.

I, for one, appreciate the spirit in which you have come here today.

Mr. SCHULTZ. Thank you, sir.

The CHAIRMAN. Mr. Schultz, the Chair certainly appreciates the spirit of your testimony. You have been very helpful. I think I speak for every member of the subcommittee when I say we are grateful.

Senator KEFAUVER. Mr. Chairman, may I ask one more question?

The CHAIRMAN. Senator Kefauver.

Senator KEFAUVER. Those who carry the seal of the code, do they advertise inside the magazine that they are complying with the code of the Comic Magazine Publishers Association?

Mr. SCHULTZ. I know of no such specific advertisement, other than the impression of the seal itself on the cover.

Senator KEFAUVER. How do people know what that seal means, then?

Mr. SCHULTZ. I really don't know. Most of the publishers who are nonmembers develop seals of their own. You find a whole series of seals which say "Good clean reading," and everything else, so that the seal has lost its imprint and its value in many ways anyhow, except for somebody who takes the trouble to look very closely at that little legend that might have some meaning to it.

Other than that I think it has no value.

Senator KEFAUVER. Thank you very much.

The CHAIRMAN. The subcommittee will stand in recess until 2 o'clock this afternoon.

(Thereupon, at 12:20 p.m., the subcommittee recessed, to reconvene at 2 p.m., same day.)

AFTERNOON SESSION

The subcommittee reconvened at 2 o'clock p.m., upon the expiration of the recess.

The CHAIRMAN. The hearing will be in order.

The first witness this afternoon will be Dr. Frederic Wertham.

Doctor, will you come forward and be sworn, please.

Do you solemnly swear that the testimony you will give this subcommittee of the Committee on the Judiciary of the United States Senate, will be the truth, the whole truth, and nothing but the truth, so help you God?

Dr. WERTHAM. I do.

TESTIMONY OF DR. FREDERIC WERTHAM, PSYCHIATRIST, DIRECTOR, LAFARGUE CLINIC, NEW YORK, N. Y.

The CHAIRMAN. Doctor, do you have a prepared statement?

Dr. WERTHAM. I have a statement of about 20 or 25 minutes.

The CHAIRMAN. All right, Doctor, you proceed in your own manner.

Dr. WERTHAM. Thank you.

The CHAIRMAN. Doctor, do you have copies of your statement?

Dr. WERTHAM. It is not written out. I have a statement of my credentials.

The CHAIRMAN. I wonder if you could not in your own way summarize this for the record. Of course, the whole statement may go in the record in its entirety.

Without objection, that will be so ordered.

(The document referred to is as follows:)

FREDERIC WERTHAM, M.D., NEW YORK, N. Y.

Specializing in neurology and psychiatry since 1922.

Certified as specialist in both neurology and psychiatry by the American Board of Psychiatry and Neurology. Have also served as examiner on the board in brain anatomy and psychiatry.

Director, Lafargue Clinic, New York City.

Consulting psychiatrist, department of hospitals, Queens Medical Center, New York City.

Psychiatric consultant and lecturer, Juvenile Aid Bureau of the New York City Police Department.

Director, Psychiatric Services and Mental Hygiene Clinic, Queens General Hospital, 1939-52.

Consulting psychiatrist, Triboro Hospital, New York City, 1939-52.

Director, Quaker Emergency Service Readjustment Center (functioning under the magistrates court), 1948-51.

Senior psychiatrist, New York City Department of Hospitals, 1932-52.

In 1932 organized and became director of the Psychiatric Clinic of the Court of General Sessions in New York, first clinic of its kind in the United States.

1933-36, assistant to the director of Bellevue Hospital; in charge of prison ward; in charge of children's psychiatric ward; in charge of alcoholic ward.

1936-39, director of the Mental Hygiene Clinic of Bellevue Hospital.

1929-31, fellow of the National Research Council of Washington, D. C., to do research in neuropathology and neuropsychiatry. First psychiatrist ever to receive this fellowship.

1922-29, psychiatrist at Phipps Psychiatric Clinic, Johns Hopkins Hospital and Johns Hopkins University.

1926-28, chief resident psychiatrist, Johns Hopkins Hospital.

1926-29, assistant in charge of the Mental Hygiene Clinic, Johns Hopkins Hospital.

Taught psychiatry, psychotherapy, and brain anatomy at Johns Hopkins Medical School.

Postgraduate studies in London, Vienna, Paris, and Munich. Invited to read scientific papers at the Medical-Psychological Society of Paris and the Research Institute of Psychiatry in Munich.

President of the Association for the Advancement of Psychotherapy, 1943-51; coeditor of the American Journal of Psychotherapy.

Member of the Committee on Ethics of the American Academy of Neurology.

Lectured at Yale Law School, New York University Law School, Massachusetts Institute of Technology, on psychiatry, criminology, and related subjects.

Reviewed books for law reviews of New York University, Buffalo Law School, Northwestern Law School, etc.

Psychiatric consultant to the Chief Censor of the United States Treasury Department.

Only psychiatrist ever employed by the city of New York who is a member of all three national neuropsychiatric associations: American Neurological Association, American Psychiatric Association, American Association of Neuropathologists. Fellow of the New York Academy of Medicine, of the American Academy of Neurology, of the American Medical Association, etc.

PUBLICATIONS

The Brain as an Organ (Macmillan, 1934), used in medical schools throughout the world, a textbook of brain pathology.

Dark Legend. A study in murder. New York, 1941, and London, 1948.

The Show of Violence (Doubleday, 1949).

The Catathymic Crisis (1937), description of a new mental disorder now included in the leading textbooks of psychiatry.

Seduction of the Innocent (Rinehart, 1954).

Articles and papers on psychology, psychiatry, neurology, brain anatomy, etc.

Dr. WERTHAM. I have practiced psychiatry and neurology since 1922. I taught psychiatry and brain pathology and worked in clinics at the Johns Hopkins Medical School from 1922 to 1929.

In 1929 I was the first psychiatrist to be awarded a fellowship by the National Research Council to do research on the brain. Some part of my research at that time was on paresis and brain syphilis. It came in good stead when I came to study comic books.

From 1932 to 1952 I was senior psychiatrist at the New York City Department of Hospitals.

I was first in charge of the Psychiatric Clinic of the Court of General Sessions examining convicted felons, making reports to the court.

In 1936 I was appointed director of the Mental Hygiene Clinic in Bellevue.

In 1939 I was appointed director of psychiatric services at the Mental Hygiene Clinic at Queens General Hospital.

In 1946 I organized and started the first psychiatric clinic in Harlem, a volunteer staff. A few years later I organized the Quaker Emergency Mental Hygiene Clinic, which functioned as a clinic for the treatment of sex offenders under the magistrates court of New York.

These are my main qualifications. I have taught psychiatry in Hopkins and New York University.

I have written both books and papers and monographs. I have reviewed psychiatric books for legal journals, like the Buffalo School Journal.

I have lectured at the Yale Law School, at the Massachusetts Institute of Technology, and in other places.

I am a fellow of the New York Academy and a member of the three national neuropsychiatric associations, the American Psychiatric Association and American Neurological Association and American Association of Neuropathologists.

I am testifying at your request on the influence of crime and horror books on juvenile delinquency.

My testimony will be in four parts. First, what is in comic books? How can one classify them clinically?

Secondly, are there any bad effects of comic books?

I may say here on this subject there is practically no controversy. Anybody who has studied them and seen them knows that some of them have bad effects.

The third problem is how farreaching are these bad effects? There is a good deal of controversy about that.

A fourth part is: Is there any remedy?

And being merely a doctor, about that I shall say only a few words.

My opinion is based on clinical investigations which I started in the winter of 1945 and 1946. They were carried out not by me alone, but with the help of a group of associates, psychiatrists, child psychiatrists, psychoanalysts, social workers, psychiatric social workers, remedial reading teachers, probation officers, and others.

In addition to material seen at the clinic both at Queens and Lafargue, we have studied whole school classes, whole classes of remedial reading clinics, over 300 children in a parochial school and private patients and consultations.

To the best of my knowledge our study is the first and only individual large-scale study on the subject of comic books in general.

The methods that we have used are the ordinary methods used in psychiatry, clinical interviews, group interviews, intelligence tests, reading tests, projective tests, drawings, the study of dreams, and so on.

This study was not subsidized by anybody. None of my associates got any money, ever. I myself have never spoken on the subject of comic books and accepted a fee for that.

This research was a sober, painstaking, laborious clinical study, and in some cases, since it has been going on now for 7 years, we have had a chance to follow for several years.

In addition to that we have read all that we could get hold of that was written in defense of comics, which is almost a more trying task than reading the comic books themselves.

What is in comic books? In the first place, we have completely restricted our-selves to comic books themselves. That leaves out newspaper comic strips entirely.

I must say, however, that when some very harmless comic strips for children printed in newspapers are reprinted for children in comic books, you suddenly can find whole pages of gun advertisements which the newspaper editor would not permit to have inserted in the newspaper itself.

There have been, we have found, arbitrary classifications of comic books according to the locale where something takes place.

We have found that these classifications don't work if you want to under-stand what a child really thinks or does.

We have come to the conclusion that crime comic books are comic books that depict crime and we have found that it makes no difference whether the locale is western, or Superman or space ship or horror, if a girl is raped she is raped whether it is in a space ship or on the prairie.

If a man is killed he is killed whether he comes from Mars or somewhere else, and we have found, therefore, two large groups, the crime comic books and the others.

I would like to illustrate my remarks by western comic books by giving you an example. This is from an ordinary western comic book. You might call it the wide open spaces.

This is from an ordinary western comic book. You see this man hitting this girl with a gun. It is a sadistic, criminal, sexual scene.

We have also studied how much time children spend on crime comic books and how much money they spend. I should like to tell you that there are thou-sands of children who spend about $60 a year on comic books.

Even poor children. I don't know where they get the money. I have seen chil-dren who have spent $75 a year and more, and I, myself, have observed when we went through these candy stores in different places, not only in New York, how 1 boy in a slum neighborhood, seemingly a poor boy, bought 15 comic books at a time.

Now, people generalize about juvenile delinquency and they have pet theo-ries and they leave out how much time, and, incidentally, how much money children spend on this commodity alone.

Now, as far as the effects on juvenile delinquency are concerned, we distin-guish four groups of delinquency:

Delinquencies against property; delinquency associated with violence; offenses connected with sex; and then miscellaneous, consisting of fire setting, drug addiction, and childhood prostitution.

I may say the latter is a very hushed-up subject. I am not referring to what young girls do with young boys, but I am referring to 10-, 11-, 12-, 13-year-old girls prostituting themselves to adults.

Now, nobody versed in any of this type of clinical research would claim that comic books alone are the cause of juvenile delinquency. It is my opinion, with-out any reasonable doubt, and without any reservation, that comic books are an important contributing factor in many cases of juvenile delinquency.

There arises the question: What kind of child is affected? I say again without any reasonable doubt and based on hundreds and hundreds of cases of all kinds, that it is primarily the normal child.

Mr. Chairman, American children are wonderful children. If we give them a chance they act right. It is senseless to say that all these people who get into some kind of trouble with the law must be abnormal or there must be some-thing very wrong with them.

As a matter of fact, the most morbid children that we have seen are the ones who are less affected by comic books because they are wrapped up in their own phantasies.

Now, the question arises, and we have debated it in our group very often and very long, why does the normal child spend so much time with this smut and trash, we have this baseball game which I would like you to scrutinize in detail.

They play baseball with a deadman's head. Why do they do that?

The CHAIRMAN. Doctor, do you want to put this up here on exhibition and explain it?

Dr. WERTHAM. Yes, sir.

Mr. Chairman, I can't explain for the reason that I can't say all the obscene things that are in this picture for little boys of 6 and 7. This is a baseball game where they play baseball with a man's head; where the man's intestines are the baselines. All his organs have some part to play.

The torso of this man is the chest protector of one of the players. There is nothing left to anybody's morbid imagination.

Mr. BEASER. That is from a comic book?

Dr. WERTHAM. That is from a comic book.

I will be glad to give you the reference later on. It is a relatively recent one.

Senator HENNINGS. Mr. Chairman, may I ask the doctor a question at that point?

The CHAIRMAN. The Senator from Missouri.

Senator HENNINGS. Doctor, I think from what you have said so far in terms of the value and effectiveness of the artists who portray these things, that it might be suggested implicitly that anybody who can draw that sort of thing would have to have some very singular or peculiar abnormality or twist in his mind, or am I wrong in that?

Dr. WERTHAM. Senator, if I may go ahead in my statement, I would like to tell you that this assumption is one that we had made in the beginning and we have found it to be wrong. We have found that this enormous industry with its enormous profits has a lot of people to whom it pays money and these people have to make these drawings or else, just like the crime comic book writers have to write the stories they write, or else. There are many decent people among them.

Let me tell you among the writers and among the cartoonists they don't love me, but I know that many of them are decent people and they would much rather do something else than do what they are doing.

Have I answered your question?

Senator HENNINGS. Yes, thank you.

Dr. WERTHAM. Now, we ask the question: Why does the normal child do that? I would say that psychology knows the answer to that.

If you consult, as we have done, the first modern scientific psychologist who lived a long time ago, you will find the answer. That psychologist was St. Augustine. This was long before the comic book era, of course, but he describes in detail how when he was a very, very young man he was in Rome and he saw these very bloody, sadistic spectacles all around him, where the gladiators fought each other with swords and daggers, and he didn't like it. He didn't want any part of it.

But there was so much going on and his friends went and finally he went and he noticed, as he expresses it, that he became unconsciously delighted with it and he kept on going.

In other words, he was tempted, he was seduced by this mass appeal, and he went.

I think it is exactly the same thing, if the children see these kinds of things over and over again, they can't go to a dentist, they can't go to a clinic, they can't go to a ward in a hospital, everywhere they see this where women are beaten up, where people are shot and killed, and finally they become, as St. Augustine said, unconsciously delighted.

I don't blame them. I try to defend them or I try to understand them.

Now, it is said also in connection with this question of who reads comic books and who is affected by them, it is said that children from secure homes are not affected.

Mr. Chairman, as long as the crime comic books industry exists in its present forms there are no secure homes. You cannot resist infantile paralysis in your own home alone. Must you not take into account the neighbor's children?

I might give one more example of the brutality in comic books. This is a girl and they are about to rip out her tongue. Now, the effect of comic books operates along four lines. While in our studies we had no arbitrary age limit, I am mostly interested in the under 16 and the first effect that is very early manifested is an effect in general on the ways of living with people.

That is to say, on theoretical development. One of the outstanding things there is in crime comic books—let me say here subject to later questions that in

my opinion crime comic books as I define them, are the overwhelming majority of all comic books at the present time. There is an endless stream of brutality.

I would take up all your time if I would tell you all the brutal things. I would like to draw your attention to one which seems to be specific almost with this literature that I have never found anywhere else, that is injuring people's eyes.

In other words, this is something now which juvenile delinquents did which I never heard of years ago. They shoot people in the eye and they throw stones and so on.

As an example, I would give you a book which nobody would testify is a crime comic book if you had not read it. You all know the novels of Tarzan which you all saw in the movies, but the comic book Tarzan which any mother would let come into her home has a story which a little boy brought me in which 22 people are blinded.

One of the 22 is a beautiful girl. They are all white people who are blinded and the man who does it is a Negro, so in addition to that it causes a great deal of race hatred.

How old are the children to whom such things are given? Dell Publishing Co., which publishes this book, boasts that this story is being read aloud to a little girl who—she is 2 years old—now, of course, many other crime comic books have this injury to the eye motive.

In other words, I think that comic books primarily, and that is the greatest harm they do, cause a great deal of ethical confusion.

I would like to give you a very brief example. There is a school in a town in New York State where there has been a great deal of stealing. Some time ago some boys attacked another boy and they twisted his arm so viciously that it broke in two places, and, just like in a comic book, the bone came through the skin.

In the same school about 10 days later 7 boys pounced on another boy and pushed his head against the concrete so that the boy was unconscious and had to be taken to the hospital. He had a concussion of the brain.

In this same high school in 1 year 26 girls became pregnant. The score this year, I think, is eight. Maybe it is nine by now.

Now, Mr. Chairman, this is what I call ethical and moral confusion. I don't think that any of these boys or girls individually vary very much. It cannot be explained individually, alone.

Here is a general moral confusion and I think that these girls were seduced mentally long before they were seduced physically, and, of course, all those people there are very, very great—not all of them, but most of them, are very great comic book readers, have been and are.

As a remedy they have suggested a formal course of sex instruction in this school.

The CHAIRMAN. What is the population of this community, Doctor?

Dr. WERTHAM. I don't know the population of the community. I know the population of the school, which is about 1,800. The town itself I don't know, but I shall give it to counsel.

The CHAIRMAN. The Senator from Tennessee.

Senator KEFAUVER. Is there something confidential about the name of the town?

Dr. WERTHAM. Yes. Publicly I don't like to give it, but I have knowledge of it, but I will give it to counsel for the information of the committee.

The CHAIRMAN. That will be in order.

Dr. WERTHAM. Now, they tried to start a course of sex instruction in this school. They have not done it. They have not started it. I wonder what they are going to do. Are the teachers going to instruct the pupils, or are the pupils going to instruct the teachers?

One reason I don't want to mention this town is because the same kind of thing happens in many other places nowadays. Maybe not quite so much, maybe a little more.

Many of these things happen and it is my belief that the comic book industry has a great deal to do with it. While I don't say it is the only factor at all, it may not be the most important one, it is one contributing factor.

I would like to point out to you one other crime comic book which we have found to be particularly injurious to the ethical development of children and those are the Superman comic books. They arose in children phantasies of sadistic joy in seeing other people punished over and over again while you yourself remain immune. We have called it the Superman complex.

In these comic books the crime is always real and the Superman's triumph over good is unreal. Moreover, these books like any other, teach complete contempt of the police.

For instance, they show you pictures where some preacher takes two policemen and bang their heads together or to quote from all these comic books you know, you can call a policeman cop and he won't mind, but if you call him copper that is a derogatory term and these boys we teach them to call policemen coppers.

All this to my mind has an effect, but it has a further effect and that was very well expressed by one of my research associates who was a teacher and studied the subject and she said, "Formerly the child wanted to be like daddy or mommy. Now they skip you, they bypass you. They want to be like Superman, not like the hard working, prosaic father and mother."

Talking further about the ethical effects of comic books, you can read and see over and over again the remark that in crime comic books good wins over evil, that law and order always prevails.

We have been astonished to find that this remark is repeated and repeated, not only by the comic books industry itself, but by educators, columnists, critics, doctors, clergymen. Many of them believe it is so.

Mr. Chairman, it is not. In many comic books the whole point is that evil triumphs; that you can commit a perfect crime. I can give you so many examples that I would take all your time.

I will give you only one or two. Here is a little 10-year-old girl who killed her father, brought it about that her mother was electrocuted. She winks at you because she is triumphant.

I have stories where a man spies on his wife and in the last picture you see him when he pours the poison in the sink, very proud because he succeeded.

There are stories where the police captain kills his wife and has an innocent man tortured into confessing in a police station and again is triumphant in the end.

I want to make it particularly clear that there are whole comic books in which every single story ends with the triumph of evil, with a perfect crime unpunished and actually glorified.

In connection with the ethical confusion that these crime comic books cause, I would like to show you this picture which has the comic book philosophy in the slogan at the beginning, "Friendship is for suckers! Loyalty—that is for Jerks."

The second avenue along which comic books contribute to delinquency is by teaching the technique and by the advertisements for weapons. If it were my task, Mr. Chairman, to teach children delinquency, to tell them how to rape and seduce girls, how to hurt people, how to break into stores, how to cheat, how to forge, how to do any known crime, if it were my task to teach that, I would have to enlist the crime comic book industry.

Formerly to impair the morals of a minor was a punishable offense. It has now become a mass industry. I will say that every crime of delinquency is described in detail and that if you teach somebody the technique of something you, of course, seduce him into it.

Nobody would believe that you teach a boy homosexuality without introducing him to it. The same thing with crime.

For instance, I had no idea how one would go about stealing from a locker in Grand Central, but I have comic books which describe that in minute detail and I could go out now and do it.

Now, children who read that, it is just human, are, of course, tempted to do it and they have done it. You see, there is an interaction between the stories and the advertisements. Many, many comic books have advertisements of all kinds of weapons, really dangerous ones, like .22 caliber rifles or throwing knives, throwing daggers; and if a boy, for instance, in a comic book sees a girl like this being whipped and the man who does it looks very satisfied and on the last page

there is an advertisement of a whip with a hard handle, surely the maximum of temptation is given to this boy, at least to have fantasies about these things.

It is my conviction that if these comic books go to as many millions of children as they go to, that among all these people who have these fantasies, there are some of them who carry that out in action.

Mr. BEASER. Doctor, may I interrupt you just a moment to go back to your Grand Central story?

Assume that is read by an otherwise healthy, normal child, with a good homelife, no other factors involved would you say that that would tempt him to go and break into a locker in Grand Central, or must there be other factors present already to give him a predisposition to steal from somebody else?

Dr. WERTHAM. I would answer that this way: I know of no more erroneous theory about child behavior than to assume that children must be predisposed to do anything wrong. I think there is a hairline which separates a boy who dreams about that, dreams about such a thing, and the boy who does it.

Now, I don't say, and I have never said, and I don't believe it, that the comic-book factor alone makes a child do anything.

You see, the comic-book factor only works because there are many, many other factors in our environment, not necessarily the homelife, not necessarily the much-blamed mother, but there are many other things; the other boys in school, the newspaper headlines where everybody accuses the other one of being a liar or thief.

There are many, many other factors in our lives, you see.

Now, actually, the answer should be put in this way: In most cases this factor works with other factors, but there are many cases that I know where such crimes have been committed purely as imitation and would have never been committed if the child hadn't known this technique.

In other words, I want to stress for you what we have found, that the temptation, and, of course, we know it from our ordinary lives—that temptation and seduction is an enormous factor. We don't have to be materially bad to do something bad occasionally, and, moreover, these children who commit such a delinquency, they don't do that because they are bad. They don't even necessarily do it to get the money or to get even, but it is a glorious deed.

You go there, you show how big you are. You are almost as big as these people you read about in crime comic books.

You see, the corruption of the average normal child has gone so far that except for those who follow this it is almost unbelievable to realize.

I would like to give you one more example. This is one I would like you to keep in mind, that the minimum edition of such a book, I think, is 300,000; probably this is distributed in a 650,000 edition.

Senator KEFAUVER. I did not understand.

Dr. WERTHAM. The minimum is 300,000.

Senator KEFAUVER. Is that a month?

Dr. WERTHAM. This is only one comic book. In order to make any kind of profit the publisher must print about 300,000 copies.

In other words, when you see a comic book you can always assume that more than 300,000 copies of this particular comic book have been printed.

In other words, you would not go far wrong if you assumed that this comic book is read by half a million children, for this reason, that when they are through with it and have read it, they sell it for 6 cents and 5 cents and then sell it for 4 cents and 2 cents.

Then you can still trade it.

So these comic books have a long, long life. We have studied this market. We know there is a great deal of this trading going on all over.

Now, this is a heroine. This is a woman who kills a man. You see, he has blood coming all over the man's face and she says, "I want you to suffer more and more and more and more."

Then the final triumph, she takes this man's organs and serves them up as dishes like a housewife and you see her "famous fried brains, famous baked kidneys, famous stuffed heart."

Next to that is the remainder of this man.

All I say is that quite apart from the disgust that it arouses in us—and I am a doctor, I can't permit myself the luxury of being disgusted—I think this kind of thing that children see over and over again causes this ethical confusion.

Senator KEFAUVER. That seems to be the end of that comic book story.

Dr. WERTHAM. Yes. I should add that it says here, "The End." "The End" is this glorious meal, cannibalism.

Senator KEFAUVER. So it did not have a very happy ending.

Dr. WERTHAM. Well, the comic book publishers seem to think it did. They made a lot of money.

Mr. Chairman, we have delinquency of the smallest kind. I have seen children who have stolen a quarter. I have seen children who stole $30,000. And they have to know some technique; they have to, for that.

But there are other crimes which you can commit in which you can take the ordinary kind of violence, for instance, there is an awful lot of shooting, knifing, throwing rocks, bombs, and all that, in combination.

On the Long Island Railroad at present I think three times a day children throw rocks through the windows.

Recently an innocent man was hit in the head and had a concussion of the brain and had to be taken to a hospital.

I have been for 12 years in Queens. I know these kids. I have seen quite a number of them who threw rocks. I can't see why we have to invoke highfalutin psychological theories and why we say these people have to have a mother who doesn't give them enough affection.

If they read this stuff all the time, some of them 2 and 3 hours a day reading, I don't think it is such an extraordinary event if they throw a stone somewhere where it may do some harm.

I want to add to this that my theory of temptation and seduction as I told you, is very, very vague. That is known to the comic-book publishers, too. They don't admit it when it comes to delinquency, but when it comes to selling stuff to children through the advertisements in comic books, then they have these enormous advertisements. This is from the Superman comic book. It says, "It is easier to put a yen in a youngster."

You see, I am still answering your question. It is easier to put a yen in a youngster when he comes from a normal thing. It is easier to go and commit some kind of delinquency.

Certainly it is easier to commit some kind of sexual delinquency.

Now, this leads me to the third avenue where they do harm. That is, they do harm by discouraging children. Mr. Chairman, many of these comic books, crime-comic books, and many of the other ones have ads which discourage children and give them all kinds of inferiority feelings. They are threatened with pimples. They worry the pre-adolescent kids about their breaths. They sell them all kinds of medicines and gadgets and even comic books like this one, and I am very conscious of my oath, even comic books like this have fraudulent advertisements, and I am speaking now as a medical physician. The children spend a lot of money and they get very discouraged, they think they are too big, too little, or too heavy. They think this bump is too big, or too little.

These discouraged children are very apt to commit delinquency as we know and have known for a long time.

Now, the fourth avenue I shall not go into in detail because that includes not only the crime-comic books, but that includes all comic books.

We have found—and in response to questions I will be glad to go into that—we have found all comic books have a very bad effect on teaching the youngest children the proper reading technique, to learn to read from left to right. This balloon print pattern prevents that. So many children, we say they read comic books, they don't read comic books at all. They look at pictures and every once in a while, as one boy expressed it to me, "When they get the woman or kill the man then I try to read a few words," but in any of these stories you don't have to have any words.

There is no doubt this is blood and this man is being killed. There is no doubt what they are going to do to this girl, you know, too.

In other words, the reading is very much interfered with.

The CHAIRMAN. Doctor, the original of all of those are in color?

Dr. WERTHAM. Yes, these are photostats I had made for your benefit.

Now, it is a known fact, although it is not sufficiently emphasized, that many delinquents have reading disorders, they can't read well. There have been estimates as to how many delinquents have reading disorders.

We have found over and over again that children who can't read are very discouraged and more apt to commit a delinquency and that is what Mr. Beaser meant, if there is another factor.

There is another factor.

Mr. BEASER. Many other factors.

Dr. WERTHAM. Yes, many other factors. We have isolated comic books as one factor. A doctor tries to isolate one factor and see what it does and tries to correlate it with other factors which either counteract it or help it or run parallel.

Now, Mr. Chairman, I have put the results of this investigation into several documents. One of them is an article in the Ladies Home Journal which gives a number of cases.

Another one is an article in the Reader's Digest which came out today.

The third one is a book.

I would like, Mr. Chairman, to draw your attention to the illustrations, but I would like to say that I am perfectly willing inasmuch as I have written this book with the greatest scientific care and checked and rechecked, and I am perfectly willing to repeat every word in there under oath.

The CHAIRMAN. Doctor, these documents will be made a part of the subcommittee's permanent file, without objection. Let that be exhibits Nos. 10a, 10b, and 10c.

(The documents referred to were marked "Exhibits Nos. 10a, 10b, and 10c," and are on file with the subcommittee.)

Dr. WERTHAM. Mr. Chairman, I would like to point out to you in conclusion that mine, in my own opinion, is not a minority report. I don't feel that way.

I would like to tell you that the highest psychiatric official in the Federal Government, who is also consulted when psychiatric problems come up in the Federal Government, Dr. Winfred Overholser, the Superintendent of Saint Elizabeths, has written that the evidence in my book is incontrovertible evidence of the pernicious influences on youth of crime comic books.

Prof. C. Wright Mills, a famous sociologist, a professor at Columbia, similarly agreed.

I would like to read you a word from the director of the juvenile delinquency project of the Children's Bureau in Washington, who has written:

In comic books we have a constant stream of garbage that cannot fail to pollute the minds of readers. After reading Dr. Wertham's book I visited my local newsstand and found the situation to be exactly as he reported it.

Senator KEFAUVER. Who is it that wrote that?

Dr. WERTHAM. Mr. Bertram M. Peck, the director of the current juvenile delinquency project in Washington.

The CHAIRMAN. He was before the subcommittee earlier in the hearings.

Dr. WERTHAM. Now, there are quite a number of other people who feel the same way. I would like to quote to you what the Minister of Justice of Canada said. In the beginning of this month they had two long sessions in the House of Commons, devoted almost entirely to my report on comic books and the Minister of Justice said:

I doubt if there is a single member of the House of Commons who dissents from disapproval of crime comic books.

In Canada, of course, they have the same situation. They get American comic books, not only directly, but they get them in plates. They can't help themselves.

Senator KEFAUVER. Dr. Wertham, while you are on the Canadian matter, Canada, of course, has a law, which was probably passed largely on the testimony you gave the House of Commons in Canada, which bans the shipment of certain horror and crime books.

What has been their experience with the reflection, or the result of that law upon juvenile delinquency? When was the law passed first?

Dr. WERTHAM. I am not quite sure. Maybe 1951. The information I have is based on the present official report of these debates on April 1 and 2. I judge from that that the law didn't work; that they made a list of crime comic books

and they didn't know how to supervise it, in fact, they couldn't, and I doubt it can be done in that form.

They have more bad crime-comic books than they ever had. They never could get them off the stand.

The latest proposal on the 2d of April that I have is that they want to put the crime comic-book publishers in jail, but they can't do that, for one thing—we have them.

I don't think that would work. So that experiment is not yet completely evaluated. All I know is that they are very much worried about the effect of comic books on delinquency, that they have not been able by this one amendment to the criminal code to curb this situation.

Stating that mine is not a minority report, Mr. Chairman, I would like to quote one more critic, Mr. Clifton Fadiman, who says that he senses the truth in my presentation as he sensed the truth in Uncle Tom's Cabin.

I don't know the man personally.

Now, what about the remedy? Mr. Chairman, I am just a doctor. I can't tell what the remedy is. I can only say that in my opinion this is a public-health problem. I think it ought to be possible to determine once and for all what is in these comic books and I think it ought to be possible to keep the children under 15 from seeing them displayed to them and preventing these being sold directly to children.

In other words, I think something should be done to see that the children can't get them. You see, if a father wants to go to a store and says, "I have a little boy of seven. He doesn't know how to rape a girl; he doesn't know how to rob a store. Please sell me one of the comic books," let the man sell him one, but I don't think the boy should be able to go see this rape on the cover and buy the comic book.

I think from the public-health point of view something might be done.

Now, Mr. Chairman, in conclusion, if I may speak in seriousness about one suggestion that I have, I detest censorship. I have appeared in very unpopular cases in court defending such novelties as the Guilded Hearse, and so on, as I believe adults should be allowed to write for adults. I believe that what is necessary for children is supervision.

But I would like to suggest to the committee a simple scientific experiment, if I may, in great brevity.

I am not advocating censorship, but it is the comic-book industry which at the present moment tries to censor what the parents read. This enormous industry at present exercises a censorship through power. Ever since I have expressed any opinion about comic books based on simple research done in basements on poor children whose mothers cried their eyes out, ever since then I have been told by threats, by libel suits, of damages; it is a miracle that my book was published considering how many threatening letters these lawyers and people have written to my prospective publishers. They have even threatened with a libel suit the Saturday Evening Post and even the National Parent Teachers, which is a nonprofit magazine.

Senator KEFAUVER. While you are on that subject. Dr. Wertham, may I see that thing, anybody who opposes comic books is a Red?

Dr. WERTHAM. Yes; that is part of it.

Senator KEFAUVER. I have read a number of your writings. I have read your Seduction of the Innocent. You remember a number of years ago I had several visits with you and you told me about the pressure they tried to apply on you in connection with this.

But I noticed here this thing, that anyone who opposes comic books are Communists. "The group most anxious to destroy comics are the Communists."

Then they have here the statement:

This article also quoted Gershon Legman (who claims to be a ghost writer for Dr. Frederick Wertham, the author of a recent smear against comics published in the Ladies Home Journal). This same G. Legman, in issue No. 2 of Neurotica, published in autumn 1948, wildly condemned comics, although admitting that "The child's natural character must be distorted to fit civilization * * *. Fantasy violence will paralyze his resistance, divert his aggression to unreal enemies and frustrations, and in this way prevent him from rebelling against parents and teachers * * * this will siphon off his resistance against society, and prevent revolution."

This seems to be an effort to tie you up in some way as Red or Communist. Is that part of a smear?

Dr. WERTHAM. This is from comic books. I have really paid no attention to this. I can tell you that I am not a ghost writer. Like this gentleman who criticized it severely, they know I don't have a ghost writer.

Gershon Legman is a man who studied comic books. He is a man who tried to do something against comic books, so they tried to do something about him.

That is just one of the ordinary kinds of things. But, Mr. Chairman, they do something quite different which is much more serious. The comic-book industry at the present moment and this is the experiment. I would like to suggest to you the comic-book industry at the present moment interferes with the freedom of publications in all fields. They have their hands on magazines, they have their hands on newspapers, they threaten the advertisers; they continually threaten libel suits and action for damages.

The experiment I suggest to you is the following: My book has been selected, Seduction of the Innocent, which is nothing but a scientific report on comic books in that I tried to make in understandable language, that is what it is except that it includes areas other than juvenile delinquency.

This group was selected by a group of men of unimpeachable integrity, Christopher Morley, Clifton Fadiman, Loveman, Dorothy Canfield Fisher, John P. Marquand; they selected this book on account of its truth, and I suppose its writing, and it has been announced all over the country that it is a Book of the Month Club selection.

The contracts have been signed. The question I would like to put to you is this: Will this book be distributed or will the sinister hand of these corrupters of children, of this comic-book industry, will they prevent distribution? You can very easily find that out and then you can see how difficult it is for parents to defend their children against comic books if they are not allowed to read what they contain.

Thank you.

The CHAIRMAN. Senator Kefauver, do you have any questions?

Senator KEFAUVER. Yes, I have one or two, Mr. Chairman.

Dr. Wertham, I assume more than any other psychiatrist in the United States—perhaps I should not be asking this—but you, over a long period of time, have interviewed children, you worked in hospitals, clinics, and schools, observing the reaction to crime and horror comic books.

Could you give us any estimate of how many children this study has been made from—from which you derive your conclusions?

Dr. WERTHAM. Yes. I figured out at one time that there were more than 500 children a year come to my attention, or did come to my attention during the bulk of this investigation.

Now, I cannot say, however, that every one of these children had as complete a study as I think they should have. I mean, some of them I saw a few times; some have all kinds of tests, good social services; some had been before the court; some I saw privately and considered in great detail, but by and large I would say that we have seen hundreds and hundreds of children.

Senator KEFAUVER. Any way it runs into many thousands?

Dr. WERTHAM. Some thousands. I would not say many thousands.

Senator KEFAUVER. You have actually asked and tried to develop from many of these children how it was they happened to try to commit, or how it was they happened to commit this, that, or the other crime; is that correct?

Dr. WERTHAM. Senator, that is not exactly correct. For instance, if I have a child sent to me—I remember the commissioner of the juvenile aid bureau of the police once came to visit me to see how I examined a child because he had a good report of my clinic in Queens. This was a child who had committed some delinquency. I spent an hour talking to this child. I didn't even mention the delinquency. I didn't say a word about it.

The commissioner asked me afterwards, "Why didn't you mention it?"

I said, "I don't want to put him on his guard. I don't want to tempt him to lie to me. I want to understand this child. I want to understand the whole setting."

The judgment that these comic books have an effect on children, that is not the children's judgment. They don't think that. The children don't say that this

U.S. SENATE HEARINGS

does them any harm, and that is an interesting thing because it has been so misrepresented by the comic-book industry and their spokesmen in all the biased opinions that they peddle and that they hand out to unsuspecting newspaper editors.

They say I asked the child, "Did you do that because you read a comic book?"

I don't ask the child "Why do you have the measles?", or "Why do you have a fever?" No child has ever said to me this excuse, "I did this because I read it in the comic book. I figured that out."

The children don't say that. Many of these children read the comic books and they like it and they are already so corrupt that they really get a thrill out of it and it is very difficult.

What you can get out of them is this, "For me, this does not do any harm to me, but my little brother, he really should not read it. He gets nightmares or he gets wrong ideas."

The actual proof that a child can say, "I did this because of so and so," that is not at all how my investigation worked.

Senator KEFAUVER. I do remember you showed me one example of a horror book with a child with a hypodermic needle and you related that to some crime that you had known something about.

Dr. WERTHAM. I have known children, in fact, if I may say, Your Honor, I notice in the room the reporter who brought to my attention one of the earliest cases of children—may I say who it is—Judith Crist, who works for the New York Herald Tribune. She brought to my attention a case in Long Island where children stuck pins in girls or something. I told her then that I have found where they stuck pins in much worse places than the arm.

I told her of the injury to the eyes. You can very rarely say that the boys said exactly, "That is what I did because this is what I wanted to do."

I have had children who told me they committed robberies. They followed the comic book, but they said, "That is not good enough, the comic books say you go through the transom."

"But," they said, "you go through the side door."

Children nowadays draw maps and say, "This is the street where the store is we are going to rob; this is where we are going to hide and this is how we are going to get away."

That is in many comic books, and they show me in comic books that is how they are going to do it.

I would not say in such a case this is the only reason why this child committed delinquency, but I will say that is a contributing factor because if you don't know the method you can't execute the act and the method itself is so intriguing and so interesting that the children are very apt to commit it.

Senator KEFAUVER. In some of the comic books the villain made one mistake, he almost committed the perfect crime, but he made one mistake and he got caught. We found some cases where they are trying to eliminate the one mistake so that they can make the perfect crime.

Dr. WERTHAM. That is absolutely correct. That is the whole philosophy of comic books. The point is don't make any mistakes. Don't leave the map there. Don't break the light aloud, put a towel over it.

Senator KEFAUVER. Would you liken this situation you talk about, showing the same thing over and over again until they finally believed it, to what we heard about during the last war of Hitler's theory of telling the story over and over again?

The CHAIRMAN. The "big lie" technique?

Dr. WERTHAM. Well, I hate to say that, Senator, but I think Hitler was a beginner compared to the comic-book industry. They get the children much younger. They teach them race hatred at the age of 4 before they can read.

Let me give you an example of a comic book which I think is on the stand right now. It may have disappeared the last few days.

You know at the present moment New York City and other cities have a great social problem in integrating immigrating Puerto Ricans. It is very important to establish peace in these neighborhoods where friction may arise, or has arisen.

This particular comic book that I am referring to now has a story in which a derogatory term for Puerto Ricans, which I will not repeat here, but which is a

880

common derogatory term, is repeated 12 times in one story. This greasy so and so, this dirty so and so. It is pointed out that a Spanish Catholic family moved into this neighborhood—utterly unnecessary.

What is the point of the story? The point of the story is that then somebody gets beaten to death. The only error is that the man who must get beaten to death is not a man; it is a girl.

Senator KEFAUVER. I think we ought to know the name of the comic book.

Dr. WERTHAM. I shall be glad to give it to your counsel.

Senator KEFAUVER. Can you tell us?

Dr. WERTHAM. I don't have it in my head.

Senator KEFAUVER. I am sure that Dr. Wertham is one who could tell about this, but I have heard it told that some people feel that comic books are harmless and respectable and don't pay much attention to them because they are certified to, and in some cases even recommended by high-sounding committees, with, of course, good names on the committees who give them an excellent bill of health.

Did you not make some investigation into whether or not a great many of the people on these so-called nonpartisan committees were actually in the pay of the comic book industry itself?

Dr. WERTHAM. Senator, I would have to mention individuals but I think it is to be assumed, and I suppose one knows that people whose names are on these comic books are paid—there are people who say, "Well, they are paid, they are biased."

I have a hard time understanding how any doctor or child expert or psychologist can put his name to that. That is not the important point, because the names usually are not known anyway.

What happens is that in Kalamazoo, or in North Dakota, or in the little village in Pennsylvania where I spend part of my time, they read the names of these institutions which sound very well, the so and so association, or so and so university. That is what influences the people.

Of course, these same people write articles which I have tried very hard to take at their face value. But when I found that they have misstatements, when they say articles sent out by one of the associations, the person who writes it and endorses these books for money, when they write a survey of all the comic books, you see all kinds of little ones, nothing of the real ones, it misleads the people.

But I think that is not as important a problem, Senator, as the problem right now that the industry itself is preventing the mothers of this country from having not only me, but anybody else make any criticism.

This tremendous power is exercised by this group which consists of three parts, the comic book publishers, the printers, and last and not least, the big distributors who force these little vendors to sell these comic books. They force them because if they don't do that they don't get the other things.

Mr. HANNOCH. How do you know that?

Dr. WERTHAM. I know that from many sources. You see, I read comic books and I buy them and I go to candy stores.

They said, "You read so many comic books." I talk to them and ask them who buys them. I say to a man, "Why do you sell this kind of stuff?"

He says, "What do you expect me to do? Not sell it?"

He says, "I will tell you something. I tried that one time."

The man says, "Look, I did that once. The newsdealer, whoever it is, says, 'You have to do it'."

"I said, 'I don't want to.' "

" 'Well', he says, 'you can't have the other magazine'."

So the man said, "Well, all right, we will let it go."

So when the next week came, all the other magazines were late. You see, he didn't give them the magazines. So he was later than all his competitors, he had to take comic books back.

I also know it another way. There are some people who think I have some influence in this matter. I have very little. Comic books are much worse now than when I started. I have a petition from newsdealers that appealed to me to help them so they don't have to sell these comic books.

What they expect me to do, I don't know. Of course, it is known to many other people. It also happens in Canada.

I know it for more reasons. I don't want to mention journalists, but I can tell you of big national magazines, the editors of which would very much like to push this question of comic book problems. They can't do that because they are themselves being distributed by very big distributors who also do comic books, and then they suffer through loss of advertising.

That is why I gave you one example of the Book of the Month Club because I think that could nail it down once and for all, what these people do deliberately.

The CHAIRMAN. Senator Hennings, have you any questions?

Senator HENNINGS. Thank you, Mr. Chairman. I have no questions.

The CHAIRMAN. Mr. Hannoch, do you have any questions you want to ask?

Mr. HANNOCH. No questions.

Senator HENNINGS. I must say that I have the doctor's book, and I am reading it with great interest.

The CHAIRMAN. Doctor, we are very grateful to you for appearing here this afternoon.

Dr. WERTHAM. Thank you.

Mr. BEASER. William Gaines.

The CHAIRMAN. Will you come forward, Mr. Gaines?

Will you be sworn?

Do you solemnly swear that the testimony you will give to this subcommittee of the Committee on the Judiciary of the United States Senate, will be the truth, the whole truth, and nothing but the truth, so help you God?

Mr. GAINES. I do.

TESTIMONY OF WILLIAM M. GAINES, PUBLISHER, ENTERTAINING COMICS GROUP, NEW YORK, N.Y.

The CHAIRMAN. You may proceed in your own manner.

Mr. GAINES. Gentlemen, I would like to make a short statement. I am here as an individual publisher.

Mr. HANNOCH. Will you give your name and address, for the record?

Mr. GAINES. My name is William Gaines. My business address is 225 Lafayette Street, New York City. I am a publisher of the Entertaining Comics Group.

I am a graduate of the school of education of New York University. I have the qualifications to teach in secondary schools, high schools.

What then am I doing before this committee? I am a comic-book publisher. My group is known as EC, Entertaining Comics.

I am here as a voluntary witness. I asked for and was given this chance to be heard.

Two decades ago my late father was instrumental in starting the comic magazine industry. He edited the first few issues of the first modern comic magazine, Famous Funnies. My father was proud of the industry he helped found. He was bringing enjoyment to millions of people.

The heritage he left is the vast comic-book industry which employs thousands of writers, artists, engravers, and printers.

It has weaned hundreds of thousands of children from pictures to the printed word. It has stirred their imagination, given them an outlet for their problems and frustrations, but most important, given them millions of hours of entertainment.

My father before me was proud of the comics he published. My father saw in the comic book a vast field of visual education. He was a pioneer.

Sometimes he was ahead of his time. He published Picture Stories from Science, Picture Stories from World History, and Picture Stories from American History.

He published Picture Stories from the Bible.

I would like to offer these in evidence.

The CHAIRMAN. They will be received for the subcommittee's permanent files. Let that be exhibit No. 11.

(The documents referred to were marked "Exhibit No. 11," and are on file with the subcommittee.)

Mr. GAINES. Since 1942 we have sold more than 5 million copies of Picture Stories from the Bible, in the United States. It is widely used by churches and schools to make religion more real and vivid.

Picture Stories from the Bible is published throughout the world in dozens of translations. But it is nothing more nor nothing less than a comic magazine.

I publish comic magazines in addition to picture stories from the Bible. For example, I publish horror comics. I was the first publisher in these United States to publish horror comics. I am responsible, I started them.

Some may not like them. That is a matter of personal taste. It would be just as difficult to explain the harmless thrill of a horror story to a Dr. Wertham as it would be to explain the sublimity of love to a frigid old maid.

My father was proud of the comics he published, and I am proud of the comics I publish. We use the best writers, the finest artists; we spare nothing to make each magazine, each story, each page, a work of art.

As evidence of this, I might point out that we have the highest sales in individual distribution. I don't mean highest sales in comparison to comics of another type. I mean highest sales in comparison to other horror comics. The magazine is one of the few remaining—the comic magazine is one of the few remaining pleasures that a person may buy for a dime today. Pleasure is what we sell, entertainment, reading enjoyment. Entertaining reading has never harmed anyone. Men of good will, free men, should be very grateful for one sentence in the statement made by Federal Judge John M. Woolsey when he lifted the ban on Ulysses. Judge Woolsey said:

It is only with the normal person that the law is concerned.

May I repeat, he said, "It is only with the normal person that the law is concerned." Our American children are for the most part normal children. They are bright children, but those who want to prohibit comic magazines seem to see dirty, sneaky, perverted monsters who use the comics as a blueprint for action.

Perverted little monsters are few and far between. They don't read comics. The chances are most of them are in schools for retarded children.

What are we afraid of? Are we afraid of our own children? Do we forget that they are citizens, too, and entitled to select what to read or do? We think our children are so evil, simple minded, that it takes a story of murder to set them to murder, a story of robbery to set them to robbery?

Jimmy Walker once remarked that he never knew a girl to be ruined by a book. Nobody has ever been ruined by a comic.

As has already been pointed out by previous testimony, a little, healthy, normal child has never been made worse for reading comic magazines.

The basic personality of a child is established before he reaches the age of comic-book reading. I don't believe anything that has ever been written can make a child overaggressive or delinquent.

The roots of such characteristics are much deeper. The truth is that delinquency is the product of real environment in which the child lives and not of the fiction he reads.

There are many problems that reach our children today. They are tied up with insecurity. No pill can cure them. No law will legislate them out of being. The problems are economic and social and they are complex.

Our people need understanding; they need to have affection, decent homes, decent food.

Do the comics encourage delinquency? Dr. David Abrahamsen has written:

Comic books do not lead into crime, although they have been widely blamed for it. I find comic books many times helpful for children in that through them they can get rid of many of their aggressions and harmful fantasies. I can never remember having seen one boy or girl who has committed a crime or who became neurotic or psychotic because he or she read comic books.

The CHAIRMAN. Senator Kefauver.

Senator KEFAUVER. Is that Dr. David Abrahamsen?

Mr. GAINES. That is right, sir. I can give you the source on that, if you like. I will give it to you later.

The CHAIRMAN. You can supply that later.

(The source is as follows:)

Abrahamsen, Dr. David, Who Are the Guilty, New York: Rinehart & Co., Inc., page 279.

Mr. GAINES. I would like to discuss, if you bear with me a moment more, something which Dr. Wertham provoked me into. Dr. Wertham, I am happy to say, I have just caught in a half-truth, and I am very indignant about it. He said there is a magazine now on the stands preaching racial intolerance. The magazine he is referring to is my magazine. What he said, as much as he said, was true. There do appear in this magazine such materials as "Spik," "Dirty Mexican," but Dr. Wertham did not tell you what the plot of the story was.

This is one of a series of stories designed to show the evils of race prejudice and mob violence, in this case against Mexican Catholics.

Previous stories in this same magazine have dealt with antisemitism, and anti-Negro feelings, evils of dope addiction and development of juvenile delinquents.

This is one of the most brilliantly written stories that I have ever had the pleasure to publish. I was very proud of it, and to find it being used in such a nefarious way made me quite angry.

I am sure Dr. Wertham can read, and he must have read the story, to have counted what he said he counted.

I would like to read one more thing to you.

Senator Hennings asked Dr. Peck a question. I will be perfectly frank with you, I have forgotten what he asked him, but this is the answer because I made a notation as he went along.

No one has to read a comic book to read horror stories.

Anyone, any child, any adult, can find much more extreme descriptions of violence in the daily newspaper. You can find plenty of examples in today's newspaper. In today's edition of the Daily News, which more people will have access to than they will to any comic magazine, there are headline stories like this:

Finds he has killed wife with gun.
Man in Texas woke up to find he had killed his wife with gun. She had bullet in head and he had a revolver in his hand.

The next one:

Cop pleads in cocktail poisoning.
Twenty-year-old youth helps poison the mother and father of a friend.
Court orders young hanging. Man who killed his wife will be hung in June for his almost-perfect murder.

Let us look at today's edition of the Herald Tribune.

On the front page a criminal describes how another criminal told him about a murder he had done. In the same paper the story of a man whose ex-wife beat him on the head with a claw hammer and slashed him with a butcher knife.

In the same paper, story of a lawyer who killed himself.

In another, a story of that man who shot his wife while having a nightmare.

Another, a story of a gang who collected an arsenal of guns and knives. These are very many stories of violence and crime in the Herald Tribune today.

I am not saying it is wrong, but when you attack comics, when you talk about banning them as they do in some cities, you are only a step away from banning crimes in the newspapers.

Here is something interesting which I think most of us don't know. Crime news is being made in some places. The United Nations UNESCO report, which I believe is the only place that it is printed, shows that crime news is not permitted to appear in newspapers in Russia or Communist China, or other Communist-held territories.

We print our crime news. We don't think that the crime news or any news should be banned because it is bad for children.

Once you start to censor you must censor everything. You must censor comic books, radio, television, and newspapers.

Than you must censor what people may say. Then you will have turned this country into Spain or Russia.

Mr. BEASER. Mr. Gaines, let me ask you one thing with reference to Dr. Wertham's testimony.

You used the pages of your comic book to send across a message, in this case it was against racial prejudice; is that it?

Mr. GAINES. That is right.

Mr. BEASER. You think, therefore, you can get across a message to the kids through the medium of your magazine that would lessen racial prejudice; is that it?

Mr. GAINES. By specific effort and spelling it out very carefully so that the point won't be missed by any of the readers, and I regret to admit that it still is missed by some readers, as well as Dr. Wertham—we have, I think, achieved some degree of success in combating anti-Semitism, anti-Negro feeling, and so forth.

Mr. BEASER. Yet why do you say you cannot at the same time and in the same manner use the pages of your magazine to get a message which would affect children adversely, that is, to have an effect upon their doing these deeds of violence or sadism, whatever is depicted?

Mr. GAINES. Because no message is being given to them. In other words, when we write a story with a message, it is deliberately written in such a way that the message, as I say, is spelled out carefully in the captions. The preaching, if you want to call it, is spelled out carefully in the captions, plus the fact that our readers by this time know that in each issue of shock suspense stories, the second of the stories will be this type of story.

Mr. BEASER. A message can be gotten across without spelling out in that detail. For example, take this case that was presented this morning of the child who is in a foster home who became a werewolf, and foster parents—

Mr. GAINES. That was one of our stories.

Mr. BEASER. A child who killed her mother. Do you think that would have any effect at all on a child who is in a foster placement, who is with foster parents, who has fears? Do you not think that child in reading the story would have some of the normal fears which a child has, some of the normal desires tightened, increased?

Mr. GAINES. I honestly can say I don't think so. No message has been spelled out there. We were not trying to prove anything with that story. None of the captions said anything like "If you are unhappy with your stepmother, shoot her."

Mr. BEASER. No, but here you have a child who is in a foster home who has been treated very well, who has fears and doubts about the foster parent. The child would normally identify herself in this case with a child in a similar situation and there a child in a similar situation turns out to have foster parents who became werewolves.

Do you not think that would increase the child's anxiety?

Mr. GAINES. Most foster children, I am sure, are not in homes such as were described in those stories. Those were pretty miserable homes.

Mr. HANNOCH. You mean the houses that had vampires in them, those were not nice homes?

Mr. GAINES. Yes.

Mr. HANNOCH. Do you know any place where there is any such thing?

Mr. GAINES. As vampires?

Mr. HANNOCH. Yes.

Mr. GAINES. No sir; this is fantasy. The point I am trying to make is that I am sure no foster children are kept locked up in their room for months on end except in those rare cases that you hear about where there is something wrong with the parents such as the foster child in one of these stories was, and on the other hand, I am sure that no foster child finds himself with a drunken father and a mother who is having an affair with someone else.

Mr. BEASER. Yet you do hear of the fact that an awful lot of delinquency comes from homes that are broken. You hear of drunkenness in those same homes.

Do you not think those children who read those comics identify themselves with the poor home situation, with maybe the drunken father or mother who is going out, and identify themselves and see themselves portrayed there?

Mr. GAINES. It has been my experience in writing these stories for the last 6 or 7 years that whenever we have tested them out on kids, or teen-agers, or adults, no one ever associates himself with someone who is going to be put upon. They always associate themselves with the one who is doing the putting upon.

The CHAIRMAN. You do test them out on children, do you?

Mr. GAINES. Yes.

Mr. BEASER. How do you do that?

Senator HENNINGS. Is that one of your series, the pictures of the two in the electric chair, the little girl down in the corner?

Mr. GAINES. Yes.

Senator HENNINGS. As we understood from what we heard of that story, the little girl is not being put upon there, is she? She is triumphant apparently, that is insofar as we heard the relation of the story this morning.

Mr. GAINES. If I may explain, the reader does not know that until the last panel, which is one of the things we try to do in our stories, is have an O. Henry ending for each story.

Senator HENNINGS. I understood you to use the phrase "put upon," and that there was no reader identification—with one who was put upon, but the converse.

Mr. GAINES. That is right, sir.

Senator HENNINGS. Now, in that one, what would be your judgment or conclusion as to the identification of the reader with that little girl who has, to use the phrase, framed her mother and shot her father?

Mr. GAINES. In that story, if you read it from the beginning, because you can't pull things out of context —

Senator HENNINGS. That is right, you cannot do that.

Mr. GAINES. You will see that a child leads a miserable life in the 6 or 7 pages. It is only on the last page she emerges triumphant.

Senator HENNINGS. As a result of murder and perjury, she emerges as triumphant?

Mr. GAINES. That is right.

Mr. HANNOCH. Is that the O. Henry finish?

Mr. GAINES. Yes.

Mr. HANNOCH. In other words, everybody reading that would think this girl would go to jail. So the O. Henry finish changes that, makes her a wonderful looking girl?

Mr. GAINES. No one knows she did it until the last panel.

Mr. HANNOCH. You think it does them a lot of good to read these things?

Mr. GAINES. I don't think it does them a bit of good, but I don't think it does them a bit of harm, either.

The CHAIRMAN. What would be your procedure to test the story out on a child or children?

Mr. GAINES. I give them the story to read and I ask them if they enjoyed it, and if they guessed the ending. If they said they enjoyed it and didn't guess the ending, I figure it is a good story, entertaining.

The CHAIRMAN. What children do you use to make these tests with?

Mr. GAINES. Friends, relatives.

Senator HENNINGS. Do you have any children of your own, Mr. Gaines?

Mr. GAINES. No, sir.

Senator HENNINGS. Do you use any of the children of your own family, any nieces, nephews?

Mr. GAINES. My family has no children, but if they had, I would use them.

The CHAIRMAN. You do test them out on children of your friends, do you?

Mr. GAINES. Yes.

Mr. BEASER. Mr. Gaines, in your using tests, I don't think you are using it in the same way that we are here. You are not trying to test the effect on the child, you are trying to test the readability and whether it would sell?

Mr. GAINES. Certainly.

Mr. BEASER. That is a different kind of test than the possible effect on the child. Then you have not conducted any tests as to the effects of these upon children?

Mr. GAINES. No, sir.

Mr. BEASER. Were you here this morning when Dr. Peck testified?

Mr. GAINES. I was.

Mr. BEASER. Did you listen to his testimony as to the possible effect of these comics upon an emotionally maladjusted child?

Mr. GAINES. I heard it.

Mr. BEASER. You disagree with it?

Mr. GAINES. I disagree with it.

Frankly, I could have brought many, many quotes from psychiatrists and child-welfare experts and so forth pleading the cause of the comic magazine. I did not do so because I figured this would all be covered thoroughly before I got here. And it would just end up in a big melee of pitting experts against experts.

Mr. BEASER. Let me get the limits as far as what you put into your magazine. Is the sole test of what you would put into your magazine whether it sells? Is there any limit you can think of that you would not put in a magazine because you thought a child should not see or read about it?

Mr. GAINES. No, I wouldn't say that there is any limit for the reason you outlined. My only limits are bounds of good taste, what I consider good taste.

Mr. BEASER. Then you think a child cannot in any way, in any way, shape, or manner, be hurt by anything that a child reads or sees?

Mr. GAINES. I don't believe so.

Mr. BEASER. There would be no limit actually to what you put in the magazines?

Mr. GAINES. Only within the bounds of good taste.

Mr. BEASER. Your own good taste and salability?

Mr. GAINES. Yes.

Senator KEFAUVER. Here is your May 22 issue. This seems to be a man with a bloody ax holding a woman's head up which has been severed from her body. Do you think that is in good taste?

Mr. GAINES. Yes, sir; I do, for the cover of a horror comic. A cover in bad taste, for example, might be defined as holding the head a little higher so that the neck could be seen dripping blood from it and moving the body over a little further so that the neck of the body could be seen to be bloody.

Senator KEFAUVER. You have blood coming out of her mouth.

Mr. GAINES. A little.

Senator KEFAUVER. Here is blood on the ax. I think most adults are shocked by that.

The CHAIRMAN. Here is another one I want to show him.

Senator KEFAUVER. This is the July one. It seems to be a man with a woman in a boat and he is choking her to death here with a crowbar. Is that in good taste?

Mr. GAINES. I think so.

Mr. HANNOCH. How could it be worse?

Senator HENNINGS. Mr. Chairman, if counsel will bear with me, I don't think it is really the function of our committee to argue with this gentleman. I believe that he has given us about the sum and substance of his philosophy, but I would like to ask you one question, sir.

The CHAIRMAN. You may proceed.

Senator HENNINGS. You have indicated by what—I hope you will forgive me if I suggest—seems to be a bit of self-righteousness, that your motivation was bringing "enjoyment"—is that the word you used?

Mr. GAINES. Yes, sir.

Senator HENNINGS. To the readers of these publications. You do not mean to disassociate the profit motive entirely, do you?

Mr. GAINES. Certainly not.

Senator HENNINGS. Without asking you to delineate as between the two, we might say there is a combination of both, is there not?

Mr. GAINES. No question about it.

Senator HENNINGS. Is there anything else that you would like to say to us with respect to your business and the matters that we are inquiring into here?

Mr. GAINES. I don't believe so.

Senator KEFAUVER. I would like to ask 1 or 2 questions.

The CHAIRMAN. You may proceed, Senator.

Senator KEFAUVER. Mr. Gaines, I had heard that your father really did not have horror and crime comics. When he had the business he printed things that were really funny, and stories of the Bible, but you are the one that started out this crime and horror business.

Mr. GAINES. I did not start crime; I started horror.

Senator KEFAUVER. Who started crime?

Mr. GAINES. I really don't know.

Senator KEFAUVER. Anyway, you are the one who, after you took over your father's business in 1947, you started this sort of thing here. This is the May edition of Horror.

Mr. GAINES. I started what we call our new-trend magazines in 1950.

Senator KEFAUVER. How many of these things do you sell a month, Mr. Gaines?

Mr. GAINES. It varies. We have an advertising guaranty of 1,500,000 a month for our entire group.

Senator KEFAUVER. That is for all the Entertaining Comics, of which Shock is one of them? How do you distribute these, Mr. Gaines?

Mr. GAINES. I have a national distributor. There are roughly 10 individual national distributors which handle roughly half of the magazines. The other half is handled by American News.

The 1 of the 10 that I have is Leader News Co.

Senator KEFAUVER. That is a distributor. Then do they sell to wholesalers?

Mr. GAINES. They in turn sell to seven-hundred-odd wholesalers around the country.

Senator KEFAUVER. The wholesalers then pass it out to the retailers, the drug stores, and newsstands; is that right?

Mr. GAINES. That is right.

Senator KEFAUVER. They are all sold on a consignment basis?

Mr. GAINES. They are all returnable.

Senator KEFAUVER. So your magazines along with what other wholesaler may be handling, are taken in a package to the retailer and left there and he is supposed to put them on his stand and sell them?

Mr. GAINES. Yes.

Senator KEFAUVER. And if he does not sell them, or does not display them, then he is liable to get another retailer?

Mr. GAINES. No, we cover every retailer as far as I know.

Senator KEFAUVER. You don't like things to be put back and resold. You would like them to be sold.

Mr. GAINES. I would prefer it. Comics are so crowded today, I think there are some 500 titles, that it is impossible for any retailer to give all 500 different places.

Senator KEFAUVER. I notice in this edition of May 14 the one in which you have the greasy Mexican the first page has apparently two shootings going on at the same time here, then on the next page is an advertisement for young people to send a dollar in and get the Panic for the next 8 issues. Is that not right?

Mr. GAINES. That is right.

Senator KEFAUVER. This says the editors of Panic, 225 Lafayette Street. That is you?

Mr. GAINES. That is right.

Senator KEFAUVER. Then the attraction here is "I dreamed I went to a fraternity smoker in my Panic magazine," you have dice on the floor and cigarettes, somebody getting beer out, somebody laying on his back taking a drink. Do you think that is all right?

Mr. GAINES. This is an advertisement for one of my lampoon magazines. This is a lampoon of the Maiden-Form brassiere ad, I dreamed I went to so-and-so in my Maiden-Form brassiere, which has appeared in the last 6 years in national family magazines showing girls leaping through the air in brassieres and panties.

We simply lampoon by saying "I dreamed I went to a panic smoker in my Panic magazine."

Senator KEFAUVER. I mean, do you like to portray a fraternity smoker like that?

Mr. GAINES. This is a lampoon magazine. We make fun of things.

The CHAIRMAN. You think that is in good taste?

Mr. GAINES. Yes, sir.

Senator KEFAUVER. I have looked through these stories. Every one of them seems to end with murder, practically. I have looked through this one where they have the greasy Mexican and the Puerto Rican business. I can't find any moral of better race relations in it, but I think that ought to be filed so that we can study it and see and take into consideration what Mr. Gaines has said.

The CHAIRMAN. Mr. Gaines, you have no objection to having this made a part of our permanent files, have you?

Mr. GAINES. No, sir.

The CHAIRMAN. Then, without objection, it will be so ordered. Let it be exhibit No. 12.

(The magazine referred to was marked "Exhibit No. 12," and is on file with the subcommittee.)

Senator KEFAUVER. Is Mr. Gaines a member of the association that we talked about here this morning?

Mr. GAINES. No longer. I was a member for about 2 or 3 years and I resigned about 2 or 3 years ago.

Senator KEFAUVER. How did you happen to resign, Mr. Gaines?

Mr. GAINES. Principally for financial reasons.

Senator KEFAUVER. It only has $15,000 a year for the whole operation?

Mr. GAINES. At that time my share would have been $2,000. At that time, also, about 10 percent of the publishers were represented. I was a charter member of the association. I stuck with it for 2 or 3 years.

The theory was that we were going to get all the publishers into it and then the burden of financial—

Senator KEFAUVER. Did you have any argument about censorship, about this gentleman, Mr. Schultz, who was here, not liking the kind of things you were publishing?

Mr. GAINES. No sir. Mr. Schultz and I frequently had disagreements which we would iron out and I would make the changes he required until I decided to resign.

The CHAIRMAN. Did you have any part, Mr. Gaines, in preparing that code?

Mr. GAINES. No, the code was prepared by, I believe, the first board of directors of the association. I was on the board of directors later on, but not at first.

The CHAIRMAN. Did you subscribe to the code?

Mr. GAINES. Yes, sir.

The CHAIRMAN. Did you think that publishing a magazine like this for example would still be within the code?

Mr. GAINES. No, sir.

Senator KEFAUVER. You admit none of this would come within that code?

Mr. GAINES. Certain portions of the code I have retained. Certain portions of the code I have not retained. I don't agree with the code in all points.

Senator KEFAUVER. The code that you have here, none of your stories would come in that code. You could not print any of these if you complied with the full code we read here this morning.

Mr. GAINES. I would have to study the story and study the code to answer that.

Senator KEFAUVER. How much is your monthly income from all your corporations with this thing, Mr. Gaines?

Mr. GAINES. You mean by that, my salary?

Senator KEFAUVER. No. How much do you take in a month from your publications?

Mr. GAINES. I wouldn't know monthly. We figure it annually.

Senator KEFAUVER. Let us say gross.

Mr. GAINES. I don't know.

Senator KEFAUVER. What is your best estimate annually?

Mr. GAINES. I would say about $80,000 a month gross.

Senator KEFAUVER. How many books did you say you printed a month?

Mr. GAINES. A million and a half guaranteed sale. We print about two, two and a half million.

Senator KEFAUVER. How much net do you make a month out of it, that is, the corporations?

Mr. GAINES. Last year it came to about $4,000 a month.

Senator KEFAUVER. Do you have several corporations, Mr. Gaines?

Mr. GAINES. Yes, sir,

Senator KEFAUVER. How many corporations do you have?

Mr. GAINES. I have five.

Senator KEFAUVER. Why do you have five corporations?

Mr. GAINES. Well, I don't really know. I inherited stock in five corporations which were formed by my father before his death. In those days he started a corporation, I believe, for every magazine. I have not adhered to that.

I have just kept the original five and published about two magazines in each corporation.

Senator KEFAUVER. Do you not think the trouble might have been if one magazine got in trouble that corporation would not adversely affect the others?

Mr. GAINES. Oh, hardly.

Senator KEFAUVER. You did get one magazine banned by the attorney general of Massachusetts, did you not?

Mr. GAINES. The attorney general of Massachusetts reneged and claims he has not banned it. I still don't know what the story was.

Senator KEFAUVER. Anyway, he said he was going to prosecute you if you sent that magazine over there any more.

Mr. GAINES. He thereafter, I understand, said he never said he would prosecute.

Senator KEFAUVER. That is the word you got through, that he was going to prosecute you?

Mr. GAINES. Yes.

Senator KEFAUVER. When was that?

Mr. GAINES. Just before Christmas.

Senator KEFAUVER. Which magazine was that?

Mr. GAINES. That was for Panic No. 1.

Senator KEFAUVER. Just one other question. There is some association that goes over these things. Do you make any contribution to the memberships of any associations?

Mr. GAINES. No.

Senator KEFAUVER. Any committee that supervises the industry?

Mr. GAINES. No. There is no such committee or organization aside from the Association of Comic Magazine Publishers.

Senator KEFAUVER. You said you had a guaranteed sale of a million and a half per month.

Mr. GAINES. We guarantee the advertisers that much.

Senator KEFAUVER. So that you do have some interest in seeing that the distributor and wholesaler and retailer get your magazines out because you guarantee the advertisers a million and a half sales a month?

Mr. GAINES. I have a very definite interest. Unfortunately, I don't have a thing to do with it.

Senator KEFAUVER. Thank you, Mr. Chairman.

Mr. HANNOCH. Could I ask one or two questions?

The CHAIRMAN. Mr. Hannoch.

Mr. HANNOCH. What is this organization that you maintain called the Fan and Addict Club for 25 cents a member?

Mr. GAINES. Simply a comic fan club.

Mr. HANNOCH. You advertise the children should join the club?

Mr. GAINES. Yes.

Mr. HANNOCH. What do they do? Do they pay dues?

Mr. GAINES. No.

Mr. HANNOCH. What do they send 25 cents in for?

Mr. GAINES. They get an arm patch, an antique bronze pin, a 7 by 11 certificate and a pocket card, the cost of which to me is 26 cents without mailing.

Mr. HANNOCH. After you get a list of all these kids and their families and addresses, what do you do with the list?

Mr. GAINES. I get out what we call fan and addict club bulletins. The last bulletin was principally made up of names and addresses of members who had back issues they wanted to trade with other members.

Mr. HANNOCH. Did anybody buy that list from you and use it?

Mr. GAINES. No, sir; I have never sold it.

Mr. HANNOCH. Do you know anything about this sheet called, "Are you a Red dupe?"

Mr. GAINES. Yes, sir; I wrote it.

Mr. HANNOCH. How has it been distributed?

Mr. GAINES. It has not been distributed. It is going to be the inside front cover ad on five of my comic magazines which are forthcoming.

Mr. HANNOCH. And it is going to be an advertisement?

Mr. GAINES. Not an advertisement. It is an editorial.

Mr. HANNOCH. Do other magazines have copies of this to be used for the same purpose?

Mr. GAINES. No, sir.

Mr. HANNOCH. You haven't made this available to the magazines as yet?

Mr. GAINES. No, sir; and I don't intend to.

Mr. HANNOCH. You believe the things that you say in this ad that you wrote?

Mr. GAINES. Yes, sir.

Mr. HANNOCH. That anybody who is anxious to destroy comics are Communists?

Mr. GAINES. I don't believe it says that.

Mr. HANNOCH. The group most anxious to destroy comics are the Communists?

Mr. GAINES. True, but not anybody, just the group most anxious.

The CHAIRMAN. Are there any other questions?

Mr. HANNOCH. No.

Mr. BEASER. I have some questions.

The CHAIRMAN. Mr. Beaser.

Mr. BEASER. Just to settle the point which came up before, Mr. Gaines, who is it that gets the idea for this, for one of your stories, you, your editor, the artist, the writer? Where does it come from?

Mr. GAINES. Principally from my editors and myself.

Mr. BEASER. Not from the artists?

Mr. GAINES. No.

Mr. BEASER. He just does what he is told?

Mr. GAINES. He just followed the story and illustrates it.

Mr. BEASER. He is told what to do and how to illustrate it?

Mr. GAINES. No, our artists are superior artists. They don't have to be given detailed descriptions.

Mr. BEASER. He has to be told what it is?

Mr. GAINES. It is lettered in before he draws it.

Mr. BEASER. He knows the story pretty much, so he knows what he can fit in?

Mr. GAINES. Yes.

Mr. BEASER. You said that you had a circulation of 5 million Bible storybooks.

Mr. GAINES. Yes.

Mr. BEASER. How many years is this?

Mr. GAINES. Twelve years, since 1942.

Mr. BEASER. In other words, in little over 3-1/2 months you sell more of your crime and horror than you sell of the Bible stories?

Mr. GAINES. Quite a bit more.

Mr. BEASER. They seem to go better?

Mr. GAINES. This is a 65-cent book. The crime-and-horror book is a 10-cent book. There is a difference.

Mr. BEASER. No further questions, Mr. Chairman.

The CHAIRMAN. Thank you very much, Mr. Gaines.

Mr. GAINES. Thank you, sir.

The CHAIRMAN. Will counsel call the next witness?

Mr. BEASER. Mr. Walt Kelly.

The CHAIRMAN. Mr. Kelly, do you have some associates?

Mr. KELLY. I have, sir.

The CHAIRMAN. Do you want them to come up and sit with you?

Mr. KELLY. I think I would enjoy the company.

The CHAIRMAN. Fine. We would enjoy having them up here. I will swear you all at one time.

Do you solemnly swear that the testimony you will give to this subcommittee of the Committee on the Judiciary of the United States Senate, will be the truth, the whole truth, and nothing but the truth, so help you God?

Mr. KELLY. I do.

Mr. CANIFF. I do.

Mr. MUSIAL. I do.

TESTIMONY OF WALT KELLY, ARTIST, CREATOR OF POGO, AND PRESIDENT, NATIONAL CARTOONISTS SOCIETY, NEW YORK, N.Y.; MILTON CANIFF, ARTIST, CREATOR OF STEVE CANYON, NEW YORK, N.Y.; AND JOSEPH MUSIAL, EDUCATIONAL DIRECTOR, NATIONAL CARTOONISTS SOCIETY, NEW YORK, N.Y.

Mr. HANNOCH. Will you give your name, sir?

Mr. KELLY. Walt Kelly, 2 Fifth Avenue, artist, drawer of Pogo, New York City.

Mr. BEASER. Have you a title, Mr. Kelly, in the association?

Mr. KELLY. I am the president of the National Cartoonists Society. I forgot about that. I just took office last night.

Mr. CANIFF. Milton Caniff, New York City, N.Y. I draw Steve Canyon for Chicago Sun-Times Syndicate, and King Features Syndicate.

Mr. MUSIAL. Joseph Musial. I am educational director for the King Features Syndicate. I am director for King Features Syndicate and educational director for the Cartoonists Society.

I live in Manhasset, Long Island, N.Y.

The CHAIRMAN. Thank you very much, gentlemen, you may be seated.

Mr. Counsel?

Mr. BEASER. You have a set method that you want to proceed in?

Mr. KELLY. We thought we would do a little commercial work here and show you some of the ways we proceed in our business.

However, before we get into that, I just want to take a moment to acquaint you in some degree at least with my own experience and I think it might be of use or value if the other gentleman would give you somewhat of their background.

The CHAIRMAN. I am sure it would be very helpful.

Mr. KELLY. I have been in the newspaper business and animated cartoons and cartooning generally since about 13 years of age. I regret to say that constitutes about 28 years now.

I got into the comic-book business at one time back in 1940 or 1941 and had some experience with its early days as before the 1947 debacle of so many crime magazines and so on.

In those days there was even then a taste on the part of children for things which are a little more rugged than what I drew. So that I was faced with the problem of putting into book form, into comic form, comic-book form, things which I desired to make popular, such as an American fairy story or American folklore type of stories.

I found after a while that this was not particularly acceptable.

The CHAIRMAN. Would you raise your voice just a little.

Mr. KELLY. I decided I would help clean up the comic-book business at one time, by introducing new features, such as folklore stories and things having to do with little boys and little animals in red and blue pants and that sort of thing.

So when my comic book folded, the one I started doing that with, I realized there was more to it than met the eye.

Perhaps this was the wrong medium for my particular efforts. Since then I have been in the strip business, the comic-strip business which is distinguished from the comic books.

We have found in our business that our techniques are very effective for bringing about certain moral lessons and giving information and making education more widespread.

Despite the testimony given before, I would say right offhand that cartoonists are not forced by editors or publishers to draw any certain way. If they don't want to draw the way the publisher or editor wants them to, they can get out of that business.

We have about 300 members of our society, each one of whom is very proud of the traditions and I think small nobility of our craft. We would hesitate, any one of us, to draw anything we would not bring into our home.

Not only hesitate, I don't think any one of us would do it. That is about all I have to say in that regard.

I would like very much to give one statement. May I do that now?

The CHAIRMAN. You may.

Mr. KELLY. This group here endorses a particular statement by the National Cartoonists Society. That statement is this:

The National Cartoonists Society views as unwarranted any additional legislative action that is intended to censor printed material. The society believes in local option. We believe that offensive material of any nature can be weeded from the mass of worthwhile publications by the exercise of existing city, State, and Federal laws.

Further, we believe that the National Cartoonists Society constitutes a leadership in the cartoon field which has previously established popular trends. We therefore will restrict any action we take to continually improving our own material and thus influencing the coattail riders who follow any successful idea.

We believe good material outsells bad. We believe people, even juveniles, are fundamentally decent. We believe, as parents and as onetime children ourselves, that most young people are instinctively attracted to that which is wholesome.

Our belief in this sound commercial theory is only in addition to our belief in free expression and the noble traditions of our profession. Our history abounds in stalwarts of pen and pencil who have fought for freedom for others. For ourselves as artists and free Americans we too cherish freedom and the resultant growth of ideas. We cannot submit to the curb, the fence, or the intimidating word. The United States of America must remain a land where the Govoernment follows the man.

Mr. BEASER. You are not saying that it is not possible to put into comics, crime comics and horror comics, what we have been talking about, things that might have some harmful effect?

Mr. KELLY. I think it is even entirely possible, sir. I think it is the duty of the creator of the material to see that this sort of thing does not get in there.

The creator, apart from the producer or the publisher, is personally responsible for his work.

I somewhat question the good doctor's statement before when he said in response to your question, sir, that perhaps the originators of this material might be under scrutiny, should be, as to their psychiatric situation.

We in the cartoon business sort of cherish the idea that we are all sort of screwball. We resent the implication that any man putting out that kind of stuff is not a screwball. That is another thing we fight for.

Senator HENNINGS. I would like to say to Mr. Kelly that I think your statement is admirable. I am a frustrated cartoonist myself. I wanted to be one when I was a boy and I got off the track. I have noticed the chairman of our committee doing a good deal of sketching during some of the hearings. He is really a very fine artist.

Without asking you to be invidious or to pass upon any thing ad hominem here with respect to any other publication, is it your opinion that there are certain publications being circulated and calculated to appeal to children in their formative years, their immature years, and from your understanding of the profession—and I call it one because it is; your strip is clean and enlightening as is Mr. Caniff's; the very best in the business—do you not deplore, do you gentlemen not deplore some of these things that you see purveyed to the children and in a sense pandering to the taste, or do you think those things will right themselves? Do you think sooner or later that the harm, if such exists, is outweighed by a good many other things?

Mr. KELLY. I think basically that is our position; yes, sir.

Senator HENNINGS. You realize, of course, the great danger of censorship?

Mr. KELLY. I realize, too, sir, the great danger of the magazines in question.

Senator HENNINGS. So it is a rough problem; is it not?

Mr. KELLY. We are put in a rather unpleasant position.

We don't like to be put in a position to defend what we will defend to the last breath.

The CHAIRMAN. Mr. Caniff do you feel the same way?

Mr. CANIFF. Yes, sir; but if I may, I would like to point out here because it has not been done, we first of all represent the newspaper strip as contrasted with the comic book. It is a fact, of course, as you all well know, that the newspaper strip is not only censored by each editor who buys it, precensors it, which is his right, but by the syndicate's own editors, who are many, and highly critical, and

then this censorship includes the readers themselves, who are in a position to take the editor to task for printing your material and they are quick to respond.

So we are never in doubt as to our status. There will never be any question after the fact. You almost know by the time it hits the street whether or not your material is acceptable to the reader.

So we are in this white-hot fight of public judgment, which is as it should be.

For instance, Walt's strip runs in 400 newspapers. Mine in 350, Blondie in 1,300 out of the 1,500 dailies. That means we have a daily circulation of 55 or 75 million. So that we are in front of the pack all the time and highly vulnerable, as a result.

I bring this in here because I think it is germane on this principle alone, that we also have comic books publishing our material so that we are in this field as well.

It is pointed toward perhaps a little audience in the simple sense that we hope to sell to the daily audience that reads the 10-cent book.

But we are in effect as responsible as well. Insofar as deploring individual books, that is a matter of individual taste. Some books I like which you wouldn't like. I can't say blanketly, for instance, that I dislike all crime comics or I think they are bad. I think they are only good or bad as they affect you, the individual, and by the same token the individual reader of any age group is affected relatively rather than as a group and cannot be condemned I believe, as a group.

The CHAIRMAN. That is a very fine statement.

Mr. CANIFF. Thank you very much. Would you like to add anything, Mr. Musial?

Mr. MUSIAL. I am supposed to be educational director. I can see I have to give my job over to Mr. Caniff. He presented my thoughts better than I could.

I would like to say, I think cartoons are of a sort and instead of making a speech at this particular time I brought in an editorial drawing which I made, which I think germane to the situation. I would like to place this on the board, with your permission.

The CHAIRMAN. Would you please do that.

Mr. KELLY. Mr. Chairman, we would appreciate very much showing you a few of the things that we have been doing, one of which is a series of talks that I personally have been giving before journalism students, newspaper groups, luncheon clubs, and other respectable bodies and people in search of some sort of education, trying to point out what is the basis of the philosophical workings of the comic strip.

I think I can use my own strip as an example, and you can see what thought goes into what we do and how we do it.

[Demonstrating.] In the first place, in every one of our strips we have a central character around whom we base most of our plotting and action.

In my case it happens to be a character who is supposed to look like a possum, in effect; he is a possum by trade, but he doesn't really work at it because actually he happens to be related to most of the people that read comic strips.

Now, he looks a little bit like a monster. This little character actually looks a little bit like a monster.

On the other hand, he is supposed to be a possum and he had this turned-up, dirty nose and a rather innocent expression on his face which is indicative of a little boy because we usually have more readers that are little boys than are possums.

With this innocent, sweet character are a number of rather disreputable characters. The reason I bring up most of these is that each one represents a certain facet of one man's personality, unfortunately mine.

Here is an alligator who at one time worked as a political expert for Pogo. Pogo ran for the Presidency of the United States, and, of course, didn't make it. Now, he, we thought, would make an excellent political type because he has a sort of thick alligator skin and some say a head to match, and so on. He is the sort of character that stands around street corners and smokes cigars.

Along with that character are several other unfortunate people who got into the swamp. One is a dog who is very proud of being a dog. Of course, those of you who have been dogs in your time understand his position in that.

Senator KEFAUVER. You are not talking about a doghouse, now?

Mr. KELLY. No, I am staying away from that. This particular dog is the kind of dog who feels that he knows all the answers and has a great deal of respect for his own judgment and we all know people like that.

One other character who is probably pertinent to the kind of work I try to do is a little character known as the porcupine. Now, this character is a very grumpy sort of character. He looks like most of us do when we get up in the morning. He has generally a sort of sour-faced kind of philosophy. It is a long time after lunch and I am drawing these from the side, so they may have a sort of lean to them.

He is very sour about everything, but he says, "You never should take life very seriously because it ain't permanent." These are the sources of things that go into comic strips.

When I talk before journalism people I try to tell them these are various facets of one man's personality, mine, yours, that everyone has in him the ability to be all of the cruel, unkind, unpleasant, wonderful and pitiful people that exist in the world.

That is my message to young journalism students, because they are in search of the truth. They sometimes fight it and sometimes are able to report on it.

For myself, I have never received any intimidation nor have I been dropped by editor or publisher for anything I wanted to say.

All I have ever been dropped for is because I was lousy.

This character here, for example, is known as the deacon. He is one of those busybodies who assumes that everything he has to say is of such importance that I have to letter his script in a gothic type, which is sometimes readable and sometimes not. I assure you when you can't read it, it is not because I am hiding anything; it is because I can't letter very well.

That man is willing to prescribe for everyone and whatever he believes in very firmly, having borrowed it from someone else. He is out to do you good whether it kills you or not. That is not his concern.

Then every cartoonist being somewhat dishonest—cartoonists are very much like people—we sometimes introduce into our strips things which we hope will be cute and will get the ladies to write in and say "Ah." This is a little puppy dog who shows up every once in a while, and the ladies do write in and think he is very cute.

I won't continue with this because we will run out of paper. Milt won't have any room.

But I would like to just say that in delivering a serious lecture, one which involves trying to make these young people feel that it is possible in our newspapers as they exist today to express themselves, that we still have a great heritage of freedom in our press, one which we want to keep, one which if you are good enough you can make daily use of.

Young people are somewhat intimidated before they become actual journalists so that they are a little frightened. They think that publishers and editors are going to bring great pressure to bear on them; they are not going to be able to say what they would like to say, so a word coming from a silly cartoonist on the outside, a man who has grown at least to the point where he can buy his own cigars, they are refreshed by this sort of experience.

We find as cartoonists that using our simple techniques of making drawings and making statements that the two somehow become entwined, the people are willing to listen because we are making pictures largely, but willing to listen also because we do have, I believe, a great tradition of trying to express the truth in a decent and sometimes, we hope, humorous way.

We believe that this is the way of America. We think it will continue.

I am sure you gentlemen are as much concerned with it as I. I know that is why we are here.

The CHAIRMAN. Speaking as one member of the committee, Mr. Kelly, I can say that you cartoonists do make a great contribution to this country.

Mr. KELLY. Thank you, sir.

The CHAIRMAN. I am sure my colleagues will agree with that statement.

Mr. KELLY. I would like to add one thing to probably clear up what I was doing here. It probably escaped a lot of us. It escaped me.

I was trying to show here the different facets of personality. It is my belief that each one of us contains all these horrible things which we sometimes see in crime books, not in any enlarged form, but way back in there are things. That is why I try to bring out and Milt tries to bring out and 300 other cartoonists in our society try to bring out other things which are much better than that. We believe as people read comic strips they will get to realize that all other people are very much like ourselves and that they will be rather patient and understanding in trying to judge their fellow men.

The CHAIRMAN. Thank you very much, Mr. Kelly. That is a fine presentation.

Mr. CANIFF. Mr. Chairman, I would like to follow with this: As you can see, we are attempting not to debate with Dr. Wertham, whose opinion we value very highly, but rather to make this point, that the newspaper comic strip does two things, and we think this is extremely important.

First, it is to entertain, as you saw in the case of Walt's presentation, just the presentation is entertaining, aside from his message.

Second, the public servant aspect of this thing which we want to put on the record, because the horrible stuff is much more fascinating than the good stuff, but I think you agree with us that the good stuff should be on the record, too.

Many of these are simply incidents in our daily lives, because we spend almost as much time doing the public service kind of thing as our regular strips; in fact, it becomes an enormous problem.

In this instance you will see, for instance, Mr. Musial here with Governor Dewey during a New York State Department of Health mental hygiene campaign to which he gave a great amount of time, and other artists involved in the society as well.

This is Dagwood Splits the Atom, which was prepared with the scientific views of Leslie Grove, General Dunning, and so forth.

This has to do with the bond sale during the war, the use of the comic strips.

This is a bulletin, rather a booklet, which was prepared for boys who are sent to Warwick School, to the New York State Reformatory.

This is to tell them not how to get in the reformatory, but how to get out of it on the assumption they have read comic books.

This is to show if they conduct themselves properly they will get paroled back to their parents.

This obviously is to get kids to brush their teeth, using Dennis the Menace; of course he is not a menace; the title is apocryphal. These are simply incidents of the same thing.

All the people know the Disney comics. The widest selling comic book in the whole country and in Canada is Donald Duck. It outsells every magazine on the stand; that includes Life, the Saturday Evening Post.

As a matter of fact, the Dell comic books constitute 30 percent of the comic books published. They think it is too much that they even dropped Dick Tracy because it was a crime comic.

These pictures with General Dunning, General Eisenhower, President Truman had to do with the bond campaigns in which we participated. This is in this case Steve Canyon's Air Power. It so happens, speaking of people condoning comic books or endorsing them, this is endorsed by General Doolittle.

The CHAIRMAN. I might add it is endorsed by the junior Senator from New Jersey, too.

Mr. CANIFF. Thank you, Senator. I hope just for the simple business of letting you know how the other half live, shall we say, that we will do some good with the very medium which is fighting for its life, if you will, and we think very highly of the industry as such, because of its enormous potential.

Thank you.

The CHAIRMAN. Thank you very much, Mr. Caniff.

Are there any questions, Senator Kefauver?

Senator KEFAUVER. I wondered, Mr. Kelly and Mr. Caniff, how do you feel you can get at this sort of thing? I know you don't think this is a good influence, some of these horror comics that you see and none of us like. How do you get at a situation like this?

Mr. KELLY. I don't know. I have no idea, sir. My personal philosophy on such a thing would be that we must educate people to not like that sort of thing or to at least not produce it.

How we can do that, I don't know. It does seem to me that this is a manifestation of a particularly bad world situation at this time, that these are not in themselves the originators of juvenile delinquency so much as juvenile delinquency is there and sometimes these are the juvenile delinquents' handbooks.

I would be frightened at doing anything about it, sir.

Senator KEFAUVER. Who are the men drawing these cartoons? Are they members of your society?

Mr. KELLY. If they are, and doing it under assumed names, and in very bad style—they are not very good drawings actually—when a man is admitted to our society we don't just assume he can draw.

Senator KEFAUVER. As a member of your society, is there a code that he is not supposed to draw obscene and horror stuff of this kind?

Mr. KELLY. Yes, sir; our statement of things that we believe in encompasses anything that a decent man would be proud to sign his name to.

The CHAIRMAN. You have an established code, Mr. Kelly?

Mr. KELLY. We have, sir.

The CHAIRMAN. I wonder if we could have a copy of that.

Mr. KELLY. I will be delighted to send it to you.

The CHAIRMAN. That will be filed with the subcommittee's permanent file. Let it be exhibit No. 13.

(The document referred to was marked "Exhibit No. 13," and is on file with the subcommittee.)

Senator KEFAUVER. In substance what is your code?

Mr. KELLY. In substance our code is that if any man chooses to take advantage of his position, a unique position, where he has learned to draw and so influence other people, if he wants to take advantage of that to spread indecency or obscenity or in any way prove himself to be an objectionable citizen, we don't have room for him in the society.

Senator KEFAUVER. Now, this picture here of the woman with her head cut off seems to be by Johnny Craig. Do you know him?

Mr. KELLY. I don't know him, sir.

Senator KEFAUVER. Do you think these may be assumed names?

Mr. KELLY. I would doubt it. There are so many markets for our work that it takes a man who is interested in that sort of thing to pick up the job, I would say. None of our members need the work.

Senator KEFAUVER. None of your members do things of this kind?

Mr. KELLY. I haven't examined all their work, and I can't truthfully swear they don't, but I will be surprised and we will take action if they do.

Senator KEFAUVER. What would you do if you found they did?

Mr. KELLY. They would violate our code.

Senator KEFAUVER. What would you do about it?

Mr. KELLY. I don't know. Maybe invite them outside.

Senator KEFAUVER. This one seems to be by Geans.

Mr. KELLY. There was an astronomer—not, it couldn't be him.

Senator KEFAUVER. Here is another one by Jack Davis.

Mr. KELLY. We don't know them, really.

Senator KEFAUVER. I think we all commend you gentlemen on having an organization of this kind in which you do promote ethical procedure and try to get your members to only paint wholesome pictures and ideas.

Mr. KELLY. Thank you.

The CHAIRMAN. Mr. Musial had something he wanted to add.

Mr. MUSIAL. I wanted to present all the Senators with a copy of that drawing which interprets my feeling about what can be done. When the Senator asked about what we can do, I think the important thing that can be done and must be done and the only thing that can be done, is that once the American public is aware of the things that this committee is aware of, if we can get that over to the American people, then under our kind of democracy I think action will follow in a certain direction which will guarantee results.

I hate to say this, but I suggest that the committee solicit our services.

The CHAIRMAN. We do that.

Mr. MUSIAL. Here is a story in the New York Times of last Saturday. We have already contributed a book. I would like that included in the record, if I may.

The CHAIRMAN. It will be included. Let it be exhibit No. 14.

(The information referred to was marked "Exhibit No. 14," and reads as follows:)

EXHIBIT NO. 14

(From the New York Times, April 17, 1954)

COMIC BOOKS HELP CURB DELINQUENCY

STATE SCHOOL ADOPTS IDEA TO ALLAY INMATES' FEARS—JUDGE BACKS USE

(By Murray Illson)

Comic books, often accused of causing juvenile delinquency, also can be used to help cure it, in the opinion of A. Alfred Cohen, superintendent of the State Training School for Boys at Warwick, N.Y.

Mr. Cohen was in the city yesterday with a batch of comic books that had been printed by youths committed to the institution. The books have been endorsed by John Warren Hill, presiding justice of the domestic relations court. He called them "a very helpful and constructive step."

Justice Hill has been concerned with the increase of juvenile delinquency over the years, and has made many speeches trying to get people aroused enough to do something about it.

STORY OF THE SCHOOL

The comic books that Mr. Cohen had were all alike. He presented one for inspection. It was drawn by Charles Biro, chairman of the child welfare committee of the National Cartoonists Society, which has taken a special interest in the Warwick State Training School. The book's 8 pages, printed in color, told the story of the school.

Mr. Cohen explained that the purpose of the book was to allay the fears of boys who were being committed to the school, which is in Orange County, 55 miles from New York. Probation officers in the city's children's courts, which are part of the domestic relations' court, give the books to boys who are being sent to Warwick for rehabilitation.

Warwick, Mr. Cohen noted, is 1 of the State's 2 institutions for delinquent boys. Consisting of 40 buildings and 800 acres, it now has 476 boys between the ages of 12 and 16. Ninety-nine percent of them are from New York. Sixty youngsters are in the city's detention center at Youth House, awaiting placement at Warwick.

"We get the boys who are judged by the courts to be seriously delinquent," Mr. Cohen explained. "We maintain a clinic serviced by a psychiatrist, a psychologist and caseworkers who decide when a boy is ready to be sent home. The superintendent, however, has the final decision. The average stay for younger boys is about 14 months; for the older boys it's about 11 months."

Mr. Cohen said that when he went to Warwick 9 years ago the school was getting "the gang-type youngster" who was characterized by loyalty to a gang but who was, for the most part, "normal" in that he did not have serious emotional disturbances.

TODAY'S TYPE DESCRIBED

The type now going to Warwick was described by Mr. Cohen as the "lone wolf, who is very disturbed, very suspicious, can't form relationships with people, feels the world is against him, has never known the meaning of love, and has only experienced failure." He went on to say:

"Many of these kids literally have never had a hot meal before they came to Warwick, never had a full night's sleep and have known only real conflict in the home. The amazing thing is that they behave as well as they do.

"I have never met a youngster among the 8,000 who have passed through Warwick in the time I have been there who hadn't been beaten physically by experts—drunken parents, psychotic parents, or sadistic relatives. We know from first hand that the woodshed doesn't work."

Warwick, Mr. Cohen said, is an "open institution" that does not believe in confinement. It offers boys an academic education, vocational training in farming, and various recreational activities."

Comparatively recently, five boys at the institution were admitted to the local high school, Mr. Cohen said. All completed their courses. One went on to take a premedical course, and another won a college scholarship.

Mr. MUSIAL. I got a big kick out of it, the New York Times printing comics. If any of the press want this, it is available.

Again, like the Chinese who say 1 picture is worth 10,000 words, I would like to add this to it, 1 comic artist supplies more cheer than 10,000 doctors.

The CHAIRMAN. Thank you very much, Mr. Musial.

Does counsel have any further witnesses?

Mr. BEASER. No further witnesses.

The CHAIRMAN. The subcommittee will stand in recess until 10 o'clock tomorrow morning.

(Thereupon, at 4:30 p.m., a recess was taken, to reconvene at 10 a.m., Thursday, April 22, 1954.)

*   *   *   *   *   *   *   *

(The subcommittee reconvened at 2:30 p.m., upon the expiration of the recess.)

The CHAIRMAN. This session of the subcommittee will be in order.

The subcommittee is highly honored today by the presence of a distinguished member of the Canadian Parliament, Mr. Fulton.

Mr. Fulton has had considerable experience with the problem which presently confronts the committee. If Mr. Fulton will come forward, we would like to hear the story as you have experienced it in your great country and our great neighbor, Canada.

You may be seated, Mr. Fulton.

I am going to depart from our usual procedure here in your case. We have been swearing witnesses, but we are not going to swear a member of the Canadian Parliament. You are one of us.

STATEMENT OF HON. E. D. FULTON, MEMBER, HOUSE OF COMMONS, CANADA

Mr. FULTON. I appreciate that very much.

Perhaps for the introductory words, I might stand, because I think it would be appropriate while I express on my behalf the feeling of deep appreciation I have for the honor of this invitation. I hope that my presentation may be of some assistance to you as indicating the course which your neighbor, Canada, followed in attempting to deal with this problem.

As a problem of concern in equal measure to both our countries, I assure you that although I am not a member of the government in Canada, I am quite certain that I speak for all our representatives in Parliament and for Canada as a whole when I say that they appreciate the honor of the invitation and the opportunity to come down and discuss with you these problems of such great mutual concern.

I think it is proper to suggest that this is one more example of the friendship and good neighborliness between our two countries.

I want to express to you, sir, and your colleagues on this subcommittee, my appreciation for the honor of this invitation and the opportunity to come here.

The CHAIRMAN. Thank you. We are grateful to you and grateful to Canada.

Now, Mr. Fulton, you may proceed to present your case in whatever manner you choose and think best.

Mr. FULTON. Mr. Chairman, I have first, two apologies to make. I was late this morning, owing to weather conditions over the airport here. I trust that my delay did not inconvenience your proceedings.

The second apology I have to make is that while I accept the responsibility for it myself, I should have been able to do it, I found that I didn't have sufficient notice to prepare a text, but I have made fairly extensive notes.

If it meets with your convenience, I would be prepared to make a statement outlining our approach to the problem and at the conclusion of that perhaps we could discuss it by way of any questions you might have.

The CHAIRMAN. That procedure will be entirely satisfactory to the subcommittee.

Mr. FULTON. There is one other matter I should explain. Your counsel, Mr. Beaser, asked me if it would be possible for me to arrange to have somebody from either our Federal Department of Justice or a provincial attorney general's office to be available to discuss with you the questions of enforcement of the law which we have in Canada. I regret that again owing to the time factor I was not able to arrange to have any such official with me.

The CHAIRMAN. For the record, the Chair might state that Mr. Fulton refers specifically to the law covering crime comics.

Mr. FULTON. That is correct. But I don't want the fact that no one else is here with me from any of the executive branch of government to be taken as an indication that they would not have liked to come had they been able to arrange it. The attorney general's department of the Province of Ontario expressed their regrets they could not make available a witness in the time at their disposal.

I thought perhaps at first I might make a few general remarks regarding the similarity of the problem as it appears to exist in our two countries.

But before I do so, there is one other introductory remark I would like to make, and that is as to my own position. I think in fairness it should be stated that I am not a member of the Government of Canada; nor, as a matter of fact, am I a member of the majority party.

I am a member of the opposition party. Therefore, I think I should say that nothing I say should be taken as necessarily indicating the views of the Government of Canada.

I will try, however, to the best of my ability, to summarize what I think to be the views of the Government of Canada with respect to this matter.

When I come to subjects or aspects of it in which I feel that it is not safe to indicate that this might be the general view, I shall try to remember to indicate to you that this is my own personal view. But in everything I say I think I should make it clear I am not here in a position to speak for the Government of Canada, but simply as an individual member of Parliament interested in this problem.

I think it goes probably without saying that we, our two countries, find themselves very much in the same situation with respect to this problem of crime comics and their influence on the matter of juvenile delinquency. Our two civilizations, our standards of living, our method of life, are very similar. Our reading habits are by and large similar to yours. Indeed, speaking generally, probably the majority of the reading material in the form of publications, that is, periodicals as distinguished from daily newspapers, have their origin here.

With respect to crime comics, I don't wish to be taken as saying that it is by any means one-way stream of traffic, because I understand some of those published in Canada find their way here and present you with a problem, but I think by and large with respect to the movement across the border of crime comics that is one thing where the balance of trade is somewhat in your favor.

Those features indicate that the problem is similar in both countries.

The CHAIRMAN. It would be safe to say that the balance of trade is largely in our favor in this case, would it not?

Mr. FULTON. That is my impression. You will appreciate that as much as we have enacted legislation which makes it a criminal offense to publish or sell a crime comic, there are not official statistics available as to the volume of these things published in Canada or sold in Canada because it is obvious that people trafficking in an illegal matter are not called upon and if they were, would not furnish the statistics they might be asked for.

We have in Canada examples which we feel indicated pretty clearly that crime comics were of similar nature to those circulating here have an adverse effect upon the thinking and in many cases on the actions of young boys and girls. I am not going to weary your committee with a complete catalog of cases. You probably have had many similar cases referred to you here, but there stands out in my mind a particular case which arose in Dawson Creek in the Yukon territory. One might have thought that that rather remote part of that country might be as insulated as any place might be against crime comics, but there was a case there in which one James M. Watson was murdered by two boys, ages 11 and 13.

At the trial evidence was submitted to show that the boys' minds were saturated with comic book reading. One boy admitted to the judge that he had read as many as 50 books a week, the other boy, 30.

The conclusion which the court came to after careful consideration of the evidence was that the exposure of these children to crime comics had had a definite bearing on the murder. There was no other explanation why the boys should have shot and killed the man driving past in his car. They probably didn't intend to kill him. They were imitating what they had seen portrayed day after day in crime comics to which they were exposed.

The other one is a case of more recent occurrence, reported in a local newspaper on March 11 of this year. I would like to read you the newspaper report. It originated at Westville, Nova Scotia:

Stewart Wright, 14, Wednesday told a coroner's jury how he shot his pal to death March 2, while they listened to a shooting radio program and read comic books about the Two-Gun Kid. The jury returned a verdict of accidental death and recommended that comic books of the type found at the scene be banned.

That, you appreciate, Mr. Chairman, is a case that occurred since the passage of our legislation, which indicates that we have not yet found the complete answer to this problem.

I would like everything I say to be taken subject to that understanding. I am not suggesting that the legislation we have passed is the complete answer.

I do suggest that it is a beginning in the effort to deal with this problem.

If we had the same general situation prevailing in Canada as you have in the United States, that is, a widespread body of opinion to the effect that this type of literature has a harmful influence on the minds of the young, we also had a similar conflict of opinions to that which I understand exists here. The publishers, particularly those engaged in the trade dealing with crime comics and other periodicals and magazines, as I think might be expected, were found on the whole to be on the side which held that these things were not a harmful influence on the minds of children.

I think that the explanation for that, sir, is readily available. They have an interest in the continuation of this stream of traffic. I am not saying, I don't wish to suggest, that they are all acting from improper motives. I am suggesting really that there is an obvious explanation as to why the majority of those concerned in the trade should be found on the one side, that is, on the side which says that these are not harmful.

I also have to confess that many experts and impartial experts in the field of psychiatry were found on the side of those who held that crime comics and similar publications were not harmful to children, but merely provided a useful outlet for what they called their natural violent instincts and tendencies.

Those generally were on the one side and as against them there were by and large all the community organizations, the parent-teacher associations, the federations of home and school, and similar organizations of a general community nature and those more particularly dealing with welfare work.

I would like to take this opportunity of paying here my tribute to the work that many of those organizations in Canada in arousing our people to an awareness of the problem, even if they didn't suggest in producing, as I say, a unanimous opinion as to how it should be dealt with. I say that because I believe that similar organizations here are assisting in that work.

Also on the side of those who came to the conclusion that these things were a harmful influence were the majority of our law-enforcement organizations. I think particularly of our own Federal Department of Justice where back in 1947 and 1948 when the matter was first discussed in Parliament in a concrete form, the Minister himself, speaking for the Government, expressed the view that these crime comics, of which he had been provided with samples, could have no other effect than a harmful one on the minds of young boys and girls.

That was even before we had taken any positive action to deal with the problem.

I also would like to pay my tribute to a noted expert in your own country, and, indeed, in your own city of New York, Dr. Frederic Wertham. I have read extensively from Dr. Wertham's articles and, of course, I read with great interest his latest book, Seduction of the Innocent. I have had considerable correspondence with Dr. Wertham and I think it is fair and accurate to say that insofar as I, myself, made any contribution to this matter and to the enactment of our legislation that I used and found Dr. Wertham's opinions, his quotations, of great assistance and I found they were generally accepted as authoritative in our country in a discussion of this matter.

I am not again saying that opinion was unanimous, but I think it is fair to say that Dr. Wertham's views were given great weight in our country.

The CHAIRMAN. Mr. Fulton, I might interrupt you at this point and, for the record, state that I received this morning upon my arrival here a communication from Dr. Wertham that was hand-delivered and that that communication will be made a part of the subcommittee files.

If at the conclusion of your testimony you would like to examine that letter, you may have that privilege.

Mr. FULTON. I shall be very much obliged, sir. I am looking forward, I might say, to meeting Dr. Wertham later on today.

That that survey of the general field in Canada, I would like to come to a more particular examination of the background of the present Canadian legislation.

We have had for many years—I see I am getting a little ahead of myself. There is another matter which I think I should mention, Mr. Chairman, to give you the full background picture and that is the constitutional position.

Here, I should say that although I am chairman of our own party organization, that is our own caucus committee of the Canadian Parliament dealing with matters having to do with law and law enforcement, I don't wish to pose as an expert lawyer.

The CHAIRMAN. That would compare to our Judiciary Committee, would it not?

Mr. FULTON. Yes, except that this is a committee into which our own party has organized, an opposition party, for the purpose of examining any legislation introduced by the Government having a bearing on those matters. It is because of my interest in that subject, and, to some extent, of my position in my own party, that I have been a spokesman on this matter. I mention that merely to make my position clear. I don't want to be taken as an expert.

I do now want to turn to a consideration of the constitutional position in Canada. I think I stated it correctly but I do so to some extent as an amateur. I mention it because there may be some difference in the constitutional position as between our two countries, particularly when it comes to the subject of law enforcement.

In Canada, broadly speaking, under our Constitution, which is the British-North America Act, all general criminal matters are reserved exclusively to the Federal Parliament, whereas on the other hand, all matters of local law enforcement are left exclusively to the jurisdiction of the provincial government.

When it comes to enacting criminal law, the Federal Parliament alone can act.

When it comes to enforcing that law the responsibility and the authority rests exclusively with the province. No province could enact as part of the criminal law any provision having exclusively application to its own territory.

On the other hand, everything enacted in the realm of general criminal law by the Federal Parliament is equally applicable all across the country.

As to the background of the legislation that we have, there has existed under the criminal code of Canada, which is a statute covering matters of general criminal law, for many years a section dealing with the general problem of literature, obscene literature, indecent objects, indecent exhibitions, and so on. That is found in section 207 of our criminal code.

And I should point out I have here with me a bill which has just this year been passed by the House of Commons, bill 7, which is an act entitled "An Act Respecting the Criminal Law." That is a general revision and recodification of the criminal code for the purpose of consolidating in one fresh statute the original statute, plus all the amending acts which have been passed over a period of some 50 years, since the last general revision. There are only, in a few cases, changes in principle.

Section 207, as it exists in the code now, is reenacted and will be found as section 150 in the bill, which is in the possession of your counsel. This bill has not yet become law because it has not yet passed our Senate, but it is my impression there will not be any changes in the present provisions of section 150 as passed by the House of Commons.

Section 150 incorporates section 207 of the old code, but until 1949 section 207 contained no reference to crime comics as such.

It was concerned exclusively with the matter of obscene objects, or obscure literature, indecent exhibitions, and so on.

I think it was after the last war—this is our experience at any rate—that the problem of crime comics as such came into existence. It seems to me by and large a postwar development. I am not saying it didn't exist before, but on the scale we now have it seems to be a postwar development which is probably the reason why our criminal law didn't refer to it before.

As a result of the emergency of the crime comics and the factors which I have reviewed already as to the public opinion which grew up about it, there was evidenced a considerable demand that something should be done to deal with this problem created by the crime comic. There was a campaign originated by such

organizations as I have already mentioned, the Canadian Federation of Home and Schools, various service clubs organized themselves on a nationwide basis, put on a campaign pressing for some effective action to deal with the problem of crime comics and obscene literature generally.

Parent-teachers' associations joined in this effort. There was in addition considerable work done on it in our House of Commons.

I have already mentioned that in 1947 and 1948, when the matter was drawn to the attention of the Minister of Justice he expressed himself as holding the opinion that it was desirable to do something, although he said up to that time they had not yet been able to figure out any effective measures.

In the course of the discussion as to what should be done, the usual problem arose, and that was to reconcile the conflicting desires to have on the one hand freedom of action, freedom of choice, and on the other hand to prevent the abuse of that very freedom.

The problem is, are you going to have complete freedom of action, or are you going to have a measure of control.

The measure of control, it was generally agreed, divided itself into two alternatives: One, direct censorship; the other, legislative action, legislative action which would lay down the general standards and leave it to the courts to enforce rather than by direct censorship imposed from above by any governmental body.

Just as background, I might say that in Canada there exists no federal censorship as such. There is only in one Province that I am aware of any extensive censorship of literature, and that is in the Province of Quebec.

The majority of our Provinces, if not nearly all, have a form of censorship of movies under the authority of the provincial government. But by and large I think it would be fair to say that the majority opinion in Canada is opposed to the idea of censorship of literature.

I am not saying that that feeling is unanimous, but that seemed to be the feeling that if possible we should avoid bringing in direct censorship. That was my feeling with regard to the matter, not only my individual feeling, but it was my impression of the stated public opinion and, therefore, I felt if we were to get anywhere with it the approach should be by way of legislation to amend the criminal law so as to create an offense on the basis that society regards the continued publication of this material as a danger to society itself, and that society, therefore, through its instrument, its elected representatives, taking cognizance of the problem, is entitled to decide whether it is of sufficient seriousness and danger that the problem is to be dealt with in the usual way under our principle of justice by the elected representatives defining the problem constituting the offense, providing the penalty, and then leaving it to the individual who knows the law, knows what is there, to decide whether he wishes to run the risk, if you like, of continuing in that course of action with the knowledge if he does he may expose himself to the penalty.

In other words, to some extent you might say it is the process of imposing on the individual the obligation of self-censorship instead of imposing it on him by direction from above.

So that was the course that was followed in Canada.

I should perhaps mention one another feature which we have. That is a measure of control at the customs points. I don't know whether you have it, or not. I don't want to go into this in any great detail because I know you have a busy session before you. I will try to summarize it.

In our customs law, and under the tariff items which are approved by Parliament to apply that law there is an item 1201, tariff item 1201, which reads as follows:

> It prohibits the entry into Canada of books, printed paper, drawings, prints, photographs, or representations of any kind of a treasonable or seditious or immoral or indecent character, on the grounds that our criminal code makes those an offense in the country; therefore, we are not going to permit them to come into the country while it is an offense under our law.

That tariff item has not been amended with respect to crime comics, but, by and large, I am informed that the officers of the border points, if they are of the opinion that a particular comic magazine would be an offense under the new revision in the criminal code, they will exercise their own discretion in prohib-

iting its entry, or, if they are in doubt, they will refer it to the department at Ottawa for a ruling as to whether it is admissible or not.

Mr. BEASER. Are the crime comics which go into your country printed in this country, or are the plates sent to Canada for printing?

Mr. FULTON. I am informed it is done in both ways. In some cases the finished article is imported. In other cases the plates are sent over and they are printed in Canada.

Mr. BEASER. You do not know which method predominates, do you?

Mr. FULTON. My impression is that the finished article predominates. Perhaps we could go into that a little more fully later. There is a real problem confronting the customs officials in that we have not had yet very much jurisprudence built up. There have not been many actions in our courts under the new sections with regard to crime comics and the customs officials are loath to set themselves up as censors. They have no hesitation if a particular subject or article has been declared offensive by a court decision in prohibiting its entry, but they find themselves under great difficulty when it comes to saying as to whether or not an article, which has never been the subject of any judicial process, is in fact prohibited under our criminal law.

That is one difficulty.

The other is that the volume of these things moving across the border makes it difficult for them to enforce their own regulations 100 percent, and I think it would be fair to say that customs officers exist mainly for the purpose of collecting duties, customs, and excises, and not for the purpose of indulging in any form of quasi-censoring of literature.

It is an obligation under the tariff item which they willingly undertake, but it is not their main task.

Senator HENNINGS. It may be of interest, perhaps Mr. Fulton is very well aware of this, but Assemblyman James A. Fitzpatrick told me during the recess today that many people come over the border from Canada to Plattsburg, N.Y., which happens to be his home, for the purpose of procuring some of the American published comic or horror books and that they take them back across the border, smuggling them or bootlegging them across, as it were.

Mr. FULTON. That may be so, Senator. The only comment I could make on that is that I regret to say that these things circulate with sufficient freedom in Canada that I am surprised that they find it necessary to come down here for that.

Senator HENNINGS. Like carrying coals to Newcastle.

Mr. FULTON. I think it must be a very incidental purpose of their visit. I am not in any way questioning that it does take place.

What I want to avoid is giving the impression of saying that we have dealt with this effectively in Canada and it is only you that have the problem.

My attitude toward it is that it is still a mutual problem although we have made a beginning.

Senator HENNINGS. You are certainly eminently fair, and I am sure want to be very careful in having made that statement not to cause any misunderstanding on that point.

Thank you, sir.

Mr. FULTON. That, then, in brief, is the background of the situation with respect to the nature of the problem and the actual legislation, or lack of it, up to 1949.

In the fall session of our Parliament in 1949, I introduced a bill, of which I regret I have no longer copies left in my file. There is only one copy left in the file of the Department of Justice. There are plenty of copies of the statute in the annual volume of statutes, but of the bill itself, an individual bill, there is only one copy left readily available. So I had our Department of Justice prepare typewritten facsimiles of the bill as introduced.

I shall be glad to give them to your counsel or your clerk for filing at the end of my presentation. This is as best as can be done, a reproduction of the bill with the front page. This was the inside page, explanatory notes and the back page was blank. It was a short bill. It was introduced by way of an amendment to section 207 of the code.

I think it is short enough that I can read it to you and you can understand then our approach to the problem of trying to find the method of dealing with this subject.

I won't read the introductory words, except as follows:

BILL 10

AN ACT To amend the Criminal Code (Portrayal of Crimes)

His Majesty, by and with the advice and consent of the Senate and House of Commons of Canada, enacts as follows:

Subsection 1 of secton 207 of the Criminal Code, chapter 36 of the Revised Statutes of Canada, 1927, is amended by adding thereto the following:

"(d) prints, publishes, sells, or distributes any magazine, periodical, or book which exclusively or substantially comprises matter depicting pictorially the commission of crimes, real or fictitious, thereby tending or likely to induce or influence youthful persons to violate the law or to corrupt the morals of such persons."

Section 207 in its introductory sections provided that:

Every person shall be guilty of an offense who

and then the introductory sections (a), (b), (c), cover obscene literature, obscene exhibitions and I was adding section (d) to make it a violation to print, sell, distribute a crime comic as a crime.

I would like to read an explanatory note which was submitted at the same time and forms part of the printed material with the bill:

This act is designed to amend the Criminal Code to cover the case of those magazines and periodicals commonly called crime comics, the publication of which is presently legal, but which it is widely felt tend to the lowering of morals and to induce the commission of crimes by juveniles.

The purpose is to deal with these publications not by imposing a direct censorship or by blanket prohibition, but rather by providing in general terms that the publication and distribution as defined in the act shall be illegal and thus leaving it for decision by the court and/or jury, in accordance with the normal principles prevailing at a criminal trial to determine whether or not the publication in question falls within the definition.

That bill was introduced as a private member's bill and given first reading on September 28, 1949. In the debate which followed, after I had outlined my argument in support of the legislation, the Minister of Justice, speaking for the Government, stated that the Government was anxious to take effective action to deal with this problem, they welcomed the introduction of the bill.

However, it raised certain questions with respect to enforcement and, therefore, they asked if it might be stood for the time being while they communicated its contents to the provincial attorneys general to get the benefit of their views as to whether it was necessary; if so, whether it was enforcible in its present suggested form, or whether they themselves would like to see some amendments to make it more workable.

That was done. As a result of the views and opinions offered by provincial attorneys general when the debate was brought on again in committee the bill as introduced was quite extensively amended and in effect given the form of a complete revision and reenactment of the whole of section 207.

In other words, instead of just adding a new clause they incorporated the suggestion into the clause and made it a more workable whole.

It had one more effect which I would like to mention. The amendment to the bill, in that under section 207 in its previous form it was a defense to anyone accused of committing the crime of printing or publishing any obscene literature or crime comic after the amendment carried. It was a defense to the accused person to show that he did not have any knowledge of the indecent content or nature of the publication complained of.

It was felt, particularly with respect to crime comics—you say the specimens on the board this morning—that it would be really pretty ridiculous for anyone to try to plead "Well, I don't know the nature of this thing." The nature is self-evident. It was felt by the attorneys general if we were going to make this section effective not only with respect to crime comics, but with respect to offensive literature generally, really this defense of lack of knowledge of the contents of the articles complained of should be removed.

It would still be the onus on the Crown to prove intent in the general sense of that onus under the criminal law.

Senator HENNINGS. May I ask Mr. Fulton one question? You may have suggested this earlier in your statement.

Does this relate to the publisher, the distributor, and the newsdealer?

Mr. FULTON. Yes, sir; it includes the whole field.

Senator HENNINGS. I take it it is announced in the statute in the subjunctive; is that correct?

Mr. FULTON. Yes.

Senator HENNINGS. They may be joined, in other words, they may be coindictees, they may be individually indicted?

Mr. FULTON. Or they may be proceeded against separately. One may be proceeded against without the other.

I shall have something to say on that a little later. That is an interesting legal point. I mean with respect to the matter of dealing more effectively with the publisher.

I should like, if time permits and you think it important, to say something on that later. But that defense was removed as a result of this amendment.

I have also a facsimile copy of the bill as it was amended in committee as a result of the Government's own suggestions. I shall be glad to file that.

Mr. BEASER. Mr. Fulton, am I wrong in believing that the bill as finally passed was different than the one you introduced in that it made it an offense to print, circulate, and so forth, a crime comic to anyone; whereas, as you read your original bill I got the impression it was aimed at distribution which had as its purpose the influencing of youthful people; is that right?

Mr. FULTON. You are correct. In my initial draft of the bill as first moved the words "thereby tending or likely to induce or influence youthful persons to violate the law or to corrupt the morals of such persons" was included.

Mr. BEASER. Was that for enforcement purposes?

Mr. FULTON. I think so on the basis that the nature of these things and their tendency is self-evident.

Senator HENNINGS. That becomes a jury question.

Mr. FULTON. No; those words are not included in section 207 at the present time. The crime comic as defined in the bill, bill 10, as it eventually passed, was defended as follows:

(7) In this section "crime comic" means a magazine, periodical or book that exclusively or substantially comprises matter depicting pictorially (a) the commission of crimes, real or fictitious—

Now, sir, the only defense as such which is open to an accused under our law, under this bill, is the following:

No one shall be convicted of any offense in this section mentioned if he proves that the public good was served by the acts that are alleged to have been done and that there was no excess in the acts alleged beyond what the public good required.

If he can prove to the satisfaction of a judge or magistrate or judge and jury that the crime comic in fact served the public good, then there is no conviction.

Senator HENNINGS. That is somewhat then in parallel to your English libel law that you require not only that as defense one need establish not only truth as in the United States, but that it be for the public benefit.

Mr. FULTON. I think that, sir, is in the realm of criminal liability only.

Senator HENNINGS. I meant criminal liability, of course.

Mr. FULTON. Yes.

Senator HENNINGS. It must be for the public benefit under the British law, is it not?

Mr. FULTON. I think it might be going perhaps a little beyond, but it must not go too far beyond. There must be some public interest to be served, yes. I think that would be a fair statement.

Now, when the bill came back in its amended form, as I have indicated it in the summary here, it passed the House unanimously. The House of Commons adopted it without any dissenting vote.

It then went to our Senate and there by that time the periodical publisher or some of those engaged in the trade—I shall put it that way—perhaps had only just awakened to what was going on; maybe they thought it would never pass the House of Commons.

What the reason was, I don't know, but at any rate, they made no representation to the House. They didn't ask for its reference to a committee. It goes through the Committee of the Whole House, but they didn't ask for reference to a special committee on the bill and they made no formal presentation.

Then it got to the Senate, having passed the House; they asked to be allowed to appear and make representations. So the Senate referred it to one of its standing committees.

There the publishers appeared and they made representations which took the form of some of the submissions which I have read in the newspaper comment, at any rate on your own proceedings from time to time down here, namely, that these things were not harmful to juveniles; in fact, to some extent they formed a harmless outlet for their natural violent instincts.

Senator HENNINGS. I take it, sir, in defining crime you mean felony. That is in section 7, "crime comic" means a periodical or book that exclusively or substantially comprises matter depicting pictorially the commission of crimes.

Mr. FULTON. There is another amendment I was going to come to, Senator, but I will be glad to deal with that point now.

Senator HENNINGS. I do not mean to distract and divert you.

Mr. FULTON. You are concerned with the definition given to the word "crime"?

Senator HENNINGS. Yes sir; whether you mean felony, misdemeanor; what classification of crime, if any?

Mr. FULTON. I don't think that point has come before our courts.

Senator HENNINGS. For example, if an embezzlement is depicted in a crime comic, a bank teller, let us say, taking money from his employer, or involuntary manslaughter, would, in your judgment, that sort of thing depicted in a comic book constitute a crime within the meaning and purview of your statute?

Mr. FULTON. I would not care to express an opinion on that. I think that would be a matter of individual interpretation by the courts. To my knowledge the point has not arisen.

I think it may be a very important point. I would have to say this, that in my mind in drafting and submitting the original legislation I had in contemplation the crime of violence, what you might call the crime of violence, but taking it over to amend it and amending it, the Government deleted the reference to that type of definition and I had no objection whatever. They had consulted with the law-enforcement officers and the law-enforcement officers felt that a too narrow definition might create obstacles which might create difficulties in the way of its enforcement and no substantial representations against the broadening of the definition were made and so it went through in that form.

I would not care at the moment to express an opinion as to whether the court, looking at it, would say, "Well, the intention of the legislature was to confine it to crimes of violence," or not.

Senator HENNINGS. We would have a most interesting situation, would we not, bearing in mind that the crime of carrying a concealed weapon is a felony in most of our States, having portrayed in a comic a representation indicating that someone was carrying a concealed weapon by verbiage, but the weapon could not be seen.

That would still be carrying it along the line. I certainly do not want to be frivolous or to attempt to make light of part of it but to attempt to present the difficulty this field presents.

Mr. FULTON. I would express this purely as an offhand opinion, that the wording of the statute is wide enough to cover anything which is made a crime by our criminal code. Anything covered in there whether fraud or embezzlement is covered in the criminal code then on the face of it an illustration of a crime of that nature is included in section 207.

It might be an interesting point for defense counsel to raise that as defense the section didn't contemplate that type of crime. Then the court would have to decide what was the intent of the legislature as gathered from the words they used.

So far that point has not come before our courts.

I was mentioning that when it came before our Senate it was referred to a standing committee and the representatives of the trade appeared and made representations against the bill.

Dr. Wertham has an interesting passage in his book in which he records it as having been the opinion expressed that they appeared to be making progress

until they made the mistake of producing to the Senators some examples of their wares, that when that was done their case was out of court.

I can't read the minds of our Senators. All I know is that in the result the standing committee reported the bill back to the Senate without amendment and it passed the Senate as a whole by a vote of 92 to 4.

Having passed the Senate, it then passed both Houses of our Parliament and was proclaimed and became law.

Now, our subsequent experience has been somewhat as follows and here I must say I am speaking on the basis of opinion for the reason, as I have said, statistics on this matter are hard to obtain but it is my impression, and I know this view is shared by the majority of those interested in the problem, the crime comic as such pretty well disappeared from the Canadian newsstands within a year or so following the enactment of this legislation.

But within about the same period of time alternative forms of comic magazines began to appear. Speaking in general terms, these took the form initially of an increase in the number of love and sex and girlie comics which began to hit the newsstands. And that as an interesting comment gave rise to a separate study launched by our Senate on the subject. They set up a committee to look into the sale and distribution of, I think the word they used was salacious literature.

One of the reasons why the demand for that rose so rapidly was the rapid increase in the circulation of that type of pulp magazine following the virtual disappearance of the crime comic.

I mention that merely as an interesting aside.

Then there crept back into circulation in Canada the crime comic again in its original form, but it also began to appear in other alternative forms and there the alternative form I have in mind is what I think you have described generally as the horror comic. I would venture the opinion that the reason the crime comic to a lesser extent and the horror comic to a greater extent reappeared and began to appear respectively, was in part because of the lack of prosecution of any publisher or printer or vendor under the new crime comic section. There were no prosecutions until about a year ago. And partly perhaps due to the fact that the public and myself and other similar interested persons included may have felt, now we have done our job, we can sit back and relax, with the result that there wasn't the same vigilant supervision of the newsstands to pick out offensive publications, bring them to the attention of the authorities and demand prosecution.

Whatever the reasons, anyway, the crime comic in its original form began to reappear and the horror comic in a much exhilarated form—I mean it is now circulating to an extent even greater than the present circulation of the crime comic and it is in Canada at any rate relatively newer in form and appearance. It has made its appearance later than crime comics. I think it would be fair to say it made its appearance only after the enactment of legislation in 1949.

But I have to express it again as my personal opinion that even the horror comic was in fact adequately covered by the legislation which we had enacted in 1949 because that legislation refers by definition to the commission of crimes, real or fictitious.

Now, again, it might be an interesting legal point as to whether the courts would say that a fictitious crime means merely a crime committed by a human being, the crime had not taken place in fact, whether they would confine it to that or whether it would be broad enough to cover the case of a crime committed by these fantastic beings, ghoul of the swamp and the Batman, those creatures that can have no existence in reality, but, nevertheless, commit what, if committed by a human being, would be crime.

It is interesting to speculate whether the words "crime, real or fictitious" would apply.

Senator HENNINGS. That would apply perhaps to a crime committed by Mickey Mouse, for example, a more innocuous kind of comic character.

Mr. FULTON. Yes, sir. Again it is a question, of course, whether the courts interpret the intent of the legislature as gathered from the words of the statute.

Mr. BEASER. Assuming you are able to find out how the American crime comics are getting into Canada, are you able under your statute to proceed against the publisher or distributor?

Mr. FULTON. In the United States?

Mr. BEASER. Yes.

Mr. FULTON. No. He is beyond our reach. His crime is not committed in Canada, you see. Unless he were to come and surrender himself voluntarily to the jurisdiction of our courts, I don't think there is any way; I don't think extradition proceedings would lie.

My understanding is that unless he came to Canada and committed the crime and came back here we could not use extradition proceedings.

Mr. BEASER. The question is whether under the Canadian statute Canada is able to proceed against an American publisher who publishes in this country crime and horror comics which then get into Canada, or whether they can proceed against a distributor who sends them into Canada.

Mr. FULTON. I think the first.

Senator HENNINGS. They would have no jurisdiction in the matter in the first place.

Mr. FULTON. Unless he submitted himself voluntarily to the jurisdiction of our courts, which I can't see him doing.

Senator HENNINGS. You would have no venue then?

Mr. FULTON. I think if he voluntarily submitted himself to jurisdiction we would. I think the execution of the sentence might, of course, present some interesting problems, but in effect I don't think it arises. In effect my opinion is—and I take it Senator Hennings concurs—that the first person we can deal with is the man who first imports it in Canada and there is no suggestion that we should proceed against the American publisher.

If we deal with the man who brings it in we are dealing effectively with it from our point of view. What is done here is a matter entirely for your own determination.

Mr. BEASER. Are you able to get the distributor; is it known or —

Mr. FULTON. It can be ascertained. I have to say with regret, in my view we are not proceeding sufficiently vigorously in our own country against the distributors, against the man who first puts this offensive material into circulation.

I would like to deal with that at greater length a little later.

I think that is one defect not only in our laws which exist, but in the enforcement of our law.

Now, I just was mentioning that these things have reappeared, although I think again it would be fair to say they don't circulate to the same extent as they did previous to the enactment of the legislation, but they circulate or have been circulating recently to an extent sufficient to give rise to genuine concern.

Then I would like to say a word in consequence of that about the courts and enforcement. I have expressed, I think, already the opinion that our legislation is adequate.

I would say, I think, by that opinion, unless the case comes before the courts in which the prosecution is dismissed then we would know whether or not the law was adequate, but I can see no reason why it should not cover it so I would like to discuss the problems of the courts and enforcement.

I think that first one should state what is probably a general proposition applicable equally in both our countries, that, generally speaking, one of the reasons for what I have called lack of vigorous enforcement may be the inherent dislike of taking measures which appear to be repressive with respect to the written word, with respect to literature.

Our law-enforcement authorities are reluctant, and I think properly reluctant, to launch prosecution against those in the printing and publishing business and in the distribution of literature. It is a reluctance which I think must and should be overcome where the case warrants it, but I used the words "I think it is a proper reluctance" and it is one which I think we must take into account.

In any event, there have been very few prosecutions in Canada, although this material is circulating in certainly greater quantity than I would like to see.

I would like then to refer to one or two specific cases which came before our courts. You will appreciate from your reading of the section as lawyers that there

are two alternative methods of proceeding. One is by indictment in which case it comes up before a court with a judge.

The other is by what we call summary procedure or on summary conviction, which means it comes up before a magistrate.

The principle, of course, applicable in both courts are exactly the same as to proof and so on, but the powers of the respective courts with respect to imposition of penalties are quite different. The penalty which the higher court can impose on the more formal indictment procedure is much larger than that which can be imposed by a magistrate on a summary conviction.

The first case I should like to mention came up before a magistrate in the Province of Alberta. Being in a magistrate court, it is not a reported case, but it was the case which gave us the greatest concern because the facts as I understand them were something like this: That the magazine or crime comic complained of illustrated everything right up to the actual moment of the delivery of the death blow, omitted that, and then continued with all the gruesome details immediately following that. That was the presentation at any rate as I understand it, given by the defending attorney.

The legislation refers to the commission of crimes. This does not illustrate the actual commission of the crime and, therefore, the accused is not guilty.

The magistrate dismissed the case on that ground. That looked as though we would have to amend our legislation if we wished it to be effective because you will appreciate so far as the juveniles are concerned if you are going to say everything which falls short of the actual commission of the crime at the moment of death, shall I say, that everything of that sort is all right, then you haven't really got an effective act from the point of view of what we want to accomplish.

So reconsideration was immediately given to introducing the necessary amendment. That has been done. There is a slight modification in bill 7 in the proposed section 150 over and above what there was in bill 10, which I shall come to, but even before we in the House of Commons enacted bill 7, there was another case, *Regina* v. *Rohr*.

As you know, in our country all criminal prosecutions are brought in the name of the Queen, or whoever happens to be wearing the Crown at the time being, be it the King or the Queen. *Regina* v. *Rohr*, a Manitoba case, in which the same defense was raised before the magistrate. The magistrate, however, convicted in this case.

So as a test case it was appealed to the Court of Appeals of the Province of Manitoba. The appeal court stated, after looking at the words of the statute, they were clearly of the opinion that the intent of the legislature as clearly to be gathered from those words, was to cover all these incidental arrangements for and consequence of the crime and that, therefore, the prosecution was properly launched.

I am not going to weary you with it here, but if any member of your committee might be interested in the discussion of the effect of that decision, it may be found in the Canadian Bar review for December 1953 at page 1164, where the case and its implications are discussed by the Deputy Attorney General for British Columbia, Mr. Eric Peppler.

That decision seemed to dispose of the fears which we had that the whole statute might be rendered ineffective, but nevertheless there was this amendment which had been contemplated which was still carried forward for the sake of greater certainty.

It is not a very important or far-reaching amendment, but I think it does substantiate my point that these words are now sufficient to cover even the horror comic because the definition of crime comic as it previously appeared in section 207 was in this form:

Crime comic means in this section any magazine, periodical, or book which exclusively or substantially comprises matter depicting pictorially the commission of crimes, real or fictitious.

Now, it reads in this section:

Crime comic means a magazine, periodical, or book that exclusively or substantially comprises matter depicting pictorially:
A. The commission of crimes, real or fictitious, or
B. Events connected with the commission of crimes, real or fictitious, whether occurring before or after the commission of a crime.

Mr. BEASER. You would say, Mr. Fulton, that the statute itself seems to be sufficient. The difficulty lies in the enforcement?

Mr. FULTON. In the enforcement; that is my point.

Mr. BEASER. You think if there were effective enforcement the problem that Canada faces with respect to crime and horror comics would no longer be there?

Mr. FULTON. I don't suppose it will ever disappear entirely, but it would be effectively dealt with; yes.

To conclude in a very few words, I would like to say a word or two with regard to our present experience. Our present experience is, it must be confessed, that printers and publishers still defy the laws because comics are still on our stands, whether publishers in the sense of those who actually print them in Canada, or in the sense of those who put them into circulation after they are imported from your country.

That is the view I know of our Government, that the law is there; what is necessary now is vigorous and complete enforcement.

I did suggest in a recent debate, and it is still my view, that there should be a differentiation in the penalty so that a stiffer penalty would be provided for those who, as I see it, carry the greater responsibility for putting this offensive material into circulation, what you might call gently at the printer and publisher level; that there should be a stiffer minimum penalty, one that he will really feel, one which will not be, and what so often they are, merely license fees to continue in business.

Mr. BEASER. However, if the majority of these crimes and horror comics are coming in from the United States, that sort of stiffening of penalty would not be effective, would it?

Mr. FULTON. I think it could be made effective because I am convinced an adequate definition could be worked out to cover the case of the initial distributor.

Mr. BEASER. The initial distributor would be included?

Mr. FULTON. Yes. I don't suggest for a moment you can absolve from responsibility the individual news vendor or the retail distributor. I do think they carry a very much lesser degree of responsibility for this thing than the others.

I think, therefore, there should be a lesser penalty for them, that the penalty should be in the discretion of the court and in our jurisdiction it runs an average of anywhere from $5 to $50 for the individual vendor, but I feel there should be heavy penalties for those higher up in the scale.

And that until, in fact, my view in conclusion really is that until you take effective action to deal with those who first put these things into circulation you are not going to deal with the problem.

As I have said, I do not for a moment suggest that the individual vendor and retail distributor can be absolved from responsibility. He is a very minor factor in the chain of responsibility.

I would like to see and have in fact suggested that our own code be amended to make that differentiation, but that suggestion was not accepted by the House of Commons and by the Government.

So that remains at the moment my own opinion and that of certain of my colleagues in the House.

There are a couple of cases I would like to mention, just to finish. There is one case in Canada where a publisher has been prosecuted, the Queen against the Peer Publisher, Ltd., of Toronto, and William Zimmerman, who is the man who is the principal of that firm, resulted in conviction and fine of a $1,000 and costs against the company and suspended sentence for Zimmerman. No notice of appeal has yet been served.

That was a conviction again by way of summary procedure by magistrate which may account for the relatively low fine.

There was another case against Kitchener News Co., Ltd., distributor, again in the magistrate court. They were fined $25. They appealed.

The appeals court quashed the conviction on technical ground that the indictment was incorrectly drawn. The attorney general informs me that he is proceeding with a new trial on a fresh indictment. That is, so far as I have been able to ascertain, the record of court cases dealing with this new law, relatively new law, in Canada.

I believe that the court cases show that the law is workable and effective and the problem is enforcement with, as my personal opinion, a desirability of providing heavier penalty and really effective penalties for those at the top who have the greatest responsibility in the chain of circulation.

One other interesting and encouraging result which has flowed from our legislation is that in a number of cities in Canada, particularly after the last discussion, when the amended criminal code came up before the House and we had extensive and quite interesting debate on that section, as a result of that publicity, at least I think it is partly as a result of that publicity, a number of both wholesale and retail distributors are approaching citizens' committees in some of our cities and saying, "We don't want to break the law in the first place and we certainly don't want to run the risk of prosecution. We would like you to cooperate with us by suggesting to us the offensive titles and if you will do that we would like you to get a representative committee so that it does not just reflect the minority viewpoint. If you will do that we will agree to withdraw those titles from circulation."

I think that springs in some measure from the existence of the legislation.

As I say, I regard it as a quite encouraging indication that this legislation can and will produce beneficial results in Canada, although I am afraid again I must confess that I am not suggesting that it is the complete answer or that it has yet provided a complete elimination of this type of undesirable publication.

That, Mr. Chairman, concludes the statement which I have to make.

I appreciate your having listened to me so patiently. I apologize for having taken rather lengthy time. I am very much interested in this subject.

If I have abused your hospitality by going on too long, that is because of my interest in the subject.

The CHAIRMAN. You have been very helpful and you have made a contribution.

Senator HENNINGS. I, too, want to thank you very much and apologize in turn. I was asked by some representatives of the press to get an exhibit of one of the things that was in evidence this morning. I was engaged in that effort during the latter part of your statement. I shall read with great interest the record.

The CHAIRMAN. I might add it was a very able statement, well presented.

Mr. FULTON. Thank you very much.

The CHAIRMAN. I think that Canada is fortunate in having such an able representative in its Parliament.

Counsel, do you have any questions?

Mr. BEASER. Just one, Mr. Chairman.

As you notice, this morning I have been asking a number of witnesses as to the effect on our country's relationships with other countries of these crime and horror comics.

Would you care to comment on what impression and what effect crime and horror comics in Canada are having on the children's ideas of what the United States of America is like?

Mr. FULTON. I would say that their effect in that regard is not very serious in Canada. We live too close to you not to know that our way of life and yours are very much the same.

It would be my opinion, therefore, that a Canadian child reading this type of magazine would not—reaction on him would not be what dreadful things go on in the United States of America as distinct from what goes on in Canada.

Rather, the undesirability from our point of view certainly is that it portrays these as natural and everyday occurrences.

In other words, our objection to them is not that it portrays the United States as a country, which has lower standard of moral values than our own. It is merely that they portray human society as having an entirely distorted and unreal sense of value and of moral standards.

Besides that, I would make no, I certainly wouldn't express any opinion that they have a derogatory effect on the opinion of our children toward America as such because as I have pointed out, although to a considerable lesser degree, many publications of the same type are published in Canada, a sufficient number to be alarming and disturbing.

Mr. BEASER. I have no further questions, Mr. Chairman.

The CHAIRMAN. It is your considered judgment that this statute has been extremely helpful, is it not?

Mr. FULTON. Yes, it is, Senator, although I must again repeat that I feel it has not been used to the fullest possible extent.

The CHAIRMAN. Senator Hennings?

Senator HENNINGS. I have nothing further, Mr. Chairman. Thank you.

The CHAIRMAN. Thank you again, Mr. Fulton, very much indeed.

Mr. FULTON. Thank you, Mr. Chairman.

* * * * * * * *

The CHAIRMAN. The chairman wishes to announce that today's hearing does not terminate the subcommittee's investigation into the field of crime and horror comic books. We shall continue to collect on this subject matter in this area, and if necessary further hearings will be scheduled at a later date.

All data thus far presented, plus all future facts compiled, will be studied most carefully before the subcommittee draws up its conclusions and recommendations.

The subcommittee will issue a special report upon this subject at an appropriate time, or we may make the report a part of our final report.

I think I speak for the entire subcommittee when I say that any action on the part of the publishers of crime and horror comic books, or upon the part of distributors, wholesalers, or dealers with reference to these materials which will tend to eliminate from production and sale, shall receive the acclaim of my colleagues and myself. A competent job of self-policing within the industry will achieve much.

We will adjourn now until 10 o'clock tomorrow morning.

(Thereupon, at 5 p.m., the subcommittee recessed, to reconvene at 10 a.m., Saturday, June 5, 1954.)

[Editor's Note: The hearings were never reconvened.]

Still More About the Comics

Selected Bibliography
Notes on the Contributors

Selected Bibliography

Abel, Robert H., and David Manning White, eds. *The Funnies: An American Idiom.* New York: The Free Press of Glencoe, 1963.

Aldridge, Alan, and George Perry. *The Penguin Book of Comics.* Harmondsworth, England: Penguin Books, 1967.

Becker, Stephen. *Comic Art in America.* New York: Simon & Schuster, 1959.

Berger, Arthur Asa. *The Comic-Stripped American.* New York: Walker and Company, 1974.

Couperie, Pierre, and Maurice Horn. *A History of the Comic Strip.* New York: Crown, 1968.

Craven, Thomas. *Cartoon Cavalcade.* New York: Simon & Schuster, 1943.

Daniels, Les. *Comix: A History of Comic Books in America.* New York: Outerbridge and Dienstfrey, 1971.

Davidson, Sol. *Culture and the Comic Strip.* New York: New York University Press, 1959. Ph.D. thesis.

Estren, Mark. *A History of Underground Comics.* San Francisco: Straight Arrow Books, 1974.

Feiffer, Jules. *The Great Comic Book Heroes.* New York: Dial Press, 1965.

Gifford, Denis. *The British Comic Catalogue 1874-1974.* London: Mansell, 1975.

———. *Happy Days! One Hundred Years of Comics.* London: Jupiter Books, 1975.

———. *Stap Me! The British Newspaper Strip.* Aylesbury, England: Shire Publications, 1971.

Goulart, Ron. *The Adventurous Decade.* New Rochelle, N.Y.: Arlington House, 1975.

Hirsh, Michael, and Patrick Lambert. *The Great Canadian Comic-Books.* Toronto: Peter Martin, 1971.

Horn, Maurice. *75 Years of the Comics.* Boston: Boston Book & Art, 1971.

Kempkes, Wolfgang, ed. *International Bibliography of Comics Literature.* New York: R.R. Bowker, 1974.

Lee, Stan. *Origins of Marvel Comics.* New York: Simon & Schuster, 1974.

Lupoff, Richard, and Donald Thompson, eds. *All in Color for a Dime.* New Rochelle, N.Y.: Arlington House, 1970.

———. *The Comic-Book Book.* New Rochelle, N.Y.: Arlington House, 1973.

Murrel, William A. *A History of American Graphic Humor* (2 vols.). New York: Macmillan for the Whitney Museum of American Art, 1933 and 1938.

Reitberger, Reinhold, and Wolfgang Fuchs. *Comics: Anatomy of a Mass Medium.* Boston: Little, Brown, 1972.

Robinson, Jerry. *The Comics: An Illustrated History of Comic Strip Art.* New York: Putnam, 1974.

Sheridan, Martin. *Comics and Their Creators.* Boston: Hale, Cushman and Flint, 1942 (paperback edition: Luna Press, 1971).

Steranko, James, ed. *The Steranko History of Comics.* Reading, Pa.: Supergraphics (2 vols), 1970 and 1972.

Waugh, Coulton. The Comics. New York: Macmillan, 1947 (paperback edition: Luna Press, 1974).

Wertham, Frederic. *Seduction of the Innocent.* New York: Rinehart and Co., 1954.

Books in Other Languages

Blanchard, Gérard. *La Bande Dessinée.* Verviers, Belgium: Editions Marabout, 1969.

Bono, Gianni. *Appunti sul Fumetto Italiano del Dopoguerra.* Genoa, Italy: Gli Amici del Fumetto, 1972.

Caen, Michel, with Jacques Lob and Jacques Sternberg. *Les Chefs d'Oeuvre de la Bande Dessinée.* Paris: Planète, 1967.

Caradec, François. *I Primi Eroi.* Milan: Garzanti, 1962.

Carpentier, André, ed. *La Bande Dessinée Kébécoise.* Bois-des-Filion, Qué.: La Barre du Jour, 1975.

Della Corte, Carlo. *I Fumetti.* Milan: Mondadori, 1961.

Gasca, Luis. *Los Comics en España.* Barcelona: Editorial Lumen, 1969.

————. *Los Comics en la Pantalla*. San Sebastian, Spain: Festival Internacional del Cine, 1965.

Lacassin, Francis. *Pour un le Art, la Bande Dessinée*. Paris: Union Générale d'Editions, 1971.

Lipscyc, Enrique. *La Historieta Mundial*. Buenos Aires: Editorial Lipscyc, 1958.

Marny, Jacques. *Le Monde Etonnant des Bandes Dessinées*. Paris: Editions du Centurion, 1968.

Moliterni, Claude, ed. *Histoire de la Bande Dessinée d'Expression Française*. Paris: Editions Serg, 1972.

Peignot, Joseph. *Les Copains de Votre Enfance*. Paris: Denoël, 1963.

Strazzula, Gaetano. *I Fumetti*. Florence: Sansoni, 1970.

Welke, Manfred. *Die Sprache der Comics*. Frankfurt a/Main: Dipa Verlag, 1958.

An Additional Bibliography 1976-1997

Only books dealing with some important aspect of the comics have been listed. Most are in the English language, but some foreign works of note have also been included. For a more comprehensive bibliography, refer to John A. Lent's four-volume *International Bibliography* mentioned below.

Aurrecoechea, Juan Manuel, and Armando Bartra, *Historia de la Historieta en Mexico*. 5 volumes. Mexico City: Grijalbo, 1990-1997.

Baron-Carvais, Annie. *La Bande Desinée*. Paris: Presses Universitaires de France, 1985.

Benton, Mike. *The Comic Book in America*. Dallas, Tex.: Taylor Publishing, 1990.

Blackbeard, Bill. *A Century of Comics*. 2 volumes. Northampton, Mass.: Kitchen Sink Press, 1995.

Blackbeard, Bill, and Martin Williams, eds. *The Smithsonian Collection of Newspaper Comics*. New York: Abrams, 1978.

Coma, Javier, and Roman Gubern. *Los Comics en Hollywood*. Barcelona: Plaza & James, 1988.

————. *Diccionario de los Comics*. Barcelona: Plaza & James, 1991.

Coma, Javier, and Roman Gubern, eds. *Historia de los Comics*. Barcelona: Toutain Editor, 1994.

Fossati, Franco. *I Fumetti in 100 Personaggi*. Milan: Longanesi & C., 1977.

Gasca, Luis, and Roman Gubern. *El Discurso del Comic*. Madrid: Catedra, 1988.

Gaumer, Patrick, and Claude Moliterni. *Dictionnaire Mondial de la Bande Dessinee*. Paris: Larousse, 1994.

Gifford, Dennis. *The International Book of Comics*. London: Deans International Publishing, 1984.

————. *American Comic Strip Collections*. New York: G.K. Hall, 1990.

Goulart, Ron, ed. *The Encyclopedia of American Comics*. New York: Facts on File, 1990.

————. *The Funnies: 100 Years of American Comic Strips*. Holbrook, Mass.: Adams, 1995.

————. *Ron Goulart's Great History of Comic Books*. Chicago: Contemporary Books, 1986.

Harvey, R.C. *The Art of the Funnies: An Aesthetic History of the Comic Strip*. Jackson, Miss.: University Press of Mississippi, 1995

Herner, Irene. *Mitos y Monitos*. Mexico City: Editorial Nueva Imagen, 1979.

Horn, Maurice. *Comics in the American West*. New York: Winchester Press, 1977.

Horn, Maurice, ed. *100 Years of American Newspaper Comics*. Avenel, N.J.: Gramercy, 1996.

————. *Sex in the Comics*. New York: Chelsea House, 1985.

————. *Women in the Comics*. New York: Chelsea House, 1977.

Inge, M. Thomas. *Comics as Culture*. Jackson, Miss.: University Press of Mississippi, 1990.

Jones, Gerard, and Will Jacobs. *The Great Comic Book Heroes. Revised edition*. Rocklin, Calif.: Prima, 1997.

Lent, John A. *An International Bibliography of Comic Art*. 4 volumes. Westport, Conn.: Greenwood Press, 1994-96.

Marschall, Richard. *America's Great Comic-Strip Artists*. New York: Abbeville Press, 1989.

Moya, Alvaro de. *Historia da Historia em Quadrinhos*. Saõ Paulo, Brazil: L & PM Editora, 1986.

————. *Shazam!* Saõ Paulo, Brazil: Editora Perspectiva, 1977.

O'Sullivan, Judith. *The Great American Comic Strip*. Boston: Little, Brown, and Company, 1990.

Robbins, Trina. *A Century of Women Cartoonists*. Northampton, Mass.: Kitchen Sink Press, 1994.

Ryan, John. *Panel by Panel: An Illustrated History of Australian Comics*. Melbourne: Cassell Australia, 1979.

Sabin, Roger. *Comics, Comix, and Graphic Novels*. London: Phaidon Press, 1997.

Schodt, Frederik. *Manga! Manga!: The World of Japanese Comics*. New York: Kodansha International, 1983.

————. *Dreamland Japan*. San Francisco: Stone Bridge Press, 1996.

Scott, Randall W. *Comic Books and Strips*. Phoenix, Ariz.: Oryx Press, 1988.

Tomic, Svetozar. *Strip, Poreklo i Znacaz*. Novi Sad, Yugoslavia: Forum Marketprint, 1985.

Wood, Art. *Great Cartoonists and Their Art*. Gretna, Louisiana: Pelican Publishing, 1987.

Notes on the Contributors

Maurice Horn

Maurice Horn, the editor of this encyclopedia, is an internationally recognized authority on comics and cartoons. He was co-organizer of the first exhibition held at a major museum, "Bande Dessinee et Figuration Narrative," at the Louvre in Paris. He also organized the exhibition "75 Years of the Comics" at the New York Cultural Center.

He has lectured on comics and cartoons at universities worldwide, and his European series of lectures in 1973-74 was printed in *Information et Documents*, the official publication of the American Center in Paris. He has written hundreds of articles on the subject for American and foreign magazines, and has contributed to *Collier's Encyclopedia* and to *The International Encyclopedia of Communications*. He has edited a number of reprints of classic American and European comic strips, and has received many awards and honors in the field.

Many of the books he has authored or edited have become standard reference works in their field. In addition to *The World Encyclopedia of Comics*, he has edited *100 Years of American Newspaper Comics* and the multivolume *Contemporary Graphic Artists*. He is coauthor of *A History of the Comic Strip* and author of *75 Years of the Comics*, *Women in the Comics*, *Comics of the American West*, and *Sex in the Comics*. He is currently at work on an update of *The World Encyclopedia of Cartoons*.

Manuel Auad

A native of the Philippines, Manuel Auad currently resides in California. His knowledge of the Philippines comics scene has enabled him to bring many fine Filipino artists to the attention of American comic book publishers.

Bill Blackbeard

Bill Blackbeard, a Californian, has written a number of science-fiction novels, as well as articles and stories on a variety of subjects. In 1967 he founded the San Francisco Academy of Comic Art, which is devoted to the study and preservation of the comics and other forms of popular culture.

Blackbeard is the author of *Comics* (1973), the two-volume anthology *A Century of Comics* (1995), and many articles on the subject. He edited *The Smithsonian Collection of Newspaper Comics* (1978) and has organized several exhibits in the Bay Area.

Gianni Bono

Born in Genoa, Italy, in 1949, Gianni Bono has been a comics fan since he was a child. Together with Nino Bernazzali, he founded the club "Gil Amici del Fumetto" in 1967. An editor of the fanzine *Comics World* from 1967 to 1972, Bono has written articles on the comics for such publications as *Il Secolo XIX* and *Eureka*, and is the author of *Appunti sul Fumetto Italiano del Dopoguerra* ("Observations on the Postwar Italian Comics"). Bono wrote many scripts for adventure comics, especially war comics, and edited *If*, a quarterly magazine devoted to the comics world.

Joe Brancatelli

Joe Brancatelli remembers that his first comic book was bought at the expense of an egg cream that his father had offered to buy for him. He has been reading them ever since, which is why he was qualified to contribute the bulk of the American comic book entries.

A graduate of New York University's School of Journalism, Brancatelli has been writing professionally since he was 16. He became the managing editor of *The Monster Times*, a children's horror and comics tabloid, at age 18 and went on to found *Inside Comics*, the first professional magazine about comic art in America, at age 20. Concentrating primarily on behind-the-scenes news, *Inside*

Comics quickly became a controversial publication. After leaving *Inside Comics*, Brancatelli served short stints at UPI and on a New Jersey daily newspaper before turning to freelance writing.

Mary Beth Calhoun

Mary Beth Calhoun is an associate at an Ohio research and consulting firm, as well as a freelance writer and editor. Previously she was employed as an editorial assistant for a scientific journal. While growing up, she followed the comics in the *Pittsburgh Press*, and having maintained her interest in the field since that time has contributed a number of entries to the *World Encyclopedia of Comics*, as well as to other comics-related reference works.

Javier Coma

Javier Coma has written extensively on film, jazz music, and the comics. He is the editor of the acclaimed *Historia Mundial de los Comics*, and has written a series of articles, *Comics, classicos y modernos*, for the influential daily newspaper *El Pais*. Among his many other books on the subject have been *Del gato Felix al gato Fritz*, *Los comics: Un arte del siglo XX*, *Diccionario de los comics*, and *Los comics en Hollywood* (with Roman Gubern). In 1996 he published an important study on Western movies, *La gran caravan del western*, and he is currently working on a book about Hollywood's war movies.

He also contributed to *Contemporary Graphic Artists* and has written for many other publications in the United States, Great Britain, France, Italy, and Argentina. He has received many international honors in recognition of his contributions to the field.

Bill Crouch Jr.

Bill Crouch Jr., a Connecticut Yankee, has written about cartooning since he was first published in *Cartoonist Profiles* in 1974. For that magazine he interviewed Harold Foster, Noel Sickles, and Norman Mingo (the first artist to paint Alfred E. Neuman in full color for the cover of *Mad*). He edited *Dick Tracy, America's Most Famous Detective*, and coauthored a Dick Tracy collectibles book. In addition, he was a contributor to *The World Encyclopedia of Cartoons* and *100 Years of American Newspaper Comics*. He has also written scripts for syndicated comics and humorous comic books, specifically *Yogi Bear*, *Top Cat*, *Hong Kong Phooey*, and *The Flintstones*.

Giulio Cesare Cuccolini

Giulio Cesare Cuccolini, a native of Corregio (Emilia), studied at institutions in Italy, the United States, England, and France. He has been a member of the faculty at the University of Bologna, where he taught philosophy and history, and he has written and lectured extensively on comics in Italy and abroad. He is a past president of Associazione Nazionale degli Amici del Fumetto, and has long been associated with the International Comics Salon in Lucca and with Expo-Cartoon in Rome. He wrote the introductory material to the Italian edition of *The World Encyclopedia of Comics*.

Mark Evanier

Born in 1952 in Los Angeles, California, Mark Evanier began reading at a surprisingly early age, interspersing comic books with all kinds of books and magazines. Gradually, an interest in communications developed, with emphasis on movies, television, and, of course, comic books. He became president of a local comic book collector's society and was a frequent contributor to comic book and film fanzines. In the summer of 1969 Evanier began freelancing for various magazines.

While attending the University of California at Los Angeles, Evanier worked for Marvelmania International, a mail-order firm producing Marvel Comics character merchandise, and produced four issues of the company's fanzine. He quit to work as Jack Kirby's assistant on Kirby's comics for National Periodicals (later DC), but continued freelancing magazine pieces and special material for Walt

Disney Studios. In 1972 he began writing "funny animal" stories for such Gold Key comics as *Super Goof, Mickey Mouse, Bugs Bunny, Porky Pig, Daffy Duck, Beep Beep the Road Runner, The Beagle Boys, Looney Tunes,* and *Moby Dick.*

Mark Evanier has also written underground comix scripts, foreign comic albums, ghost comics, film reviews, and book reviews. Among his recent works have been *Comic Handbuch* and *San Francisco* (with Gerhard Muller).

Wolfgang Fuchs

Wolfgang Fuchs, born in 1945, grew up and went to school in and around Munich, Germany. While attending university courses in American cultural history, journalism and communications, and English literature, Fuchs participated in a university project that led to his coauthorship of *Comics: Anatomie eines Massenmediums.* A number of assignments for television, audiovisual aids and articles followed.

Fuchs gained valuable experience in the comics field by translating a number of comics and editing a German *Peanuts* comic book in 1974-75; he has since translated *Comics: The Art of the Comic Strip* for *Graphis.* He is currently a contributing editor of *Shock!,* a regular contributor to *Jugend, Film, Fernsehen,* and is preparing special projects for both. Recently he coauthored a series of articles on comics and advertising in *werben & verkaufen.* Among his recent works are *Comic Hardbuch* and *San Francisco* with Gerhard Müller.

Luis Gasca

Luis Gasca is a native of San Sebastian, Spain, and a graduate of Saragossa Law School (1955). He has been the manager of several advertising agencies and has taught at the School of Tourism of San Sebastian.

The writer of a number of books on a variety of subjects, his publications in the field of comic art include: *Los Comics en la Pantalla* ("Comics on the Screen"), *Imagen y Ciencia Ficción* ("Image and Science Fiction"), and *Los Comics en España* ("The Comics in Spain").

Gasca has been extremely active in the fields of comics and the movies; in fact, he is an executive board member of the San Sebastian Film Festival and of various comics conventions. He is currently the general editor of *Pala,* a San Sebastian-based publishing house specializing in books of and about comics.

Denis Gifford

Denis Gifford, the contributor of the entries about British comic characters and cartoonists in this encyclopedia, is Britain's leading authority on the comics. A collector of comics since the age of three, Gifford now has over 20,000 comics. His first ambition was to draw and edit comics, so at age 12 he printed and published his own comic, *Junior.* He turned professional at 14, drawing *Sammy and His Sister* for *All Fun Comic,* and then he took over such standing characters as *Pansy Potter* in *Beano* and *Our Ernie* in *Knockout.* His first regular job was as a junior cartoonist on the Sunday paper *Reynold's News.* During national service in the RAF (1946), he freelanced, drawing superheroes in the American style for *Streamline Comics* (1947).

Gifford has edited a series of comic books for Modern Fiction, including *Amazing Comics* (1949); he created *Steadfast McStaunch* (1950) and *Flip and Flop* (1954), among others, and was one of the artists on *Marvelman* (1955). In 1956 he created the daily *Telestrip,* the first newspaper strip to satirize current television shows. In 1960 he drew the complete *Classics Illustrated of Baron Munchausen.*

Gifford changed careers to take up writing and show business in the 1960s. He created a nostalgic panel game for BBC radio called *Sounds Familiar* (1966-74) and a television version, *Looks Familiar,* in 1972. Another of his ideas was the first panel game for cartoonists, *Quick on the Draw* (1974). Gifford has also written several books on the comics: *Discovering Comics* and *Stap Me! The British Newspaper Strip* (1971); *Six Comics of World War One* (1973, reprint); *Victorian Comics, The British Comic Catalogue,* and *Happy Days: One Hundred Years of Comics* (1975). Gifford is also the author of the acclaimed *British Film Catalogue.* Among his

recent works are *The International Book of Comics* and *American Comic Strip Collections*.

Robert Gerson

Robert Gerson is a book designer and painter whose creative influences are drawn from the comic art medium. In 1970 he published and edited the limited-edition art magazine *Reality*. Devoted to comic book art and fantasy illustration from the artist's perspective, *Reality* featured the early works of artists Jeffrey Jones, Michael Kaluta, Kenneth Smith, and Howard Chaykin. Robert has collected original comic book, comic strip, and illustration art since 1970. His collection features artwork dating back to 1893.

As a book designer his most notable work is the 1987 edition of Ansel Adams's *The Mural Project*. He studied at the School of Visual Arts in Manhattan and the Pennsylvania Academy of the Fine Arts in Philadelphia. Robert paints in the fantasy art tradition reminiscent of the period of art known as the "golden age of illustration." He currently lives in the Brandywine River valley in Pennsylvania.

Paul Gravett

Born in Chelmsford, Paul Gravett completed studies in the law at Cambridge University. He edited the magazine *Escape* with Peter Stanbury, and has written many articles on the comics and lectured at comics conventions in Europe and the United States. He is the director of the Cartoon Art Trust in London.

Peter Harris

Peter Harris of Toronto is the editor of one of the largest weekly magazines in Canada, *Star Week*, the TV and entertainment supplement of the *Toronto Star*. At the same time, he was also the editor of the smallest, *Captain George's Penny Dreadful*, a nostalgia-oriented newsletter issued every Friday by the Vast Whizz-bang Organization for many years.

Hongying Liu-Lengyel

Hongying Liu-Lengyel was born in Beijing, China, and graduated from Anhui University in Hefei in 1982. After marrying an American in the mid-1980s she moved to the United States, where she received a Ph.D. in communication from Temple University. She has written on comic art for various Chinese journals and has done a great number of book reviews on Chinese cartoons and comics for the U.S. publications *Wings* and *WittyWorld*.

She has lectured widely on the subject at Chinese and American universities. She has authored several books, including *Chinese Cartoons as Mass Communication: The History of Cartoon Development in China* (1993).

Pierre L. Horn

Pierre L. Horn is professor of French at Wright State University in Dayton, Ohio, where he also holds the Brage Golding Distinguished Professorship in Research. He has written extensively on French literature and civilization, and his works include biographies of Louis XIV and Lafayette. In addition, he has lectured on popular culture and contributed numerous entries to *The World Encyclopedia of Cartoons*, the multivolume series *Contemporary Graphic Artists*, and *100 Years of American Newspaper Comics*. He also edited the *Handbook of French Popular Culture*, and is the advisor for the multivolume *Guides to the World's Cinema*, published by Greenwood Press.

In 1978 he was decorated with the rank of Chevalier dans l'Ordre des Palmes Académiques by the French government.

Slobodan Ivkov

Born in 1959 in Subotica (northern Serbia), Slobodan Ivkov pursued postgraduate studies at the Faculty of Philosophy in Belgrade. He has been drawing comics and cartoons since 1977, and has also written scripts for many eminent

Yugoslav authors. He has published a number of comic books and has been comics editor for several publications. He has also been active in cartoons and graphic design, and has participated in some 70 exhibitions in Yugoslavia and abroad.

He is the organizer of the great retrospective exhibition "60 Years of Serbian Comics (1936-1995)," and the author of the accompanying 320-page catalogue. He has written articles on comics and cartoons for every leading magazine in Serbia and for many publications abroad. He has had a book of his cartoons, *Zid* ("The Wall"), and a collection of his science-fiction stories, *At Book's Edge*, published. He is a member of the Association of Applied Artists and of the Association of Journalists of Yugoslavia, and is the recipient of many honors and awards for his works in the field of comics.

Bill Janocha

Bill Janocha is a freelance artist who has been studio assistant to Mort Walker on *Beetle Bailey* since 1987. He has contributed articles to *Nemo*, *Inks*, Comicana books, and *Mad* magazine. Editor of the 1988 and 1996 editions of *The National Cartoonists Society Album*, Janocha helped with the development of the 1995 "Comic Strip Classics" U.S. postage stamps and with exhibitions for the Newspaper Features Council and for the International Museum of Cartoon Art. He was also a contributor to *100 Years of American Newspaper Comics*.

Orvy Jundis

A native of the Philippines, Orvy Jundis was born in 1943 and came to the United States in 1954, where he attended San Francisco Junior College, San Francisco State, and the University of San Francisco. An active leader in the Philippine American Collegiate Endeavor (PACE, a group responsible for originating and establishing Asian-American study programs), Jundis received a special commendation from the California state legislature and the Philippine Consulate.

Jundis was the first Filipino to promote and exhibit Philippine comic art outside of the Philippines. Actively involved in comics, science fiction, and fantasy fandom, Jundis founded the Philippine Comic Archives in 1968. In 1971 he returned to the Philippines to do extensive research on Filipino comics, but three years later he was back in the United States working with Marvel Comics and founding the Philippine Science-Fantasy Society. That same year (1974) Jundis brought the Philippines' talented Alex Niño to the United States.

A very prolific writer, editor, and artist, Jundis has written newspaper articles for the *San Francisco Phoenix*, the *Philippine News*, and the *Mabuhay Republic*, and his fanzine articles have appeared in *Jasoomian* and *Destiny*. He has contributed artwork to *Amra*, *ERBania*, *Collector's Showcase*, and *Stoned*, and his poetry has been published in *Kapatid*, *Kalayaan International*, *Filipino Heart-Throbs*, *Liwanag* (where he is an art editor), and *Time to Greeze* (an anthology of Third World arts and writing). He was a collaborator in *The Showcase of Fantasy Art*, edited by Emile Petaja, with an introduction by Ray Bradbury.

Hisao Kato

Hisao Kato was born in Oiso, Japan, on December 16, 1951. After graduation from the College of Foreign Studies in 1970, he entered the Tokyo Academy of Design, where he studied basic editorial design. In 1972 Kato attended the Japanese School for Editors and, after graduation in 1973, started on a promising editorial career.

A knowledgeable student of the comics, Kato has written several articles on the subject, as well as scripts for comic book companies. He read and carefully studied a great number of comic books, magazines, graphic publications, newspapers, and Ukiyo-e books as background material for the Japanese entries to this encyclopedia.

John A. Lent

Dr. John A. Lent, a professor at Temple University, has authored or edited 49 books, including *Asian Popular Culture* and *An International Bibliography of Comic*

Art, a four-volume reference work. He is chair of the Comic Art Working Group of the International Association for Mass Communication Research, the Asian Popular Culture Group of the Popular Culture Association, and the Asian Cinema Studies Society; he is also the editor of *Asian Cinema* and *Berita*, and the managing editor of *WittyWorld*. He has interviewed cartoonists and lectured on comic art on every continent, and was a contributor to *100 Years of American Newspaper Comics*.

Lent's nearly 40-year career includes a Fulbright scholarship to the Philippines, directorship of the first academic program in mass communication in Malaysia, pioneering research in Asia and the Caribbean, and study at universities in Norway, Mexico, Japan, and India.

Richard Marschall

Richard Marschall has devoted his life to the study and collection of comic strips and cartoons. His collection includes more than 3,000 original drawings, bound runs of the early humor magazines, and voluminous amounts of published and unpublished miscellany about cartoons and cartoonists.

Born in 1949 in Ridgewood, New York, he started drawing cartoons at an early age, and formed friendships with many cartoonists. He received degrees in American Studies and History from the American University in Washington, D.C., writing his master's thesis on the early American humor and cartoon magazines. While in school he began freelancing editorial cartoons to many of the nation's leading conservative journals.

In 1972 Marschall joined the staff of the Palisades Newspapers in Englewood, New Jersey, as a reporter and cartoonist. He shifted later in the year to the *Connecticut Sunday Herald* in Norwalk and served in the same capacities before rising to the positions of feature editor and magazine editor. Thereafter followed brief stints as associate editor of United Feature Syndicate and associate editor for comics of the Chicago Tribune-New York News Syndicate. In September 1975 he assumed his duties at Field in Chicago.

Marschall has exhibited major portions of his collection and has spoken on the comics extensively, as well as having assisted on several books on the subject. His areas of specialization are early magazine cartoons, early humor strips, American illustration, and the political cartoon. He credits his father's interest in cartoons with exciting his own proclivities.

He is now a freelance writer, and his works on the comics include *America's Great Comic-Strip Artists* (1989).

Alvaro de Moya

Alvaro de Moya is the foremost Brazilian authority on comics and cartoons. He has organized a number of important exhibitions of comic art in Brazil and South America, and has lectured extensively on the subject in America and in Europe. He has been a member of numerous international juries. Among the books he has written are *Shazam!*, *Historia da Historia em Quadrinhos*, and *O Mundo de Disney*.

Kalman Rubovszky

Born in Kisvarda, in northeastern Hungary, in 1942, Kalman Rubovszky is a professor at Debrecen University. He started research in the comics in the 1980s and gave a series of lectures on Hungarian comics at the International Comics Salon in Lucca, Italy, in 1982. He has also organized scientific conferences on comics. He has written many essays on the comics and has published two books on the subject, *Apropos comics!* (1988) and *A képregény* ("Novels in Pictures," 1989).

Ervin Rustemagić

Born in Ilidž, Yugoslavia, in 1952, Ervin Rustemagić worked as an illustrator for the children's newspaper *Male novine* in Sarajevo after his graduation from high school. In November 1971 he founded the comics magazine *Strip Art*, which he also edited for two years.

Rustemagić regularly attends many international comics conventions as the head of the Yugoslav delegation and a member of the juries of Angoulême (France) and Gijon (Spain). He is the author of the first book on comic art ever published in Yugoslavia, *The Professional Secrets of the Comics*. His lecture, which he presented at Angoulême 1, "La Bande Dessinée Yougoslave," was the first lecture on Yugoslav comics ever given anywhere.

John Thomas Ryan

A collector of vintage comics and original artwork, John Thomas Ryan was born in 1931 in Cowra, N.S.W., Australia. He contributed many articles, including some for the well-known *Bid gee* series, to amateur magazines relating to the comics.

In 1964 Ryan published Australia's first comic fanzine, *Down Under*, and its lead article, "With the Comics Down Under," won the Alley Award for the best article. In 1979, he published *Panel by Panel: An Illustrated History of Australian Comics*, the definitive work on the subject. He died in 1980.

Matthew Allen Thorn

Matt Thorn is a cultural anthropologist, writer, and translator who lives and works in Kyoto, Japan. He has translated thousands of pages of Japanese comics into English for Viz Comics, including Hayao Miyazaki's *Nausicaä of the Valley of Wind*, Rumiko Talahashi's *Mermaid* saga, and Hagio Moto's *They Were Eleven*. The author of numerous articles and essays on *shojo manga*, or Japanese girls' and women's comics, he is currently working on an ethnographic book on the subject. He also maintains a World Wide Web site known as "The Shojo Manga Home Page."

Dennis Wepman

Dennis Wepman has taught English at the City University of New York and held the post of cultural affairs editor of the *New York Daily News*. The holder of a graduate degree in linguistics from Columbia University, he is the author of 12 volumes of biography and has contributed to numerous publications in linguistics, literature, art, and popular culture, as well as to several standard reference books on cartooning. He has been a contributor to the multivolume *Contemporary Graphic Artists*, to *The Encyclopedia of American Comics*, and to *100 Years of American Newspaper Comics*. He is the chief review editor of *WittyWorld*, the international cartoon magazine.

Appendices

Code of the Comics Magazine Association of America

Institutions

In general, recognizable national, social, political, cultural, ethnic and racial groups, religious institutions, and law enforcement authorities will be portrayed in a positive light. These include the government on the national, state, and municipal levels, including all of its numerous departments, agencies, and services; law enforcement agencies such as the FBI, the Secret Service, the CIA, etc.; the military, both United States and foreign; known religious organizations; ethnic advancement groups; foreign leaders and representatives of other governments and national groups; and social groups identifiable by lifestyle, such as homosexuals, the economically disadvantaged, the economically privileged, the homeless, senior citizens, minors, etc.

Socially responsible attitudes will be favorably depicted and reinforced. Socially inappropriate, irresponsible, or illegal behavior will be shown to be specific actions of a specific individual or group of individuals, and not meant to reflect the routine activity of any general group of real persons.

If, for dramatic purposes, it is necessary to portray such a group of individuals in a negative manner, the name of the group and its individual members will be fictitious, and its activities will not clearly be identifiable with the routine activities of any real group.

Stereotyped images and activities will not be used to degrade specific national, ethnic, cultural, or socioeconomic groups.

Language

The language in a comic book will be appropriate for a mass audience that includes children. Good grammar and spelling will be encouraged. Publishers will exercise good taste and a responsible attitude as to the use of language in their comics. Obscene and profane words, symbols, and gestures are prohibited.

References to physical handicaps, illnesses, ethnic backgrounds, sexual preferences, religious beliefs, and race, when presented in a derogatory manner for dramatic purposes, will be shown to be unacceptable.

Violence

Violent actions or scenes are acceptable within the context of a comic book story when dramatically appropriate. Violent behavior will not be shown as acceptable. If it is presented in a realistic manner, care should be taken to present the natural repercussions of such actions. Publishers should avoid excessive levels of violence, excessively graphic depictions of violence, and excessive bloodshed or gore. Publishers will not present detailed information instructing readers how to engage in imitable violent actions.

Characterizations

Character portrayals will be carefully crafted and show sensitivity to national, ethnic, religious, sexual, political, and socioeconomic orientations. If it is dramatically appropriate for one character to demean another because of his or her sex, ethnicity, religion, sexual preference, political orientation, socioeconomic status, or disabilities, the demeaning words or actions will be clearly shown to be wrong or ignorant in the course of the story. Stories depicting characters subject to physical, mental, or emotional problems or with economic disadvantages should never assign ultimate responsibility for these conditions to the characters themselves. Heroes should be role models and should reflect the prevailing social attitudes.

Substance abuse

Healthy, wholesome lifestyles will be presented as desirable. However, the use and abuse of controlled substances, legal and illicit, are facts of modern existence, and may be portrayed when dramatically appropriate.

The consumption of alcohol, narcotics, pharmaceuticals, and tobacco will not be depicted in a glamourous way. When the line between the normal, responsible consumption of legal substances and the abuse of these substances is crossed, the distinction will be made clear and the adverse consequences of such abuse will be noted.

Substance abuse is defined as the use of illicit drugs and the self-destructive use of such products as tobacco (including chewing tobacco), alcohol, prescription drugs, over-the-counter drugs, etc.

Use of dangerous substances both legal and illegal should be shown with restraint as necessary to the context of the story. However, storylines should not be detailed to the point of serving as instruction manuals for substance abuse. In each story, the abuser will be shown to pay the physical, mental, and/or social penalty for his or her abuse.

Crime

While crimes and criminals may be portrayed for dramatic purposes, crimes will never be presented in such a way as to inspire readers with a desire to imitate them nor will criminals be portrayed in such a manner as to inspire readers to emulate them. Stories will not present unique imitable techniques or methods of committing crimes.

Attire and Sexuality

Costumes in a comic book will be considered to be acceptable if they fall within the scope of contemporary styles and fashions. Scenes and dialogue involving adult relationships will be presented with good taste, sensitivity, and in a manner which will be considered acceptable by a mass audience. Primary human sexual characteristics will never be shown. Graphic sexual activity will never be depicted.

Administrative Procedure

I

All comics which member publishers wish to bear the Comics Code Seal will be submitted to the Code administrator for review prior to publication. The administra-

tor will review them according to the guidance he has received from the permanent committee and will either approve them to bear the seal, or return them to the publisher with his comments. The responsible editor from the publisher will either revise the comic, in accordance with those comments, or discuss with the administrator the concerns raised with him and reach agreement on how the comic can properly bear the Code Seal either without being revised or with a mutually agreeable set of alternative revisions. In the event no agreement can be reached between the editor and the administrator, the matter will be referred to the permanent committee, which will act promptly to determine if, or under what conditions, the comic in question can bear the Code Seal. Decisions of the permanent committee will be binding on the publishers, who agree not to place the Code Seal on any comic on which it is not authorized.

II

The members of the Comics Magazine Association of America include publishers who elect to publish comics that are not intended to bear the Code Seal, and that therefore need not go through the approval process described above. Among the comics in this category may be titles intended for adult readers. Member publishers hereby affirm that we will distribute these publications only through those distribution channels in which it is possible to notify retailers and distributors of their content, and thus help the publications reach their intended audiences. The member publishers agree to refrain from distributing these publications through those distribution channels that, like the traditional newsstand, are serviced by individuals who are unaware of the content of specific publications before placing them on display.

III

Recognizing that no document can address all the complex issues and concerns that face our changing society, the member publishers have established a permanent committee composed of the senior editor of each member's staff. This committee will meet regularly to review those issues and concerns as they affect our publications, and to meet with and guide the administrator of the Comics Code, and will replace the previous written guidelines of the Comics Code.

Appendix B
Reuben Award Winners

In April of each year the National Cartoonists Society awards the Reuben—so named in honor of Rube Goldberg, the NCS's first president—to an outstanding cartoonist for his or her achievements during the preceding year. (From 1946-53 it was called the Billy DeBeck Award.)

1946: **Milton Caniff**
1947: **Al Capp**
1948: **Chic Young**
1949: **Alex Raymond**

1950: **Roy Crane**
1951: **Walt Kelly**
1952: **Hank Ketcham**
1953: **Mort Walker**
1954: **Willard Mullin**
1955: **Charles Schulz**
1956: **Herbert Block (Herblock)**
1957: **Hal Foster**
1958: **Frank King**
1959: **Chester Gould**
1960: **Ronald Searle**

1961: **Bill Mauldin**
1962: **Dik Browne**
1963: **Fred Lasswell**
1964: **Charles Schulz**
1965: **Leonard Starr**
1966: **Otto Soglow**
1967: **Rube Goldberg**
1968: **Johnny Hart and Pat Oliphant (tied)**
1969: **Walter Berndt**
1970: **Alfred Andriola**
1971: **Milton Caniff**
1972: **Pat Oliphant**
1973: **Dik Browne**
1974: **Dick Moores**
1975: **Bob Dunn**
1976: **Ernie Bushmiller**
1977: **Chester Gould**
1978: **Jeff MacNelly**

1979: **Jeff MacNelly**
1980: **Charles Saxon**
1981: **Mell Lazarus**
1982: **Bil Keane**
1983: **Arnold Roth**
1984: **Brant Parker**
1985: **Lynn B. Johnston**
1986: **Bill Watterson**
1987: **Mort Drucker**
1988: **Bill Watterson**
1989: **Jim Davis**
1990: **Gary Larson**
1991: **Mike Peters**
1992: **Cathy Guisewite**
1993: **Jim Borgman**
1994: **Gary Larson**
1995: **Garry Trudeau**
1996: **Sergio Aragones**

Appendix C
Directory of Newspaper Syndicates

Chronicle Features
870 Market Street
San Francisco, CA 94102

Creators Syndicate
5777 W. Century Boulevard, Suite 700
Los Angeles, CA 90045

Editors Press Service
330 W. 42nd Street
New York, NY 10036

King Features Syndicate
235 E. 45th Street
New York, NY 10017

Los Angeles Times Syndicate
218 S. Spring Street
Los Angeles, CA 90012

Newspaper Enterprise Association
200 Madison Avenue
New York, NY 10016

Toronto Star Syndicate
1 Yonge Street
Toronto, ON M5E 1E6
Canada

Tribune Media Services
435 N. Michigan Avenue, Suite 1500
Chicago, IL 60611

United Feature Syndicate
200 Madison Avenue
New York, NY 10016

Universal Press Syndicate
4520 Main Street, Suite 700
Kansas City, MO 64111-7701

Washington Post Writer's Group
1150 15th Street NW
Washington, DC, 20071-9200

Appendix D
Directory of Comic Book Publishers

Acclaim Entertainment
One Acclaim Plaza
Glen Cove, NY 11542-2708

Caliber Comics
225 N. Sheridan Road
Plymouth, MI 48170

Comico Comics
119 W. Hubbard Street
Chicago, IL 60610

Dark Horse Comics
10956 SE Main Street
Milwaukie, OR 97222

DC Comics
1700 Broadway
New York, NY 10019

Fantagraphics
7563 Lake City Way NW
Seattle, WA 98113

Harris Comics
1115 Broadway
New York, NY 10010

Image Comics
1440 N. Harbor Boulevard, Suite 305
Fullerton, CA 92635

Kitchen Sink Press
320 Riverside Drive
Northampton, MA 01060

Marvel Entertainment Group
387 Park Avenue South
New York, NY 10016

Topps Comics
One Whitehall Street
New York, NY 10004

Warp Graphics
43 Haight Avenue
Poughkeepsie, NY 12601

Indices

A

Aasnes, Håkon, 75
Abuli, Enrique Sanchez, 771
Ache, Jean (pseud. of Huet, Jean), 98-99
Ackerman, Forrest, 787
Adams, Art, 292
Adams, George Matthew, 180, 271
Adams, Neal, 77, 104, 117, 131, 212, 344, 356, 357, 534, 583, 757, 821
Adams, Scott, 249-50, 716-17
Addison. *See* Walker, Addison Mortimer (pseud. of)
Adkins, Dan, 260, 759, 818, 821
Afonski, Nicholas (pseud. Afonsky, N.), 499, 535-36, 537, 686, 806, 813
Aguila, Dani, 79-80
Aguirre, Vir, 350
Ahern, Gene, 80-81, 322, 589-90, 660
Aidans, Edouard, 647
Ainsworth, Ed, 370
Aizen, Adolfo, 83
Akatsuka, Fujio, 38, 84, 588
Alan, Jay, 820
Albano, John, 735
Alber, Wolfgang, 632
Albert, Louis. *See* Régnier, Michel (pseud. of)
Albertarelli, Rino, 86, 143, 266, 344, 449, 543, 548, 603
Alberti, Mario, 562
Albertson, Ward, 550
Alcala, Alfredo P., 32, 86-87, 350, 462, 510, 651, 726, 793
Alcala, Larry, 32, 462, 674, 705-6, 772, 793
Alcazar, Victor. *See* Mora, Victor (pseud. of)
Alcover, Jaume Vidal, 717
Alessandrini, Giancarlo, 516-17, 575
Alexander, F. O., 322, 366
Alexandre, Arsene, 168
Alfieri, Janet, 732-33
Alger, Edwin, Jr. (pseud. of Williams, Jay Jerome), 613-14
AL G (pseud. of Gérard, Alexandre), 286
Allain, Marcel, 293
Allard, John, 335
Allen, Dale. *See* Connor, Dale; Saunders, Allen
Allen, J. B., 110, 393
Aloisi, Franco, 587, 765
Altman, Gerry, 219
Alvarado, Pete, 122, 261
Ambrosi, L., 522
Ambrosini, Carlo, 273
Ambrosio, Raffaele, 278
Ambrosio, Zaragoza Miguel (pseud. Ambros), 178
Amorsolo, Fernando, 773
Amos, Hart, 82

An Chung-min, 393-94
Anderson, Carl Thomas, 91-92, 185, 378-79, 382, 630
Anderson, Frank, 808
Anderson, Harold, 97, 454, 541, 593, 728
Anderson, Lyman, 92, 402-3, 581
Anderson, Murphy, 78, 92, 117, 159, 160, 374, 400, 683, 718, 736
Andersson, Oskar Emil (pseud. O. A.), 93, 510
Andreasson, Rune, 94, 479-80
Andrews, Jim, 423
Andriola, Alfred (pseud. James, Alfred), 94-95, 189, 195-96, 233, 440
Andru, Ross, 689, 718, 821
Angiolini, Sandro, 111, 404-5
Angissola, Giana, 614
Anglo, Mick, 95-96, 517, 544, 808
Angoletta, Bruno, 513-14
Anthony, Ed, 632
Anzi, Rino, 227
Aparo, Jim, 117, 344, 612
Appleby, Barry and Dobs, 332-33
Aragonés, Sergio, 99, 400
Arambula, Roman, 532
Arbeau, Jacques (pseud. Jacarbo), 286, 615
Archibald, Joe, 185
Arenas, Rafael, 89
Arikawa, Asakazu, 399
Aristides, Othon (pseud. Fred), 36, 527, 613
Armstrong, Mick, 364
Armstrong, Robb, 426-27
Armstrong, Roger, 162, 281, 486, 625
Armstrong, Stanley, 709
Arnal, Claude (pseud. of Cabrerero Arnal, José), 617, 621
Arnao, Gabriel (pseud. Gabi), 416, 694
Arnold, "Busy," 206, 219, 303, 364
Arrabal, Juan, 289
Arranz, Juan, 813
Arriola, Gus, 101, 351-52
Arthur, Paul. *See* Caniff, Milton; Terry, John
Asbury, Martin, 335
Aschmeier, Stan (pseud. Asch, Stan), 257, 258-59, 422, 541
Ashley, Frank and Jimmy, 621
Aso, Yutaka, 575-76
Asō, Yutaka, 766
Aston, Julian, 109
Attanasio, Dino, 100, 141, 352
Austin, Adam. *See* Colan, Eugene (pseud. of)
Austin, Steve, 404, 718
Austin, Terry, 481
Avai, Cesare. *See* Caesar, Kurt (pseud. of)
Avery, Fred ("Tex"), 162, 218, 231, 625

Avison, Al, 95, 357
Away, Caesar. *See* Caesar, Kurt (pseud. of)
Ayers, Richard, 104-5, 337, 424, 641, 689, 690

B

Baba, Tatsuo, 452
Backer, Henk, 107, 163, 773-74
Bäckmann, Axel, 282
Badert, A. G., 615
Baer, Stanley, 564
Baggioli, Vincenzo, 246-47
Bagnoli, Enrico, 327
Bailey, Ray, 158-59, 386, 728
Bails, Dr. Jerry, 756
Baily, Bernard, 318, 718, 791, 796
Bajeff, Igor Artz (pseud. of Micheluzzi, Attilio), 273, 530-31, 575
Baker, A. Z., 514
Baker, George, 27, 107-8, 122, 539, 669-70
Baker, Julius Stafford, 22, 188, 317, 761
Baker, Kyle, 204
Baker, Mart, 400
Baker, Matt, 204, 306, 379
Bakker, Jon, 372
Bakshi, Ralph, 324
Bald, Kenneth (pseud. Bruce, K.), 108, 257
Ball, Murray, 42, 311-12
Bancks, James Charles, 109-10, 343-44
Banger, Edgar Henry, 110, 246
Bara (pseud. of Herzog, Guy), 382, 523-24
Barbera, Joseph, 766, 773
Barbieri, Renzo, 111, 161, 404-5
Barker, Clive, 674
Barker, Gary, 333
Barker, Tom, 569
Barks, Carl, 111-12, 225, 253, 260-61, 324-25, 535, 648, 664, 744
Barlog, 325-326
Barreiro, Richard, 341, 714
Barrett, Monty, 411
Barrier, Mike, 214
Barrow, Hank, 820
Barry, Daniel, 115, 141, 222, 233, 308, 319, 376, 378, 443, 474, 698, 748
Barry, Lynda Jean, 115-16
Barry, Seymour (Sy), 75, 116, 308, 612, 683
Barth, Karl-Heinz, 459
Bartholomew, Harry Guy, 161, 498, 544
Bartier, Pierre, 418
Barton, Bob, 159

Index A

Proper Names Index

Barton, Les, 133
Bartsch, Art, 532
Bastianoni, Dante, 562
Batchelor, C. D., 550
Bateman, Henry Mayo, 116-17
Bates, Cary, 160, 378, 430, 490
Batet, Francisco, 217
Batho, H. O., 265
Batiuk, Tom, 326-27
Batsford, Ben, 482
Battaglia, Dino, 103, 118, 189, 602
Battaglia, Laura, 118
Battaglia, Roberto, 118, 509
Baxendale, Leo, 118-19, 242
Baxter, W. G., 89
Bea, José-Maria, 120
Beard, Cecil, 122, 162, 315-16, 316
Beardsley, John, 819
Bech, Carlos, 291
Beck, Charles Clarence, 26, 120-21,
   133, 164, 182-83, 223, 518,
   723-24
Beck, Frank Hem, 121, 806
Becker, Franziska, 121-22
Becker, Stephen, 599
Beek, Ton, 454
Beker, Žarko, 123, 327
Belale, Seg, 462
Belardinelli, Massimo, 103
Belbin, Phil, 82
Bell, Steve, 123-24
Bell, Walter, 124-25
Bellamy, Frank, 36, 61, 123, 125,
   232, 335, 368
Bellavitis, Giorgio, 103, 118
Belson, Jerry, 122, 231
Bender, Jack, 88, 368
Benedicto, Fernández, 631
Benejam, Marino, 291
Bennett, James Gordon, 497
Bennett, Spencer Gordon, 152, 158
Benoit, Ted, 137
Bentley, Stephen R., 379
Berardi, Giancarlo, 439-40
Beretta, Vincenzo, 516
Berg, David, 125-26
Berg, Vivian Lipman, 126
Bergdahl, Gustav Victor, 126-27
Bergèse, Francis, 159
Bergua, Erique Jarnés. See Jarber
   (pseud. of)
Berhard, Manfred, 131
Berndt, Walter, 127, 550, 712
Bernet, Jordi, 41, 771
Bernet, Jorge, 94
Beroth, Leon A., 263
Berrill, Jack, 127-28
Bertelot, Hector, 607
Bertolini, Mario, 286
Bess, Gordon, 128, 643-44
Bestall, Alfred, 666
Bester, Alfred, 357, 804
Betts, Frank, 807

Bevère, Maurice de (pseud. Morris),
   29, 129-30, 318, 339, 352,
   492-93
Bianconi, Renato, 715
Biassoni, Marco, 731
Bibber, Max van, 150, 813
Biggers, Earl Derr, 94
Biggs, Walter, 92
Bignot, Franco, 327
Bignotti, Franco, 177
Bilal, Enki, 40, 131-32
Billingsley, Ray, 228-29
Billon, Daniel, 111
Binder, Eando. See Binder, Otto O.
   (pseud. of)
Binder, Earl, 133
Binder, Jack, 133, 135, 164, 223, 233,
   234, 257, 302, 518, 678, 691, 693
Binder, Otto O. (pseud. Binder,
   Eando), 117, 133-34, 164, 183,
   184, 185, 223, 368, 399, 518,
   541, 683, 726, 732, 734-35, 804,
   827
Binet, Christian, 134
Biro, Charles, 81, 134-35, 137, 219,
   222, 233, 443-44, 726
Bishop, Wally, 552
Bisi, Carlo, 23, 717-18
Bisley, Simon, 424
Bissette, Stephen, 461, 738
Bjarre, Torsten, 282, 314, 479
Blackaller, 596
Blackton, J. Stuart, 66
Blair, Joe, 379
Blaisdel, Philip (Tex), 627
Blake, Bud, 760
Blake, Everett. See Everett, Bill
   (pseud. of)
Blake, William. See Everett, Bill
   (pseud. of)
Blanc, Mel, 162
Blanco, Manuel Lopez, 341, 514
Blasco, Adriano, 138
Blasco, Alejandro, 138
Blasco, Jesus, 96-97, 137-38, 179,
   229-30, 361
Bleach, James, 282, 518
Blik. See Dowling, Frank; Dowling,
   Steve
Blonay, Paulette, 286
Blosser, Merrill, 140, 320, 414
Blotta, Oscar, 140
Bluhm, Hans, 285, 525
Blum, Alex, 140, 204, 399
Blumenfield, R. D., 665
Blummer, Jon, 302, 693
Blyth, Harry, (pseud. Meredyth, Hal),
   690-91
Bobic, Ljubinka, 512
Bocquet, José-Louis, 415
Bogdanović, Dusan, 830
Boivin, René, 196
Boldman, Craig, 100
Bolland, Brian, 424, 547

Bolland, Bruce, 395
Bolle, Frank, 222, 376, 628, 813
Bom, Michel de, 200
Bonato, Armando, 161, 603
Bonazzi, Germano, 562
Bond, J. Harvey (pseud. of
   Winterbotham, Russ), 791, 814
Bonelli, Gianluigi, 327, 449
Bonelli, Giovanni Luigi, 91, 118, 143,
   202, 753-54
Bonelli, Sergio, 143, 273, 301, 516,
   754
Bonvicini, Franco (pseud. Bonvi), 18,
   37, 144-45, 731
Booth, Walter, 146-47, 657, 808
Bordillo, Jun, 350
Boring, Wayne (pseud. Harmon,
   Jack), 147-48, 462, 736-37, 804
Boscarato, Carlo, 575
Bostwick, Sals, 660
Bottaro, Luciano, 148-49, 198, 227,
   587-88, 606, 644
Bouchard, Gerry, 730
Boucq, François, 40, 149
Bourgeois, Albéric, 607
Bowen, Major T. E., 185
Boyce, D. W., 517
Boyette, Pat, 344, 809
Bozzoli, Flavio, 245
Brabner, Joyce, 91
Bradley, Marvin, 231, 649-50
Brady, Pat, 661-62
Brand, Nat, 243
Brandoli, Anna, 150
Brandon, Barbara, 806-7
Brandon, Brumsic, 778
Brangwyn, Frank, 87
Branner, Martin, 21, 127, 157, 313,
   616, 706, 790, 813, 820
Brant, Remington. See Briefer,
   Richard (pseud. of)
Braun, Caspar, 277
Bray, J. R., 309
Breathed, Berke, 39, 139-40, 591-92
Breccia, Alberto, 41, 123, 150, 286,
   549, 552, 580, 714
Breger, David, 27, 150-51, 538-39
Breisacher, George, 556, 711
Brennan, T. Casey, 787
Brent, Bob, 426
Bresciani, Andrea, 768
Bretecher, Claire, 122, 192
Briault, Louis, 188
Briefer, Richard (pseud. Brant,
   Remington; Norman, Richard;
   Stein, Frank N.), 152-53, 316-17
Briggs, Austin, 153, 308, 354, 427,
   576, 623, 641, 686, 813
Briggs, Clare, 17, 97-98, 153-54, 187,
   304, 429, 498, 538, 555, 728,
   762, 806
Briggs, Raymond, 154
Brigman, June, 152, 154
Brindisi, Bruno, 273

Brinkerhoff, Robert Moore, Jr., 155, 802
Brinkerhoff, Robert Moore, 155
Brion, Marcel, 299
Brisbane, Arthur, 20, 498
Broberg, Krister, 297
Broca, Nicolas, 721
Brödl, Günter, 633
Broenland, Piet-Hein, 149
Broome, John, 104, 307, 316, 357, 430, 683
Broos, Piet, 156-57, 707
Brown, Albert Thacker ("Bertie"), 157, 386
Brown, Bob, 104, 338, 641
Brown, Cliff, 797
Brown, Gary, 756
Brown, Leonard, 758-59
Brown, Wasdale, 650
Brown, William F., 189
Browne, Bob, 383
Browne, Chris, 158
Browne, Dik, 34, 157-58, 365-66, 383, 385, 632
Browne, Tom, 83, 124, 125, 157, 158, 187, 205, 801, 812, 823
Bruce, K. (pseud. of Bald, Kenneth), 108, 257
Bruggman, Alfred, 346
Brugman, Cideon, 372
Brunel, Adrian, 145
Brunner, Frank, 260
Bryant, Al, 260
Brydner, Janne, 348
Büchi, Werver, 346
Buck, Frank, 427, 749
Buckler, Rich, 307, 705
Buell, Marjorie Henderson (pseud. Margie), 485-86
Buendía, Fausto, Jr., 600
Buettner, Carl, 162, 218
Buffolente, Lina, 161, 162, 202, 476, 684
Bugg, Bob, 267
Buigas, Joaquin, 291
Bulanadi, Danny, 163, 462
Bülow, Bernhard-Victor von (pseud. Loriot), 163-64
Bunker, Max. *See* Secchi, Luciano (pseud. of)
Bun Lour Utsahajit, 165
Burgon, Sid, 166
Burgos, Carl, 26, 166, 287, 397
Burnley, Jack, 430, 724-25, 804
Burns, Charles, 719
Burns, John, 686
Burvik, Mabel Odin, 247, 801
Bus, Bert, 707
Buscema, John, 103, 104, 166-67, 212, 292, 395, 397, 568, 610, 704, 705, 748, 757, 821
Buscema, Sal, 104, 182, 338, 732

Busch, Wilhelm, 12, 121, 167-68, 253, 277, 285, 437, 504, 524, 579, 581, 770
Bushmiller, Ernest, 168, 481, 560-61, 685
Busino, Orlando, 548
Bustos, Luis, 552
Butschkow, Peter, 169
Butterworth, Jenny, 36, 760
Butze Oliver, German, 169
Butze Oliver, Valdemar, 169
Buylla (pseud. of Rodriguez, Braulio), 249
Buzzelli, Guido, 170
Byck, Sylvan, 179, 376, 383, 538
Byrne, John, 104, 118, 170-71, 182, 292, 397, 404, 718, 726, 736, 809, 821
Byrnes, Eugene, 171-72, 646-47

C

C. F. (pseud. of Folkard, Charles), 18, 317
Cabrera, Jesus Acosta, 201
Cabrerero Arnal, José (pseud. Arnal, Claude), 617, 621
Cabuhat, Mauro, 675
Cady, Harrison, 611
Caesar, Kurt (pseud. Avai, Cesare; Away, Caesar), 173, 603, 609, 659-60
Calcaterra, Ivan, 562
Calkins, Dick, 23, 92, 159, 173, 438, 645, 708
Calvo, Edmond-François, 174-75
Camerata, Al, 137
Campagna, Hal, 155
Campani, Paul, 539
Campbell, Cliff, 368
Campbell, E. Simms, 778
Campbell, Eddy, 547
Canale, Antonio, 91, 175, 792
Cance, Louis, 617
Caniff, Milton, 24, 27, 28, 62, 63, 71, 94, 158, 159, 175-76, 179, 213, 215, 247, 354, 391, 506-7, 529, 539, 579, 593, 627, 684, 700, 725, 727-28, 729-30, 751-52, 801, 820
Cannellas Casals, José, 669
Canzio, Decio, 162
Capadonio, Giuseppe, 162
Caparas, Carlo J., 163
Caplin, Alfred Gerald. *See* Capp, Al (pseud.)
Caplin, Deborah, 478
Caplin, Elliot, 75, 130, 179, 231-32, 267, 376-77, 490, 554
Caplin, Jerry, 179
Capp, Al (pseud. of Caplin, Alfred Gerald), 24, 30, 61, 75, 179-80,

249, 280, 284, 294-95, 304, 319, 420, 445, 470, 478-79, 490, 492, 501, 788
Caprioli, Franco, 180
Caravana, Nemesio, 659
Caravana, Tony, 32, 350, 793
Cardy, Nick, 278, 400
Cardy (pseud. of Viskardy, Nicholas), 748
Caregaro, Giuseppe, 227
Carew, Kate, 271
Carey, Ed, 185-86, 804
Carey, John, 162, 231, 625
Carillo, Fred, 32, 350
Carillo, Manuel, 32
Carleton, Henry Guy, 499
Carlson, Wallace A., 186, 383, 564
Carpenter, John Alden, 457
Carpi, Giovanni Battista, 198, 587, 715
Carpinteri, Giorgio, 521
Carr, Eugene, 186, 581
Carr, Sir William, 302
Carr, Thomas, 152, 158
Carreño, Albert, 186-87
Carroll, Les, 147, 516, 590
Carroll, Ruth, 632
Carter, Augustus Daniels (pseud. Carter, Ad) 187, 212, 429, 569, 647
Carter, Reg, 187
Carteret, John, 387
Cartier, Edd, 257, 400, 691
Casarotti, Gino, 111
Casertano, Giampiero, 273, 517
Casin, Stefano, 562
Casquel, Miguel Gonzalez, 359
Casson, Melvin, 95, 189, 404, 644
Cassone, John, 801
Cassone, Sandro, 344
Castelli, Alfredo, 189-90, 508, 516, 608, 658
Castellini, Claudio, 562
Castrillo, Amado S., 573
Castrillo, Ding S., 793
Catalano, Roberto, 228
Caumery (pseud. of Languereau, Maurice), 120, 617
Cauvin, Raoul, 721
Cavazzano, Giorgio, 191, 617
Cavedon, Giorgio, 404
Cazanave, Raymond, 176
Cazeneuve, Art, 135, 357
Cazeneuve, Lou, 725
Celardo, John (pseud. Lardo, John C.), 170, 191-92, 267, 748
Certa, Joe, 184, 257
Cézard, Jean, 192-93
Chaffin, Glen, 311, 438, 743-44
Chai Rachawat, 193-94
Chaland, Yves, 194-95, 721
Chang, Eric, 540
Chaplain, Frederick, 666
Chapman, C. H., 132

Index A
Proper Names Index

Chapman, Steve, 209
Charlebois, J., 607
Charlier, Jean-Michel, 159, 196, 241, 345, 396, 476-77, 529, 647, 781
Charteris, Leslie, 686
Chartier, Albert, 196-97
Chatterton, George, 631
Chatto, Keith, 82
Chaulet, George (pseud. Georges, François), 217
Chaykin, Howard, 40, 197-98, 212, 726
Chayrin, Jerome, 149
Chendi, Carlo, 149, 198, 228, 587, 606, 644, 765
Chen Ping, 674
Chéret, André, 638-39
Chiaverotti, Claudio, 273
Chiba, Akio, 199, 370
Chiba, Tetsuya, 38, 101, 198-99
Chierchini, Giulio, 587, 715
Chiletto, Franco, 143, 266, 549
Chmielewski, Henryk Jerzy (pseud. Chimel), 200
Christensen, Bert, 684
Christensen, Don, 122, 162, 231, 625
Christiansen, Anne, 346
Christiansen, Arthur, 210
Christin, Pierre (pseud. Linus), 131, 527, 745, 786
Christman, Bert, 200, 673, 820
Christophe. *See* Colomb, Georges (pseud. of)
Chu, Ronald (pseud. of Chu Teh-Yung), 200-201
Chua, Enrie, 212
Chu Hsiang-chun, 393-94
Chung-chien, Lu, 345
Chu Teh-Yung (pseud. Chu, Ronald), 200-201
Cifre, Guillermo, 202
Cilino, Frank, 309
Cimpellin, Leone, 162, 202-3, 602, 603
Cinco, Terry, 418
Ciocca, Walter, 203, 481
Clampett, Bob, 162, 625
Claremont, Chris, 397, 568
Clark, George, 354
Clark, Jim, 386
Clark, Peter, 797
Class, Alan, 236
Coching, Francisco V., 32, 350, 400, 462
Cochran, John, 787
Cochran, Ned, 592, 810
Cochran, Russ, 401
Cocking, Percy (pseud. Daw, Jack), 205-6, 801
Cockrum, Dave, 821
Coelho, E. T., 215
Cohl, Emile, 501, 567, 616

Colan, Eugene (pseud. Austin, Adam), 104, 118, 182, 183, 206, 233, 260, 395, 403, 534, 732
Colantuoni, Tiberio, 227, 715, 765
Cole, Jack (pseud. Johns, Ralph), 26, 206, 364, 471, 621-22
Coletta, Vince, 732
Coll, Charles, 557, 693
Colletta, Vince, 735
Colley, Ed, 732-33
Collins, Dennis, 608
Collins, Max Allan, 489
Collins, Ray (pseud. Zappietto, Eugenio), 239, 249, 441, 552
Colomb, Georges (pseud. Christophe), 12, 206-8, 290, 292, 399, 770
Colquhoun, Joe, 208-9
Combe, William, 663
Comés, Didiet, 211
Condre, J., 438
Conleys, Eugene, 728
Connell, Del, 485
Connelly, Joe, 485
Conner, Dale, 518-19
Connolly, Joseph, 638
Connor, Dale, 677
Conselman, Bill, 280-81
Conte, Brigitte, 346
Conti, Oscar (pseud. Oski), 213
Conway, Gerald, 233, 397, 404, 718, 757
Cooke, Brian, 468
Cooper, Robert St. John, 468
Corbella, Ferdinando, 132, 562, 659
Corben, Richard Vance, 213-14
Corbett, Bertha, 271, 632
Cordwell, Frederick, 795
Cores, Carlos, 480-81
Coria, Francisco, 141
Cornelius, Cosper, 87, 300
Corno, Andrea, 459
Cornwell, Bruce, 232
Cornwell, Dean, 87
Corteggiani, François, 191
Cortez, Jayme, 215
Cory, Fanny Young, 215-16, 348, 632
Cosgriff, Jack, 122
Cossio, Carlo, 161, 216, 228, 246-47, 327, 659
Cossio, Vittorio, 216, 247
Costanza, Pete, 120, 723
Coulson, Juanita, 135, 693
Counihan, Bud, 129
Coutelis, Alexandre, 529
Covarrubias, Miguel, 187
Cowan, Denys, 356
Cox, Erle, 592
Cox, Palmer, 441, 628
Craenhals, François (pseud. Hals, F.), 36, 198, 217-18
Craft, Jerry, 218
Craig, Chase, 162, 218-19, 625
Craig, John, 219, 331, 404

Crammond, Harry, 574
Crandall, Reed, 136, 219-20, 260, 303, 308, 331, 364, 379, 400, 401, 458, 471, 587, 759, 818, 819
Crane, Royston Campbell (Roy), 27, 158, 169-70, 220, 322, 727, 777, 799-800
Cravath, Glen, 749
Craveri, Sebastiano (pseud. Pin-Tin), 221
Crawford, Arthur, 150
Crawford, Mel, 270
Crenshaw, George, 685
Crepax, Guido, 37, 39, 61, 221-22, 627, 785
Cretti, Glauco, 245
Crooks, Bill, 800
Crosby, Leo, 740
Crosby, Percy Leo, 222-23, 325, 552, 647, 707-8
Cross, Stanley George, 223, 625, 666, 797
Crouch, Bill, 635
Crowley, Wendell, 183, 223
Cruikshank, George, 223-24
Crumb, Charles, 323
Crumb, Robert, 36, 39, 91, 224-26, 284, 289, 323-24, 449, 463, 481, 540-41, 694
Cruse, Howard, 40, 226-27
Cruz, Gemma, 659
Cubbino, Mario, 190
Cubie, Alex, 666
Cudlipp, Hugh, 418
Cueto, Francisco, 348
Cuidera, Chuck, 136, 219, 622
Čukli, Marcel, 738
Culliford, Pierre (pseud. Peyo), 36, 228, 318, 680
Culliford, Thierry, 680
Cusso, Miguel, 94
Cuti, Nick, 809
Cutrate, Joe. *See* Spiegelman, Arthur (pseud. of)
Cuvelier, Paul, 214

D

Daix, Andre, 630
Dale, Allen. *See* Connor, Dale; Saunders, Allen (pseud. of)
Daley, Brian, 726
Dallis, Nicholas, 32, 97, 231-32, 424-26, 454, 649-50
Dalmasso, Giacomo, 111
Dalton, Cal, 162, 315
D'Ami, Rinaldo (pseud. D'Amy, Roy), 510
Damiani, Damiano, 103
Damonte Taborda, Raul, 232
Daniel, Vincent, 657
D'Antonio, Gino, 118, 602, 771

Dany (pseud. of Henrotin, Daniel), 127, 647
Darien. *See* Dingle, Adrian (pseud. of)
Darnis, Francisco, 407
Darrow, Geoff, 534
Darthel, J. (pseud. of Velter, Robert), 339, 630, 721, 790-91
Darthl, J., 630
David, Peter, 718
Davies, George, 302
Davies, Roland (pseud. Pip), 210-11, 236, 691, 749
Davis, Art, 625
Davis, Jack, 129, 236-37, 278, 315, 316, 331, 361, 401, 458, 463, 481, 641, 812
Davis, Jim, 39, 237, 333-34, 667
Davis, Martha, 238
Davis, Phil, 24, 237-38, 290-91, 321, 508-9
Davis, Roy, 166, 797
Daw, Jack (pseud of. Cocking, Percy), 205-6, 801
Dawkins, Colin, 690
Day, Gene, 519
Daziell, Gilbert, 89
Dean, Allen, 370, 446
Dean, Roger, 433
De Angelis, Ottavio, 150
De Angelis, Robert, 562
De Beck, Billy, 22, 114, 165, 196, 238, 352, 469, 547, 554, 600, 809, 813
Debrix, J. R., 66
De Carlo, Dan, 100, 131
DeCesare, Angelo, 437
Decker, Dwight, 704
De Dios, Greg Igna, 675
De Falco, Tom, 646
Deitch, Kim, 284
Delač, Vladimir, 238-39
DeLara, Phil, 122, 162, 231, 625
Del Castillo, Arturo, 33, 161, 239, 462, 580, 663
Del Duca, Alceo, 734
Del Duca, Domenico, 314, 629, 734
De Leo, Giovanni, 143
Dell'Acqua, Edgardo, 176, 342, 344
Dell'Agnol, Piero, 273
Delmasso, Gian Giacoma, 596
Delporte, Yves, 680
Del Principe, Nicolino, 715
Del Río, Eduardo (pseud. Ríus), 79, 735
DeLuca, Gianni, 211, 240-41
De Moor, Bob, 137
Dennett, Joe, 669, 711
Dennis, C. J., 364
Dent, Lester, 257
Derib (pseud. of Ribeaupierre, Claude de), 647
Dern, Marion, 651
De Souza, Maurico, 41, 215, 243
Devescovi, Franco, 517

Devil, Nicholas, 670
De Vine, Albert, 535
De Vita, Pier Lorenzo, 602
Devlin, Johnny, 233
Diamond, H. Louis, 110, 245-46
Dibble, Bernard, 182, 375
Dickens, Frank, 36, 155
Dickenson, Fred, 246, 308, 627, 653
Dickson, Don, 729-30
Dierckx, Rik, 161
Dijkstra, Waling, 372
Dill, Klaus, 128
Dillin, Dan, 429
Dimitrijevic, Mica, 512
Ding Cong (pseud. Xiao Ding), 250-51
Dingle, Adrian (pseud. Darian), 251-52, 565, 606, 649
Ding Song, 250
Dionnet, Jean-Pierre, 131
DiPreta, Tony, 81, 233, 420, 650
Dirgo, Ray, 809
Dirks, Gus, 514
Dirks, John, 182
Dirks, Rudolph, 14, 19, 168, 182, 233, 252-53, 317, 375, 436-37, 448, 504
Disney, Walt, 253, 261, 353, 531-32, 554, 734, 755
Ditko, Steve, 35, 140, 253-54, 259-60, 344, 400, 403, 472, 527, 612, 660, 718, 759, 818
Divito, Guillermo, 254-55, 257-58, 291, 399
Dixon, Chuck, 560
Dixon, John Dangar, 81-82, 255
Dixon, Les, 141
Dobrić, Milorad, 256
Dodd, Edward Benton, 512-13
Dodd, Howell, 684
Dodd, Maurice, 608
Doisy, Jean, 339
Donahey, Joe, 709
Donahue, Don, 224, 540
Donatelli, Franco, 143, 327
Donnenfeld, Harry, 26, 524, 735
Dorfman, Leo, 735
Dorgan, Thomas Aloysius (Tad), 264-65, 360
Dorne, Al, 267
Dovniković, Borivoj, 239, 266
Dowling, Frank, 267, 665
Dowling, Steve, 123, 266-67, 334-35, 429, 665
Downs, Sarah, 463
Doya, Ippei, 399
Doyle, Larry, 623
Drake, Stanley, 32, 267, 376-77, 722, 725, 812
Drappier, Franz, 415
Drayton, Grace (pseud. Wiedersheim, Grace), 267-68, 271, 631-32
Drucker, Mort, 270, 316
Druillet, Philippe, 269
Duan Jifu, 269-70

Dubois, Gaylord, 748
Dubois, Pierre, 303
Dubos, Danie, 614
Duchateau, André-Paul, 335, 436, 650-51, 663
Duffy, J. C., 327-28
Duga, Giovanni, 715
Dugmore, Harry, 503
Du Jianguo, 269
Dumas, Gerald, 144, 270, 673, 796
Dumas, Jacques (pseud. François, Jacques; Marijac), 175, 176, 270-71, 345, 361, 415-16, 624, 774
Dumm, Frances Edwina, 180, 271-72
Dunbar, Geoff, 666
Dunkley, Jack, 468
Dunn, Bob, 360, 483, 755
Dunn, Harvey, 92
Dupanloup, Luc (pseud. Dupa), 227
Durbridge, Francis, 599
Durham, Robert C., 451
Duval, Marie (pseud of. Tessier, Emilie de), 88
Duval, Yves, 788
Duvall, Earl, 532
Dwiggins, Clare Victor, 272-73, 349, 514
Dworkins, Leon, 159
Dyer, Bill, 598
Dyson, Will, 569

E

Eade, Charles, 210
Earrol, Paul (pseud. of Gustafson, Paul), 364
Eastman, Kevin, 749-50
Eaton, Mal, 610
Ebara, Shin, 199
Ebner, Marijan (pseud. of Kalmarevic, Dragan), 473
Echeverria, Carlos, 359
Ed, Carl Frank Ludwig, 275, 370-71, 392
Eden, Eric, 232
Edgar, James, 161
Edgington, Frank, 231, 649
Edgren, Bob, 711
Edson, Gus, 262, 275-76, 362, 373, 481
Edward, Scott. *See* Kane, Gil (pseud. of)
Egan, John, 535
Egerbrandt, Nils, 572
Eguillor, Juan Carlos, 512
Eisenberg, Harvey, 767
Eisman, Hy, 437, 483, 755, 756
Eisner, Will, 26-27, 40, 71, 83, 92, 102, 133, 260, 277-78, 295, 303, 391, 400, 454, 692, 693, 720, 727, 818

Index A
Proper Names Index

Elder, William W., 237, 278, 319, 331, 378, 463, 481, 690
Eleuteri Serpieri, Paolo, 278-79
Elias, Leopold, 78, 135, 185, 280, 307
Ellis, Frank, 411
Ellis, Warren, 787
Ellison, Harlan, 397
Ellsworth, Whitney, 117, 434
Elrod, Jack, 513
Elworth, Lennart, 282, 314
Embleton, Ronald S., 282, 518
Englehart, Steve, 104, 260, 397, 519
Ernst, Kenneth, 263, 285, 519, 677
Ernsting, Volker, 285, 533-34
Erwin, Will. *See* Eisner, Will (pseud. of)
Escher, Reinhold, 169, 285-86, 525, 648
Escobar, Josep, 186
Esposito, Mike, 689
Essegesse (pseud. of Sinchetto, Sartoris, Guzzon), 177, 446-47
Estrada, Ric, 308, 690
Estren, Mark, 224
Evanier, Mark, 122, 162, 231, 625
Evans, George, 81, 204, 219-20, 286-87, 331, 686, 690
Everett, Bill (pseud. Blake, Everett; Blake, William), 26, 90, 131, 166, 206, 233, 260, 287, 731-32
Ewer, Raymond Crawford, 19, 709
Ezquerra, Carlos, 424

F
_____

Facciolo, Enzio, 245
Fagarazzi, Daniele, 190
Fago, Vincent, 611
Fajardo, Perez, 311
Falk, Lee, 24, 238, 290-91, 321, 361, 399, 508-9, 611-12, 677
Fallberg, Carl, 162
Fasani, Angelo, 587
Fauche, Xavier, 493
Faustinelli, Mario, 102, 627
Fawcett, Gene, 185
Fawcett, Robert, 87, 267
Fawkes, Wally (pseud. Trog), 29, 310
Fazekas, Attila, 294
Feiffer, Jules, 33, 62, 295-96, 775, 807, 816
Feign, Larry, 296-97
Feininger, Lyonel, 14, 16, 19, 63, 71, 297, 444-45, 525, 628, 804
Feldmann, Andi, 805
Feldmann, Rötger (pseud. Brösel), 805
Feldstein, Al, 126, 237, 297, 331, 400, 401, 458, 818
Fenderson, Mark, 499
Feng Zikai, 300
Fera, A. C., 281-82, 740, 813

Ferdinand, Ron, 242, 441
Ferguson, Fred, 370
Fernandez, Fernando, 41, 301, 793
Fernandez, Jim, 32, 343
Ferrer, Manuel, 239
Ferrier, Arthur, 301-2
Ferro, Ted, 113, 474
Figueras, Alfonso, 102, 302
Filho, Manoel Victor, 83
Filippucci, Lucio, 517
Fine, Louis (pseud. Berold, Basil; Cortez, Jack; Lectron, E.; Lewis, Kenneth), 26, 77, 86, 92, 133, 135-36, 303, 364, 379, 400, 471, 622, 720
Finger, Bill, 117, 303, 357, 434, 656, 804
Finne, Jalmari, 604
Fischer, Ludwig, 305
Fischer, Margot, 497
Fisher, Hammond Edward, 179, 255, 303-4, 420, 478, 531
Fisher, Harry Conway (Bud), 16-17, 66, 98, 201, 304-5, 419, 555-56
Fisher, William, 317
Fitzgerald, Owen, 316
Flagg, James Montgomery, 347, 395
Flanders, Charles, 306-7, 446, 490, 686, 763, 813
Flax (pseud. of Palacio, Lino), 263, 595
Fleischer, Dave, 309
Fleischer, Max, 129, 309, 755
Fleisher, Michael, 424
Flessel, Craig, 673
Fletcher, Frank, 155, 249, 309
Fletcher, Rick, 489, 582
Fletcher, Wendy, 279-80
Flinders, Evelyn, 309-10, 704
Flinton, Ben, 104
Flooglebuckle, Al. *See* Spiegelman, Arthur (pseud. of)
Florese, Rudy, 462
Floyd, Dick, 617-18
Flynt, Larry, 809
Fogelberg, Ola (pseud. Fogeli), 603-4
Fogelberg-Kalia, Toto, 604
Folkard, Charles (pseud. C. F.), 18, 317, 749
Folkard, Harry, 749
Folwell, Arthur, 538
Forest, Jean-Claude (pseud. Valherbe, Jean), 36, 39, 110-11, 313, 722, 746, 787
Forman, Tom, 379, 551
Formhals, Henry, 140, 320, 420
Forrest, Hal, 24, 743-44
Forsythe, Vic, 419-20
Fortess, Karl, 61
Forton, Louis, 22, 130, 141-42, 256, 313-14, 615, 829
Forza, John, 314
Fosgrave, Les, 563
Fossati, Franco, 672

Foster, Bob, 261
Foster, Harold, 23, 71, 86, 125, 147, 213, 215, 220, 287, 315, 347, 348, 374, 389, 400, 411, 427, 457, 460, 467, 510, 524, 525, 554, 628-29, 645, 662, 678, 716, 738, 747, 748, 752
Foster, Warren, 315
Fournier, Jean-Claude, 721
Foust, Felix, 429
Fox, Fontaine Talbot, Jr., 316, 600, 647, 768-69
Fox, Fred, 218, 281
Fox, Gardner (pseud. Cooper, Jefferson; Sommers, Bart), 78, 104, 117, 212, 257, 307, 316-17, 319, 357, 374, 376, 422, 429, 430, 673, 683, 718, 724
Fox, Gil, 136, 267, 673
Foxwell, Herbert, 22, 317, 749, 761
Fradon, Ramona, 152, 154, 527
Franchi, C., 830-31
Francis, Stephen, 503
Francisco, Carlos, 32
François, André, 559
François, Jacques. *See* Dumas, Jacques (pseud. of)
Franićević, Andra, 256
Franklin, Robert. *See* Goodwin, Archie (pseud. of)
Franquin, André, 318-19, 337, 339, 721
Frazetta, Frank, 160, 212, 220, 308, 319-20, 331, 337, 401, 432, 481, 587, 787, 811
Fredericks, Fred, 509
Fredericks, Harold, 321
Fred (pseud. of Aristides, Othon), 36, 527, 613
Freeman, Don, 161, 544
Freghieri, Gianni, 273
Frehm, Paul, 749, 813
Frehm, Walter, 813
Freixas, Carlos, 579, 619-20
Freixas, Emilio, 177, 197
Freleng, Fritz, 162, 231, 625
Fremon, Jess, 806
Frescura, Franco, 228, 765
Freyse, Bill, 322, 590
Friedrich, Gary, 338, 397, 404, 689
Friedrich, Mike, 430
Frink, George, 709
Frise, James Llewellyn, 322-23
Frollo, Leone, 111
Frost, A. B., 499
Fry, Christopher, 208
Fry, Michael, 593-94
Fuchs, Erika, 324-25
Fuchs, Wolfgang, 680
Fuente, Victor de la, 37, 343, 375
Fuji, Bob, 443
Fujiko, Fujio, 755
Fujitani, Bob, 222, 368
Fukui, Eiichi, 83, 399

Fukumoto, Kazuya, 199
Fukushima, Tetsuji, 669
Fukuzawa, Yukichi, 448
Fuller, Ralph Briggs, 325, 579
Fung, Paul, 271, 322, 326, 624, 813
Fung, Paul, Jr., 139, 326
Furness, Ed, 321-22
Furtinger, Zvonimir, 123, 327, 380, 638
Fusco, Ferdinando, 754
Fyfe, Hamilton, 372

G

Gabi (pseud. of Arnao, Gabriel), 416, 694
Gabriele, Al, 135, 827
Gabrielsen, D., 137
Gago, Manuel, 361
Gahlin, Torvald, 450, 480
Gaiman, Neil, 500, 674, 744
Gaines, William M., 126, 219, 297, 331-32, 401, 458, 472, 587, 690, 735, 818
Gajō, 745
Galleppini, Aurelio, 29, 753-54
Gamba, Francisco, 754
Gamba, Pietro, 111, 446, 603
Gambiotta, Giorgio, 609
Gamblin, Len, 311
Gamboli, Mario, 145
Gammidge, Henry, 409
Gammidge, Ian, 311, 665
Gan, Steve, 350, 462
García Lopez, José Luis, 424, 663
García Lopez, Ricardo (pseud. K-Hito), 23, 497
Garland, Nicholas, 36
Garnier, Max Massimino, 539
Garofalo, Romano, 203
Gascard, Gilbert (pseud. Tibet), 335, 650
Gattia, Alarico, 245
Gaty, Christian, 241
Gavioli, Gino, 273
Georges, François (pseud. of Chaulet, George), 217
Gérard, Alexandre (pseud. AL G), 286
Gerber, Steve, 394-95
Gertenaar, Piet, 768
Gey, Moum (pseud. of Solovjev, Sergej), 715-16
Ghastly. *See* Ingels, Graham (pseud. of)
Gherlizza, Egidio, 688-89, 765
Giacoia, Frank, 183, 400, 430, 827
Giardino, Vittorio, 41, 338-39
Gibbons, Dave, 40, 232, 534, 547, 800
Gibbs, Cecilia May, 130, 339
Gibbs, Ron, 429
Gibson, Charles Dana, 325, 469, 514

Gibson, Ian, 424
Gibson, Walter Brown (pseud. Grant, Maxwell), 691
Giella, Joe, 104, 307, 519
Giffey, René, 286
Gifford, Denis (pseud. Kol), 96, 518, 545, 590, 608, 693, 729, 750
Gil, Hugo, 286
Gilchrist, Brad and Guy, 561
Gill, Joe, 379
Gill, Tom, 490, 705
Gillain, John (pseud. Jijé), 33, 241, 318, 339, 345, 415, 529, 663, 721
Gillain, Laurent (pseud. Lorg), 241, 339
Gillain, Philippe, 339, 415
Gillon, Paul, 302-3
Gillray, James, 11, 224, 339-40, 663
Gimenez, Carlos, 37, 239, 341, 359-60, 514, 663
Gimenez, Juan, 341
Giner, Eugenio, 402
Giolitti, Alberto, 103, 161
Giordano, Richard, 136, 344, 429, 583
Giovannini, Ruggero, 575
Giraud, Jean (pseud. Gir), 36, 196, 345, 476-77
Gire, Eugène, 606
Giunta, John, 319, 759
Giussani, Angela and Luciana, 37, 245
Glackens, Louis, 395
Glanzman, Sam, 90
Glass, Jack, 345-46
Glass, Montague, 76
Glenn, Bill St. John, 749
Gloria (pseud.), 123
Glut, Don, 625
Godfrey, Bob, 123
Godwin, Francis, 24, 30, 147, 212-13, 347-48
Godwin, Frank, 557, 666-67, 788
Godwin, Harold, 666
Gog (pseud. of Hogg, Gordon), 390, 625
Gohs, Rolf, 348, 557-58
Goldberg, Reuben Lucius, 19, 22, 145-46, 272, 275, 348-49, 360, 362, 400, 481, 533, 804, 805
Golon, Anne and Serge, 404
Gomez, Dominador, 350
Gomez, Pablo, 32, 163, 350, 573, 675
Gonano, Gian Luigi, 211
Gonick, Larry, 350-51
Gonzales, Deo, 350
Gonzales, José, 787
Gonzales, Manuel, 532
Gonzalez, Deo, 32
Gonzalez, Rafael, 259, 402
Gooch, Stanley J., 376
Good, Edmond, 252, 649, 684
Goodman, Arthur and Martin, 472

Goodwin, Archie (pseud. Franklin, Robert), 351, 377, 397, 404, 686, 726, 748, 787, 811
Goosens, Roland, 562
Gordon, John, 210
Gortatowsky, J. P., 247
Goscinny, René, 103, 129, 335, 352-53, 415, 493, 606, 647, 781
Gotlib, Marcel, 36, 331
Gottfredson, Floyd, 253, 261, 353, 531-32, 744, 831
Gotto, Ray, 594
Götze, Michael, 657
Goulart, Ron, 434
Gould, Chester, 24, 69, 71, 248, 294, 295, 353-54, 400, 416, 434, 489, 582
Gould, Will, 354, 642
Gowans, Alan, 390
Grace, Bud, 284, 547
Graddon, Bernard, 428-29
Graff, Mel, 354, 576, 582, 598, 686, 777, 800
Graham, Alex, 320-21
Graham, Walt, 411
Granberry, Ed, 170, 220
Grandenetti, Jerry, 690
Grant, Alan, 424
Grant, Bob, 744
Grant, Maxwell (pseud. of Gibson, Walter Brown), 691
Grant, Skeeter. *See* Spiegelman, Arthur (pseud. of)
Graton, Jean, 529-30
Graue, Dave, 88, 368
Gray, Clarence, 24, 30, 152, 315, 354-55, 576, 653
Gray, Harold, 22, 34, 61, 62-63, 71, 165, 179, 220, 355, 400, 484, 487-88, 712
Grecchi, Luigi, 161, 314
Greco, Guiseppe, 198
Green, Justin, 719
Greenall, Jack, 608
Greene, Joe, 307
Greene, Side, 104
Greene, Valette, 237, 333
Greene, Vernon van Atta, 155, 309, 356, 600, 692, 813
Greening, H. C., 628
Greg. *See* Régnier, Michel (pseud. of)
Grell, Mike, 307, 356, 359
Griffith, Bill, 39, 359, 719
Griffiths, Sal, 807
Grignon, Claude-Henri, 197
Gringle, Paul, 592
Groening, Matt, 115, 477-78, 547
Groot, Bob de, 200, 493
Gross, Milton, 19, 22, 109, 127, 168, 216-17, 233, 236, 360, 474, 575
Gross, Tom, 392
Grosz, George, 552
Grover, Monty, 109
Gruber, Frank, 500

Index A

Proper Names Index

Grundeen, Frank, 261
Gruskin, Ed, 737
Guard, William J., 682
Guardineer, Frederic, 360-61
Guilford, James. *See* Swinnerton, James Guilford (pseud. of)
Guisewite, Cathy, 190, 423
Gulacy, Paul, 81, 519
Gulbransson, Jan, 535
Guljevic, Vsevolud, 473
Gunnis, Louis, 362-63
Gurney, Alexander George, 141, 363-64
Gusso, Miguel, 361
Gustafson, Bob, 144, 762, 806
Gustafson, Nils, 364
Gustafson, Paul (pseud. Earrol, Paul), 90, 95, 364
Gutu (pseud. of Vargas, Agustin), 291
Guvreaux, Emil, 474
Gwynne (pseud. of Price, Cyril), 628

H

H. (pseud. of Horrabin, James Frances), 265, 412-13
Haenigsen, Harry, 286, 365
Hager, Dok, 582
Hagio, Moto, 366
Hales, John, 352, 611
Hall, Bob, 513
Hall, Kenneth F., 683
Hall, Richard, 598
Hall, Robert, 295
Hallgren, Gary, 584
Hals, F. (pseud. of Craenhals, François), 36, 198, 217-18
Hama, Larry, 812
Hamilton, Bob, 410, 441
Hamilton, Edmond, 137, 683, 735, 804
Hamilton, Marcus, 242
Hamlin, Vincent T., 88, 367-68
Hammett, Dashiell, 641, 685-86
Hammond, Carl, 263
Hampson, Frank, 33, 125, 232, 368, 778
Hanato, Kobako, 542
Hand, David, 369, 393
Hannah, Jack, 111
Hannah, William, 766
Hansen, Carla, 639
Hansen, Vilhelm, 639
Hao Shih, 393-94
Harburger, Edmund, 579
Hardaway, Ben ("Bugs"), 162
Hardman, Joe, 620
Hargreaves, Harry, 369-70, 375, 501
Harley, Donald, 232
Harman, Fred, 156, 370, 645
Harmon, Jack. *See* Boring, Wayne (pseud. of)

Harmsworth, Alfred, 158, 823
Harper, Alpine, 316
Hart, Johnny, 33, 34, 119-20, 269, 371-72, 438, 503, 532, 556, 597, 610, 814
Hartog van Banda, Lo, 100-101, 372, 436, 493, 519
Hartt, Cecil, 223
Harvey, R. C., 91
Hasegawa, Machiko, 677
Haselden, W. K., 372
Hasen, Irwin, 262, 275-76, 357, 372-73, 430, 804
Hatlo, James, 373-74, 483, 755
Haupt, Daniel, 579
Hayashi, Hisao, 560
Haydon, Percival Montagu, 690
Heade, R. C. W., 691
Hearst, William Randolph, 13, 122, 130, 153, 168, 182, 185, 238, 244, 247, 253, 265, 354, 378, 395, 437, 450, 457, 485, 537, 552, 553, 585, 590-91, 611, 682, 714, 740, 755, 796, 805
Heath, George, 377, 490
Heath, Michael, 377
Heath, Russ, 377-78, 481, 690
Heath, Russell, 377-78
Heck, Don, 403, 821
Heck, John, 104
Hefner, Hugh, 463
Heilman, Dan, 231, 424-25
Heimdahl, Ralph, 162-63
Heinzer, Peter, 346
Held, John, Jr. (pseud. Held, Myrtle), 378
Henrotin, Daniel (pseud. Dany), 127, 647
Henson, Teny, 32
Herbert, Bill, 267, 608
Hergé. *See* Rémi, Georges (pseud. of)
Hermann. *See* Huppen, Hermann (pseud. of)
Hernandez, Antonio, 195
Hernandez, Luis Carlos, 293
Herriman, George, 18-19, 57, 62, 63, 127, 174, 185, 215, 225, 250, 289, 380-81, 446, 457, 709, 711, 727
Herron, France Edward, 183, 184, 381, 541, 637
Hershfield, Harry, 76, 244, 381-82, 740, 802
Herzog, Guy (pseud. Bara), 382, 523-24
Heskes, W., 163
Hess, Dirk, 103, 161, 609
Hess, Sol, 186, 382-83, 564, 712
Hethke, Norbert, 702
He Youzhi, 375-76
Hibbard, E. E., 307
Hicks, Reginald Ernest (pseud. Hix), 383-84, 592
Hidajat, Johnny, 42, 255

Hidalgo, Francisco (pseud. Roy, Yves), 259, 384
Hiéris, B., 286
Hierl, Werner, 305
Higgins, Lewis, 693
Hildebrandt, Greg and Tim, 159, 384-86, 752
Hill, Albert, 386
Hill, Bert, 246
Hill, Frank, 583, 699
Hill, Tom, 513
Hinds, Bill, 745
Hirai, Kazumasa, 276
Hirata, Hiroshi, 26, 38, 69, 71, 387
Hix (pseud. of Hicks, Reginald Ernest), 383-84, 592
Hoban, Walter C., 388, 414-15, 563, 712
Hodgins, Dick, Jr., 367, 379, 441
Hodgson, Ralph, 83, 124
Hoest, Bill, 388-89
Hoest, Bunny, 389
Hogarth, Burne, 24, 28, 30, 39, 61, 69, 71, 125, 212, 213, 220, 315, 329, 348, 389-90, 510, 524, 639, 747-48, 763, 811, 818
Hogarth, William, 11, 339, 390
Hogg, Gordon (pseud. Gog), 390, 625
Hokusai, Katsushika, 390-91, 438
Holdaway, James, 36, 391, 543, 686
Hollander, Nicole, 391-92
Holley, Lee, 625
Holloway, Ray, 260
Holman, Bill, 299, 388, 392-93, 712-13, 721-22
Holmes, Fred, 393
Holroyd, Bill, 393, 648
Homan, Harry, 420
Hoover, Rick, 532
Hopf, Angela, 495
Horak, Yaroslav (Larry), 409-10
Horie, Taku, 750
Horn, Maurice, 301
Horner, Arthur, 208
Horner, W. G., 66
Horrabin, James Francis (pseud. H), 265, 412-13
Howard, Greg (pseud. Howard), 672-73
Howard, Robert E., 35, 211-12, 646, 756, 757
Howarth, F. M., 395, 493, 514, 628
Ho Yu-chih, 345
Hsü Chin, 141
Hubbard, Michael, 410
Hubinon, Victor, 159, 196, 241, 396
Huet, Jean (pseud. Ache, Jean), 98-99
Huet, Pierre, 398
Huffman, Art, 350
Hughes, Richard, 137, 302
Huizinga, Dirk, 283
Hulton, Edward, 232, 363
Humphries, Barry, 116

Huppen, Hermann (pseud. Hermann), 36, 127, 209, 398, 647
Hurtubise, Jacques (pseud. Zyx), 398

I

Ianiro, Abel, 399
Ibañez, Francisco, 549
Iger, Samuel Maxwell ("Jerry"), 26, 185, 204, 297, 306, 400, 526, 693
Ignjacevic, Milutin S., 473, 829
Ikeda, Riyoko, 41
Ikegami, Ryōchi, 452
Ikeuchi, Seiichi, 697
Ille, Eduard, 524, 579
Imoto, Suimei, 26, 559
Infantino, Carmine, 78, 81, 92, 95, 117, 147, 307, 316, 357, 376, 397, 400-401, 422, 430, 526, 587, 683
Ingels, Graham (pseud. Ghastly), 204, 331, 401-2, 458, 587
Inoue, Yasuji, 451
Inwood, G. Burr, 647
Irving, Jay, 404
Isabella, Tony, 233, 338
Ishii, Masami, 387
Ishikawa, Fumiyasu, 670
Ishikawa, Kyûta, 442-43
Ishimori, Shōtarō, 41, 230, 405, 755
Isidro, Marcelo B., 573
Ito, Masami, 367
Ivie, Larry, 758-59
Ivković, Aleksandar J., 715, 829-30
Iwasawa, Masaru, 350
Iwerks, Ub, 253, 370, 531, 625

J

Jacarbo (pseud. of Arbeau, Jacques), 286, 615
Jacobs, Edgar Pierre, 29, 63, 137, 407
Jacobsson, Oscar, 77, 87, 300, 407-8
Jacovitti, Benito, 205, 408, 519, 618
Jaffee, Allan, 278, 408, 481
Jagelitz, Rasmus, 759
James, Alfred. *See* Andriola, Alfred (pseud. of)
Janković, Djordje, 411-12
Jannin, Frederic, 319
Janocha, Bill, 796
Jansson, Lars, 412
Jansson, Tove, 412, 546
Jarber (pseud. of Bergua, Erique Jarnés), 249
Javinal, Federico, 32

Jaxon, Jack, 224
Jehorak, Steve, 673
Jelicic, Djuradj M., 473
Jenner, Arthur, 801
Jepsen, Paul H., 187
Jeva, Lino, 245, 314
Jijé. *See* Gillain, John (pseud. of)
Jippes, Daan, 532, 535
Jodloman, Jess M., 32, 418-19
Jodloman, Venancio, Jr., 419
Jodorowski, Alexandro, 96, 149, 289, 341, 345, 589
Johns, Harold, 232
Johns, Ralph. *See* Cole, Jack (pseud. of)
Johnson, A. E., 158
Johnson, Crockett (pseud. of Leisk, David Johnson), 27, 112-13, 474
Johnson, Ferd, 422-23, 547, 753, 810
Johnson, Frank, 144, 155
Johnson, Tom, 423
Johnson, Will, 561
Johnston, Lynn B., 312, 423
Johnston, Will B., 155
Jones, Bruce, 514
Jones, Charles M., 122, 162, 231, 625, 812
Jones, Jeff, 320, 432, 612
Jones, Kelley, 674
Jones, Ralston, 144, 538
Jonsson, Per Anders, 348
Jordan, John, 541
Jordan, Sydney, 33, 414
Jori, Marcello, 521
Joyce, Major J. L., 693
Judge, Malcolm (pseud. Mal), 424
Judson, E. Z. C., 161
Juhre, William, 748
Jukes, John L., 426
Julino, Florian, 305
Julius, Harry, 534-35
Jundis, Edna, 462

K

Kabashima, Kasuichi (pseud. Tōfujin), 697
Kahles, Charles William, 14, 23, 82, 244, 322, 366, 431, 709, 789, 826
Kajiwara, Ikki, 465
Kalenbach, Dieter, 431-32
Kalmarevic, Dragan (pseud. Ebner, Marijan), 473
Kaluta, Michael Wm., 318, 320, 432-33, 583
Kame, Al. *See* Kane, Gil (pseud. of)
Kamen, Jack, 306
Kanda, Takeshi, 670
Kane, Bob, 26, 117, 303, 400, 656
Kane, Gil (pseud. Edward, Scott; Kame, Al; Stack, Gil), 92, 104, 197, 212, 320, 351, 357, 359,

397, 434, 462, 718, 735, 748, 757, 759, 818
Kane, Robert, 434-35
Kanigher, Robert, 183, 357, 374, 422, 430, 435, 460, 660, 689-90, 726
Kanō, Douhahu, 438
Kanter, Albert L., 204
Karabajic, Branco, 305
Karp, Bob, 744
Karp, Hubert, 315-16
Kasprzak, Zbigniew (pseud. Kas), 436
Kästner, Erich, 581
Kata, Koji, 542, 580
Kato, Yoshirou, 436
Kauka, Rolf, 38, 94, 178, 305, 437-38, 493-94, 566
Kavanagh, Bill, 155, 309
Kawanabe, Gyōsai (pseud. Shuran-sairaisui), 391, 438, 776, 783
Kawasaki, Noboru, 463
Kawashima, Mitsuhiro, 133
Kawauchi, Yasunori, 337
Keaton, Russell, 160, 173, 311, 438, 708-9
Keefe, Tim, 308
Keeley, James, 196, 297, 444, 687
Kefauver, Sen. Estes, 32, 219, 331
Keller, Jack, 641
Kelly, A. J., 590, 729
Kelly, Bill, 468
Kelly, Cecilia May Ossoli Gibs. *See* Gibbs, Cecilia May
Kelly, Selby, 623
Kelly, Stephen, 623
Kelly, Walt, 29, 33, 61, 62, 63, 71, 174, 253, 438, 470, 594, 622-23, 698, 767, 789
Kemsley, James, 344
Kennedy, Cam, 726
Kent, Jack, 440, 445-46
Kent, John, 208, 704
Ketcham, Henry King, 32, 242, 367, 440-41, 445
Khalid, Mohamed Nor (pseud. Lat), 42, 442
Khing, The Tjong, 100-101, 372
K-Hito (pseud. of García Lopez, Ricardo), 23, 497
Kida, Fred, 81, 426, 443-44
Kiefer, Henry, 204, 257
Kieth, Sam, 674
Kievit, C. J., 163
Kijkstra, Jan Walin, 283
Kilian, Michael, 249, 489
Killeen, Bill, 694
Kimbrell, Woody, 485-86
Kim (pseud. of Price, Cyril), 628
Kim Song Hwan, 444
King, Fay, 271
King, Frank, 62, 286, 312, 320, 335-36, 351, 419, 445
King, Joe, 749
King, Robert Drew, 445
King, Warren, 819

Index A
Proper Names Index

Kirby, Jack, 26, 27, 35, 95, 104, 105, 133, 134, 140, 141, 149, 164, 167, 180-82, 183, 196, 233, 292, 320, 381, 396-97, 401, 403, 418, 447-48, 472, 476, 526-27, 541, 568, 641, 673-74, 689, 690, 705, 726-27, 756-57, 811, 818, 821, 827

Kirby, Robin, 186

Kirby, Rollin, 581

Kirkman, Rick (pseud. of Scott, Jerry), 685

Kita, Kyōta, 350

Kitazawa, Rakuten, 16, 776

Kitchen, Denis, 449-50

Kitzawa, Rakuten, 448-49

Kiyo-chan (pseud. of Shimizu, Kiyoshi), 696

Klein, Fritz, 570

Klein, H. Arthur, 12

Klein, Isidore, 533

Kley, Heinrich, 709

Kling, Ben, 711

Kling, Ken, 354, 419

Kmochk, Ladislaus (pseud. Kmoch, Ludwig), 731, 765-66

Knerr, Harold H., 19, 182, 252, 437, 450, 813

Knight, Clayton, 451

Knight, "Tack," 647

Knott, W. A., 517

Knox, Sir Errol, 293

Kobayashi, Kiyochika, 451, 776

Koenigsberg, Moe, 97-98

Kōgo, Tsuguo, 560

Kohloff, Will, 656

Kohlsaat, Roland, 417, 451

Koike, Kazuo, 350, 452, 454

Kojima, Goseki, 26, 38, 452, 454, 534, 676

Kojima, Koo, 38, 452

Kol. See Gifford, Denis (pseud. of)

Komatsuzaki, Shigeru, 231

Kondō, Hidezō, 581, 825

König, Ralf, 452-53

Kostanjsek, V., 305

Kostuk, Al, 420

Koth, Brett, 333

Kotzky, Alex, 97, 231, 454, 812

Kotzky, Brian, 97

Koyama, Haruo, 452, 464, 697

Kozlak, Jon, 104

Kramsky, Jerry, 521

Krantz, Steve, 324

Kraus, Ruth, 474

Krenkel, Ray, 308, 432, 811

Kresse, Hans G., 29, 283, 457-58, 461, 792

Kressy, Ed, 490

Krigstein, Bernard, 331, 458-59, 622, 727

Krisp, Peter, 495

Kromschröder, Gerhard, 285

Krüger, Hans Martin (pseud. Martin, Hans), 459

Kruis, Jan, 616, 707

Kubert, Andy, 338, 736-37

Kubert, Joe, 40, 92, 135, 192, 222, 257, 307, 338, 357, 374, 378, 424, 459-61, 527, 690, 725, 748, 809

Kuhn, Pieter Joseph, 435-36, 461-62

Kuniyushi, Osato, 115

Kuragane, Shōsuke, 97

Kure, Henning, 786

Kurganski, Vadim, 489

Kurtzman, Harvey, 129, 224, 237, 278, 297, 319, 323, 331, 351, 378, 408, 458, 462-63, 481, 496, 690, 694, 750, 818

Kusenberg, Kurt, 789

Kusonoki, Shōhei, 697

Kusunoki, Takahuru, 464

Kuwata, Jirō, 276, 337, 463-64

Kuyten, Anton, 491

Kuznjecov, Konstantin, 464-65, 473

Kyōsai, Shōjō (pseud. of Kawanabe, Gyōsai), 438

L

Laborne, Daniel, 467

Lacroix, Pierre, 130

Laffond, José, 343

Laird, Peter, 749-50

Laloux, René, 345

Lamb, Bertram, 619

Lampert, Harry, 219, 307

Landolfi, Lino, 575, 630

Lane, John, 791

Langmead, Donald, 610

Languereau, Maurice (pseud. Caumery), 120, 617

Lansky, Mark, 561

Lanteri, Arturo, 18, 23, 263, 564-65

Lanyi, Ronald Levitt, 653

Lanzelotti, José, 641

Lardner, Ring, 762

Lardo, John C.. See Celardo, John (pseud. of)

Larkman, G., 246

Larraz, José Ramon, 217, 361

Larsen, Erik, 718

Larsen, Knud V., 258, 468

Larson, Gary, 468

Laser, Heinrich, 346

Lasswell, Fred, 101, 114-15, 165, 238, 469-70

Lat (pseud. of Khalid, Mohamed Nor), 42, 442

Lau, Chris, 818

Lau, Johnny, 540

Lavado, Joaquin (pseud. Quino), 470, 502-3

LaVarre, William, 422

Lavezzolo, Andrew, 162, 342, 446, 768

Law, David, 241-42

Lawrence, Don, 518

Lawrence, James, 160, 260, 322, 409, 800

Lawson, Len, 535

Lay, Arthur, 468

Lazarus, Mel (pseud. Fulton; Mell), 289, 438, 470, 537-38, 543-44

Lazenby, Frank, 590

Leach, Garry, 518

Leav, Mort, 376, 400, 470-71

Lebeck Oskar, 502

Le Blanc, Andre, 83

Lécureux, Roger, 29, 302-3, 623, 638-39

Ledesma, Francisco Gonzalez, 402

LeDoux, Harold, 231, 425

Lee, Elaine, 432

Lee, Jim, 338, 471-72, 476, 821

Lee, Stan, 35, 104, 105, 126, 131, 167, 180-81, 183, 206, 233, 254, 259-60, 267, 292, 345, 396-97, 401, 403, 447, 458, 472, 500, 641, 660, 689, 690, 704, 718, 722, 726, 732, 756-57, 821, 827

Leff, Moe, 304, 420

Leff, Sam, 147, 192, 420, 502

Leffingwell, Ed, 355, 484

Leffingwell, Robert, 355, 484

Lefort, Michel, 630

LeGoff, Pierre, 303, 630

Lehner, René (pseud. René), 472-73, 678

Lehner, Sebastijan, 473

Lehning, Walter, 702

Lehti, John, 473-74, 748

Leiber, Fritz, 159

Leibowitz, Jack, 524

Leiderman, Al, 420

Leisk, David Johnson (pseud. Johnson, Crockett), 27, 112-13, 474

Lensen, Wim, 768

Leonard, Frank (Lank), 474-75, 531

Leone, Mario, 103

Leone, Sergio, 188

Leonidez, Nestor, 32

Leporini, Bernardo, 175, 176

Lessing, Bruno, 450

Letteri, Guglielmo, 754

Léureux, Roger, 618

Levin, Al, 263, 532

Lewis, Bob. See Lubbers, Robert (pseud. of)

Lewis, Kenneth (pseud. of Fine, Louis), 77, 86, 92, 133, 135-36, 303

Lewis, T., 593-94

Leyendecker, J. C., 87

Lhote, André, 55

Liang Hsin, 642

Liao Bingxiong, 475

Liberatore, Gaetano (pseud. Liberatore, Tanino), 41, 475-76, 600, 601

Lichtenstein, Roy, 593
Lieber, Larry, 403, 641, 756
Lieberson, Will, 183
Liefeld, Rob, 182, 476, 547, 568
Light, Norman, 518
Lignante, Bill, 594, 612
Lilley, Les, 678, 686
Lim, Yu Cheng, 540
Lindroth, Petter, 572
Lindsay, Norman, 223, 535, 569
Liney, John, 92, 379
Link, Stanley J., 275, 481, 712
Lin Tzu-shun, 642
Linus (pseud. of Christin, Pierre), 131, 527, 786
Lips, Robert, 346
Liquois, Pierre, 361
Li Shuong, 300
Liverpool, Billy, 305, 556, 711
Llanuza, Pete, 420
Lloyd, David, 547
Lloyd, Dick, 617-18
Lloyd, Harold, 168, 561
Lob, Jacques, 415, 614, 781-82
Lobačev, Jurij (Djordje) (pseud. Strip, George), 488-89
Locher, Richard, 249, 489
Lockman, Vic, 122, 625
Lohmann, Willy, 454-57
London, Bobby, 584, 756
Longaron, Jorge, 322
Lööf, Jan, 297-98, 490-91
Looman, Jos, 491
Lorg (pseud. of Gillain, Laurent), 241, 339
Loriot (pseud. of Bülow, Bernhard-Victor von), 163-64
Losfeld, Eric, 269, 670
Loubert, Deni, 192
Low, David, 535
Lozano, José Suárez, 89
Lubbers, Robert (pseud. Lewis, Bob), 179, 185, 192, 267, 280, 376, 490, 492, 686, 748, 808, 811
Lucenay, Martin de, 195
Ludvigsen, Viggo, 77
Ludwig, Heinz, 525
Luk, George B., 824
Luna, Othon, 89
Lundqvist, Ruben, 480
Lundström, Janne, 557
Lynch, Jay, 463, 496
Lynde, Stan, 496, 651
Lynder, Frank, 244, 651
Lyon, Carl, 223, 797
Lyttelton, Humphrey, 310

M

Ma, Wing-Shing, 818
McAdam, Charles V., 304
McBride, Clifford, 497, 561-62
McCabe, Norman, 625

McCall, Ted, 321-22, 655
McCay, Robert, 487
McCay, Winsor (pseud. Silas), 14, 16, 19, 39, 61, 63, 66, 69, 71, 76, 126, 127, 164, 171, 174, 268-69, 486-87, 497-98, 569, 709
McClelland, Hugh, 418, 498-99, 619
McClure, Darrell, 482-83, 499, 789
McCoy, Tim, 691
McCoy, Wilson, 116, 491, 612
McCutcheon, George Barr, 682, 709, 806
McCutcheon, John, 153
McDonnell, Patrick, 556
McDougall, Walter Hugh, 499
McEvoy, Joseph Patrick, 255, 500, 730
McEvoy, Renny, 500
McFadden, Bernard, 474
McFarlane, Todd, 397, 476, 500, 568, 674, 718
McGee, Ernest, 514, 709
McGeean, Ed, 379
McGill, Angus, 205
MacGillivray, R., 125, 691
McGuire, Jack W., 411, 644
Macherot, Raymond, 199-200
MacIntosh, Craig, 672-73
Mack, Ed, 711
Mackenzie, Sir Compton, 310
McKimson, Robert, 162, 231, 625
McKimson, Tom, 162
McKuen, Rod, 608
McLeans, Bill, 807
McLeod, Bob, 645
McLoughlin, Denis, 500-501
McLusky, John, 409-10
McMahon, Mike, 424
McManus, George, 14, 18-19, 62, 63, 66, 154, 206, 309, 356, 375, 501-2, 567, 568-69, 595-96, 662, 820
McNamara, John, 599
McNeill, Hugh, 119, 369, 502, 590, 596, 650, 729, 807
MacNelly, Feff, 697-98
McNelly, Jeff, 39
McNitt, Virgil V., 218, 552
McRae, Alex, 364
McWhirter, William, 301-2
McWilliams, Alden, 192, 233-34, 502-3, 628, 677
Madgič, Vlado, 305
Madsen, Peter, 786-87
Maetani, Koremitsu, 657
Mager, Charles Augustus (Gus), 374-75, 504-5, 505-6
Magni, Enzo, 596
Magnus. *See* Raviola, Roberto (pseud. of)
Magsino, Frank, 462, 505
Mahoney, Roger, 333
Mairowitz, David, 226
Maitland, Lester J., 173, 708

Maki, Miyako, 521, 542
Makino, Taisei, 559
Makins, Clifford, 125, 232
Malang (pseud. of Santos, Malang), 32, 675
Malaya, 506
Mal (pseud. of Judge, Malcolm), 424
Maltese, Michael, 122
Man, Fuentes, 178
Manara, Maurilio, 41, 507-8, 633
Manca, Giovanni, 616
Manchette, Jean-Patrick, 746
Mancuso, Antonio, 132
Mandel, George, 95, 115, 141
Maneely, Joe, 472, 641
Manfrin, Umberto, 227, 764-65
Manning, Jack, 122, 231, 748
Manning, Russell, 510-11, 720, 726
Manubu, Oyama, 560
Marato, Esteban, 663
Marc, Ralph (pseud. of Marcello, Raffaelo Carlo), 511, 754
Marceau, Marcel, 99
Marcello, Raffaelo Carlo (pseud. Marc, Ralph), 511, 754
Marcelo, P. Z., 32
Marcoux, George, 737
Marcus, Sid, 162
Marechal, Gigi, 396
Marek, Jan, 346
Margie (pseud. of Buell, Marjorie Henderson), 485-86
Mari, Nicola, 562
Maria, Guido de, 145
Marijac. *See* Dumas, Jacques (pseud. of)
Marin, Antonio Torralbo, 197
Marković, Momcilo-Moma, 512
Marlette, Doug, 39, 461
Maroto, Esteban, 37, 71, 120, 177-78, 203, 212, 514
Marquez, Fermin, 293
Marriner, William, 514-15, 795
Marsh, Jesse Mace, 510, 748
Marsh, Norman, 232-33
Marston, William Moulton (pseud. Moulton, Charles), 515, 816
Martin, Arthur, 133
Martin, Edgar Everett, 147, 515-16
Martin, Hans (pseud. of Krüger, Hans Martin), 459
Martin, Henry, 411
Martin, Jacques, 29, 87
Martin, Keith, 364
Martin, Menny Eusobio, 32, 516, 793
Martina, Guido, 118, 203, 602
Martinek, Frank V., 263
Martinez, Agustin, 293
Martinez, Osets, 178
Martini, Amedeo, 247, 344
Mas, René, 617
Masaoka, Tashiya, 199
Mashiko, Zenroku, 825
Massey, Tom, 763, 826

Mastroserio, Rocco, 587
Matena, Dick, 100, 372, 458, 519-20
Matera, Frank, 729
Matshisa, Yû, 464
Matsumoto, Reiji, 520-21, 755
Mattioli, Massimo, 41, 600, 601
Mattotti, Lorenzo, 521-22
Mauldin, Bill, 122, 151, 539, 782
Maurer, Norman, 222, 233
Maurović, Andrija, 522
Mavrides, Paul, 290
Maxon, Rex, 524, 747-48
Maxwell, Bob, 417, 736
Maxwell, Rod, 306
Mayer, Henry (Hy), 386, 514
Mayer, Sheldon, 141, 219, 400, 430,
    524-25, 773
Mayerick, Val, 395
Mazucchelli, David, 534
Mazure, Alfred, 246, 391, 410
Mazzanti, Attilio, 228
Meagher, Fred, 161
Medda, Michele, 562
Medici, Amilcare, 161, 177
Medina, Manuel, 359
Meggendorfer, Lothar, 524
Meglin, Nick, 237, 408
Meji, Miguel, 291
Melendez, Bill, 334
Melho, Messias de, 215
Mell. *See* Lazarus, Mel (pseud. of)
Melly, George, 310
Melouah, Sid Ali, 42, 525-26
Mendelson, Lee, 334
Mendez, Phil, 809
Mendez, Rafael, 462
Mendiola, José Maria, 240
Mendizabal, Guillermo, 293
Mendl, Wolfgang, 678
Meredyth, Hal (pseud. of Blyth,
    Harry), 690-91
Mesina, Ruding, 350
Meskin, Morton (pseud. Morton,
    Mort, Jr.), 137, 302, 400, 460,
    526-27, 656, 693, 725
Messerli, Joe, 231
Messick, Dale, 151-52, 154, 270, 527,
    587
Messmer, Otto, 299
Metcalf, Greg, 567
Meulen, Ever, 719
Mevin, Bill, 608
Meyer, Larry, 261
Mézières, Jean-Claude, 345, 527, 786
Miao Di, 527-28
Michael de Jong, Adrianus, 163
Michelinie, David, 738
Micheloni, Saverio, 161, 245
Micheluzzi, Attilio (pseud. Bajeff,
    Igor Artz), 273, 530-31, 575
Michman, J., 749
Mignacco, Luigi, 273
Mik, Al. *See* Plastino, Al (pseud. of)
Mikkelsen, H. Dahl, 87, 300-301, 382

Milani, Milo, 508, 530
Milazzo, Ivo, 439-40
Milgrom, Al, 183-84
Millar, Jeff, 745
Miller, Anthony, 517
Miller, Arnold, 96
Miller, David, 235-36
Miller, Dean, 791
Miller, Frank (1898-1949), 534, 563
Miller, Frank (1957-   ), 40, 85,
    113-14, 118, 182, 233, 260, 397,
    534, 726
Miller, Jack, 77
Miller, Sydney Leon, 534-35, 569,
    658
Mills, Pat, 209, 424
Mills, Tarpe, 190, 537
Milton, Freddy, 535
Minnitt, Frank, 132, 536
Misuki, Shigeru, 542
Mitchell, Harry, 110
Mitchell, Hutton, 132
Mitchell, J. A., 325
Mitrovic, Zika, 473
Miyaji, Masahiro, 387
Miyao, Shigeo, 581
Miyaya, Kazuhiko, 560
Miyazaki, Hayao, 562-63
Miyazaki, Tsutomu, 350
Mizuki, Shigeru, 366-67
Mizuno, Hideko, 542, 755
Mizushima, Shinji, 26, 542
Moberg, Rune, 479
Moench, Doug, 519
Mogenson, Jørgen, 87, 300
Moldoff, Sheldon, 374
Molino, Walter, 143, 176, 449, 543,
    603, 792
Moliterni, George (Jorge), 424
Mondadori, Arnoldo, 180, 266, 549,
    602
Moneypenny, David, 791
Moniquet, Marcel, 413
Monk, Jack, 160-61, 544
Monkhouse, Bob, 96, 544-45, 808
Montana, Bob, 99-100, 137, 545-46
Montanari, Giuseppe, 111, 273
Monti, Roberto, 818
Mooney, Jim, 338, 735, 804
Moore, Alan (pseud. Vile, Curt), 40,
    118, 500, 547, 738, 800
Moore, Bob, 262, 352, 611
Moore, Don, 308
Moore, Ed, 263
Moore, Ray, 24, 612
Moore, Willfred, 184
Moores, Richard, 336, 416-17, 445
Mora, Angel José, 89, 195, 600
Mora, Ulises, 195
Mora, Victor (pseud. Alcazar, Victor),
    178, 239, 259, 341, 384, 402, 407
Morales, Paolo, 517
Mordillo, Guillermo, 459, 548

Moreira, Ruben (pseud. Rubimor),
    185, 748
Mori, Kōtāro, 350
Morley, Allan, 442, 536, 807
Morley, Jack, 113, 474
Moroni-Celsi, Guido (pseud. Sterny),
    344, 548-49
Morris. *See* Bevère, Maurice de
    (pseud. of)
Morris, John Milt, 325, 684
Morris, Rev. Marcus, 232, 368
Morrison, Tom, 378, 533
Morrow, Gray, 131, 160, 308, 322,
    423, 424, 628
Mortimer, Winslow, 725, 735
Mosley, Zack, 549-50, 708, 710
Motomitsu, K., 350
Motton, David, 232
Mouchot, Pierre, 143
Moulton, Charles (pseud. of Marston,
    William Moulton), 515, 816
Mouly, François, 719
Mount, Douglas, 310
Moya, Alvaro de, 215
Mundo, Clodualdo del, 32, 419, 573
Muñoz, José, 41, 85, 534, 552, 719
Munsey, Frank, 317, 779
Muraoka, Eiichi, 560
Murdoch, Rupert, 677-78
Murdoch, Sir Keith, 110, 223
Murit, Robert, 184
Murphy, James Edward, 552-54,
    769-70
Murphy, Joe Callen, 130-31
Murphy, John Cullen, 315, 554, 629
Murphy, Matthew, 524, 778
Murray, Doug, 560, 692
Murry, Paul, 324
Musial, Joseph, 437, 554, 813
Mussino, Attilio, 132, 635
Muster, Miki, 554-55
Muzzi, Virgilio, 754
Myers, Russell, 156, 556-57

N

Nabi, Rafiqun (pseud. Ranabi), 42,
    766
Nadon, Pascal, 398
Nagai, Gō, 559
Nagamatsu, Takeo, 580
Nagasaki, Batten, 449
Nagashima, Shinji, 38, 39, 328-29,
    559-60, 755
Nagayasu, Takami, 452
Nakajima, Kikuo, 373, 452
Nakazawa, Keiji, 42
Nankivel, Frank A., 448
Nash, Meg, 629
Nast, Thomas, 499
Natsume, Sōseki, 581
Navojev, Nikola, 715, 829-30

Naylor, Bob, 534, 813
Naylor, Frank, 113
Naylor, Robert, 563-64
Nebres, Rudy, 748, 787
Neebe, Joseph H., 315, 747
Neels, Marc (pseud. Sleen, Marc),
     564, 566
Neill, Noel, 490
Nemeth, Gabriel "Tschap," 535
Nestor, Virgilio, 645
Neugebauer, Norbert, 566, 661
Neugebauer, Walter, 239, 266, 305,
     327, 566-67, 813
Neville, Dennis, 374
Newell, Peter, 628
Newhouse, Don, 620, 812
Newman, Paul S., 490, 567-68, 778
Nicholas, Charles, 140
Nicholls, Sydney Wentworth, 293-94,
     569
Nicholson, Basil, 498
Nicholson, Major, 524
Nickel, George, 495
Nickel, Helmut, 570, 655-56, 813
Nicolle, Patrick, 393
Nicolo, Erio, 734, 754
Nidasio, Grazia, 785-86
Niebres, Rudy, 260
Nilsson, Börje, 348
Niño, Alex N., 32, 350, 462, 573-74
Nishigawa, Tatsumi, 449
Nishimura, Tsuyako, 452
Nivolo, Erio, 314
Nixon, Robert, 492, 574-75
Nizzi, Claudio, 530, 575, 754
Noble, Joe, 807
Nodell, Martin, 357
Norman, Barry, 310
Norman, Richard. *See* Briefer, Richard
     (pseud. of)
Norris, Paul, 98, 152, 308, 355, 427,
     576-77, 582, 748, 791, 813
Novick, Irv, 137, 357, 368, 690,
     694-95, 726, 801
Nowlan, Philip, 159, 160, 173, 577
Nussbaumer, Erich, 632-33
Nye, Bill, 499

O

O. A. (pseud. of Andersson, Oskar
     Emil), 93, 510
O'Bannon, Dan, 345
Oberländer, Adolf, 524, 579
Ocampo, Abe, 350, 773
Ocampo, Tuning, 32
Ochiai, Yoshiiku, 775-76, 783
O'Connor, B., 104
Oda, Shousei, 697
O'Donnell, Peter, 36, 391, 543
O'Donoghue, Michael, 614, 722-23

Oesterheld, Hector German, 150,
     239, 284-85, 286, 549, 579-80,
     627, 714
Oesterheld, Jorge, 580
Offenstadt, Georges, 313, 605
Ogawa, Jihei, 449
Ogawa, Tetsuo, 328, 449
Ogle, Bob, 231, 625
Ohser, Erich (pseud. Plauen, E. O.),
     580-81, 789-90
Okamoto, Ippei, 581, 696
O'Keefe, Neil, 92, 247-48, 403,
     581-82
Oksner, Bob, 735
Olazo, Flor Afable, 418
Oliphant, Pat, 372
Oliveira, Reynaldo de, 215
Olivera, Nestor, 285
Ollivier, Jean, 511, 621
Omagap, Bello Rico, 32
O'Malley, Michael, 791
O'Neal, Frank, 583, 698-99
O'Neal, Rose, 271
O'Neil, Dennis (pseud. O'Shaug-
     nessey, Sergius), 77, 260, 344,
     356, 357, 429, 430, 583, 692, 817
O'Neil, Robert, 818
O'Neill, Dan, 583-84, 584
O'Neill, Harry, 161
O'Neill, Rose Cecil, 441-42, 584, 632
Ongaro, Alberto, 103, 580
Ongaro, Paolo, 245
Opper, Frederick Burr, 13, 18, 19, 63,
     89, 93-94, 186, 317, 368-69, 390,
     448, 514, 585-86
Oriolo, Joe, 188-89, 299
Orlando, Joe, 204, 206, 233, 472, 587
Ormes, Jackie, 587
Orr, Carey, 518, 550
Orr, Martha, 518, 677
Ortolani, Attilio, 765
Osanai, Ryû, 825
Osete, Martinez, 407
O'Shaughnessey, Sergius. *See* O'Neil,
     Dennis (pseud. of)
Oshima, Yumiko, 366, 588
Oski (pseud. of Conti, Oscar), 213
Osted, Torben, 787
Otomo, Katsuhiro, 588-89
Otto, Max A., 730-31
Outcault, Richard Felton, 13, 168-69,
     196, 390, 448, 590-91, 682, 687,
     824-25
Outcault, Richard Felton, Jr., 591
Outen, Shimokawa, 449
Overgard, John, 728-29
Overgard, William Thomas, 593,
     728-29
Oxton, J. G., 819

P

Paape, Eddy, 647
Packer, Robert Clyde, 223
Packer, Tom, 162, 625
Pai, Anant, 595
Palacio, Lino (pseud. Flax), 263, 595
Palacios, Antonio Hernandez, 511
Palais, Rudy, 136
Palmiotti, Jimmy, 787
Paludetti, Franco, 245, 684
Palumbi, Nino, 198
Palumbo, Guiseppe, 517
Panaligan, Noly, 32, 350, 424,
     599-600
Panter, Gray, 719
Paparella, Raffaele, 602
Papp, George, 355-56
Paprocki, Tom, 820
Parker, Al, 267
Parker, Bill, 120, 182, 183, 399, 723
Parker, Brant, 34, 371, 556, 597, 814
Parker, Eric, 393, 691
Parker, R., 517
Parlett, George, 518
Parlett, Reg, 133, 166, 590
Pasini, Andrea, 516
Pataruzú, 597-98
Patrick, Terence, 282
Patterson, Captain Joseph Medill, 17,
     20-21, 127, 151, 175, 248, 275,
     336, 353, 355, 362, 370, 445,
     487, 547, 711, 712, 809
Patterson, Russell, 598-99
Patterson, Willy, 414
Payne, A. B., 22, 619
Payne, Charles M., 600, 647
Payne, G. M., 157, 302, 812
Payne, Laurence, 691
Paynter, Bob, 574, 797
Pazienza, Andrea (pseud.
     Traumfabrik), 476, 600-601
Pearson, Bill, 809
Pease, A. T., 133
Peddy, A., 613
Pedrazza, Augusto, 84
Pedrocchi, Federico, 176, 344, 449,
     543, 603, 677, 792
Peeters, Benoit, 680
Pekar, Harvey, 40, 90
Pellaert, Guy, 418, 722
Pellerin, Patrice, 241
Pellos, René, 24, 329, 604-5, 615
Peña, Alfredo Cardona, 293
Penalva, Bosch, 703
Peñamora, Jorge, 350
Peña Rego, Jesus (pseud. Suso), 203,
     360
Peñarroya, José, 261-62
Peng Guoliang, 605
Penteado, Miguel, 215
Pepper, Frank S. (pseud. Wilton, Hal),
     209
Perelman, S. J., 714

Index A
Proper Names Index

Perera, Camillus, 607
Perez, George, 104, 292, 359, 817
Perez, Johnny, 462
Perini, Carlo, 190
Perkins, S. K., 246
Peroni, Carl, 608, 702
Perré, Aristide, 615
Perrott, Reg, 608-9, 650
Perry, Bill, 336, 445
Persson, Elov, 572
Pesch, Jean-Louis, 615
Peter, H. G., 515, 816
Peters, Mike, 39, 550-51
Petersen, Professor Wilhelm, 525
Petersson, Rudolf, 282, 314, 572
Petkovic, S., 473
Pett, Norman, 410
Peynet, Raymond, 559
Peyo (pseud. of Culliford, Pierre), 36, 228, 318, 680
Pezzin, Giorgio, 191
Pfeufer, Carl, 262, 352, 399, 611
Phillips, Irving, 730
Phillips, Nat, 364
Phipps, Julian, 686, 760
Piccatto, Luigi, 273
Pichard, Georges, 40, 614, 781-82
Pierotti, John, 179
Pierre, Michel, 215
Piët, Frans, 157, 616, 706
Piffarerio, Paolo, 685
Pinchon, Jean-Pierre, 120, 617
Pini, Richard, 279-80
Pini, Wendy, 812
Pinson, Paul, 233
Pin-Tim (pseud. of Craveri, Sebastiano), 221
Pip. *See* Davies, Roland (pseud. of)
Piper, Lloyd, 344
Pisu, Silverio, 508
Pitt, Reginald, 621
Pitt, Stanley John, 620-21, 703-4
Pitz, Henry C., 700
Pizarro, Garcia, 514
Plastino, Al (pseud. Mik, Al), 301, 381, 561, 735, 804
Platt, Kin, 538
Plauen, E. O. (pseud. of Ohser, Erich), 580-81, 789-90
Ploog, Mike, 204, 318, 338
Plumb, Charlie, 280-81
Plymell, Charles, 224, 540
Poblete, Ric, 163
Pocci, Count, 579
Poelsma, Dominic, 205
Poïvet, Raymond, 29, 618, 623, 663
Polese, Renato, 575
Pope, Wilson, 265
Posen, Al, 739-40
Post, Howard, 269, 400
Potter, Jack, 96
Potts, Arthur (pseud. Spot), 749
Powell, Bob, 257, 278, 691, 693
Powell, Paul, 348

Power, Paul, 82
Powers, Gregg, 379
Pran Kumar Sharma, 42, 626-27
Pratt, Hugo, 37, 71, 102, 108, 215, 284, 508, 579, 627
Prentice, John, 246, 502, 627-28, 652, 811
Price, Cyril (pseud. Gwynne; Kim; Spike), 628
Price, Garrett, 808
Principe, Nicolino Del, 177
Protheroe, Glyn, 631
Pruneda, Alvaro, 631
Pruneda, Salvado, 631
Puck, Peter, 664-65
Puerto, Juan B., 654
Puigmiquel, Angel, 177
Pulitzer, Joseph, 13
Pultizer, Ralph, 499
Putato, Cesarina, 162
Putzker, Ronald Alfred, 632-33
Pyle, Howard, 87

Q

Queirolo, Renato, 150
Quesada, Joe, 787
Quimby, Fred, 766
Quinlan, Chris, 190-91
Quino (pseud. of Lavado, Joaquin), 470, 502-3
Quinterno, Dante, 254, 598, 768
Quinto, Nadir, 575

R

Raab, Charles, 598
Raab, Fritz, 637, 651, 746-47
Raboy, Emanuel (Mac), 115, 133, 164, 184, 308, 381, 399, 518, 541, 637
Radilović, Julio, 327, 380, 637-38
Rajković, Zivko V., 411
Rallic, Le, 624
Ramello, G., 771
Ramón, Lopez, 663
Ramos, Luis, 407
Ranabi (pseud. of Nabi, Rafiqun), 42, 766
Rancke-Madsen, Hans, 786
Randall, Albertine, 271, 806
Randall, Neville, 760
Rapela, Enrique, 639
Rasmussen, Ole Munk, 299
Ravelo, Mars, 32, 163, 462, 675, 772
Raviola, Roberto (pseud. Magnus), 85, 459, 639-41, 685
Rawlings, Leo, 518
Raymond, Alex, 24, 28, 30, 39, 92, 153, 173, 184, 202, 209, 213,

215, 220, 243, 246, 287, 306, 308, 315, 348, 354, 374, 407, 411, 427, 447, 460, 554, 576, 620, 623, 627, 637, 641, 645, 651-53, 659, 678, 685-86, 703, 725, 738, 762, 763, 788, 811
Raymond, Jack, 554
Raymond, Jim, 139
Raymond, Robert, 310
Rebuffi, Giorgio, 198, 227, 228, 642, 764-65
Recagno, Carlo, 516
Rechin, Bill, 597
Redler, Thierry, 529
Redondo, Frank, 350
Redondo, Nestor, 32, 163, 350, 462, 644-45, 738, 793
Redondo, Virgilio, 32, 659, 743, 793
Reed, Ron, 183, 203, 666, 671
Reese, Ralph, 308
Reggie, 646
Régnier, Michel (pseud. Greg; Albert, Louis), 36, 76-77, 127, 159, 209, 214, 335, 398, 647, 788, 829
Rehr, Henry, 301
Reiche, Volker, 525, 535, 647-48
Reid, Ken, 242, 648
Reilly, Frank, 535, 725
Reiner, John, 389
Reinicke, Emil, 524
Reinman, Paul, 104, 641, 725, 748, 759
Reisenstein, Charles, 258
Reit, Sy, 188-89
Reitberger, Reinhold, 680
Reith, B. J., 707
Reizenstein, Charles, 541
Rémi, Georges (pseud. Hergé), 24, 62, 407, 648-49, 721, 737, 739, 764, 788, 829
Rendondo, Virgilio, 462
René (pseud. of Lehner, René), 472-73, 678
Rensie, Willis. *See* Eisner, Will (pseud. of)
Renzi, Roberto, 85, 228, 642, 764
Repetto, Mirco, 598
Rexroth, Kenneth, 437, 651
Reyes, Francisco, 32, 462
Reyna, José S., 293
Reyna, Ricardo, 89
Reynaud, Emile, 66
Reynolds, Basil, 650, 808
Reynolds, Len, 110
Reynolds, Warwick, 650
Rhein, Eduard, 285, 525
Ribeaupierre, Claude de (pseud. Derib), 647
Rice, Norm, 141
Richards, Frank, 132, 796
Richards, Ted, 584
Richmond, Kane, 724
Richter-Johnsen, Friedrich-Wilhelm, 244, 637, 651, 746-47

Rickard, Jack, 470
Rico, Don, 135, 140, 233, 234, 260, 397, 827
Ridgeway, Frank, 538
Rigby, Clarence, 709
Rinaldi, Ricardo, 305
Rissack, Eddy, 680
Ritt, William, 152, 354-55, 653
Ritter, Jörg, 459
Ríus (pseud. of del Río, Eduardo), 79, 735
Rival, Rico, 32, 350
Robbins, Athena, 582
Robbins, Frank, 24, 27, 117, 158, 280, 307, 338, 420-22, 583, 653, 684, 692, 820
Robbins, Trina, 653-54, 787, 812
Roberg, Syllas, 215
Roberge, Frank, 270, 809
Robinson, Fred, 166, 590, 656
Robinson, James, 787
Robinson, Jerry, 117, 212, 223, 253, 302, 357, 435, 526-27, 656-57
Robinson, Paul, 286
Robinson, W. Heath, 349
Robles, Javier, 195
Roca, Luis, 678
Roche, Ruth, 306
Rockwell, Dick, 176, 728
Rodriguez, Braulio (pseud. Buyulla), 249
Rodriguez, Emilio D., 658-59
Roger (pseud. of Toutain, José), 239, 341, 771
Rogers, Barksdale, 271
Rogers, W. A., 499
Roi, Corrado, 273
Rollin, Jean, 670
Romero, Enrique, 543, 639
Romero, Rubén Lara and Jorge, 293, 543
Romita, John, 167, 206, 233, 292, 660, 705, 718
Romita, John, Jr., 660
Rosales, Rene, 32
Roscher, Franz, 305, 528-29, 660-61
Rosenthal, David H., 771
Rosi, Sergio, 405
Rosinski, Grzegorz, 41, 436, 662-63
Roso, Vincent, 310-11
Ross, Charles Henry, 88-89
Ross, Charles Henry, Jr., 89
Ross, Harold, 713-14
Ross, Russell, 411
Rosso, Gustavo, 266
Rostagno, Marco, 189
Rosy, Maurice, 680
Roth, Arnold, 481
Roth, Werner, 641
Roume, Carlos, 580
Roussos, George, 426, 725
Rowlandson, Thomas, 11, 224, 663
Royer, Mike, 748
Royle, Tony, 123, 429

Rubbo, Datillo, 109
Rubichek, Dorothy, 820
Rubino, Antonio, 23, 86, 635, 664
Rubio, Adolfo Lopez, 343
Ruiz, Carlos, 818
Russell, Clarence D., 611, 666
Russell, James Newton, 223, 625-26, 666
Ryan, John, 312
Ryan, Paul, 292
Ryan, Tom K., 237, 333, 667, 776
Ryssack, Edouard, 149-50, 707

S
_____

Saaf, Art, 185, 735
Sachs, Bernard, 78, 259, 376
Sack, Steve, 672
Sagendorf, Bud, 675, 756, 813
Sailer, Anton, 571
Saint-Ogan, Alain, 21-22, 545, 605, 647, 648, 670, 829, 831
Saio, Alfredo, 765
Saio, Andrea, 765
Saitō, Takao, 38, 349-50, 670-71
Saitō, Yuzuro, 670
Sajem, Johnny, 796
Salem, Lee, 42
Salemme, Antonio, 629
Salinas, Alberto, 672, 818
Salinas, José K., 380, 671-72
Salinas, José-Luis, 32, 203
Salisbury, Allan, 42, 713
Sammarini, Umberto, 405
Sampayo, Carlos, 41, 85, 552, 714
Samson, Jacques, 398
Sanderhage, Per, 299
Sansom, Arthur, 148, 791
Sansom, Chip, 148
Santiago, Cirio H., 32
Santiago, Hal, 350
Santos, Angel Ad, 659
Santos, Jesse F., 32, 253, 350, 462, 674-75
Santos, Malang (pseud. Malang), 32, 675
Santos, Sabala, 32
Saporito, Alf, 166
Sardinian Trio (pseud. of Goosens, Medda, Serra and Vigna), 562
Sato, Takao, 41
Satonaka, Machiko, 676
Saudek, Karel, 41
Saunders, Allen, 231-32, 285, 424, 440, 502, 518, 593, 649, 677, 728-29
Saunders, John, 233-34, 519, 677, 729
Saura, Carlos, 375
Saxon, Charles, 796
Saylor, Dick, 367
Scaduto, Al, 755

Scancarelli, Jim, 336
Scarbo, George, 810
Scarpa, Romano, 191, 198
Scarpelli, Henry, 100
Scerbanendo, Giorgio, 211
Schacheri, Rico, 503
Schaffenberger, Kurt (pseud. Wahl, Lou), 399, 490, 678, 735, 804
Scheuer, Chris, 678
Scheyer, Ernst, 297
Schiele, J. K., 346
Schiff, Jack, 117
Schlensker, Harry, 170, 220
Schlensker, Leon, 625
Schlesinger, Leon, 162, 231
Schmich, Maria, 152, 154
Schmidt, Charles, 638
Schmidt, Heiri, 346
Schmidt, Manfred, 571-72, 678-80
Schneider, Howie, 276
Schodt, Frederik, 84, 109, 387, 452, 559
Schoenke, Bob, 411
Schomburg, Alex, 135, 137, 302, 397, 827
Schubel, Heinz, 495
Schuiten, François, 680-81
Schuiten, Luc, 680
Schultheiss, Matthias, 41, 678, 681-82
Schultze, Carl Edward, 317, 395, 556, 682-83
Schulz, Charles Monroe, 33, 60, 63, 227, 352, 445, 470, 478, 496, 556, 559, 601-2, 683, 687, 708, 777, 803
Schwartz, Julius, 92, 117, 316, 356, 357, 400, 429, 583, 683, 736, 756
Schwartz, Sayre, 813
Schweizer, Rinaldo, 472
Schwind, Moritz von, 579
Sclavi, Tiziano, 191, 273
Scolari, Giovanni, 603, 677
Scott, Jerry (pseud. Kirkman, Rick), 685
Scott, Thurman, 185
Scott, Walt, 488, 814
Scozzari, Filippo, 600, 601
Scudellari, Giorgio, 247
Secchi, Luciano (pseud. Bunker, Max), 85, 459, 639, 685
Secchi, Ricardo, 685
Segar, Elzie Crisler, 22, 67, 127, 186, 196, 206, 225, 238, 309, 352, 626, 675, 687, 755-56, 809, 813
Segrelles, Vicente, 687-88
Sekine, Giichi, 452
Sekowsky, Mike, 397, 429, 735, 759, 827
Seldes, Gilbert, 457
Sels, Frank, 128
Senich, Joe, 437
Serra, Antonio, 562
Serres, Patrice, 529

Severin, John Powers, 105, 278, 331, 689, 690
Severin, Marie, 260, 397, 690, 732
Shahn, Ben, 559
Sharp, Hal, 541
Shaw, Ernest, 693, 749
Shearer, Ted, 228, 635, 778
Shelton, Gilbert, 36, 289-90, 463, 481, 694
Shen Pei (Peijin), 694-95
Sherman, Howard, 257, 725
Shifrin, Sol, 311
Shimada, Keizo, 143
Shimizu, Kiyoshi (pseud. Kiyo-chan), 696
Shimizu, Kon, 325, 452, 581, 696
Shimoyama, Chohei, 399
Shirato, Sanpei, 26, 38, 433-34, 452, 572-73, 675-76, 696-97, 775
Shishido, Sakō, 718
Shores, Syd, 397, 827
Shorten, Harry, 136-37, 694-95
Shuransairaisui (pseud. of Kawanabe, Gyōsai), 391, 438, 776, 783
Shuster, Joe, 26, 35, 147, 233, 434, 489, 526, 699-700, 735-37
Shwe Min Thar, 700
Sickles, Noel, 24, 94, 200, 212, 354, 579, 598, 684, 700-701, 773, 820
Siegel, Jerome, 26, 35, 147, 233, 489, 695, 700, 701, 718, 725, 735-37, 804
Sienkiewicz, Bill, 534, 547, 568, 726
Silas. See McCay, Winsor (pseud. of)
Sileo, Dom, 189
Silver Kane (pseud. of Ledesma, F. Gonzalez), 259
Silvestri, Guido (pseud. Silver), 494-95
Sim, David, 40, 41, 192
Simmonds, Posy, 704
Simmons, R., 209
Simon, Joseph, 27, 95, 140-41, 149, 180, 196, 447, 472, 527, 541, 568, 673-74, 690, 704-5, 827
Simonson, Louise, 154
Simonson, Walt, 117, 118, 212, 292, 351, 395, 397, 726, 757, 821
Sims, Tom, 756
Sindall, Alfred, 599
Sinnott, Joe, 292, 705
Sío, Enric, 37, 79, 470, 577
Sironi, Mario, 543
Skeates, Steve, 735, 759
Skinn, Dez, 518
Sleen, Marc (pseud. of Neels, Marc), 564, 566
Slesinger, Stephen, 370, 594
Slott, Mollie, 527, 820
Small, Jon, 164
Small, Louis, Jr., 787
Smith, Al, 201-2, 305, 556, 710-11, 721-22
Smith, Barry, 167, 212, 292, 821

Smith, Col. Orlando Jay, 499
Smith, Dan, 535, 569
Smith, Frank, 261
Smith, Robert Sidney, 711-12
Smith, Ron, 424
Smith, Sidney, 186, 275, 336, 355, 362, 383, 481, 582
Smith, Wyn, 162, 531
Smythe, Reginald, 95
Snelgrove, Charles R., 655
Soglow, Otto, 67, 162, 485, 713-14
Solano López, Francisco, 285, 286, 579, 714-15
Solano López, Gabriel, 714
Solini, Cesare, 91
Solovjev, Sergej (pseud. Gey, Moum; Solo, S.), 715-16
Sommer, Paul, 315
Sonoyama, Shunji, 38, 716-17
Souster, Eric, 96
Souter, D. H., 343
Souvestre, Pierre, 293
Soyer, Ralph, 115
Sparling, Jack, 160, 257, 821
Speed, Jim, 411
Speer, Tony, 650
Spenceley, Edgar, 749
Spicer, William, 816
Spiegelman, Arthur (pseud. Cutrate, Joe; Flooglebuckle, Al; Grant, Skeeter), 40, 522-23, 719-20, 739
Spiegle, Dan, 81, 386, 720, 752
Spike (pseud. of of Price, Cyril), 628
Spillane, Mickey, 622, 732
Spitzweg, Carl, 524, 579
Spot (pseud. of Potts, Arthur), 749
Sprang, Richard, 722
Springer, Frank, 356, 614, 722-23
Sremac, Stevan, 411
St. John, J. Allen, 133, 220, 315, 747
Staack, Kirsten, 805
Stack, Frank, 91
Stack, Gil. See Kane, Gil (pseud. of)
Stäheli, Jakob, 346
Stallman, Manny, 759
Stallworth, Clarke, 226
Stamm, Russell, 403
Stangenberg, Knut, 282, 572
Stanley, John, 485-86, 724
Stano, Angelo, 273
Stapel, Gerrit, 101
Stark, Sheldon, 92, 402
Starlin, Jim, 118, 183-84, 519
Starr, Leonard, 32, 78, 351, 376, 488, 584-85, 722, 725
Statler, Warren, 809
Staton, Joe, 809
Steeman, Jan, 372, 616, 707
Stein, Frank N.. See Briefer, Richard (pseud. of)
Stein, Harry, 376, 471
Steinberg, Saul, 491, 826
Steinigans, William, 186

Steranko, James, 35, 133, 182, 223, 443, 448, 692, 700, 726-27, 821
Stern, Charles, 278
Stern, Roger, 718
Sternecky, Neal, 623
Sterrett, Cliff, 21, 127, 326, 388, 446, 600, 623-24, 727
Stevenson, Richard, 66
Stevenson, Thorne, 306, 749
Stoddard, Colonel Henry, 804
Stoffel, Al, 162
Stone, Chi, 759
Sto (pseud. of Tofano, Sergio), 23, 701-2
Storm, George, 141-42, 368, 420, 598, 613-14
Storm, Robert. See Trell, Max (pseud. of)
Stranks, Alan, 232
Strebel, Werner, 346
Streibel, Renny, 730
Striebel, John H., 255, 500, 730
Striker, Fran, 307, 490, 567
Strip, George (pseud. of Lobačev, Jurij (Djordje)), 488-89
Strnad, Jan, 104, 214
Strobi, Tony, 532
Stuck, Franz, 524
Studdy, George E., 145, 386, 807
Sugiura, Shigeru, 733, 825
Sugiura, Yukio, 581
Su Lang, 733-34
Sullivan, Ed, 592, 638
Sullivan, Pat, 299, 734
Sullivant, T. S., 395
Sultan, Charles, 136, 724
Sung Yu-chieh, 642
Suresh, James, 540
Suso (pseud. of Peña Rego, Jesus), 203, 360
Sutter, Linda, 152, 527
Sutton, Tom (pseud. Todd, Sean), 318, 338, 376, 689, 787
Suzuki, Ichirō, 580
Svirčić, Zdenko, 327, 738
Swan, Charles, 92, 736, 804
Swan, Gerald G., 205, 631
Swarte, Joost, 41, 719, 738-39
Swayze, Marc, 311
Swift, Howard, 315
Swinnerton, James Guilford (pseud. Guilford, James), 13, 317, 381, 483-84, 499, 514, 539-40, 548, 582, 740-41, 761
Sylvere, Jean, 605

T

Tabary, Jean, 352
Tabrett, Mike, 82
Tacconi, Ferdinando, 190, 614, 684
Tagawa, Suihou, 576, 733

Taguchi, Beisaku, 451
Takahashi, Rumiko, 41, 506
Takamori, Asao, 101
Takano, Yoshiteru, 399
Takemiya, Keiko, 366
Takemoto, Saburō, 670
Takeuchi, Tsunayoshi, 83
Talbot, Bryan, 744
Taliaferro, Charles Alfred, 260-61, 702, 744
Tamburini, Stefano, 41, 476, 600, 601
Tardi, Jacques, 719, 745-46
Tashlin, Frank, 162, 231, 315-16, 625
Taylor, Alfred H., 691
Taylor, C. J., 499
Taylor, Jack, 162
Taylor, R. W., 185
Taylor, Zachary, 200
Tchao Hong-pen, 706
Tchernia, Pierre, 129
Tebbel, John, 602
Teixido, Emili, 470, 717
Tempesti, Mario, 344
Templeton, Ben, 379, 551
Terenghi, Antonio, 227, 603, 765
Terry, Hilda, 286
Terry, John, 684, 700
Terry, Paul, 189, 378, 533, 684
Tessier, Emilie de (pseud. Duval, Marie), 88
Tettamanti, A., 521
Tezuka, Osamu, 33, 38, 78-79, 366, 386-87, 399, 405, 427-28, 463, 520, 542, 559, 573, 582-83, 589, 670, 676, 697, 752-53, 754-55, 775
Thatcher, George, 306
Thies, Flores, 239
Thomas, Bert, 535
Thomas, Roy, 104, 140, 212, 233, 260, 292, 351, 397, 646, 689, 718, 726, 732, 756, 812, 821
Thomas, W. F., 12, 89, 125
Thomas, William, 693
Thompson, Bud, 184
Thompson, Ray, 557
Thorne, Frank, 646, 757-58, 812
Thornton, John, 306
Thurber, James, 155, 478, 714
Thwaites, Ted, 353
Tibet (pseud. of Gascard, Gilbert), 335, 650
Ticci, Giovanni, 754
Tidy, Bill, 36, 315
Tillieux, Maurice, 762
Tinsley, Bruce, 507
Tippit, Jack, 379
Todd, Sean. See Sutton, Tom (pseud. of)
Tofano, Sergio (pseud. Sto), 23, 701-2
Tōfujin (pseud. of Kabashima, Katsuichi), 697
Tomaselli, Gino, 211

Tomi, Shinzō, 387
Tomlinson, Barrie, 209
Tonna, Giancarlo, 587
Took, Barry, 310
Toonder, Jan Gerhard, 768
Toonder, Marten, 283, 370, 372, 435-36, 453-54, 457, 461, 519, 595, 630, 767-68
Toonder, Phiny, 768
Töpffer, Rodolphe, 26, 224, 387-88, 770
Topor, Roland, 289
Toppi, Sergio, 770-71
Torelli, Bubi, 111, 683
Torelli, Tristano, 111, 614
Torrens, Ramon, 203
Torres, Angelo, 131, 628
Torres, Daniel, 41, 771-72
Torres, Elpidio, 32, 462, 516, 772-73
Torres, Jess, 516
Torti, Rodolfo, 517, 575
Toth, Alexander, 259, 280, 357, 422, 430, 435, 692, 771, 773, 820, 821
Toth, Werner, 821
Totleben, John, 738
Tourret, Pat, 36, 760
Tourtel, Herbert, 665
Tourtel, Mary, 22, 665-66
Toutain, José (pseud. Roger), 239, 341, 771
Townley, Langton, 157
Towntree, Harry, 535
Trachte, Don, 92, 379
Trapani, Sal, 344
Traumfabrik (pseud. of Paziena, Andrea), 476, 600-01
Trell, Max (pseud. Storm, Robert), 247-48, 354, 582, 686
Trevisan, Giorgio, 440
Triberti, Carlo, 202
Trillo, Carlos, 301, 341
Trimpe, Herb, 397, 560, 689
Trinidad, Celso, 439
Trinidad, Sonny, 462
Trog (pseud. of Fawkes, Wally), 29, 310
Trubert, Jean, 120
Trudeau, Garry, 34, 264, 775
Truman, Timothy, 461
Tschernegg, Markus, 632, 678
Tsien Siao-Tai, 706
Tsuge, Yoshiharu, 697, 775
Tsukikage, Ken, 387
Tsukioka, Yoshitoshi, 391, 775-76, 783
Tsukiyama, Mito, 387
Tuazon, Larry, 675
Tufts, Warren, 188, 467-68, 773, 776
Tuis, Sergio, 189
Tully, Tom, 125
Turner, John R., 544
Turner, Leslie, 220, 322, 776-77, 800
Turner, Lloyd, 122, 162, 231, 625
Turner, Morrie, 635, 777-78, 803

Turner, Ron, 584, 778
Tuska, George, 137, 159, 160, 222, 338, 359, 379, 404, 759, 821
Tuthill, Harry J., 164-65, 778-79

U

Udall, Ted, 104, 541
Uderzo, Albert, 103, 196, 339, 352, 459, 529, 647, 781
Uggeri, Mario, 658, 754
Uggetti, Maria Luisa, 227, 765
Ugolini, Loredano, 132, 658
Uhlik, J., 473
Ulmer, Allan, 140
Umemoto, Sachio, 199
Ungaro, Alberto, 627
Usero, Adolfo, 203, 239, 663
Uslan, Michael, 385, 752
Utagawa, Kuniyoshi, 391, 438, 775-76, 783

V

Vadim, Christian, 529
Vadmand, Per, 786
Valdés, Alfredo, 293
Valherbe, Jean. See Forest, Jean-Claude (pseud. of)
Valle, Jo, 286
Vallet, Andre, 286
Van Buren, Dick, 192
Van Buren, Raeburn, 75, 76, 179, 787-88
Vance, William, 141, 159, 345, 477, 647, 788
Van der Born, Bob, 630
Van der Elst, André (pseud. Willi), 200
Van der Heide, Dorul, 437
Vandersteen, Willy, 29, 128, 161, 738, 788-89
Van Erp, Jan, 491
Van Hamme, Jean, 137, 214, 662
Van Melkebeke, Jacques, 214, 407
Vaño, Eduardo, 654
Van Raemdonck, George, 163
Vargas, Agustin (pseud. Gutu), 291
Vargas, Gabriel, 291
Vasilovich, Guy, 593
Veitch, M. C., 188
Veitch, Rick, 461, 738
Veitch, Tom, 726
Vel, Rob. See Velter, Robert (pseud. of)
Velasquez, Damy, 32, 253, 674
Velasquez, Tony, 32, 438-39, 674
Velter, Robert (pseud. Darthel, J.; Vel, Rob), 339, 630, 721, 790-91
Ventosa, José Maria Huertas, 197
Verbeck (a.k.a Verbeek), Gustave, 751, 782-83, 791

Index A

Proper Names Index

Verdier, Ed (pseud. Verd), 481-82
Vernes, Henri, 141
Verschuere, Karel, 128, 161
Vess, Chales, 674
Vichi, Ferdinando, 228
Vidal, Guy, 493
Vidal, Jaimie, 32
Vidić, Branko, 411, 715-16, 829-30
Vidler, Edward A., 592
Vierhout, Lou, 157, 616
Vigil, Guillermo, 600
Vigil, Luis, 120
Vigna, Bepi, 562
Vile, Curt. See Moore, Alan (pseud. of)
Villa, Virgo, 573
Vincent, Alf, 569
Viskardy, Nicholas (pseud. Cardy), 748
Vivian, Ron, 344
Voight, Charles A., 128, 347, 365, 792-93
Von Eeden, Trevor, 574
Vukadinović, Ljubomir, 266

W

Wagner, John, 424
Wahl, Lou. See Schaffenberger, Kurt (pseud. of)
Wakefield, George William, 125, 795-96, 798
Wakefield, Terry, 656
Walduck, Desmond, 232
Walker, Addison Mortimer (pseud. Addison), 32, 122-23, 143-44, 158, 170, 270, 383, 445, 532, 673, 796
Walker, Brian, 300, 383, 796-97
Walker, Greg, 300, 383, 796
Walker, Joseph, 691, 798
Walker, Morgan, 300
Walker, Neal, 796
Walling, Dow, 707
Walsh, Bill, 532, 535-36
Walsh, Brandon, 481-82, 499
Walsh, Jim, 450
Walthéry, Francois, 562
Wan Chia-ch'un, 141
Wang Sunpei, 706
Ward, Norman, 729, 798
Ward, Terry, 242
Ward, William A., 145, 807
Warkentin, Tom, 308
Warnes, Carlos (pseud. Bruto, César), 213
Warren, James, 120, 224, 320, 463, 787
Wäscher, Hansrudi, 161, 569-70, 702, 759-60, 798-99
Watanabe, Masako, 542
Watkins, Dudley D., 244, 492, 574, 585

Watso. See Mager, Charles Augustus (Gus) (pseud. of)
Watson, Keith, 232
Watt, John Millar, 22, 390, 624-25
Watterson, Bill, 39, 173-74, 503, 556
Waugh, Coulton, 29, 55-56, 147, 158, 180, 186, 200, 247, 315, 422, 801
Wead, Frank, 311, 438
Webb, Jack, 597
Webb, R. H., 306
Weber, Bob, Jr., 548, 709-10
Weber, Bob, Sr., 547-48
Webster, Harold Tucker, 168, 220, 762-63, 802, 806
Webster, Tom, 693, 802-3
Wein, Len, 429, 430, 587, 738
Weisinger, Mort, 98, 147, 355-56, 417, 576, 683, 734-35, 736, 804
Weiss, Mort, 420, 474, 531
Wejp-Olsen, Werner, 299
Welch, John J., 644
Wellington, Charles H., 185, 186, 804-5
Wellman, Manly Wade, 399, 804
Wells, Bob, 426
Wells, Peter, 113
Wells, Sam, 364
Wentworth, John, 422
Werkman, Evert, 435, 461
Wertham, Dr. Frederic, 32, 135, 219, 331, 515, 613, 816-17
Wesley, Jeff, 333
West, Russ, 641
Westover, Russell, 128, 555, 761-62, 805-6
Wexler, Elmer, 791
Wheelahan, Paul, 621
Wheelan, Edgar, 414, 536-37, 687, 755, 789, 806
Wheeler, John, 383, 647, 669
Wheelis, Mark, 350
White, Brian, 442, 574, 803, 807
White, Doris, 686
White, E. B., 714
White, Hugh Stanley, 808
White, Stanley, 146, 518, 650
Whitney, Otto, 759
Whittock, Colin, 166
Wickersham, Bill, 315
Wiechmann, Peter, 177, 178
Wiedersheim, Grace. See Drayton, Grace (pseud. of)
Wiese, Ellen, 387
Wijn, Piet, 372, 436
Wilder, Don, 597
Wildey, Doug, 690, 748, 808-9
Wildman, George, 612, 809
Wildman, Karl, 809
Willard, Frank Henry, 196, 422-23, 546-47, 660, 796, 809-10
Willard, Rodlow, 684
Williams, Gaar, 739, 806
Williams, James Robert, 592, 740, 810-11

Williams, Jay Jerome (pseud. Alger, Edwin, Jr.), 613-14
Williams, Roy L., 348, 532
Williamson, Al, 131, 280, 308, 319, 331, 338, 351, 401, 432, 472, 587, 612, 628, 686, 726, 811
Williard, Frank, 753
Willi (pseud. of Van der Elst, André), 200
Wilshire, Mary, 646, 811-12
Wilson, Colin, 345, 477
Wilson, Gahan, 204
Wilson, Harry Leon, 584
Wilson, Roy, 119, 426, 620, 628, 812
Wilson, Woody, 426, 650
Wilton, Hall (pseud. of Pepper, Frank S.), 209
Windsor-Smith, Barry, 432
Wingert, Dick, 395-96
Winner, Charles H. (Doc), 252, 281-82, 437, 484, 539, 554, 812-13
Winterbotham, Russ (pseud. Bond, J. Harvey), 791, 814
Wirgman, Charles, 451
Witham, Ben, 608
Woggon, Elmer, 593, 677, 728-29
Wolfe, George, 711
Wolinski, Georges, 62, 814-16
Wolverton, Basil, 78, 225, 472, 626, 733, 816
Wong, Tony, 817-18
Wood, Bob, 135, 222, 233, 463, 545
Wood, Dave, 447
Wood, Dick, 447
Wood, Lawson, 285
Wood, Otis F., 186
Wood, Robin, 41, 818
Wood, Wallace, 105, 197, 206, 237, 254, 331, 447, 612, 673, 720, 723, 758-59, 818
Woolcock, Peter, 761
Woolfolk, William, 117, 136, 183, 368, 376, 399, 818-20
Wostkoski, C., 827
Wren, John, 809
Wright, Bill, 532
Wright, Karran, 316
Wrightson, Berni, 118, 318, 320, 432, 587, 692, 738
Wroblewski, Jerzy, 41, 820
Wunder, George, 159, 287, 378, 722, 752, 820
Wust, Theodore, 499
Wu Tcheng-en, 706
Wyeth, N. C., 87

X

Xiao Ding (pseud. of Ding Cong), 250-51

Y

Yager, Rick, 159, 160, 173
Yajima, Riichi, 133
Yamagami, Tatsuhiko, 38, 332
Yamagishi, Ryōko, 366
Yamakawa, Soji, 698
Yamamoto, Junya, 366
Yamanaka, Minetarō, 697
Yandoc, Reuben, 32, 793
Yates, Bill, 189, 445, 644
Yeates, Tom, 461
Yeats, Jack B., 823
Ye Gongzhuo, 300
Yeh Hung Chia, 823-24
Ye Quianyu, 42, 798
Yoe, Craig, 131
Yokoi, Fukujirō, 325, 328, 825
Yokoyama, Mitsuteru, 84, 752
Yokoyama, Ryūichi, 325, 696, 825-26

Yokoyama, Taizō, 826
Yoshida, Akimi, 108-9
Young, Bob, 763, 826
Young, Dean, 139
Young, Lyman, 228, 344, 763, 826
Young, Murat (Chic), 138, 208, 271, 326, 826-27
Yue Xiaoying, 827

Z

Zaboly, Bela, 675, 756, 813
Zagat, Samuel, 341-42
Zahn, Brian, 540
Zambrano, R. R., 89
Zamora, Noly, 462

Zamperoni, Guido, 143, 639
Zaniboni, Sergio, 189, 245, 575
Zapiain, Pedro, 89, 195
Zappietto, Eugenio (pseud. of Collins, Ray), 239, 249, 441, 552
Zarate, Oscar, 85
Zavattini, Cesare, 676-77
Zeck, Mike, 809
Zee, Donald, 315
Zekely, Zeke, 356
Zetterström, Hasse, 407
Zhang Leping, 42, 674
Zhu Youlan, 300
Ziegler, Bill, 519
Zolnerowich, Dan, 379
Zorad, Ernö, 830
Zucconi, Guglielmo, 202
Zuñiga, Tony, 32, 163, 424, 462
Zyx (pseud. of Hurtubise, Jacques), 398

A

A. Piker Clerk, 17, 97-98, 153, 304, 555
Abbie an'Slats, 75-76, 179, 301, 788
Abdul Jones, 447
Abelarda, 715
Abie the Agent, 20, 76, 382
Absent Minded Abner, 499
Abu Fakir, 408
Abu-san, 542
Academia Waltz, 139
According to Hoyle, 382
Ace Drummond, 451
Ace McCoy, 319
Ace Malloy, 96
Ace no Jōken, 542
Achille Talon, 36, 76-77, 647
Active Jim, 251
Adam and Eva, 807
Adam Eterno, 209, 714
Adamson, 18, 23, 77, 87, 300, 407-8
Adam Strange, 78, 92, 147, 280, 316, 400, 683
Addy, 110
Adèle Blanc-Sec, 746
Adieu Brindavoine, 745
Adolf, 78-79, 754
Adolf, Hermann and Musso, 666
Adolphus, 107
Adventure in Ujar, 294
Adventures of Big Boy, 131
Adventures of Bobby Crusoe, The, 273
Adventures of Hedley Kase, 722
Adventures of Larry Steele, The, 25, 285, 383
Adventures of Luther Arkwright, The, 744
Adventures of Matt, The, 363
Adventures of Patsy, The, 354, 598, 700
Adventures of Phoebe Zeit-Geist, The, 614, 722-23
Adventures of the Noah Family, The, 412
Adventures of Tom Sawyer, The, 575
Adventures of Ulysses, The, 575
Affairs of Jane, The, 826
Afghanistan, 530
African Adventures for Plavi Vjesnik, 638
Afričke pustolovine, 327
Agachados, Los, 79, 735
Aga od Rudnika, 411
Agatha Blue, 521
Agatha Crumm, 389
Agente Allen, 273
Agent SS018, 639
Aghardi, 79
Aglaya, 632
Ahiruga Oka 77, 452
Ahoy McCoy, 499
Ain't it a Grand and Glorious Feeling?, 153, 806
Air Ace Library, 714

Airboy, 81, 115, 135, 443, 567
Air-Fighters, 81
Air Hawk and the Flying Doctors, 34, 81-82, 255
Air Heroes, 286
Air Mail, 529
Air Pirates, 584
Airship Man, The, 82-83
Airwave, 804
Airy Alf and Bouncing Billy, 16, 83, 124, 158, 801
Ai Tua Lek, 166
Aizo no Hissatsuken, 387
Akadō Suzunosuke, 33-34, 83-84
Akage no Hitotsu, 520
Akai Hana, 775
Akai Kagebōshi, 452
Akakke ponii, 542
Akihiko kaku katariki, 588
Akiko, 676
Akim, 84-85, 759-60
Akira, 588-89
Ako Si Abraham, 163
Akumakun, 542
Alack Sinner, 41, 85, 534, 552
Aladin and His Magic Lamp, 464
Alan Ford, 85-86, 639, 685
Alan Mistero, 177
Alas y azar, 771
Albi Costellazione, 408
Album di Pippo, L', 548
Alec the Great, 271
Alert, The, 354
Ale tran tran, 521
Alex, 514
Alexander Smart, Esq., 282, 813
Alexandre Newski, 221
Alfie, Auntie & Annabel, 245
Alfie the Air Tramp, 426
Alfredo, 87, 300
Alf Wit the Ancient Brit, 393
Ali and His Baba, 424
Alias, 150
Alias Ego, 520
Ali Baba, 157, 408
Ali Baba and 40 Thieves, 464
Ali Barber, the Whisker Wizard of Old Bagdad, 536
Alice brum Brum, 521
Alice in Cartoonland, 253
Alice in Wonderland, 226, 575
Alien, 294
Aliens, 171
Ali Haha, 648
Alix l'Intrépide, 29, 87
All at Sea, 110
Alley Oop, 24, 88, 367-68, 449
All in a Lifetime, 121
All Sorts Stores, 110
All-Star Squandron, 524, 756
All the Comforts of Home, 186
All Winners, 731
Ally Sloper, 12, 88-89, 124, 483, 650, 734, 795

Alma and Oliver, 501
Alma Grande, 38, 89, 195
Alpha Flight, 40, 471
Alphonse, 335
Alphonse and Gaston, 89-90, 93, 585
Altai & Jonson, 191, 273
Alter Alter, 601
Always Belittlin', 708
A-Man, 90, 364
Amanda, 818
Amapola Negra, 714
Amapolo Nevera, 202
Amargo, 514
Amateur Etiquette, 173
Amateur Night, 360
Amazing Adventures, 821
Amazing Man, 90, 287
Amazing Spider-Man, 472, 500. See also *Spider-Man*
Ambassador, The, 485, 714
Ambler, 809
Ambrose and Al, 656
Ambrosius, 372
Ambush, 236
American Eagle, 690
American Flagg!, 40, 197-98
American Splendor, 40, 90-91
Amleto, 241
Amok, 91, 175
Amor Amor!!, 341
Amours de M. Vieuxbois, Les, 387
Ana, 714
Anac il distruttore, 240
Anatole, 740
And Her Name Was Maud, 93-94, 664
Andrax, 94
Android Pini, 463
And Then The Fun Began, 127, 360
Andy Benjamin, 656
Andy Capp, 34, 38, 95, 547
Angel, The, 95, 189, 364
Angel Caido, El, 771
Angel Dark, 685
Angélique, 170
Ang Rosas na Itim, 418
Anibal 5, 96, 289
Animaland, 370, 544
Animalaughs, 535
Animalie, 731
Animal Land, 749
Anita Diminuta, 96-97, 137
Anjinho, 243
Anmitsu Hime, 97
Anna della Jungla, 627
Annalise and the Devil, 170
Anna Stein, 632
Anne Shelton, 377
Annie Oakley, 96
Ano Eka Kūn, 452
Anthony Fury, 620
Anvil, The, 368
Apartment 3-G, 97, 232, 454
Aphrodite, 772
Apple Mary, 518, 677

Aquaman, 98, 344, 576
Aquile de Roma, Le, 180
Arabelle la Sirène, 98-99
Arad en Maya, 372, 707
Aram, 372
Arashio Koete, 84
Arbre-Coeur, L', 211
Archer Highwayman, The, 609
Archie, 67, 77, 99-100, 545-46, 567, 695, 802
Archie Andrews, 426
Arcibaldo e Petronilla, 664
Arden, 411
Are You One of These Spineless Creatures¿, 762
Argonautjes, De, 100, 372, 519
Argo Under the Ocean, 243
Arizona Kid, 377
Arkubs, The, 412
Ar Little Uns, 797
Armageddon 2419, 577
Arman en Ilva, 100-101
Aroldo, 148
Arrow, The, 364, 492
Arthur le Fantome, 193
Arthur Prince and Jim, 798
Arys Buck, 781
Arzach, 345
As de Pike, 341
Asesinato a 64 imagenes por segundo, 771
Ashita no Joe, 38, 101-2
Ashta Kagayaku, 676
As I Saw It, 581
Asparagus Tipps, 354
Aspirino y Colodion, 102, 302
Asso di Picche, 102-3, 118, 539, 627
Astérix, 34, 67, 103, 137, 285, 352, 353, 494, 529, 781, 805
Asthma Simpson, the Village Queen, 556
Astonishing Stunts, 187
Astronauta, Nico Demo, 243
Astronave Pirata, L', 221
Atlan, 103-4
Atlantic Patrol, 502
Atom, The, 92, 104, 316, 434, 583, 773
Atoman, 656
Atom and Hawkman, 374
Atomas, 605
Atomic Knights, 92
Atomic Mouse, 533
Atom's Daughter, 676
Atom-Taishi, 752, 754
At the Circus in Hogan's Alley, 824
Auf den Hund gekommen, 163
Augustus Topping, 812
Automan, 280
Auxillo social, 341
Aux Médianes de Cymbiola, 680
Avenger, The, 104, 400
Avengers, The, 104, 167, 171, 180, 379, 404, 476, 660, 689, 756

Avenging World, 254
Aventura en la India, Una, 138
Aventuras del F.B.I., Las, 514
Aventures de Barbe-Rouge, Les, 396
Aventures de Franck et Jéremie, 345
Aventures de Seraphin Laricot, Les, 313
Avonturen van Brom, 157
Avonturen van detectief Van Zwam, De, 564, 566
Avonturen van Knobbeltje Knop, 157
Avonturen van Rikki en Wiske, 789
Avonturen van Tom Texan, De, 457
Avonturen von Koenrad, La, 335
Avontuur van Pinkeltree, 157
Avventura sull'Orinoco, 241
Avventure di Spinarello, MocColino e Zaratustra, 221

B

Babbling Brooks, 217, 360
Babe Bunting, 216, 348
Bab El Mandeb, 530
Babou, 175
Baby, 166
Baby, The, 363
Baby Blues, 685
Babyettes, 222
Baby Marie Osborne, 796
Baby Snookums, 501
Baby Snoots, 219
Back Home Again, 260, 512-13
Bad Baby, 556
Badd Lads, The, 424
Bad Dream That Made Billy a Better Boy, 186
Bad Mans, 740
Baffels, 110
Baghongi il Pagliaccio, 86
Baileys, The, 481
Bajke A. S. Pushkina, 489
Bakropsuit, 166
Baldo, 148
Ballata del Mare Salato, Una, 37, 108, 215
Ball Boy, 424
Balloon Buster, 435
Bamse, 94
Banana Bunch, 118
Banana Fish, 108-9
Banana Oil, 109, 360
Bande Des Pieds-Nickeles, La. See Pieds-Nickeles, Les
Bantam Prince, 611
Baptistou le Lièvre, 271
Barbacucco, 664
Barbarella, 36, 110-11, 313, 614, 722, 723, 787
Barbaverde, 522
Barbe-Rouge, 339
Barbie, 154, 654, 812
Barbiere della Prateria, 205, 408

Barb Wire, 40
Barker, The, 206
Barnaby, 27, 112-13, 310
Barney Baxter, 22, 113-14, 534, 563, 564
Barney Google, 101, 114, 165, 238, 468, 469, 547, 554, 813
Baron Bean, 251, 381
Baron De Cuff and the Hon. Samuel Shiney, 795
Baron Mooch, 381
Baron Munchausen, 437, 489, 566
Baron vampir, 464
Barrio, 341
Barrio Breeze, 80
Barry Appleby's Gambols. See Gambols, The
Barry McKenzie, 36, 71, 116
Barry Noble, 301
Barry the Boob, 687
Bascule à Charlot, La, 746
Bash Street Kids, 118
Basil and Bert, 812
Basura, 341
Bat Lash, 99, 400
Batman, 26, 40, 77, 92, 117-18, 171, 219, 285, 303, 316, 351, 385, 400, 432, 434, 526, 534, 539, 541, 547, 583, 653, 656, 683, 696, 722, 744, 773, 808, 830
Bat Masterson, 77, 381, 656
Battle, 96
Battle Action, 209
Bazurka en Jampie Hoed, 455
B.C., 33, 119-20, 269, 371, 597, 814
Beach Boys, 453
Beany and the Gang, 222
Bear, 704
Bear Creek Folks, 600
Beat Group, 514
Beauregard, 237
Bebe Cyanure, 313
Bebe Daniels, 377
Bécassine, 16, 120, 617
Beelzebub Jones, 498
Beep Beep the Road Runner, 122
Beetle Bailey, 32, 122-23, 144, 236, 313, 796, 809
Beezer, 118
Beggar King, The, 825
Belette, La, 211
Believe It or Not, 192
Belinda, 221
Belinda Blue Eyes, 123, 267, 498
Belles and Wedding Bells, 727
Bellman, 491
Belloy l'Invulnérable, 781
Bell's Theorem, 41
Benben Monogatari, 436
Ben & Bert the Kid Cops, 426
Ben Bowie, 593
Ben Bowyang, 364
Ben Bur, 294
Ben Casey, 77, 206

Benchley, 270
Ben Hur, 511
Benjamin Beetroot, 187
Benjamin et Benjamine, 352, 781
Benjamin Pampe, 326
Ben Lyon, 377
Benny & Buster, 609
Bentley Prince, 243
Ben Turpin, 796
Ben Webster's Career, 613
Bernard Prince, 36, 127, 209, 398, 647
Bertha, 146
Beryl the Peril, 242
Beside the Sea, 812
Bessie, 236
Bessy, 128, 789
Bête Est Morte, La, 175
Betsy and Me, 206
Betsy's Buddies, 463
Better or Worse, 678
Betty, 128-29, 365, 792
Betty and Bob, 383
Betty and Veronica, 100
Betty Boop, 129, 309, 447
Betty Boop and Felix, 129, 300
Betty & Brian, 386
Between Love and Fatherland, 465
Bewegte Mann, Der, 453
Beyond Mars, 280
Bianca, 37, 221
Bib and Bub, 130, 339
Biberce, 489
Bibi e Bibo, 664
Bibi Fricotin, 22, 130, 314
Bible Bee, 356
Bibor, 790
Bicot, 313
Biddy's Beastly Bloomers, 166
Bidochon, Les, 40, 134
Bidu and Franjinha, 243
Biff Bang Bella, 596
Biff Benbow, 209
Biffo the Bear, 241
Big Ben Bolt, 77, 130-31, 179, 454,
  554, 796
Big Boy, 131
Big Chief Wahoo, 196, 593, 677, 728
Big Flame, 282
Big Game Gannon, 393
Biggles, 789
Bigh Hugh and You, 393
Big Hit Swift, 501
Big Kid, 716
Big Mounty, 778
Big Numbers, 547
Big Sister, 563
Big Tom, 198
Big Top, 806
Big Town, 474
Big X, 754
Bilbolbul, 16, 132
Bill, 146
Bill Bailey, 823
Bill Body, 472-73, 678

Bill de Clown, 271
Bill Mauldin's Cartoon, 782
Billoo, 626
Bill the Office Boy, 712
Billville Birds, 392
Billy Banks, 536
Billy Bis, 132
Billy Bounce, 431
Billy Bunter, 132-33, 536
Billy Make Believe, 420
Billy Muggins, 812
Billy Pack, 133
Billy Rock, 111
Billy the Baby Beetle, 650
Billy the Kid, 138, 393, 423, 811
Billy the Office Boy, 127
Billy Whizz, 424
Bimbo Bambus, 566
Bimbo Goes to the Moon, 544
Bing Bang Benny, 648
Binky and Granpop, 502
Bint el Hadra, 123
Bionic Woman, The, 809
Birdseye Center, 322, 323
Birre Beer, 454
Bitter Olive, 201
Biyak Na Bato, 350
Bizzy Beaver, 650
Blackbow, 138
Black Buccaneer, 447
Black Bull, 462, 690
Black Canary, 280, 400, 725
Black Cat, 135, 280
Black Condor, 135-36, 303
Black Dagger, 282
Black Diamond, 593
Black Fury, 537
Blackhawk, 81, 134, 136, 149, 198,
  219, 282, 303, 344, 381, 454,
  471, 500, 819
Black Hood, 136-37, 545, 819
Black Jack, 754
Black Kiss, 198
Black Lion, 282
Black Magic, 527
Blackmark, 351, 434
Black Marvel, 472
Black Mask-Lord Warwick, 716
Black Orchid, 163, 525, 573
Black Owl, 108, 223
Black Panther, The, 364
Blackstone the Magician, 434
Black Terror, 137, 526, 656
Black Tulip, The, 511
Black Venus, 462
Black Widow, 167
Blade Runner, 811
Blake et Mortimer, 29, 137, 407
Blanche Epiphanie, 614
Blazing Combat, 351, 690
Blimps, The, 110
Blondie, 21, 138-39, 267, 271, 325,
  326, 377, 493, 677, 809, 826-27
Blondin et Cirage, 339, 352, 396

Bloodstar, 214
Blook, 372
Bloom County, 39, 139-40, 591
Blue Beetle, 115, 140, 187, 191, 254,
  344, 435, 447, 705
Blue Bolt, 115, 140-41, 447, 704
Blue Jacket, 745
Blue Phantom, The, 321
Blue Raven, The, 252, 606
Blue Sea and Red Heart, 141
Bluey and Curley, 28, 141, 364
Bo, 121
Bobbie & Bertie Bruin, 609
Bobbie Blake, 267
Bobby, 306, 400
Bobby Benson and the B-Bar-B Riders,
  104
Bobby Bounce, 632
Bobby Brain, 544
Bobby Dare, 363
Bobby Make-Believe, 445
Bobby Thatcher, 141-42, 220, 524, 614
Bob Crack, 246
Bob Mallard, 384
Bob Morane, 142-43, 788
Bobo Baxter, 348-49
Bob Phantom, 526
Bob Stay, 110
Bob's Your Uncle, 536
Bob the Bugler, 187
Bōken Dankichi, 143
Boksingera, 675
Bokutō kun, 399
Bold Adventures, 574
Bomben, 348
Bombola, 255
Bonachi Bushido, 452
Bon Bon, 405
Bondying, 773
Boner's Ark, 143-44, 796
Boney Prince Charlie, 110
Boney & Stoney, 110
Bongo, 715
Bonifazio, 548
Bon Jan, El, 302
Bonnie, 678
Bonnie and Boo-Boo, 709-10
Bonzo, 145, 807
Boob McNutt, 19, 145-46, 348, 349,
  533
Boobs Abroad, 348
Books of Magic, The, 432
Bookworm, 166
Booma, 773
Boomer, 189
Boomerang Burke, 346
Boots and Her Buddies, 147, 515-16
Bo-Peep, 808
Bornéo Joe, 614
Born Loser, The, 148
Botchan, 542
Botond, 294
Bouboule, 196
Bouche du Diable, 149

Index B
Title Index

Bouncer, 110, 246
Bound to Win, 613-14
Bourchier-Walkeley Episode in Four
    Scenes, 372
Box-a-Tricks, 797
Boy Animal Trainer, The, 445
Boy Buddies and Black Witch, 460
Boy Comics, 135
Boy Commandos, 149, 381, 447, 568,
    705
Boy King, 443
Boy's Ranch, 705
Boy Who Breathed on Glass at the
    British Museum, 116
Bozo Blimp, 404
Braccobaldo, 608
Brad and Dad, 349
Brainy Bowers, 185
Brammetje Bram, 149-50, 707
Brave and the Bold, 356
Bravo for Adventure, 773
Breezy Ben, 536
Breezy Moments on Wurzel Farm, 386
Brenda Starr, 27, 151-52, 154, 270,
    527, 587
Brick Bradford, 24, 40, 137, 152,
    354-55, 576-77, 592, 653
Briganti, I, 640
Briggs the Butler, 321
Brik, 193
Bring 'em Back Alive, 427, 749
Bringing Up Father, 17, 19, 21, 26, 62,
    67, 69, 154-55, 306-7, 309, 356,
    501-2, 567, 569, 581, 603, 624,
    662, 664
Bristow, 36, 155-56
Broncho Bill, 161
Bronc Peeler, 156, 370
Broom Hilda, 156, 556-57, 699
Broons, The, 585
Brother of the Spears, 675
Brother Power, The Geek, 705
Brouillard au Pont de Tolbiac, 746
Brownies, 441, 628
Bruce Forsyth, 812
Bruce Gentry, 158-59
Brum, 94, 480
Bruno Brazil, 159, 647, 788
Bruno Lionel, 656
Brusel, 680
Buck Danny, 159, 196, 241, 396
Buck John, 514
Buck Jones, 285
Buck Nix, 582, 711
Buck Rogers, 23, 24, 92, 137, 152,
    159-60, 173, 409, 427, 438, 488,
    502, 550, 577, 592, 677, 708, 792
Buck Ryan, 25, 160-61, 498, 544
Buckskin Benson, 627
Bud Abbott and Lou Costello, 798
Buddha, 754
Buddy, 186
Budge & Co, 370
Bud Smith, 381

Bufalo Bil, 716
Bufalo Bill, 161, 216
Buffalo Bill, 138, 161-62, 393, 500,
    511, 798-99, 808
Bugei Kikou, 671
Bughouse Fables, 165, 326
Bugs Bunny, 162-63, 218, 625
Bulaklak, 163
Bullenklöten, 453
Bullet Benton, 411
Bulletje en Bonestaak, 18, 163
Bulletman, 108, 134, 164, 223, 678
Bull Rocket, 286, 714
Bull's Eye Bill, 458
Bumbazine and Albert the Alligator, 438
Bumper Snickers, 389
Bungle Family, The, 164-65, 538, 647,
    778-79
Bunky, 165, 468, 554
Bunny the Rabbit, 812
Buntala, 462
Burke's Law, 206
Burre Busse, 572
Bussi Bär, 566
Bussola of Turin, La, 221
Buster, 95
Buster & Bones, 609
Buster Brown, 26, 168-69, 564, 591
Buster Brown and Tige, 795
Buster Button, 246
Buster Crabbe, 811
Butch the Butcher's Boy, 431
Buy-tonic Boy, The, 574
Buz Sawyer, 27, 58, 158, 159, 169-70,
    192, 220, 777, 800

C

Caça aos Tubaroes, 215
Calamity Jane, 162
Calata di Mac Similiano, La, 221
Caleb King's Mine, 246
Calico Kid, 104
Calimero, 608
Call of the West, 377
Cal McCord, 391
Calvin and Hobbes, 39, 173-74, 556,
    593
Camelot 3000, 40
Camillusge Gajaman Sama Sathsiri,
    607
Camilusge Don Sethan, 607
Campbell Kids, The, 268
Canadiens, Les, 197
Canal Choc, 527
Candid Camera, 508
Candy, 434, 587
Canecaldo, 521
Canyon Kiddies, 484, 740, 741
Can You Beat It?, 544
Capitaine Babedure, 271
Capitaine Fantôme, Le, 176

Capitalists, 201
Capitan Caribe, 580
Capitan Cormorand, 627
Capitan Erik, 529, 575
Capitan l'Audace, 176, 543
Capitan Miki, 161, 176-77
Capitan Misterio, El, 177
Capitano di 15 anni, Un, 575
Capitan Terror, 177-78
Capitan Trueno, El, 34, 178-79, 407
Cap Stubbs and Tippie, 180, 271
Captain, the Kid, and the Cook, The,
    812
Captain America, 27, 105, 134,
    180-82, 206, 321, 381, 397,
    447-48, 471, 472, 476, 526, 653,
    660, 678, 695, 705, 727, 732, 819
Captain and the Kids, The, 19, 182,
    233, 252, 375, 437, 504. See also
    Katzenjammer Kids, The
Captain Atom, 254
Captain Battle, 108, 223
Capt. Billy Whiz Bang, 218
Captain Cutler, 574
Captain Easy, 40, 220, 322, 409, 488,
    777, 800, 814. See also Wash
    Tubbs
Captain Fear, 573
Captain Fibb, 431
Captain Flag, 27, 502
Captain Frank Hawks, 502
Captain Gin, 175
Captain Harlock, 520
Captain Jet Dixon of the Space
    Squadron, 649
Captain Justice, 96
Captain Ken, 351, 754
Captain Marvel, 26, 87, 96, 108,
    120-21, 126, 133, 148, 166, 167,
    182-84, 223, 381, 400, 435, 447,
    490, 517, 518, 541, 567, 583,
    678, 683, 819
Captain Marvel Jr., 96, 133, 164, 184,
    187, 381, 517, 518, 637, 819
Captain Midnight, 115, 134, 184-85
Captain Miracle, 96
Captain Moonlight, 146
Captain Power, 592, 620
Captain Savage and His Leatherneck
    Raiders, 689
Captain Scarlet, 282
Capt. Storm, 435
Captain Strato Comics, 255
Captain Terry Thunder, 492
Captain Thunder, 182
Captain Tootsie, 120
Capt. Triumph, 219
Captain Universe, 254
Captain Valiant, 96
Captain Victory and the Galactic
    Rangers, 448
Captain Video, 286
Captain Vigour, 391
Captain West, 192

Captain Wings, 185, 280, 492
Captain Zbik, 820
Carev Štitonoša, 716
Caribu, 227
Caricatures by Robinson, 656
Carlomango, 659
Carlo the Jester, 823
Carmen, 614
Carnivora, 278
Caroline Choléra, 614
Carpanta, 186
Carrière Militaire d'Onésim Baluchon,
    La, 313
Carrie the Girl Chaplin, 796
Carson of Venus, 432
Carson's Cubs, 393
Cartoccino dei Piccoli, 86
Carton Guide to (Non) Communication,
    The, 350
Cartoon Guide to Genetics, The, 350
Cartoon Guide to Physics, The, 350
Cartoon Guide to U.S. History, The,
    350
Cartoon History of the Universe, The,
    350
Casa Matta, La, 37, 221
Casey Court, 125, 187-88
Casey Ruggles, 188, 202, 467, 773,
    775
Casper, 188-89
Caste des metabarons, La, 341
Castle of Terror, 631
Cat and the Canary, 789
Cathy, 39, 190, 423, 672, 733
Cat-Man, The, 190-91
Cato Zulu, 627
Cattivik, 145
Cave Carson, 280
Cebolinha, 243
Cellulite, 192
Centaure Vezelay, Le, 174, 175
110 pillole, Le, 640
Century 21, 778
Cent Vingt-Six Métiers de Caramel, 313
Cerebus, 40, 41, 192
Cerro de la Plata, El, 771
César, 762
Césarin, 271
C'était la Guerre des Tranchées, 746
Chacal de Bir Jerari, El, 138
Chacha Chaudhary, 626
Chakkari Densuke, 825
Challengers of the Unknown, 381, 447
Chameleon, 287
Chame to Dekobo, 448
Chanoc, 195
Chao Yang Gou, 375, 376
Charley's War, 209
Charlie Chan, 24, 95, 195-96, 440,
    611
Charlie Chaplin's Comic Capers, 157,
    196, 619, 686
Charlie Chasem, 236
Charlie Chuckle, 386

Charlie Conscript, 356
Charlie McCarthy, 218
Charlie Mensuel, 678
Charlie Sprint, 202
Charlot, 313
Charterhouse of Parma, The, 511
Chatillo y Federico, 197
Checca, La, 664
Cheekichap the Jap, 110
Cheerful Charley, 501
Cheeverwood, 593
Chef, De, 246
Chesty Bond, 535
Chevalier Ardent, 36, 198, 217
Chicchirichi, 408
Chick, 656
Chick Bill, 335
Chico Bento, 243
Chief Chucklehead, 812
Chigley and Trumpton, 656
Chikaino Makyû, 199
Chikyu S.O.S., 698
Children of Doom, 583
Children of the Mayflower, 363
Chimp and the Imp, 628
Chimpo's Circus, 812
Chimps, The, 386
Chip and Jerry, 812
Chip Collins, Adventurer, 653
Chisholm Kid, 611
Chispita, 138
Chlorophylle, 199-200
Chōhen Dai Roman, 452
Chōken Leap, 464
Choo Choo Charlie, 724
Choose Your Own Adventures, 154
Chouchou, 313
Chris Crusty, 281
Chriss Lean, 508
Christmas Eve, 464
Christophe Cofumb, 623
Chris Welkin, 814
Chroniqu des Tifous, La, 319
Chubb-Lock Homes, 823
Chubb & Tubb, 110
Chubby and Lulu, 317
Chubby & the Christmas Star, 544
Chuckler, 110, 246
Chuck White, 587
Chuko Szu-lang, 823
Chu Liu Chu, 200-201
Chums of the Circus, 363
Chupamirto, 23, 201
Chūsingura, 452
Cicero's Cat, 201-2, 711, 721-22
Cid, El, 511
Cinco por Infinito, 37, 203, 514
Cinque della Selena, I, 118
Cinque su Marte, 118
Cip e Zagar, 408
Circus Solly, 709
Cirilo El Audaz, 639
Cisco Kid, The, 32, 203, 380, 672
Cité interdite, La, 525

Cités Obscures, Les, 680
Citizen Smith, Son of the Unknown
    SOlder, 372
Città, La, 771
Ciudad, 341
Clancy Kids, The, 222
Clarence, 693
Clarence the Cop, 431
Clarissa's Chances, 740
Clark Gable, 377
Classics Illustrated, 83, 96, 204,
    219-20, 401
Classics Illustrated Junior, 204
Claude Duval, the Laughing Chevalier,
    393
Claude Duval and the Traitor Cavalier,
    393
Claws of the Cat, 778
Cliff McCoy, 391
Clifford, 295
Cliff Rendall, 707
Clift Steele, 251
Clip Carson, 303, 434
Clipper Kirk, 206
Clive, 204-5
Cloggies, The, 315
Cloris and Clare, 812
Clumsy Claude, 431
Coal Black Joens, 110
Cobra, El, 239
Cocco Bill, 34, 205, 408
Coccobill, 608
Cock and Bull, The, 80
Coco, Facho & Co., 341
Code of the Northland, 609
Codinzolo, 202
Cody Starbuck, 197
Coeur couronné, Le, 345
Coeurs Vaillants, 345
Coffee Nerves, 700
Collana Freccia, 177
Collana Prateria, 177
Collegio 1a Delizia, Il, 664
Collezionista, Il, 771
Col. Gilfeather, 179
Colonel Crackpot's Circus, 424
Colonel Pewter, 208
Colonel Potterby and the Duchess, 208,
    827
Colonnello Caster Bum, Il, 575
Colorado Kid, 162
Colorful Road, The, 827
Comanche, 36, 209, 398, 647
Combat Kelly, 105, 126, 689
Come On, Steve!, 210-11, 236
Comforts of Bath, The, 663
Comic Wonder, 96
Commandante Mark, 162, 177
Commander Cockle, 544
Commander Mantell, 657
Commander Steel, 321
Commando Gibbs, 125
Commando Ranger, 492
Commando Yank, 27, 115

Commando York, 611
Commissario Spada, Il, 211, 240-41
Committed, 593
Compagnia dei Sette, La, 603
Compagnia dell Forca, La, 640
Conan, 35, 99, 167, 192, 211-12, 319, 432, 434, 505, 573, 646, 690, 757, 778
Condor y el Bebé, El, 138
Congressman Kalog, 705
Connie, 24, 128, 147, 212-13, 228, 347, 348, 557
Conquerer, 287
Conquesta di Mompracem, La, 549
Constable Cuddlecook, 205
Contes de la Barque Saoule, 313
Continuity, 755
Contract with God, A, 40
Contrary Mary, 236
Convict, 823
Cookney Sportsman, 340
Cool McCool, 435
Coon Hollow Folks, 600
Copperclock the Desert Cop, 386
Corchito, 606
Corentin, 214
Cornets d'Humour, Les, 149
Corrier Boy, 508
Corsaro Nero, Il, 86
Corto Maltese, 37, 215, 627
Cosacco, Il, 818
Cosmine, 507
Costo Chien Policier, 271
Cotton Carver, 473
Countdown, 686
Count Screwloose of Tooloose, 19, 109, 216-17, 236, 360, 575
Courageous Cat, 435
Cowboy Charlie, 377
Coyote, El, 111, 217, 500
Cracker Jack, the Wonder Whip Man, 346
Crash Carew, 243
Crasy Castle, 656
Crazy Cowboy, 548
Crazy Kink the Goofy Gangster, 386
Crazyman, 77
Creatura, 278
Creeper, Hawk and Dove, 344
Creepy Creations, 648
Cricri Souris d'Appartement, 175
Cries of London, The, 663
Crime and Punishment, 204
Crimebuster, 115, 135, 222, 593
Crime Detective, 567
Crime Does Not Pay, 135, 444
Crimson Avenger, The, 473
Crimson Pirate, The, 576
Cristoforo Colombo, 508
Critical Error, 171
Crni ataman, 716
Crock, 597
Croisière des Oubliés, La, 131
Cro-Magnon, 382

Cronache d'armi, di giullari, di briganti e militari, 770
Croquemulot, 175
Crossfire, 720
Crow, The, 40, 449
Cruise of the Sea Hawk, 146
Crusaders, The, 321
Crusader's Christmas, 609
Cuba 1942, 150
Cubitus, 227
Cucciolo, 189, 227-28
Cucciolo e Beppe, 642
Cuore Garibaldino, 228
Curiosities, 535
Curley Harper, 228
Curly Crusoe, 110
Curly Kayoe, 420
Curtis, 39, 218, 228-29, 379
Cuthbert the Carpenter, 812
Cuties, 778
Cuto, 25, 137, 229-30
Cyborg 009, 230, 405
Cyril the Sporty Scout, 693

D

Daabu, 626
Daffy Doodles, 813
Daffy Duck, 231
Dagar, 675
Dago, 818
Dagwood Splits the Atom, 554
Daiheigenji, 231, 698
Daihikyō, 463
Dai Machine, The, 752
Dainihon Meishō Kagami, 775
Daiya Majin, 669
Dakota Jim, 180
Dale Arden, 703
Daleks, The, 778
Dambanang Putik, 675
Damon and Pythias, 727
Dan Dakota, 239
Dan Dare, 33, 125, 232, 368, 778
Dan Doofer, 498
Dan Dunn, 95, 232-33, 440
Dandy McQueen, 243
Dan Hastings, 360
Daniël, 157
Daniel Boone, 321, 511
Daniel Dole and Oscar Outofwork, 187
Dani Futuro, 37, 341
Dan Jensen, 138
Dan Leno, 158
Danny Dingle, 233
Danny Dreamer, 538
Danny Hale, 233
Danny Longlegs, 393
Dan O'Neill's Comics and Stories, 584
Dar Aguila, 675
Dare-a-Day Davy, 648

Daredevil, 40, 115, 135, 171, 206, 233-34, 472, 534, 593, 660, 811, 818
Daredevil Barry Finn, 537
Daring Deeds of Buck Wilson, The, 346
Dark Empire, 726
Darkie and Dick, 536
Dark Knight Returns, The, 118
Dark Shadows, 108
Darna, 645
Daruma-kun, 399
Dateline: Danger!, 234-35, 502, 729
Date with Judy, A, 567
Dauntless Durham of the U.S.A., 244, 382
Dave, 235-36
Dave O'Flynn, 335
Dave's Delicatessen, 217, 236
Davor, 239
Davy Crockett, 96, 143, 381, 391
Davy Jones, 147, 502
Daydreaming Don, 812
Days of Real Sport, The, 153, 806
Dazzler, 110
Dchikai no Makyū, 199
Deadly Hands of Kung Fu, 519
Deadman, 77
Deadshot Sue, 502
Dear Dollink, 360
Death Patrol, 125, 206
Debbie, 384
Debbie Deere, 408
Déchéance du Professeur Adamus, La, 313
Declic, Le, 508
Decouverte du monde en B.D., La, 771
Dedalito, 302
Deed-a-Day Danny, 502, 798, 807
Deerslayer, 383
Defenders, The, 259
De Groyte Pyr, 100
Delta 99, 37, 239-40, 341
Démon des Caraïbes, Le, 196, 241, 396
Demonja, 123
Demonyo Made Me Do It, The, 646
Den, 214
Den II, 214
Denkō Ozma, 520
Dennis the Menace (G.B.), 118, 166, 596
Dennis the Menace (U.S.), 32, 40, 58, 241-42, 367, 441
Densuke, 825
Derek Roy, 812
Derickson Denie, 27, 242-43
De rode Ridder, 789
Desmond Durham, 382
Desperate Dan, 243-44
Desperate Desmond, 76, 244, 366, 382
Destroyer, 133, 472
Destroyer 171, 502
Destroyer Duck, 99
Detective, 432
Detektive Schmidtchen, 244-45, 651

Devilman, 559
Devil's Angel, The, 757-58
Devlin, 462
DI 13, 253, 674
D.I., The, 689
Diablo, The, 423, 435
Diabolik, 37, 189, 245, 459, 639
Diary of a Bad Boy, 110
Dick Bos, 246
Dick Fulmine, 28, 111, 216, 246-47, 255
Dick Hercules, 391, 414
Dickie Dare, 175, 247, 248, 700, 751, 801
Dick Peter, 215
Dick's Adventures in Dreamland, 247-48, 582
Dick Sanders, 384
Dick's Quick Tricks, 798
Dick Tracy, 24, 26, 40, 161, 232, 248-49, 289, 294-95, 353-54, 402, 403, 416, 417, 434, 489, 571, 582, 642, 679
Dick Turpin, 393
Diego Valor, 249, 361
DI Jr, 674
Dilbert, 39, 249-50, 672, 716-17
Dili Ako Mahadlok, 506
Dimple and Dumpling, 812
Dinah Mite, 110, 426
Dingbat Family, The, 251, 290, 381, 457
Dingbats, The, 693
Ding Dong Belle, 393
Dinglehoofer und His Dog Adolph, 252, 450
Dinoceras, 573
Dippy Duck, 582
Dirk the Demon, 287
Dirk the Dog Detective, 823
Discontinued Stories, 388, 415
Discs a Go Go, 370
Dispettieri, I, 642
Diwani, 462
Dixie Dugan, 255, 304, 500, 730
Djon Domino, 42, 255-56
Dobol Trobol, 773
Doc Savage, 108, 115, 255, 256-57, 737
Doc Strange, 108
Docteur Gaudeamus, Le, 352
Docteur Justice, 511
Dr. 13, 163
Dr. Bobbs, 179
Dr. Destine, 321
Doctor Doodah, 205
Dr. Fate, 257, 316, 460
Doctor Faust, Il, 86
Dr. Gnome of Gnomansland, 693
Dr. Guy Bennett, 757
Dr. Hee-Haw, 798
Dr. Jekyll and Mr. Hyde, 221
Dr. Kildare, 108, 179, 257
Doctor Merengue, El, 255, 257-58

Dr. Merling, 258, 468
Dr. Mid-Nite, 258-59, 773
Doctor Niebla, 259, 384
Dr. Occult, 699
Dr. Patent, 823
Dr. Sabak en His Monster, 705
Dr. Spektor, 675
Dr. Strange, 254, 259-60, 351, 472
Dr. Up-To-Dayte's Academy, 823
Doctor Who, 778
Dr. Wonder, 105
Doc Wright, 146, 349
Dödens fågel, 348
Doggy Officer, 605
Doings at Whackington School, 158
Doings of the Duffs, 482
Dolliwogs' Dolls' House, 317
Doll Man, 134, 192, 219, 260, 297, 454, 471
Dolly Dimples, 632
Dolly Drake, 267
Dominatori dell'Abisso, 175
Domu, 588
Donald Duck, 67, 111-12, 148, 219, 253, 260-61, 324, 525, 535, 642, 648, 703, 744
Don Antonio della Mancia, 543
Don Ataulfo Clorato y su Sobrino Renato, 695
Doña Tremebunda, 595
Don Berrinche, 261-62
Don Catarino, 18, 631
Doncia, 16
Dondi, 262, 275-76, 373
Don Dixon and the Hidden Empire, 262, 352, 611
Don Fulgencio, 262-63, 595
Doninki, 452
Don Julian de Monte Pío, 597
Donnie, 499
Don Pancho Talero, 21, 263
Don Pascual, 118
Don Pedro, 570
Don Placído, 302
Don Quickshot, 370
Don Quixote, 408, 464
Don Quixote de Tintogs, 158
Don Tele, 202
Don Terrible Banuelos, 302
Don Winslow of the Navy, 24, 263-64, 285, 611, 725
Doodle Family, The, 482
Doomsday + 1, 171
Doonesbury, 34, 264, 503, 507
Dororo, 754
Doshako, 825
Dos Hermanos, 138
Dot and Carrie, 21, 265-66, 412
Dot and Dash, 727
Dottor Faust, Il, 25, 266
Dottor Nefasto, 521
Dotty and Scotty, 656
Double Trouble, 807
Down Main Street, 711

Down on the Farm, 369
Down the Road, 121
Dōyō Sanbusaku, 559
Dracula, 41, 206, 301, 818
Dragamuffin, 812
Drago, 28, 267, 389
Drake & Drake, 341
Dream Dope, 80
Dreamer, The, 40
Dreams of the Rarebit Fiend, 14, 268-69, 498
Drei Musketiere, Die, 50
Dropouts, The, 269
Dropsie Avenue, 40, 278
Druka, 217
Druuna, 278
Dub-Dabs, 233
Dude Dawson, 631
Dudley D., 760
Dudley Dudd the Dud Detective, 110
Due Tamburini, I, 603
Duke Handy, 454
Dull Care, 498
Dumagit, 462
Dumb Bunnies, The, 806
Dumb Dora, 271, 322, 326, 826
Dumbo, 253, 438
Durango Kid, 360
Durga-Rāni, 605
Dutchy & Dolly, 426
Dve sirotice, 830
Dylan Dog, 273, 516, 530
Dysebel, 773
Dzarto, Prehistoric Hero, 473
Dzjengis Khan, 38, 273, 491
Džungla Ved, 411

E

Eagle Scout Roy, 348
Eclipso, 280
Edgar Allen Poe, 214
Edokko Ken-chan. See Fuku-chan
Edward and the Jumblies, 138
Eek and Meek, 276
Eerie, 120
Eggbert and Philbert, 823
Ehon Musha Burui, 391
8-man, 276-77, 463
Eimei Nijuhasshuk, 775
Eisele und Beisele, 277
Ejecucion, La, 150
Electropolis, 604
Elektra Assassin, 534
Elements of Skating, 340
Elfquest, 279-80
Ella Cinders, 280-81
Elmer, 281-82, 554, 740, 813
Elmer Fudd, 231
E-Man, 809
Embarassing Moments, 381
Emergency!, 171

Emil und die Detektive, 451
Empire's End, 726
Empire Strikes Back, The, 726, 811
Enemigo del Hombre, El, 254
Enemy Ace, 460-61, 757
Enfance, L', 338
Enfants, C'est l'Hydragon Qui Passe, 313
Engholm, Kaj, 282-83
En Los Dominios de los Sioux, 361
Enoch Hard, 110
En un lugar de la mente, 120
Ephémère, 382
Ephraim Broadbeamer, 823
Episode Banal de la Guerre des Tranchées, 745-46
Episodios de Guerra, 137
Eppo, 638
Ergun L'Errant, 211
Eric de Noorman, 29, 283, 457-58, 792
Ernest Ringard, 319
Ernie, 284
Ernie Pike, 284-85, 580, 627, 714
Ernie Pook's Comeek, 115-16
Erwin, 283, 458
Escuadrilla de la Muerte, La, 137
Esky Mo, 574
Esopo Minore, 642
Espana Grande, 341
Espana Libre!, 341
Espana Una, 341
Espesial Komiks, 86
Espiègle Lili, L', 286
Espionage, 192, 460
Esteban, 350
Estrella Negra, La, 341
Eternals, The, 447
Eternauta, El, 150, 286, 580, 714
Etta Kett, 286
Et Voila, 731
Eulenspiegel, 437
Eva, 211
Evaristo, 714-15
Eva Sedlitzky, 632
Events Leading Up to the Tragedy, The, 762
Evermores, The, 796
Ever Since Adam and Eve, 189
Everyday Dreams, 504
Evil Eye, 797
Exploits d'Isidore MacAron and Anatole Fricotard, Les, 313
Exploring, 110
Exterminateur 17, 131
Extraordinaire Aventure de Monsieur Faust, L', 527

F

Fable about Little Golden Rooster, 464
Fablettes, 482
Fabulas de klokkendokter, 372

Fabulosas ciudades de Arizona, Las, 771
Fabulous Furry Freak Brothers, 36, 289-90, 694
Fabulus Panicas, 289
Faceache, 648
Face de Lune, 149
Facéties du Père Passe-Passe, 193
Facéties du Sapeur Camember, Les, 206, 290, 399
Fairytale about Tzar Saltan, 464
Falcon, The, 377
Falk, 798-99
Fallutelli, 255, 291
Famiglia Cristiana, 221
Familia Burron, La, 22, 291
Familia Ulises, La, 22, 291
Familie Snoek, De, 789
Famille Amulette, La, 617
Famille Fenouillard, La, 206, 290, 292, 399
Famille Petitou, La, 335
Family Foursome, The, 826-27
Family Man, 384
Family Theatre, 377
Family Upstairs, The, 251, 457. See also Dingbat Family, The
Famous Churches of the World, 389
Fandango the Hoss, 823
Fantasia, 438, 441
Fantastic Four, 167, 171, 292-93, 396, 447, 472, 689, 704, 705, 732, 756, 757
Fantomas, 293
Fantomen, 348
Fantomette, 218
Far Side, The, 468
Fat Chance, 128
Fat Freddy's Cat, 290
Fathead Fritz, 80
Father, 186
Father Christmas, 154
Fatman, The Human Flying Saucer, 121
Fatty Arbuckle, 796
Fatty Felix, 499
Fatty Finn, 293-94, 569
Fatty Fitt, 110
Faust, 623
Fax from Sarajevo, 461
FBI Story, The, 773
Fearless Fosdick, 249, 294-95, 478
Federal Men, 699
Fée Aveline, La, 352
Feiffer, 33, 189, 295
Feitlebaum Family, The, 109
Felix, 297-99, 491, 762
Felix Mendelssohn and his Hawaiian Serenaders, 377
Felix O'Fan, 354
Felix the Cat, 67, 299-300, 473, 617, 734
Femme-Piège, La, 131
Femmine incantate, Le, 640
Ferarella, 608
Ferdinand the Fire Fighter, 187

Ferd'nand, 87, 300-301, 301
Ferrier's World Searchlight, 302
Fido, 110
Fiery Mask, 705
Fièver d'Urbicande, La, 680
Fiffige Alf, 297, 491
Fighting American, 447
Fighting Frazers, The, 393
Fighting Yank, 27, 302, 526, 656, 678
Filipino and the Chick, The, 91
Filipino Food, 646
Filleter Fish, 187
Fillum Fables, 353, 806
Film Fannie, 302
Fils de Chine, 302-3
Fin, The, 287
Find Six Differences, 709
Fiordistella, 162
Fire!, 542
Fireball, 588
Firehair, 280, 492
Firestar, 812
First Aid Freddie, 693
Fitz and Startz, 628
Five-Fifteen, The, 675, 687
Fix und Foxi, 305-6, 437-38, 493-94, 566, 661
Flag-Man, 460
Flame, The, 303
Flamingo, 306, 400
Flash, The, 104, 259, 307-8, 316, 357, 358, 372, 373, 400, 401, 407, 422, 460, 524, 653, 683
Flash Gordon, 24, 40, 83, 115, 116, 137, 152, 153, 160, 170, 209, 220, 243, 262, 308-9, 319, 378, 407, 427, 432, 434, 443, 444, 474, 502, 576, 592, 618, 620, 637, 641, 676, 686, 703, 716, 757, 809, 811, 818
Flashing Through, 808
Flash Point, 209
Flèche Noire, La, 313
Flenheimer Kids, The, 450
Flexo, 133
Flic et Piaf, 271
Flint, 791
Flint Baker, 152
Flintstones, The, 149, 657, 809
Flip, 646
Flip en Flop, 163
Flipper the Skipper, 125, 656
Flippity and Flop, 315
Flirting Flora, 186
Flook, 29, 208, 310, 418
Florita, 310-11
Flossie and Phyllis the Fascinating Flappers, 796
Flubs and Fluffs, 656
Flutters, The, 311
Fly, The, 447, 705
Flygande hunden, Den, 490
Flygsoldat 113 Bom, 282, 314, 479
Flying Dutchman, 223

Flying House, The, 498
Flyin' Jenny, 311, 438
Flynn, 520
Foire aux Immortels, 131
Folio the Page, 812
Folly Bololy, 476
Foolish Ferdinand, 514
Foolish Questions, I'm the Guy, 348, 349
Football Family Robinson, 209
Footrot Flats, 42, 311-12
For Better or For Worse, 39, 312-13, 423, 733
Ford Sterling, 796
Ford T, 762
Foreign Correspondent, 598
Forest of Fear, 377
Forgotten City, 282
For This We Have Daughters?, 623, 727
Fort Navajo. See Lieutenant Blueberry
Fortune in the Desert, 377
Fortunello, 664
Forza John, 658
Fosdyke Saga, The, 36, 311, 314-15
Fouce, un Uomo nella Revoluzione, 685
Four Aces, The, 744
4 As, Les, 217
Fox, The, 372, 545
Fox and the Crow, The, 315-16
Foxy Grandpa, 26, 317, 395, 682
Franca, 216
Francis Drake, 570
François Veyrac l'Emigrant, 271
Frankenstein, 152, 317-18
Frankie Doodle, 482
Frankie Stein, 574, 648
Franz Fazakerly, Space Ace of the Future, 744
Frazer of Africa, 36, 125
Freccia d'Argente, La, 216
Freccia nera, La, 241
Freckles and His Friends, 140, 320
Fred, 704
Fred and Freda, 812
Fred Basset, 320-21
Freddie Flap and Uncle Bunkle, 796
Freddie Freewheel, 386
Freddie & His Flying Flea, 110
Freddy and Fred, 339
Freddy Flipperfeet, 187
Freddy Lombard, 194
Fredrik, 450, 480
Freelance, 321-22
Frenchy, 360
Friday Foster, 322
Fridolf Celinder, 282, 572
Frisco Jim, 162
Fritzi Ritz, 168, 233, 560-61
Fritz the Cat, 36, 323-24, 539
Frog Prince, 465
Froid Equateur, 131
Frolic in the Far West, 386
Frolicomic, 96
From Hell, 547

From 9 to 5, 711
Frontline Combat, 377, 462
Fudge the Elf, 648
Fuerte Argentino, 203, 480
Fugaku Hyakkei, 391
Fugaku Sanjūrnkkei, 391
Fuku-chan, 325, 825
Fukushū no Semushiotoko, 198
Fukuwajutsushi, 775
Fuller Gusto, 205
Fuller Humor, 325
Fulmine. See Dick Fulmine
Fulmine, 255
Fūma, 696
Fūma Ninpūden, 696
Fumetti verità, 770
Fumetto dell realta, Il, 507
Fun and Frolic at Fitzpip Hall, 812
Fun Fear, 797
Fünf Schreckensteiner, Die, 325-26, 581
Fungus the Bogeyman, 154
Funky Winkerbean, 326-27
Funny Fauna, 808
Funny Folk of Meadow Bank, 110
Funnyman, 700, 701
Funnymen, 104
Fuochi, 522
Furio Almirante, 216, 327
Furio Mascherato, 162
Fury's Family, 501
Fusco Brothers, The, 327-28
Fushigina Kuni no Putchā, 29, 328
Fūten, 328-29
Fūten, 559
Futuropolis, 24, 329, 604, 605

G

G. Whizz, 812
G. Whizz Jr., 392
Gabby Hayes, 611
Gabriel, 685
Gaikotsu no Buyō, 438
Gai Luron, 36, 331
Gaki Deka, 38, 71, 332
Galaxus, 714
Gambalesta, 608
Gambols, The, 332-33
Games and Gimmicks, 504
Gamin and Patches, 796
Ganbare Gonbe, 716
Gangbusters, 502
Garage hermétique, La, 345
Garfield, 39, 237, 333
Garfield and Friends, 333-34
Garth, 125, 267, 334-35, 657
Gas Buggies, 121
Gasoline Alley, 21, 22, 62, 69, 312, 335-37, 419, 445, 617, 733
Gaston Lagaffe, 34, 319, 337
Gateway to Glory, 778
Gatto Silvestro, 608

Gaucho, Il, 508
Gaucho, The, 627
Gay Goblins, The, 317, 693
Gay Gordons, The, 393
Gay Honor, 593
Gay Thirties, The, 175
Gazeta Juvenil, 215
Gejigeji Tarō Gyōjōki, 436
Gekkō Kamen, 337, 463
Geky Dor, 768
Gems, The, 575
Gen 13, 472
Genius, Jolanda de Almaviva, 507
Genma Taisen, 405
Gen of Hiroshima, 42
Gentiluomo di 16 Anni, 86
Gentle Jim, 154
George Formby, 796, 798
George the Jolly Gee Gee, 426, 812
Georgie's Germs, 628
Gerald McBoing-Boing, 514
Gertie, the Trained Dinosaur, 498
Gertie and Gladys, 795
Gertie Gladeyes, 796
Gertie Goodsort, 795
Gert Jörg, 798-99
Gervasio, 608
Gesebel, 639
Ghigno il Maligno, 408
Ghost Patrol, 400
Ghost Rider, 104, 319, 337-38, 653
Ghost Train, 797
G.I. Combat, 689
G.I. Daddy, 600
G.I. Joe, 27, 151, 539, 567
Giacinto Corsaro Dipinto, 408
Gianconiglio, 608
Gianni e Luciano, 344
Giant-Man, 166
Giant Robot, 752
Gibernetta, 202
Gibi, 83
Gigante italiano, Il, 150
Gigetto, Pirata Picoletto, 608
Gigi Bizz, 202
Gihyō no Tabi, 826
Gilgamesh, 818
Gil Jourdan, 33, 762
Gil Thorp, 127-28
Gimpel Beinish the Matchmaker, 341-42
Gim Toro, 342
Ginesito, 342-43
Ginger Meggs, 23, 109-10, 293, 294, 343-44, 569
Ginger Nick the Whaler, 808
Gingham & Polkadot, 693
Ginjar the Turk, 245
Gink and Boob, 499
Gin no hanbira, 542
Gino e Gianni, 25, 86, 344, 603
Gino e Piero, 180
Gioco, Il, 508
Gioietta Portafortuna, 86
Gionni e Geppina, 227

Giornalino, Il, 221
Giornalino di Gian Burrasca, Il, 241
Giorni dell'impero, I, 241
Giorno per caso, Un, 771
Gipsy, 608
Girafone, 221
Girl from the People's Commune, The, 345
Girls & Boys, 115-16
Girls in Apartment 3-G. See Apartment 3-G
Give It a Whirl, 373
Give Me Liberty, 534
Gladiator, 726
Gladsome Gladys, 109
Gli Aristocratici, 190, 731
Gli ultimi della Terra, 240
Globi, 346
Globine, 346
Globul le Martien, 335
Gloops, 346-47
Gloria Sagrada, 163
Glugg, 390
Gnidén, 283
Gnomo Pimentón, El, 140
Gnorm Gnat, 237
Gnuffen, 535
Gog, 773
Gohikino Yōjimnō, 520
Goldbergs, The, 373
Golden Arrow, 319, 458, 609
Golden Eagle, 609
Golden Gladiator, 377
Golden Penny, The, 245
Goldilocks, 317
Goldrake, 111
Golf, 153
Golf Bug, The, 552
Golgo 13, 38, 41, 349-50, 671
Golondrino Perez, 202
Gonzales, 350
Good Friends, 605
Good God Almighty, 123
Good Guys, The, 791, 814
Goodies, The, 209
Good Knight Gilbert, 812
Good Morning, Boss, 662
Gordo, 101, 351-52
Gordon, Soldier of Fortune, 228, 352, 611
Gorgo, 254
Gorin e Obi, 608
Gospodar sveta, 473
Go West!, 647
Graham's Golf Club, 321
Grama Gramelloni, 608
Grande Blek, 177
Grande Caccie di Gino e Gianni, 344
Grand Hotel, 543
Grandi del giallo, I, 770
Grandpa, 574, 648
Grandpa and Grandson, 528
Grand Trésor, Le, 525
Graves, Inc., 661

Great Aventure, The, 368
Great Gusto, The, 728
Great Guston, The, 677
Great Scientist, The, 740
Green Arrow, 77, 280, 355-56, 583, 804
Green Berets, 192, 461
Green Hornet, 280, 356-57, 372, 656, 757
Green Lama, The, 637
Green Lantern, 77, 92, 104, 171, 280, 316, 356, 357-59, 372, 373, 400, 434, 524, 583, 683, 773
Gremlins, 166
Grifagno Sparagno, 642
Griffu, 746
Grifo, Il, 508
Grillo il Balillino, 549
Grimbledon Down, 315
Gringo, 359-60
Grizzly Gus the Tricky Trapper, 386
Grock, 796
Grofica Margo, 464
Gross Exaggerations, 360
Grossly Xaggerated, 217, 360
Grote Pyr, De, 519-20
Groucho the Monk, 504, 505
Gruaga, 462, 573
Grünes Blatt, 730
Guardsman Who Dropped It on Parade, 116
Guerilleros, Les, 361
Guerra de los Antartes, 580
Guerre à la Terre, 361
Guerrero del Antifaz, El, 361-62
Guerrilleros, 138
Gueule de Bois en Plomb, Une, 746
Gulliver of Mars, 148
Gully Foyle, 621
Gumdrop, 685
Gumnut Babies, 339
Gumps, The, 17, 21, 186, 275, 355, 362, 383, 481, 487, 538, 553, 564, 582, 711-12
Gums, 574
Gumshoe Gus, 434
Gun Gallon, 162
Gun Grontier, 520
Gunhawks, 96
Gunmaster, 443, 704
Gunner, 672
Gunn's Gully, 364
Guremono, 452
Gusari na Atlantiku, 738
Gusarsko Blago, 566
Gussy the Gas Meter Manipulator, 187
Guy from Grand Rapids, A, 326
Guy Lebleu, 623
Guy Powers Secret Agent, 251
Gyatoruzu, 38, 716
Gyōsai Donga, 438
Gyōsai Gadan, 438
Gyōsai Gashū, 438
Gyōsai Suiga, 438

H

Hadži Murat, 464
Hägar the Horrible, 34, 158, 365-66
Hagen, Fagin and O'Toole, 155
Hagibis, 462
Hagio Moto sakuhinshuū, 366
Haiiroguma no Denki, 696
Haikara Kidoro no Shippai, 448
Hairbreadth Harry, 83, 244, 322, 366, 431, 789
Hair Raising Voyage, A, 609
Hajimeningen Gon, 716
Hakaba no Kitarō, 26, 366-67, 542
Halcon, 243
Half-Hitch, 367, 441
Half-Holiday, 89
Hall of Fame of the Air, The, 451
Hamfatto the Monk, 504
Hamlet, 241, 537
Hammerhead Hawley, 377
Hana no Kakarichō, 716
Hana no nijuyonen gumi, 542
Handsome Hautrey, 499
Hangman, The, 368, 443
Hank, 801
Hank the Hermit and His Animal Friends, 499
Hans, 395, 436, 662-63
Hans and Fritz, 19, 182, 253, 437
Hansje Teddybeer en Mimie Poezekat, 107, 773
Hanzo Nomon, 452
Hap Hooper, 301
Happy Andy and His Playful Pets, 812
Happy Bob Harriday, 377
Happy Daze, 400
Happy Family, 317, 812
Happy Hambone, 205
Happy Harry and Sister Sue, 812
Happy Hooligan, 62, 67, 93, 146, 335, 368-69, 585, 664, 702
Happy Yank, The, 96
Hard Boiled, 534
Hard Hearted Hicky, 499
Harenchi Gakuen, 559
Harisu no Kaze, 38, 199, 370
Harlot's Progress, A, 390
Harold Hare, 147, 370, 502
Harold Teen, 275, 370-71
Haroun El Poussah, 352
Harry Secombe, 812
Hashita no Joe, 199
Hashmark, 468
Hatanosuke Hinomaru, 25, 373
Haunted Tank, The, 435, 690
Haunted Wood, The, 166
Haut et Puissant Seigneur Baron de Cramoisy, Le, 207
Have a Go Jo, 393
Hawk, and The Dove and The Creeper, The, 254
Hawk, The, 192, 306

Hawkman, 92, 104, 134, 219, 316, 374, 460, 461, 583
Hawk of the Seas, 278
Hawkshaw the Detective, 374-75, 504, 506
Hawkworld, 374
Haxtur, 37, 375
Hayseeds, 370, 375
Hazañas de Tarpon, 579
Heap, The, 115, 376, 435
Heap Big Beef, 426
Heart of Juliet Jones, The, 32, 179, 267, 376-77, 454, 722
Heavy Metal, 214, 341
Heckle and Jeckle, 378
Hector, 693
Hein Daddel, 533
Hein Ei, 285
Heitere Fridolin, Der, 326
He Knew How To Do It, 158
Hellblazer, 744
Hello Jim, 162
Help Wanted, 360
Hem and Amy, 121
Henery Hawk, 231
Heno Heno Moheji, 542
Henpecko the Monk, 504
Henri Duval, 699
Henry, 91-92, 378-79, 630
Herb & Jamaal, 39, 218, 379
Herby, 127, 712
Hercules, 192, 379-80
Hércules Paput, 302
Hercules Unchained, 287
Herculoids, The, 773, 809
Her Daughter Kitty, 798
Here, Gentlemen, Is Polly!, 623
Here Comes Motorcycle Mike!, 445
Herlock Sholmes, 38, 327, 380, 638, 695
Hermit, 351
Hernàn el Corsario, 25, 380, 671
Heroes of American History, 535
Heros the Spartan, 36, 125
Herr des Dschungels, 759
Herr Knatt, 480
Herr Spiegelberger, the Amateur Cracksman, 91
Hey Coach, 379
Hey Look, 462
Hi and Lois, 144, 158, 383, 796
Hidamari no Ki, 754
High Jinks at High School, 245
Highway Days/Dick Turpin, 502
Hi Hopper, 445
Hilarion Leiva, 203, 480
Hillman, 704
Hime Ga Yuka, 676
Himitsu no Akko chan, 84
Hi no Tori, 38, 386-87
Hinotori, 583, 754
Hip Pip and Hoo Ray, 205
Hippo and Hookey, 179
Hiram B. Boss, 823

Hiram Hick, 434
Hire a Horror, 574
Hishū no Tachi, 387
His Name Is Savage, 351, 434
Histoire d'Albert, L', 387
Histoire de Chine, L', 508
Histoire de France en B.D., L', 508, 771
Histoire de Jacques, L', 387
Histoire de M. Jabot, 387
Histoire du Far West en B.D., 278
Histoires en Estampes, 26, 387-88, 770
Histoires Inventées, 815
Historias de la Taberna Galactica, 120
Historias tristes, 714
Hitch Your Wagon, 451
Hite and Mite, 807
Hit-Parades, 815
Hiwaga Komiks, 86
Hogan's Alley, 590-91, 824-25
Hokusai Manga, 391
Hollywood Hams, 218
Hom, 341
Home, Sweet Home, 164, 779
Homeless Hector, 244, 382
Hondo, 143
Honeybunch's Hubby, 600
Honey Potts, 812
Hong Kong Phooey, 809
Hook, Line and Singer, 812
Hop, Skip, and Jack, 424
Hopalong Cassidy, 206, 567, 611, 720, 808
Hoppy, The Marvel Bunny, 183
Hops und Stops, 305
Horace Horseradish, 187
Horacio, 243
Hormiga Negra, 480
Horror, 435
Hoshi no tategoto, 542
Hosteen Crotchety, 741
Hot Jerry, 570, 813
Hot on the Trail, 393-94
Hotspur, The, 346
Hotsy-Totsy, 271, 769
Hot Wheels, 773
House of Mystery, 432, 574, 627
House of Secrets, 87, 432, 574
How a Mosquito Operates, 498
Howard Flynn, 788
Howard Huge, 389
Howard the Duck, 394-95
How to Draw, 709
How To Start the Day Wrong, 538
How to Torture Your Wife (Husband), 762
HP e Giuseppe Bergman, 508
Hua Tuo, 375-76
Hubert, 395-96
Huckleberry Finn, 521
Huckleberry Hollow, 488
Huckleberry Hound, 454
Hugh Fowler, 648
Hulk, The, 105, 167, 171, 259, 321, 396-97, 434, 472, 500, 690, 756

Human Bomb, The, 364
Human Flying Saucer, The, 223
Human Top, 152
Human Torch, The, 26, 95, 105, 166, 287, 397-98, 611, 725, 731, 732, 819
Hunchback of Notre Dame, 152, 287
Hungarian Rhapsody, 41
Hungry Henrietta, 498
Hungry Horace, 393, 442
Hunter Keene, 233
Hurricane Hawk, 709
Hurricane to the Rescue, 489
Hu Sheng Hua Ji, 300
Hyakki Yakō Byōbu, 438
Hyaku Baka, 825
Hyakumensō, 451
Hyaku Monogatori, 391
Hyakusen Hyakushō, 451
Hydroman, 287
Hylda Baker's Diary, 608

I

Ian on Mu, 808
Ibis the Invincible, 120, 187, 399, 611, 637
Ice Cream for All, 798
Ice Même, 746
Idaten Santa, 542
Idée Fixe du Savant, Cosinus, L', 206-7, 399
If . . . , 123
Igaguri-kun, 399
Iglesia de los Agachados, La, 79
Ii Tairō Sōnanzu, 775
Ikeybod & Tinribs, 693
Ikkai Zuihitsu, 775
Iliad, 204
Il N'y A Pas Que la Politique Dans la Vie, 815
Ils Ne Pensent Qu'à Ca, 815
Impero del sole, L', 240
Imps, The, 609
Inazuma-kun, 399
In Biblis ist die H'lle los, 648
Incedenti, 521
Incredible Hulk, The. See Hulk, The
Indestructible Man, The, 138
Indiana Jones, 115, 254, 720
Indian Summer, 627
Indio, El, 400
Indio Suarez, 286, 579
Indoor Sports, 265
Inferior Man, 408
Inferno, 755
Infinity, Inc., 756
Inhabitants of Planet Monip, 473
In Jungle Land, 504
Innocent Hing, 326
Innocents on the River, 801
Inspector Dan, El, 402

Index B

Title Index

Inspector Dayton, 306, 400
Inspector Hayden, 391
Inspector Hector the Crime Detector, 816
Inspector Jellicoe, 544
Inspector Slop the Plain Clothes Cop, 386
Inspector Wade, 92, 402-3, 544, 581
Inspektor Burnadz, 632
Inspirasiyon, 675
Institution, L', 134
Intervallo, 408
In the Days of Drake, 808
In The Good Old Days, 740
In the Kingdom of Apes, 464
In the Wild West, 464
Into Strange Lands, 282
Into Unknown Worlds, 808
Intrepido, L', 162
Inu Yahsa, 506
Invisible Monster, The, 166
Invisible Scarlet O'Neil, 403
Ippei Zenshū, 581
Iris, 100-101, 211
Iron Ace, 443
Iron Devil, The, 757
Iron Fish, The, 346
Ironfish, The, 393
Iron Fist, 171
Iron Man, 219, 351, 403-4, 404, 435, 472
Iron Skull, 166
Iron Teacher, The, 346
Iron Vic, 233
Isabella, 111, 404-5
Isabelle, 319
Isometrics, 414
I Spy, 502, 797
Italino e Kartoffel Otto, 664
It Happens in the Best Regulated Families, 538
It's a Great Life If You Don't Weaken, 172, 646
It's Me Dilly, 95, 189
It's Papa Who Pays, 553, 769
It's the Gremlins, 656
Ivanhoe, 118, 537, 716
Ivan il Vegente, 162
I've Got News For You, 383
Ivica Bucko, 239
Ivor Lott and Tony Broke, 166, 574
Ivory Elephant, The, 363
I Vow Vengeance, 377
Ivy Hemmanhaw, 389
Izumi i otkrića, 638
Izzy Human, 360

J

J. Fillien Wilberfloss, 272
J. Worthington Blimp, 524
Jabato, El, 407
Jacht naar geluk, 491

Jack and Jill, 147, 678
Jack and the Beanstalk, 204
Jack Frost, 400, 472
Jack & His Baby Jet, 236
Jackie and Sammy, 205
Jackie Coogan, 796
Jack Mandolino, 408
Jacko and Jerry, 812
Jack O'Spades, 536
Jack Sprat and Tubby Tadpole, 812
Jack Warner, 377
Jack Webster's Dictionary, 185
Jaken Yaburetari, 387
Jak-ki und Paff, 459
Jakun of the Jungle, 631
James Bond, 408-10
James Cagney, 377
Jamie McPheters, 638
Jane, 27-28, 267, 410
Jane and Laredo, 411
Jane Arden, 128, 411
Jane Eyre, 511
Janne Ankkanen, 604
Jann of the Jungle, 693
Jan Perewiet, 157
Japan, Inc., 41
Japhet and Happy, 208, 265, 412-13
Japie Makreel, 768
Jason, 408
Jasper the Grasper, 648
Jazzamentos, 521
Jean de la Marinica, 150
Jean des Flandres, 413
Jean-Jacques Ardent, 604
Jean-Jean et Gigi, 335
Jean Valhardi, 196, 339
Jeep, 762
Jeff Crockett, 189
Jeff Hawke, 33, 413-14, 592
Je Ne Veux Pas Mourir Idiot, 815-16
Jeremiah, 398
Jerom, 789
Jerry, Jenny and Joe, 812
Jerry Lewis, 812
Jerry on the Job, 388, 414-15, 563, 712
Jerry Spring, 33, 339, 345, 352, 415, 663
Jest a Second, 434
Jester, The, 364
Jester Theatre Royal, 823
Jest Laffs, 434
Jesuit Joe, 627
Jet Scott, 656
Jetsons, The, 809
Jeune Albert, Le, 194
Jeunesse de Blueberry, La, 345
Jeux pour Mourir, 746
Jill Joy the Tomboy, 798
Jimbo the Jungle Boy, 110
Jim Boum, 270, 415-16
Jim Bowie, 96
Jim Clopin Clopan, 271
Jim el Terrible, 138
Jim Erizo, 416, 695

Jim et Joe, 271
Jim Hardy, 416-17
Jim Jam, 426
Jim Minimum, 193
Jimmy and Jumbo, 536
Jimmy das Gummipferd, 417, 451, 747
Jimmy Gimmicks, 499
Jimmy in Java, 808
Jimmy Jog the Juggler, 823
Jimmy Jolly's Magic Brolly, 812
Jimmy Olsen, 417-18, 568
Jimpy, 418, 498
Jingle's Jolly Circus, 146
Jinglet, 740
Jinx, 126, 648
Jippi der Indianerboy, 730
Jo, Zette et Jocko, 649
Jocke, Nicke och Majken, 572
Jodelle, 418, 722
Joe and Asbestos, 419
Joe and Willie, 151
Joe Bing, 271
Joe E. Brown, 796, 798
Joe Jinks, 419-20
Joe Palooka, 40, 130, 179, 255, 303-4, 409, 420, 478, 479
Joe Prep, 378
Joe Quince, 419
Joe Runt, 360
Joe's Car, 419
Joe Zonda, 714
Johan et Pirlouit, 228, 680
Johhny Thunder, 435
John Byrne's Next Men, 171
John Difool, 345
John Duff-Pie, 823
John Irons, 808
Johnny Bostonbeans, 504
Johnny Carey, 282
Johnny Cloud, 690
Johnny Comet, 319
Johnny Dekker, 96
Johnny Focus, 529
Johnny Hazard, 27, 158, 420-22, 653
Johnny Logan, 202, 203
Johnny Peril, 116
Johnny Quest, 808-9
Johnny Quick, 460, 526, 656
Johnny-Round-the-World, 422
Johnny Thunder, 373, 400, 422
Johnny Wise, 265
John Parade, 511
John Wayne, 811
Joke Book, 100
Joker, 166
Jollity Farm, 426
Jolly Jacko, 812
Jolly Jinky, 807
Jolly Rover, The, 796
Jolly Tom the Menagerie Man, 205
Jolly Western, 96
Jonah, 648
Jonah Hex, 105, 163, 423-24, 809
Jonas Fink, 338

Jones Boys, The, 186
Jon Fury, 773
Jon Jarl, 133
Jonque Fantome Vue de l'Orchestre, La, 313
Jopie Slim en Dikkie Bigmans, 107
Jose Rizal, 163
Jossie Jovel, 616
Journal Tigers, 13
Jours de France, 352
Joyland Express, 812
Juan Cuello, 480
Judd Saxon, 108
Judge Dredd, 40, 171, 424, 744, 778
Judge Parker, 32, 97, 231, 424-26, 454, 649
Judge Wright, 426
Judgment Day, 547
Jughead, 100
Jugurtha, 398
Jūichigatsu no gimunajiumu, 366
Jūichinin iru!, 366
Jules Barigoule, 271
Juliette, 221
Julios abenteuerliche Reisen. See Jimmy das Gummipferd
Julius Caesar, 287
Jumbo, 146, 303
Jumbo and Jim, 317
Jumpstart, 39, 218, 379, 426-27
Jungle Book, The, 236, 463
Jungle Emporer, The, 676
Jungle Jim, 24, 83, 153, 177, 427, 576, 593, 641, 749, 757
Junglemen, 118, 627
Jungle Tales of Tarzan, 748
Jungle Tatei, 427-28, 583, 754
Jungle Twins, The, 219
Junior and Happy, 628
Juniper Junction, 323
Jurassic Park, 434
Jusei, 588
Just Boy, 281-82
Justice League of America, 316, 373, 422, 429-30, 583
Justice Society of America, 316, 356, 429, 430
Justine, 221
Just Jake, 428-29, 498
Just Judy, 544
Just Kids, 187, 429, 569, 647

K

K-51, 278
Kaanga, 192
Kabibble Kaberet, 76
Kabul de Bengala, 580
Kador, 134
Kafka, 226
Kaidai Hyakusensō, 775
Kai Hua Lok, 166

Kaiketsu Harimao, 405
Kaiki Seidan, 463
Kalabog en Bosyo, 705
Kalayaan International, 506
Kamagong, 80
Kama-Sutra, 614
Kam et Rah, les Terribles, 606
Kampung Boy, 42, 442
Kamui Den, 38, 433-34, 696, 697
Kanraku, 581
Kansas Kid, 161, 631
Kapetan Leš, 716
Kapetan Leši, 638
Kapitein Rob, 435, 436, 461
Kappa, 34, 452
Kappa no Kawatarō, 696
Kappa no Sanpei, 542
Kappie, 372, 435-36, 768
Kapten Groggs, 126-27
Karan, 217
Karl May, 789
Katakumba, 163
Katzenjammer Kids, The, 13, 19, 20, 26, 62, 67, 69, 167, 182, 252, 253, 317, 335, 436-37, 444, 450, 524, 554, 615, 664, 813. See also Captain and the Kids, The
Katzies, The, 813
Kawaite Soro, 452
Kayo Kirby, 297
Ka-Zar, 105, 167, 812
Kaze no Ishimaru, 696
Keeper Nyon, 812
Keeping Up With the Joneses, 267
Keesje Slim, 157
Kelly Green, 725
Kelly Kids, The, 431, 826
Kelly Pool, 806
Kelly's Eye, 714
Kelot, 516
Kelpie, 686
Ken Brady, 206
Kendall, 663
Kenkoy, 32, 438-39
Ken Maynard, 611
Ken Parker, 439-40
Ken Winston, 701
Kerry Drake, 95, 440
Kerry Kross, 685
Kevin the Bold, 441
Kewpies, The, 441-42, 584, 632
Keyhole Kate, 442, 807
Khan y Khamar, 514
Kibaō, 442-43
Kića, 411
Kid, El, 118
Kid Chameleon, 209
Kid Cody, 809
Kid Colt, 641
Kid Colt Outlaw, 377
Kiddo the Boy King, 536
Kiddyfun, 110
Kiddyfun Circus, 110
Kid Eternity, 471

Kid Kartoons, 186
Kid King, 574
Kid Kong, 574
Kidlat, 674
Kid Marvelman, 517
Kidnappers from Space, 778
Kid Sister, The, 228, 763, 826
Kiiroi Namida, 38, 329
Kilabot Ng Persia, 573
Kilroy, 315, 348
Kim Devil, 196
Kin-der-Kids, The, 14, 297, 444-45, 804
King, The, 219
King Aroo, 440, 445-46
King Arthur, 125
King Arthur and the Frights of the Round Table, 574
King Harold's Sun, 609
King Kong, 175
King Kull, 690
King Leonardo, 321
King of the Highway, 393
King of the Khyber Rifles, 204
King of the Royal Mounted, 24, 307, 370, 446
King Robot, 752
Kings of the Air, 609
King Solomon's Mines, 502
King's Treasure, 383
King Toot, 656
Kinney B. Alive, 360
Kinowa, 446-47
Kiroskewero the Detective, 823
Kit and Kompany, 729
Kit Carson, 25, 86, 449, 543, 603
Kitties, The, 656
Kitty Higgins, 547
Kitty's Kapers, 383
Kiwi, 193
Kiyochika Punch, 451
Klaik Sa Apoy, 350
Klotjohan, 450
Knjaz Miloš, 464
Knocko the Monk, 504, 505
Kobau, 444
Kōga Bugeichō, 696
Koko the Pup, 110
Kolumbus, 632
Komedy Kids, 628
Kometjakten, 412
Komikku Showa-shi, 542
Kondom des Grauens, 453
Kong Que Dong Nan Fei, 797
Koning Hollewijn, 372, 453-54, 768
Konrad und Paul, 453
Kon Rosa, 283
Konulawang, 166
Korak, 462, 573, 720, 757, 809
Korky the Cat, 442
Koroshiya, 775
Kōsenga, 451
Kosme the Cop, 675

Kōsoku Esper, 520
Köter & Co., 285
Kozure Okami, 38, 452, 454
Kraaienhove, 454-57, 455
Kraljević Marko, 464
Krazy Kat, 17, 19, 20, 22, 57, 67, 76, 120, 251, 290, 381, 457
Kriminal, 37, 459, 639, 685
Kroz minula stoljeća, 327, 638
Krvavo nasledstvo, 489
Kubidai Hikiukenin, 387
Kudzu, 39, 461
Kuif de onverschrokkene, 157
Kulafu, 462
Kul-Hebra, 138
Kuma o Tazunete, 581
Kurir Fića, 255
Kuroi Hanabira, 520
Kuroneko Don, 452
Kwikkie Kwiek, 157
Kyoiku Iroha Tango, 451
Kyojin no Hoshi, 465
Kyoshin no Hoshi, 199

L

Laatsch and Bommel, 326
Laber Boy, 705
Labryinths, The, 170
Lad and His Lass, A, 395, 628
Lady Ann, 676
Lady Bountiful, 186
Lady Luck, 278
Lala Palooza, 349
Lance, 467-68, 776
Lancelot, 788
Land of Silent Perils, 377
Land of the Lost People, 609
Land Unknown, The, 773
Lann, 757
Lao Ma's Adventures, 269-70
Laredo, 411
Lariat Pete, 381
Lariflette, 467
Larks, The, 468
Larrigan, 239
Larry and Len, 386
Larry Leopard, 236
Larry Semon, 796
Larry Steele, 25, 285, 383
Larry Yuma, 575
Lash LaRue, 808
Lassie, 474, 656
Last of the Mohicans, The, 733
Late Late War, The, 321
Latigo, 496
Laugh Parade, 389
Laurel and Hardy, 410, 796, 798
Lavinia 2.016, 470
Lawrence of Arabia, 757
Lazo Kid, 690
Leap Year Lizzie, 272

Learn Cantonese the Hard Way, 296
Leatherface, 346
Leçons du Professeur Bouremou, Les, 149
Lederstrumpg, 161
Left wa Shinazu, 542
Lefty Louie, 617
Legends Along the Silk Road, 734
Leggenda di Italianino Liberatore, La, 476
Legija prokletib, 715
Legionnaire Terry's Desert Quest, 209
Lem Dart, 341
Lemmy Caution, 621
Lemon Kid, 754
Lena Pry, 411
Leo Roa, 341
Let George Do It, 501
Lex Brand, 246
Lex Knight, 391
Leyenda do los cuatro sombras, La, 301
Liang Shanbo yu Zhu Yingtai, 797
Liberty Kid, 162, 476
Liberty Scout, 492
Licketty Switch, 823
Liebe, 647
Lieutenant Blueberry, 36, 196, 209, 345, 476-77
Lieut. Daring and Jolly Roger, 812
Lt. Larry Rock, 690
Life in Hand, 393
Life in Hell, 115, 477-78
Life of Ben Hogan, The, 282
Life of Pope John Paul II, 705
Life on Other Worlds, 92
Life's Darkest Moment, 762, 802
Life's Little Comedies, 322
Lifetime in the Sky, 451
Life with Robinson, 656
Lightening Comics, 500
Li'l Abner, 24, 30, 61, 71, 179-80, 280, 284, 294, 295, 304, 420, 445, 449, 470, 478-79, 490, 492, 816
Lilla Fridolf, 479
Lille Rickard och hans Katt, 94, 479-80
Lillo, Lallo e Lello, 608
L'il Mose, 168
Lil Ole Orvie, 539
L'il One, 470
Li'l Wolf and Danny the Lamb, 650
Linda Denim, 632
Lindor Covas, 203, 480-81
Line, 214
Line et Zoum, 271
Lionelle e Nerone, 664
Lion King, 676
Li Sheng San Ji, 376
Li Shuangshuang, 375, 376
Litening, 282
Little Angel Face, 648
Little Annie Fanny, 237, 278, 319, 378, 408, 463, 481, 499

Little Annie Rooney, 481-83, 535, 537, 789
Little Bears and Tykes, 483, 740
Little Boy Pink, 823
Little Dog Guaiguai, 605
Little Hiawatha, 703
Little Hut, 516
Little Iodine, 373, 483, 554, 755
Little Jim from Nowhere, 363
Little Jimmy, 483-84, 539, 548, 740
Little Joe, 355, 484
Little King, The, 67, 484-85, 714, 740
Little Leaders, 191
Little Lost Bear, The, 665
Little Lulu, 485-86, 724
Little Man with the Eyes, 474
Little Mary Mixup, 155
Little Master of the Swooping Monster, 346
Little Mermaid, The, 654
Little Miss Muffet, 216
Little Monsters, The, 166, 219
Little Nemo in Slumberland, 14, 69, 132, 248, 268, 345, 486-87, 488, 498, 501, 569, 628, 750-51
Little Obelia, 339
Little Orphan Annie, 17, 21, 22, 26, 34, 61, 62, 71, 123, 141, 165, 179, 220, 233, 238, 289, 355, 463, 473, 481, 484, 487-88, 585, 725
Little Pals, 605
Little People, The, 488
Little Plum Your Redskin Chum, 118, 574
Little Ragged Blossom, 339
Little Red School House, The, 431
Little Sammy Sneeze, 14, 498
Little Stowaways, 823
Little Taotao, 605
Little Tough Guy, 807
Little White Rabbit and Big Grey Wolf, 605
Little Willy and Tiny Tim, 158, 801
Ljuba Truba, 255
Loana, 511
Lobo, 360
Lockhorns, The, 389
Lois Lane, 489-90, 678, 804
Lola, Nasolungo, 148
Lola and Otello, 588
Lola e Lalla, 664
Lollipop Gnomes, 110
Lolly Pop, 166
Lone Fighter, 808
Lone Ranger, The, 307, 378, 490, 567, 568, 778
Lone Sloane, 269
Lone Spaceman, The, 776
Long Sam, 179, 490, 492
Long Tomorrow, The, 345
Looie the Lawyer, 150
Look-A-Like Boys, The. See Mike and Ike

Loony, 302
Loony Lyrics or Lulu, The, 791
Looping The Loop, 687
Looy Dot Dope, 109, 233
Lord Jim, 287
Lord of the Rings, The, 384, 385
Lord Pampa, 714
Lord Snooty and His Pals, 491-92, 574
Lo Scimiotto, 508
Loser, The, 474
Lost World, 754
Lou Ah Shu, 375
Love is Hell, 478
Love Me Forever, 498
Loves of Edwy, The, 584
Lovey Dovey, 422, 753, 810
Luchtrovers van Hoitika, De, 616
Luck of the Legion, 609
Luck Star O'Hara, 627
Lucky Luke, 29, 67, 129-30, 352,
    492-93, 753
Lucky Starr, 301
Luc Tremplin, 217
Lulu and Leander, 395, 493
Lumak, 608
Lupino Lane, 796
Lupo, 493-94
Lupo Alberto, 494-95
Lupo Pugacioff, 642
Lurchis Abenteuer, 495
Lustige Kapoentjes, De, 564
Luther, 778, 807
Luther Arkwright, 744
Lysistrata, 453

M

Maboroshi Kozō, 463
Macaco, 23, 497
Macaronis, De, 100
Macbeth, 204
McCall of the Wild, 270
Māchan no Nikkichō, 754
Mack Swain, 796
Mac the Med, 356
Madam and Eve, 42, 503
Mad Artist, 87
Mafalda, 38, 470, 503-4, 534
Mager's Monks, 504-5
Maggie and Jigs. See Bringing Up
    Father
Maggie's Farm, 123
Magic Flute, The, 464, 623
Magician's Wife, 40, 149
Magic Man, 678
Magicman, 726
Magirus, 123
Magno, 364, 462
Magnus, Robot Fighter, 219, 720
Mago da Vinci, Il, 240
Maha Sanuk, 166
Mainichi ga natsu yasumi, 588

Main Street, 375, 504, 505-6
Maiopi, 148
Maison Ikkoku, 506
Maitres du temps, Les, 345
Majin Garon, 754
Major Ozone's Fresh Air Crusade, 381
Major Victory, 27
Makić, 123
Makisig, The Little Hero of Mactan, 659
Malaya, 506
Male Call, 27, 175, 506-7
Maligno, 573
Mali moreplovac, 830
Mallard Fillmore, 507
Mama no Violin, 199
Mama's Boyz, 218
Mamie, 599
Mammoth Flower, 542
Manayome Sensei, 676
Mandrago il Mago, 408
Mandragola, 278
Mandrake the Magician, 24, 83, 170,
    177, 238, 291, 321, 360, 399,
    408, 508-9, 716
Mandrie sulla sabia, 521
Man from the Past, The, 631
Man from UNCLE, 502
Mangaka Zankoku Monogatori, 329,
    559
Mang Ambo, 705
Man-Gods, 573
Mangucho y Meneca, 118, 509
Manhunter, 351, 705
Manhuntress, 514
Mani in Alto!, 509-10
Man in the Brown Derby, The, 763,
    802
Man in the Iron Mask, The, 239
Manly, 514
Mannen från Claa, 348
Mannen som gör vad som faller honom
    in, 93, 408, 510
Mann of India, 537
Manos Kelly, 511
Man Who Dared to Feel Seasick on the
    Queen Mary, The, 117
Man Who Owned the Moon, The, 778
Many Fascinating Islands, The, 163
Mao Dangā, 464
Mappirakun, 436
Marabini, 462
Marameo, 148
Marc Dacier, 196
Marcela y Kiki, 138
Marcel Labrume, 529
Marc Lebut, 762
Marco e Andrea, 344
Marco Polo, 125, 282
Marc Reynes, 623
Marginal, 366
Mari Aguirre, 512
María Luz, 118
Marie-Gabrielle, 614

Marie Jade, 678
Marie Math, 313
Marina, 239
Marinette Cheftaine, 271
Mario e Furio, 344
Marion Delorme, 623
Mark Merlin, 527
Marksman, 360
Mark Trail, 260, 512-13
Mark Trent, 623
Marmittone, 513-14
Marriage à la Mode, 11
Married Life, 114, 238
Marshal Blueberry, 345
Marsupilami, La, 319
Martha's Monster Makeup, 648
Martín a Bordo, 118
Martin Mystere, 190, 203, 516-17
Marvel Family, The, 96, 133, 517, 518
Marvelman, 96, 517-18
Marvelman Family, 96, 517
Marvel Super-Heroes, 809
Marvin il detective, 440
Mary and Her Little Lamb, 514
Mary Jane and Sniffles, 218
Mary Marvel, 133, 517, 518
Mary's Home From College, 381
Mary Worth, 32, 62, 285, 376, 518-19,
    677
Mask, The, 40
Masked Ballerina, The, 310
Masked Lady, 356
Master Key, 303, 649
Master Man, 541
Master of Kung Fu, 519
Master Race, 458-59
Masters of the Universe, 657
Match no Bou, 581
Matho Tonga, 458
Maud, 369, 585, 586
Maus, 40, 522-23, 719-20
Maverick, 720
Maw Green, 355
Max, 34, 382, 523-24
Maxmagnus, 639, 685
Max Miller, 796
Max und Moritz, 12, 167, 253, 437,
    524
Maxwell the Cat, 547
Mayonakano Genshijin, 716
Mazinger Z, 559
Meanderings of Minnie, 271
Mecki, 285, 525, 534, 648
Meddlesome Matty, 424
Medieval Castle, The, 315, 525
Meet Misty, 654
Mefistofele, 86
Megamex, 589
Melvin Monster, 724
Memoirs of a Don Juan, 614
Memo Migaja, 169
Mendo Mendovic', 266
Meng Jiang Nu, 797
Mercenary, The, 688

Merely Margy, 378
Merlin, 360, 361
Merlino, 818
Mermaid Saga, 506
Merry Marcelene, 501
Merry Margie the Invisible Mender, 536
Merry Merlin, 317
Merry Mike's Ice Cream Bike, 426
Merry Nobles Three, The, 431
Métal Hurlant, 131
Metamorphosis, 226
Metropolitan Movies, 581
Mga Kuwento Ni Kenkoy, 439
Mga Matang Naglilivab, 462, 573
Michel, 528-29, 661
Michel Strogoff, 671
Michel Tanguy, 34, 196, 529, 781
Michel Vaillant, 529-30
Mickey Finn, 474, 531
Mickey Mouse, 67, 180, 219, 246, 253,
  261, 353, 531-32, 584, 593, 642,
  702, 744, 831
Micky Maus, 305, 324, 325, 437,
  566-67
Micky the Merry Midget, 245
Micky the Mouse, 812
Middy Malone, 293, 569
Midget Movies, 414, 537, 687, 755,
  806
Midi et Soir, 313
Midnight, 206, 364
Midsummer Night's Dream, 715
Mighty Hercules, The, 474
Mighty Man of Yesterday, 321
Mighty Mighter, The, 773, 809
Mighty Mouse, 378, 532-33
Mighty Samson, 757
Mike and Ike, 145, 348, 349, 533
Mike Macke, 285, 533-34
Mike Spike & Greta, 426
Mike Steel, 410
Mike the Mule, 386
Miki, 239
Milady, 640
Millionbucks and Kandykiddo, 375
Million Pound Mutt, 544
Milly and Billy, 798
Milly O'Nare and the Penny Less, 166
Milo Marat, 145
Ming Foo, 482, 535-36
Minnie the Minx, 118, 242
Mino e Dario, 180
Minouche, 623
Minute Movies, 536-37, 789, 806
Minwa, 559
Miracle Jones, 389
Miracleman, 518
Mireille, 311
Mirobolantes Aventures du Professeur
  Pipe, Les, 192-93
Mischa, 305
Miserable Moments, 677, 728
Misérables, Les, 162
Miseries of Life, The, 663

Misery Buckets, 797
Mishiranu Hitobito, 775
Miss Doron Ototo, 452
Miss Fury, 537
Missing Millionaire, The, 690
Mission Impossible, 687
Miss Mimi, 614
Miss Peach, 470, 537-38
Miss Tarantula, 138
Mistakes Will Happen, 381
Mr. A., 254
Mr. A. Mutt. See Mutt and Jeff
Mr. Abernathy, 538
Mr. and Ms., 97, 153-54, 538
Mr. and Ms. Dillwater, 693
Mr. and Ms. Peter Rabbit, 804
Mr. and Ms. Pott, 666
Mr. Batch, 740
Mr. Breger, 151, 538-39
Mr. Croc's School, 317
Mr. Dooley, 802
Mr. Dough and Mr. Dubb, 369
Mr. Dubb, 369
Mr. E. Z. Mark, 504
Mister Ed, 321
Mr. Enry Noodle, 807
Mister Fantasy, 476
Misteri della Giungla Nera, I, 549
Misterio de Susurro, El, 771
Misterix, 539
Mr. Jack, 539-40, 582, 740
Mr. Kiasu, 540
Mr. Melbourne Day by Day, 110
Mr. Midnight, 621
Mr. Moneybags, 538
Mr. Mum, 699
Mr. Mystic, 77, 278
Mr. Natural, 36, 540-41
Mister No, 575
Mr. Nutt, 740
Mr. Satan, 526
Mr. Scarlet, 133, 381, 541, 637
Mr. Simkins On His Holiday, 372
Mr. Stankey Deadstone and Company,
  158
Mr. Subito, 790
Mr. Terrific, 541-42
Mrs. Bunty's Boarding House, 317
Mrs. Fitz's Flats, 144, 270, 796
Mrs. Lyons' Cubs, 472
Mrs. Spiker's Boarding House, 823
Mitos de Cthulu, Los, 150, 549
Mitou et Toti, 670
Mitsubahi no Bōken, 520
Mitti Pisawang, 166
Mitzi McCoy, 441
Mixed Singles, 189
Miyamoto Musashino Kujirataiji, Sōma
  no Furudairi, 783
Mladi Bartulo, 830
Moby Dick, 180
Moco, 87
Modeste et Pompon, 318
Modesty Blaise, 36, 344, 391, 543

Moeurs et las Caricature, Les, 387
Mohawk Trail, 282
Mohican Zokuno Saigo, 733
Molly and Mick, 812
Molly Manderling, 529
Molo the Mighty, 535
Momma, 470, 543-44
Mom's Homemade Comics, 449
Mondo Lumace, 608
Mondo Quino, 470
Mongtongguri, 444
Monica, 243
Monk and Jaff, 812
Monki, 707
Mononiyusan, 581
Monsieur Cryptogame, 387
M. le Minstre, 134
M. Pencil, 387
Monsieur Petipon, 604
Monsieur Poche, 545, 670
Monsieur Toudou, 192
Montezuma's Daughters, 138
Montgomery of Alamein, 125
Monty Carstairs, 125
Moomin, 412, 546
Moon Mullins, 21, 62, 420, 422, 423,
  498, 546-47, 753, 809-10
Moonshine McJuggs, 757
Moose, 709
Moose Miller, 547-48
Morbus Gravis, 278
Morecambe and Wise, 812
Moretsu Ataro, 84
Morfar är sörövare, 490
Mortadelo y Filemon, 34, 549
Mort Cinder, 150, 549, 580
Moschettieri del Aeroporto Z, I, 173
Mossoo Marmalade, 812
Mostly Malarkey, 186
Motemote Ojisan, 436
Mother Goose and Grimm, 39, 550-51
Mother Goose Treasury, The, 154
Motley's Crew, 379, 551-52
Mount Ararat, 483, 740
Mousqueton, Rouletabille, 162
Moustache et Trotinette, 175
Moustique, 604
Moutette, La, 396
Movie of a Man, 153
Movies Featuring Haphazard Helen, 238
Mozzo del Sommergibile, Il, 28, 173
Mu-fu, un Detective Oriental, 150
Muggs and Skeeter, 552
Mulberry Flats, 205
Mumin. See Moomin
Muminpappans Bravader, 412
Munro, 296
Munsters, The, 321
Murailles de Samaris, 680
Muralla, La, 120
Musical Box, 656
Musical Paintbox, 370, 544
Music Master, 287
Music to the Ear, 220

Musō Ogidachi, 387
Muss'em Up Donovan, 278
Musso the Wop, 27
Mutant Sabu, 405
Muteki Dump Guy, 542
Mutt and Jeff, 16-17, 26, 67, 98,
    201-2, 244, 304-5, 555-56, 581,
    711
Mutts, 556
Muyōnosuke, 671
My Date, 447
My Friend Irma, 472
Mylene, 511
My Name is Natsuko, 452
Myoukai Kou Goju Sanbiki, 783
Myra North, 557
My Son John, 389
Mysteries of Chicago, 464
Mysteries of Paris, The, 162
Mysterieuse Matin, 313
Mysterious Driver No. 13, 411
Mysterious Island, The, 575
Mysterious Island in the Pacific, 473
Mystery Eve, 520
Mystery Wood, 363
Mystic Moot and His Magic Snoot, 816
Mystiska 2:an, 348, 557-58
Mysto, 302

N

Nagagutsu no Sanjûshi, 26, 559
Nakimushi Dera no Yawa, 581
'Nam, 560
Namachan, 84
Namora, 287
Nanar et Jujube, 331
Nancy, 168, 560-61, 685
Nancy and Sluggo, 809
Nancy Parker, 656
Nanny the Nursemaid, 536
Napolean, 497
Napoleon, 561-62, 716
Narciso Putiferio, 562
Nard n' Pat, 496
Nasredin Hodža, 411, 566
Natacha, 562
Nat del Santa Cruz, 111, 683
Nathaniel Nodd, 187
Nathan Never, 562
Nature's Way, 468
Naufragés du Temps, Les, 313
Nausicaä of the Valley of Wind, 562-63
Naval Stowaways, 209
Nazi Spy Ring, 243
Nazo, 775
Nazz, The, 744
Nebbs, The, 186, 383, 553, 564
Necron, 640
Neddy the Cuddy, 236
Needlenose Noonan, 388, 415
Negro Raul, El, 18, 262, 564-65

Nelvana of the Northern Lights, 251,
    252, 565
Nemesis, 678
Nemesis the Warlock, 744
Nero, 564, 566
Nervo the Monk, 504
Nervy Nat, 395
Neutron, 221
Never Never Nelson, the Circus Scout
    Who Never Fails, 346
Neverwhere, 214
Neverworld, 214
Nevista živog Bude, 716
New Fun, 92
New Hotspur, 346
New Jersey's Patriots, 321
New Kids on the Block, 218
Newlyweds, The, 14, 501, 567
New Mutants, 40, 812
New Mutants, The, 476, 568
Newsboy Legion, 447, 460, 568, 705
New Scientist, 315
News of the World, 302
New Tales of the Arabian Nights, 214
New Terrytoons, 378
Neznanac iz svermira, 327
Nezumi, 775
Nibelunzi, 473
Nibsy the Newsboy, 501, 568-69, 596
Nick, 798-99
Nick Carter, 145
Nick der Weltraumfahrer, 569-70
Nick Fury, Agent of SHIELD, 689, 726
Nick Knatterton, 34, 571-72, 679-80
Nick Raider, 575
Nick Reporter, 162
Nickum the Nigger, 536
Nicodemus O'Malley, 187
Nicoletta, 575
Night Rider. See Ghost Rider
Nih on no Kaāchan, 452
Nikyu Tenshi, 405
Nils Grant, Private Investigator, 251
Ninja Bugeichō, 26, 34, 572-73, 696
Ninja Zankokushou, 573
Nipper, 272, 574, 714, 807
Nippur de Lagash, 818
Nizar, 798-99
Nize Baby, 19, 109, 216, 360, 575
Noah's Ark, 656
Nobby the Enchanted Bobby, 393
Nobody Wants Billy Bunter. See Billy
    Bunter
Nobody Works Like Father, 186
Nonkina Tousan, 18, 575-76, 766
Norakuro, 28, 576
Norman and Henry Bones, 236
Norman Wisdom, 426
Nosey Parker, 442
Notari Matsutaro, 199
Now Listen, Mabel, 381
Nubbin, 760
Nuja, 166
Numa, 775

Numskulls, The, 424
Nuovo Sceriffo, Il, 614
Nus, 37, 470, 577
Nut Brothers, The, 80, 589-90
Nuts and Jolts, 392
Nutty Noodle, 650
Nyoka, 458, 693

O

Oaky Doaks, 24, 325, 579
Oboro Jūninchō, 452
Oddbod, 155
Odd Bodkins, 218, 583-84
Odd Occupations and Strange Accidents,
    389
Odettojō no Niji, 198-99
Odinah, 350
O'Doo and O'Don't, 536
Odyssée d'Alix, L', 87
Odyssey, 614
Oeuf, L', 382
Officer Clancy, 206
Og, 462
O.G. Whiz, 724
Oggle & Woggle, 110
Ogon Bat, 580
Ogon no Trunk, 754
O Guarany, 215
Oh! Margy, 378
Oh Sidney Not the Walnut Tree, 321
Oil and Claw, 808
Ojisama Daimiyō, 436
Ōkami Kazō, 696
Okanda, Det, 557
Okkie en Knokkie, 157
Oklahoma, 203
Olaf Noort, 707
Old Boy, 797
Old Doc Yak, 582, 711
Old Glory Story, The, 582
Old Kobau, 444
Old Man Muffaroo, 791
Old Mickey, 566
Old Mother Riley, 798
Old Phibber, 236
Old Timer, The, 713
Old Witch, 192
Ole Opey Dildock-the Storyteller, 395
Olimpiastri, 731
Oliver Twist, 511, 575
Olivier Rameau, 647
Ollie the Alley Cat, 370
O'Malley's Mystery Page, 650
O-Man, 582-83, 754
Ombra, L', 190
Ombre du Corbeau, L', 211
O Mirim, 83
Onboro Jinsei, 436
One Eyed Joe, 502
120 Rue de la Gare, 746
One Note Man, The, 116

One Pound Gospel, 506
Onerevole Tarzan, L', 408
Onésime, 196-97
Onésime Pellicule, 271
Onikagejo Hishi, 696
Onkel Toldi, 326
Only a Poor Old Duck, 112
Only Waiting for the Torch, 372
Onmitsu Yūreijō, 452
On Stage, 32, 262, 351, 488, 584-85,
  722, 725
On the Farm, 807
On the Wing, 550, 710
00 Ongoy, 462
Oor Wullie, 585
Oozee the Wonder Bird, 812
Operacija palac, 123
Ophelia, 272
Optimist, The, 369, 792
Optimistic Oswald, 431
Oretacha Rival Da!, 452
Ore wa Obake dazo, 436
Ore was Yaru, 542
Ore wa Teppei, 199
Orient Express, 464
Orient Gateway, 41
Ornladinski borac, 239
Orphans of the Sea, 146
Orsolino Director, 118
Orvie, 539-40
Oscar, 587-88
Oscar Dientes de Leche, 254
Oscar e Tango, 191
Os Dois Amigos, 215
Oskar, 479
Osomatsu-kun, 38, 84, 588
Ossie Oddsocks, 205
Ostrvo s blagom, 716
Oswald the Rabbit, 253
Oswold the Oddjob Man, 187
Otasukekun, 84
Otoko Doahou Koushien, 542
Otoko Oidon, 520
Otto Kruntz, 190
Oumaga Tsuji, 452
Oumpah Pah le Peau-Rouge, 352, 781
Our Antediluvian Ancestors, 369
Our Bill, 321, 365
Our Boarding House, 80, 322, 515,
  589-90, 660
Our Bobbie, 363
Our Dumb Blonde, 302
Our Ernie, 502, 590, 656
Our Fighting Forces, 690
Our Gang, 766-67
Our Silly Cinema, 650
Outland, 140, 591-92, 727
Outlaw, The, 435
Outlaw Kid, The, 105, 808
Outlaw Trail, 377
Out of the Silence, 383, 592
Out Our Way, 592-93, 810-11
Outtaluck Club, The, 809
Ovaltiney's Own Comic, 246

Over the Hedge, 593-94
Over There, 110
Ozark Ike, 594

P

P. C. Blossom, 812
Paddy Payne, 209
Paese dell'Alfabeto, Il, 198, 644
Pagbabalik Ng Lawin, 350
Påhittiga Johansson, 282
País del Oro Negro, El, 137
Paja Patak, 473
Pals and Gals, 100
Pancho Lopez, 150
Pancho Talero, 565
Panda, 370, 372, 595, 768
Pandora, 676
Panhandle Pete, 14, 501, 569, 595-96
Pansy Potter, 369, 502, 596
Pantera Bionda, 596-97
Panthères, Les, 647
Pantomime, 730
Pa Perkins, 734
Papero Grosso e Fiorello, 202
Papi Papero, 148, 198
Paracuellos, 341
Parade, 166
Parlor, Bedroom and Sink, 165, 238
Parola alla giuria, La, 508
Partie de Chasse, 131
Partizanen, Die, 638
Pasha the Persian, 360
Pasqualino e Pasqualone, 408
Pasquino, 731
Pa's Son-in-Law, 186, 804
Patatras, 22, 617
Patches, 471
Pat O'Cake, 536
Patoflor, 302
Patoruzú, 597-98
Patos Enfant de la Brousse, 271
Pat Patrick, 384
Pat Rick, 335
Patriot, The, 287
Patsy, 598, 700
Patsy & Tim, 691
Patsy Walker, 567
Pattuglia senza Paura, La, 143
PattyJo 'n Ginger, 587
Paula, 675
Paul Bunyan, 192
Paulette, 614
Pauli, 305
Pauline and Patsy, 317
Pauline McPeril, 470
Paul Temple, 599
Paulus, 241
Pavel Biri, 123
Payaso, 599-600
Payo, El, 600
Pean, 166

Peanut and Doughboy, 33, 812
Peanuts, 34, 38, 60, 67, 189, 334, 496,
  559, 601-2, 683, 708
Peck's Bad Boy, 499
Pecky the Penguin, 656
Pecos Bill, 118, 602-3
Pedrito El Drito, 189, 603
Pedro, 236
Peer Viking, 100
Pee Wee, 306, 400
Peewee Throttle, 206
Peggy and Peter in Toyland, 146
Peggy the Peeress, 795
Pekka Puupää, 23, 603-4
Peko-chan, 825
Pellefant, 94, 480
Pelle Svanslös, 348
Penadinho, 243
Penguin, The, 251, 252, 606
Penn and Chris, 720
Penny, 286, 365
Pension Radicelle, La, 606
Pentonino, 221
Pepe el Inquieto, 169
Pepito, 148, 149, 198, 227, 606-7, 765
Pep Morgan, 360
Pequeñno Professor Pin y su Ayudante
  Freddy, El, 695
Pera Pešak, 255
Per Atoomraket naar Mars, 457
Percival the Perky Page, 110
Percy the Mechanical Man-Brains He
  Has Nix, 628
Percy the Policeman, 236
Percy Thggins, 656
Père Ladébauche, Le, 607-8
Perils of Submarine Boating, The, 431
Perishers, The, 608
Perramus, 41, 150
Perry, 173, 609-10
Perry Mason, 356, 757
Personal Love, 319
Pescatori de Perle Yukon, I, 180
Pesma južnog vetra, 716
Pete and Pinto, 150
Pete Madden, 236
Peter in Pygmy Land, 808
Peterkin Pottle, 724
Peter mit dem Mikrophon, 285
Peter og Perle, 299
Peter O'Pencil, 191
Peter Pan, 236
Peter Pat, 420
Peter Penguin, 187
Peter Piltdown, 610
Peter Pranky, 536
Peter Pupp, 434
Peter Puppet, 650, 656
Peter Rabbit, 611
Peter Scratch, 77, 303
Peter seltsame Reisen, 570, 813
Peter the Pussy Policeman, 812
Pete's Pup, 611, 666
Pete the Tramp, 554, 611, 666

Petey Dink, 792
Petit Essai de Physiognomie, 388
Petit Nicolas, Le, 352
Petits Belges, 339
Petko, 239
Petra Chérie, 529
Petrified Valley, The, 393
Petto de Pollo, 162
Petzi, Pelle, Pingo, 639
Phalanges de l'Ordre Noir, Les, 131
Phantom, The, 24, 40, 75, 116, 170,
    177, 291, 611-12, 716, 809,
    829-30
Phantom City, 808
Phantom Clipper, 443
Phantom Lady, 460, 612-13
Phantom of the Forest, The, 138
Phantom Stranger, 116, 163, 318
Phil and Bert, 812
Philémon, 36, 613
Phil Fumble, 168, 561
Phil Hardy, 141, 613-14
Phoebe Zeit-Geist, 614, 722-23
Phool Phan Phables, 360
Phyllis, 186
Pia no Shōzo, 676
Piccola Eva, 603
Piccolo Dente, 575
Piccolo Ranger, Il, 162
Piccolo Re, 162
Piccolo Sceriffo, Il, 111, 161, 614
Pickles the Puppy, 812
Pieces of Eight, 389
Pieds-Nickelés, Les, 16, 22, 67, 120,
    130, 313, 314, 605, 615-16, 774,
    829
Pied Tendre, 228
Pier Cloruro De'Lambicchi, 616
Pierino e il Burattino, 664
Pierre et Pierrette, 598
Pierrot of Bab El Oued, 525
Piet Fluwijn en Bolleke, 564
Pif le Chien, 191, 616-17, 621, 642
Pigglys, The, 709
Pik e Pok, 198
Pik Pok, 148
Piltdown-the Almost Human, 610
Pilul, 192
Pinco Pallino, 221
Ping en Ming, 157
Ping e Pong, 608
Ping the Elastic Man, 502
Pinito Pinole, 169
Pinkerton Jr., 638
Pinki and Uncle Sulemani, 626
Pinko e Ponko, 148-49
Pinky Green, 333
Pinky Rankin, 617-18
Pinocchio, 253, 441, 522
Pino e Pina, 664
Pino il Mozzo, 180
Pinoy Moreno, 80
Pintados, Los, 418-19
Pioneer Western, 96

Pionniers de l'Espérance, Les, 29, 618,
    623, 663
Pip, Squeak and Wilfred, 22, 418, 498,
    618-19
Piper Maiopi, 588
Pippo, 408, 618
Pippo Cow Boy, 205
Pippotto ed il Ca prone, 664
Pirate's Secret, The, 146
Pirati del Pacifico, I, 86
Pista dei Quattro, La, 118
Pistol Jim, 619-20
Pitch and Toss, 620, 812
Piwo, 788
Placid et Muzo, 617, 621
Plain Jane, 797
Plane Crash, 451
Planeta Misterioso, El, 137
Planeta X, 773
Planet Eye, 773
Plastic Man, 26, 206, 377, 454,
    621-22, 756
Plavi Vjesnik, 566
Playbox, The, 317
Plick and Plock, 207
Plisch und Wisch, 451
Plop, 661
Pluggers, 697, 698
Plumber, The, 116
Plum Duffy, 807
Plum MacDuff, the Highlandman Who
    Never Gets Enough, 393
Pluto, 434, 703
P.M. Barnaby, 474
Pochita Morfoni, 255
Pogo, 29, 33, 34, 61, 71, 438, 488,
    622-23, 787, 789
Poker Portraits, 802
Poldino, 603
Polletje Pluim, 100, 519
Polly, 804
Polly and Her Pals, 21, 128, 147, 326,
    356, 388, 515, 623-24, 727
Polly Sleepyhead, 628
Polonius, 746
Polop le Caid, 467
Pom et Teddy, 217
Pompeo, 601
Poncho Libertas, 624
Pō no ichizoku, 366
Pon Pon, 149, 198
Pookie, 610
Poor Jake, 498
Poor Jones, 740
Poor Li'l Mose, 591, 825
Poor Little Lone Girl, 363
Poor Peggy, 363
Poo Yai Ma Kap Tung Ma Muen,
    193-94
Pop, 22, 390, 624-25, 665
Pop C'ira I pop Spira, 411
Popeye, 40, 67, 196, 309, 447, 755-56,
    809, 813

Popol et Virginie ou Pays des Lapinos,
    649
Pop Parade, 390
Poppo of the Popcorn Theatre, 135
Pops, 711
Pora no namida, 588
Porky Pig, 162, 218, 231, 625
Porta d'Oriente, La, 338
Posapiano, 145
Positive Polly. See Polly and Her Pals
Post Atom, 393
Pototo y Boliche, 695
Pot T. Pot and his Pet Patient, Piecan,
    245
Potters, The, 500, 730
Potts, The, 18, 21, 223, 625-26, 666
Pottsy, 404
Poupon la Peste, 134
Pour la Horde, 313
Povratak Starog Mačak, 522
Powerhouse Pepper, 626, 816
Powerman, 192
Power Nelson, Futureman, 576
Power of the Atom, 104
Power Pack, 154, 812
Power the Danger Ranger, 501
Pravda, 418
Precinto 56, 552
Predator, 206
Predator and Prey, 811
Premier, 96
Press Guardian, 133
Pretending Percy, 431
Pretty Baby, 453
Pretty Peggy, 812
Prez, 705
Priča s Rubašume, 566
Priceless Percy, 187
Prima Angelica, La, 375
Primus et Musette, 217
Princ Bialco, 473
Prince and the Pauper, The, 529
Prince Errant, 628
Prince on the Flying Horse, The, 346
Prince Pippin, 795
Prince Rollin, 781
Prince Valiant, 24, 131, 147, 217, 315,
    441, 462, 467, 525, 528, 554,
    628-29, 716, 731, 747, 818
Princeza Ru, 489
Principe Azzurro, 629
Príncipe de Rodas, El, 514
Prinz Waldemar, 731
Prisoner of Zenda, The, 204
Prison Ship, 514
Private Billy Muggins, 620
Private Breger, 150-51, 538-39
Private Lives, 355
Private Potts, 628
Private Ramrod, 146
Private Strong, 447, 705
Procopio, 630
Prode Anselmo, 731
Professeur Nimbus, Le, 18, 630, 790

Professor Cerebus, 642
Professor Doodle's, 672
Professor Knix, 740
Professor P. Nutts, 502
Professor Pechmann, 326
Professor Pi, 630-31
Professor Pienterbult, 156-57
Professor Poosum, 544
Professor Potash, 146
Professor Simple, 317
Professor Snip Snap, 157
Profumo dell'invisible, Il, 508
Progress of Flight, 744
Prora vichinga, 240
Prosper l'Ours, 670
Protagonisti, I, 86
P'tit Gus, 623
Public Enemies Through the Ages, 638
Puckville Pranks, 386
Pudden, 797
Pulcinella nel Bosco, 216
Pultos, 202
Punisher, 167, 811
Puny Peter Pieface, 205
Puppet Land, 393
Purapinta, 399
Purple Zombie, The, 537
Pu-san, 826
Puss Gets the Boot, 766
Pussycat Princess, The, 268, 631-32
Put ka slavi, 716
Put oko sveta, 411
Puž and Pužek, 566
Pvt. Pippin, 126

Q

Quackie the Duck, 656
Quadratino, 23, 635, 664
Quan Buzhi, 269
Quark, 787
Queen of Spades, The, 464
Queen of the Seas, 648
Quest for Fire, The, 511
Question, The, 254, 344
Quick et Flupke, 649
Quicksilver, 206, 303, 360
Qui la Legionc, 818
Quincy, 39, 228, 635, 778

R

R. Hudi Junior, 606
Rabbits Rafferty, 270
Racconti della vita, I, 770-71
Racconti del vento della sera, I, 771
Racketty Row, 205
Radio Buggs, The, 499
Radio Patrol, 24, 473, 638

Radio Squad, 699
Raffles and Bunny, 91
Rahan, 638-39
Rah! Rah! Rosalie, 378
Raimondo il Vagabondo, 408
Rainbow, The, 381
Rainbow Duffy, 415
Rajah, The, 158
Rakes' Progress, The, 11, 390
Rake's Progress at the University, The,
    340
Raman and Bhagat Ji, 626
Ram and Rod, 146
Ramir, 418
Ramona, 262, 595
Ranch, 111
Randall, 33, 161, 239, 462, 580
Randall's Vandals, 346
Ranger, The, 282
Ranji's Ruby, 808
Ranma 1/2, 41, 506
Ran-Tan-Plan, 129, 493
Ranxerox, 41, 476
Rapsodia ungherese, 338
Rasika, 607
Rasmus Klump, 38, 639
Rastus Brown, 538
Rattler, 110
Raven on the Wing, 714
Rawhide Kid, 105, 641
Ray, The, 219, 303
Rayomondo o Cangaceiro, 641
Rayon U, Le, 407
Rayos y centellas, 552
Ray Regan, 282
Ray Ringo, 788
Real Folks at Home, 153
Rebellenclub, 616
Rectangle, The, 445
Red and the Black, The, 511
Red Barry, 354, 642
Red Comet, 192
Red Detachment of Women, The, 642-43
Reddy and Caruso, 186
Redeye, 128, 189, 643-44
Red Gaucho, 187
Red Grainger, 535
Red Gregory, 535
Red Hawk, 434
Redipicche, 149, 642, 644
Red Knight, The, 644
Red Man's Gold, 377
Red Ray, Space Raynger, 236
Red Rider, The, 391, 609
Red Ryder, 24, 156, 173, 370, 594,
    645, 814
Red Skull, The, 381
Red Sonja, 646, 757, 812
Red Tide, 727
Reef Kinkaid, 492
Reel Comedies, 812
Reflection of the Society, 250
Regazzo nel Oeste, Un, 143
Reggie van Twerp, 701

Reg'lar Fellers, 172, 646-47, 740
Reg Varney, 812
Reine Margot, La, 623
Reinhold das Nashorn, 163-64
Remember When, 711
Rémy et Ghislaine, 217
Renkin Jutsu, 542
Reno Kid, 161
Repent Harlequin, Siad the Tick Tock
    Man, 573
Reporter Tribulete que en Todas Partes
    se Mete, 202
Rescue from the Roundheads, 393
Rescuer's Reward, 609
Respiro e il sogno, Il, 440
Return of Captain Trueno, The, 138
Return of the Jedi, 726, 811
Rêve du requin, Le, 682
Revija na dvoristu, 239
Rex, 116
Rex Baxter, 28, 251, 649
Rex Dexter of Mars, 152
Rex Morgan, M.D., 32, 97, 231, 424,
    454, 649-50, 722
Rhymo the Monk, 504, 505
Ribambelle, La, 762
Ribit, 757
Ribon no Kishi, 754
Richard Long, 150
Richard Venna, MD, 631
Ric Hochet, 33, 335, 650-51
Rick O'Shay, 87, 496, 651
Rico Tipo, 399
Ridder Roodhart, 100, 372, 519
Riding Mystery at Moorland School,
    The, 310
Rikke en Wiske, 737-38
Rima, 462, 645
Rina, 199
Ring of the Nibelung, The, 434, 756
Ringo Kid, 444
Rip Carson, 492
Rip Kirby, 28, 202, 246, 285, 502,
    627-28, 641, 651-53, 811
Riri, Gogo et Lolo, 604
Risk, 820
Rista Sportista, 512
Rivals at the Alpine School, 310
Rivals of the Spanish Main, 377
River Queen, 162
Rivolta dei Racchi, La, 170
Road to Rome, 609
Robby Robijn, 457
Rob Conway, 368
Roberta, 772
Roberto Alcazar y Pedrín, 654-55
Robina, 462, 773
Robin Hood, 125, 174, 175, 307, 575,
    716, 812
Robin Hood and Company, 655
Robin Hood of Sherwood, 393
Robin Malone, 490, 492, 568
Robinson, 655-56, 813
Robinson Crusoe, 383, 623

Robinson Crusoe Esquire, 158
Robot Imperium, 657
Robotman, 705, 765
Robot Santōhei, 657
Robot Smith, 648
Rob Roy, 393
Rob the Rover, 146, 657, 808
Rocco Vargas, 771-72
Rock Derby, 647
Rocket, 110, 246
Rocket Man, 542
Rocketman, 303, 649
Rocket Tarō, 463
Rockfist the Jungle Ruler, 110
Rock Mastard, 149
Rockwood, 796
Rocky and Bullwinkle, 656
Rocky Mason, 484
Rocky Rider, 314, 658
Rocky Stoneaxe, 610
Rod Craig, 384, 535, 658
Roddy the Road Scout, 236
Rod Rian of the Sky Police, 187
Rody, 302
Rog: 2000, 809
Rogers' Rangers, 282
Roger the Dodger, 242, 574, 648
Rolan Aquila, 562
Roland Butter and Hammond Deggs, 812
Roland Eagle, 659
Roland el Corsario, 580
Rollicking Ranch, 110
Rollicking Rollo, 317
Rollo the Gypsy Boy, 393
Rolo, el marciano adoptivo, 714
Roly Poly, 609
Roly Poly's Tours, 823
Rom, 254
Romano Il Legionario, 28, 659-60
Romeo, 186
Romeo and Juliet, 241, 286, 716
Romeo Brown, 391
Romeo e Giulietta, 241
Romeo Lancia, 642
Ronin, 534
Ronnie Rich, 390
Rook, The, 280
Room and Board, 80-81, 590, 660
Rosaspina, 664
Rosco & Sonny, 575
Rose is Rose, 661-62, 733
Rose of Versailles, The, 41
Rosie and Rex, 812
Rosie Romance, 152
Rosie's Beau, 501, 569, 662
Rosso Stenton, 529
Rosy-Posy-Grandma's Girl, 381
ROTC, 675
Roudoudou, 617
Rouletabosse, 271
Rowlf, 214
Roy Carson, 500
Roy Mann, 273, 530

Roy of the Rovers, 209, 393
Roy Powers, 348
Roy Renk, 123
Roy Rogers, 167, 567
Roy Tiger, 38, 663-64
Rozana, Schoolgirl of Mystery, 310
Rozet Cochon de Lait, 271
Rubber, the Canine Cop, 382
Rube Goldberg's Sideshow, 349
Rubin and Rut, 302
Rudi, 664-65
Rudy, 593, 729
Rufus. See Flook
Rufus DeBree, 278
Ruggles, 267, 498, 665
Rumeurs su le Rouergue, 745
Rumic World, 506
Rupert, 22, 665-66
Rural Delivery, 711
Ruru to Mimi, 366
Rusty and His Pals, 303, 434
Rusty Riley, 348, 666-67

S

Sabaku no Maō, 669, 698
Saber, 209, 501
Sabio Megaton, El, 202
Sabotage!, 771
Sabotage and War, 243
Sacred Eye of Satpura, 377
Sad Experiences of Big and Little Willie, The, 372
Sadhú, 669
Sad Sack, The, 27, 107-8, 122, 151, 669-70
Safari, 575, 789
Saga de los Menendez, La, 341
Saga de Xam, 670
Sahara, 282
Saint, The, 95, 237, 808
Salesman Sam, 220
Sally, 236
Sally Forth, 672-73, 723, 733
Salty Ranks, 321
Sam and His Laugh, 740
Sam and Silo, 796
Sambo and His Funny Noises, 514, 795
Sambo Remo, 538
Sammy and Sausage, 807
Sammy Spry, 386
Sammy Squirrel, 370
Sammy the Scout, 693
Sam Pezzo, 338
Sam Scatterem, 426
Samson, 435
Sam's Strip, 144, 270, 673, 699, 796
Sam the Skipper, 317
Samuel Johnson, 734
Sandab, 823
Sand e Zeos, 608

Sandman, The, 200, 434, 576, 673-74, 705, 744
Sandman Mystery Theater, 674
Sandra, 535
Sandy, 693
Sandy and Muddy, 798
Sandy Cove, 110
Sandy Highflier, the Airship Man, 431
Sandy's Steam Man, 798
San Mao, 674
Sanshōuo, 775
Santincielo, 731
Santo Domingo, 350
Santos Vega, 203, 480
Sapeur Camember, Le. See Facéties du Sapeur Camember, Les
Sappo, 675
Sargento Kirk, 579-80
Sarge Snorkle, 809
Sarge Steele, 344
Sargon, 462
Sarutobi Sasuke, 733
Sasuke, 38, 675-76
Sasurai no Gambler, 716
Satanik, 639, 685
Sathsiri, 607
Saturna Contro la Terra, 476, 676-77, 792
Saxxon, 771
Sayonara Nihon, 588
Sazae-san, 22, 29, 677
Scamp, 370
Scarlet Avenger, 434
Scarlet O'Neil, 403
Scarth, 677-78
Scary William, 450, 600
Scenes of Malaysian Life, 442
Sceriffo Fox, Il, 227, 642
Scheletrino, 189
Schmit der Sphy, 666
Schnoox, The, 354
School Days, 272, 310
School on the Island, 363
Schtroumpes, Les, 36, 67, 228, 680, 809
Sciuscià, 111, 162, 683-84
Sconosciuto, Lo, 640
Scooby Doo, 809
Scoop, 656
Scoop Donovan, 778
Scoop Scuttle, 816
Scoop Smithy, 631
Scorchy Smith, 24, 114, 200, 212, 252, 325, 420, 421, 649, 653, 684-85, 700
Scorpions du Désert, Les, 627
Scott Lanyard, 499
Scott Rand, 133
Scream Inn, 797
Screwy Scrapbook with Pop Cornish, 628
Scribbly, 219, 524-25
Sea Devils, 378
Sea Foam, 609

Sea Shanties, 187
Seaside Comic, The, 125
Secondamano, 521
Secret Agent X-9, 24, 40, 153, 287, 307, 351, 354, 490, 492, 554, 576, 598, 621, 641, 642, 685-86, 811
Secret Angent Corrigan. See Secret Agent X-9
Secret in the Sands, 125
Secret Life of Pigs, The, 593-94
Secret of Monte Cristo, 691
Secret of the Manor, 609
Secret Six, 344
Secte des Assassins, La, 525
Seekers, The, 686-87
Segreto del castello, 575
Seidel og Tobran, 75
Senbiki no Ninja, 436
Sengoku Zouhyō, 696
Sennin Buraku, 452
Señor Burron o Vida de Perro, El, 291
Señor Conejo, El, 695
Sentinel Louie, 485, 714
Septimus and His Space Ship, 650
Serafino, 227, 688-89
Séraphin, 197
Sergeant Craig, 729
Sgt. Fury, 105, 689
Sgt. Kirk, 627
Sgt. O'Malley of the Redcoat Patrol, 473
Sergeant Pat of the Radio Patrol, 638
Sgt. Rock, 378, 435, 460, 474, 689-90, 809
Sergeant Spook, 502
Seton Dōbutsuki, 696
Seven Soldiers of Victory, 356
Sexaroid, 520
Sexton Blake, 236, 690-91
Sfinge nera, La, 240
Shadow, The, 198, 255-56, 356, 400, 432, 583, 653, 691-93, 737
Shadow Troop, The, 734
Shakai Gihyō, 826
Shakespeare in Possumville, 591
Shan Gou le de Nu Xiou Cai, 375
Shan Xiang Ju Bian, 376
Shattuck, 197
Shazam!, 121, 183, 184, 518
Sheena, Queen of the Jungle, 297, 303, 344, 400, 511, 526, 693-94
Sheepy, 236
She Hawk, 154
She-Hulk, The, 171
Shenanigan Kids, The. See Katzenjammer Kids, The
Shepherd King, 125
Sheriff Sockeye, 110
Sherlock Holmes, 185, 571, 608, 695, 757
Sherlock Holmes und das Geheimnis der blauen Erbse, 285, 533
Sherlock Lopez, 695

Sherlocko the Monk, 374, 504, 505, 695
Sherlock Time, 150, 580
Sherriff, The, 96
Sheshiva, 678
Shibire no Skatan, 84
Shidenkai no Taka, 199
Shield, The, 526, 695-96, 819
Shigatsu kaidan, 588
Shinban Sanju ni Mensō, 451
Shinigami Shōnen Kim, 696
Shining Knight, 319
Shin Mizu ya Sora, 581
Shin Takarajima, 670, 754
Shipwrecked, The, 464
Shiver & Shake, 166, 648
Shōchan no Bōken, 697
Shoe, 39, 697-98
Shokoku Meikyō Kiran, 391
Shōnen Dōmei, 405
Shōnen Gahō, 84
Shōnen Kenya, 698
Shōnen Oja, 29, 698
Short Ribs, 583, 698-99
Shorty, 666, 807
Shot Basky, 138
Show Girl. See Dixie Dugan
Shrimatiji, 626
Shuang Hsiang Pao, 200-201
Shuffled Symphonies, 650
Siberian Girl, 716
Sidonie en Vacances, 271
Siegfried, 169, 534
Siete Vidas, 120
Sigfrid, 473
Siggi un Babarras, 494
Sigi the Frank, 382
Sign of Freedom, The, 251
Signor Bonaventura, Il, 23, 701-2
Signor McCoy the Circus Hoss, 823
Signor Spaghetti, 352
Signor Spartaco, Il, 521
Sigurd, 702, 798-99
Silang and Zhenping, 823-24
Silas Finn, 191, 273
Silent Knight, 377
Silent Sam. See Adamson
Silent Three, The, 309, 310
Silk Hat Harry's Divorce Suit, 265
Silly Symphonies, 253, 261, 621, 702-3, 744
Silver Linings, 462
Silver Metal Lover, The, 654
Silver Roy, 703
Silver Smutt, 536
Silver Star, 448
Silver Starr in the Flame World, 592, 620, 621, 703-4
Silver Streak, 135, 206, 233
Silver Surfer, The, 167, 206, 345, 704
Si Mamat, 442
Simon Simple, 185-86
Simon the Simple Sleuth, 502
Simple Simon, 502

Simp O'Dill, 383
Sinbad, 272
Sinbad the Sailor, 464
Sin City, 85, 534
Sindbad de Zeerover, 788
Sinking of the Lusitania, The, 498
Sinner, 85
Siopawman, 705-6
Sir Balantime, 678
Sir Butch, 126
Sir Leo, 120
Sir Roger de Coverlet, 609
Sir Toby Tinribs, 812
Sister's Little Sister's Beau, 498
Siulauman, 817
Six Million Dollar Man, The, 809
Si Yeoo Ki, 706
Sjors en Sjimmie, 157, 616, 706-7
S.K. 1, 549
Skeets, 707
Skid Davis, 502
Skilled, 384
Skilly the Convict, 823
Skippy, 222-23, 552, 707-8, 740
Skit, Skat and the Captain, 333, 650
Skull Valley, 808
Skylark, 728
Skyman, 316
Skymasters, 105, 447, 818
Sky Rangers, 92
Skyroads, 173, 438, 550, 708-9
Sky Rocket Steele, 287
Slam Bradley, 147, 699
Slave of the Screamer, The, 138
Slavuj Gliša, 255
Slicksure, 110
Slim and Tubby, 411, 644
Slim Jim, 19, 709
Slot-Barr, 714
Slylock Fox, 548, 709-10
Small Change, 478
Small Fox with Big Feet, 605
Smalto & Jonny, 191
Smarty, 812
Smash, 119
Smash and Grab, 628
S'Matter, Popċ, 600
Smiley O'Hara, 138
Smilin' Jack, 550, 710
Smith's Vaudevillians, 223, 666
Smitty, 127, 414, 420, 550, 712
Smokey Stover, 388, 392, 393, 415, 590, 712-13, 722
Smurfs, The. See Schtrouompes, Les
Snake Tales, 42, 713
Snapshot Bill, 805
Snookums, 567, 662
Snoozer, 501
Snorks, The, 809
S no Taiyō, 520
Snowfire, 236
Snowman, The, 154
Snow White, 253
Snugglepot and Cuddlepie, 339

Soccer Spook, 648
Socko the Seadog, 447
Soggy the Sea Monster, 574
Soldino, 715
Solitario dei Dakya, Il, 175
Sombre Vilain, Le, 398
Somebody's Stenog, 265
Someone's Always Taking the Joy Out of Life, 153, 806
Song Cartoons, 807
Song of the Sword, 609
Sonnysayings, 216
Son of Dracula, 757
Son of Tomahawk, 435
Sons of the Sword, 609
Sooper Dooper, 321
Sooty and Sweep, 656
Sorang, 37, 470, 577, 717
Soregashi Kojikini Arazu, 387
Sor Pampurio, 23, 717-18
South Sea Girl, 306
South with the Hover-car, 346
Space 1999, 171, 809
Space Accident, The, 778
Space Age, 778
Space Cadet, 474, 568
Space Cadets, 502
Space Comics, 96
Space Family Robinson, 720
Space Ghost, 722, 773
Spacehawk, 78, 816
Space Patrol, 383, 592
Space Patrolman, 511
Space Pirates, 778
Space Rangers, 280
Spaceship to the Moon, 609
Space Voyagers, 573
Spare Ribs and Gravy, 501, 569, 596
Sparks & Flash, 236
Sparky, 189
Spawn, 500
Spawn of Frankenstein, 318
Specialiste, Le, 339
Spectre, The, 316
Speed Saunders, 360
Speed Tarō, 718
Spider, 796
Spider-Man, 67, 83, 171, 254, 259, 434, 472, 500, 660, 718-19, 756, 812
Spies in Action, 470
Špilijko, 123
Spinal Comics, 115
Spinball Slaves, 778
Spirit, The, 26-27, 102, 278, 295, 454, 642, 720-21, 818
Spirit of Frankenstein, 318
Spirou, 318, 319, 337, 721, 790
Spitfire, 502
Spooks of St. Luke's, The, 628
Spooktacular Seven, 797
Spooky, 392, 713, 721-22
Sporting Life, The, 551
Sportograms, 360

Spotlight on Sally, 302
Spring and Autumn in Cat Kingdom, 475
Spugna, 608
Spy, 147, 699
Spyman, 726
Spy Smasher, 27, 120, 134, 153, 723-24
Square Eyes, 424
Squirrel Cage, The, 81, 590
Squirrel Food, 80
Squirt, 379
Stage School, 574
Stainless Steel, 403
Stainless Stephen, 536
Stan Laurel and Oliver Hardy, 796, 798
Stanley and His Monster, 316
Stanley the Station Master, 110
Star Ballerina, 511
Stari Mačak, 25, 522
Starman, 40, 316, 526, 724-25
Star Pirate, 92
Star Reach Classics, 574
Stars My Destination, The, 197
Star Spangled Kid, 222, 725
StarStruck, 432
Star Struck Sam, 656
Star Trek, 103, 502, 778
Star Wars, 87, 154, 197, 294, 351, 385, 510, 725-26, 811
Statyetten, 348
Steel Claw, The, 138
Steel Sterling, 134, 435, 545, 726
Stenyka Razyn, 464
Steve and Stumpy, 812
Steve Canyon, 28, 58, 62, 158, 159, 175-76, 454, 529, 539, 593, 685, 727-28, 778
Steve Conrad, Adventurer, 473
Steve Ditko's Avenging Tales, 254
Steve Malone, 316
Steve Roper, 593, 677, 728-29
Steve Samson, 243, 391
Steve Wood, 502
Stewart McPherson, 377
Stiffy & Mo, 364
Stingray, 282, 778
Stips, 730
Stojadin, 512
Stonehenge Kit the Ancient Brit, 729, 798
Stoney Dawson, 166
Stony Craig of the Marines, 729-30
Stoogie, 110
Storia d'Italia a fumetti, 508
Storie d'oro e di frontiera, 771
Stormwatch, 472
Stormy Foster, 303
Story of Flight, 451
Story of O, 221
Strain on the Family Tie, A, 739, 740
Strange Adventures of Mr. Weed, 524
Strange World of Mr. Mum, The, 730

Straordinarie avventure di Penthotal, Le, 601
Stratosphere Jim, 502
Strega, La, 150
Streken van Reintje de Vos, 157
Stropke en Flopke, 564
Stroppie, 157
Stuck Rubber Baby, 40, 226
Student Life, 80
Stumble Inn, 381
Stups, 730-31
Sturmtruppen, 18, 37, 71, 144, 731
Stymie and His Magic Wishbone, 812
Sub-Mariner, The, 26, 90, 95, 98, 166, 167, 206, 287, 351, 397, 404, 472, 611, 725, 731-32, 819
Submerman, 614
Sub-Zero, 287
Sueurs de Métèques, 552
Sugar and Spike, 525
Suicide Brigade, 206
Suicide Smith, 92, 192, 280
Suikoden Nishikie, 783
Sun, 110
Sunbeam and the Innocent, 205
Sunbonnet Babies, 632
Sunshine, 110, 246
Sunshine Falls, 498
Suparnici, 123
Superbone, 734
Super Fan, 237, 551
Supergirl, 154, 734-35, 804
Superlocos, Los, 291
Supermachos, Los, 79, 735
Superman, 26, 35, 40, 77, 83, 92, 134, 147, 218, 233, 242, 285, 309, 417, 422, 434, 489, 515, 526, 533, 541, 547, 567, 571, 583, 678-79, 683, 694, 699-700, 701, 722, 725, 734, 735-37, 804, 830
Superman Family, 418
Supermouse, 533
Supersabios, Los, 169
Super Sam, 648
Supersnipe, 222, 737
Supreme, 547
Surburban Cowgirls, 732-33
Surprise, 110
Suske en Wiske, 29, 737-38
Suzie Snaffle, 628
Svernirko, 239
Swamp Thing, The, 547, 587, 645, 738
Sweeney and Son, 739-40
Sweet 16, 218
Sweethearts and Wives, 727
Sweet Hortense, 245
Sweet Little Katy, 740
Sweet Rosie O'Grady, 812
Swift Morgan, 500
Swineskin Gulch, 373
Swiss Family Robinson, 125, 204
Sword of the Atom, 104
Sylvia, 391-92

T

Tabibito-Kun, 559
Tad of the Tanbark, 262, 352, 611
Tagalog Klassiks, 86
Tagisan Ng Mga Agimat, 743
Taifu Goro, 671
Tailspin Tommy, 24, 114, 220, 311, 743-44
Tajne abisinskih gudura, 411
Takaou, 542
Taking Her to the Ball Game, 80
Tale of One Bad Rat, The, 744
Tales from the Great Book, 474
Tales of Asgard, 757
Tales of the Black Freighter, 800
Tales of the Jungle Imps, 497
Tallulah, 701
Tama no Kashi Monagotari, 452
Tamburino del Re, Il, 202
Tango the Terrier, 812
Tanguy et Laverdure, 529
Tanjo, 588
Tank, 216
Tank McNamara, 745
Tanku Tankurō, 745
Tanpō Gashu, 581
Tanteiō, 463
Tap Room Tales, 795
Taras Bulba, 830
Targa the Tiger Man, 609
Target, 110, 246
Taró, 637, 651, 746-47
Tarzan, 23, 24, 83, 84-85, 115, 167, 192, 218, 246, 285, 315, 319, 389, 401, 427, 457, 461, 462, 474, 490, 492, 510-11, 524, 570, 573, 629, 693, 698, 720, 747-48, 752, 757, 778, 809
Tarzanetto, 603
Tarzan no Himitsukichi, 463
Tatamidori Kasajin, 452
Tatave, 467
Teacher Trotter, 796
Team 7, 472
Teddy in Africa, 499
Teddy Sberla, 765
Teddy Spring, 608
Teddy Tail, 18, 317, 748-49
Teddy Ted, 384
Teddy Turner & his Television, 110
Tedious Pastimes, 538
Ted Strong, 187
Ted Towers, 749
Teena, 286
Teenage Mutant Ninja Turtles, 40, 749-50
Teen Titans, 40, 77, 154
Teknophage, 744
Telerompo, 507
Telestrip, 750
Teletoons, 750
Televisor, El, 714
Tele Wischen, 451

Tempest, The, 241
Tempesta, La, 241
Tempio delle genti, Il, 240
Tenebrax, 614
Tenente Marlo, Il, 575
Tenpei Tenma, 750
Tensai Bakabon, 84
Tenth Player, The, 379
Tere Creuse, La, 680
Terrible Tales of Captain Kiddo, 268
Terror, 507
Terror in the Tall Tower, 501
Terror Keep, 161, 402, 544
Terrors of the Tiny Tads, 750-51, 791
Terry and the Pirates, 24, 27, 40, 81, 83, 159, 175, 247, 280, 287, 378, 384, 385, 386, 488, 507, 685, 700, 703?, 722, 727, 728, 729-30, 751-52, 818, 820
Terry the Troubador, 370
Terry Thomas, 812
Testamenti di Sant'Ambrogio, 150
Tetsujin 28gō, 752
Tetsuwan-Atom, 33, 67, 583, 752-53, 754
Tex, 575
Texas Slim, 422-23, 753, 810
Texas Willer, 753-54
Tex Revolver, 205
Tex Willer, 29, 91, 143, 449, 509, 511
Thatcher, 140-41
That's Different, 127
That's My Pop, 217, 360
Their Only Child, 501, 567, 569
Them Days Is Gone Forever, 740
Them Was the Happy Days, 272
Théorème de Bell, 682
There's at Least One in Every Office, 153
There Was an Old Woman Who Lived in a Shoe, 147
They'll Do It Everytime, 373, 483, 755
Thick Black Kiss, 198
Thimble Theater, 22, 196, 554, 687, 755-56, 806, 809, 813
Things That Never Happen, 171
Thirteen, 724
13 rue de l'Espoir, 303
This is America, 554
Thor, 83, 167, 259, 447, 472, 756-57
Thorgal, Fils des Etoiles, 436, 662
Thoughts of Citizen Doe, 208
Three Aces, The, 200
Three Bears, The, 118
Three Brothers, 278
3 Jolly Sailorboys, 812
Three Little Pigs, The, 253
Three Musketeers, The, 204, 239, 287, 671, 715
Three Story Stan, 797
Thriller, 574
Thrill o Ajiwan Otoko, 542
Thrill that Comes Once in a Lifetime, The, 762

Thudor, 282
Thun'da, 319
THUNDER Agents, 220, 434, 758-59, 818
Thunderbirds, 125
Thunderbolt Jaxon, 502
Thunderbolts, 773
Thundercats, 725
Tiamotti, 476
Tibor, 759-60, 798-99
Tich, 267
Tich and Snitch, 807
Tickle and Tootle, 812
Tick Tock Tony, 393
Ticonderoga, 286, 580
Tiddlewink Family, 812
Tif et Tondu, 762
Tiffany Jones, 36, 760
Tiga Sekawan, 442
Tiger, 760
Tiger Joe, 196
Tiger Man, 192, 286
Tiger Tim, 22, 748, 760-61
Tiger Time, 317
Tightrope Tim, 383-84
Tightwaddo the Monk, 504
Tigri di Sumatra, I, 180
Tijl Uilenspiegel, 789
Tiki, 440
Tillie the Toiler, 21, 147, 271, 554, 641, 761-62, 805-6
Tim, 148
Timber Jack, 111
Time², 198
Times Five, 778
Time Top, The, 355
Time Tunnel, The, 464
Tim Holt, 319
Timid Soul, The, 762-63, 802
Tim McCoy, 377
Timothy Titan, 191
Tim Tyler's Luck, 24, 228, 306, 344, 641, 763-64, 826
Tim Valour Comics, 255
Tinklebell Tree, 317
Tin-Pot Foreign General and Old Iron Woman, The, 154
Tintin, 25, 67, 99, 137, 159, 648-49, 737, 764
Tintin-Selection, 99
Tinwhiskers the Pirate, 205
Tiny Tim, 481
Tiny Tots, 650
Tiny Toy Boys, The, 317
Tipin, 705
Tip & Topper, 110
Tiramolla, 189, 642, 764-65
Tiriel, 623
Tishy and Steve, 803
Titanus, 570
Titi et Tutu, 335
Tito and His Burrito, 315
TNT, 576
Tobias Seicherl, 731, 765-66

Toby and Tinker, 317
Todano Bonji, 766
Toddles, 222
Toffs and the Toughs, The, 166
Togosaku to Mokubē no Tokyo
    Kenbutsu, 448
Tokai, 42, 766
Tokyō Senichi ya Monogatari, 696
Tom, Dick, and Harry, 809
Tomador, 675
Tomahawk, 381, 435, 757
Tom and Jerry, 766-67
Tōma no shinzō, 366
Tomato Khan, 628
Toma Vank, 239
Tom ba de los Dioses, La, 514
Tom & Biber, 437
Tom Bill, 162
Tom Corbett, 568, 757
Tom et Nelly, 781
Tom Jones, 511
Tommie's avonturen, 157
Tom Mix, 161, 162, 174, 175, 611
Tommy Handley, 812
Tommy of the Big Top, 474
Tommy's Avonturen, 707
Tommy's Clockword Brother, 393
Tommy Trinder, 426
Tommy Trot the Tudor Tramp, 386
Tommy Walls, 368
Tom o'London, 282
Tom Poes, 372, 436, 767-68
Tom Sawyer and Huck Finn, 272
Tom the Ticket of Leave Man, 205
Tom Tip & Tim Top the Tramps, 386
Tom und Biber, 305, 566
Tom und Klein Biberherz, 305
Tonda Haneko, 16
Tontote y Cia, 138
Tony, 221
Tony Falco, 768
Toodles, 268
Toonerville Folks, 316, 768-69
Toon Okkernoot, 157
Toots and Casper, 553, 554, 769-70
Top Cat, 809
Topical Breezes, 807
Topolino, 189, 302
Topple Twins, 236
Tops, 135
Tor, 360, 361, 460
Torcy Brown, 587
Tori, 788
Tornado, 111, 544, 808
Tornado Tom, 110
Torpedo 1936, 41, 771, 773
Totor, chef de la patrouille des
    Hannetons, 648, 737, 788
Touch and Go, 219
Tough But Tender Tex, 798
Tough Kid Squad, 827
Tough Teddy, 445
Tough Tod & Happy Annie, 502
Touitoui, 670

Tour, La, 680
Tour of Dr. Syntax in Search of the
    Picturesque, 663
Towers of Bois-Maury, The, 398
Tóxico y Biberón, 399
Toys of Doom, 714
Trac et Boum, 670
Tracy Twins, 383
Tragg, 675
Tram Tram Rock-Tram Tram Waltz,
    521
Tramvajko, 239
Travelin' Gus, 485
Treasure Chest, Classics Illustrated, 401
Treasure Island, 575, 716
Tres Inseparables, Les, 137
Tres Mosqueteros en el Oeste, Los, 239
Tres por la Ley, 580
Trial, The, 226
Tribar, 790
Tribunzio, 202
Trigan Empire, 282
Trinet et Trinette, 339
Tripje en Liezenbertha, 107, 773-74
Tripudio, 595
Triton, 771
Tri života, 464
Trois Mousquetaires du Maquis, Les,
    271, 774
Trolldrycken, 126
Trollkarlens hatt, 412
Trollkarl i Stockholm, En, 297, 490
Trolls, The, 236, 502
Tron, 345
Tropical Tricks, 110
Trottolino, 715
Troubles of Mr. Jack, The, 539
Trucker, 682
Trudi, 705
Trudy and Hazel, 396
True Life Adventures, 650
True Love, 704, 773
Tsannga Rannga, 462, 573
Tsuki Hyakusha, 775
Tsunde ha kuzushi, 387
Tsuri, 696
Tubby & Trot, 110
Tucker Twins, The, 666
Tuckwells, The, 686
Tuer de Cafards, 746
Tumbleweeds, 237, 333, 669, 699, 776
Turi and Tolk, 432
Turn of the Screw, 221
Turok, Son of Stone, 103, 524, 567,
    778
Tutto ricominciò con un estate indiana,
    508
T.V. Heroes, 96
T.V. Tornado, 96
Twiddle and Nobb, 812
Twilight Zone, 220, 287
Twin Earths, 502, 592
Two-Fisted Tales, 462
Two-Gun Kid, The, 105, 567, 641

Two Little Wanderers, 377
2000 A.D., 778
2001 Space Odyssey, 447
Two Toof Tom, 502
Two True Friends, 377
Tytus, Romek, and Tomek, 200
Tzar's Shieldbearer, 716

U

Uchi no Yomehan, 452
Uchū Senkan Yamato, 520
Udarnik Ratko, 266
Ufo, 657
Ugly Duckling, The, 204
Uk en Puk, 768
Ulceda, 549
U ledenoj pustinji, 738
Ulf, 798-99
Ullao, 765
Ultra, 280
Ultra-Man, 524
Ulysse, 781-82
Ulysses, 614
Uma-Uma, 579, 714
Una Ballata del Mare Salato, 627
Unbesiegbaren, Die, 459
Uncanny X-Men, 821
Uncle Crabapple, 186
Uncle Jonathan's Will, 363
Uncle Sam, 126, 192, 219, 303, 471
Underground Front, 820
Unfortunate Fate of a Well-Intentioned
    Dog, 499
United Continental, 349
Unknown Rider, 511
Unknown Soldier, The, 27, 462, 653
Unlucky Georgie, 798
Unlucky Wally Twenty Years On, 154
Unmei, 775
Uomini che non ebbero paura, 770
Uomo alla finestra, L', 522
Uomo che uccise Ernesto "Che"
    Guevara, L,' 640
Uomo del Khyber, L', 529
Uomo delle Filippine, L', 440
Uomo delle nevi, L', 508
Uomo del Messico, L', 771
Uomo del Nilo, L', 771
Uomo del paludi, L', 771
Uomo del Tanganyka, L', 529
Uomo di carta, L', 508
Uomo di Cuba, L', 301
Up Anchor, 441
Up Front, 782
Upside Downs of Little Lady Lovekins
    and Old Man Muffaroo, The,
    782-83, 791
Urhunden, 93
Ursurak, 385
Urusei yatsura, 506
U.S. Acres, 237, 333

U.S. Rangers, 492
Useless Eustace, 608
Us Fellers, 109, 293, 343, 569
Us Girls, 535, 658
Ushitsuki, 542
Us Husbands, 381
Usura Retsuden, 329

V

Vacanze fatali, 338
Vaillant, 193
Vaillant-Pif: Les Rigouis et les Tristus, 193
Vaisseau de Pierre, Le, 131
Valentina, 37, 189, 221, 785
Valentina Melaverde, 785-86
Valérian, 527, 786
Valeria the She-Bat, 574
Valhalla, 41, 786-87
Valiant, 133
Valle del terrore, La, 640
Vampire, 754
Vampirella, 120, 301, 432, 759, 787
Vangelo sconosciuto, Il, 771
Van Helsing, 190, 608
Vanilla and the Villians, 482, 499, 789
Van Swaggers, The, 806
Varoomschka, 208, 704
Vater und Sohn, 22, 325, 581, 730, 789-90
Velika utakmica, 266
Veliki Miting, 239, 566
Veliki turner, 255
Vendicatore del Oeste, Il, 143
Veneziano Telgtammi, 608
Vengador, El, 150
Vengeance du Corsaire, La, 173-74, 174-75
Venus in Furs, 221
Verdugo Ranch, 286
Veritable Histoire de M. Crépin, La, 387
Vernon the Villain, 812
Versos y Noticias de César Bruto, 213
V for Vendetta, 547
Viaggi e Avventure, 86
Viaggio a Tulum, 508
Vic Flint, 791, 814
Vic Jordan, 576, 791
Victor, 236
Vida del Che, La, 150
Vidocq, 458, 792
Vie des Grands Fauves, La, 617
Vie des Hommes Illustres, La, 617
Vigilante, The, 526, 656
Viki and Niki, 239
Viking Prince, 461
Ville qui n'Existait Pas, La, 131
Villiams Verden, 535
Virtue of Vera Valiant, 722
Virus, Il Mago della Foresta Morta, 25, 175, 543, 603, 792

Virus Psik, 685
Vision, 434
Viso nascosto, 771
Vita Col Gatto, 198, 642
Vita da cani, 273
Vita di un Commesso Viaggiatore, 198, 642
Vitellini in Citta, 111
Vito Nervio, 150
Vjerenica mača, 522
Volpone Dulcamara, 642
Voltar, 38, 793
Voltfeder, 657
Volton, 460
Voorwarts, 107
Vorg, 657
Voyages et Aventures du Docteur Festus, Les, 387
Voyageurs, Les, 436
Vuna Kic'o orasi Mic'o, 239

W

W 3, 754
Wags, the Dog that Adopted a Man, 514, 795
Wahre Geschichten erlogen von Loriot, 163
Wakamontachi, 559
Walkie & Talkie, 191
Wally and the Major, 223, 797
Walt Disney's Donald Duck. See Donald Duck
Walt Disney's Silly Symphonies. See Silly Symphonies
Walter Forde, 796
Walt Kelly's Pogo. See Pogo
Wanda the Wonder Girl, 110
Wandering Willie, 393
Wang Shuhui, 797
Wang Xiansheng He Xiao Chen, 797-98
Warlock, 167
Warlord, 476
Warlords of Han, The, 577
War on Crime, 348
Warp (play), 77
Waru Waru World, 84
Washable Jones, 179
Wash Tubbs, 23, 141, 220, 777, 799-800. See also Captain Easy
Wata no kunihoshi, 588
Watari, 696
Watashi no Joni, 676
Watchmen, 40, 547, 800-801
Way Out West, 420
Weary Willie and the Count de Main, 343
Weary Willie and Tired Tim, 16, 83, 125, 158, 205, 801
Weather Pup, 807
Web, The, 435, 801-2
Wee Eck and his Elephant, 536

Wee Georgie Wood, 798
Wee Hughie, 321
Wee Macs, The, 693
Wee Pals, 39, 635, 777, 803
Wee Tusky, 544
Wee Willie Winkie's World, 14, 297, 804
Wee Women, 470
Welcome to Springville, 440
Wendel, 226
Werewolf, 214
Werner, 805
Wesley Barry, 796
West Coast Avengers, 171
Western Brothers, The, 377
Western Kid, 660
Western Penman, The, 153
Western Willie the Cowboy Coughdrop, 386
West of Eden, 627
Wet Blanket, 347
Wetworks, 472
Wham, 118
What a Guy!, 389
What's Cooking, 236
What's This?, 360
What the Dickens, 155
Wheeler and Woolsey, 796
Wheeling, 627
Wheels of Fortune, 609
When a Feller Needs a Friend, 97, 153, 728, 806
When a Man's Married, Before and After, 727
When I Was Short, 593
When the Bell Rings, 118
When the Wind Blows, 154
When Worlds Collide, 286
Where I'm Coming From, 218, 587, 806-7
Where in the World is Carmen San Diego?, 154
Whiskers Club, The, 628
Whisk the Squirrel, 628
Whisky e Gogo, 148, 198, 642, 765
White Boy, 808
White Cloud, 609
White King of Arabia, 609
White Streak, 287
Whizzer, 472
Whodidit, 823
Whole Blooming Family, The, 501, 662
Whoopee Hank, 236
Wicked Wanda, 282
Wide Awake Willie, 646
Wild Batson, 138
Wild Bill Pecos, Wanted, 471
Wildcat, 434, 526
WildC.A.T.S. Covert Action Teams, 472
Wildfire, 209
Wildfire, the War Horse, 346
Wildflower and Little Elf, 812
Wild Yukon, 180
Will Bragg, 364

Will Hay, 386, 536
Willie and Joe, 122, 395, 782
Willie Doodle, 404
Willie Evergrow, 812
Willie Lumpkin, 472
Willie Scribble the Pavement Artist, 386
Willie Wart & Wally Warble, 386
Willie Wise, 186
Willie Write, 110
Willi Wiedehopf, 648
Will Sparrow, 173
Willy and Wally, 383
Willy Nilly, 321
Wilson the Wonder Man, 346
Windy and Paddles, 417
Windy Riley, 419
Wings of Fortune, 609
Wing Tips, 206
Winks, The, 223
Winnetou, 566, 570, 813
Winnie the Pooh in Disneyland, 236
Winnie Winkle, 21, 22, 127, 147, 150, 157, 313, 461, 706, 712, 790, 813-14
Winston Churchill, 125
Wireless Willie and Bertie Broadcast, 187
Wise Little Hen, The, 261
Wise Quacks, 392
Witching Hour, The, 773
With the Willits, 810
Witness, The, 472
Wizard, 526
Wizard of Id, The, 34, 156, 189, 192, 371, 597, 699, 814
Wizard of Oz, The, 150, 489, 499
Wizards Anonymous, 797
Wolf, 395
Wolff, 37, 514
Wolverine, 167
Wonder Boy, 192
Wonder Car, 778
Wonderman, 96
Wonder Wart-Hog, 289, 694
Wonder Woman, 348, 515, 524, 541, 583, 654, 693, 816-17
Wonder Zoo, The, 426
Woody Woodpecker, 535
World of Lily Wong, The, 296-97
World Wide Weirdies, 648
Wott and Nott, 796
Wo Wang en Simmie, 616

Wrath of the Gods, 282, 686
Wulf the Briton, 282
Wuzzy Wiz, Magic is his Biz, 393
Wyatt Earp, 105, 138

X

Xalanta's Secret, 649
X-Force, 476
Xiang Gege, 269
Xiao Hou's Adventures, 528
Xiaohuzi, 694-95
Xiao Moli, 269
Xiao Peng You, 674
Xiaotu Feifei, 269
Xiaoxioing he Xiaoxiaoxiong, 269
X-1 il Pugile Misterioso, 216, 327
Xi Xiang Ji, 797
X-Men, 40, 77, 95, 171, 471-72, 568, 727, 821

Y

Yagyū Ningun, 452
Yajikita Saikou, 581
Yakyūkyō no Uta, 542
Yang Men Nu Jiang, 797
Yank and Doodle, 576
Yarmak Comics, 621
Yarrowstalks, 540
Yarzael ou la Fin des Temps, 269
Yellow Kid, The, 13, 26, 58, 62, 168, 188, 252, 590-91, 824-25
Yennie Yonson, 600
Yeux du chat, Les, 345
Yoebje en Achmed, 107, 163, 773
Yogi Bear, 809
Yojigen Sekai, 520
Yornsorn, 166
Yosemite Sam, 162
Yottsu no Hanzai, 775
You and Me, 21, 223, 666
Young Adventurers, 377
Young Allies, 434, 472, 705, 827
Youngblood, 476
Young Buffalo Bill, 161

Young King Cole, 502
Young Knight: A Tale of Medieval Times, The, 525
Young Marvelman, 96, 517, 808
Young Strongarm, the Axe Man, 346
Yoyo, 335
Yuki, 825
Yukino Taiyō, 199
Yuma Kid, 143
Yūrei Ikka, 366, 542
Yureisen, 405

Z

Zagor, 511
Zanardi, 601
Zankoku na kami ga shihai suru, 366
Zarga, Man of Mystery, 209
Zatanna, 514
Zatara, 316, 360, 361, 460
Zaviša, 123
Zeffy & Cerry, 765
Zembla, 162
Zero, 192
Zero Pilot, 520
Zibillo e l'Orso, 216
Zig et Puce, 21-22, 545, 647, 670, 829, 831
Zigfrid, 473
Zigomar, 829-30
Zi Kai Man Hua, 300
Zilzelub, 170
Zio Boris, 189, 608, 731
Zip, 801
Zip Nolan, 209
Zippy the Pinhead, 39, 359
Zodiac, 215
Zoo Film, 221
Zoo-Illogical Snapshots, 450
Zoolandia, 221
Zora, 161, 301
Zorro, 170, 458, 567, 705, 773
Zorro della Metropoli, 603
Zorry Kid, 408
Zozo, 830-31
Zrak smrti, 489
Zvitorepec, 554
ZX-5, 470

Advertising campaigns

Arabelle la Sirène (France), 98-99
Big Boy (U.S.), 131
Browne, Dik, and, 157-58
Buster Brown (U.S.), 169
Capitan Trueno, El (Spain), 178
Captain and the Kids, The (U.S.), 252
Captain Tootsie (U.S.), 120
Cavazzano, Giorgio, and, 191
Chai Rachawat, and, 194
Chanoc (Mexico), 195
Chartier, Albert, and, 197
Chesty Bond (Australia), 535
Cocco Bill (Italy), 205
Coffee Nerves (U.S.), 700
Commando Gibbs (G.B.), 125
Cossio, Carlo, and, 216
De Souza, Maurico, and, 243
Dowling, Steve, and, 267
Duke Handy (U.S.), 454
Dylan Dog (Italy), 273
Jerry on the Job (U.S.), 388
Khalid, Mohamed Nor (pseud. Lat), and, 442
Locher, Richard, and, 489
Lurchis Abenteuer (Germany), 495
Manara, Maurilio, and, 508
Mattotti, Lorenzo, and, 522
Mortadelo y Filemon (Italy), 549
Pazienza, Andrea (pseud. Traumfabrik), and, 601
Shimizu, Kiyoshi (pseud. Kiyo-chan), and, 696
Tom Poes (Netherlands), 767
Tripje en Liezebertha (Netherlands), 107, 774

Animated films

Ahiruga Oka 77 (Japan), 452
Akadō Suzunosuke (Japan), 84
Akira (Japan), 589
Alan Ford (Italy), 685
Aquaman (U.S.), 98
Ashita no Joe (Japan), 102
Astérix (France), 103
Barks, Carl, and, 111-12
Barnaby (U.S.), 113
Barney Google (U.S.), 114
Batman (U.S.), 118, 119
B.C. (U.S.), 120
Beep Beep the Road Runner (U.S.), 122
Beetle Bailey (U.S.), 123
Bell, Steve and, 124
Bergdahl, Gustav Victor, and, 126-27
Betty Boop (U.S.), 129, 309
Bevère, Maurice de (pseud. Maurice), and, 129-30

Blotta, Oscar, and, 140
Bonvicini, Franco (pseud. Bonvi), and, 144-45
Bonzo (G.B.), 145
Briggs, Clare, and, 154
Bringing Up Father (U.S.), 155
Bugs Bunny (U.S.), 162
Bülow, Bernhard-Victor von (pseud. Loriot), and, 164
Captain America (U.S.), 182
Carlson, Wallace A., and, 186
Casper (U.S.), 188-89
Cathy (U.S.), 190
Come On, Steve! (G.B.), 210
Cool McCool (U.S.), 435
Corben, Richard Vance, and, 213-14
Corto Maltese (France/Belgium), 215
Cossio, Carlo, and, 216
Courageous Cat (U.S.), 435
Craig, Chase, and, 218
Crepax, Guido, and, 221
Cubitus (Belgium), 227
Culliford, Pierre, and, 228
Cyborg 009 (Japan), 230
Daffy Duck (U.S.), 231
Damonte Taborda, Raul (pseud. Copi), and, 232
Davies, Roland (pseud. Pip), and, 236
Delac, Vladimir, and, 239
Dennis the Menace (G.B.), 242
De Souza, Maurico, and, 243
Dick Tracy (U.S.), 249
Disney, Walt, and, 253
Donald Duck (U.S.), 260-61, 744
Dovniković, Borivoj, and, 266
Dreams of the Rarebit Fiend (U.S.), 269
Du Jianguo and, 269
8-man (Japan), 277
Escobar, Josep, and, 186
Fazekas, Attila, and, 294
Feiffer, Jules, and, 296
Feign, Larry, and, 296
Felix (Sweden), 298, 491
Felix the Cat (U.S.), 299-300, 734
Fix und Foxi (Germany), 305
Flash Gordon (U.S.), 308
Fleischer, Max, and, 309
Forest, Jean-Claude, and, 313
For Better or For Worse (U.S.), 313
Fox and the Crow, The (U.S.), 315
Fred (G.B.), 704
Fritz the Cat (U.S.), 324
Garfield (U.S.), 333
Gekkō Kamen (Japan), 337
Gimenez, Juan, and, 341
Giraud, Jean (pseud. Gir), and, 345
Gordo (U.S.), 101
Gottfredson, Floyd, and, 353
Gumps, The (U.S.), 362
Gyatoruzu (Japan), 716
Hakaba no Kitarō (Japan), 367

Hanii Haniino sutekina boken (Japan), 542
Happy Hooligan (U.S.), 369
Hargreaves, Harry, and, 369-70
Harisu no Kaze (Japan), 370
Heathcliff the Cat (U.S.), 296
Heckle and Jeckle (U.S.), 378
Himitsu no Akko chan (Japan), 84
Jansson, Lars, and, 412
Jungle Tatei (Japan), 428
Kane, Robert, and, 435
Katzenjammer Kids, The (U.S.), 437
Kauka, Rolf, and, 437
Kelly, Walt, and, 438
Ketcham, Henry King, and, 441
Khalid, Mohamed Nor (pseud. Lat), and, 442
Kid Power (U.S.), 777
Kirby, Jack, and, 447
Konrad und Paul (Germany), 453
Krazy Kat (U.S.), 457
Kyojin no Hoshi (Japan), 465
Lao Ma's Adventures (China), 270
Larson, Gary, and, 468
Lehner, René (pseud. René), and, 472
Lehti, John, and, 474
Leonard, Frank (Lank), and, 474
Li'l Abner (U.S.), 479
Little Dog Guaiguai (China), 605
Little Lulu (U.S.), 486
Little Nemo in Slumberland (U.S.), 487
Lubbers, Bob (pseud. Lewis, Bob), and, 492
Lucky Luke (Belgium), 129, 493
Lupo Alberto (Italy), 495
McCay, Winsor (pseud. Silas), and, 498
by McDougall, Walter Hugh, and, 499
Mafalda (Argentina), 504
Maria D'Oro (Germany), 305
Marie Math (France), 313
Mazinger Z (Japan), 559
Mecki (Germany), 285, 525
Mickey Mouse (U.S.), 531
Mighty Hercules, The (U.S.), 474
Mighty Mouse (U.S.), 532-33
Miller, Sydney Leon, and, 534-35
Mr. Kiasu (Singapore), 540
Mizuki, Shigeru, and, 542
Monkhouse, Bob, and, 544
Moretsu Ataro (Japan), 84
Mortadelo y Filemon (Italy), 549
Mother Goose and Grimm (U.S.), 551
Munro (U.S.), 296
Muster, Miki, and, 555
Mutt and Jeff (U.S.), 556
Nausicaä of the Valley of Wind (Japan), 563
Neugebauer, Walter, and, 566-67
Nick Knatterton (Germany), 571, 679-80

Norakuro (Japan), 576
Ogon Bat (Japan), 580
Osomatsu-kun (Japan), 84, 588
Paese dei Ranocchi, Il (Italy), 664
Pa Perkins (U.S.), 734
Patoruzú (Argentina), 598
Peanuts (U.S.), 334, 602
Perishers, The (G.B.), 608
Peroni, Carl, and, 608
Pieds-Nickelés, Les (France), 616
Pip, Squeak and Wilfred (G.B.), 619
Pogo (U.S.), 623
Popeye (U.S.), 309, 755-56
Porky Pig (U.S.), 625
Procopio (Italy), 630
Professeur Nimbus, Le (France), 630
Rahan (France), 639
Rasmus Klump (Denmark), 639
Régnier, Michel (pseud. Greg), and, 647
Reiche, Volker, and, 648
Ribon no Kishi (Japan), 754
Rubino, Antonio, and, 664
Rupert (G.B.), 666
Sasuke (Japan), 676
Sazae-san (Japan), 677
Schtroumpes, Les (Belgium), 680
Silly Symphonies (U.S.), 703
Smitty (U.S.), 712
Snookums (U.S.), 567
Snowman, The (G.B.), 154
Space Angel (U.S.), 773
Space Ghost (U.S.), 722
Spawn (U.S.), 500
Sullivan, Pat, and, 734
Superman (U.S.), 309, 736, 737
Tales from the Great Book (U.S.), 474
Taliaferro, Charles Alfred, and, 744
Teenage Mutant Ninja Turtles (U.S.), 749
Tensai Bakabon (Japan), 84
Terry, Paul, and, 378
Tetsujin 28gō (Japan), 752
Tetsuwan-Atom (Japan), 753, 754
Tezuka, Osamu, and, 754
Thundercats (U.S.), 725
Tintin (Belgium), 647, 764
Tom and Jerry (U.S.), 766
Tom Poes (Netherlands), 768
Toonder, Marten, and, 768
Toppi, Sergio, and, 770
Toth, Alex, and, 773
Tumbleweeds (U.S.), 776
Upa en Apuros (Argentina), 140
Valhalla (Denmark), 787
Webster, Tom, and, 802-3
Wee Pals (U.S.), 803
Werner (Germany), 805
When the Wind Blows (G.B.), 154
White, Brian, and, 807
Wildey, Doug and, 808-9
Wildman, George, and, 809
Yokoyama, Ryûichi, and, 825
Zig et Puce (France), 829

Ballets

Krazy Kat (U.S.), 457
Mutt and Jeff (U.S.), 556
Red Detachment of Women, The (China), 642

Books

Adamson (Sweden), 77
Adolf (Japan), 79
Albertarelli, Rino, and, 86
Alice brum Brum (Italy), 521
Alphonse and Gaston (U.S.), 89-90
American Splendor (U.S.), 91
Andy Capp (G.B.), 95
Anita Diminuta (Spain), 97
Arabelle la Sirène (France), 99
Archie (U.S.), 100
Aristides, Othon (pseud. Fred), and, 613
Backer, Henk (Netherlands), 107
Banana Oil (U.S.), 109
Barbarella (France), 111-12, 313
Barbieri, Renzo, and, 111
Barks, Carl, and, 112
Barnaby (U.S.), 113
Barney Google (U.S.), 115
Barry, Lynda Jean, and, 115-16
Barry McKenzie (Australia), 116
Bateman, Henry Mayo, and, 117
Batman (U.S.), 118
B.C. (U.S.), 120
Bea, José-Maria, and, 120
Bécassine (France), 120
Beetle Bailey (U.S.), 123
Belinda Blue Eyes (G.B.), 123
Bell, Steve, and, 124
Bellamy, Frank, and, 125
Berg, David, and, 125-26
Bernard Prince (Belgium), 127
For Better or For Worse (U.S.), 313
Betty Boop (U.S.), 129
Bibi Fricotin (France), 130
Binder, Otto O. (pseud. Binder Eando), and, 134
Biro, Charles, and, 135
Blake et Mortimer (Belgium), 137
Blondie (U.S.), 139
Bobby Thatcher (U.S.), 141-42
Bob Morane (France/Belgium), 143
Bonelli, Giovanni Luigi, and, 143
Bonzo (G.B.), 145
Born Loser, The (U.S.), 148
Bouche du Diable (France/U.S.), 149
Brandoli, Anna, and, 150
Breger, David, and, 151
Briggs, Raymond, and, 154
Bringing Up Father (U.S.), 155
Bristow (G.B.), 156
Bruno Brazil (Belgium), 159
Buck Danny (Belgium), 159

Buck Rogers (U.S.), 159, 160
Bulletje en Bonestaak (Netherlands), 163
Bungle Family, The (U.S.), 165
Busch, Wilhelm, and, 167-68
Buster Brown (U.S.), 169
Byrnes, Eugene, and, 172
Calvin and Hobbes (U.S.), 174
Caniff, Milton, and, 176
Capitan Trueno, El (Spain), 178
Caprioli, Franco, and, 180
Captain America (U.S.), 182
Captain and the Kids, The (U.S.), 182
Captain Midnight (U.S.), 185
Casson, Melvin, and, 189
Cathy (U.S.), 190
Cavazzano, Giorgio, and, 191
Cellulite (France), 192
Cerebus (Canada), 192
Charlier, Jean-Michel, and, 196
Charlie's War (G.B.), 209
Chevalier Ardent (Belgium), 198
Chiba, Tetsuya, and, 199
Chlorophylle (Belgium), 199-200
Chu Teh-Yung, and, 200-201
Clive (G.B.), 205
Colonel Pewter (G.B.), 208
Come On, Steve! (G.B.), 211
Cortez, Jayme, and, 215
Corto Maltese (France/Belgium), 215
Cory, Fanny Young, and, 216
Coyote, El (Spain), 217
Craig, Chase, and, 218
Crandall, Reed, and, 220
Craveri, Sebastiano (pseud. Pin-Tin), and, 221
Crepax, Guido, and, 221
Crosby, Percy Leo, and, 222
Cruikshank, George, and, 223-24
Cubitus (Belgium), 227
Cuto (Spain), 230
Dan Dare (G.B.), 232
Dan Dunn (U.S.), 233
Davies, Roland (pseud. Pip), and, 236
Dennis the Menace (G.B.), 242
Desperate Dan (G.B.), 243-44
Dick Tracy (U.S.), 249
Dilbert (U.S.), 250
Ding Cong (pseud. Xiao Ding), and, 250-51
Doc Savage (U.S.), 257
Dodd, Edward Benton, and, 260
Don Winslow of the Navy (U.S.), 264
Doonesbury (U.S.), 264
Dot and Carrie (G.B.), 266
Drayton, Grace (pseud. Wiedersheim, Grace), and, 267-68
Dreams of the Rarebit Fiend (U.S.), 268
Dropouts, The (U.S.), 269
Druillet, Philippe, and, 269

Dumas, Gerald, and, 270
Dumm, Frances Edwina, and, 272
Dylan Dog (Italy), 273
Eek and Meek (U.S.), 276
Eisner, Will (pseud. Erwin, Will;
 Rensie, Willis), and, 278
Elfquest (U.S.), 280
Ella Cinders (U.S.), 280
Ernie (U.S.), 284
Ernsting, Volker, and, 285
Escher, Reinhold, and, 285-386
Espiègle Lili, L' (France), 286
Fabulous Furry Freak Brothers (U.S.),
 290
Famille Fenouillard, La (France), 292
Far Side, The (U.S.), 468
Fazekas, Attila, and, 294
Fearless Fosdick (U.S.), 295
Feiffer, Jules, and, 296
Feiffer (U.S.), 295
Feng Zikai, and, 300
Ferrier, Arthur, and, 302
Flash Gordon (U.S.), 308-9
Flinders, Evelyn, and, 310
Flook (G.B.), 310
Fosdyke Saga, The (G.B.), 315
Fox, Gardner, and, 316
Foxy Grandpa (U.S.), 317
Fred Basset (G.B.), 321
Frise, James Llewellyn, and, 323
Fritz the Cat (U.S.), 323
Fūten (Japan), 329
Gambols, The (G.B.), 333
Garfield (U.S.), 333
Garth (G.B.), 335
Gasoline Alley (U.S.), 336
Gaston Lagaffe (Belgium), 337
Gekkō Kamen (Japan), 337
Gibbs, Cecilia May, and, 130, 339
Girl from the People's Commune, The
 (China), 345
Globi (Switzerland), 346
Glossary of McKenzie-isms
 (Australia), 116
Golgo 13 (Japan), 350
Gomez, Pablo, and, 350
Good Times Are Killing Me, The
 (U.S.), 116
Gordo (U.S.), 352
Gross, Milton, and, 360
Gumnut Babies (Australia), 130
Gumps, The (U.S.), 362
Gurney, Alexander George, and,
 364
Happy Hooligan (U.S.), 369
Harman, Fred, and, 370
Harold Teen (U.S.), 275
Haselden, W. K., and, 372
Hayseeds (G.B.), 375
And Her Name Was Maud (U.S.), 94
Hershfield, Harry, and, 382
High Camp Superheroes (U.S.), 696
Hildebrandt, Greg and Tim, and,
 384-86

Hogarth, Burne, and, 389, 390
Hot on the Trail (China), 394
Idée Fixe du Savant, Cosinus, L'
 (France), 399
Iglesia de los Agachados (Mexico), 79
Ishimori, Shōtarō, and, 405
Jacobs, Edgar P., and, 407
Jacovitti, Benito, and, 408
Jaffee, Allan, and, 408
Jane (G.B.), 410
Jansson, Tove, and, 412
Japhet and Happy (G.B.), 413
Jimpy (G.B.), 418
Jippi der Indianerboy (Germany), 730
Jodelle (France), 418
Johnston, Lynn B., and, 423
JumpStart (U.S.), 427
Just Jake (G.B.), 429
Kabashima, Katsuichi (pseud.
 Tōfujin), and, 697
Kamui Den (Japan), 434
Kane, Robert, and, 435
Kanigher, Robert, and, 435
Kapitein Rob (Netherlands), 461-62
Kelly, Walt, and, 438
Kent, Jack, and, 440
Ketcham, Henry King, and, 441
Kewpies, The (U.S.), 584
Khalid, Mohamed Nor (pseud. Lat),
 and, 442
King Aroo (U.S.), 446
Kitazawa, Rakuten, and, 448
Kit Carson (Italy), 449
Kozure Okami (Japan), 454
Krazy Kat (U.S.), 457
Kurtzman, Harvey, and, 463
Kyojin no Hoshi (Japan), 465
Lao Ma's Adventures (China), 270
Lazarus, Mel (pseud. Mell), and,
 470
Leisk, David Johnson (pseud.
 Johnson, Crockett), and, 474
Liberatore, Gaetano (pseud.
 Liberatore, Tanino), and, 476
Life is Hell (U.S.), 476
Li'l Abner (U.S.), 479
Little Annie Fanny (U.S.), 481
Little Dog Guaiguai (China), 605
Little Iodine (U.S.), 483
Little Jimmy (U.S.), 484
Little Lulu (U.S.), 486
Little Nemo in Slumberland (U.S.),
 487
Lone Ranger, The (U.S.), 490
Lucky Luke (Belgium), 493
Lupo Alberto (Italy), 495
Lynch, Jay, and, 496
McDonnell, Patrick, and, 556
McEvoy, Joseph Patrick, and, 500
McLoughlin, Denis, and, 500-501
Madam and Eve (South Africa), 503
Mager, Charles Augustus, and, 375
Magician's Wife (France/U.S.), 149
Male Call (U.S.), 507

Manara, Maurilio, and, 508
Mary Worth (U.S.), 519
Mattotti, Lorenzo, and, 522
Maus (U.S.), 522-23, 719
Max (Belgium), 524
Mecki (Germany), 285, 525
Metropolitan Movies (Kid Cartoons)
 (U.S.), 186
Miao Di, and, 528
Michel Tanguy (France), 529
Mickey Mouse (U.S.), 531
Miss Peach (U.S.), 538
Mizuki, Shigeru, and, 542
Mizuno, Hideko, and, 542
Modesty Blaise (G.B.), 543
Momma (U.S.), 544
Moomin (Finland/G.B.), 546
Moon Mullins (U.S.), 547, 810
Mother Goose and Grimm (U.S.), 5
51
Musial, Joseph, and, 554
Mutt and Jeff (U.S.), 556
Napoleon (U.S.), 561-62
Nicholls, Sydney Wentworth, and,
 569
Nipper (G.B.), 574
Nonkina Tousan (Japan), 576
Norakuro (Japan), 576
Oberländer, Adolf, and, 579
Odd Bodkins (U.S.), 584
Okamoto, Ippei, and, 581
O-Man (Japan), 583
O'Neill, Rose Cecil, and, 584
Opper, Frederick Burr, and, 586
Oscar (Italy), 588
Oshima, Yumiko, and, 588
Our Cancer Year (U.S.), 91
Out of the Silence (Australia), 592
Out Our Way (U.S.), 592-93
Overgard, John, and, 593
Paul Temple (G.B.), 599
Peanuts (U.S.), 602
Pekka Puupää (Finland), 604
Pepito (Italy), 607
Perishers, The (G.B.), 608
Phantom, The (U.S.), 291, 612
Phoebe Zeit-Geist (U.S.), 614
Piccolo Sceriffo, Il (Italy), 614
Pieds-Nickelés, Les (France), 615-16
Pip, Squeak and Wilfred (G.B.), 619
Pogo (U.S.), 623
Polly and Her Pals (U.S.), 624
Pop (G.B.), 625
Poppo of the Popcorn Theatre (U.S.),
 135
Potters, The (U.S.), 500
Pratt, Hugo, and, 627
Prince Valiant (U.S.), 629
Private Breger (U.S.), 538-39
Professeur Nimbus, Le (France), 630
Protheroe, Glyn, and, 631
Pruneda, Salvado, and, 631
Quadratino (Italy), 635
Quincy (U.S.), 635

Raab, Fritz, and, 637
Radilović, Julio, and, 638
Ranxerox (Italy), 476
Rapela, Enrique, and, 639
Reg'lar Fellers (U.S.), 647
Régnier, Michel (pseud. Greg), and, 647
Reid, Ken, and, 648
Ric Hochet (Belgium), 651
Rick O'Shay (U.S.), 651
Ritt, William, and, 653
Robbins, Trina, and, 654
Robinson, Jerry, and, 657
Rodriguez, Emilio D., and, 659
Rowlandson, Thomas, and, 663
Sad Sack, The (U.S.), 107
Saint-Ogan, Alain, and, 670
Sam's Strip (U.S.), 673
San Mao (China), 674
Sazae-san (Japan), 677
Schtroumpes, Les (Belgium), 680
Schultheiss, Matthias, and, 682
Schulz, Charles Monroe, and, 683
Sciuscià (Italy), 684
Secchi, Luciano (pseud. Bunker, Max), and, 685
Segrelles, Vicente, and, 688
Sexton Blake (G.B.), 691
Shaw, Ernest, and, 693
Sherlock Holmes und das Geheimnis der blauen Erbse (Germany), 285
Shimizu, Kiyoshi (pseud. Kiyo-chan), and, 696
Short Ribs (U.S.), 699
Skyroads (U.S.), 709
Smitty (U.S.), 712
Smokey Stover (U.S.), 713
Snake Tales (Australia), 713
Sonoyama, Shunji, and, 716
Spider-Man (U.S.), 718
Star Wars (U.S.), 726
Strange World of Mr. Mum, The (U.S.), 730
Sturmtruppen (Italy), 731
Superman (U.S.), 736
Swinnerton, James Guilford (pseud. Guilford, James), and, 741
Sylvia (U.S.), 392
Tank McNamara (U.S.), 745
Tarzan (U.S.), 748
They'll Do It Everytime (U.S.), 755
Thimble Theater (U.S.), 755
Tillie the Toiler (U.S.), 805
Tillieux, Maurice, and, 762
Timid Soul, The (U.S.), 762-63
Tintin (Belgium), 648-49, 764
Tobias Seicherl (Austria), 766
Tom Poes (Netherlands), 767
Toonerville Folks (U.S.), 769
Töpffer, Rodolphe, and, 770
Torres, Daniel, and, 772
Trois Mousquetaires du Maquis, Les (France), 774
Trudeau, Garry, and, 775

Tumbleweeds (U.S.), 776
Up Front (U.S.), 782
Upside Downs of Little Lady Lovekins and Old Man Muffaroo, The (U.S.), 783
Valentina (Italy), 785
Valérian (Italy), 786
Vater and Sohn (Germany), 789
Virus, Il Mago della Foresta Morta (Italy), 792
Vitellini in Citta (Italy), 111
Voltar (Philippines), 793
Watchmen (U.S.), 801
Waugh, Coulton, and, 801
Web, The (U.S.), 802
Webster, Harold Tucker, and, 802
Webster, Tom, and, 803
Wee Pals (U.S.), 803
Weisinger, Mort, and, 804
Werner (Germany), 805
What the Dickens (G.B.), 155
When a Feller Needs a Friend (U.S.), 806
Where I'm Coming From (U.S.), 807
White, Brian, and, 807
Wildman, George, and, 809
Woolfolk, William, and, 819
Xiao Peng You (China), 674
Yamagami, Tatsuhiko, and, 332
Yeats, Jack B. (Ireland), and, 823
Zig et Puce (France), 829
Zippy the Pinhead (U.S.), 359

Films

Ace Drummond (U.S.), 451
Ako Si Abraham (Philippines), 163
Alan Ford (Italy), 685
Ally Sloper (G.B.), 89
Alma Grande (Mexico), 89
Anmitsu Hime (Japan), 97
Bamse (Sweden), 94
Barbarella (France), 111, 313
Barney Google (U.S.), 114
Barry McKenzie (Australia), 116
Batman (U.S.), 117-18, 385, 435
Bécassine (France), 120
Bewegte Mann, Der (Germany), 453
Bibi Fricotin (France), 130
Bidochon, Les (France), 134
Bilal, Enki, and, 131
Blackhawk (U.S.), 136
Blondie (U.S.), 138-39
Brenda Starr (U.S.), 151
Brick Bradford (U.S.), 152
Briggs, Clare, and, 154
Bringing Up Father (U.S.), 155
Bruce Gentry (U.S.), 159
Buck Rogers (U.S.), 160
Bulanadi, Danny, and, 163
Bülow, Bernhard-Victor von (pseud. Loriot), and, 164

Bushmiller, Ernest, and, 168, 561
Buster Brown (U.S.), 169
Captain America (U.S.), 182
Captain Midnight (U.S.), 185
Chai Rachawat, and, 194
Chanoc (Mexico), 195
Charlie Chan (U.S.), 195
Charlie Chaplin's Comic Capers (U.S.), and, 196
Charlier, Jean-Michel, and, 196
Cisco Kid, The (U.S.), 203
Conan (U.S.), 212
Coyote, El (Spain), 217
Crow, The (U.S.), 449
Crumb, Robert, and, 226
Declic (Italy), 508
Dennis the Menace (U.S.), 242
De Souza, Maurico, and, 243
Dick Tracy (U.S.), 249, 489
DI 13 (Philippines), 253
Disney, Walt, and, 253
Dixie Dugan (U.S.), 255
Doc Savage (U.S.), 257
Dr. Kildare (U.S.), 257
Dondi (U.S.), 262, 275
Don Fulgencio (Argentina), 263
Don Pancho Talero (Argentina), 263
Don Winslow of the Navy (U.S.), 264
Dreams of the Rarebit Fiend (U.S.), 268-69
Ella Cinders (U.S.), 280
Fabulous Furry Freak Brothers (U.S.), 290
Facéties du Sapeur Camember, Les (France), 290
Famille Fenouillard, La (France), 292
Fatty Finn (Kid Stakes) (Australia), 569
Feiffer, Jules, and, 296
Flash Gordon (U.S.), 308
Fleischer, Max, and, 309
Forest, Jean-Claude, and, 313
Fritz the Cat (U.S.), 324
Gasoline Alley (U.S.), 336
Gekkō Kamen (Japan), 337
Gimenez, Juan, and, 341
Ginesito (Spain), 343
Gohs, Rolf, and, 348
Golgo 13 (Japan), 350
Gomez, Pablo, and, 350
Gross, Milton, and, 360
Gumps, The (U.S.), 362
Hairbreadth Harry (U.S.), 366
Harold Teen (U.S.), 275, 371
Hershfield, Harry, and, 382
Hildebrandt, Greg and Tim, and, 385
Howard the Duck (U.S.), 395
James Bond (G.B.), 409
Jane (G.B.), 410
Jodorowski, Alexandro, and, 289
Joe Palooka (U.S.), 420
Judge Dredd (G.B.), 424
Jungle Jim (U.S.), 427

Kapetan Lesi (Yugoslavia), 638
Kenkoy (Philippines), 439
King of the Royal Mounted (U.S.),
   446
Kondom des Grauens (Germany),
   453
Konrad und Paul (Germany), 453
Kozure Okami (Japan), 454
   Lee, Stan, and, 472
Li'l Abner (U.S.), 479
Lindor Caovas (Argentina), 481
Little Iodine (U.S.), 483
Little Orphan Annie (U.S.), 488
Lone Ranger, The (U.S.), 490
Mandrake the Magician (U.S.), 509
   Mèziéres, Jean-Claude, and, 527
Mickey McGuire (U.S.), 769
Modesty Blaise (G.B.), 543
   Muster, Miki, and, 555
   Neels, Marc (pseud. Sleen, Marc),
      and, 564
Nick Knatterton (Germany), 571
Ninja Bugeichō (Japan), 573
   Niño, Alex N. and, 573
Nipper (G.B.), 574
Nonkina Tousan (Japan), 576
Norakuro (Japan), 576
Og (Philippines), 462
Old Doc Yak (U.S.), 582
   Oshima, Yumiko, and, 588
   Panaligan, Noly, and, 600
Paul Temple (G.B.), 599
Payo, El (Mexico), 600
Pekka Puupää (Finland), 604
Perry (Germany), 610
Phantom, The (U.S.), 291, 612
Piccolo Sceriffo, Il (Italy), 614
Pieds-Nickelés, Les (France), 616
Poo Yai Ma Kap Tung Ma Muen
   (Thailand), 194
Popeye (U.S.), 296, 756
Prince Valiant (U.S.), 629
Pu-san (Japan), 826
   Raab, Fritz, and, 637
Radio Patrol (U.S.), 638
Red Barry (U.S.), 642
Red Detachment of Women, The
   (China), 642
Red Ryder (U.S.), 645
Red Sonja (U.S.), 646
Reg'lar Fellers (U.S.), 647
Sad Sack, The (U.S.), 107, 670
   Schuiten, François, and, 680
Secret Agent X-9 (U.S.), 686
Sexton Blake (G.B.), 690
Sheena, Queen of the Jungle (U.S.),
   694
Signor Bonaventura, Il (Italy), 702
   Simmonds, Posy, and, 704
Skippy (U.S.), 707, 708
Smilin' Jack (U.S.), 710
Spawn (U.S.), 500
Spooky (U.S.), 708
Spy Smasher (U.S.), 724

Star Wars (U.S.), 725-26
Sturmtruppen (Italy), 145
Supergirl (U.S.), 735
Supermachos, Los (Mexico), 735
Superman (U.S.), 736-37, 804
Tailspin Tommy (U.S.), 744
Tarzan (U.S.), 748
Teenage Mutant Ninja Turtles (U.S.),
   749
Terry and the Pirates (U.S.), 752
Tiffany Jones (G.B.), 760
Tillie the Toiler (U.S.), 762, 805
Tim Tyler's Luck (U.S.), 764
Tintin (Belgium), 764
Toonerville Folks (U.S.), 769
Toots and Casper (U.S.), 553
   Tufts, Warren, and, 776
Werner (Germany), 805

___

Film strips

Nipper (G.B.), 574

___

Movies and Movie serials. *See* Films

Musical comedies

   Bancks, James Charles, and, 110
Blue Mountain Medley (Australia),
   110
Casey Court (G.B.), 188
Coyote, El (Spain), 217
   Khalid, Mohamed Nor (pseud. Lat),
      and, 442
Li'l Abner (U.S.), 479
Little Nemo in Slumberland (U.S.),
   487
Little Orphan Annie (U.S.), 488
Lucky Luke (Belgium), 493
Mutt and Jeff (U.S.), 556
Newlyweds, The (U.S.), 567
Peanuts (U.S.), 602
Pieds-Nickelés, Les (France), 616
Sylvia (U.S.), 392
Tumbleweeds (U.S.), 776

___

Operas

Red Detachment of Women, The
   (China), 642

___

Orchestral works

Superman (U.S.), 737

Radio ads

Buster Brown (U.S.), 169

___

Radio programs

Adolf (Japan), 79
Akadō Suzunosuke (Japan), 84
Anita Diminuta (Spain), 97
Archie (U.S.), 100, 545
Batman (U.S.), 118
Bécassine (France), 120
Billy Pack (Japan), 133
Blackhawk (U.S.), 136
Blake et Mortimer (Belgium), 137
Blue Beetle (U.S.), 140
Buck Rogers (U.S.), 160
Captain Midnight (U.S.), 184-85,
   185
Cuto (Spain), 230
Dan Dare (G.B.), 232
Date with Judy, A (U.S.), 567
Dick Tracy (U.S.), 249
Diego Valor (Spain), 249
Don Fulgencio (Argentina), 263
Don Winslow of the Navy (U.S.), 264
   Falk, Lee, and, 291
Flash Gordon (U.S.), 308
   Furtinger, Zvonimir, and, 327
Gasoline Alley (U.S.), 336
   Greene, Vernon van Atta, and, 356
   Gross, Milton, and, 360
Hairbreadth Harry (U.S.), 366
   Hershfield, Harry, and, 382
   Hicks, Reginald Ernest, and, 383
Igaguri-kun (Japan), 399
Joe Palooka (U.S.), 420
Jungle Jim (U.S.), 427
Little Orphan Annie (U.S.), 488
Lone Ranger, The (U.S.), 490
Lorenzo Jones (U.S.), 113
Mr. and Ms. (U.S.), 154
Mr. Kiasu (Singapore), 540
Moon Mullins (U.S.), 810
   Newman, Paul S., and, 568
Paul Temple (G.B.), 599
   Raab, Fritz, and, 637
Radio Patrol (U.S.), 638
Reg'lar Fellers (U.S.), 647
Rod Craig (Australia), 535
   Saint-Ogan, Alain, and, 670
Secret Agent X-9 (U.S.), 686
Shadow, The (U.S.), 691
Superman (U.S.), 736
Terry and the Pirates (U.S.), 752
Tetsujin 28gō (Japan), 752
That's My Pop (U.S.), 360
   Tufts, Warren, and, 776
Zig et Puce (France), 829

Index C
Media Index

Records

Akadō Suzunosuke (Japan), 84
Archie (U.S.), 100
Bécassine (France), 120
Bessy (Germany), 128
Blake et Mortimer (Belgium), 137
Coyote, El (Spain), 217
Crumb, Robert, and, 449
Diego Valor (Spain), 249
Familia Ulises, La (Spain), 291
Fix und Foxi (Germany), 305
Hatanosuke Hinomaru (Japan), 373
Kozure Okami (Japan), 454
Lucky Luke (Belgium), 493
Norakuro (Japan), 576
Perry (Germany), 610
Pogo (U.S.), 438
Porky Pig (U.S.), 625
Procopio (Italy), 630
Spider-Man (U.S.), 718
Taró (Germany), 747
Zig et Puce (France), 829

Songs

Akadō Suzunosuke (Japan), 84
Alley Oop (U.S.), 88
Ally Sloper (G.B), 89
Archie (U.S.), 100
Barney Google (U.S.), 114
Bécassine (France), 120
Drago (U.S.), 267
Gekkō Kamen (Japan), 337
Happy Hooligan (U.S.), 369
Hatanosuke Hinomaru (Japan), 373
Lucky Luke (Belgium), 493
Mutt and Jeff (U.S.), 556
Newman, Paul S., and, 568
Nonkina Tousan (Japan), 576
Pip, Squeak and Wilfred (G.B.), 619
Pogo (U.S.), 438

Stage plays

Bidochon, Les (France), 134
Bringing Up Father (U.S.), 155
Bristow (G.B.), 155-56, 156
Buster Brown (U.S.), 169
Casson, Melvin, and, 189
Coyote, El (Spain), 217
Craveri, Sebastiano (pseud. Pin-Tin), and, 221
Damonte Taborda, Raul (pseud. Copi), and, 232
Diego Valor (Spain), 249
by Falk, Lee, 291
by Feiffer, Jules, 296
Feiffer (U.S.), 295

Ginger Meggs (Australia), 109-10, 344
Gomez, Pablo, and, 350
Happy Hooligan (U.S.), 369
Je Ne Veux Pas Mourir Idiot (France), 815-16
Katzenjammer Kids, The (U.S.), 437
Kyojin no Hoshi (Japan), 465
Little Orphan Annie (U.S.), 488
McDougall, Walter Hugh, and, 499
McEvoy, Joseph Patrick, and, 500
Newman, Paul S., and, 568
Potters, The (U.S.), 500, 730
Red Detachment of Women, The (China), 642
Red Ryder (Belgium), 645
Sazae-san (Japan), 677
Signor Bonaventura, Il (Italy), 702
Simulatore, Il (Italy), 86
StarStruck (U.S.), 432
Sturmtruppen (Italy), 145, 731
Supermachos, Los (Mexico), 735
Superman (U.S.), 736
Tintin (Belgium), 764
Tumbleweeds (U.S.), 776
Warp (U.S), 77
When the Wind Blows (G.B.), 154
Wolinski, Georges, and, 815-16
Yeats, Jack B., and, 823
Zig et Puce (France), 829

Television

Ahiruga Oka 77 (Japan), 452
Akadō Suzunosuke (Japan), 84
Andreasson, Rune, and, 94
Anmitsu Hime (Japan), 97
Aquaman (U.S.), 98
Archie (U.S.), 100
Aristides, Othon (pseud. Fred), and, 613
Barnaby (U.S.), 113
Barney Google (U.S.), 114
Batman (U.S.), 118, 683
B.C. (U.S.), 120
Bea, José-Maria, and, 84, 120
Bell, Steve, and, 124
For Better or For Worse (U.S.), 313
Billy Pack (Japan), 133
Biro, Charles (U.S.), 134-35
Blondie (U.S.), 139
Bob Morane (France/Belgium), 143
Bonvicini, Franco (pseud. Bonvi), and, 145
Buck Rogers (U.S.), 160
Bülow, Bernhard-Victor von (pseud. Loriot), and, 164
Butschkow, Peter, and, 169
Carpanta (Spain), 186
Casson, Melvin, and, 189
Castelli, Alfredo, and, 190
Chai Rachawat, and, 194

Charlier, Jean-Michel, and, 196
Chaykin, Howard, and, 198
Cisco Kid, The (Mexico), 203
Cool McCool (U.S.), 435
Corto Maltese (France/Belgium), 215
Courageous Cat (U.S.), 435
Crepax, Guido, and, 221
Cubitus (Belgium), 227
Cyborg 009 (Japan), 230
Dennis the Menace (G.B.), 242
Dennis the Menace (U.S.), 242
De Souza, Maurico, and, 243
Dick Tracy (U.S.), 249
Diego Valor (Spain), 249
Dr. Kildare (U.S.), 257
Donald Duck (U.S.), 261
Dondi (U.S.), 262
Du Jianguo, and, 269
Facéties du Sapeur Camember, Les (France), 290
Fantastic Four, The (U.S.), 809
Feign, Larry, and, 296
Felix (Sweden), 298, 491
Felix the Cat (U.S.), 299
Flash Gordon (U.S.), 308
Fleischer, Max, and, 309
Forest, Jean-Claude, and, 313
Furtinger, Zvonimir, and, 327
Garfield and Friends (U.S.), 333-34
Gekkō Kamen (Japan), 337
Globi (Switzerland), 346
Golgo 13 (Japan), 350
Gomez, Pablo, and, 350
Green Hornet (U.S.), 357
Hairbreadth Harry (U.S.), 366
Hakaba no Kitarō (Japan), 367
Hanii Haniino sutekina boken (Japan), 542
Hargreaves, Harry, and, 370
Heathcliff the Cat (U.S.), 296
Herculoids, The (U.S.), 809
Hulk (U.S.), 397
Jansson, Lars, and, 412
Joe Palooka (U.S.), 420
Johnny Quest (U.S.), 808-9
Jungle Jim (U.S.), 427
Jungle Tatei (Japan), 428
Kane, Robert, and, 435
Kappa no Kawatarō (Japan), 696
Kato, Yoshirou, and, 436
Kid Power (U.S.), 777
Konrad und Paul (Germany), 453
Kozure Okami (Japan), 454
Lao Ma's Adventures (China), 270
Leav, Mort, and, 471
Lee, Stan, and, 472
Lehner, René (pseud. René), and, 472
Liberatore, Gaetano (pseud. Liberatore, Tanino), and, 476
Little Dog Guaiguai (China), 605
Lois Lane (U.S.), 490
Lööf, Jan, and, 491
Lucky Luke (Belgium), 129

Lupo Alberto (Italy), 495
Mafalda (Argentina), 504
Marie Math (France), 313
Marvel Super-Heroes (U.S.), 809
Mecki (Germany), 525
Michel Tanguy (France), 529
Mighty Mighter, The (U.S.), 809
Mighty Mouse (U.S.), 533
Miss Peach (U.S.), 538
Monkhouse, Bob, and, 545
Mother Goose and Grimm (U.S.), 551
Muster, Miki, and, 555
Oshima, Yumiko, and, 588
Osomatsu-kun (Japan), 588
Panahon (Philippines), 350
Paul Temple (G.B.), 599
Peanuts (U.S.), 602
Perishers, The (G.B.), 608
Peroni, Carl, and, 608
Pogo (U.S.), 623
Poo Yai Ma Kap Tung Ma Muen
(Thailand), 194
Popeye (U.S.), 756
Procopio (Italy), 630
Quark (Denmark), 787
Raab, Fritz, and, 637
Rahan (France), 639

Rasmus Klump (Denmark), 639
Régnier, Michel (pseud. Greg), and,
647
Reiche, Volker, and, 648
Rupert (G.B.), 666
Saint-Ogan, Alain, and, 670
Sazae-san (Japan), 677
Schmidt, Manfred, and, 680
Schtroumpes, Les (Belgium), 680
Schulz, Charles Monroe, and, 683
Sexton Blake (G.B.), 691
Shaw, Ernest, and, 693
Sheena, Queen of the Jungle (U.S.),
694
Simmonds, Posy, and, 704
Simpsons, The (U.S.), 115, 478
Space Angel (U.S.), 773
Space Ghost (U.S.), 722
Steve Canyon (U.S.), 728
Sturmtruppen (Italy), 731
Sub-Mariner, The (U.S.), 809
Superman (U.S.), 490, 736, 737, 804
Teenage Mutant Ninja Turtles (U.S.),
749
Tenpei Tenma (Japan), 750
Terry and the Pirates (U.S.), 752
Tetsujin 28gō (Japan), 752

Tetsuwan-Atom (Japan), 753, 754
Tezuka, Osamu, and, 754
Thunderbirds (G.B.), 125
Thundercats (U.S.), 725
Tidy, Bill, and, 315
Tintin (Belgium), 647
Tom Poes (Netherlands), 768
Toth, Alex, and, 773
Tufts, Warren, and, 776
Tumbleweeds (U.S.), 776
Valentina (Italy), 785
Wee Pals (U.S.), 803
Wildey, Doug, and, 808-9
Wonder Woman (U.S.), 817
Woolfolk, William, and, 819
Young, Murat (Chic) and, 827

Videos

Dennis the Menace (G.B.), 242
Laswell, Fred, and, 470
Mr. Kiasu (Singapore), 540
Nick Knatterton (Germany), 571

Auad, Manuel

Alcala, Alfredo P., 86-87
Redondo, Nestor, 644-45
Santos, Malang (pseud. Malang), 675

Blackbeard, Bill

A. Piker Clerk, 97-98
Abie the Agent, 76
Ahern, Gene, 80-81
Alphonse and Gaston, 89-90
Anderson, Carl Thomas, 91-92
Arriola, Gus, 101
Baker, George, 107-8
Banana Oil, 109
Barks, Carl, 111-12
Barney Google, 114
Beck, Frank Hem, 121
Bobby Thatcher, 141-42
Boob McNutt, 145-46
Breger, David, 150-51
Bungle Family, The, 164-65
Bunky, 165
Bushmiller, Ernest, 168
Buster Brown, 168-69
Buz Sawyer, 169-70
Capp, Al, 179-80
Carter, Augustus Daniels, 187
Casey Ruggles, 188
Charlie Chaplin's Comic Capers, 196
Cicero's Cat, 201-2
Count Screwloose of Tooloose, 216-17
Crane, Royston Campbell, 220
Crosby, Percy Leo, 222-23
Dan Dunn, 232-33
Danny Dingle, 233
Dave's Delicatessen, 236
De Beck, Billy, 238
Desperate Desmond, 244
Dingbat Family, The, 251
Donald Duck, 260-61
Dorgan, Thomas Aloysius, 264-65
Dumb Dora, 271
Dwiggins, Clare Victor, 272-73
Ed, Carl Frank Ludwig, 275
Edson, Gus, 275-76
Ella Cinders, 280-81
Elmer, 281-82
Fearless Fosdick, 294-95
Fisher, Hammond Edward, 303-4
Fisher, Harry Conway, 304-5
Fox, Fontaine Talbot, Jr., 316
Foxy Grandpa, 317
Freckles and His Friends, 320
Freyse, Bill, 322
Fung, Paul, 326
Gasoline Alley, 335-37
Goldberg, Reuben Lucius, 348-49
Gordo, 351-52
Gottfriedson, Floyd, 353

Gray, Harold, 355
Gross, Milton, 360
Gumps, The, 362
Happy Hooligan, 368-69
Harold Teen, 370-71
Hatlo, James, 373-74
Hawkshaw the Detective, 374-75
And Her Name Was Maud, 93-94
Herriman, George, 380-81
Hershfield, Harry, 381-82
Hoban, Walter C., 388
Jerry on the Job, 414-15
Joe Palooka, 420
Johnson, Ferd, 422-23
Kewpies, The, 441-42
Krazy Kat, 457
Lance, 467-68
Leonard, Frank, 474-75
Li'l Abner, 478-79
Link, Stanley J., 481
Little Annie Rooney, 481-83
Little Bears and Tykes, 483
Little Jimmy, 483-84
Little Joe, 484
Mager, Charles Augustus, 504
Mager's Monks, 504-5
Main Street, 505-6
McBride, Clifford, 497
McEvoy, Joseph Patrick, 500
Mickey Finn, 531
Mickey Mouse, 531-32
Mike and Ike, 533
Moon Mullins, 546-47
Mr. and Mrs., 538
Mr. Breger, 538-39
Mr. Jack, 539-40
Murphy, James Edward, 552-54
Mutt and Jeff, 555-56
Nancy, 560-61
Napolean, 561-62
Nibsy the Newsboy, 568-69
Nize Baby, 575
Old Doc Yak, 582
O'Neill, Rose Cecil, 584
Opper, Frederick Burr, 585-86
Our Boarding House, 589-90
Outcault, Richard Felton, 590-91
Out Our Way, 592-93
Panhandle Pete, 595-96
Peter Rabbit, 611
Phil Hardy, 613-14
Polly and Her Pals, 623-24
Room and Board, 660
Rosie's Beau, 662
Sappo, 675
Schultze, Carl Edward, 682-83
Segar, Elzie Crisler, 687
Silly Symphonies, 702-3
Smith, Robert Sidney, 711-12
Smitty, 712
Spooky, 721-22
Sterrett, Cliff, 727
Striebel, John H., 730
Sweeney and Son, 739-40

Swinnerton, James Guilford (pseud. Guilford, James), 740-41
Texas Slim and Dirty Dalton, 753
They'll Do It Everytime, 755
Thimble Theater, 755-56
Timid Soul, The, 762-63
Toonerville Folks, 768-69
Toots and Casper, 769-70
Turner, Leslie, 776-77
Tuthill, Harry J., 778-79
Up Front, 782
Vanilla and the Villians, 789
Wash Tubbs, 799-800
Webster, Harold Tucker, 802
Westover, Russell, 805-6
When a Feller Needs a Friend, 806
White Boy, 808
Willard, Frank Henry, 809-10
Williams, James Robert, 810-11
Yellow Kid, The, 824-25

Bono, Gianni

Akim, 84-85
Alan Ford, 85-86
Albertarelli, Rino, 86
Amok, 91
Asso di Picche, 102-3
Barbieri, Renzo, 111
Battaglia, Dino, 118
Bilbolbul, 132
Billy Bis, 132
Bonelli, Giovanni Luigi, 143
Bonvicini, Franco (pseud. Bonvi), 144-45
Bottaro, Luciano, 148-49
Bufalo Bill (Italy), 161
Buffolente, Lina, 162
Buzzelli, Guido, 170
Caesar, Kurt (pseud. Avai, Cesare; Away, Caesar), 173
Canale, Antonio, 175
Capitan L'Audace, 176
Capitan Miki, 176-77
Caprioli, Franco, 180
Castelli, Alfredo, 189-90
Chendi, Carlo, 198
Cimpellin, Leone, 202-3
Cocco Bill, 205
Commissario Spada, Il, 211
Craveri, Sebastiano (pseud. Pin-Tin), 221
Cuore Garibaldino, 228
Diabolik, 245
Dottor Faust, Il, 266
Forza, John, 314
Furio Almirante, 327
Gim Toro, 342
Gino e Gianni, 344
Isabella, 404-5
Jacovitti, Benito, 408
Kinowa, 446-47
Kit Carson, 449

Kriminal, 459
Liberty Kid, 476
Mani in Alto!, 509-10
Marmittone, 513-14
Misterix, 539
Moroni-Celsi, Guido (pseud. Sterny), 548-49
Narciso Putiferio, 562
Oscar, 587-88
Pantera Bionda, 596-97
Pecos Bill, 602-3
Pedrito El Drito, 603
Pepito, 606-7
Peroni, Carlo, 608
Piccolo Sceriffo, Il, 614
Pier Cloruro De'Lambicchi, 616
Pippo, 618
Principe Azzurro, 629
Procopio, 630
Quadratino, 635
Rebuffi, Giorgio, 642
Redipicche, 644
Rocky Rider, 658
Roland Eagle, 659
Romano Il Legionario, 659-60
Rubino, Antonio, 664
Saturna Contro la Terra, 676-77
Sciuscià, 683-84
Serafino, 688-89
Signor Bonaventura, Il, 701-2
Soldino, 715
Sor Pampurio, 717-18
SturmTruppen, 731
Superbone, 734
Texas Willer, 753-54
Tiramolla, 764-65
Valentina Melaverde, 785-86
Virus, Il Mago della Foresta Morta, 792

Brancatelli, Joe

Adams, Neal, 77
Adam Strange, 78
Airboy, 81
Amazing Man, 90
Anderson, Murphy, 92
Angel, The, 95
Aquaman, 98
Archie, 99-100
Avengers, The, 104
Ayers, Richard, 104-5
Beck, Charles Clarence, 120-21
Berg, David, 125-26
Binder, Jack, 133
Binder, Otto O. (pseud. Binder Eando), 133-34
Biro, Charles, 134-35
Black Cat, 135
Black Condor, 135-36
Blackhawk, 136
Black Hood, 136-37
Black Terror, 137

Blue Beetle, 140
Blue Bolt, 140-41
Boring, Wayne (pseud. Harmon, Jack), 147-48
Boy Commandos, 149
Briefer, Richard, 152-53
Bulletman, 164
Burgos, Carl, 166
Buscema, John, 166-67
Captain America, 180-82
Captain Marvel, 182-84
Captain Marvel Jr., 184
Captain Midnight, 184-85
Captain Wings, 185
Cat-Man, The, 190-91
Colan, Eugene (pseud. Austin, Adam), 206
Cole, Jack (pseud. Johns, Ralph), 206
Conan, 211-12
Corben, Richard Vance, 213-14
Craig, John, 219
Crandall, Reed, 219-20
Crimebuster, 222
Crowley, Wendell, 223
Daredevil, 233-34
Davis, Jack, 236-37
Ditko, Steve, 253-54
Doc Savage, 256-57
Doctor Strange, 259-60
Doll Man, 260
Dr. Fate, 257
Dr. Mid-Nite, 258-59
Elder, William W., 278
Elias, Leopold, 280
Evans, George, 286-87
Everett, Bill (pseud. Blake, Everett; Blake, William), 287
Fabulous Furry Freak Brothers, 289-90
Feldstein, Albert, 297
Fighting Yank, 302
Fine, Louis, 303
Finger, Bill, 303
Fox, Gardner (pseud. Cooper, Jefferson; Somers, Bart), 316-17
Frankenstein, 317-18
Frazetta, Frank, 319-20
Fritz the Cat, 323-24
Gaines, William M., 331-32
Giordano, Richard, 344
Goodwin, Archie (pseud. Franklin Robert), 351
Green Arrow, 355-56
Green Hornet, 356-57
Guardineer, Frederic, 360-61
Gustafson, Paul (pseud. Earrol, Paul), 364
Hangman, The, 368
Hawkman, 374
Heap, The, 376
Heath, Russell, 377-78
Hercules, 379-80
Herron, France Edward, 381

Hulk, The, 396-97
Human Torch, The, 397-98
Ibis the Invincible, 399
Iger, Sumeul Maxwell, 400
Infantino, Carmine, 400-401
Ingels, Graham (pseud. Ghastly), 401-2
Jaffee, Allan, 408
Jimmy Olsen, 417-18
Johnny Thunder, 422
Justice Society of America, 430
Kane, Gil (pseud. Edward, Scott; Kane, Al; Stack, Gil), 434
Kane, Robert, 434-35
Kanigher, Robert, 435
Kida, Fred, 443-44
King, Frank O., 445
Kirby, Jack, 447-48
Kitchen, Denis, 449-50
Krigstein, Bernard, 458-59
Kubert, Joe, 459-61
Kurtzman, Harvey, 462-63
Leav, Mort, 470-71
Lee, Stan, 472
Little Annie Fanny, 481
Lois Lane, 489-90
Lynch, Jay, 496
Marston, William Moulton (pseud. Moulton, Charles), 515
Mary Marvel, 518
Mayer, Sheldon, 524-25
Meskin, Morton (pseud. Morton, Mort, Jr.), 526-27
Montana, Bob, 545-46
Mr. Natural, 540-41
Mr. Scarlet, 541
Mr. Terrific, 541-42
Newsboy Legion, 568
O'Neil, Dennis, 583
O'Neill, Dan, 583-84
Orlando, Joe, 587
Phantom Lady, 612-13
Phanton, The, 612
Plastic Man, 621-22
Powerhouse Pepper, 626
Raboy, Emanuel, 637
Robinson, Jerry, 656-57
Romita, John, 660
Sandman, 673-74
Schaffenberger, Kurt (pseud. Wahl, Lou), 678
Schwartz, Julius, 683
Severin, John Powers, 690
Shadow, The, 691-92
Sheena, Queen of the Jungle, 693-94
Shelton, Gilbert, 694
Shield, The, 695-96
Shuster, Joe, 699-700
Siegel, Jerome, 701
Silver Surfer, 704
Simon, Joseph, 704-5
Sinnott, Joe, 705
Spectre, The, 718
Spider-Man, 718-19

Spy Smasher, 723-24
Starman, 724-25
Star Spangled Kid, 725
Steel Sterling, 726
Steranko, James, 726-27
Sub-Mariner, The, 731-32
Superman, 735-37
Supersnipe, 737
Tarzan, 748
Thomas, Roy, 756
Thor, 756-57
Vampirella, 787
Web, The, 801-2
Weisinger, Mort, 804
Williamson, Al, 811
Wolverton, Basil, 816
Wonder Woman, 816-17
Wood, Wallace, 818
Woolfolk, William, 818-20
Young Allies, 827

Calhoun, Mary Beth

For Better or For Worse, 312-13
JumpStart, 426-27

Coma, Javier

Bea, José-Maria, 120
Fernandez, Fernando, 301
Gimenez, Carlos, 341
Gimenez, Juan, 341
Muñoz, José, 552
Segrelles, Vicente, 687-88
Solano López, Francisco, 714-15
Torres, Daniel, 771-72

Crouch, Bill, Jr.

Brigman, June, 154
Craft, Jerry, 218
Curtis, 228-29
Dave, 235-36
Fusco Brothers, The, 327-28
Herb & Jamaal, 379
Hildebrandt, Greg and Tim, 384-86
Kudzu, 461
Locher, Richard, 489
Mallard Fillmore, 507
Moose Miller, 547-48
Motley's Crew, 551-52
Mutts, 556
Old Glory Story, The, 582
Ormes, Jackie, 587
Over the Hedge, 593-94
Rose is Rose, 661-62
Sally Forth, 672-73
Shoe, 697-98
Springer, Frank, 722-23

Surburban Cowgirls, 732-33
Where I'm Coming From, 806-7
Wildman, George, 809
Wilshire, Mary, 811-12

Cuccolini, Giulio Cesare

Brandoli, Anna, 150
Cavazzano, Giorgio, 191
De Luca, Gianni, 240-41
Dylan Dog, 273
Eleuteri Serpieri, Paolo, 278-79
Giardino, Vittorio, 338-39
Ken Parker, 439-40
Liberatore, Gaetano (pseud. Tanino), 475-76
Lupo Alberto, 494-95
Manara, Maurilio, 507-8
Martin Mystere, 516-17
Mattotti, Lorenzo, 521-22
Micheluzzi, Attilio (pseud. Bajeff, Igor Artz), 530-31
Nathan Never, 562
Nizzi, Claudio, 575
Pazienza, Andrea, 600-601
Raviola, Roberto (pseud. Magnus), 639-41
Toppi, Sergio, 770-71

Evanier, Mark

Aragonés, Sergio, 99
Beep Beep the Road Runner, 122
Bugs Bunny, 162-63
Casper, 188-89
Craig, Chase, 218-19
Daffy Duck, 231
Fox and the Crow, The, 315-16
Ghost Rider, 337-38
Heckle and Jeckle, 378
Iron Man, 403-4
Little Lulu, 485-86
Mighty Mouse, 532-33
Porky Pig, 625
Rawhide Kid, 641
Sgt. Fury, 689
Sgt. Rock, 689-90
Stanley, John, 724
Taliaferro, Charles Alfred, 744
Thunder Agents, 758-59
Tom and Jerry, 766-67
Toth, Alexander, 773
Wildey, Doug, 808-9

Fuchs, Wolfgang

Aasnes, Håkon, 75
Adamson, 77
Alfredo, 87

Andersson, Oskar Emil (pseud. O. A.), 93
Andrax, 94
Andreasson, Rune, 94
Argonautjes, De, 100
Atlan, 103-4
Backer, Henk, 107
Becker, Franziska, 121-22
Bergdahl, Gustav Victor, 126-27
Bessy, 128
Brammetje Bram, 149-50
Broos, Piet, 156-57
Buffalo Bill (Germany), 161-62
Bulletje en Bonestaak, 163
Bülow, Bernhard-Victor von (pseud. Loriot), 163-64
Busch, Wilhelm, 167-68
Butschkow, Peter, 169
Capitan Terror, 177-78
Detektive Schmidtchen, 244-45
Dick Bos, 246
Dr. Merling, 258
Dzjengis Khan, 273
Eisele und Beisele, 277
Elworth, Lennart, 282
Engholm, Kaj, 282-83
Eric de Noorman, 283
Ernsting, Volker, 285
Escher, Reinhold, 285-86
Felix, 297-99
Ferd'nand (Denmark), 300-301
Fix und Foxi, 305-6
47:an Löken, 314
Fuchs, Erika, 324-25
Fünf Schreckensteiner, Die, 325-26
Globi, 346
Gohs, Rolf, 348
Hartog van Banda, Lo, 372
Jacobsson, Oscar, 407-8
Jansson, Lars, 412
Jansson, Tove, 412
Jimmy das Gummipferd, 417
Kalenbach, Dieter, 431-32
Kapitein Rob, 435
Kappie, 435-36
Kauka, Rolf, 437-38
Klotjohan, 450
Kohlsaat, Roland, 451
König, Ralf, 452-53
Koning Hollewijn, 453-54
Kraaienhove, 454-57
Kresse, Hans G., 457-58
Krüger, Hans Martin (pseud. Martin, Hans), 459
Kuhn, Pieter Joseph, 461-62
Kulafu, 462
Larsen, Knud V., 468
Lehner, René (pseud. René), 472-73
Lilla Fridolf, 479
Lille Rickard och hans Katt, 479-80
Lööf, Jan, 490-91
Looman, Jos, 491
Lupo, 493-94
Lurchis Abenteuer, 495

Mannen som gör vad som faller honom in, 510
Matena, Dick, 519-20
Max und Moritz, 524
Mecki, 525
Michel, 528-29
Mike Macke, 533-34
Milton, Freddy, 535
Mystiska 2:an, 557-58
Neels, Marc (pseud. Sleen, Marc), 564
Nero, 566
Neugebauer, Walter, 566-67
Nick der Weltraumfahrer, 569-70
Nickel, Helmut, 570
Nick Knatterton, 571-72
91 Karlsson, 572
Oberländer, Adolf, 579
Ohser, Erich (pseud. Plauen, E. O.), 580-81
Palacio, Lino (pseud. Flax), 595
Panda, 595
Pekka Puupää, 603-4
Perry, 609-10
Piët, Frans, 616
Professor Pi, 630-31
Putzker, Ronald, 632-33
Raab, Fritz, 637
Rasmus Klump, 639
Reiche, Volker, 647-48
Richter-Johnsen, Friedrich-Wilhelm, 651
Robinson, 655-56
Robot Imperium, 657
Roscher, Franz, 660-61
Roy Tiger, 663-64
Rudi, 664-65
Scheuer, Chris, 678
Schmidt, Manfred, 678-80
Schultheiss, Matthias, 681-82
Sigurd, 702
Sjors en Sjimmie, 706-7
Stups, 730-31
Suske en Wiske, 737-38
Swarte, Joost, 738-39
Taró, 746-47
Tibor, 759-60
Tobias Seicherl, 765-66
Tom Poes, 767-68
Tony Falco, 768
Toonder, Marten, 768
Tripje en Liezenbertha, 773-74
Valhalla, 786-87
Vandersteen, Willy, 788-89
Vater and Sohn, 789-90
Vidocq, 792
Wäscher, Hansrudi, 798-99
Werner, 805
Winnetou, 813

Gasea, Luis

Agachados, Los, 79
Aghardi, 79
Alma Grande, 89
Anibal 5, 96
Anita Diminuta, 96-97
Aspirino y Colodion, 102
Battaglia, Roberto, 118
Bea, José-Maria, 120
Blasco, Jesus, 137-38
Blotta, Oscar, 140
Breccia, Alberto, 150
Capitan Misterio, El, 177
Capitan Trueno, El, 178-79
Carpanta, 186
Chanoc, 195
Chatillo y Federico, 197
Cifre, Guillermo, 202
Cinco por Infinito, 203
Ciocca, Walter, 203
Conti, Oscar (pseud. Oski), 213
Coyote, El, 217
Cuto, 229-30
Damonte Taborda, Raul, 232
Del Castillo, Arturo, 239
Delta 99, 239-40
Diego Valor, 249
Divito, Guillermo, 254-55
Doctor Merengue, El, 257-58
Doctor Niebla, 259
Don Berrinche, 261-62
Don Fulgencio, 262-63
Don Pancho Talero, 263
Ernie Pike, 284-85
Eternauta, El, 286
Fabulus Panicas, 289
Fallutelli, 291
Familia Burron, La, 291
Familia Ulises, La, 291
Fantomas, 293
Figueras, Alfonso, 302
Florita, 310-11
Ginesito, 342-43
Gringo, 359-60
Guerilleros, Les, 361
Guerrero del Antifaz, El, 361-62
Haxtur, 375
Hernan el Corsario, 380
Ianiro, Abel, 399
Inspector Dan, El, 402
Jabato, El, 407
Jim Erizo, 416
Lavado, Joaquin (pseud. Quino), 470
Lavinia 2.016, 470
Lindor Caovas, 480-81
Macaco, 497
Mafalda, 503-4
Mangucho y Meneca, 509
Manos Kelly, 511
Mari Aguirre, 512
Maroto, Esteban, 514
Mordillo, Guillermo, 548

Mortadelo y Filemon, 549
Mort Cinder, 549
Negro Raul, El, 564-65
Nus, 577
Patoruzú, 597-98
Payo, El, 600
Pistol Jim, 619-20
Rapela, Enrique, 639
Roberto Alcazar y Pedrín, 654-55
Sadhú, 669
Sherlock Lopez, 695
Silver Roy, 703
Sorang, 717
Supergirl, 734-35
Supermachos, Los, 735

Gerson, Robert

Kaluta, Michael Wm., 432-33

Gifford, Denis

Airy Alf and Bouncing Billy, 83
Ally Sloper, 88-89
Andy Capp, 95
Anglo, Mick, 95-96
Banger, Edgar Henry, 110
Barry McKenzie, 116
Bateman, Henry Mayo, 116-17
Baxendale, Leo, 118-19
Belinda Blue Eyes, 123
Bell, Steve, 123-24
Bell, Walter, 124-25
Bellamy, Frank, 125
Billy Bunter, 132-33
Bonzo, 145
Booth, Walter, 146-47
Bristow, 155-56
Brown, Bertie, 157
Browne, Tom, 158
Buck Ryan, 160-61
Burgon, Sid, 166
Carter, Reg, 187
Casey Court, 187-88
Clive, 204-5
Cocking, Percy (pseud. Daw, Jack), 205-6
Colonel Pewter, 208
Colquhoun, Joe, 208-9
Come On, Steve!, 210-11
Dan Dare, 232
Davies, Roland (pseud. Pip), 236
Dennis the Menace (G.B.), 241-42
Derickson Denie, 242-43
Desperate Dan, 243-44
Diamond, H. Louis, 245-46
Dot and Carrie, 265-66
Dowling, Steve, 266-67
Embleton, Ronald S., 282
Ferrier, Arthur, 301-2
Flinders, Evelyn, 309-10
Flook, 310

Flutters, The, 311
Fosdyke Saga, The, 314-15
Foxwell, Herbert, 317
Fred Basset, 320-21
Gambols, The, 332-33
Garth, 334-35
Glass, Jack, 345-46
Gloops, 346-47
Gunnis, Louis, 362-63
Hampson, Frank, 368
Hargreaves, Harry, 369-70
Haselden, W. K., 372
Hayseeds, 375
Heath, George, 377
Hill, Albert, 386
Hogg, Gordon (pseud. Gog), 390
Holdaway, James, 391
Holmes, Fred, 393
Holroyd, Bill, 393
James Bond, 408-10
Jane, 410
Japhet and Happy, 412-13
Jeff Hawke, 413-14
Jimpy, 418
Judge, Malcolm (pseud. Mal), 424
Jukes, John L., 426
Just Jake, 428-29
Keyhole Kate, 442
Larks, The, 468
Lord Snooty and His Pals, 491-92
Marvelman, 517-18
McClelland, Hugh, 498-99
McLoughlin, Denis, 500-501
McNeill, Hugh, 502
Minnitt, Frank, 536
Modesty Blaise, 543
Monk, Jack, 544
Monkhouse, Bob, 544-45
Moomin, 546
Nipper, 574
Nixon, Robert, 574-75
Oor Wullie, 585
Our Ernie, 590
Pansy Potter, 596
Paul Temple, 599
Perishers, The, 608
Perrot, Reg, 608-9
Pip, Squeak and Wilfred, 618-19
Pitch and Toss, 620
Pop, 624-25
Price, Cyril (pseud. Gwynne, Kim, and Spike), 628
Protheroe, Glyn, 631
Reid, Ken, 648
Reynolds, Basil, 650
Robinson, Fred, 656
Rob the Rover, 657
Ruggles, 665
Rupert, 665-66
Scarth, 677-78
Seekers, The, 686-87
Sexton Blake, 690-91
Shaw, Ernest, 693
Stonehenge Kit the Ancient Brit, 729

Teddy Tail, 748-49
Telestrip, 750
Tiffany Jones, 760
Tiger Tim, 760-61
Turner, Ron, 778
Wakefield, George William, 795-96
Walker, Brian, 796-97
Ward, Norman, 798
Weary Willie and Tired Tim, 801
Webster, Tom, 802-3
White, Brian, 807
White, Hugh Stanley, 808
Wilson, Roy, 812
Yeats, Jack B., 823

Gravett, Paul

Briggs, Raymond, 154
Judge Dredd, 424
Simmonds, Posy, 704

Harris, Peter

Bloom County, 139-40
Dingle, Adrian (pseud. Darian), 251-52
Freelance, 321-22
Frise, James Llewellyn, 322-23
Nelvana of the Northern Lights, 565
Penguin, The, 606
Rex Baxter, 649

Hongying Liu-Lengyel

Ding Cong (pseud. Xiao Ding), 250-51
Duan Jifu, 269-70
Du Jianguo, 269
Feng Zikai, 300
He Youzhi, 375-76
Liao Bingxiong, 475
Miao Di, 527-28
Peng Guoliang, 605
San Mao, 674
Shen Pei, 694-95
Su Lang, 733-34
Wang Shuhui, 797
Wang Xiansheng He Xiao Chen, 797-98
Yue Xiaoying, 827

Horn, Maurice

Achille Talon, 76-77
Adams, Neal, 77
Adolf, 78-79
Airboy, 81
Airship Man, The, 82-83

Alack Sinner, 85
Alix l'Intrépide, 87
Alley Oop, 88
Andriola, Alfred (pseud. James, Alfred), 94-95
Apartment 3-G, 97
Arabelle la Sirène, 98-99
Aragonés, Sergio, 99
Archie, 100
Arman en Ilva, 100-101
Astérix, 103
Atom, The, 104
Avengers, The, 104
Ayers, Richard, 105
Bald, Kenneth (pseud. Bruce, K.), 108
Ballata del Mare Salato, Una, 108
Banana Fish, 108-9
Barbarella, 110-11
Barks, Carl, 112
Barney Baxter, 113-14
Barney Google, 115
Barry, Daniel, 115
Barry, Seymour, 116
Batman, 117-18
B.C., 119-20
Bécassine, 120
Beetle Bailey, 123
Bernard Prince, 127
Berndt, Walter, 127
Berrill, Jack, 127-28
Bess, Gordon, 128
Betty, 128-29
Betty Boop, 129
Bevère, Maurice de (pseud. Maurice), 129-30
Bibi Fricotin, 130
Big Ben Bolt, 131
Big Boy, 131
Bilal, Enki, 131-32
Binet, Christian, 134
Blackhawk, 136
Blake et Mortimer, 137
Blondie, 138-39
Blosser, Merrill, 140
Blue Sea and Red Heart, 141
Bob Morane, 142-43
Boner's Ark, 144
Boots and Her Buddies, 147
Boucq, François, 149
Branner, Martin, 150
Brenda Starr, 151-52
Brick Bradford, 152
Briggs, Austin, 153
Bringing Up Father, 154-55
Brinkerhoff, Robert Moore, 155
Bronc Peeler, 156
Broom Hilda, 156
Browne, Dik, 157-58
Bruce Gentry, 158-59
Bruno Brazil, 159
Buck Danny, 159
Buck Rogers, 159-60
Buscema, John, 167

Butze Oliver, German, 169

Buz Sawyer, 170

Byrne, John, 170-71

Byrnes, Eugene, 171-72

Calkins, Richard, 173

Calvin and Hobbes, 173-74

Calvo, Edmond-François, 174-75

Caniff, Milton, 175-76

Capitaine Fantôme, Le, 176

Cap Stubbs and Tippie, 180

Captain America, 182

Captain and the Kids, The, 182

Carlson, Wallace A., 186

Carr, Eugene, 186

Carreño, Albert, 186-87

Casson, Melvin, 189

Cellulite, 192

Cerebus, 192

Cézard, Jean, 192-93

Chaland, Yves, 194-95

Charlie Chan, 195-96

Charlier, Jean-Michel, 196

Chartier, Albert, 196-97

Chaykin, Howard, 197-98

Chevalier Ardent, 198

Chlorophylle, 199-200

Christman, Bert, 200

Chupamirto, 201

Cisco Kid, The, 203

Classics Illustrated, 204

Colomb, Georges (pseud. Christophe), 206-8

Colonel Potterby and the Duchess, 208

Comanche, 209

Comés, Didiet, 211

Conan, 212

Connie, 212-13

Corben, Richard Vance, 214

Corentin, 214

Corto Maltese, 215

Cory, Fanny Young, 215-16

Cossio, Carlo, 216

Craenhals, François (pseud. Hals, F.), 217-18

Crepax, Guido, 221-22

Cruikshank, George, 223-24

Crumb, Robert, 224-26

Cruse, Howard, 226-27

Cubitus, 227

Cucciolo, 227-28

Culliford, Pierre, 228

Curley Harper, 228

Daredevil, 234

Dateline: Danger!, 234-35

Davis, Phil, 237-38

Démon de Caraïbes, Le, 241

Dennis the Menace (U.S.), 242

Dickenson, Fred, 246

Dick Fulmine, 246-47

Dickie Dare, 247

Dick's Adventures in Dreamland, 247-48

Dick Tracy, 248-49

Dinglehoofer und His Dog Adolph, 252

Dirks, Rudolph, 252-53

Disney, Walt, 253

Ditko, Steve, 254

Dixie Dugan, 255

Doc Savage, 257

Doctor Strange, 260

Dodd, Edward Benton, *260*

Donald Duck, 261

Don Dixon and the Hidden Empire, 262

Don Winslow of the Navy, 263-64

Doonesbury, 264

Dr. Kildare, 257

Drago, 267

Drayton, Grace (pseud. Wiedersheim, Grace), 267-68

Dreams of the Rarebit Fiend, 268-69

Dropouts, The, 269

Druillet, Philippe, 269

Dumas, Gerald, 270

Dumas, Jacques (pseud. François, Jacques; Marijac), 270-71

Eek and Meek, 276

Eisner, Will (pseud. Erwin, Will; Rensie, Willis), 277-78

Elfquest, 279-80

Ernst, Kenneth, 285

Espiègle Lili, L', 286

Etta Kett, 286

Fabulous Furry Freak Brothers, 290

Facéties du Sapeur Camember, Les, 290

Falk, Lee, 290-91

Famille Fenouillard, La, 292

Fantastic Four, The, 292-93

Feiffer, 295

Feiffer, Jules, 295-96

Feininger, Lyonel, 297

Felix the Cat, 299-300

Fils de Chine, 302-3

Flamingo, 306

Flanders, Charles, 306-7

Flash, 307-8

Flash Gordon, 308-9

Fleischer, Max, 309

Flyin' Jenny, 311

Footrot Flats, 311-12

Forest, Jean-Claude (pseud. Valherbe, Jean), 313

Forton, Louis, 313-14

Foster, Harold, 315

Frankenstein, 318

Franquin, André, 318-19

Fredericks, Harold, 321

Friday Foster, 322

Futuropolis, 329

Gai Luron, 331

Garfield and Friends, 333-34

Gascard, Gilbert (pseud. Tibet), 335

Gaston Lagaffe, 337

Ghost Rider, 338

Gillain, John (pseud. Jijé), 339

Gillray, James, 339-40

Gimpel Beinish the Matchmaker, 341-42

Giraud, Jean (pseud. Gir), 345

Girl from the People's Commune, The, 345

Godwin, Francis, 347-48

Gonick, Larry, 350-51

Goodwin, Archie, 351

Gordon, Soldier of Fortune, 352

Goscinny, René, 352-53

Gould, Chester, 353-54

Gould, Will, 354

Graff, Mel, 354

Gray, Clarence, 354-55

Green Arrow, 356

Green Hornet, 357

Green Lantern, 357-59

Guerre à la Terre, 361

Haenigsen, Harry, 365

Hairbreadth Harry, 366

Hamlin, Vincent, 367-68

Harman, Fred, 370

Hart, Johnny, 371-72

Hasen, Irwin, 372-73

Held, John, Jr. (pseud. Held, Myrtle), 378

Henry, 378-79

Herzog, Guy (pseud. Bara), 382

Hess, Sol, 382-83

Hidalgo, Francisco (pseud. Roy, Yves), 384

Histoires en Estampes, 387-88

Hoest, Bill, 388-89

Hogarth, Burne, 389-90

Hogarth, William, 390

Holman, Bill, 392-93

Hot on the Trail, 393-94

Howard the Duck, 394-95

Hubinon, Victor, 396

Huppen, Hermann (pseud. Hermann), 398

Hurtubise, Jacques (pseud. Zyx), 398

Idée Fixe du Savant Cosinus, L', 399

Infantino, Carmine, 401

Inspector Wade, 402-3

Invisible Scarlet O'Neil, 403

Iron Man, 404

Irving, Jay, 404

Jacobs, Edgar-Pierre, 407

Jean des Flandres, 413

Jerry Spring, 415

Jim Boum, 415-16

Jim Hardy, 416-17

Jodelle, 418

Joe and Asbestos, 419

Joe Jinks, 419-20

Johnny Hazard, 420-22

Johnny-Round-the-World, 422

Jonah Hex, 423-24

Judge Wright, 426

Jungle Jim, 427

Justice League of America, 429-30

Just Kids, 429
Kahles, Charles William, 431
Katzenjammer Kids, The, 436-37
Keaton, Russell, 438
Kelly, Walt, 438
Kerry Drake, 440
Ketcham, Henry King, 440-41
Kin-der-Kids, The, 444-45
King of the Royal Mounted, 446
Knerr, Harold H., 450
Knight, Clayton, 451
Laborne, Daniel, 467
Lasswell, Fred, 469-70
Lazarus, Mel (pseud. Mell), 470
Lee, Jim, 471-72
Lee, Stan, 472
Liefeld, Rob, 476
Lieutenant Blueberry, 476-77
Little Annie Fanny, 481
Little Iodine, 483
Little Nemo in Slumberland, 486-87
Little Orphan Annie, 488
Lois Lane, 490
Lone Ranger, The, 490
Lubbers, Robert (pseud. Lewis,
    Bob), 492
Lucky Luke, 492-93
Lynde, Stan, 496
Male Call, 506-7
Mandrake the Magician, 508-9
Manning, Russell, 510-11
Marcello, Raffaelo Carlo (pseud.
    Marc, Ralph), 511
Maroto, Esteban, 514
Mary Worth, 518-19
Master of Kung Fu, 519
Maus, 522-23
Max, 523-24
Maxon, Rex, 524
McCay, Winsor (pseud. Silas),
    497-98
McClure, Darrell, 499
McFarlane, Todd, 500
McManus, George, 501-2
McWilliams, Alden, 502-3
Medieval Castle, The, 525
Melouah, Sid Ali, 525-26
Messick, Dale, 527
Mézières, Jean-Claude, 527
Michel Tanguy, 529
Michel Vaillant, 529-30
Mickey Mouse, 532
Miller, Frank (1898-1949), 534
Miller, Frank (1957-   ), 534
Ming Foo, 535-36
Miss Fury, 537
Miss Peach, 537-38
Molino, Walter, 543
Monsieur Poche, 545
Moore, Alan (pseud. Vile, Curt),
    547
Musial, Joseph, 554
Myers, Russell, 556-57
Myra North, 557

Nagai, Gō, 559
'Nam, 560
Natacha, 562
Naylor, Robert, 563-64
Nebbs, The, 564
Newlyweds, The, 567
Newman, Paul S., 567-68
New Mutants, The, 568
Norris, Paul, 576-77
Nowlan, Philip, 577
Oesterheld, Hector German, 579-80
O'Keefe, Neil, 581-82
O'Neal, Frank, 583
O'Neill, Dan, 584
Otomo, Katsuhiro, 588-89
Outland, 591-92
Patsy, 598
Patterson, Russell, 598-99
Peanuts, 601-2
Pedrocchi, Federico, 603
Pellos, René, 604-5
Pension Radicelle, La, 606
Père Ladébauche, Le, 607-8
Pete the Tramp, 611
Pfeufer, Carl, 611
Phanton, The, 611-12
Philémon, 613
Phoebe Zeit-Geist, 614
Pichard, Georges, 614
Pieds-Nickelés, Les, 615-16
Pif le Chien, 616-17
Pinchon, Jean-Pierre, 617
Pinky Rankin, 617-18
Pionniers de l'Espérance, Les, 618
Placid et Muzo, 621
Pogo, 622-23
Poïvet, Raymond, 623
Poncho Libertas, 624
Pratt, Hugo, 627
Prince Valiant, 628-29
Professeur Nimbus, Le, 630
Pruneda, Salvado, 631
Quincy, 635
Radio Patrol, 638
Raymond, Alex, 641
Rayomondo o Cangaceiro, 641
Red Barry, 642
Red Detachment of Women, The,
    642-43
Redeye, 643-44
Red Knight, The, 644
Red Ryder, 645
Red Sonja, 646
Régnier, Michel (pseud. Greg,
    Albert, Louis), 647
Rémi, Georges (pseud. Hergé),
    648-49
Ric Hochet, 650-51
Rick O'Shay, 651
Rip Kirby, 651-53
Ritt, William, 653
Robbins, Frank, 653
Robbins, Trina, 653-54
Robin Hood and Company, 655

Rosinski, Grzegorz, 662-63
Rowlandson, Thomas, 663
Russell, Clarence D., 666
Rusty Riley, 666-67
Ryan, Tom K., 667
Saga de Xam, 670
Saint-Ogan, Alain, 670
Salinas, José K., 671-72
Saunders, Allen, 677
Schtroumpes, Les, 680
Schuiten, François, 680-81
Schulz, Charles Monroe, 683
Scorchy Smith, 684-85
Secchi, Luciano (pseud. Bunker,
    Max), 685
Secret Agent X-9, 685-86
Shadow, The, 692-93
Short Ribs, 698-99
Sickles, Noel, 700-701
Si Yeoo Ki, 706
Skippy, 707-8
Skyroads, 708-9
Smilin' Jack, 710
Smokey Stover, 712-13
Snake Tales, 713
Spiegelman, Arthur, 719-20
Spiegle, Dan, 720
Spirit, The, 720-21
Spirou, 721
Sprang, Richard, 722
On Stage, 584-85
Star Wars, 725-26
Steve Canyon, 727-28
Stony Craig of the Marines, 729-30
Strange World of Mr. Mum, The, 730
Sullivan, Pat, 734
Superman, 737
Swamp Thing, 738
Tailspin Tommy, 743-44
Talbot, Bryan, 744
Tank McNamara, 745
Tanku Tankurō, 745
Tardi, Jacques, 745-46
Tarzan, 747-48
Ted Towers, 749
Teenage Mutant Ninja Turtles,
    749-50
Terrors of the Tiny Tads, 750-51
Terry and the Pirates, 751-52
Thimble Theater, 756
Thomas, Roy, 756
Thorne, Frank, 757-58
Tiger, 760
Tillie the Toiler, 761-62
Tim Tyler's Luck, 763-64
TinTin, 764
Töpffer, Rodolphe, 770
Torpedo 1936, 771
Trois Mousquetaires du Maquis, Les,
    774
Trudeau, Garry, 775
Tumbleweeds, 776
Turner, Morrie, 777-78
Turok, Son of Stone, 778

Uderzo, Albert, 781
Ulysse, 781-82
Upside Downs of Little Lady Lovekins and Old Man Muffaroo, The, 782-83
Valentina, 785
Valérian, 786
Vampirella, 787
Vance, William, 788
Velter, Robert (pseud. Dathel, J.; Rob-Vel), 790-91
Verbeck (a.k.a. Verbeek), Gustave, 791
Vic Jordan, 791
Walker, Addison Mortimer (pseud. Addison), 796
Watchmen, 800-801
Waugh, Coulton, 801
Wee Pals, 803
Wee Willie Winkie's World, 804
Wildey, Doug, 809
Williamson, Al, 811
Winnie Winkle, 813-14
Wizard of Id, The, 814
Wolinski, Georges, 814-16
Wonder Woman, 817
Wood, Robin, 818
X-Men, 821
Young, Lyman, 826
Young, Murat, 826-27
Zig et Puce, 829
Zozo, 830-31

Horn, Pierre L.

Cathy, 190
Dilbert, 249-50
Funky Winkerbean, 326-27
Momma, 543-44
Mother Goose and Grimm, 550-51
Scott, Jerry (pseud. Kirkman, Rick), 685

Ivkov, Slobodan

Janković, Djordje, 411-12
Kuznjecov, Konstantin, 464-65
Lehner, Sebastijan, 473
Lobačev, Jurij (Djordje) (pseud. Strip, George), 488-89
Marković, Momcilo-Moma, 512
Solovjev, Sergej (pseud. Gey, Moum; Solo, S), 715-16

Janocha, Bill

Born Loser, The, 148
Davis, Jim, 237
Ernie, 284

Garfield, 333
Johnston, Lynn B., 423
Larson, Gary, 468
Peter Piltdown, 610
Skeets, 707
Slylock Fox and Comics for Kids, 709-10

Jundis, Orvy

Aguila, Dani, 79-80
Bulandi, Danny, 163
DI 13, 253
Gomez, Pablo S., 350
Indio, El, 400
Jodloman, Jess M., 418-19
Kenkoy, 438-39
Magsino, Frank, 505
Malaya, 506
Martin, Menny Eusobio, 516
Niño, Alex N., 573-74
Payaso, 599-600
Reggie, 646
Rodriguez, Emilio D., 658-59
Santos, Jessie F., 674-75
Siopawman, 705-6
Tagisan Ng Mga Agimat, 743
Torres, Elpidio, 772-73
Voltar, 793

Kato, Hisao

Akadō Suzunosuke, 83-84
Akatsuka, Fujio, 84
Anmitsu Hime, 97
Ashita no Joe, 101-2
Billy Pack, 133
Bōken Dankichi, 143
Chiba, Tetsuya, 198-99
Chikaino Makyû, 199
Cyborg 009, 230
Daiheigenji, 231
8-man, 276-77
Fuku-chan, 325
Fushigina Kuni no Putchā, 328
Fûten, 328-29
Gaki Deka, 332
Gekkō Kamen, 337
Golgo 13, 349-50
Hakaba no Kitarō, 366-67
Harisu no Kaze, 370
Hatanosuke Hinomaru, 373
Hi no Tori, 386-87
Hirata, Hiroshi, 387
Hokusai, Katsushika, 390-91
Igaguri-kun, 399
Ishimori, Shōtarō, 405
Jungle Tatei, 427-28
Kamui Den, 433-34
Kato, Yoshirou, 436

Kawanabe, Gyōsai (Shuransairaisu), 438
Kibaō, 442-43
Kitzawa, Rakuten, 448-49
Kobayashi, Kiyochika, 451
Kojima, Goseki, 452
Kojima, Koo, 452
Kozure Okami, 454
Kuwata, Jirō, 463-64
Kyojin no Hoshi, 465
Matsumoto, Reiji, 520-21
Misuki, Shigeru, 542
Mizushima, Shinji, 542
Nagagutsu no Sanjûshi, 559
Nagashima, Shinji, 559-60
Ninja Bugeichō, 572-73
Nonkina Tousan, 575-76
Norakuro, 576
Ogon Bat, 580
Okamoto, Ippei, 581
O-Man, 582-83
Osomatsu-kun, 588
Robot Santōhei, 657
Sabaku no Maō, 669
Saitō, Takao, 670-71
Sasuke, 675-76
Sazae-san, 677
Shimizu, Kon, 696
Shirato, Sanpei, 696-97
Shōchan no Bōken, 697
Shōnen Oja, 698
Sonoyama, Shunji, 716-17
Speed Tarō, 718
Sugiura, Shigeru, 733
Tenpei Tenma, 750
Tetsujin 28gō, 752
Tetsuwan-Atom, 752-53
Tezuka, Osamu, 754-55
Todano Bonji, 766
Tsuge, Yoshiharu, 775
Tsukioka, Yoshitoshi, 775-76
Utagawa, Kuniyoshi, 783
Yokoyama, Ryûichi, 825-26
Yokoyama, Taizō, 826

Lent, John A.

Bun Lour Sarn, 165-66
Chai Rachawat, 193-94
Chu Teh-Yung, 200-201
Djon Domino, 255-56
Feign, Larry, 296-97
Khalid, Mohamed Nor (pseud. Lat), 442
Kim Song Hwan, 444
Madam and Eve, 503
Mr. Kiasu, 540
Pai, Anant, 595
Perera, Camillus, 607
Pran Kumar Sharma, 626-27
Satonaka, Machiko, 676
Shwe Min Thar, 700
Tokai, 766

Wong, Tony, 817-18
Wroblewski, Jerzy, 820
Yeh Hung Chia, 823-24

Marschall, Richard

Abbie an'Slats, 75-76
Anderson, Lyman, 92
Barnaby, 112-13
Beetle Bailey, 122-23
Big Ben Bolt, 130-31
Boner's Ark, 143-44
Briggs, Clare, 153-54
Caplin, Elliot, 179
Carey, Ed, 185-86
Casson, Melvin, 189
Celardo, John (pseud. Lardo, John C.), 191-92
Dallis, Nicholas, 231-32
Dondi, 262
Drake, Stanley, 267
Dumas, Gerald, 270
Dumm, Frances Edwina, 271-72
Ferd'nand (U.S.), 301
Fletcher, Frank, 309
Fuller, Ralph Briggs, 325
Greene, Vernon van Atta, 356
Hägar the Horrible, 365-66
Half-Hitch, 367
Heart of Juliet Jones, The, 376-77
Hi and Lois, 383
Howarth, F. M., 395
Hubert, 395-96
Jane Arden, 411
Judge Parker, 424-26
Kent, Jack, 440
Kevin the Bold, 441
King Aroo, 445-46
Kotzky, Alex, 454
Lehti, John, 473-74
Leisk, David Johnson (pseud. Johnson, Crockett), 474
Little King, The, 484-85
Little Orphan Annie, 487-88
Little People, The, 488
Long Sam, 490
Lulu and Leander, 493
Mark Trail, 512-13
Marriner, William, 514-15
Martin, Edgar Everett, 515-16
McDougall, Walter Hugh, 499
Minute Movies, 536-37
Mosley, Zack, 549-50
Mr. Abernathy, 538
Muggs and Skeeter, 552

Murphy, John Cullen, 554
Oaky Doaks, 579
Overgard, William Thomas, 593
Ozark Ike, 594
Parker, Brant, 597
Payne, Charles M., 600
Prentice, John, 627-28
Prince Errant, 628
Pussycat Princess, 631-32
Reg'lar Fellers, 646-47
Rex Morgan, M.D., 649-50
Sad Sack, The, 669-70
Sam's Strip, 673
Slim Jim, 709
Smith, Al, 710-11
Soglow, Otto, 713-14
Starr, Leonard, 725
Steve Roper, 728-29
Van Buren, Raeburn, 787-88
Vic Flint, 791
Voight, Charles A., 792-93
Wags, the Dog that Adopted a Man, 795
Walker, Addison Mortimer (pseud. Addison), 796
Wellington, Charles H., 804-5
Wheelan, Edgar, 806
Winner, Charles H., 812-13
Winterbotham, Russell (pseud. Bond, J. Harvey), 814
Wunder, George, 820

Moya, Alvaro de

Aizen, Adolfo, 83
Cortez, Jayme, 215
De Souza, Maurico, 243

Rubovszky, Kalman

Chmielewski, Henryk Jerzy (pseud. Chimel), 200
Fazekas, Attila, 294
Kasprzak, Zbigniew (pseud. Kas), 436
Zorad, Ernö, 830

Rustemagić, Ervin

Beker, Žarko, 123
Delač, Vladimir, 238-39

Dobrić, Milorad, 256
Dovniković, Borivoj, 266
Furtinger, Zvonimir, 327
Herlock Sholmes, 380
Maurović, Andrija, 522
Muster, Miki, 554-55
Radilović, Julio, 637-38
Svirčić, Zdenko, 738
Tillieux, Maurice, 762
Tufts, Warren, 776

Ryan, John Thomas

Air Hawk and the Flying Doctors, 81-82
Bancks, James Charles, 109-10
Bib and Bub, 130
Bluey and Curley, 141
Cross, Stanley George, 223
Dixon, John Dangar, 255
Fatty Finn, 293-94
Gibbs, Cecilia May, 339
Ginger Meggs, 343-44
Gurney, Alexander George, 363-64
Hicks, Reginald Ernest (pseud. Hix), 383-84
Miller, Sydney Leon, 534-35
Nicholls, Sydney Wentworth, 569
Out of the Silence, 592
Pitt, Stanley John, 620-21
Potts, The, 625-26
Rod Craig, 658
Russell, James Newton, 666
Silver Starr in the Flame World, 703-4
Wally and the Major, 797

Thorn, Mattew Allen

Hagio, Moto, 366
Maison Ikkoku, 506
Mizuno, Hideko, 542
Nausicaä of the Valley of Wind, 562-63
Oshima, Yumiko, 588

Wepman, Dennis

American Splendor, 90-91
Barry, Lynda Jean, 115-16
Hollander, Nicole, 391-92
Life in Hell, 477-78

Algeria

Melouah, Sid Ali, 525-26

Argentina

Alack Sinner, 85
Battaglia, Roberto, 118
Blotta, Oscar, 140
Ciocca, Walter, 203
Conti, Oscar (pseud. Oski), 213
Dan Dare, 232
Divito, Guillermo, 254-55
Doctor Merengue, El, 257-58
Don Fulgencio, 262-63
Don Pancho Talero, 263
Ernie Pike, 284-85
Eternauta, El, 286
Fallutelli, 291
Hernan el Corsario, 380
Ianiro, Abel, 399
Lavado, Joaquin (pseud. Quino),
 470
Lindor Caovas, 480-81
Mafalda, 503-4
Mangucho y Meneca, 509
Mordillo, Guillermo, 548
Mort Cinder, 549
Muñoz, José, 552
Negro Raul, El, 564-65
Oesterheld, Hector German, 579-80
Palacio, Lino (pseud. Flax), 595
Patoruzú, 597-98
Rapela, Enrique, 639
Salinas, José K., 671-72
Solano López, Francisco, 714-15
Wood, Robin, 818

Australia

Air Hawk and the Flying Doctors,
 81-82
Bancks, James Charles, 109-10
Bib and Bub, 130
Bluey and Curley, 141
Crowley, Wendell, 223
Dixon, John Dangar, 255
Fatty Finn, 293-94
Ginger Meggs, 343-44
Miller, Sydney Leon, 534-35
Nicholls, Sydney Wentworth, 569
Out of the Silence, 592
Pitt, Stanley John, 620-21
Potts, The, 625-26
Rod Craig, 658
Russell, James Newton, 666
Silver Starr in the Flame World,
 703-4
Snake Tales, 713
Wally and the Major, 797

Austria

Putzker, Ronald, 632-33
Scheuer, Chris, 678
Tobias Seicherl, 765-66

Bangladesh

Tokai, 766

Belgium

Alix l'Intrépide, 87
Bernard Prince, 127
Bessy, 128
Bevère, Maurice de (pseud.
 Maurice), 129-30
Blake et Mortimer, 137
Bob Morane, 142-43
Bruno Brazil, 159
Buck Danny, 159
Chaland, Yves, 194-95
Charlier, Jean-Michel, 196
Chevalier Ardent, 198
Chlorophylle, 199-200
Comanche, 209
Commissario Spada, Il, 211
Corentin, 214
Corto Maltese, 215
Craenhals, François (pseud. Hals,
 F.), 217-18
Cubitus, 227
Culliford, Pierre, 228
Franquin, André, 318-19
Gascard, Gilbert (pseud. Tibet), 335
Gaston Lagaffe, 337
Gillain, John (pseud. Jijé), 339
Guerilleros, Les, 361
Herzog, Guy (pseud. Bara), 382
Hubinon, Victor, 396
Huppen, Hermann (pseud.
 Hermann), 398
Jacobs, Edgar-Pierre, 407
Jean des Flandres, 413
Jerry Spring, 415
Lucky Luke, 492-93
Max, 523-24
Michel Vaillant, 529-30
Nathan Never, 562
Neels, Marc (pseud. Sleen, Marc),
 564
Nero, 566
Régnier, Michel (pseud. Greg,
 Albert, Louis), 647
Rémi, Georges (pseud. Hergé),
 648-49
Ric Hochet, 650-51
Rosinski, Grzegorz, 662-63
Schtroumpes, Les, 680
Schuiten, François, 680-81
Spirou, 721

Suske en Wiske, 737-38
Tillieux, Maurice, 762
TinTin, 764
Vance, William, 788
Vandersteen, Willy, 788-89
Zozo, 830-31

Brazil

Aizen, Adolfo, 83
Cortez, Jayme, 215
De Souza, Maurico, 243
Rayomondo o Cangaceiro, 641

Burma

Shwe Min Thar, 700

Canada

Byrne, John, 170-71
Cerebus, 192
Chartier, Albert, 196-97
Dingle, Adrian (pseud. Darian),
 251-52
Freelance, 321-22
Frise, James Llewellyn, 322-23
Hurtubise, Jacques (pseud. Zyx),
 398
Johnston, Lynn B., 423
Nelvana of the Northern Lights, 565
Penguin, The, 606
Père Ladébauche, Le, 607-8
Rex Baxter, 649
Robin Hood and Company, 655

Chile

Del Castillo, Arturo, 239

China

Blue Sea and Red Heart, 141
Ding Cong (pseud. Xiao Ding),
 250-51
Duan Jifu, 269-70
Du Jianguo, 269
Feng Zikai, 300
Girl from the People's Commune, The,
 345
He Youzhi, 375-76
Hot on the Trail, 393-94
Liao Bingxiong, 475
Miao Di, 527-28
Peng Guoliang, 605

Red Detachment of Women, The, 642-43
San Mao, 674
Shen Pei, 694-95
Si Yeoo Ki, 706
Su Lang, 733-34
Wang Shuhui, 797
Wang Xiansheng He Xiao Chen, 797-98
Yue Xiaoying, 827

Denmark

Alfredo, 87
Dr. Merling, 258
Engholm, Kaj, 282-83
Felix, 297-99
Ferd'nand, 300-301
Larsen, Knud V., 468
Milton, Freddy, 535
Rasmus Klump, 639
Valhalla, 786-87

Finland

Jansson, Lars, 412
Jansson, Tove, 412
Moomin, 546
Pekka Puupää, 603-4

France

Achille Talon, 76-77
Alack Sinner, 85
Arabelle la Sirène, 98-99
Astérix, 103
Barbarella, 110-11
Bécassine, 120
Bibi Fricotin, 130
Bilal, Enki, 131-32
Binet, Christian, 134
Bob Morane, 142-43
Boucq, François, 149
Calvo, Edmond-François, 174-75
Capitan L'Audace, 176
Cellulite, 192
Cézard, Jean, 192-93
Colomb, Georges (pseud. Christophe), 206-8
Corto Maltese, 215
Démon de Caraïbes, Le, 241
Druillet, Philippe, 269
Dumas, Jacques (pseud. François, Jacques; Marijac), 270-71
Espiègle Lili, L', 286
Facéties du Sapeur Camember, Les, 290
Famille Fenouillard, La, 292
Fils de Chine, 302-3

Forest, Jean-Claude (pseud. Valherbe, Jean), 313
Forton, Louis, 313-14
Futuropolis, 329
Gai Luron, 331
Giraud, Jean (pseud. Gir), 345
Goscinny, René, 352-53
Guerre à la Terre, 361
Idée Fixe du Savant, Cosinus, L', 399
Jim Boum, 415-16
Jodelle, 418
Laborne, Daniel, 467
Lieutenant Blueberry, 476-77
Mézières, Jean-Claude, 527
Michel Tanguy, 529
Monsieur Poche, 545
Pellos, René, 604-5
Pension Radicelle, La, 606
Philémon, 613
Pichard, Georges, 614
Pieds-Nickelés, Les, 615-16
Pif le Chien, 616-17
Pinchon, Jean-Pierre, 617
Pionniers de l'Espérance, Les, 618
Placid et Muzo, 621
Poïvet, Raymond, 623
Poncho Libertas, 624
Professeur Nimbus, Le, 630
Rahan, 638-39
Saga de Xam, 670
Saint-Ogan, Alain, 670
Tardi, Jacques, 745-46
Trois Mousquetaires du Maquis, Les, 774
Uderzo, Albert, 781
Ulysse, 781-82
Valérian, 786
Velter, Robert (pseud. Dathel, J.; Rob-Vel), 790-91
Wolinski, Georges, 814-16
Zig et Puce, 829

Germany

Andrax, 94
Atlan, 103-4
Becker, Franziska, 121-22
Bessy, 128
Buffalo Bill, 161-62
Bülow, Bernhard-Victor von (pseud. Loriot), 163-64
Busch, Wilhelm, 167-68
Butschkow, Peter, 169
Capitan Terror, 177-78
Detektive Schmidtchen, 244-45
Eisele und Beisele, 277
Ernsting, Volker, 285
Escher, Reinhold, 285-86
Fix und Foxi, 305-6
Fuchs, Erika, 324-25
Fünf Schreckensteiner, Die, 325-26
Jimmy das Gummipferd, 417
Kalenbach, Dieter, 431-32

Kauka, Rolf, 437-38
Kohlsaat, Roland, 451
König, Ralf, 452-53
Krüger, Hans Martin (pseud. Martin, Hans), 459
Lupo, 493-94
Lurchis Abenteuer, 495
Max und Moritz, 524
Mecki, 525
Michel, 528-29
Mike Macke, 533-34
Nick der Weltraumfahrer, 569-70
Nickel, Helmut, 570
Nick Knatterton, 571-72
Oberländer, Adolf, 579
Ohser, Erich (pseud. Plauen, E. O.), 580-81
Perry, 609-10
Raab, Fritz, 637
Reiche, Volker, 647-48
Richter-Johnsen, Friedrich-Wilhelm, 651
Robinson, 655-56
Robot Imperium, 657
Roscher, Franz, 660-61
Roy Tiger, 663-64
Rudi, 664-65
Schmidt, Manfred, 678-80
Schultheiss, Matthias, 681-82
Sigurd, 702
Stups, 730-31
Taró, 746-47
Tibor, 759-60
Vater and Sohn, 789-90
Wäscher, Hansrudi, 798-99
Werner, 805
Winnetou, 813

Great Britain

Airy Alf and Bouncing Billy, 83
Ally Sloper, 88-89
Andy Capp, 95
Anglo, Mick, 95-96
Banger, Edgar Henry, 110
Barry McKenzie, 116
Bateman, Henry Mayo, 116-17
Baxendale, Leo, 118-19
Belinda Blue Eyes, 123
Bell, Steve, 123-24
Bell, Walter, 124-25
Bellamy, Frank, 125
Billy Bunter, 132-33
Bonzo, 145
Booth, Walter, 146-47
Briggs, Raymond, 154
Bristow, 155-56
Brown, Bertie, 157
Browne, Tom, 158
Buck Ryan, 160-61
Burgon, Sid, 166
Carter, Reg, 187

Casey Court, 187-88
Clive, 204-5
Cocking, Percy (pseud. Daw, Jack), 205-6
Colonel Pewter, 208
Colquhoun, Joe, 208-9
Come On, Steve!, 210-11
Cruikshank, George, 223-24
Damonte Taborda, Raul, 232
Davies, Roland (pseud. Pip), 236
Dennis the Menace, 241-42
Derickson Denie, 242-43
Desperate Dan, 243-44
Diamond, H. Louis, 245-46
Dot and Carrie, 265-66
Dowling, Steve, 266-67
Embleton, Ronald S., 282
Ferrier, Arthur, 301-2
Flinders, Evelyn, 309-10
Flook, 310
Flutters, The, 311
Fosdyke Saga, The, 314-15
Foxwell, Herbert, 317
Fred Basset, 320-21
Gambols, The, 332-33
Garth, 334-35
Gibbs, Cecilia May, 339
Gillray, James, 339-40
Gloops, 346-47
Gunnis, Louis, 362-63
Gurney, Alexander George, 363-64
Hampson, Frank, 368
Hargreaves, Harry, 369-70
Haselden, W. K., 372
Hayseeds, 375
Heath, George, 377
Hicks, Reginald Ernest (pseud. Hix), 383-84
Hill, Albert, 386
Hogarth, William, 390
Hogg, Gordon (pseud. Gog), 390
Holdaway, James, 391
Holmes, Fred, 393
Holroyd, Bill, 393
Howarth, F. M., 395
James Bond, 408-10
Jane, 410
Japhet and Happy, 412-13
Jeff Hawke, 413-14
Jimpy, 418
Judge, Malcolm (pseud. Mal), 424
Judge Dredd, 424
Jukes, John L., 426
Just Jake, 428-29
Keyhole Kate, 442
Larks, The, 468
Lord Snooty and His Pals, 491-92
Marriner, William, 514-15
Marvelman, 517-18
McLoughlin, Denis, 500-501
McNeill, Hugh, 502
Minnitt, Frank, 536
Modesty Blaise, 543
Monk, Jack, 544

Monkhouse, Bob, 544-45
Moomin, 546
Moore, Alan (pseud. Vile, Curt), 547
Nipper, 574
Nixon, Robert, 574-75
Oor Wullie, 585
Our Ernie, 590
Pansy Potter, 596
Paul Temple, 599
Perishers, The, 608
Perrot, Reg, 608-9
Pip, Squeak and Wilfred, 618-19
Pitch and Toss, 620
Pop, 624-25
Price, Cyril (pseud. Gwynne, Kim, and Spike), 628
Protheroe, Glyn, 631
Reid, Ken, 648
Reynolds, Basil, 650
Robinson, Fred, 656
Rob the Rover, 657
Rowlandson, Thomas, 663
Ruggles, 665
Rupert, 665-66
Scarth, 677-78
Seekers, The, 686-87
Sexton Blake, 690-91
Shaw, Ernest, 693
Simmonds, Posy, 704
Stonehenge Kit the Ancient Brit, 729
Talbot, Bryan, 744
Teddy Tail, 748-49
Telestrip, 750
Tiffany Jones, 760
Tiger Tim, 760-61
Turner, Ron, 778
Wakefield, George William, 795-96
Walker, Brian, 796-97
Ward, Norman, 798
Weary Willie and Tired Tim, 801
Webster, Tom, 802-3
White, Brian, 807
White, Hugh Stanley, 808
Wilson, Roy, 812

Hong Kong

Wong, Tony, 817-18

Hungary

Fazekas, Attila, 294
Zorad, Ernö, 830

India

Pai, Anant, 595
Pran Kumar Sharma, 626-27

Indonesia

Djon Domino, 255-56

Ireland

Yeats, Jack B., 823

Italy

Akim, 84-85
Alack Sinner, 85
Alan Ford, 85-86
Albertarelli, Rino, 86
Amok, 91
Asso di Picche, 102-3
Ballata del Mare Salato, Una, 108
Barbieri, Renzo, 111
Battaglia, Dino, 118
Bilbolbul, 132
Billy Bis, 132
Bonelli, Giovanni Luigi, 143
Bonvicini, Franco (pseud. Bonvi), 144-45
Bottaro, Luciano, 148-49
Brandoli, Anna, 150
Bufalo Bill, 161
Buffolente, Lina, 162
Buzzelli, Guido, 170
Caesar, Kurt (pseud. Avai, Cesare; Away, Caesar), 173
Canale, Antonio, 175
Capitaine Fantôme, Le, 176
Capitan Miki, 176-77
Caprioli, Franco, 180
Castelli, Alfredo, 189-90
Cavazzano, Giorgio, 191
Chendi, Carlo, 198
Cimpellin, Leone, 202-3
Cocco Bill, 205
Comés, Didiet, 211
Cossio, Carlo, 216
Craveri, Sebastiano (pseud. Pin-Tin), 221
Crepax, Guido, 221-22
Cucciolo, 227-28
Cuore Garibaldino, 228
De Luca, Gianni, 240-41
Diabolik, 245
Dick Fulmine, 246-47
Dottor Faust, Il, 266
Dylan Dog, 273
Eleuteri Serpieri, Paolo, 278-79
Forza, John, 314
Furio Almirante, 327
Giardino, Vittorio, 338-39
Gim Toro, 342
Gino e Gianni, 344
Isabella, 404-5
Jacovitti, Benito, 408
Ken Parker, 439-40

Kinowa, 446-47
Kit Carson, 449
Kriminal, 459
Liberatore, Gaetano (pseud. Tanino), 475-76
Liberty Kid, 476
Lupo Alberto, 494-95
Manara, Maurilio, 507-8
Mani in Alto!, 509-10
Marcello, Raffaelo Carlo (pseud. Marc, Ralph), 511
Marmittone, 513-14
Martin Mystere, 516-17
Mattotti, Lorenzo, 521-22
Micheluzzi, Attilio (pseud. Bajeff, Igor Artz), 530-31
Misterix, 539
Molino, Walter, 543
Moroni-Celsi, Guido (pseud. Sterny), 548-49
Narciso Putiferio, 562
Natacha, 562
Nizzi, Claudio, 575
Orlando, Joe, 587
Oscar, 587-88
Pantera Bionda, 596-97
Pazienza, Andrea, 600-601
Pecos Bill, 602-3
Pedrito El Drito, 603
Pedrocchi, Federico, 603
Pepito, 606-7
Peroni, Carlo, 608
Piccolo Sceriffo, Il, 614
Pier Cloruro De'Lambicchi, 616
Pippo, 618
Pratt, Hugo, 627
Principe Azzurro, 629
Procopio, 630
Quadratino, 635
Raviola, Roberto (pseud. Magnus), 639-41
Rebuffi, Giorgio, 642
Redipicche, 644
Rocky Rider, 658
Roland Eagle, 659
Romano Il Legionario, 659-60
Rubino, Antonio, 664
Saturna Contro la Terra, 676-77
Sciuscià, 683-84
Secchi, Luciano (pseud. Bunker, Max), 685
Serafino, 688-89
Signor Bonaventura, Il, 701-2
Soldino, 715
Sor Pampurio, 717-18
SturmTruppen, 731
Superbone, 734
Texas Willer, 753-54
Tiramolla, 764-65
Tony Falco, 768
Toppi, Sergio, 770-71
Valentina, 785
Valentina Melaverde, 785-86

Virus, Il Mago della Foresta Morta, 792

Japan

Adolf, 78-79
Akadō Suzunosuke, 83-84
Akatsuka, Fujio, 84
Anmitsu Hime, 97
Ashita no Joe, 101-2
Banana Fish, 108-9
Billy Pack, 133
Bōken Dankichi, 143
Chiba, Tetsuya, 198-99
Chikaino Makyû, 199
Cyborg 009, 230
Daiheigenji, 231
8-man, 276-77
Fuku-chan, 325
Fushigina Kuni no Putchā, 328
Fûten, 328-29
Gaki Deka, 332
Gekkō Kamen, 337
Golgo 13, 349-50
Hagio, Moto, 366
Hakaba no Kitarō, 366-67
Harisu no Kaze, 370
Hatanosuke Hinomaru, 373
Hi no Tori, 386-87
Hirata, Hiroshi, 387
Hokusai, Katsushika, 390-91
Igaguri-kun, 399
Ishimori, Shōtarō, 405
Jungle Tatei, 427-28
Kamui Den, 433-34
Kato, Yoshirou, 436
Kawanabe, Gyōsai, 438
Kibaō, 442-43
Kitzawa, Rakuten, 448-49
Kobayashi, Kiyochika, 451
Kojima, Goseki, 452
Kojima, Koo, 452
Kozure Okami, 454
Kuwata, Jirō, 463-64
Kyojin no Hoshi, 465
Maison Ikkoku, 506
Matsumoto, Reiji, 520-21
Misuki, Shigeru, 542
Mizuno, Hideko, 542
Mizushima, Shinji, 542
Nagagutsu no Sanjûshi, 559
Nagai, Gō, 559
Nagashima, Shinji, 559-60
Nausicaä of the Valley of Wind, 562-63
Ninja Bugeichō, 572-73
Nonkina Tousan, 575-76
Norakuro, 576
Ogon Bat, 580
Okamoto, Ippei, 581
O-Man, 582-83
Oshima, Yumiko, 588
Osomatsu-kun, 588

Otomo, Katsuhiro, 588-89
Robot Santōhei, 657
Sabaku no Maō, 669
Saitō, Takao, 670-71
Sasuke, 675-76
Satonaka, Machiko, 676
Sazae-san, 677
Shimizu, Kon, 696
Shirato, Sanpei, 696-97
Shōchan no Bōken, 697
Shōnen Oja, 698
Sonoyama, Shunji, 716-17
Speed Tarō, 718
Sugiura, Shigeru, 733
Tanku Tankurō, 745
Tenpei Tenma, 750
Tetsujin 28gō, 752
Tetsuwan-Atom, 752-53
Tezuka, Osamu, 754-55
Todano Bonji, 766
Tsuge, Yoshiharu, 775
Tsukioka, Yoshitoshi, 775-76
Utagawa, Kuniyoshi, 783
Yokoyama, Ryûichi, 825-26
Yokoyama, Taizō, 826

Korea

Kim Song Hwan, 444

Malaysia

Khalid, Mohamed Nor (pseud. Lat), 442

Mexico

Agachados, Los, 79
Alma Grande, 89
Anibal 5, 96
Aragonés, Sergio, 99
Butze Oliver, German, 169
Chanoc, 195
Chupamirto, 201
Fabulus Panicas, 289
Familia Burron, La, 291
Fantomas, 293
Payne, Charles M., 600
Pruneda, Salvado, 631

Myanmar. See Burma

Netherlands

Argonautjes, De, 100
Arman en Ilva, 100-101

Backer, Henk, 107
Brammetje Bram, 149-50
Broos, Piet, 156-57
Bulletje en Bonestaak, 163
Dick Bos, 246
Dzjengis Khan, 273
Eric de Noorman, 283
Hartog van Banda, Lo, 372
Kapitein Rob, 435
Kappie, 435-36
Koning Hollewijn, 453-54
Kraaienhove, 454-57
Kresse, Hans G., 457-58
Kuhn, Pieter Joseph, 461-62
Looman, Jos, 491
Matena, Dick, 519-20
Panda, 595
Piët, Frans, 616
Professor Pi, 630-31
Sjors en Sjimmie, 706-7
Swarte, Joost, 738-39
Tom Poes, 767-68
Toonder, Marten, 768
Tripje en Liezenbertha, 773-74
Vidocq, 792

New Zealand

Footrot Flats, 311-12

Norway

Aasnes, Håkon, 75

Philippines

Aguila, Dani, 79-80
Alcala, Alfredo P., 86-87
Bulandi, Danny, 163
DI 13, 253
Gomez, Pablo S., 350
Indio, El, 400
Jodloman, Jess M., 418-19
Kenkoy, 438-39
Kulafu, 462
Magsino, Frank, 505
Malaya, 506
Martin, Menny Eusobio, 516
Niño, Alex N., 573-74
Payaso, 599-600
Redondo, Nestor, 644-45
Reggie, 646
Rodriguez, Emilio D., 658-59
Santos, Jessie F., 674-75
Sappo, 675
Siopawman, 705-6
Tagisan Ng Mga Agimat, 743
Torres, Elpidio, 772-73
Voltar, 793

Poland

Chmielewski, Henryk Jerzy (pseud. Chimel), 200
Kasprzak, Zbigniew (pseud. Kas), 436
Wroblewski, Jerzy, 820

Singapore

Mr. Kiasu, 540

South Africa

Madam and Eve, 503
McClelland, Hugh, 498-99

Spain

Aghardi, 79
Alack Sinner, 85
Anita Diminuta, 96-97
Aspirino y Colodion, 102
Bea, José-Maria, 120
Blasco, Jesus, 137-38
Capitan Misterio, El, 177
Capitan Trueno, El, 178-79
Carpanta, 186
Chatillo y Federico, 197
Cifre, Guillermo, 202
Cinco por Infinito, 203
Coyote, El, 217
Cuto, 229-30
Delta 99, 239-40
Diego Valor, 249
Doctor Niebla, 259
Don Berrinche, 261-62
Familia Ulises, La, 291
Fernandez, Fernando, 301
Figueras, Alfonso, 302
Florita, 310-11
Gimenez, Carlos, 341
Gimenez, Juan, 341
Ginesito, 342-43
Gringo, 359-60
Guerrero del Antifaz, El, 361-62
Haxtur, 375
Hidalgo, Francisco (pseud. Roy, Yves), 384
Inspector Dan, El, 402
Jabato, El, 407
Jim Erizo, 416
Lavinia 2.016, 470
Macaco, 497
Manos Kelly, 511
Mari Aguirre, 512
Maroto, Esteban, 514
Mortadelo y Filemon, 549
Nus, 577

Pistol Jim, 619-20
Roberto Alcazar y Pedrín, 654-55
Sadhú, 669
Segrelles, Vicente, 687-88
Sherlock Lopez, 695
Silver Roy, 703
Sorang, 717
Torpedo 1936, 771
Torres, Daniel, 771-72

Sri Lanka

Perera, Camillus, 607

Sweden

Adamson, 77
Andersson, Oskar Emil (pseud. O. A.), 93
Andreasson, Rune, 94
Bergdahl, Gustav Victor, 126-27
Elworth, Lennart, 282
47:an Löken, 314
Gohs, Rolf, 348
Jacobsson, Oscar, 407-8
Klotjohan, 450
Lilla Fridolf, 479
Lille Rickard och hans Katt, 479-80
Lööf, Jan, 490-91
Mannen som gör vad som faller honom in, 510
Mystiska 2:an, 557-58
91 Karlsson, 572

Switzerland

Globi, 346
Histoires en Estampes, 387-88
Lehner, René (pseud. René), 472-73
Töpffer, Rodolphe, 770

Taiwan

Chu Teh-Yung, 200-201
Yeh Hung Chia, 823-24

Thailand

Bun Lour Sarn, 165-66
Chai Rachawat, 193-94

United States

A. Piker Clerk, 97-98
Abbie an' Slats, 75-76

Abie the Agent, 76
Adams, Neal, 77
Adam Strange, 78
Ahern, Gene, 80-81
Airboy, 81
Airship Man, The, 82-83
Alley Oop, 88
Alphonse and Gaston, 89-90
Amazing Man, 90
American Splendor, 90-91
Anderson, Carl Thomas, 91-92
Anderson, Lyman, 92
Anderson, Murphy, 92
Andriola, Alfred (pseud. James, Alfred), 94-95
Angel, The, 95
Apartment 3-G, 97
Aquaman, 98
Archie, 99-100, 100
Arriola, Gus, 101
Atom, The, 104
Avengers, The, 104
Ayers, Richard, 104-5
Baker, George, 107-8
Bald, Kenneth (pseud. Bruce, K.), 108
Banana Oil, 109
Barks, Carl, 111-12
Barnaby, 112-13
Barney Baxter, 113-14
Barney Google, 114
Barry, Daniel, 115
Barry, Lynda Jean, 115-16
Barry, Seymour, 116
Batman, 117-18
B.C., 119-20
Beck, Charles Clarence, 120-21
Beck, Frank Hem, 121
Beep Beep the Road Runner, 122
Beetle Bailey, 122-23
Berg, David, 125-26
Berndt, Walter, 127
Berrill, Jack, 127-28
Bess, Gordon, 128
For Better or For Worse, 312-13
Betty, 128-29
Betty Boop, 129
Big Ben Bolt, 130-31
Big Boy, 131
Binder, Jack, 133
Binder, Otto O. (pseud. Binder Eando), 133-34
Biro, Charles, 134-35
Black Cat, 135
Black Condor, 135-36
Blackhawk, 136
Black Hood, 136-37
Black Terror, 137
Blondie, 138-39
Bloom County, 139-40
Blosser, Merrill, 140
Blue Beetle, 140
Blue Bolt, 140-41
Bobby Thatcher, 141-42

Boner's Ark, 143-44
Boob McNutt, 145-46
Boots and Her Buddies, 147
Boring, Wayne (pseud. Harmon, Jack), 147-48
Born Loser, The, 148
Boy Commandos, 149
Branner, Martin, 150
Breger, David, 150-51
Brenda Starr, 151-52
Brick Bradford, 152
Briefer, Richard, 152-53
Briggs, Austin, 153
Briggs, Clare, 153-54
Brigman, June, 154
Bringing Up Father, 154-55
Brinkerhoff, Robert Moore, 155
Bronc Peeler, 156
Broom Hilda, 156
Browne, Dik, 157-58
Bruce Gentry, 158-59
Buck Rogers, 159-60
Bugs Bunny, 162-63
Bulletman, 164
Bungle Family, The, 164-65
Bunky, 165
Burgos, Carl, 166
Buscema, John, 166-67
Bushmiller, Ernest, 168
Buster Brown, 168-69
Buz Sawyer, 169-70
Byrnes, Eugene, 171-72
Calkins, Richard, 173
Calvin and Hobbes, 173-74
Caniff, Milton, 175-76
Caplin, Elliot, 179
Capp, Al, 179-80
Cap Stubbs and Tippie, 180
Captain America, 180-82
Captain and the Kids, The, 182
Captain Marvel, 182-84
Captain Marvel Jr., 184
Captain Midnight, 184-85
Captain Wings, 185
Carey, Ed, 185-86
Carlson, Wallace A., 186
Carr, Eugene, 186
Carreño, Albert, 186-87
Carter, Augustus Daniels, 187
Casey Ruggles, 188
Casper, 188-89
Casson, Melvin, 189
Cathy, 190
Cat-Man, The, 190-91
Celardo, John (pseud. Lardo, John C.), 191-92
Charlie Chan, 195-96
Charlie Chaplin's Comic Capers, 196
Chaykin, Howard, 197-98
Christman, Bert, 200
Cicero's Cat, 201-2
Cisco Kid, The, 203
Classics Illustrated, 204

Colan, Eugene (pseud. Austin, Adam), 206
Cole, Jack (pseud. Johns, Ralph), 206
Colonel Potterby and the Duchess, 208
Conan, 211-12
Connie, 212-13
Corben, Richard Vance, 213-14
Cory, Fanny Young, 215-16
Count Screwloose of Tooloose, 216-17
Craft, Jerry, 218
Craig, Chase, 218-19
Craig, John, 219
Crandall, Reed, 219-20
Crane, Royston Campbell, 220
Crimebuster, 222
Crosby, Percy Leo, 222-23
Cross, Stanley George, 223
Crumb, Robert, 224-26
Cruse, Howard, 226-27
Curley Harper, 228
Curtis, 228-29
Daffy Duck, 231
Dallis, Nicholas, 231-32
Dan Dunn, 232-33
Danny Dingle, 233
Daredevil, 233-34
Dateline: Danger!, 234-35
Dave, 235-36
Dave's Delicatessen, 236
Davis, Jack, 236-37
Davis, Jim, 237
Davis, Phil, 237-38
De Beck, Billy, 238
Dennis the Menace, 242
Desperate Desmond, 244
Dickenson, Fred, 246
Dickie Dare, 247
Dick's Adventures in Dreamland, 247-48
Dick Tracy, 248-49
Dilbert, 249-50
Dingbat Family, The, 251
Dinglehoofer und His Dog Adolph, 252
Dirks, Rudolph, 252-53
Disney, Walt, 253
Ditko, Steve, 253-54
Dixie Dugan, 255
Doc Savage, 256-57
Doctor Strange, 259-60
Dodd, Edward Benton, 260
Doll Man, 260
Donald Duck, 260-61
Dondi, 262
Don Dixon and the Hidden Empire, 262
Don Winslow of the Navy, 263-64
Doonesbury, 264
Dorgan, Thomas Aloysius, 264-65
Dr. Fate, 257
Dr. Kildare, 257
Dr. Mid-Nite, 258-59
Drago, 267

Drake, Stanley, 267
Drayton, Grace (pseud.
  Wiedersheim, Grace), 267-68
Dreams of the Rarebit Fiend, 268-69
Dropouts, The, 269
Dumas, Gerald, 270
Dumb Dora, 271
Dumm, Frances Edwina, 271-72
Dwiggins, Clare Victor, 272-73
Ed, Carl Frank Ludwig, 275
Edson, Gus, 275-76
Eek and Meek, 276
Eisner, Will (pseud. Erwin, Will;
  Rensie, Willis), 277-78
Elder, William W., 278
Elfquest, 279-80
Elias, Leopold, 280
Ella Cinders, 280-81
Elmer, 281-82
Ernie, 284
Ernst, Kenneth, 285
Etta Kett, 286
Evans, George, 286-87
Everett, Bill (pseud. Blake, Everett;
  Blake, William), 287
Fabulous Furry Freak Brothers, 289-90
Falk, Lee, 290-91
Fantastic Four, The, 292-93
Fearless Fosdick, 294-95
Feiffer, 295
Feiffer, Jules, 295-96
Feign, Larry, 296-97
Feininger, Lyonel, 297
Feldstein, Albert, 297
Felix the Cat, 299-300
Ferd'nand, 301
Fighting Yank, 302
Fine, Louis, 303
Finger, Bill, 303
Fisher, Hammond Edward, 303-4
Fisher, Harry Conway, 304-5
Flamingo, 306
Flanders, Charles, 306-7
Flash, 307-8
Flash Gordon, 308-9
Fleischer, Max, 309
Fletcher, Frank, 309
Flyin' Jenny, 311
Foster, Harold, 315
Fox, Fontaine Talbot, Jr., 316
Fox, Gardner (pseud. Cooper,
  Jefferson; Somers, Bart), 316-17
Fox and the Crow, The, 315-16
Foxy Grandpa, 317
Frankenstein, 317-18
Frazetta, Frank, 319-20
Freckles and His Friends, 320
Fredericks, Harold, 321
Freyse, Bill, 322
Friday Foster, 322
Fritz the Cat, 323-24
Fuller, Ralph Briggs, 325
Fung, Paul, 326
Funky Winkerbean, 326-27

Fusco Brothers, The, 327-28
Gaines, William M., 331-32
Garfield, 333
Garfield and Friends, 333-34
Gasoline Alley, 335-37
Ghost Rider, 337-38
Gimpel Beinish the Matchmaker,
  341-42
Giordano, Richard, 344
Glass, Jack, 345-46
Godwin, Francis, 347-48
Goldberg, Reuben Lucius, 348-49
Gonick, Larry, 350-51
Goodwin, Archie (pseud. Franklin
  Robert), 351
Gordo, 351-52
Gordon, Soldier of Fortune, 352
Gottfriedson, Floyd, 353
Gould, Chester, 353-54
Gould, Will, 354
Graff, Mel, 354
Gray, Clarence, 354-55
Gray, Harold, 355
Green Arrow, 355-56
Greene, Vernon van Atta, 356
Green Hornet, 356-57
Green Lantern, 357-59
Griffith, Bill, 359
Gross, Milton, 360
Guardineer, Frederic, 360-61
Gumps, The, 362
Gustafson, Paul (pseud. Earrol,
  Paul), 364
Haenigsen, Harry, 365
Hägar the Horrible, 365-66
Hairbreadth Harry, 366
Half-Hitch, 367
Hamlin, Vincent, 367-68
Hangman, The, 368
Happy Hooligan, 368-69
Harman, Fred, 370
Harold Teen, 370-71
Hart, Johnny, 371-72
Hasen, Irwin, 372-73
Hatlo, James, 373-74
Hawkman, 374
Hawkshaw the Detective, 374-75
Heap, The, 376
Heart of Juliet Jones, The, 376-77
Heath, Russell, 377-78
Heckle and Jeckle, 378
Held, John, Jr. (pseud. Held,
  Myrtle), 378
Henry, 378-79
Herb & Jamaal, 379
Hercules, 379-80
And Her Name Was Maud, 93-94
Herriman, George, 380-81
Herron, France Edward, 381
Hershfield, Harry, 381-82
Hess, Sol, 382-83
Hi and Lois, 383
Hildebrandt, Greg and Tim, 384-86
Hoban, Walter C., 388

Hoest, Bill, 388-89
Hogarth, Burne, 389-90
Hollander, Nicole, 391-92
Holman, Bill, 392-93
Howard the Duck, 394-95
Hubert, 395-96
Hulk, The, 396-97
Human Torch, The, 397-98
Ibis the Invincible, 399
Iger, Sumeul Maxwell, 400
Infantino, Carmine, 400-401
Ingels, Graham (pseud. Ghastly),
  401-2
Inspector Wade, 402-3
Invisible Scarlet O'Neil, 403
Iron Man, 403-4
Irving, Jay, 404
Jaffee, Allan, 408
Jane Arden, 411
Jerry on the Job, 414-15
Jim Hardy, 416-17
Jimmy Olsen, 417-18
Joe and Asbestos, 419
Joe Jinks, 419-20
Joe Palooka, 420
Johnny Hazard, 420-22
Johnny-Round-the-World, 422
Johnny Thunder, 422
Johnson, Ferd, 422-23
Jonah Hex, 423-24
Judge Parker, 424-26
Judge Wright, 426
JumpStart, 426-27
Jungle Jim, 427
Justice League of America, 429-30
Justice Society of America, 430
Just Kids, 429
Kahles, Charles William, 431
Kaluta, Michael Wm., 432-33
Kane, Gil (pseud. Edward, Scott;
  Kane, Al; Stack, Gil), 434
Kane, Robert, 434-35
Kanigher, Robert, 435
Katzenjammer Kids, The, 436-37
Keaton, Russell, 438
Kelly, Walt, 438
Kent, Jack, 440
Kerry Drake, 440
Ketcham, Henry King, 440-41
Kevin the Bold, 441
Kewpies, The, 441-42
Kida, Fred, 443-44
Kin-der-Kids, The, 444-45
King, Frank O., 445
King Aroo, 445-46
King of the Royal Mounted, 446
Kirby, Jack, 447-48
Kitchen, Denis, 449-50
Knerr, Harold H., 450
Knight, Clayton, 451
Kotzky, Alex, 454
Krazy Kat, 457
Krigstein, Bernard, 458-59
Kubert, Joe, 459-61

Kudzu, 461
Kurtzman, Harvey, 462-63
Lance, 467-68
Larson, Gary, 468
Lasswell, Fred, 469-70
Lazarus, Mel (pseud. Mell), 470
Leav, Mort, 470-71
Lee, Jim, 471-72
Lee, Stan, 472
Lehti, John, 473-74
Leisk, David Johnson (pseud. Johnson, Crockett), 474
Leonard, Frank, 474-75
Liefeld, Rob, 476
Life in Hell, 477-78
Li'l Abner, 478-79
Link, Stanley J., 481
Little Annie Fanny, 481
Little Annie Rooney, 481-83
Little Bears and Tykes, 483
Little Iodine, 483
Little Jimmy, 483-84
Little Joe, 484
Little King, The, 484-85
Little Lulu, 485-86
Little Nemo in Slumberland, 486-87
Little Orphan Annie, 487-88
Little People, The, 488
Locher, Richard, 489
Lois Lane, 489-90
Lone Ranger, The, 490
Long Sam, 490
Lubbers, Robert (pseud. Lewis, Bob), 492
Lulu and Leander, 493
Lynch, Jay, 496
Lynde, Stan, 496
Mager, Charles Augustus, 504
Mager's Monks, 504-5
Main Street, 505-6
Male Call, 506-7
Mallard Fillmore, 507
Mandrake the Magician, 508-9
Manning, Russell, 510-11
Mark Trail, 512-13
Marston, William Moulton (pseud. Moulton, Charles), 515
Martin, Edgar Everett, 515-16
Mary Marvel, 518
Mary Worth, 518-19
Master of Kung Fu, 519
Maus, 522-23
Maxon, Rex, 524
Mayer, Sheldon, 524-25
McBride, Clifford, 497
McCay, Winsor (pseud. Silas), 497-98
McClure, Darrell, 499
McDougall, Walter Hugh, 499
McEvoy, Joseph Patrick, 500
McFarlane, Todd, 500
McManus, George, 501-2
McWilliams, Alden, 502-3
Medieval Castle, The, 525

Meskin, Morton (pseud. Morton, Mort, Jr.), 526-27
Messick, Dale, 527
Mickey Finn, 531
Mickey Mouse, 531-32
Mighty Mouse, 532-33
Mike and Ike, 533
Miller, Frank (1898-1949), 534
Miller, Frank (1957-   ), 534
Ming Foo, 535-36
Minute Movies, 536-37
Miss Fury, 537
Miss Peach, 537-38
Momma, 543-44
Montana, Bob, 545-46
Moon Mullins, 546-47
Moose Miller, 547-48
Mosley, Zack, 549-50
Mother Goose and Grimm, 550-51
Motley's Crew, 551-52
Mr. Abernathy, 538
Mr. and Mrs., 538
Mr. Breger, 538-39
Mr. Jack, 539-40
Mr. Natural, 540-41
Mr. Scarlet, 541
Mr. Terrific, 541-42
Muggs and Skeeter, 552
Murphy, James Edward, 552-54
Murphy, John Cullen, 554
Musial, Joseph, 554
Mutt and Jeff, 555-56
Mutts, 556
Myers, Russell, 556-57
Myra North, 557
'Nam, 560
Nancy, 560-61
Napolean, 561-62
Naylor, Robert, 563-64
Nebbs, The, 564
Newlyweds, The, 567
Newman, Paul S., 567-68
New Mutants, The, 568
Newsboy Legion, 568
Nibsy the Newsboy, 568-69
Nize Baby, 575
Norris, Paul, 576-77
Nowlan, Philip, 577
Oaky Doaks, 579
O'Keefe, Neil, 581-82
Old Doc Yak, 582
Old Glory Story, The, 582
O'Neal, Frank, 583
O'Neil, Dennis, 583
O'Neill, Dan, 583-84, 584
O'Neill, Rose Cecil, 584
Opper, Frederick Burr, 585-86
Ormes, Jackie, 587
Our Boarding House, 589-90
Outcault, Richard Felton, 590-91
Outland, 591-92
Out Our Way, 592-93
Overgard, William Thomas, 593
Over the Hedge, 593-94

Ozark Ike, 594
Panhandle Pete, 595-96
Parker, Brant, 597
Patsy, 598
Patterson, Russell, 598-99
Payo, El, 600
Peanuts, 601-2
Peter Piltdown, 610
Peter Rabbit, 611
Pete the Tramp, 611
Pfeufer, Carl, 611
Phantom Lady, 612-13
Phanton, The, 611-12
Phil Hardy, 613-14
Phoebe Zeit-Geist, 614
Pinky Rankin, 617-18
Plastic Man, 621-22
Pogo, 622-23
Polly and Her Pals, 623-24
Porky Pig, 625
Powerhouse Pepper, 626
Prentice, John, 627-28
Prince Errant, 628
Prince Valiant, 628-29
Pussycat Princess, 631-32
Quincy, 635
Raboy, Emanuel, 637
Radio Patrol, 638
Rawhide Kid, 641
Raymond, Alex, 641
Red Barry, 642
Redeye, 643-44
Red Knight, The, 644
Red Ryder, 645
Red Sonja, 646
Reg'lar Fellers, 646-47
Rex Morgan, M.D., 649-50
Rick O'Shay, 651
Rip Kirby, 651-53
Ritt, William, 653
Robbins, Frank, 653
Robbins, Trina, 653-54
Robinson, Jerry, 656-57
Romita, John, 660
Room and Board, 660
Rose is Rose, 661-62
Rosie's Beau, 662
Russell, Clarence D., 666
Rusty Riley, 666-67
Ryan, Tom K., 667
Sad Sack, The, 669-70
Sally Forth, 672-73
Sam's Strip, 673
Sandman, 673-74
Santos, Malang (pseud. Malang), 675
Saunders, Allen, 677
Schaffenberger, Kurt (pseud. Wahl, Lou), 678
Schultze, Carl Edward, 682-83
Schulz, Charles Monroe, 683
Schwartz, Julius, 683
Scorchy Smith, 684-85

Scott, Jerry (pseud. Kirkman, Rick), 685
Secret Agent X-9, 685-86
Segar, Elzie Crisler, 687
Severin, John Powers, 690
Sgt. Fury, 689
Sgt. Rock, 689-90
Shadow, The, 691-93
Sheena, Queen of the Jungle, 693-94
Shelton, Gilbert, 694
Shield, The, 695-96
Shoe, 697-98
Short Ribs, 698-99
Shuster, Joe, 699-700
Sickles, Noel, 700-701
Siegel, Jerome, 701
Silly Symphonies, 702-3
Silver Surfer, 704
Simon, Joseph, 704-5
Sinnott, Joe, 705
Skeets, 707
Skippy, 707-8
Skyroads, 708-9
Slim Jim, 709
Slylock Fox and Comics for Kids, 709-10
Smilin' Jack, 710
Smith, Al, 710-11
Smith, Robert Sidney, 711-12
Smitty, 712
Smokey Stover, 712-13
Soglow, Otto, 713-14
Spectre, The, 718
Spider-Man, 718-19
Spiegelman, Arthur, 719-20
Spiegle, Dan, 720
Spirit, The, 720-21
Spooky, 721-22
Sprang, Richard, 722
Springer, Frank, 722-23
Spy Smasher, 723-24
On Stage, 584-85
Stanley, John, 724
Starman, 724-25
Starr, Leonard, 725
Star Spangled Kid, 725
Star Wars, 725-26
Steel Sterling, 726
Steranko, James, 726-27
Sterrett, Cliff, 727
Steve Canyon, 727-28
Steve Roper, 728-29
Stony Craig of the Marines, 729-30
Strange World of Mr. Mum, The, 730
Striebel, John H., 730
Sub-Mariner, The, 731-32
Sullivan, Pat, 734
Supergirl, 734-35
Superman, 735-37

Supersnipe, 737
Surburban Cowgirls, 732-33
Swamp Thing, 738
Sweeney and Son, 739-40
Swinnerton, James Guilford (pseud. Guilford, James), 740-41
Tailspin Tommy, 743-44
Taliaferro, Charles Alfred, 744
Tank McNamara, 745
Tarzan, 747-48
Ted Towers, 749
Teenage Mutant Ninja Turtles, 749-50
Terrors of the Tiny Tads, 750-51
Terry and the Pirates, 751-52
Texas Slim and Dirty Dalton, 753
They'll Do It Everytime, 755
Thimble Theater, 755-56
Thomas, Roy, 756
Thor, 756-57
Thorne, Frank, 757-58
Thunder Agents, 758-59
Tiger, 760
Tillie the Toiler, 761-62
Timid Soul, The, 762-63
Tim Tyler's Luck, 763-64
Tom and Jerry, 766-67
Toonerville Folks, 768-69
Toots and Casper, 769-70
Toth, Alexander, 773
Trudeau, Garry, 775
Tufts, Warren, 776
Tumbleweeds, 776
Turner, Leslie, 776-77
Turner, Morrie, 777-78
Turok, Son of Stone, 778
Tuthill, Harry J., 778-79
Up Front, 782
Upside Downs of Little Lady Lovekins and Old Man Muffaroo, The, 782-83
Vampirella, 787
Van Buren, Raeburn, 787-88
Vanilla and the Villians, 789
Verbeck (a.k.a Verbeek), Gustave, 791
Vic Flint, 791
Vic Jordan, 791
Voight, Charles A., 792-93
Wags, the Dog that Adopted a Man, 795
Walker, Addison Mortimer (pseud. Addison), 796
Wash Tubbs, 799-800
Watchmen, 800-801
Waugh, Coulton, 801
Web, The, 801-2
Webster, Harold Tucker, 802
Wee Pals, 803

Wee Willie Winkie's World, 804
Weisinger, Mort, 804
Wellington, Charles H., 804-5
Westover, Russell, 805-6
Wheelan, Edgar, 806
When a Feller Needs a Friend, 806
Where I'm Coming From, 806-7
White Boy, 808
Wildey, Doug, 808-9
Wildman, George, 809
Willard, Frank Henry, 809-10
Williams, James Robert, 810-11
Williamson, Al, 811
Wilshire, Mary, 811-12
Winner, Charles H., 812-13
Winnie Winkle, 813-14
Winterbotham, Russell (pseud. Bond, J. Harvey), 814
Wizard of Id, The, 814
Wolverton, Basil, 816
Wonder Woman, 816-17
Wood, Wallace, 818
Woolfolk, William, 818-20
Wunder, George, 820
X-Men, 821
Yellow Kid, The, 824-25
Young, Lyman, 826
Young, Murat, 826-27
Young Allies, 827

Uruguay

Breccia, Alberto, 150

Yugoslavia

Beker, Žarko, 123
Delač, Vladimir, 238-39
Dobrić, Milorad, 256
Dovniković, Borivoj, 266
Furtinger, Zvonimir, 327
Herlock Sholmes, 380
Janković, Djordje, 411-12
Kuznjecov, Konstantin, 464-65
Lehner, Sebastijan, 473
Lobačev, Jurij (Djordje) (pseud. Strip, George), 488-89
Marković, Momcilo-Moma, 512
Maurović, Andrija, 522
Muster, Miki, 554-55
Neugebauer, Walter, 566-67
Radilović, Julio, 637-38
Solovjev, Sergej (pseud. Gey, Moum; Solo, S), 715-16
Svircić, Zdenko, 738
Zigomar, 829-30

A

A. Piker Clerk, 98
Abbie an'Slats, 75
Abie the Agent, 76
Achille Talon, 76
Acosta, Jesus, 201
Adams, Austin (pseud. of Colan, Eugene), 207, 394
Adams, Scott, 249
Adamson, 77
Adam Strange, 78
Addison (pseud. of Walker, Addison Mortimer), 62, 122, 144, 383
Adolf, 78
Adventures of Phoebe Zeit-Geist, The, 723
Afonski, Nicholas (pseud. Afonsky, N.), 536
Agachados, Los, 79
Aguila, Dani, 80
Ahern, Gene, 80, 590
Airboy, 81
Air Burst, 463
Air Hawk and the Flying Doctors, 82
Airship Man, The, 82
Airy Alf and Bouncing Billy, 83
Akadō Suzunosuke, 83
Akim, 84
Alack Sinner, 85, 553
Alan Ford, 86
Albert, Louis (pseud. of Régnier, Michel), 127, 209, 646
Alcala, Alfredo P., 793
Alcala, Larry, 705
Alcazar, Victor (pseud. of Mora, Victor), 178
Alfieri, Janet, 733
Alfred, James (pseud. of Andriola, Alfred), 195, 440
Alfredo, 87
Alix, 87
Alley Oop, 88
Ally Sloper, 88
Alma Grande, 89
Alphonse and Gaston, 89
Altai & Jonson, 191
American Splendor, 90
Anderson, Lyman, 92, 402
Andersson, Oskar Emil (pseud. O. A.), 93, 510
Andreasson, Rune, 480
Andriola, Alfred (pseud. James, Alfred), 195, 440
Andy Capp, 95
Angoletta, Bruno, 513
Anita, 221
Anita Diminuta, 96
Anmitsu Hime, 97
Anzi, Rino, 227
Appleby, Barry and Dobs, 333
Apple Mary, 47
Archie, 99, 545
Argonautjes, De, 100

Aristides, Othon (pseud. Fred), 613
Arman en Ilva, 101
Armstrong, Robb, 427
Arnal, Claude (pseud. of Cabrerero Arnal, José), 617, 621
Arriola, Gus, 352
Ashita no Joe, 102
Asso di Picche, 102
Astérix, 57, 103
Atomas, 604
Avenger, The, 433
Ayers, Richard, 337
Ayos, 516

B

Backer, Henk, 774
Bailey, Ray, 158
Bajeff, Igor Artz (pseud. of Micheluzzi, Attilio), 530
Baker, George, 107, 669
Baker, Matt, 306
Bald, Kenneth (pseud. Bruce, K.), 257, 724
Ball, Murray, 312
Ballata del Mare Salato, Una, 108
Banana Oil, 109
Bancks, James, 46
Bandolero, 340
Bara (pseud. of Herzog, Guy), 523
Barbarella, 37, 110
Barks, Carl, 112
Barney Baxter, 113, 564
Barney Google, 22, 114
Barrett, Monty, 411
Barry, Daniel, 115
Barry, Lynda Jean, 116
Bartsch, Art, 532
Bascule à Charlot, 746
Bateman, Henry Mayo, 117
Batiuk, Tom, 327
Batman, 117
Battefield, Ken, 164
Baxendale, Leo, 119, 124
B.C., 50, 119
Beautiful Bab, 827
Beck, Charles Clarence, 183
Becker, Franziska, 121
Beelzebub Jones, 498
Beetle Bailey, 62, 122
Beker, Žarko, 123
Bell, Steve, 124
Ben Hur, 512
Berardi, Giancarlo, 439
Berg, David, 126
Bernard Prince, 127
Berndt, Walter, 712
Bess, Gordon, 643
Bessy, 128
Bestall, Alfred, 665
Betty, 129
Betty Boop, 129

Bevère, Maurice de (pseud. Morris), 493
Bibi Fricotin, 130
Bidochon, Les, 134
Big and Little Willie, 372
Big Ben Bolt, 131
Billingsley, Ray, 229
Billy Bunter, 132
Binder, Jack, 518
Binet, Christian, 134
Bishop, Wally, 552
Bisi, Carlo, 717
Bjarre, Torsten, 479
Blackaller, 596
Blackhawk, 136
Blake, Bud, 760
Blake and Mortimer, 29
Blasco, Jesus, 96, 229
Blondie, 138
Bloom County, 139
Blosser, Merrill, 320
Bluey and Curley, 364
Bobby Bubble, 386
Bobby Thatcher, 142
Bob Fish, 194
Bōken Dankichi, 143
Boner's Ark, 144
Bonvicini, Franco (pseud. Bonvi), 144, 731
Bonzo, 145
Boob McNutt, 145
Booth, Walter, 657
Boots and Her Buddies, 147, 515
Boring, Wayne (pseud. Harmon, Jack), 736
Born Loser, The, 148
Bottaro, Luciano, 148, 606, 644
Bourgeois, Albéric, 607
Bradley, Marvin, 649
Brady, Pat, 661
Brammetje Bram, 149
Brand, Nat, 243
Brandon, Barbara, 807
Branner, Martin, 814
Braun, Caspar, 277
Breathed, Berke, 139
Breccia, Alberto, 549, 580
Breger, David, 151
Brenda Starr, 151
Bresciani, Andrea, 768
Bretecher, Claire, 192
Brick Bradford, 152
Briggs, Clare, 98, 153, 806
Bringing Up Father, 18, 155
Bronc Peeler, 156
Broom Hilda, 156
Broos, Piet, 157
Brösel (pseud. of Feldmann, Rötger), 805
Browne, Chris, 654
Browne, Dik, 53, 365, 383
Browne, Tom, 158
Bruce, K. (pseud. of Bald, Kenneth), 257, 724

Bruce Gentry, 158
Brunner, Frank, 259
Buck Danny, 159
Buck Rogers, 25, 160
Buck Ryan, 160
Buell, Marjorie Henderson (pseud. Margie), 486
Bugs Bunny, 162
Bulletje en Bonestaak, 17, 163
Bulletman, 164
Bungle Family, The, 165
Bunker, Max (pseud. of Secchi, Luciano), 86, 685
Burns, John, 686
Busch, Wilhelm, 12, 167
Bushmiller, Ernest, 560
Buster Brown, 168
Butterworth, Jenny, 760
Buyulla (pseud. of Rodriguez, Braulio), 249
Buz Sawyer, 169
Buzzelli, Guido, 170
Byrne, John, 171
Byrnes, Eugene, 171

C

C. F. (pseud. of Folkard, Charles), 18, 317, 749
Cabrerero Arnal, José (pseud. Arnal, Claude), 617, 621
Caesar, Kurt (pseud. Avai, Cesare; Away, Caesar), 659
Calkins, Dick, 25, 160, 708
Calvin and Hobbes, 174
Canale, Antonio, 175
Caniff, Milton, 29, 247, 271, 507, 728, 751
Capitaine Fantôme, Le, 176
Capitan Miki, 177
Capitan Misterio, El, 177
Capitan Terror, 178
Capitan Trueno, El, 178
Capp, Al (pseud. of Caplin, Alfred Gerald), 294, 478
Captain America, 28, 181
Captain and the Kids, The, 182
Captain Easy, 777
Captain Marvel, 183
Captain Marvel Jr., 184
Captain Midnight, 184
Carroll, Ruth, 632
Carter, Ad, 429
Casa Mana, La, 60
Casey Court, 188
Castelli, Alfredo, 517
Cathy, 190
Cattivik, 144
Cavazzano, Giorgio, 191
Cazanave, Raymond, 176
Cellulite, 192
Centaure Vezelay, Le, 174

Cerebus, 193
Chai Rachawat, 193
Chaland, Yves, 194
Chanoc, 195
Charlie Chan, 195
Charlier, Jean-Michel, 529
Chartier, Albert, 197
Chéret, André, 638
Chevalier Ardent, 198
Chiba, Akio, 199
Chiba, Tetsuya, 101
Chikaino Makyû, 199
Chlorophylle, 199
Christin, Pierre (pseud. Linus), 786
Christophe (pseud. of Colomb, Georges), 292
Chubb-Lock Homes, 823
Chuckle Our Own Clown, 245
Chupamirto, 201
Chu Teh-Yung, 201
Cicero's Cat, 202
Cimpellin, Leone, 203
Cinco por Infinito, 203
Ciocca, Walter, 480
Cisco Kid, The, 50, 204
Clarence the Cop, 431
Clive, 204
Cocco Bill, 205
Cocking, Percy (pseud. Daw, Jack), 800
Colan, Eugene (pseud. Austin, Adam), 207, 394
Cole, Jack (pseud. Johns, Ralph), 621
Coll, Charles, 557
Colley, Ed, 733
Collins, Dennis, 608
Collins, Kreigh, 441
Colomb, Georges (pseud. Christophe), 292
Colonel Pewter, 208
Colonel Potterby and the Duchess, 208
Comanche, 209, 398
Come On, Steve!, 210
Comés, Didiet, 210
Commissario Spada, Il, 211
Conan, 212
Connie, 213
Conselman, Bill, 281
Corben, Richard Vance, 213
Cornelius, Cosper, 87
Cortez, Jayme, 215
Corto Maltese, 215
Cosmic Ray Bomb Explosion, The, 332
Cossio, Carlo, 246
Count Screwloose of Tooloose, 216
Couple, The, 201
Coyote, El, 217
Craenhals, François (pseud. Hals, F.), 198
Craft, Jerry, 218
Crandall, Reed, 136, 219, 260
Crane, Royston Campbell (Roy), 169, 220, 799
Crepax, Guido, 37, 60, 221, 785

Crockett, Johnson (pseud. of Leisk, David Johnson), 112
Crosby, Percy Leo, 222, 707
Cruikshank, George, 224
Crumb, Robert, 36, 225, 324, 541
Cruse, Howard, 226
Crystal Sett, 654
Cubitus, 227
Cucciolo, 227
Cuestion de Tiempo, 342
Culliford, Pierre (pseud. Peyo), 680
Curtis, 229
Cuto, 229
Cyborg 009, 230

D

Daix, Andre, 630
Dallis, Nicholas, 649
Dalmasso, Giacomo, 597
Dan Dunn, 233
Daredevil, 207, 234
Darian (pseud. of Dingle, Adrian), 565
Darthel, J. (pseud. of Velter, Robert), 790
Dateline: Danger!, 235
Dave, 235
Davies, Roland (pseud. Pip), 210
Davis, Jack, 53, 237
Davis, Phil, 509
Daw, Jack (pseud. of Cocking, Percy), 800
Death, 226
De Beck, Billy, 22, 114
DeCarlo, Dan, 98
Deed-a-Day Danny, 502
Delač, Vladimir, 238
Del Castillo, Arturo, 34
Dell'Acqua, Edgardo, 343
Delta 99, 239
De Luca, Gianni, 211, 240
Demonyo Made Me Do It, The, 646
Dennis the Menace (U.S.), 242
Dennis the Menace (G.B.), 241
Derickson Denie, 242
De Souza, Maurico, 243
Desperate Dan, 243
Desperate Desmond, 244
Devil's Angel, 758
DI 13, 253
Diabolik, 245
Diamond, H. Louis, 245
Dick Fulmine, 246
Dickie Dare, 247
Dick's Adventures in Dreamland, 248
Dick Tracy, 24, 248
Diego Valor, 249
Dilbert, 249
Dimples, 268
Dingbat Family, The, 251
Ding Cong (pseud. Xiao Ding), 250

Dingle, Adrian (pseud. Darian), 565
Dinglehoofer und His Dog Adolph, 252
Dirks, Gus, 182
Dirks, Rudolph, 12, 252
Disney, Walt, 532
Ditko, Steve, 254
Divito, Guillermo, 254, 258
Dixie Dugan, 255
Dixon, John Dangar, 82
Djon Domino, 256
Dobrić, Milorad, 256
Doc Savage, 256, 433
Doctor Merengue, El, 258
Doctor Niebla, 259
Doctor Strange, 259
Dodd, Edward Benton, 513
Doll Man, 260
Domu, 589
Donald Duck, 261
Don Catarino, 631
Dondi, 262
Don Dixon, 262
Don Winslow, 264
Doonesbury, 34, 264
Dorgan, Thomas Aloysius, 265
Dot and Carrie, 265
Dottor Faust, Il, 266
Double Trouble, 807
Dovniković, Borivoj, 266
Dowling, Steve, 334, 665
Dr. Kildare, 257
Dr. Merling, 258
Drago, 267
Drake, Stanley, 377
Drayton, Grace (pseud. Wiedersheim, Grace), 268
Dreams of the Rarebit Fiend, 268
Druillet, Philippe, 269
Duan Jifu, 54, 270
Duffy, J. C., 328
Dugmore, Harry, 503
Dumas, Gerald, 416, 673
Dumas, Jacques (pseud. François, Jacques; Marijac), 774
Dumb Dora, 271
Dumm, Frances Edwina, 272
Dunkley, Jack, 468
Dupanloup, Luc (pseud. Dupa), 227
Duval, Marie, 87

E

Eaton, Mal, 610
Ed, Carl Frank Ludwig, 371
Edson, Gus, 275
Eek and Meek, 276
8-man, 276
Eisele und Beisele, 277
Eisner, Will, 48, 721
Eleuteri Serpieri, Paolo, 279
Elfquest, 279
Ella Cinders, 281

Elmer, 281
Elworth, Lennart, 314
Endrody, Istvan, 61
Eric, 283
Eric de Noorman, 458
Ernie, 284
Ernie Pike, 284
Ernst, Kenneth, 519
Ernsting, Volker, 534
Essegesse (pseud. of Sinchetto, Sartoris, Guzzon), 177
Eternauta, El, 580
Etta Kett, 56, 286
Evaristo, 714
Everett, Bill (pseud. Blake, Everett; Blake, William), 287, 732
Ewer, Raymond Crawford, 709

F

Fabulous Furry Freak Brothers, 290
Fabulus Panicas, 289
Falk, Lee, 509, 612
Famille Fenouillard, La, 292
Fantastic Four, 448
Fantomas, 293
Far Side, The, 469
Fatty Finn, 294
Fawkes, Wally (pseud. Trog), 310
Fearless Fosdick, 294
Feiffer, 63, 295
Feiffer, Jules, 295
Feign, Larry, 296
Feininger, Lyonel, 14
Feldmann, Rötger (pseud. Brösel), 805
Feldstein, Al, 297, 332
Felix, 299
Felix the Cat, 299
Fera, A. C., 281
Ferd'nand (Denmark), 300
Fernandez, Fernando, 301
Ferrier, Arthur, 302
Filippucci, Lucio, 517
Fine, Louis, 379
Finzioni, 601
Fisher, Hammond Edward, 304, 420
Fisher, Harry Conway (Bud), 16, 304, 555
Fix und Foxi, 305
Flamingo, 306
Flanders, Charles, 490
Flash, 307
Flash Gordon, 115, 308, 620
Flax (pseud. of Palacio, Lino), 263
Fleischer, Max, 129, 309
Flook, 310
Floyd, Dick, 618
Flutters, The, 311
Flying Machine, The, 458
Fogelberg, Ola (pseud. Fogeli), 604

Folkard, Charles (pseud. C. F.), 18, 317, 749
For Better or For Worse, 312, 423
Forest, Jean-Claude (pseud. Valherbe, Jean), 37, 110, 313
Forman, Tom, 551
Forrest, Hal, 743
Forton, Louis, 16, 130, 616
47:an Löken, 314
Foster, Harold, 24, 59, 629, 748
Fox, Fontaine Talbot, Jr., 769
Foxwell, Herbert, 761
Foxy Grandpa, 682
Franchi, C., 831
Francis, Stephen, 503
François, Jacques (pseud. of Dumas, Jacques), 774
Franklin, (pseud. of Goodwin, Archie), 351
Franquin, André, 318, 336
Frazetta, Frank, 319
Freckles and His Friends, 320
Fred (pseud. of Aristides, Othon), 613
Freelance, 321
Freixas, Carlos, 619
Freyse, Bill, 590
Friday Foster, 323
Fritz the Cat, 324
Fry, Michael, 593
Fujitani, Bob, 356
Fuku-chan, 325, 825
Fukui, Eüchi, 83
Fulmine, 254
Funky Winkerbean, 327
Furness, Ed, 321
Fusco Brothers, The, 328
Fûten, 328

G

Gahlin, Torvald, 450
Gai Luron, 331
Gaines, William M., 332
Gajō, 745
Gaki Deka, 332
Galleppini, Aurelio, 754
Gamba, Pietro, 603
Gamblin, Len, 311
Gambols, The, 333
Garfield, 53, 334
Garth, 334
Gascard, Gilbert (pseud. Tibet), 650
Gasoline Alley, 21, 335, 445
Gaston Lagaffe, 337
Gertie, the Trained Dinosaur, 497
Ghastly (pseud. of Ingels, Graham), 402
Gherlizza, Egidio, 688
Ghost Rider, 337
Giardino, Vittorio, 338
Gibbons, Dave, 800
Gifford, Denis (pseud. Kol), 750

Gillain, John (pseud. Jijé), 415, 721
Gillray, James, 43
Gimenez, Carlos, 239, 340
Gim Toro, 343
Ginesito, 343
Ginger Meggs, 46
Gin Lane, 11
Giolitti, Alberto, 609
Giraud, Jean (pseud. Gir), 477
Girl from the People's Commune, The, 345
Gir (pseud. of Giraud, Jean), 477
Giussani, Angela and Luciana, 245
Globi, 346
Gloops, 347
Gloria (pseud.), 123
Godwin, Francis, 213, 347, 667
Gohs, Rolf, 557
Goldberg, Reuben Lucius, 19, 145, 349
Golgo 13, 52, 350
Gonzales, José, 787
Goodwin, Archie (pseud. Franklin, Robert), 351
Gordo, 352
Goscinny, René, 57, 103
Gotlib, Marcel, 331
Gottfredson, Floyd, 261
Gotto, Ray, 594
Gould, Chester, 24, 58, 248
Gould, Will, 642
Grace, Bud, 284
Graddon, Bernard, 428
Graff, Mel, 598
Graton, Jean, 530
Gray, Clarence, 152
Gray, Harold, 355, 487
Green Arrow, 356
Greene, Vernon van Atta, 692
Green Lantern, 358
Greg (pseud. of Régnier, Michel), 127, 209, 646
Griffith, Bill, 359
Groening, Matt, 477
Gross, Milton, 19, 109, 216
Guerrero del Antifaz, El, 362
Guilford, James (pseud. of Swinnerton, James Guilford), 484, 539, 740
Guisewite, Cathy, 190
Gumps, The, 21, 363
Gurcka Vjestica, 522
Gurney, Alexander George, 364
Gyatoruzu, 38, 716

H

H. (pseud. of Horrabin, James Francis), 265, 412
Hägar the Horrible, 53, 365
Hairbreadth Harry, 44
Hajduk Velijko, 488

Hakaba no Kitarō, 367
Hall, Harry, 71
Hals, F. (pseud. of Craenhals, François), 198
Hamlin, Vincent T., 87
Hansen, Vilhelm, 639
Hao Shih, 394
Happy Hooligan, 13, 369
Hargreaves, Harry, 375
Harman, Fred, 48, 156, 645
Harmon, Jack (pseud. of Boring, Wayne), 736
Harold Teen, 371
Hart, Johnny, 50, 119, 815
Haselden, W. K., 372
Hasen, Irwin, 262
Hatlo, James, 373, 483
Hawkman, 374
Hayseeds, 375
Heap, The, 376
Heart of Juliet Jones, The, 377
Hef's Pad, 36
Heilman, Dan, 425
Hercules, 379
Hergé (pseud. of Rémi, Georges), 25, 764
Herlock Sholmes, 380
Hermann (pseud. of Huppen, Hermann), 127, 209, 398
Hernán el Corsario, 671
Herriman, George, 18, 251, 456
Hershfield, Harry, 76, 244, 382
Herzog, Guy (pseud. Bara), 523
Hi and Lois, 383
Hicks, Reginald Ernest (pseud. Hix), 384
Hidajat, Johnny, 256
Hidalgo, Francisco, 385
Hidalgo, Francisco (pseud. Roy, Yves), 259
Hill, Albert, 386
Hi no Tori, 387
Hirai, Kazumasa, 276
Hix (pseud. of Hicks, Reginald Ernest), 384
Hoban, Walter C., 388, 414
Hodgson, Ralph, 83
Hogarth, Burne, 70, 267, 389, 747
Hogarth, William, 11, 390
Holdaway, James, 36, 391
Hollander, Nicole, 392
Holman, Bill, 392, 713, 722
Hopalong Cassidy, 720
Horie, Taku, 750
Horner, Arthur, 208
Horrabin, James Francis (pseud. H), 265, 412
Hot on the Trail, 394
Howard, Greg (pseud. Howard), 672
Howard, John, 425
Howard the Duck, 394
Howarth, F. M., 493
Ho Yu-chih, 343
Hubert, 395

Hubinon, Victor, 159
Hulk, The, 396
Human Torch, The, 397
Huppen, Hermann (pseud. Hermann), 127, 209, 398

I

I Briganti, 640
Incredible Hulk, The, 171
Indoor Sports, 265
Infantino, Carmine, 78, 401
Ingels, Graham (pseud. Ghastly), 402
Ingrid the Bitch, 449
Inspector Wade, 402
Inspektor Burnadz, 633
Iron Man, 403
Irving, Jay, 404
Ishimori, Shōtarō, 230, 405
Ivanhoe, 715

J

Jacobs, E. P., 29
Jacobsson, Oscar, 77
Jacovitti, Benito, 205
Jaffee, Allan, 409
James Bond, 410
Jane, 410
Jane Arden, 411
Jansson, Tove, 546
Japhet and Happy, 413
Jean des Flandres, 413
Jeff Hawke, 413
Jerry on the Job, 388, 414
Jerry Spring, 415
Jijé (pseud. of Gillain, John), 415, 721
Jim Boum, 416
Jimmy das Gummipferd, 417
Jimpy, 418
Jodorowski, Alexandro, 289
Joe Jinks, 419
Joe Palooka, 420
Johnny Focus, 530
Johnny Hazard, 421
Johnny Logan, 203
Johns, Ralph (pseud. of Cole, Jack), 621
Johnston, Lynn B., 312, 423
Jordan, Sydney, 413
Judge Dredd, 425
Judge Parker, 425
JumpStart, 427
Jungle Drums, 384
Jungle Jim, 219, 427
Jungle Tatei, 428
Justice League of America, 430
Just Jake, 428
Just Kids, 429

K

Kabashima, Kasuichi (pseud. Tōfujin), 697
Kahles, Charles William, 44, 82, 431
Kaluta, Michael Wm., 433
Kane, Bob, 117
Kane, Gil (pseud. Edward, Scott; Kame, Al; Stack, Gil), 212
Kapitein Rob, 435
Kappa Tengoku, 696
Kappie, 436
Katzenjammer Kids, The, 12, 57, 437
Kauka, Rolf, 178, 305, 494
Kawasaki, Noboru, 463
Kelly, A. J., 729
Kelly, Walt, 33, 622
Ken Parker, 439
Kent, Jack, 446
Kerry Drake, 440
Ketcham, Henry King, 242
Kevin the Bold, 441
Keyhole Kate, 442
Khalid, Mohamed Nor (pseud. Lat), 443
Khing, The Tjong, 101
Kida, Fred, 81
Kim Song Hwan, 444
Kin-der-Kids, The, 14
King, Frank O., 445
King Aroo, 446
King of the Royal Mounted, 447
Kirby, Jack, 28, 51, 448
Kitchen, Denis, 449
Klotjohan, 450
Kmochk, Ladislaus (pseud. Kmoch, Ludwig), 765, 766
Knerr, Harold H., 57, 252, 437
Kobau, 444
Kohlsaat, Roland, 417
Kojima, Goseki, 455
Kojima, Koo, 452
Kol (pseud. of Gifford, Denis), 750
König, Ralf, 453
Koning Hollewijn, 454
Kraaienhove, 455
Krazy Kat, 18, 55, 456
Kresse, Hans G., 283, 458, 792
Krigstein, Bernard, 458
Kriminal, 459
Kubert, Joe, 460, 689
Kudzu, 39
Kuhn, Pieter Joseph, 435
Kuragane, Shōsuke, 97
Kurtzman, Harvey, 463
Kuwata, Jirō, 276, 463
Kuznjecov, Konstantin, 464
Kyojin no Hoshi, 465

L

Laborne, Daniel, 467

Landolfi, Lino, 575
Lanteri, Arturo, 565
Lao Ma's Adventures, 54, 270
Lariflette, 467
Larks, The, 468
Larsen, Knud V., 258
Larson, Gary, 469
Lat (pseud. of Khalid, Mohamed Nor), 443
Lau, Johnny, 540
Laurel and Hardy, 795
Lavado, Joaquin (pseud. Quino), 504
Lavezzolo, Andrew, 343, 768
Lavinia 2.016, 470
Law, David, 241
Lawrence, Don, 517
Lazarus, Mel (pseud. Mell), 537, 544
Leav, Mort, 376
Lécureux, Roger, 617
Lee, Jim, 471
Lee, Stan, 35
Legends along the Silk Road, 734
Lehner, René (pseud. René), 473
Leisk, David Johnson (pseud. Johnson, Crockett), 112
Lena the Hyena, 816
Leonard, Frank (Lank), 531
Lewis, Bob (pseud. of Lubbers, Robert), 491
Lewis, T., 593
Liao Bingxiong, 475
Liberatore, Gaetano (pseud. Liberatore, Tanino), 475
Lieutenant Blueberry, 477
Life in Hell, 477
Li'l Abner, 479
Lilla Fridolf, 479
Lille Rickard och hans Katt, 480
L'indiana blanca, 279
Lindor Caovas, 480
Lin Tzu-shun, 643
Linus (pseud. of Christin, Pierre), 786
Lips, Robert, 346
Little Annie Rooney, 482
Little Bears, The, 740
Little Dog Guaiguai, 605
Little Iodine, 483
Little Jimmy, 484
Little King, The, 485
Little Lulu, 486
Little Nemo in Slumberland, 15, 61, 486
Little Orphan Annie, 487
Little Plum, 119, 124
Little Stranger, A, 402
Ljuba Truba, 256
Lob, Jacques, 781
Lobačev, Jurij (Djordje) (pseud. Strip, George), 488
Lohmann, Willy, 455
Lone Ranger, The, 490
Lone Sloan, 269
Longaron, Jorge, 322
Long Sam, 490
Lööf, Jan, 299

Looy Dot Dope, 19
Lord Snooty and His Pals, 492
Lozano, José Suárez, 89
Lubbers, Robert (pseud. Lewis, Bob), 491
Lucky Luke, 493
Lulu and Leander, 493
Lump of Innocence, A, 663
Lupo, 494
Lupo Alberto, 494
Lurchis Abenteuer, 495
Lynch, Jay, 36
Lynde, Stan, 496, 652

M

M. Crépin, 770
Macaco, 47
McBride, Clifford, 561
McCall, Ted, 321
McCay, Winsor (pseud. Silas), 15, 61, 267, 468, 497
McClelland, Hugh, 498
McClure, Darrell, 482, 789
McEvoy, Joseph Patrick, 255
Macherot, Raymond, 199
MacIntosh, Craig, 672
McManus, George, 18, 155, 501, 567, 568, 596, 662
McNamara, John, 599
McNeill, Hugh, 502, 590
MacNelly, Feff, 697
McWilliams, Alden, 235
Madam and Eve, 503
Mafalda, 504
Mager, Charles Augustus (Gus), 505
Mager's Monks, 505
Magni, Enzo, 597
Magnus (pseud. of Raviola, Roberto), 86, 640
Magrius, 123
Male Call, 507
Mama's Boyz, 218
Manara, Maurilio, 508
Mandrake the Magician, 509
Mannen som gör vad som faller honom in, 93, 510
Manos Kelly, 511
Mantena, Dick, 100
Marc, Ralph (pseud. of Marcello, Raffaelo Carlo), 511
Marcello, Raffaelo Carlo (pseud. Marc, Ralph), 511
Margie (pseud. of Buell, Marjorie Henderson), 486
Marijac (pseud. of Dumas, Jacques), 774
Marina, 238
Mark Trail, 513
Marlette, Doug, 39
Marmittone, 513
Maroto, Esteban, 203

Marsh, Norman, 233
Marston, William Moulton (pseud. Moulton, Charles), 515, 816
Martin, Edgar Everett, 147, 515
Martin, Jacque, 87
Martin, Menny Eusobio, 516
Martinek, Frank V., 264
Martin Mystere, 517
Marvelman, 517
Mary Marvel, 518
Mary Worth, 519
Matena, Dick, 520
Matsumoto, Reiji, 520
Mattotti, Lorenzo, 521
Maurović, Andrija, 522
Maus, 41, 523
Max, 523
Max und Moritz, 12
McCall, Ted, 71
Mell (pseud. of Lazarus, Mel), 537, 544
Melouah, Sid Ali, 526
Men of the Mounted, 71
Men Who Broke the Tube, The, 117
Mercenario, El, 688
Meskin, Morton (pseud. Morton, Mort, Jr.), 694
Messick, Dale, 151, 527
Mézières, Jean-Claude, 786
Miao Di, 528
Michel, 529
Michel Tanguy, 529
Micheluzzi, Attilio (pseud. Bajeff, Igor Artz), 530
Michel Vaillant, 530
Mickey Finn, 531
Mickey Mouse, 532
Mike Macke, 534
Mikkelsen, H. Dahl, 300
Milazzo, Ivo, 439
Millar, Jeff, 745
Miller, David, 235
Miller, Frank, 113
Miller, Sydney Leon, 658
Ming Foo, 536
Minnitt, Frank, 132
Minute Movies, 537
Miss Peach, 537
Miyazaki, Hayao, 563
Mizuki, Shigeru, 367
Moco, 85
Modeste et Pompon, 318
Modesty Blaise, 36
Mogenson, Jørgenson, 87
Momma, 544
Monica, 243
Moniquet, Marcel, 413
Monsieur Poche, 545
Montana, Bob, 545
Moomin, 546
Mooney, Jim, 719
Moon Mullins, 546, 810
Moore, Alan, 548
Moore, Alan (pseud. Vile, Curt), 800

Moore, Ray, 612
Moores, Richard, 21, 335
Mora, Angel José, 195
Mora, Victor (pseud. Alcazar, Victor), 178
Mordillo, Guillermo, 548
Morley, Allan, 442
Moroni-Celsi, Guido (pseud. Sterny), 549
Morris (pseud. of Bevère, Maurice de), 493
Mort Cinder, 549
Morton, Mort, Jr. (pseud. of Meskin, Morton), 694
Mosley, Zack, 711
Mother Goose and Grimm, 550
Motley's Crew, 551
Moulton, Charles (pseud. of Marston, William Moulton), 515, 816
Mr. and Mrs., 538
Mr. and Mrs. Dillwater, 693
Mr. Jack, 539
Mr. Kiasu, 540
Mr. Natural, 541
M Subito, 790
Muggs and Skeeter, 552
Muñoz, José, 85, 553
Murphy, James Edward, 554
Muster, Miki, 555
Mutt and Jeff, 16, 66, 555
Muttersorgen, 453
Myers, Russell, 156
Myra North, 557
Mystérieuse Matin, Midi et Soir, 313
Mystiska 2:an, 557

N

Nagashima, Shinji, 328, 560
Nancy, 560
Napolean, 561
Nausicaä of the Valley of Wind, 563
Navojev, Nikola, 830
Naylor, Robert, 564
Neels, Marc (pseud. Sleen, Marc), 566
Negro Raul, El, 565
Nelvana, 565
Nero, 566
Newlyweds, The, 567
Nibsy the Newsboy, 568
Nicholls, Sydney Wentworth, 294
Nick, 569
Nickel, Helmut, 571, 656
Nick Fury, 64-65, 67
Nick Knatterton, 571
Nidasio, Grazia, 786
91 Karlsson, 572
Ninja Bugeichō, 26, 572
Niño, Alex N., 573
Nipper, 574
Nizzi, Claudio, 575
Norakuro, 576

Norris, Paul, 791
Nowlan, Philip, 25, 160

O

O. A. (pseud. of Andersson, Oskar Emil), 93, 510
Occhio di Luna, 575
O'Donnell, Peter, 36
O'Donoghue, Michael, 723
Oesterheld, Hector German, 580
Ohser, Erich (pseud. Plauen, E. O.), 581, 790
Okamoto, Ippei, 581
O'Keefe, Neil, 248
O'Neal, Frank, 699
O'Neill, Dan, 583
Onésime, 197
On Stage, 585
Oor Wullie, 585
Opper, Frederick Burr, 13, 89, 369, 586
Orr, Martha, 47
Otoko Oidon, 520
Otomo, Katsuhiro, 589
Otto, Max A., 731
Our Boarding House, 590
Our Ernie, 590
Outcault, Richard Felton, 44, 168, 591, 824
Out Our Way, 592, 810
Overgard, John, 728
Over the Hedge, 593
Ozark Ike, 594

P

Palacio, Lino (pseud. Flax), 263
Palacios, Antonio Hernandez, 511
Panaligan, Noly, 599
Panhandle Pete, 596
Pansy Potter, 596
Pantera Bionda, 597
Parker, Brant, 815
Pa's Son-in-Law, 804
Patoruzú, 597, 598
Patsy, 598
Paulette, 615
Paul Temple, 599
Payaso, 599
Payne, A. B., 619
Payo, El, 601
Pazienza, Andrea, 601
Peanuts, 33, 60, 602
Pease, Charlie, 188
Pecos Bill, 603
Pedrazza, Augusto, 84
Pedrito El Drito, 603
Pekar, Harvey, 90

Pekka Puupää, 604
Pellos, René, 604
Peng Guoliang, 605
Pepito, 606
Père Ladébauche, Le, 607
Perishers, The, 608
Perry, 609
Peter Piltdown, 610
Peters, Mike, 550
Petersson, Rudolf, 572
Pete the Tramp, 611
Pett, Norman, 410
Peyo (pseud. of Culliford, Pierre), 680
Pfeufer, Carl, 262, 611
Phantom, The, 612
Philémon, 613
Pichard, Georges, 615, 781
Pieds-Nickelés, Les, 16, 616
Pif le Chien, 617
Pini, Wendy, 279
Pinky Rankin, 618
Pinoy Moreno, 80
Pionniers de l'Espérance, Les, 49, 618
Pip, Squeak and Wilfred, 619
Pip (pseud. of Davies, Roland), 210
Pistol Jim, 620
Pitt, Reginald, 620
Pitt, Stanley John, 620
Placid et Muzo, 621
Plastic Man, 621
Platt, Kin, 538
Plauen, E. O. (pseud. of Ohser, Erich), 581, 790
Plumb, Charlie, 281
Poelsma, Dominic, 204
Pogo, 33, 622
Poïvet, Raymond, 49, 617
Polly and Her Pals, 624
Pop, 624
Popeye, 67
Potts, The, 22, 625
Powerhouse Pepper, 626
Pratt, Hugo, 101, 108, 215, 284
Prince Valiant, 59, 629
Private Berger, 151
Professeur Nimbus, Le, 630
Professor Pi, 631
Pruneda, Salvado, 631
Puck, Peter, 664
Pussycat Princess, 632
Putzker, Ronald, 633

Q

Quincy, 635
Quino (pseud. of Lavado, Joaquin), 504
Quinterno, Dante, 597, 598

R

Raboy, Emanuel (Mac), 184
Radilović, Julio, 380
Radio Patrol, 638
Rahan, 638
Randall, 34
Ranxerox, 475
Rasmus Klump, 639
Raviola, Roberto (pseud. Magnus), 86, 640
Raymond, Alex, 28, 308, 427, 652, 686
Rebuffi, Giorgio, 642, 765
Red Barry, 642
Red Detachment of Women, The, 643
Redeye, 643
Redipicche, 644
Redondo, Virgilio, 743
Red Ryder, 48, 645
Reed, Rod, 50
Reggie, 646
Régnier, Michel (pseud. Greg; Albert, Louis), 127, 209, 646
Reiche, Volker, 647
Rémi, Georges (pseud. Hergé), 25, 764
René (pseud. of Lehner, René), 473
Rex Morgan, M.D., 649
Reynolds, Basil, 650
Ric Hochet, 650
Rick O'Shay, 652
Rip Kirby, 28
Ritt, William, 152
Rivolta dei Racchi, La, 170
Robbins, Frank, 421
Robbins, Trina, 654
Roberto Alcazar, 655
Robin Hood and Company, 655
Robinson, 656
Robinson, Fred, 166, 590, 656
Robinson, Paul, 56
Robinson Crusoe Esq., 158
Rob the Rover, 657
Roca, Luis, 677
Rocco Vargas, 772
Rod Craig, 658
Rodriguez, Braulio (pseud. Buyulla), 249
Romano Il Legionario, 659
Romeo Brown, 391
Romita, John, 35, 719
Room and Board, 80
Roscher, Franz, 529
Rose is Rose, 661
Rosie's Beau, 662
Ross, Charles, 87
Ross, Russell, 411
Rosso, Gustavo, 266
Rowlandson, Thomas, 663
Rowlf, 213
Roy, Yves (pseud. of Hidalgo, Francisco), 259
Rubio, Adolfo Lopez, 343

Rudi, 664
Ruggles, 665
Rupert, 23, 665
Russell, Clarence D., 611
Russell, James Newton, 22, 625
Rusty Riley, 347, 667
Ryan, Tom K., 776
Ryssack, Edouard, 149

S

Sad Sack, The, 107, 669
Saint-Ogan, Alain, 545, 670, 829
Saitō, Takao, 52, 350, 671
Salinas, Alberto, 204
Salinas, José K., 671
Salinas, José-Luis, 50
Sally Forth, 672
Sampayo, Carlos, 85, 552, 553, 714
Sam Pezzo, 338
Sam's Strip, 673
Sansom, Arthur, 148
Sasuke, 676
Saturna Contro la Terra, 676
Saunders, Allen, 519
Saunders, John, 235
Scarth, 677
Scenes of Malaysian Life, 443
Sceriffo Fox, Lo, 642
Schacheri, Rico, 503
Scheuer, Chris, 679
Schmidt, Charles, 638
Schmidt, Manfred, 571
Schneider, Howie, 276
Schtroumpfes, Les, 680
Schubel, Heinz, 495
Schultheiss, Matthias, 681
Schultze, Carl Edward, 682
Schulz, Charles Monroe, 33, 60, 602
Sclavi, Tiziano, 191
Scolari, Giovanni, 676
Scorchy Smith, 56, 684
Secchi, Luciano (pseud. Bunker, Max), 86, 685
Secret Agent X-9, 686
Seekers, The, 686
Segar, Elzie Crisler, 687, 755
Segrelles, Vicente, 688
Sennin Buraku, 452
Serafino, 688
Sergio Amazonas, 215
Sexton Blake, 691
Sgt. Fury, 689
Sgt. Rock, 689
Shadow, The, 433, 692
Shaw, Ernest, 693
Shearer, Ted, 635
Sheena, 694
Shelton, Gilbert, 290
Shen Pei, 695
Shimada, Keizo, 143
Shimizu, Kon, 696

Shirato, Sanpei, 572, 676
Shōchan no Bōken, 697
Shoe, 697
Shōnen Oja, 698
Short Ribs, 699
Shuster, Joe, 27, 699
Sickles, Noel, 56, 684
Siegel, Jerry, 27
Signor Bonaventura, Il, 45, 701
Sigurd, 702
Silas (pseud. of McCay, Winsor), 267, 468
Silly Symphonies, 703
Silver Surfer, The, 448
Silvestri, Guido (pseud. Silver), 494
Sim, David, 193
Simon, Joe, 28
Sinner, 351
Sío, Enric, 470
Siopawman, 705
Si Yeoo Ki, 706
Skeates, Steve, 394
Skeets, 707
Skippy, 707
Skit and Skat, 650
Skyroads, 708
Slam Bradley, 699
Sleen, Marc (pseud. of Neels, Marc), 566
Slim Jim, 709
Slylock Fox, 710
Smilin' Jack, 711
Smith, Al, 202
Smith, Sidney, 21, 363
Smitty, 712
Smokey Stover, 713
Smythe, Reginald, 95
Snelgrove, Charles R., 655
Soglow, Otto, 485
Solano López, Francisco, 714
Solovjev, Sergej, 715
Sonoyama, Shunji, 38, 716
Sor Pampurio, 717
Spider-Man, 35, 719
Spiegelman, Arthur, 41, 523, 720
Spiegle, Dan, 720
Spirit, The, 48, 721
Spirou, 721
Spooky, 722
Spotlight on Sally, 302
Spring and Autumn in Cat Kingdom, 475
Springer, Frank, 723
Spy Smasher, 724
Starr, Leonard, 585
Steranko, James, 64-65, 67, 181, 726
Sterny (pseud. of Moroni-Celsi, Guido), 549
Sterrett, Cliff, 624
Steve Canyon, 29, 728
Steve Roper, 728
Stonehenge Kit, 729
Sto (pseud. of Tofano, Sergio), 701
Storm, George, 142

Striebel, John H., 255
Strip, George (pseud. of Lobačev, Jurij (Djordje)), 488
Studdy, George E., 145
Stups, 731
SturmTruppen, 731
Sub-Mariner, The, 287, 732
Sugiura, Shigeru, 733
Su Lang, 734
Sullivan, Ed, 638
Sullivan, Pat, 299
Sung Yu-chieh, 643
Superman, 27, 69, 548, 736
Surburban Cowgirls, 733
Suske en Wiske, 737
Swamp Thing, 739
Swan, Charles, 548
Swan, Curt, 548
Swarte, Joost, 739
Swinnerton, James Guilford (pseud. Guilford, James), 484, 539, 740
Sylvia, 392

T

Tagawa, Suihou, 576
Tagisan Ng Mga Agimat, 743
Tailspin Tommy, 743
Tales of Wonder, 43
Taliaferro, Charles Alfred, 703
Tank McNamara, 745
Tanku Tankurō, 745
Tardi, Jacques, 746
Tarzan, 24, 70, 460, 747, 748
Taylor, Alfred H., 691
Tchao Hong-pen, 706
Teddy Ted, 385
Telestrip, 750
Templeton, Ben, 551
Tenpei Tenma, 750
Terrors of the Tiny Tads, 751
Terry and the Pirates, 751, 820
Tetsujin 28gō, 752
Tetsuwan-Atom, 33, 753, 754
Texas Willer, 754
Tezuka, Osamu, 33, 78, 387, 428, 753, 754
That's My Pop, 19
Their Only Child, 501
They'll Do It Every Time, 373
Thimble Theater, 687, 755
Thor, 51, 757
Thorne, Frank, 758
Three Lives, 464
Thunderjet, 773
Tianus, 571
Tibet (pseud. of Gascard, Gilbert), 650
Tibor, 759
Tiffany Jones, 760
Tiger, 760
Tiger Tim, 761

Tigri de Mompracem, Le, 549
Tillie the Toiler, 762
Timid Soul, The, 763
Tim Tyler's Luck, 763, 826
Tintin, 25, 764
Tippie, 272
Tiramolla, 765
Tobias Seicherl, 765, 766
Tofano, Sergio (pseud. Sto), 701
Tōfujin (pseud. of Kabashima, Kasuichi), 697
Tommie's Avonturen, 157
Tom Poes, 767
Tony Falco, 768
Toonder, Jan Gerhard, 436
Toonder, Marten, 454, 520, 767
Toonerville Folks, 769
Toots and Casper, 554
Töpffer, Rodolphe, 770
Toppi, Sergio, 45, 770
Torres, Victor, 772
Toth, Alexander, 773
Touareg, The, 526
Tourret, Pat, 760
Tourtel, Mary, 23
Tower of Shadows, 726
Tripje en Liezenbertha, 774
Trog (pseud. of Fawkes, Wally), 310
Trois Mousquetaires du Maquis, Les, 774
Trucker, 681
Trudeau, Garry, 34, 264
Tsien Siao-Tai, 706
Tumbleweeds, 776
Turner, Leslie, 777
Turner, Morrie, 803
Tuthill, Harry J., 164

U

Uderzo, Albert, 57, 103, 529
Ulysse, 781
Uncle Scrooge, 112
Upside Downs, The, 782
U Zemlji Lijepog Nogometa, 266

V

Valentina, 37, 785
Valentina Melaverde, 786
Valérian, 786
Valherbe, Jean (pseud. of Forest, Jean-Claude), 37, 110, 313
Vampirella, 787
Van Buren, Raeburn, 75, 788
Van der Born, Bob, 631
Vandersteen, Willy, 128, 737
Vanilla and the Villians, 789
Vaño, Eduardo, 655
Van Raemdonck, George, 17, 163

Vater und Sohn, 581, 790
Vecchia America, 175
Vel, Rob (pseud. of Velter, Robert), 790
Velasquez, Tony, 253
Velter, Robert (pseud. Darthel, J.; Vel, Rob), 790
Verbeck (a.k.a Verbeek), Gustave, 751, 782
Vic Jordan, 791
Vidić, Branko, 830
Vidocq, 792
Vigil, Guillermo, 601
Vile, Curt (pseud. of Moore, Alan), 800
Voight, Charles A., 129
Voltar, 793

W

Wakefield, George William, 795
Walker, Addison Mortimer (pseud. Addison), 62, 122, 144, 383
Walling, Dow, 707
Walsh, Brandon, 482, 536
Wäscher, Hansrudi, 570, 759
Wash Tubbs, 799
Watchmen, 800
Watkins, Dudley D., 244, 492, 585
Watt, John Millar, 624
Watterson, Bill, 174

Weary Willie and Tired Tim, 801
Weber, Bob, Jr., 710
Webster, Harold Tucker, 762, 802
Webster, Tom, 803
Wee Pals, 803
Wein, Len, 739
Weird Science, 819
Wellington, Charles H., 804
Werner, 805
Westover, Russell, 762
Wheelan, Edgar, 537
When a Feller Needs a Friend, 806
Where I'm Coming From, 807
White, Brian, 574, 807
White Indian, 319
Whole Blooming Family, The, 501
Wiedersheim, Grace (pseud. of Drayton, Grace), 268
Willard, Frank Henry, 546, 810
Williams, James Robert, 592, 810
Williamson, Al, 811
Williamson, Skip, 36
Willi Wiederhopf, 647
Wingert, Dick, 395
Winnie Winkle, 814
Wizard of Id, The, 815
Wolinski, Georges, 615, 815
Wolverton, Basil, 626, 816
Wonder Woman, 515, 817
Wood, Wallace, 819
World of Lily Wong, The, 296
Wrightson, Berni, 739
Wunder, George, 820

X

Xiao Ding (pseud. of Ding Cong), 250
Xiao Hou's Adventures, 528
X-Men, 471, 821

Y

Yamagami, Tatsuhiko, 332
Yamakawa, Soji, 698
Yeats, Jack B., 823
Yellow Kid, The, 44, 824
Yokoyama, Mitsuteru, 752
Yokoyama, Ryūichi, 325, 825
Young, Lyman, 763, 826
Young, Murat (Chic), 138, 208, 827
Yue Xiaoying, 827

Z

Zig et Puce, 829
Zigomar, 830
Zippy, 359
Zoon van de Zon, De, 520
Zozo, 831
Zvitorepec, 555

A

Aardvark (U.S.) (college magazine), 496

A.B.C. (Belgium) (magazine), 407

ABC Comics (Arnold Book Company), 96

ABC (Spain) (newspaper), 341

Acclaim Comics (Valiant Comics) (U.S.), 204, 778

Ace Comics (U.S.), 206, 319, 462

Ace Publications (Philippines), 32, 86, 126, 659, 675, 772

ACG Comics (U.S.), 167, 219, 318, 364, 678, 811

Acme Features Syndicate (U.S.), 478

ACME (Italy) (publisher), 494

Action Comics (Germany), 94, 178, 462

Adams and Fidler Agency, 608-9

Admiralty Publishing, 246

Adult comics/strips
Chūsingura, 452
Crepax, Guido, and, 221
Diabolik, 245
Embleton, Ronald S., and, 282
Fazekas, Attila, and, 294
Isabella, 404-5
Kojima, Koo, and, 452
Kuroneko Don, 452
Little Annie Fannie, 481
Little Ego, 338
Melouah, Sid Ali, and, 525
Miss Doron Ototo, 452
Sennin Buraku, 452
Tops, 135
Wicked Wanda, 282
See also Erotic comics/strips;
Underground comix

Adventure strips, 23-25, 33-34
Adventures of Bobby Crusoe, The, 273
Adventures of Larry Steele, The, 592
Adventures of Luther Arkwright, 744
African Adventures for Plavi Vjesnik, 638
Air Hawk and the Flying Doctors, 81-82, 255
Airship Man, The, 82-83
Airy Alf and Bouncing Billy, 83
Akadō Suzunosuke, 83-84
Alan Ford, 85-86, 685
Alix l'Intrépide, 87
Alma Grande, 89
Arabelle la Sirène, 98-99
Argonautjes, De, 100
Arys Buck, 781
Astérix, 352, 781
Ballata del Mare Salato, Una, 108
Barbe-Rouge, 339
Benjamin et Benjamine, 352, 781
Ben Webster's Career, 613
Bernard Prince, 127, 398, 647
Big Kid, 716
Bimbo Bambus, 566

Black Lion, 282
Black Mask-Lord Warwick, 716
Blondin et Cirage, 339
Blue Sea and Red Heart, 141
Bobby Thatcher, 141-42, 614
Bob Morane, 142-43, 788
Bōken Dankichi, 143
Botond, 294
Bound to Win, 613-14
Brick Bradford, 152, 354, 576
Bronc Peeler, 156
Bruce Gentry, 158-59
Bruno Brazil, 159, 647, 788
Bulletje en Bonestaak, 163
Capitan l'Audace, 176, 543
Capitan Trueno, El, 178-79
Captain Easy, 777, 800
Carev štitonoša, 716
Chatillo y Federico, 197
Chevalier Ardent, 198, 217
Chip Collins, Adventurer, 653
Chuck White, 587
Clip Carson, 303, 434
Connie, 212-13
Corentin, 214
Crimebuster, 222
Cuore Garibaldino, 228
Cuto, 229-30
Daabu, 626
Dago, 818
Dateline: Danger!, 234-35, 502, 677
Dauntless Durham of the U.S.A., 382
Dick Fulmine, 246-47
Dickie Dare, 247-48, 801
Drago, 267
Druka, 217
Dzjengis Khan, 273, 491
Enfance, L', 338
Eric de Noorman, 283, 457-58
Famille Fenouillard, La, 292
Felix, 297-99
Fiffige Alf, 297, 491
Flamingo, 306
Forza John, 314
4 As, Les, 217
Freddy and Fred, 339
Gaucho, Il, 508, 627
Gim Toro, 342
Gino e Gianni, 344
Gli Aristocratici, 190, 731
Gordon, Soldier of Fortune, 228, 352, 611
Gorin e Obi, 608
Grote Pyr, De, 519-20
Guerrero del Antifaz, El, 361-62
Hakaba no Kitarō, 366-67
Harisu no Kaze, 370
Hatanosuke Hinomaru, 373
Haxtur, 375
Hernàn el Corsario, 380
Hoshi no tategoto, 542
Indio, El, 400
Jabato, El, 407
Jean des Flandres, 413

Jean Valhardi, 196, 339
Jo, Zette et Jocko, 649
Jonas Fink, 338
Jon Fury, 773
Kabul de Bengala, 580
Kaiketsu Harimao, 405
Kevin the Bold, 441
Kilabot Ng Persia, 573
Legija prokletib, 715
Liberty Kid, 476
Lindor Covas, 480-81
Luc Tremplin, 217
Mark Merlin, 527
Max, 523-24
Mercenary, The, 688
Michel Tanguy, 529
Michel Vaillant, 529-30
Mike Steel, 410
Ming Foo, 482, 535-36
Miss Fury, 537
Myra North, 557
Mysteries of Chicago, 464
Mysterious Driver No. 13, 411
Mystiska 2:an, 557-58
Nagagutsu no Sanjûshi, 559
Narciso Putiferio, 562
Natacha, 562
Nero, 564, 566
Nippur de Lagash, 818
O.G. Whiz, 724
Ombra, L', 190
Panhandle Pete, 595
Pauline McPeril, 470
Payo, El, 600
Pepito, 606-7
Père Ladébauche, Le, 607-8
Peter Pat, 420
Peter seltsame Reisen, 570, 813
Phantom, The, 611-12
Phil Hardy, 141, 613-14
Pier Cloruro De'Lambicchi, 616
Pinky Rankin, 617-18
Pippo, 408, 618
Pom et Teddy, 217
Prince Errant, 628
Prince Valiant, 628-29
Pultos, 202
Rahan, 638-39
Ramir, 418
Red Detachment of Women, The, 642-43
Red Gregory, 535
Red Knight, The, 644
Ridder Roodhart, 100, 372, 519
Rip Kirby, 627-28
Roberto Alcazar y Pedrín, 654-55
Rob the Rover, 657
Rod Craig, 384, 535, 658
Rolan Aquila, 562
Roland Eagle, 659
Roy Mann, 273, 530
Rusty and His Pals, 303, 434
Rusty Riley, 666-67
Sabaku no Maō, 669

Safari, 575, 789
Sahara, 282
Samson, 435
Sand e Zeos, 608
Sarge Steele, 344
Schtroumpes, Les, 680
Sciuscià, 683-84
Segreto del castello, 575
Siberian Girl, 716
Siegfried, 534
Signor Bonaventura, Il, 701-2
Silver Roy, 703
Slim and Tubby, 644
Smitty, 712
Smokey Stover, 712-13
Soldino, 715
Speed Tarō, 718
Spirou, 721
Suske en Wiske, 737-38
Taró, 637, 746
Terry and the Pirates, 751-52, 820
Three Brothers, 278
Tightrope Tim, 383-84
Tim Tyler's Luck, 763-64, 826
Tintin, 648-49, 764
Tony Falco, 768
Tough Tod & Happy Annie, 502
Trucker, 682
Turok, Son of Stone, 103, 524,
    567-68, 778
Unbesiegbaren, Die, 459
Uomo delle nevi, L', 508
Wash Tubbs, 220, 777, 799-800
White Boy, 808
Zig et Puce, 829
See also Jungle strips; Science
    fiction strips
Advertising strips
Big Boy, 131
Campbell Soup Kids, 632
Captain Tootsie, 120
Chesty Bond, 535
Commando Gibbs, 125
Duke Handy, 454
Globi, 346
Johnson, Ferd, and, 423
Lurchis Abenteuer, 495
Mister Coffee Nerves, 700
for Phillips Stickasoles, 544
Pitt, Stanley John, and, 620
Sammy Squirrel, 370
Advocate, The (U.S.) (magazine), 226
African-American strips
Candy, 587
Curtis, 228-29
Cuties, 778
Friday Foster, 322
Herb & Jamaal, 379
Jumpstart, 426-27
Lookin' Fine, 229
Luther, 778, 807
Mama's Boyz, 218
PattyJo 'n Ginger, 587
Quincy, 228, 635, 778

Torchy Brown, 587
Where I'm Coming From, 806-7
See also Ethnic strips; Integrated
    strips
After Schock (U.S.) (underground
    comic), 654, 812
Aftonbadet (Sweden) (newspaper), 480
Agostino della Casa (Italy)
    (publisher), 91
Aidelaide News (Australia)
    (newspaper), 364
Ajax comics, 400, 613
Albi d'Oro (Italy) (comic book), 602,
    792
Albi le Piú Belle Avventure (Italy)
    (magazine), 539
Albo dell'Intrepido (Italy) (magazine),
    603
Alcala Fight Komix (Philippines), 705,
    793
Alcala Komix (Philippines) (comic
    book), 573
Alchemy Press (Germany)
    (underground comics), 744
Alcotan (Spain) (magazine), 138
Alfred Harmsworth comic weeklies
    (G.B.), 823
Algemeen Dagblad (Netherlands)
    (newspaper), 456
Algerie-Actualites (Algeria) (weekly),
    525
Ali Baba (Italy) (magazine), 785
Allers (Sweden) (magazine), 94, 480
All Hands (U.S.) (magazine), 499
Allied Newspapers (U.S.), 544
All Sports (G.B.), 693
Allt för Alla (Sweden) (newspaper),
    572
Alter Alter (Italy) (magazine), 150,
    521-22, 530, 771
Alter-Ego (U.S.) (fanzine), 756
Alterlinus (Italy) (magazine), 170, 508,
    600
Amalgamated Press (G.B.)
    Bell, Walter, and, 125
    Booth, Walter, and, 146
    Cocking, Percy (pseud. Daw, Jack),
        and, 205-6
    Colquhoun, Joe, and, 209
    Derickson Denie, 243
    Diamond, H. Louis, and, 245-46
    Embleton, Ronald S., and, 282
    Flinders, Evelyn, and, 310
    Foxwell, Herbert, and, 317
    Gunnis, Louis, and, 363
    Heath, George, and, 377
    Hill, Albert, and, 386
    Jukes, John L., and, 426
    McNeill, Hugh, and, 502
    Minnitt, Frank, and, 536
    Perrott, Reg, and, 609
    Price, Cyril, and, 628
    Reid, Ken, and, 648
    Reynolds, Basil, and, 650

Robinson, Fred, and, 656
Sexton Blake, 690
Shaw, Ernest, and, 693
Turner, Ron, and, 778
Wakefield, George William, and,
    795-96
Walker, Brian, and, 797
White, Hugh Stanley, and, 808
Wilson, Roy, and, 812
See also Fleetway Productions;
    Fleetway Publications
Ambassador Press (U.S.), 816
American Comics Group (U.S.), 315
American Humorist (U.S.)
    (supplement), 436-37, 582, 586,
    824
American Press Association (U.S.),
    499
American Visual Corporation (U.S.),
    278
America's Humor (U.S.) (magazine),
    816
Ang Bali tang Pilipino (Philippines)
    (newspaper), 646
Anglo-American Publishing
    Company, 321-22
Anglo Comics, 96
Animal strips
Atomic Mouse, 533
Bamse, 94
Beep Beep the Road Runner, 122
Billville Birds, 392
Boner's Ark, 142-43
Buck Nix, 582, 711
Chlorophylle, 199-200
Cicero's Cat, 201-2
Coconino County, 381
Come On, Steve!, 210-11
Copyright, 313
Cricri Souris d'Appartement, 175
Damon and Pythias, 727
Dippy Duck, 582
Discontinued Stories, 388, 415
Donald Duck, 260-61, 535, 744
Dot and Dash, 727
Eek and Meek, 276
Fix und Foxi, 305-6
Fox and the Crow, The, 315
Funny Fauna, 808
Gnuffen, 535
Groucho the Monk, 504, 505
Hagen, Fagin and O'Toole, 155
Hamfatto the Monk, 504
Hayseeds, 370, 375
Heckle and Jeckle, 378
Henpecko the Monk, 504
And Her Name Was Maud, 93-94
Huckleberry Hollow, 488
Japhet and Happy, 412-13
In Jungle Land, 504
Kibaō, 442-43
In the Kingdom of Apes, 464
Knocko the Monk, 504, 505
Köter & Co., 285

Krazy Kat, 381, 457
Little Bears and Tykes, 483
Little People, The, 488
Little White Rabbit and Big Grey Wolf, 605
Lo Scimiotto, 508
Lupo, 493-94
Lupo Alberto, 494-95
Mager's Monks, 504-5
Maus, 522-23, 719
Mecki, 285, 525, 534, 648
Mickey Mouse, 531-32, 744
Mighty Mouse, 532-33
Mr. Jack, 539-40, 740
Mount Ararat, 483, 740
Mutts, 556
Nervo the Monk, 504
Old Doc Yak, 582, 711
Oscar, 587-88
Otto and Blotto, 360
Over the Hedge, 593-94
Panda, 370, 595
Pellefant, 94
Peter Rabbit, 611
Pif le Chien, 616-17, 642
Pigglys, The, 709
Pip, Squeak and Wilfred, 618-19
Placid et Muzo, 617, 621
Playbox, The, 317
Pogo, 438, 622-23
Polletje Pluim, 100, 519
Popol et Virginie ou Pays des Lapinos, 649
Porky Pig, 625
Priča s Rubašume, 566
Prosper l'Ours, 670
Puž and Pužek, 566
Rasmus Klump, 639
Rhymo the Monk, 504, 505
Rudy, 593, 729
Rupert, 665
Sherlocko the Monk, 374, 504, 505, 695
Shipwrecked, The, 464
Shoe, 697-98
Slylock Fox and Comics for Kids, 709
Small Fox with Big Feet, 605
Snake Tales, 713
Spring and Autumn in Cat Kingdom, 475
Supermouse, 533
Teddy Tail, 317, 748-49
Tiger Tim, 760-61
Tiger Time, 317
Tightwaddo the Monk, 504
Tom and Jerry, 766-67
U.S. Acres, 237, 333-34
Ushitsuki, 542
In the Wild West, 464
Wise Quacks, 392
Woody Woodpecker, 535
Zoo Film, 221
Zoo-Illogical Snapshots, 450
Zoolandia, 221

Zozo, 830-31
Zvitorepec, 554
See also Cat strips; Dog strips
Animation, 66-67
A Noite (Brazil) (newspaper), 83
Answers (G.B.) (magazine), 693
Anvil, The (G.B.) (magazine), 368
A.P. Comics (G.B.). *See* Amalgamated Press
Arcade (U.S.) (underground comic), 719
Archie-Radio Group/MLJ (U.S.)
   Archie, 99-100, 545-46
   Berg, David, and, 126
   Binder, Jack, and, 133
   Biro, Charles, and, 134
   Black Hood, 136-37
   Giordano, Richard, and, 344
   Hangman, The, 368
   Hercules, 379
   Kane, Gil, and, 433
   Kanigher, Robert, and, 435
   Kida, Fred, and, 443
   Kirby, Jack, and, 447
   Krigstein, Bernard, and, 458
   Kubert, Joe, and, 460
   Leav, Mort, and, 471
   Meskin, Morton (pseud. Morton, Mort, Jr.), and, 526
   Montana, Bob, and, 545
   S. M. Iger Studios and, 400
   Shadow, The, 692
   Shield, The, 695-96, 696
   Simon, Joseph, and, 705
   Steel Sterling, 726
   Teenage Mutant Ninja Turtles, 749
   THUNDER Agents, 759
   Web, The, 801-2, 802
   Woolfolk, William, and, 818-19
Arena (Yugoslavia) (magazine), 239
Ares Publications (Philippines), 773
Året Runt (Sweden) (newspaper), 572
Argentinian Ediciones Record, 239
Argentovivo (Italy) (weekly), 86, 170, 180
Armand Colin (France) (publisher), 290, 292
Armed services strips
   Barry the Boob, 687
   Beetle Bailey, 122-23, 796
   Bluey and Curley, 141, 364
   Buz Sawyer, 169-70
   Crock, 597
   Don Winslow of the Navy, 263-64
   Eisner, Will, and, 278
   Elworth, Lennart, and, 282
   Facéties du Sapeur Camember, Les, 290
   Flygsoldat 113 Bom, 282, 314, 479
   47:an Löken, 282, 314, 572
   G.I. Joe, 539
   Gibernetta, 202
   Half-Hitch, 367, 441
   Hubert, 395-96

   Male Call, 506-7
   Marmittone, 513-14
   Mr. Breger, 538-39
   91 Karlsson, 282, 572
   Private Billy Muggins, 620
   Robot Santōhei, 657
   Sad Sack, The, 669-70
   Salty Ranks, 321
   Sturmtruppen, 731
   Up Front, 782
   Wally and the Major in, 797
   See also War strips
Army Motors (U.S.) (magazine), 278
Arnold Book Company (ABC Comics), 96
Arthur J. LaFave Syndicate, 497, 561, 757
Asahigraph (Japan) (magazine), 436, 696, 697
Asahi (Japan) (newspaper), 325, 581, 697, 766
Asian Newsweekly Examiner (Philippines) (newspaper), 80
Asino, L' (Italy), 513
Aspirante, L' (Italy) (weekly), 221, 608
Associated Editors Syndicate, 389
Associated Newspapers (G.B.)
   Foxwell, Herbert, and, 317
   Moomin, 412
   Paul Temple, 599
   Tiffany Jones in, 760
Associated Newspapers Ltd. (Australia), 110, 620
Associated Press Newsfeatures
   Caniff, Milton, and, 175
   Capp, Al (pseud. of Caplin, Alfred Gerald), and, 179
   Christman, Bert, and, 200
   Dickenson, Fred, and, 246
   Dickie Dare, 247, 801
   Hicks, Reginald Ernest (pseud. Hix), and, 383-84
   Hodgins, Dick, Jr., and, 367
   Oaky Doaks, 325, 579
   Patsy, 354, 598
   Scorchy Smith, 653, 684-85
   Sickles, Noel, and, 700
   Waugh, Coulton, and, 801
   Wunder, George, and, 820
Asso di Picche (Italy), 118
Astral (G.B.) (fanzine), 232
A Suivre (France) (magazine), 85, 508
Atlanta Constitution (U.S.) (newspaper), 461
Atlas. *See* Marvel/Timely/Atlas group
Atlas/Seaboard
   Severin, John Powers, and, 690
Atlas/Seaboard Company, 757
Atlas/Seabord Company, 809
Audace, L' (Italy) (magazine)
   Albertarelli, Rino, and, 86
   American adventure strips in, 676
   Bonelli, Giovanni Luigi, and, 143, 327

Canale, Antonio, and, 175
Capitan l'Audace in, 176
Cossio, Carlo, and, 216
Dick Fulmine in, 247
Dottor Faust, Il in, 266
Furio Almirante in, 327
Virus, Il Mago della Foresta Morta in, 792
Aum Divine Truth cult, 563
Aussie (Australia) (magazine), 535
Automobile strips
  Bumper Snickers, 389
  Gasoline Alley, 335-36, 445
  Joe Jinks, 419-20
  Marc Lebut, 762
  Rosalie, 175
Aventuras (Argentina) (weekly), 239, 619
Aviation Press (U.S.), 297
Aviation strips
  Ace Drummond, 451
  Airboy, 81, 443
  Air Hawk and the Flying Doctors, 81-82, 255
  Airship Man, The, 82-83, 431
  Alfie the Air Tramp, 426
  Barney Baxter, 113-14, 534, 563-64
  Black Venus, 462
  Bob Mallard, 384
  Bruce Gentry, 158-59
  Buck Danny, 159, 396
  Buz Sawyer, 169-70, 220, 777, 800
  Captain Wings, 185, 280
  As de Pike, 341
  Elias, Leopold, and, 280
  Enemy Ace, 460-61, 757
  Evans, George, and, 287
  Flyin' Jenny, 311, 438
  Four Aces, The, 744
  Golden Eagle, 609
  Hall of Fame of the Air, The, 451
  Hurricane Hawk, 709
  Johnny Hazard, 420-22, 653
  Keaton, Russell, and, 438
  Kings of the Air, 609
  Knight, Clayton, and, 451
  Lord Pampa, 714
  Luchtrovers van Hoitika, De, 616
  Michel Tanguy, 529
  Mosley, Zack, and, 550
  Paddy Payne, 209
  Petra Chérie, 529
  Progress of Flight, 744
  Romano il Legionario, 659
  Scorchy Smith, 653, 684-85, 700
  Skylark, 728
  Skyroads, 438, 708-9
  Smilin' Jack, 550, 710
  Steve Canyon, 727-28
  Tailspin Tommy, 743-44
  On the Wing, 550, 710
  Wings of Fortune, 609
Avivato (Argentina) (magazine), 595

Avon Comics
  Fox, Gardner, and, 316
  Frazetta, Frank, and, 319
  Heath, Russell, and, 377
  Kubert, Joe, and, 460
  Orlando, Joe, and, 587
  Wood, Wallace, 818
AVRO-bode (Netherlands) (weekly), 767
Avventure Western (Italy), 111
Avventuroso, L' (Italy) (weekly), 676, 792
Awantura (Poland) (magazine), 820

B

Baberiba (Netherlands) (magazine), 491
Baily Comics, 319
Baily Shop, 433
Balilla, Il (Italy) (weekly), 86, 664
Ballantine (U.S.) (publisher), 323-24
Ballyhoo (U.S.) (magazine), 325, 647
Baltimore American (U.S.) (newspaper), 140
Baltimore Sun (U.S.) (newspaper), 419
Bancarella, La (Italy) (magazine), 521
Bannawag (Philippines) (magazine), 462
Bardon Art Studios (Spain), 94, 177
Barnett Press (G.B.), 125
Baroud (Algeria) (magazine), 525
Barrett Publishing (U.S.), 96
Baseball strips
  Abu-san, 542
  Ace no Jōken, 542
  Chikaino Makyū, 199
  Kyojin no Hoshi, 465
  Mizushima, Shinji, and, 542
  Otoko Doahou Koushien, 542
  Ozark Ike, 594
  Yakyūkyō no Uta, 542
Bastei Verlag (Germany) (publisher), 128, 663, 798
Beano (G.B.)
  Baxendale, Leo, and, 118
  Carter, Reg, and, 187
  Davies, Roland (pseud. Pip), and, 236
  Dennis the Menace (G.B.) in, 241-42
  Hargreaves, Harry, and, 369
  Holroyd, Bill, and, 369
  Judge, Malcolm (pseud. Mal), and, 424
  Lord Snooty and His Pals in, 491-92
  McNeill, Hugh, and, 502
  Nixon, Robert, and, 574
  Pansy Potter in, 595
  Reid, Ken, and, 648
Beaverbrook Newspapers (G.B.), 282
Beck-Constanza studio, 223
Belang van Limburg (Belgium), 128

Bell Features and Publishing Company (Canada), 251-52, 565, 606, 649
Bell-McClure Syndicate. *See* United Features Syndicate
Bell Syndicate
  Barnaby, 113
  Beautiful Bab, 826
  Bobby Thatcher, 142
  Cicero's Cat, 202
  Don Winslow of the Navy, 263
  Flyin' Jenny, 311
  Funnyman, 700
  King Aroo, 446
  Looie the Lawyer, 150
  Miss Fury, 537
  Mutt and Jeff, 305, 556
  Nebbs, The, 564
  Phil Hardy, 613
  Pop, 625
  Reg'lar Fellers, 647
  Sad Sack, The, 669
  S'Matter, Pop? in, 600
  Smith, Al, and, 711
  Tailspin Tommy, 743
  Toonerville Folks, 316, 768
  Wheeler, John, and, 383
  Young, Murat (Chic), and, 826
Benjamin (France) (weekly), 670, 829
Benton and Bowles Advertising Agency, 471
Berit Minggu (Malaysia), 442
Berkley Books (U.S.) (publisher), 204
Berliner Illustrirte (Germany), 325-26, 581, 789
Berlingske Tidende (Denmark) (newspaper), 258, 468
Bertoldo, Il (Italy) (magazine), 86, 543
Better Comics, 137
  See also Nedor Group; Standard Group
B.& H. White Publications (G.B.), 807
Bhang (Italy) (magazine), 685
Biblical strips
  Redondo, Nestor, and, 645
  Rodriguez, Emilio D., and, 659
  Sinnot, Joe, and, 705
  Tales from the Great Book, 474
  Wolverton, Basil, and, 816
Biblipop (France) (magazine), 521
Bicitra (Bangladesh) (weekly), 766
Big Ass (U.S.) (comic book), 224
Big Comic Gold (Japan) (magazine), 559
Big Comic (Japan) (magazine), 349, 671
Big Comic Original (Japan) (magazine), 452
Big Comic Spirits (Japan) (weekly), 506
"Big-foot" comic art style
  Cimpellin, Leone, and, 203
  Cole, Jack, and, 206, 622
  Hägar the Horrible, 365

Kane, Robert, and, 434
Nard n' Pat and, 496
Walker, Addison Mortimer (Mort; also pseud. Addison), and, 796
Bijou (U.S.) (magazine), 449, 463, 496
Bilderbogen, 326, 774
Bild und Funk (Germany) (weekly), 459
Bild-Zeitung (Germany) (newspaper), 244-45, 651
Bilingual strips
Canadiens, Les, 197
Bimbo (Belgium) (magazine), 407, 762
Binder Shop, 433
Binghamton Press (U.S.) (newspaper), 597
Birmingham Sports Argus (G.B.) (newspaper), 802
Birmingham Weekly Post (G.B.), 393
Bituin Komiks (Philippines) (comic book), 86
Bizarre (France) (magazine), 232
Bizarre Sex (U.S.) (magazine), 90, 449, 719
Black-and-white comic books/ magazines
Aghardi, 79
Cerebus, 192
Dylan Dog, 273
Elder, William W., and, 278
Evans, George, and, 287
Feldstein, Al, and, 297
Kane, Gil, and, 433
Kurtzman, Harvey, and, 278, 463
Master of Kung Fu, 519
Nathan Never, 562
Nelvana of the Northern Lights, 565
Psycho, 318
Severin, John Powers, and, 690
Vampirella, 787
See also *Creepy; Eerie; Vampirella;* Warren Publishing
Black comic strips. See Fumetto nero (black comic strips)
Blade (U.S.) (newspaper), 155
Blighty (G.B.) (magazine), 302
Bluebook (U.S.) (magazine), 371
Boardman Comics (G.B.), 500
Bocaccio (Italy) (magazine), 548
Bodljikavo prase (Yugoslavia) (magazine), 465
Bōken Katsugeki Bunko (Japan) (magazine), 580
Bōkenō (Japan) (monthly), 399, 669
Bokura (Japan) (magazine), 463, 669
Boliche (Spain) (magazine), 137, 229
Bolton Evening News Buff (G.B.) (newspaper), 544
Bonelli Publishing (Italy). See Sergio Bonelli
Bonnes Soirees (Belgium) (weekly), 228
Bonnet-Brown Company, 389
Borba (Yugoslavia) (newspaper), 256

Boston Daily Record (U.S.) (newspaper), 638
Boston Globe (U.S.) (newspaper), 561
Boston Traveler (U.S.) (newspaper), 792
Boxing strips
Ashita no Joe, 101-2
Big Ben Bolt, 130-31, 179, 454, 554, 796
Furio Almirante (X-1 il Pugile Misterioso), 216, 327
Joe Palooka, 420
Left wa Shinazu, 542
Muyōnosuke, 671
Box of Curios (Japan) (magazine), 448
Boys and Girls Daily Mail, The (G.B.) (supplement), 317, 749, 808
Boy's Life Magazine (Japan) (magazine), 671
Boy's Life (U.S.) (magazine), 383, 610, 801
Boy strips
Bibi Fricotin, 130
Bobby Dare, 363
Bud Smith, 381
Cap Stubbs and Tippie, 180, 271
Cascão, 243
Cebolinha, 243
Chiba, Tetsuya, and, 198-99
Chikaino Makyū, 199
Cuto, 229-30
Elmer, 281-82
Ginesito, 342-43
Hakaba no Kitarō, 366-67
Harisu no Kaze, 370
Hatanosuke Hinomaru in, 373
Henry, 379
Lille Rickard och hans Katt, 479-80
Little Jimmy, 483-84
Little Joe, 355
Little Sammy Sneeze, 498
Osomatsu-kun, 588
Peter Pat, 420
Sabaku no Maō, 669
San Mao, 674
Scribbly, 219, 524-25
Sjors en Sjimmie, 706-7
Skeets, 707
Boy's World (G.B.) (magazine), 282
Brave and the Bold (comic book), 690
Bravo (Belgium/France) (magazine), 407, 588, 609, 788
Bremer Nachrichten (Germany) (newspaper), 651, 678
Bridgeport Post (U.S.) (newspaper), 438
Bristol Evening Post (G.B.) (newspaper), 797
Bristol Evening World (G.B.) (newspaper), 426, 609, 628
Brivido, Il (Italy) (weekly), 408
Bronx Home News (U.S.) (newspaper), 354

Brooklyn Eagle (U.S.) (newspaper), 262, 352, 611
"Brussells school," 649
Bulaklak (Philippines) (magazine), 163, 418, 505, 772
Bulletin, The (Australia) (newspaper), 109, 364, 534-35, 569
Bulletin des Agriculteurs (Canada) (newspaper), 196
Bull's Press Service, 75, 682
Bungeishunjii Publishing Company (Japan), 696
Bun Lour Sarn (Thalaind), 165-66
Business life strips
Dilbert, 249-50, 672, 716-17
From 9 to 5, 711
Butcher's Film Distributors, 210

C

Cadence Industries, 449
Cadet-Revue (France) (magazine), 545, 829
Cairo (Spain) (magazine), 771
Caliber Press, 318
Calson Studios, 186
Camillus Publications, 607
Campeon, El (Spain) (magazine), 259, 261
Camp Lejeune Globe (U.S.), 321
Camp Newspaper Service, 506-7
Canecaldo (Italy) (magazine), 521
Caniff style, 286
Cannibale (Italy) (magazine), 476, 600
Can You Top This? (radio program), 382
Capp Enterprises, 179
Captain Walter (Italy) (comic book), 608
Caricatures
Angoletta, Bruno, and, 513
Brown, Bertie, and, 157
Gascard, Gilbert (pseud. Tibet), and, 335
Gillray, James, and, 339-40
Ianiro, Abel, and, 399
Leav, Mort, and, 471
Okamoto, Ippei, and, 581
Robinson, Jerry, and, 656
Russell, James Newton, and, 666
Shinjinbutsu Gihyō, 826
Wolverton, Basil, and, 816
Carlsen Verlag (Germany) (publisher), 678
Carroccio (Italy) (publisher), 603
Cartoon (Germany) (television program), 163
Cartoonists and Writers Syndicate (U.S.), 656-57
Cartoon News (Korea) (magazine), 444
Cartoons (U.S.) (magazine), 713
Cartoon Weekly (China), 823

Casa Editrice ARC (Italy) (publisher), 162, 596
Casa Editrice Idea (Italy) (publisher), 327
Casa Editrice Universo (Italy) (publisher), 132, 162, 734
Catalan Communication (U.S.), 771
Cat strips
  Cicero's Cat, 201-2, 711
  Felix the Cat, 299-300, 617, 734
  Fred, 704
  Fritz the Cat, 323-24
  Garfield, 237, 333
  Gloops, 346-47
  Pelle Svanslös, 348
  Poussy, 228
  Pussycat Princess, 631-32
  Spooky, 392, 713, 721-22
  Spring and Autumn in Cat Kingdom, 475
C.C. Beck studio, 133
Celebrity strips
  Charlie Chaplin's Comic Capers, 157, 196, 619, 686
  Heath, George, and, 377
  Hylda Baker's Diary, 608
  Jukes, John L., and, 426
  Minnitt, Frank, and, 536
  Stainless Stephen, 536
  Stiffy & Mo, 364
  Wakefield, George William, and, 796
  Ward, Norman, and, 798
  Will Hay, 386, 536
Censorship of comics
  in China, 249, 300, 475, 797
  Crumb, Robert, and, 224
  in Germany, 759
  in Hungary, 830
  in Italy, 228, 246
  König, Ralf, and, 453
  Malaya, and, 506
  O'Neil, Dan, and, 584
  in Russia, 489
  in Yugoslavia, 411-12
Centaur comics
  Amazing Man, 90
  Burgos, Carl, and, 166
  Cat-Man, The, 190
  Guardineer, Frederic, and, 360
  Gustafson, Bob, and, 364
  Herron, France Edward, and, 381
  Lubbers, Robert (pseud. Lewis, Bob), and, 492
  McWilliams, Alden, and, 502
Central Press Association (U.S.), 152, 354, 552, 653
  See also King Features Syndicate
Century, The (U.S.) (magazine), 586
Ce Soir (France) (magazine), 467
Chamaco Chinco (Mexico), 169
Chamaco Grande (Mexico), 169
Champion (G.B.) (weekly), 209, 693

Chapel Hill Weekly (U.S.) (college newspaper), 698
Charlatan (U.S.) (magazine), 694
Charleton (U.S.) (college magazine), 496
Charlie (France) (magazine), 170, 278, 678, 781, 815-16
Charlton Comics
  Atomic Mouse, 533
  Ayers, Richard, and, 104
  Blue Beetle, 140
  Buscema, John, and, 167
  Byrne, John, and, 171
  Colan, Eugene (pseud. Austin, Adam), and, 206
  Ditko, Steve, and, 254
  Flash Gordon, 308
  Giordano, Richard, and, 344
  Hercules, 380
  Hustler and, 809
  King Features Syndicate and, 809
  O'Neil, Dennis (pseud. O'Shaugnessey, Sergius), 583
  Orlando, Joe, and, 587
  Pfeufer, Carl, and, 611
  Phantom, The, 612
  Popeye, 809
  Screen Gems and, 809
  Severin, John Powers, and, 690
  Sinnott, Joe, and, 705
  Tarzan, 748
  Thomas, Roy, and, 756
  Wildman, George, and, 809
  Williamson, Al, and, 811
  Wood, Wallace, 818
Chat Noir (France) (magazine), 467
Chiaroscuro technique, 138, 549
Chicago American (U.S.) (newspaper)
  A. Piker Clerk in, 97-98, 153
  Ed, Carl Frank Ludwig, and, 275
  Fillum Fables in, 353
  Gould, Chester, and, 353
  King, Frank O., and, 445
  Looping The Loop in, 687
  Segar, Elzie Crisler, and, 687
  Willard, Frank Henry, and, 809
Chicago Daily News (U.S.) (newspaper)
  Carreño, Albert, and, 187
  Circus Solly in, 709
  Hershfield, Harry, and, 382
  Schultze, Carl Edward, and, 682
  Webster, Harold Tucker, and, 802
Chicago Defender (U.S.) (newspaper), 587
Chicago Examiner (U.S.) (newspaper)
  A. Piker Clerk in, 97-98
  Briggs, Clare, and, 153
  Calkins, Dick, and, 173
  De Beck, Billy, and, 238
  Hershfield, Harry, and, 382
  King, Frank O., and, 445
  Smith, Robert Sydney, and, 711
  Smith, Sydney, and, 582

Chicago Herald (U.S.) (newspaper)
  Charlie Chaplin's Comic Capers in, 196, 687
  De Beck, Billy, and, 238
  Married Life in, 114
  Segar, Elzie Crisler, and, 687
  Willard, Frank Henry, and, 809
Chicago Inter-Ocean (U.S.) (newspaper), 186, 802
Chicago Post (U.S.) (newspaper), 316, 792
Chicago Reader (U.S.) (newspaper), 115
Chicago Record-Herald and Inter-Ocean (U.S.) (newspaper). See Chicago Herald
Chicago Seed (U.S.) (newspaper), 496
Chicago Sun-Times Syndicate, 112, 206, 403
Chicago Sun-Times (U.S.) (newspaper), 760
Chicago Tribune-New York News Syndicate
  Ambler, 809
  Brenda Starr, 151, 154
  Broom Hilda, 156, 556
  Celardo, John (pseud. Lardo, John C.), and, 192
  Dickie Dare, 247
  Dick Tracy, 248, 353
  Dondi, 262, 275
  Edson, Gus, and, 275
  Friday Foster, 322
  Gil Thorpe, 127
  Gray, Harold, and, 355
  Green Berets, 461
  Gumps, The, 275
  Link, Stanley J., 481
  Little Joe, 484
  Little Lulu, 485-86
  Little Orphan Annie, 355
  Messick, Dale, and, 527
  Moon Mullins, 809
  Mosley, Zack, and, 550
  My Son John, 389
  Old Glory Story, The, 582
  Pottsy, 404
  Rick O'Shay, 496, 651
  Smilin' Jack, 710
  Smitty, 127, 712
  Smokey Stover, 392, 712
  On Stage, 584, 725
  still life, 656
  Terry and the Pirates, 507, 751, 820
  Tiny Tim, 481
  Winnie Winkle, 150, 813
  See also Tribune Media Services
Chicago Tribune (U.S.) (newspaper)
  Bobby Make-Believe in, 445
  Briggs, Clare, and, 153
  Feininger, Lyonel, and, 297
  Gasoline Alley in, 335, 445
  Gasoling Alley in, 445
  Gray, Harold, and, 355

Gumps, The in, 275, 362, 711-12
Harold Teen in, 275, 370
Howarth, F. M., and, 395
Johnson, Ferd, and, 422-23
Kin-der-Kids, The in, 444-45
King, Frank O., and, 445
Little Joe in, 484
Little Orphan Annie in, 355
Locher, Richard, and, 489
Lovey Dovey in, 753
Lulu and Leander in, 493
McBride, Clifford, and, 497
McEvoy, Joseph Patrick, and, 500
Moon Mullins in, 546-47, 809
Mosley, Zack, and, 550
Murphy, John Cullen, and, 554
O'Keefe, Neil, and, 581
Old Doc Yak in, 711
Rectangle, The in, 445
Smith, Sydney, and, 582
Spooky in, 722
Sweeney and Son in, 739
Texas Slim and Dirty Dalton in, 753
Wee Willie Winkie's World in, 804
When a Feller Needs a Friend in, 806
White Boy in, 808
Chicos (Spain) (weekly)
    Blasco, Jesus, and, 137
    Capitan Misterio, El in, 177
    Chatillo y Federico in, 197
    Cuto in, 137, 229
    Figueras, Alfonso, and, 302
    Jim Erizo in, 416
    Sadhú in, 669
Children Journals Publishing House
    (China), 269
Children's strips
    Anmitsu Hime, 97
    Baby Blues, 685
    Barbaverde, 522
    Bib and Bub, 130, 339
    Billy Bunter, 132-33, 536
    Bobbie Blake, 267
    Burgon, Sid, and, 166
    Campbell Kids, The, 268
    Crosby, Percy Leo, and, 222
    De Souza, Maurico, and, 243
    Dingbats, The, 693
    Dolly Dimples, 268
    Dolly Drake, 267
    Drayton, Grace (pseud.
        Wiedersheim, Grace), and, 268
    Du Jianguo, and, 269
    Feng Zikai and, 300
    Flook, 310
    Flubs and Fluffs, 656
    Fudge the Elf, 648
    Good Friends, 605
    Hargreaves, Harry, and, 370
    Hill, Albert, and, 386
    Hogg, Gordon (pseud. Gog), and,
        390
    Japhet and Happy, 412-13
    Jimpy, 418

Kewpies, The, 441-42, 584
    Kitty's Kapers, 383
    Larry and Len, 386
    Little Bears and Tykes, 740
    Little Pals, 605
    Little Taotao, 605
    Mayer, Sheldon, and, 525
    Melouah, Sid Ali, and, 525
    Nic, 398
    Paese dell'Alfabeto, Il, 644
    Peng Guoliang and, 605
    Pip, Squeak and Wilfred, 618-19
    Pussycat Princess, The, 268, 631-32
    Quadratino, 635
    Quan Buzhi, 269
    Rasmus Klump, 639
    Redipicche, 644
    Robinson, Fred, and, 656
    Rupert, 665
    Sjors en Sjimmie, 706-7
    Slylock Fox and Comics for Kids,
        709-10
    Sugar and Spike, 525
    Superbone, 734
    Tanku Tankurō, 745
    Teddy Tail, 317, 748-49
    Terrible Tales of Captain Kiddo, 268
    Tiger Tim, 760-61
    Tiger Time, 317
    Tiny Tim, 481
    Tobias Seicherl, 731
    Tom Poes, 767, 768
    Trinet et Trinette, 339
    Tripje en Liezenbertha, 773-74
    U.S. Acres, 237
    Wakefield, George William, and,
        795-96
    Walker, Brian, and, 797
    White, Brian, and, 807
    White, Hugh Stanley, and, 808
    Wilson, Roy, and, 812
    Xiang Gege, 269
    Xiaohuzi, 694-95
    Xiao Moli, 269
    Xiaotu Feifei, 269
    Xiaoxioing he Xiaoxiaoxiong, 269
    Yeats, Jack B., and, 823
    Yue Xiaoying, and, 827
    Zhang Leping, and, 674
    See also Boy strips; Girl strips; Kid
        strips; Nursery strips
China Times (Taiwan) (newspaper),
    200-201
Chine Artists Association, 475
Chinese Children and Juvenile
    Publisher, 605
Chinese Juvenile Journal (China), 693
Chinese Literature Publishing House,
    734
Chiquitito (Spain) (weekly), 197
Chito (Spain) (magazine), 97, 137-38,
    230, 669
Chouchou (France) (magazine), 313
Chronicle Features, 468

Cimoc (Spain) (magazine), 688
Cincinnati Post (U.S.) (newspaper),
    155, 802
Cincinnati Times-Star (U.S.)
    (newspaper), 497
Cinema, and comics, 63-66
Circus (France) (magazine), 521
Citta Futura, Il, 338
City Sun (U.S.) (newspaper), 218
"clear line" style, 771
Cleveland Leader (U.S.) (newspaper),
    155
Cleveland Plain Dealer (U.S.)
    (newspaper), 140
Cleveland Press (U.S.) (newspaper),
    621, 653
Cleveland Shopping News (U.S.)
    (newspaper), 701
Coeurs Vaillants (France) (magazine),
    270, 345, 415
Collano Freccia (Italy), 177
Collano Prateria (Italy), 177
Collano Scudo (Italy), 177
College Humor (U.S.) (magazine), 325
Collier's (U.S.) (magazine)
    Anderson, Carl Thomas, and, 91
    Cole, Jack (pseud. Johns, Ralph),
        and, 206
    Dirks, John, and, 252
    Fuller, Ralph Briggs, and, 325
    Haenigsen, Harry, and, 365
    Hart, Johnny, and, 371
    Held, John, Jr. (pseud. Held,
        Myrtle), and, 378
    Hoest, Bill, and, 388
    Holman, Bill, and, 392
    Irving, Jay, and, 404
    Kent, Jack, and, 440
    Knight, Clayton, and, 451
    Leisk, David Johnson (pseud.
        Johnson, Crockett), and, 474
    Murphy, John Cullen, and, 130
    Van Buren, Raeburn, and, 788
    Woolfolk, William, and, 818
Columbia (U.S.) (magazine), 554
Columbus Daily Monitor (U.S.)
    (newspaper), 271
Columbus Dispatch (U.S.) (newspaper),
    175
Comic Art (Italy) (magazine), 150,
    338, 439, 530, 771
Comic books
    Canadian embargo of U.S., 251-52,
        321-22, 565, 606
    formats of, 391, 569, 614, 702, 798
    history of, 26-27, 35, 40
Comic book supplements, 278, 314,
    317, 658, 761, 795
Comic Companion (G.B.) (supplement),
    795
Comic Forum (Austria) (fanzine), 678
Comic Forum (Austria) (fanzines), 632
Comic House, 233
    See also Lev Gleason

Comico Company, 757
Comicon (Spain), 178
Comic Reader (Germany), 682
Comics
  advertising and, 58
  cinema and, 63-66
  Cinematic technique in, 526
  color in, 824
  as communication, 57-58
  criticism on, 58-60, 67-68
  critics of, 38-39
  definition of, 55-57
  as dramatic form, 62-63
  as graphic art, 60-61
  history of, 11-16
  internationalization of, 40-42
  language of, 57
  as narrative, 61-62
  post-war, 28-34
  during the 1920s, 22-23
  during the 1960s, 34-38
  since the 1970s, 38-39
  Senate Judiciary Commitee
    Hearings on, 32, 219, 331
  space and time in, 66-69
  stylistics of, 71
  themes of, 69-71
  during World War II, 27-28
Comic strips
  color in, 499
  daily, 16-18
  history of, 18-20
  revival of classic comics, 488
Comix Book (U.S.) (underground
  comic), 91, 449
Comixene (Germany) (fanzine), 472,
  727
Comix International (Argentina)
  (magazine), 341
COM (Japan) (magazine), 328, 386
Commercial Daily (Taiwan), 201
Commercial Tribune (U.S.)
  (newspaper), 497
Company and Sons (U.S.), 584
Computer-aided comics
  Bottaro, Luciano, and, 149
  Robot Imperium, 657
Consolidated Press Ltd. (Australia),
  110, 620
Continuity Associates (U.S.), 77
Cookham Studio (G.B.) (animation
  studio), 544
Coq Hardi (France) (magazine)
  Dumas, Jacques (pseud. François,
    Jacques; Marijac), and, 271
  Guerre à la Terre in, 361
  Jim Boum in, 416
  Lariflette in, 467
  Poncho Libertas in, 624
  Trois Mousquetaires du Maquis, Les
    in, 774
Corbeau Déchainé (France)
  (newspaper), 271, 774

Correo Español-El Pueblo Vasco (Spain)
  (magazine), 512
Corrier Boy (Italy) (magazine), 508
Corriere dei Piccoli, Il (Italy) (weekly)
  Ballata del Mare Salato, Una in, 108
  Barbaverde in, 522
  Battaglia, Dino, and, 118
  Bilbolbul in, 132
  Bonelli, Giovanni Luigi, and, 143
  Canale, Antonio, and, 175
  Caprioli, Franco, and, 180
  Cavazzano, Giorgio, and, 191
  Cimpellin, Leone, and, 202
  Cocco Bill in, 205
  Happy Hooligan in, 702
  Pier Cloruro De'Lambicchi in, 616
  Jacovitti, Benito, and, 408
  Lupo Alberto in, 494
  Marmittone in, 513
  Moroni-Celsi, Guido (pseud.
    Sterny), and, 548-49
  Pedrocchi, Federico, and, 603
  Pratt, Hugo, and, 627
  Quadratino in, 635
  Redipicche in, 644
  Rubino, Antonio, and, 664
  Signor Bonaventura, Il in, 701
  Sor Pampurio in, 717
  Toppi, Sergio, and, 770
  Valentina Melaverde in, 786
  Wizard of Oz in, 150
Corriere dei Ragazzi, Il (Italy)
  (magazine)
  Castelli, Alfredo, and, 190
  Fumetto dell realta, Il in, 507
  Jacovitti, Benito, and, 408
  Manara, Maurilio, and, 507-8
  Micheluzzi, Attilio (pseud. Bajeff,
    Igor Artz), and, 530
  Nick Carter in, 145
  Sturmtruppen in, 144
  Toppi, Sergio, and, 770
  Valentina Melaverde in, 785
Corrierino (Italy) (weekly), 221
Corto Maltese (Italy) (magazine), 338,
  508, 771
Cosmopolitan (U.S.) (magazine), 347,
  514, 788
Cottonwood Graphics (U.S.), 496,
  651
Country-Wide Comics (U.S.), 166,
  183
Coyote, El (Spain), 111, 138
Cracked (U.S.) (magazine), 496, 690
Craft Publications (Philippines). *See*
  Redondo Komix
Crazy (U.S.) (magazine), 812
Creators Syndicate
  Archie, 100
  Momma, 544
  Teenage Mutant Ninja Turtles, 750
  Wee Pals, 803
  Wizard of Id, The, 814
Credo (Netherlands), 157

Creepy (U.S.) (magazine)
  Bea, José-Maria, and, 120
  Corben, Richard Vance, and, 214
  Evans, George, and, 287
  Orlando, Joe, and, 587
Crestwood Group, 447-48, 690, 705
Crime strips
  Badd Lads, The, 424
  Banana Fish, 108-9
  Billy Bis, 132
  Buck Ryan, 160-61
  Commissario Spada, Il, 211, 240-41
  Crime Does Not Pay, 135
  Dateline: Danger!, 234-35, 502, 677
  Dick Fulmine, 246-47
  Docteur Justice, 511
  Elder, William W., and, 278
  Fantomas, 293
  Feldstein, Al, and, 297
  Giardino, Vittorio, and, 338
  Golgo 13, 349-50, 671
  Jim Hardy, 416-17
  Judge Wright, 426
  Nick Raider, 575
  Public Enemies Through the Ages, 638
  Seekers, The, 686-87
  Terror Keep, 402
  Torpedo 1936, 771, 773
  Tres por la Ley, 580
  Vacanze fatali, 338
  War on Crime, 348
Critters (U.S.) (magazine), 535
Croc (Canada) (magazine), 398
Crown comics (U.S.), 400
Cryptic Comics (U.S.), 297
Cuatro Patas (Argentina) (magazine),
  232
Cubilete (Spain) (magazine), 302
Cucciolo (Italy) (comic book), 688,
  764-65
Cult strips. *See* Intellectual strips
Custom Comics (U.S.), 678

D

Dagens Nyheter (Sweden)
  (newspaper), 408, 450
Da Gong (China) (newspaper), 674
Daily Chronicle (G.B.) (newspaper),
  125
Daily Citizen (G.B.) (newspaper), 802
Daily Express Children's Own (G.B.)
  (supplement), 236, 665
Daily Express (G.B.) (newspaper), 332,
  413-14, 543, 544
Daily Graphic (G.B.) (newspaper),
  625, 628
  See also Daily Sketch
Daily Illustrated Mirror (G.B.)
  (newspaper), 372
Daily Mail (G.B.) (newspaper)
  Colonel Pewter in, 208

Flook in, 310
Fred Basset in, 320-21
Hogg, Gordon (pseud. Gog), and, 390
Nipper in, 574, 807
Teddy Tail in, 748-49
Tiffany Jones in, 760
Webster, Tom, and, 803
Daily Mirror (G.B.) (newspaper)
  Andy Capp in, 95
  Buck Ryan in, 160
  Burgon, Sid, and, 166
  Dowling, Steve, and, 266-67
  Flutters, The in, 311
  Fosdyke Saga, The in, 315
  Garth in, 125, 334
  Holdaway, James, and, 391
  Jane in, 410
  Jimpy in, 418
  Just Jake in, 428
  Larks, The in, 468
  McClelland, Hugh, and, 498
  Monk, Jack, and, 544
  Perishers, The in, 608
  Pip, Squeak and Wilfred in, 619
  Pratt, Hugo, and, 627
  Ruggles in, 665
  Tiger Tim in, 760
Daily News (G.B.) (newspaper), 412, 686-87
Daily News (Philadelphia) (U.S.) (newspaper), 327
Daily News (Thailand) (newspaper), 193-94
Daily Oklahoman (U.S.) (newspaper), 782
Daily Record (G.B.) (newspaper), 301
Daily Sketch (G.B.) (newspaper)
  Ferrier, Arthur, and, 302
  Hogg, Gordon (pseud. Gog), and, 390
  McClelland, Hugh, and, 498, 499
  Pop in, 624
  Reynolds, Basil, and, 650
  Seekers, The in, 686
  Tiffany Jones in, 760
  Webster, Tom, and, 803
  See also Daily Graphic
Daily Telegraph (Australia) (newspaper), 535, 713
Daily Telegraph (G.B.) (newspaper), 166
Daily Worker (U.S.) (newspaper), 617-18
Daim Press (Italy), 86, 754
Dante Quinterno (Argentina) (publisher), 118, 140, 254
Dargaud International (France), 647
Dark Horse Comics
  Adventures of Luther Arkwright, 744
  Barry, Daniel, and, 115
  Brigman, June, and, 154
  Byrne, John, and, 171

Colan, Eugene (pseud. Austin, Adam), and, 206
  Doc Savage, 257
  Kaluta, Michael Wm., and, 432
  Martin Y, 517
  Miller, Frank (1957-), and, 534
  Shadow, The, 693
  Star Wars, 726
  Tarzan, 748
David Hand Studio, 393
Dayton Daily News (U.S.) (newspaper), 576
Dayton Journal (U.S.) (newspaper), 175
D.C. Thomson (G.B.) (publisher)
  Banger, Edgar Henry, and, 110
  Baxendale, Leo, and, 118
  Carter, Reg, and, 187
  Davies, Roland (pseud. Pip), and, 236
  Dennis the Menace (G.B.), 241
  Desperate Dan, 244
  Diamond, H. Louis, and, 245
  Glass, Jack, and, 345-46
  Graham, Alex, and, 321
  Hargreaves, Harry, and, 369-70
  Holroyd, Bill, and, 393
  Judge, Malcolm (pseud. Mal), and, 424
  Keyhole Kate, 442
  McNeill, Hugh, and, 502
  Minnitt, Frank, and, 536
  Monk, Jack, and, 544
  Nixon, Robert, and, 574
  Oor Wullie, 585
  Pansy Potter, 595
  Reid, Ken, and, 648
  Walker, Brian, and, 797
DC Comics. *See* National Periodical Publications/DC Comics
DDT (Spain), 102
Deka (Japan) (magazine), 559
Dell/Western/Gold Key Publishing
  Beep Beep the Road Runner, 122
  Berg, David, and, 126
  Buck Rogers, 160
  Bugs Bunny, 162
  Buscema, John, and, 167
  Captain Midnight, 184-85
  Celardo, John (pseud. Lardo, John C.), and, 192
  Charlie Chan, 196
  Craig, Chase, and, 218
  Crandall, Reed, and, 220
  Daffy Duck, 231
  Dennis the Menace (U.S.), 242
  Ditko, Steve, and, 254
  Doc Savage, 257
  Donald Duck, 111-12
  Elias, Leopold, and, 280
  Ernst, Kenneth, and, 286
  Evans, George, and, 287
  Fredericks, Harold, and, 321
  Giordano, Richard, and, 344

Greene, Vernon van Atta, and, 356
Green Hornet, 357
Heckle and Jeckle, 378
Hercules, 380
Hildebrandt, Greg and Tim, and, 384
Kelly, Walt, and, 438
Lehti, John, and, 474
Little Lulu, 485-86, 724
McWilliams, Alden, and, 502
Manning, Russell, and, 510-11
Maxon, Rex, and, 524
Mayer, Sheldon, and, 524-25
Mighty Mouse, 533
Miller, Frank (1957-), 534
Niño, Alex N., and, 573
Overgard, William Thomas, and, 593
Pfeufer, Carl, and, 611
Phantom, The, 612
Pitt, Stanley John, and, 621
Porky Pig, 625
Robinson, Jerry, and, 656
Santos, Jesse F., and, 675
Sinnott, Joe, 705
Spiegle, Dan, and, 720
Springer, Frank, and, 722
Stanley, John, and, 724
Steve Canyon, 728
Tarzan, 510, 748
Thorne, Frank, and, 757
Tom and Jerry, 766-67
Toth, Alexander, and, 773
Turok, Son of Stone, 524, 778
Wildey, Doug, and, 808, 809
Williamson, Al, and, 811
Wood, Wallace, and, 818
Demócrata, El (Mexico) (newspaper), 631
Denver Post (U.S.) (newspaper), 534, 561, 802
Denver Republican (U.S.) (newspaper), 802
Derniere Heure, La (Belgium) (newspaper), 228
Des Moines Register and Tribune (U.S.) (newspaper), 411
Detective Comics (U.S.) (New Fun Comics), 699, 701
Detective strips
  Alack Sinner, 85, 552
  Angel Dark, 685
  Aphrodite, 772
  Avonturen van detectief Van Zwam, De, 564, 566
  Billy Pack, 133
  Bob Fish, 194
  Brouillard au Pont de Tolbiac, 746
  Buck Ryan, 160-61, 544
  Charlie Chan, 195-96
  Chubb-Lock Homes, 823
  Dan Dunn, 232-33
  Detektive Schmidtchen, 244-45, 651
  DI 13, 253, 674

Dick Bos, 246
Dick Peter, 215
Dick Tracy, 248, 489
Doctor Niebla, 259, 384
8-man, 276-77, 463
Emil und die Detektive, 451
Falcon, The, 377
Gekkō Kamen, 337, 463
Gueule de Bois en Plomb, Une, 746
Gunner, 672
Hawkshaw the Detective, 374-75
Hércules Paput, 302
Herlock Sholmes, 380, 638, 695
Hot on the Trail, 393-94
Inspector Dan, El, 402
Inspector Hayden, 391
Inspector Wade, 402-3
Inspektor Burnadz, 632
John Difool, 345
Kerry Drake, 440
Lex Knight, 391
Luck Star O'Hara, 627
Maboroshi Tantei, 463
Martin Mystere, 516-17
Mike Macke, 533-34
Millionbucks and Kandykiddo, 375
Mosqueton, Rouletabille, 162
Muss'em Up Donovan, 278
Nero, 564, 566
Nick Knatterton, 571-72, 679
Nick Silver, 511
Nils Grant, Private Investigator, 251
120 Rue de la Gare, 746
Paul Temple, 599
Peter og Perle, 299
Pinkerton Jr., 638
Ric Hochet, 335
Roy Carson, 500
Sam Pezzo, 338
Seekers, The, 686-87
Sexton Blake, 236, 690-91
Sherlock Holmes, 608
Sherlock Lopez, 695
Sherlocko the Monk, 374, 504, 505, 695
Sin City, 534
Taifu Goro, 671
Tanteiō Gorō, 463
Terror Keep, 544
Vic Flint, 791
Vidocq, 792
See also Crime strips; Police strips; Spy strips
Detroit Free Press (U.S.) (newspaper), 173, 379, 806
Detroit Journal (U.S.) (newspaper), 322
Detroit Times (U.S.) (newspaper), 322
Dialect strips
Broons, The, 585
Oor Wullie, 585
Werner, 805
Diamond Comics (India), 627
Diario da Noite, O (Brazil) (daily), 215
DIC Studios, 296

Dimanche Illustré (France) (weekly), 545, 670, 829
Diogenes (Switzerland) (publisher), 163
Direct Action (Australia) (magazine), 569
Disney Productions. See Walt Disney Productions
Doctor strips. See Medical strips
Dog strips
Alec the Great, 271
Auf den Hund gekommen, 163
Bessy, 128
Bo, 121
Bonzo, 145
Cubitus, 227
Cucciolo e Beppe, 642
Dirk the Dog Detective, 823
Doggy Officer, 605
Dumm, Frances Edwina, and, 271
Fred Basset, 320-21
Gai Luron, 331
Hershfield, Harry, and, 382
Homeless Hector, 382
Howard Huge, 389
Kador, 134
Little Dog Guaiguai, 605
Norakuro, 576
Pif le Chien, 616-17, 642
Ran-Tan-Plan, 493
Rubber, the Canine Cop, 382
Rudi, 664-65
Sam the Skipper, 317
Serafino, 688-89
Sinbad, 272
Wags, the Dog that Adopted a Man, 514, 795
Dokuritsu Mangaha (Japan) (cartoonists group), 452
Dolce Vita, La (U.S.) (magazine), 520-21
Domenica dei Fanciulli (Italy) (magazine), 548
Domenica del Corriere (Italy) (magazine), 543, 603
Domestic strips. See Family strips
Dope Comix (U.S.) (underground comic), 226
Double Action group (U.S.), 473
Drag (U.S.) (underground comic), 694
Dream strips
Dickie Dare, 247, 801
Dick's Adventures in Dreamland, 247-48, 582
Dreams of the Rarebit Fiend, 268-69, 498
Little Nemo in Slumberland, 486-87
Negro Raul, El, 564-65
Nibsy the Newsboy, 501, 568-69, 596
Procopio, 630
Drummonds of Stirling (G.B.) (publisher), 393

Duga-Film (Yugoslavia), 566
Dynamic Comics (U.S.), 303

E

Eagle (G.B.) (weekly), 125, 232, 368, 686, 778
Eastern Color Printing Company (U.S.)
Berrill, Jack, and, 127
Everett, Bill, and, 287
Iger, Samuel Maxwell ("Jerry"), and, 400
Ingels, Graham (pseud. Ghastly), and, 401
Napoleon, 562
Williamson, Al, and, 811
Eastern Daily Press (G.B.), 110
Eastern Echo (South Africa) (newspaper), 155
Eastman Color Printing Company (U.S.), 773
East Village Other (U.S.) (underground comic), 224, 540, 653
Ebony (U.S.) (magazine), 218
E.C. Comics
Berg, David, and, 126
Binder, Otto O. (pseud. Binder, Eando), and, 134
Colan, Eugene (pseud. Austin, Adam), and, 206
Craig, John, and, 219
Crandall, Reed, and, 219
Davis, Jack, and, 237
Elder, William W., and, 278
Evans, George, and, 286-87
Feldstein, Al, and, 297
Fox, Gardner, and, 316
Frazetta, Frank, and, 319
Gaines, William M., and, 331
Heath, Russell, and, 377
Ingels, Graham (pseud. Ghastly), and, 401
Krigstein, Bernard, and, 458
Kurtzman, Harvey, and, 462
Orlando, Joe, and, 587
S. M. Iger Studios and, 400
science fiction strips by, 78
Severin, John Powers, and, 690
Toth, Alexander, and, 773
Williamson, Al, and, 811
Wood, Wallace, and, 587, 818
Echo de la Mode, L' (France) (magazine), 781
Echo des Savanes, L' (France) (magazine), 111, 345, 508, 682, 816
Eclipse Comics (U.S.), 81
Edifumetto RG (Italy) (publisher), 111
Ediperiodici (Italy) (publisher), 405
Editions Aventures et Voyages (France) (publisher), 162

Editions Dargaud (France) (publisher), 352-53, 647, 678

Editions de Fleures (France) (publisher), 527

Editions du Lombard (Belgium) (publisher), 335, 436

Editions Hachette (France) (publisher), 218

Editions Lombard (Belgium) (publisher), 662

Editions Opta (France) (publisher), 345

Editora Las Selva (Brazil) (publisher), 215

Editorial Abril (Argentina) (publisher), 83, 539, 579, 627

Editorial Bruguera (Spain) (publisher), 202, 259, 302, 549

Editorial cartoons
  Goldberg, Reuben Lucius, and, 349
  MacNelly, Jeff, and, 697
  Ohser, Erich (pseud. Plauen, E. O.), and, 580-81

Editoriale Corno (Italy) (publisher), 247, 459, 494, 685

Editoriale Meridiano S.A. (Mexico), 735

Editoriale per Ragazzi (Italy) (publisher), 768

Editorial Frontera (Argentina), 552, 580, 627

Editorial Senda (Mexico) (publisher), 600

Editors
  Barbieri, Renzo, 111
  Biro, Charles, 134-35
  Bonelli, Giovanni Luigi, 143
  Craig, Chase, 218-19
  Crowley, Wendell, 223
  Diamond, H. Louis, 245-46
  Dumas, Jacques (pseud. François, Jacques; Marijac), and, 270-71
  Feldstein, Al, 297
  Fuchs, Erika, 324-25
  Gaines, William M., 331-32
  Giordano, Richard, 344
  Goscinny, René, 352
  Herron, France Edward, 381
  Herzog, Guy (pseud. Bara), 382
  Iger, Samuel Maxwell ("Jerry"), 400
  Kanigher, Robert, 435
  Kauka, Rolf, 437-38
  Kirby, Jack, 447-48
  Kubert, Joe, 459-61
  Kurtzman, Harvey, 462-63
  Lee, Stan, 472
  Mayer, Sheldon, 524-25
  Miao Di, 527-28
  O'Neil, Dennis (pseud. O'Shaugnessey, Sergius), 583
  Schwartz, Julius, 683
  Secchi, Luciano (pseud. Bunker, Max), 685

  Severin, John Powers, 690
  Simon, Joseph, 704-5
  Thomas, Roy, 756
  Weisinger, Mort, and, 804
  Winterbotham, Russell (pseud. Bond, J. Harvey), 814
  Woolfolk, William, 818-20

Editors Press Service (U.S.), 400, 470, 693

Editrice Cenisio (Italy) (publisher), 642

Editrice Dardo (Italy) (publisher), 111, 177

Edizioni Alpe (Italy) (publisher)
  Bonvicini, Franco (pseud. Bonvi), and, 145
  Bottaro, Luciano, and, 148
  Buffolente, Lina, and, 162
  Caprioli, Franco, and, 180
  Pecos Bill, 603
  Pepito, 607
  Rebuffi, Giorgio, and, 642
  Soldino, 715

Edizioni Audace (Italy) (publisher), 118, 162, 202, 509, 754

Edizioni del Vascello (Italy) (publisher), 111

Edizioni RG (Italy) (publisher), 111, 405

Educational Classics (U.S.), 573

Educational strips
  Amar Chitra Katha, 595
  Classics Illustrated, 204
  Dick's Adventures in Dreamland, 247-48, 582
  Gonick, Larry and, 350-51
  Heroes of American History, 535
  Johnny-Round-the-World, 422
  Lupo Alberto, 494-95
  Musial, Joseph, and, 554
  Old Glory Story, The, 582
  Piccolo Centauro, Il, 597
  Treasure Chest, 401, 575

Eerie (U.S.) (magazine), 120, 287, 514

Ehe (Japan) (magazine), 826

Eisner-Iger Studio. *See* S. M. Iger Studios

Elliot Publishing (U.S.), 204

emma (Germany) (magazine), 121

English Illustrated Magazine (G.B.), 363

Epatant, L' (France) (weekly), 614

Epic Comics, 500

Eppo (Netherlands) (magazine), 638

Erotic comics/strips
  Blanche Epiphanie, 614
  Candid Camera, 508
  Caroline Choléra, 614
  Declic, Le, 508
  Devil's Angel, The, 757-58
  Femmine incantate, Le, 640
  Gioco, Il, 508
  Ils Ne Pensent Qu'à Ca, 815
  Iron Devil, The, 757
  Kojima, Koo, and, 452

  Lann, 757
  Little Ego, 338
  Manara, Maurilio, and, 508
  Marie-Gabrielle, 614
  Moonshine McJuggs, 757
  Paulette, 614
  Pichard, Georges, and, 614
  Profumo dell'invisible, Il, 508
  Ribit!, 757
  Thorne, Frank, and, 757
  Wolinski, Georges, and, 814-16

Eshinbun Nipponchi (Japan) (magazine), 438

Espesial Komiks (Philippines), 86, 516, 573

Espresso, L' (Italy) (daily), 338

Esquire Syndicate (U.S.), 218

Esquire (U.S.) (magazine), 327, 788

Eternauta, El (Italy) (monthly), 278, 286

Ethnic strips
  Abie the Agent, 76, 382
  Gimpel Beinish the Matchmaker, 341-42
  Gordo, 101
  Gross, Milton, and, 360
  Innocent Hing, 326
  Nize Baby, 360, 575
  See also American strips; Integrated strips

Eulenspiegel (Germany) (comic book), 305, 437

Eureka (Italy) (magazine), 144, 494, 521, 685

Evening Chronicle (G.B.) (newspaper), 544

Evening News (G.B.) (newspaper), 236, 266, 370, 375, 686, 807

Evening Standard (G.B.) (newspaper), 204, 543

Evening Star, The (G.B.) (newspaper), 807

Evening World (G.B.) (newspaper), 797

Evening World (U.S.) (newspaper), 155

Everbody's Weekly (G.B.), 302

Evergreen Review (U.S.) (magazine), 614, 722

Everybody's Weekly (G.B.), 392

Evviva (Italy), 684

Exciting Comics (U.S.), 137

Exlex (Sweden) (newspaper), 408

Expansion, L' (France), 149

Expressen (Sweden) (newspaper), 557

Express Weekly (G.B.), 282

Extra! (U.S.) (comic book), 219

Extreme Studios (G.B.), 547

F

Fact strips
  Can You Beat It?, 544

Fairy-tale strips
  Krüger, Hans Martin (pseud.
    Martin, Hans), and, 459
  Kuznjecov, Konstantin, and, 464
  Lurchis Abenteuer, 495
  Patsy, 598
  Schtroumpes, Les, 680
  See also Fantasy strips
Faisani (Italy), 148
Family Journal (G.B.), 693
Family strips, 20-22
  According to Hoyle, 382
  Baby Snookums, 501
  Belles and Wedding Bells, 727
  Betsy and Me, 206
  For Better or For Worse, 312-13, 423
  Bidochon, Les, 134
  Blondie, 138-39, 826-27
  Boots and Her Buddies, 147
  Born Loser, The, 148
  Bringing Up Father, 154-55, 356,
    501-2
  Bungle Family, The, 164-65, 778-79
  Committed, 593
  Curtis, 228-29
  Dingbat Family, The, 251.381
  Don Pancho Talero, 263
  Familia Burron, La, 291
  Familia Ulises, La, 291
  Famille Fenouillard, La, 292
  Family Foursome, The, 826-27
  Family Man, 384
  Far till fyra, 283
  Ferd'nand, 300-301
  Flutters, The, 311
  Fosdyke Saga, The, 314-15
  Fuku-chan, 325, 825
  Gambols, The, 332-33
  Gasoline Alley, 335-37, 445
  Gumps, The, 362, 711-12
  Herb & Jamaal, 379
  Hi and Lois, 383
  Home, Sweet Home, 164, 779
  Honeybunch's Hubby, 600
  I Shoulda Ate the Eclair, 360
  It's Papa Who Pays, 553, 769
  Jumpstart, 426-27
  Kenkoy, 438-39
  Lariflette, 467
  Larks, The, 468
  Li'l Abner, 478-79
  Lilla Fridolf, 479
  Little Iodine, 483
  Lockhorns, The, 389
  Lovey Dovey, 753
  Main Street, 375, 504, 505-6
  Mama's Boyz, 218
  Man in the Brown Derby, The, 802
  Married Life, 238
  Mr. and Ms., 538
  Mr. and Ms. Dillwater, 693
  Momma, 470, 543-44
  Moose Miller, 547-48
  Motley's Crew, 551-52

Nebbs, The, 383, 564
Newlyweds, The, 501, 567
Nize Baby, 575
Pa's Son-in-Law, 804
Polly and Her Pals, 623-24
Polly and Her Pals in, 727
Pop, 624-25
Potters, The, 500, 730
Potts, The, 625-26, 666
Rose is Rose, 661-62
Rosie's Beau, 501, 569, 662
Ruggles, 665
Sally Forth, 672
Sappo, 675
Sazae-san, 677
Shuang Hsiang Pao, 200
Snookums, 567, 662
Sor Pampurio, 717
Suburban Cowgirls, 732-33
Sweethearts and Wives, 727
Their Only Child, 501, 567, 569
For This We Have Daughters?, 623
Toots and Casper, 552-54, 769-70
Us Husbands, 381
Van Swaggers, The, 806
Wang Xiansheng He Xiao Chen,
  797-98
Whole Blooming Family, The, 501,
  662
Famous Funnies (U.S.), 127, 647
Famous Studios (animation studio),
  188-89, 486
Fanfan la Tulipe (France) (weekly),
  617
Fantagraphics, 85
Fantasy Quarterly (U.S.), 280
Fantasy strips
  Adieu Brindavoine, 745
  Aghardi, 79
  Arzach, 345
  Baron Bean, 251, 381
  Baron vampir, 464
  Dingbats, The, 693
  Dyesebel, 772
  Elfquest, 279-80
  Fukuwajutsushi, 775
  Grofica Margo, 464
  Gruaga, 573
  Haxtur, 375
  Hi no Tori, 386-87
  Jimmy das Gummipferd, 417, 451
  Kappa, 452
  Klotjohan, 450
  Loony Lyrics of Lulu, The, 791
  Lucky Starr, 301
  Macaco, 497
  Manly, 514
  Maxmagnus, 639, 685
  Moomin, 412, 546
  Nus, 577
  Olivier Rameau, 647
  Paese dell'Alfabeto, Il, 644
  Patsy, 598
  Philémon, 613

Plop, 661
P'tit Gus, 623
Redipicche, 644
Schtroumpes, Les, 680
Segrelles, Vicente, and, 688
Shōchan no Bōken in, 697
Si Yeoo Ki, 706
Soldino, 715
Spirou, 721
Strange World of Mr. Mum, The, 730
Tagisan Ng Mga Agimat, 743
Terrors of the Tiny Tads, 750-51, 791
Tiriel, 623
Towers of Bois-Maury, The, 398
Tripje en Liezenbertha, 773-74
Tri života, 464
*Upside Downs of Little Lady Lovekins
  and Old Man Muffaroo, The*,
  782-83, 791
Ursurak, 385
Valentina, 785
Valhalla, 786-87
Voltar, 793
Wee Willie Winkie's World, 297, 804
Wolff, 514
See also Sword-and-sorcery strips
Fanzines
  Astral, 232
  Comic Forum (Austria), 678
  Comixene, 472
  Corben, Richard Vance, and, 214
  Funnyworld, 214
  Lynch, Jay, and, 496
  Monster Times, 171
  Putzker, Ronald Alfred, and,
    632-33
  Schwartz, Julius, and, 683
  Stripschrift, 461
  Thomas, Roy, and, 756
  Time Traveller, The (U.S.), 683
  Voice of Comicdom, 214
Farrell Comics, 254, 400
Far West (France) (magazine), 345
FarWorks (U.S.), 468
Father-and-son strips
  Elmer, 281-82, 554, 740, 813
  Kyojin no Hoshi, 465
  Skippy, 552, 707-8, 740
  Strain on the Family Tie, A, 739, 740
  Sweeney and Son, 739-40
  Vater und Sohn, 581, 789-90
Faune, Le (Belgium) (weekly), 382
Fawcett Publications
  Anglo, Mick, and, 96
  Bald, Kenneth (pseud. Bruce, K.),
    and, 108
  Barry, Daniel, and, 115
  Beck, Charles Clarence, and, 120
  Berg, David, and, 126
  Binder, Jack, and, 133
  Binder, Otto O. (pseud. Binder,
    Eando), and, 133-34
  Bulletman, 164
  Captain Marvel, 182-83, 541

Captain Marvel Jr., 184
Captain Midnight, 184
Carreño, Albert, and, 187
comic book formats experimented
   by, 164
Crowley, Wendell, and, 223
Don Winslow of the Navy, 264
Evans, George, and, 286
Finger, Bill, and, 303
Frazetta, Frank, and, 319
Herron, France Edward, and, 381
holiday specials, 164
Ibis the Invincible, 399
Kanigher, Robert, 435
Krigstein, Bernard, and, 458
Mary Marvel, 518
Master Man, 541
Mr. Scarlet, 541
Pfeufer, Carl, and, 611
Raboy, Emanuel (Mac), and, 637
Schaffenberger, Kurt (pseud. Wahl,
   Lou), and, 678
Spy Smasher, 723-24
Starr, Leonard, 725
Wildey, Doug, and, 808
Wolverton, Basil, and, 816
Woolfolk, William, and, 819
F.E. Howard Publications (Canada),
   565
Feds and Heads (U.S.) (underground
   comic), 289, 694
Felix (Germany), 128
Femmes d'Aujourd'hui (France), 142,
   788
Fiction House
   Anderson, Murphy, and, 92
   Berg, David, and, 126
   Briefer, Richard, and, 152
   Captain Wings, 185
   Celardo, John (pseud. Lardo, John
      C.), and, 192
   Colan, Eugene (pseud. Austin,
      Adam), and, 206
   Crandall, Reed, and, 219
   Elias, Leopold, and, 280
   Evans, George, and, 286
   Feldstein, Al, and, 297
   Frazetta, Frank, and, 319
   Giordano, Richard, and, 344
   Ingels, Graham (pseud. Ghastly),
      and, 401
   Kane, Robert, and, 434
   Kubert, Joe, and, 460
   Leav, Mort, and, 470
   Lubbers, Robert (pseud. Lewis,
      Bob), and, 492
   Meskin, Morton (pseud. Morton,
      Mort, Jr.), 526
   science fiction strips by, 78
   Sheena, Queen of the Jungle, 693
Field Syndicate
   Funky Winkerbean, 326
   Latigo, 496
   Mark Trail, 513

Momma, 544
Rex Morgan, M.D., 722
Sally Forth, 672, 673
Steve Canyon, 727
Fierro (Argentina) (magazine), 714
Filipino Komiks (Philippines) (comic
   book), 86
Filipino Reporter (Philippines)
   (newspaper), 80
Fillette (France) (weekly), 286
Fiordistella (Italy), 162
Firmousse (France) (magazine), 271
First Comics (U.S.), 198
First Publishing (U.S.), 204
Fishing World (U.S.) (magazine), 351
Fix und Foxi (Germany) (comic book),
   661
Flamed-Out Funnies (U.S.), 90
Flapper strips
   Boots and Her Buddies, 147, 515-16
   Dumb Dora, 271
   Fritzi Ritz, 168, 233, 560-61
   Gertie and Gladys, 795
   Gertie Goodsort, 795
   Held, John, Jr. (pseud. Held,
      Myrtle), 378
   Merely Margy, 378
   Oh! Margy, 378
   See also Girl Strips; Girl strips
Flechas y Pelayos (Spain) (magazine),
   695
Fleetway Publications (G.B.)
   Breccia, Alberto, and, 150
   Caesar, Kurt (pseud. Avai, Cesare;
      Away, Caesar), and, 173
   Canale, Antonio, and, 175
   Del Castillo, Arturo, and, 239
   Pratt, Hugo, and, 627
   Price, Cyril, and, 628
   See also Amalgamated Press
Fliegenden Blätter (Germany)
   (magazine), 167, 276, 524, 579
Florita (Spain) (magazine), 138,
   310-11
Fluide Glacial (France) (magazine),
   149, 331
Folha de S. Paulo (Brazil) (newspaper),
   243
Football strips
   Swineskin Gulch, 373
Fort Worth Record (U.S.) (newspaper),
   367
Fort Worth Star Telegram (U.S.)
   (newspaper), 367
45th Division News (U.S.)
   (newspaper), 782
Fox Comics
   Blue Beetle, 140
   Briefer, Richard, and, 152
   Carreño, Albert, and, 187
   Craig, John, and, 219
   Feldstein, Al, and, 297
   Kanigher, Robert, and, 435
   Phantom Lady, 613

   S. M. Iger Studios and, 400
   Simon, Joseph, and, 705
Fra Diavlo (Italy) (magazine), 86
France-Soir (France), 98-99, 303, 313,
   382, 523, 829
Francisco Coching comic style,
   658-59
Francs-Jeux (France) (magazine), 192
Frank Johnson Publications
   (Australia), 620
Frank Markey Syndicate (U.S.), 349
Frew Publications (Australia), 255
Frigidaire (Italy) (magazine), 476, 601
Fripounet (France) (magazine), 527
Frontera (Argentina) (publisher), 150,
   552, 580, 627
Fujio Productions (Japan), 84
Fujokai (Japan) (magazine), 581
Fules (Hungary) (magazine), 294, 830
Fumetti per adulti, 404-5
Fumetto nero (black comic strips), 37,
   245, 459, 498, 639, 685
Funkwacht (Germany) (weekly), 417
Funnies, The (U.S.) (comic book), 184
Funny Aminals(sic) (U.S.), 522, 719
Funnyworld (U.S.) (fanzine), 214
Future Comics (U.S.) (comic book),
   677

G

G. Miranda & Sons Publishing
   Company (Philippines), 675
Gabriele Gioggi (Italy) (publisher),
   170
Gag strips
   Alphonse and Gaston, 89-90
   Banana Oil, 109, 360
   Bertha, 146
   Bill, 146
   Bon Bon, 405
   Boob McNutt, 144-45, 348, 349
   Bumper Snickers, 389
   Carpanta, 186
   Clive, 204-5
   Croquemulot, 175
   Cubitus, 227
   Discontinued Stories, 388, 415
   Doctor Merengue, El, 257-58
   Don Berrinche, 261-62
   Ephémère, 382
   Foolish Questions, I'm the Guy, 348,
      349
   Goldberg, Reuben Lucius, and,
      348-49
   Gumdrop, 685
   Hey Look, 462
   Hotsy-Totsy, 769
   Hubert, 395-96
   Inferno, 755
   In Jungle Land, 504
   Larks, The, 468

Laugh Parade, 389

Little Joe, 484

Lulu and Leander, 493

Macaco, 497

McBride, Clifford, and, 497

Mager, Charles Augustus (Gus),
and, 504

Married Life, 238

Maw Green, 355

Mike and Ike, 533

Mistakes Will Happen, 381

Mr. Abernathy, 538

Monsieur Poche, 545, 670

Mostly Malarkey, 186

Music to the Ear, 220

Napoleon, 497, 561-62

Outcault, Richard Felton, and, 589

Pantomime, 730

Pete the Tramp, 611, 666

Primus et Musette, 217

Protheroe, Glyn, and, 631

Quick et Flupke, 649

Rosy-Posy-Grandma's Girl, 381

Ruggles, 267

Signor Spaghetti, 352

They'll Do It Everytime, 373, 755

Thimble Theater, 687

Timid Soul, The, 762-63, 802

Wet Blanket, 347

When a Feller Needs a Friend, 806

Galantuomo, Il (Italy) (magazine), 86

Gansu Daily (China) (newspaper), 733

Gansu People's Publishing House
(China), 733

Gansu Pictorial (China), 733

Ganze Woche, Die (Austria)
(newspaper), 632

Garo (Japan) (monthly), 432

Gauthier-Languereau (France)
(publisher), 617

Gavroche (France) (weekly), 293

Gay Comix (U.S.), 226

Gay/lesbian strips

Cruse, Howard, and, 225-26

Kerry Kross, 685

König, Ralf, and, 452-53

Mystiska 2:an and, 558

Gazeta Esportiva (Brazil), 215

Gazeta Juvenil (Brazil), 215

Gazetta di Parma (Italy), 144-45

Gazet van Antwerpen (Belgium), 128

Geillustreerde Pers (Netherlands)
(publisher), 100, 454

GEIS (Italy) (publisher), 111

General Features Syndicate, 594

George Matthew Adams Service, 187,
271, 474, 806

Gerald G. Swan (G.B.) (publisher),
110, 205, 386, 536, 631

Gibi (Brazil) (comic book), 83

Gift (U.S.), 164

Gilberton Publications (U.S.), 204

Giolitti Studio (Italy), 161

Giornalino, Il (Italy) (magazine)

Caesar, Kurt (pseud. Avai, Cesare;
Away, Caesar), and, 173

Caprioli, Franco, and, 180

Cavazzano, Giorgio, and, 191

Cocco Bill in, 205

Commissario Spada, Il in, 211

DeLuca, Gianni, and, 240-41

Jacovitti, Benito, and, 408

Nizzi, Claudio, and, 575

Peroni, Carl, and, 608

Procopio in, 630

Toppi, Sergio, and, 770

Giorni (Italy)

Bonvicini, Franco (pseud. Bonvi),
and, 144-45

Giorno, Il (Italy) (newspaper), 408,
616, 731

Giorno dei Ragazzi (Italy)
(supplement), 205

Girl Fight Comics (U.S.) (underground
comic), 654

Girl (G.B.), 236

Girl strips

Affairs of Jane, The, 826

Anita Diminuta, 96-97

Arabelle la Sirène, 98-99

Babe Bunting, 216, 348

Bamse, 94

Beautiful Bab, 826

Bebe Cyanure, 313

Bécassine, 120, 617

Belinda Blue Eyes, 123

Betty, 128-29, 792

Bib and Bub, 130

Bilbolbul, 132

Bōken Dankichi, 143

Casper, 188-89

Chiba, Tetsuya, and, 198-99

Connie, 212-13, 347-48

Dixie Dugan, 255, 500, 730

Dumb Dora, 826

Ella Cinders, 280-81

Espiègle Lili, L', 286

Ferrier, Arthur, and, 302

Film Fannie, 302

Florita, 310-11

Gertie Gladeyes, 796

Hagio, Moto, and, 366

Hungry Henrietta, 498

Jane, 410

Keyhole Kate, 442

Kitty Higgins, 547

Kuroi Hanabira, 520

Lille Rickard och hans Katt, 94

Little Iodine, 483

Little Mary Mixup, 155

Little Miss Muffet, 216

Little Orphan Annie, 355, 487-88

Mafalda, 470

Male Call, 506-7

Meanderings of Minnie, 271

Meddlesome Matty, 424

Minouche, 623

Modesty Blaise, 543

Monica, 243

Myra North, 557

Natacha, 562

Our Dumb Blonde, 302

Panthères, Les, 647

Patsy, 354

Peggy the Peeress, 795

Pellefant, 94

Penny, 365

Polly and Her Pals, 623-24

Polly and Her Pals in, 727

Poupon la Peste, 134

Rah! Rah! Rosalie, 378

Ribon no Kishi, 754

Rosie's Beau, 501, 569, 662

Rosy-Posy-Grandma's Girl, 381

Silent Three, The, 704

S no Taiyō, 520

Tillie the Toiler, 761-62, 805-6

Valentina Melaverde, 785-86

Wakefield, George William, and,
795

Winnie Winkle, 706, 813-14

Young, Murat (Chic), and, 826-27

See also Flapper strips; Heroines

Gladstone Publishing (U.S.), 261

Glas Slavonije (Yugoslavia), 266

Glenat Italia (Italy) (publisher), 494

Globus (Yugoslavia) (magazine), 239

Gobuji Chushingura (Japan), 783

Golden Comics Digest (U.S.), 162

Golden Gate Syndicate, 440, 446

Gold Star Publishing Co.
(Philippines), 675

Golf Illustrated (G.B.) (magazine), 802

Good Housekeeping (U.S.) (magazine),
484, 584, 741, 812

Gorrion, El (Argentina), 150

Göteborgs Handels-Och Sjöfarstidning
(Sweden) (newspaper), 450

Gothic Blimp Works (U.S.)
(underground comic), 653

Gower Studios (G.B.), 96, 517

GPD Press Service (Netherlands), 595

Gran Chicos (Spain) (magazine), 97,
177, 619

Grande Firme, Le (Italy) (magazine),
86

Graphic Arts Inc. (Philippines), 675

Graphic novels

Air Mail, 529

Boucq, François, and, 149

Bulanadi, Danny, and, 163

Carlomango, 659

Cité interdite, La, 525

Comés, Didiet, and, 211

Contract with God, A, 40, 278

Dreamer, The, 40, 278

Dropsie Avenue, 40, 278

Eisner, Will, and, 278

Fazekas, Attila, and, 294

Gaucho, Il, 508, 627

Gomez, Pablo, and, 350

To the Heart of the Storm, 278
HP e Giuseppe Bergman, 508
Indian Summer, 627
Jodelle, 418
Ken Parker, 439
Melouah, Sid Ali, and, 525
Micheluzzi, Attilio (pseud. Bajeff,
    Igor Artz), and, 530
Modesty Blaise, 344
Molly Manderling, 529
Niño, Alex N., and, 573
Outland, 727
Paulus, 241
Payaso, 599-600
Pierrot of Bab El Oued, 525
Predator and Prey, 811
Red Tide, 727
Rêve du requin, Le, 682
Rosso Stenton, 529
Secte des Assassins, La, 525
Silver Metal Lover, The, 654
Tagisan Ng Mga Agimat, 743
Théorème de Bell, 682
Tony Falco, 768
True Love, 704, 773
Tutto ricomincio con un estate indiana,
    508
Uomo del Khyber, L', 529
Uomo delle Filippine, L', 440
Uomo del Tanganyka, L', 529
Voltar, 793
Graphic Story Magazine (U.S.)
    (magazine), 816
Green Book (U.S.) (magazine), 788
Green Lantern/Green Arrow series, 77,
    356, 357, 400, 583, 683
Greeting cards
    Duffy, J. C., and, 327
    Hollander, Nicole, and, 392
    Kent, Jack, and, 440
    Little Nemo in Slumberland, 487
    Messick, Dale, and, 527
    Mordillo, Guillermo, and, 548
    Myers, Russell, and, 556
    Where I'm Coming From, 807
Grifo, Il (Italy) (magazine), 508
Grüne Post (Germany) (newspaper),
    730
Guangzhou Literature Federation
    Publishing Department, 475
Guardian, The (Australia)
    (newspaper), 130, 293, 364
Guardian, The (G.B.) (newspaper),
    123, 208, 704
Guernsey Star (G.B.) (newspaper), 386

H

H. John Edwards Publishing
    Company (Australia), 255
Halaklak (Philippines) (comic book),
    674

Hallmark Company, 548, 556
Hall Syndicate
    Barnaby, 113
    Casson, Melvin, and, 189
    Dennis the Menace, 441
    Dennis the Menace (U.S.), 242
    It's Me Dilly, 189
    Mark Trail, 260
    Pogo, 622
Hamburger Anzeiger (Germany)
    (newspaper), 285
Hamburger Illustrierte (Germany)
    (weekly), 285
Hana no nijūyonen gumi (Japan), 366,
    542, 588
Handelsblad (Netherlands), 454
Hanna-Barbera studios, 608, 680,
    722, 773, 808-9
Hara-Kiri (France) (magazine), 345,
    815
Harper's (U.S.) (magazine), 325, 499,
    584, 586
Harris Publications (U.S.), 787
Harry "A" Chesler Shop
    Binder, Jack, and, 133
    Binder, Otto O. (pseud. Binder,
      Eando), 133
    Biro, Charles, and, 134
    Cole, Jack (pseud. Johns, Ralph),
      and, 206
    Ernst, Kenneth, and, 286
    Guardineer, Frederic, and, 360
    Gustafson, Bob, and, 364
    Herron, France Edward, and, 381
    Kubert, Joe, and, 459
    Meskin, Morton (pseud. Morton,
      Mort, Jr.), and, 526
    Raboy, Emanuel (Mac), and, 637
Harry (Germany) (magazine), 702
Hartentroef (Netherlands), 157
Harvey Comics
    Black Cat, 135
    Casper, 188-89
    Craft, Jerry, and, 218
    Elias, Leopold, and, 280
    Flash Gordon, 308
    Goodwin, Archie (pseud. Franklin,
      Robert), and, 351
    Green Hornet, 357
    Kirby, Jack, and, 447-48
    Kubert, Joe, and, 460
    Robinson, Jerry, and, 656
    S. M. Iger Studios and, 400
    Severin, John Powers, and, 690
    Simon, Joseph, and, 705
    Steranko, James, and, 726
    Tom and Jerry, 767
    Williamson, Al, and, 811
Hasmin (Philippines) (magazine), 418
H.C. Fisher Inc. (U.S.), 202
Hearst Publications
    Afonsky, Nicolas, and, 537
    Alphonse and Gaston, 89
    Bringing Up Father, 154

    Goldberg, Reuben Lucius, and, 349
    Gross, Milton, and, 360
    Happy Hooligan, 368-69
    Howarth, F. M., and, 395
    Krazy Kat, 381, 457
    Little Jimmy, 483-84
    Little King, The, 714
    Little Nemo in Slumberland, 487
    Lulu and Leander, 493
    McCay, Winsor, and, 498
    Mr. Jack, 539-40
    Muggs and Skeeter, 552
    Mutt and Jeff, 555-56
    Newlyweds, The, 567
    Opper, Frederick Burr, and, 586
    Pussycat Princess, 632
    Rosie's Beau, 662
    See also King Features Syndicate;
      specific newspapers
Heavy Metal (U.S.) (magazine)
    Basura in, 341
    Cruse, Howard, and, 226
    Lann in, 757
    Robbins, Trina, and, 654
    Rocco Vargas in, 772
    Segrelles, Vicente, and, 688
    Wilshire, Mary, and, 812
    Zora in, 301
Heitere Fridolin, Der (Germany)
    (bi-weekly), 326
Help! (U.S.), 224, 237, 278, 463, 694
Help! (U.S.) (magazine), 323
Helsingein Sanomt (Finland)
    (newspaper), 468
Herald and Weekly Times, Ltd.
    (Australia) (newspaper), 141, 625,
    666, 797
Herald-Examiner (U.S.) (newspaper),
    114
Heraldo Cultural (Mexico)
    (newspaper), 289
Heraldo de Mexico, El (Mexico)
    (newspaper), 631
Herald-Tribune Syndicate
    B.C., 119, 371
    Briggs, Clare, and, 153
    Casson, Melvin, and, 189
    G. Whizz Jr., 392
    Haenigsen, Harry, and, 365
    Hart, Johnny, and, 371
    Jeff Crockett, 189
    Our Bill, 365
    Voight, Charles A., and, 792-93
    Willie Doodle, 404
    Wizard of Id, The, 597
    See also Publishers-Hall Syndicate
Heroic-Albums (Belgium), 217, 335,
    413, 762
Heroines
    Aphrodite, 772
    Durga-Rāni, 605
    Gesebel, 639
    Milady, 640
    Petra Chérie, 530

Phoebe Zeit-Geist, 614, 722-23
Red Sonja, 812
Saga de Xam, 670
Satanik, 639, 685
Seekers, The, 686-87
Tiffany Jones, 760
Valentina, 785
Vampirella, 787
High Times (U.S.) (magazine), 654
Hillbilly strips
  G.I. Daddy, 600
  Lena Pry, 411
  Li'l Abner, 478-79
  Long Sam, 490, 492
  Payne, Charles M., and, 600
Hillborough Studio (Canada), 565
Hillman Publications
  Airboy, 81, 443
  Barry, Daniel, and, 115
  Briefer, Richard, and, 152
  Crowley, Wendell, and, 223
  Elias, Leopold, and, 280
  Everett, Bill, and, 287
  Guardineer, Frederic, and, 360
  Heap, The, 376, 471
  Kida, Fred, and, 443
  Kirby, Jack, and, 447-48
  Krigstein, Bernard, and, 458
  Prentice, John, and, 627
  S. M. Iger Studio and, 471
  Simon, Joseph, and, 705
Hinz und Kunz (Germany) (magazine),
  647
Historical strips
  Agachados, Los, 79
  Alix l'Intrépide, 87
  Astérix, 352, 781
  Barbe-Rouge, 339
  Botond, 294
  Briganti, I, 640
  Capitan l'Audace, 176, 543
  Capitan Trueno, El, 178-79
  Carev štitonoša, 716
  Centaure Vezelay, Le, 175
  Cerro de la Plata, El, 771
  Chevalier Ardent, 198, 217
  Chuko Szu-lang, 823
  Compagnia dell Forca, La, 640
  Corentin, 214
  Cuore Garibaldino, 228
  Dago, 818
  DeLuca, Gianni, and, 240
  Dickie Dare, 247-48, 801
  Don Furcio Buscabollos, 202
  Dororo, 754
  Druka, 217
  Due Tamburini, I, 603
  Dzjengis Khan, 273, 491
  Eric de Noorman, 283, 457-58
  Evermores, The, 796
  Fabulosas ciudades de Arizona, Las,
    771
  Fouche, un Uomo nella Revoluzione,
    685

Gaucho, Il in, 508, 627
Gilgamesh, 818
Gin no hanbira, 542
Guerrero del Antifaz, El, 361-62
Hägar the Horrible, 365-66
Hidamari no Ki, 754
Indio, El, 400
Jabato, El, 407
Jean des Flandres, 413
Jugurtha, 398
Kamui Den, 432-33
Kevin the Bold, 441
Kilabot Ng Persia in, 573
Knjaz Miloš, 464
Kraljevic' Marko, 464
Kroz minula stoljec'a, 638
Lad and His Lass, A, 395, 628
Late Late War, The, 321
Legends Along the Silk Road, 734
Majka, 464
Manly, 514
Medieval Castle, The, 315, 525
New Jersey's Patriots, 321
Oaky Doaks, 325, 579
Parola alla giuria, La, 508
Payaso, 599-600
Prince Valiant, 315, 628-29
Road to Rome, 609
Ronin, 534
Siegfried, 534
Sigi the Frank, 382
Song of the Sword, 609
Under the Stars and Bars, 321
Suikoden Nishikie, 783
Tiriel, 623
Toppi, Sergio, and, 770
Towers of Bois-Maury, The, 398
Tutto ricomincio con un estate indiana,
  508
Unknown Rider, 511
Uomo che uccise Ernesto "Che"
  Guevara, L,' 640
Vidocq, 792
Wheeling, 627
White Boy, 808
Wolff, 514
See also Pre-historic strips
Historietas (Spain) (magazine), 177
Hiwaga Komiks (Philippines) (comic
  book), 86, 350
Hobo News (U.S.), 690
Hógar, El (Argentina) (magazine), 258,
  263, 564, 672
Holyoke Publications
  Barry, Daniel, and, 115
  Blue Beetle, 140
  Cat-Man, The, 190-91
  Green Hornet, 356-57
  Hasen, Irwin, and, 372
  Heath, Russell, and, 377
  Kubert, Joe, and, 459-60
  S. M. Iger Studios and, 400
Home (G.B.), 693
Home Grown (U.S.) (magazine), 449

Hong Kong Business News
  (newspaper), 693
Hong Kong Standard (newspaper), 296
Hōpo (Japan) (magazine), 826
Hora Cero (Argentina) (magazine),
  284-85, 286, 580
Horizons (Algeria) (newspaper), 525
Horizontov Zabavnik (Yugoslavia)
  (magazine), 266
Horror comics/strips
  banned in U.S., 215
  Capitaine Fantôme, Le, 176
  Corben, Richard Vance, and, 214
  Davis, Jack, and, 237
  Devilman, 559
  Ditko, Steve, and, 254
  Dracula, 818
  Dylan Dog, 273
  Elder, William W., and, 278
  Elias, Leopold, and, 280
  Feldstein, Al, and, 297
  Frankenstein, 317-18
  Gog, 773
  Ibis the Invincible, 399
  Ingels, Graham (pseud. Ghastly),
    and, 401
  Jacht naar geluk, 491
  Kappa no Sanpei, 542
  Mizuki, Shigeru, and, 542
  Mort Cinder, 549
  Orlando, Joe, and, 587
  Pō no ichizoku, 366
  Rocket Man, 542
  Swamp Thing, The, 547, 587, 645,
    738
  Vampire, 754
  Vampirella, 787
  Zio Boris, 608
Horror (Italy) (magazine), 145, 189-90
Horwitz Publications (Australia), 255
Hör zu (Germany) (magazine)
  Butschkow, Peter, and, 169
  Ernsting, Volker, and, 285, 534
  Escher, Reinhold, and, 285
  Krüger, Hans Martin (pseud.
    Martin, Hans), and, 459
  Mecki in, 285, 525, 648
  Mike Macke in, 533
Hot Rod Cartoons (U.S.), 694
Houston Chronicle (U.S.) (newspaper),
  745
Houston Press (U.S.), 593
Hudibras (Denmark) (magazine), 87
Hull & Daily Mail (G.B.) (newspaper),
  693
Hull & Yorkshire Times (G.B.)
  (newspaper), 693
Hulton Press (G.B.), 232, 368
Humanité, L' (France) (newspaper),
  617, 816
Humbug (U.S.) (magazine), 278, 408,
  463
Humor and Satire (China)
  (supplement), 527-28

Humor strips, 34, 39
  Abbie an'Slats, 75-76, 788
  Abie the Agent, 76, 382
  Achille Talon, 76-77, 647
  Aga od Rudnika, 411
  Agatha Crumm, 389
  Airship Man, The, 82-83
  Akatsuka, Fujio, and, 84
  Alan Ford, 85-86, 685
  Alfie the Air Tramp, 426
  Alley Oop, 88, 367-68
  Ally Sloper, 88-89
  Alphonse and Gaston, 89-90
  Andy Capp, 95
  Argonautjes, De, 100
  Arnao, Gabriel (pseud. Gabi), and,
    695
  Arthur le Fantome, 193
  Aspirino y Colodion, 102, 302
  Astérix, 103
  Badd Lads, The, 424
  Barney Google, 114
  B.C., 119-20, 371
  Ben Bowyang, 364
  For Better or For Worse, 423
  Bidochon, Les, 134
  Birdseye Center, 322-23
  Blondie, 138-39
  Bloom County, 139
  Bob Fish, 194
  Bondying, 773
  Boner's Ark, 142-43
  Boob McNutt, 144-45
  Boobs Abroad, 348
  Born Loser, The, 148
  Botond, 294
  Brad and Dad, 349
  Brammetje Bram, 149-50
  Bringing Up Father, 154-55, 356
  Bristow, 155-56
  Bronc Peeler, 156
  Broom Hilda, 156, 556-57
  Bulletje en Bonestaak, 163
  Bunky, 165
  Calvin and Hobbes, 173-74, 446,
    556, 593
  Captain Easy, 777, 800
  Casey Court, 187-88
  Cathy, 190
  Cellulite, 192
  César, 762
  Charlie Chaplin's Comic Capers, 196
  Chlorophylle, 199-200
  Chu Liu Chu, 200-201
  Chupamirto, 201
  Clive, 204-5
  Colonel Crackpot's Circus, 424
  Colonel Pewter, 208
  Colonel Potterby and the Duchess,
    208, 827
  Count Screwloose of Tooloose, 216-17
  Cro-Magnon, 382
  Danny Dingle, 233
  Dave, 235-36

Dave's Delicatessen, 235
Dedalito, 302
Desperate Dan, 243-44
Desperate Desmond, 244, 382
Dilbert, 249-50
Ding Cong (pseud. Xiao Ding),
  and, 250-51
Dinglehoofer und His Dog Adolph,
  252
Djon Domino, 255-56
Dobol Trobol, 773
Don Catarino, 631
Don Fulgencio, 262-63
Don Placído, 302
Don Terrible Banuelos, 302
Doonesbury, 264
Dot and Carrie, 265-66
Dropouts, The, 269
Ernie, 284
Facéties du Sapeur Camember, Les,
  290
Fallutelli, 291
Far Side, The, 468
Fazekas, Attila, and, 294
Figueras, Alfonso, and, 302
Flip, 646
Footrot Flats, 311-12
Foxy Grandpa, 317
Fünf Schreckensteiner, Die, 325-26,
  581
Fusco Brothers, The, 327-28
Gaki Deka, 332
Ganbare Gonbe, 716
Garfield, 237, 333
Gaston Lagaffe, 337
Gnidén, 283
Gordo, 101, 351-52
Go West!, 647
Gunn's Gully, 364
Gyatoruzu, 716
Hägar the Horrible, 365-66
Happy Hooligan, 368-69, 586
Hawkshaw the Detective, 374-75
Herb & Jamaal, 379
Hércules Paput, 302
Herlock Sholmes, 380, 638
Holroyd, Bill, and, 393
Janković, Djordje, and, 411
Jim Erizo, 416
Juniper Junction, 323
Just Jake, 428-29
Kane, Robert, and, 434
Kelot, 516
Keyhole Kate, 442
Kića, 411
Kudzu, 461
Lao Ma's Adventures, 269-70
Lazarus, Mel (pseud. Fulton; Mell),
  and, 470
Learn Cantonese the Hard Way, 296
Li'l Abner, 478-79
Loony, 302
McNeill, Hugh, and, 502
MacNelly, Jeff, and, 697

Major Ozone's Fresh Air Crusade,
  381
Mangucho y Meneca, 509
*Mannen som gör vad som faller honom
  in*, 93, 510
Marc Lebut, 762
Michel, 528-29, 661
Mike and Ike, 533
Millionbucks and Kandykiddo, 375
Miracle Jones, 389
Miserable Moments, 677, 728
Mixed Singles, 189
Momma, 470
Monsieur Petipon, 604
Monsieur Poche, 545, 670
Monsieur Toudou, 192
Moose Miller, 547-48
Mutt and Jeff, 555-56, 711
Mysto, 302
Nasredin Hodža, 566
Needlenose Noonan, 388, 415
Nonkina Tousan, 575-76
Numskulls, The, 424
Oaky Doaks, 579
Onésime, 196-97
Oor Wullie, 585
Otto Kruntz, 190
Our Boarding House, 322, 589-90
Our Ernie, 589
Outland, 591-92
Outtaluck Club, The, 809
Over the Hedge, 593-94
Patoflor, 302
Patoruzú, 597-98
Pension Radicelle, La, 606
Pepito, 606-7
Pitch and Toss, 620
Polop le Caid, 467
Poo Yai Ma Kap Tung Ma Muen,
  193-94
Prince Errant, 628
Purapinta, 399
Ramona, 262, 595
Redeye, 128, 643-44
Rick O'Shay, 496, 651
Ridder Roodhart, 100, 372, 519
Rody, 302
Room and Board, 660
Rube Goldberg's Sideshow, 349
Rubin and Rut, 302
Sad Sack, The, 669
Sally Forth, 672
Sam's Strip, 270, 673
Seidel og Tobran, 75
Shoe, 697-98
Short Ribs, 583, 698-99
Shuang Hsiang Pao, 200
Siegfried, 169
Sigi the Frank, 382
Silk Hat Harry's Divorce Suit, 265
Silly Symphonies, 702-3, 744
Simeon Batts, 365
Simon Simple, 185-86
Simp O'Dill, 383

Slim Jim, 709
Smokey Stover, 392-93, 712-13
Spirou, 721
Stojadin, 512
Stonehenge Kit the Ancient Brit, 729
Stumble Inn, 381
Suburban Cowgirls, 732-33
Texas Slim, 422-23
Texas Slim and Dirty Dalton, 753
They'll Do It Everytime, 373
Thimble Theater, 687, 755-56
Tiramolla, 642, 764-65
Toonerville Folks, 316, 768-69
Tóxico y Biberón, 399
Tri bekrije, 411
Tumbleweeds, 667, 776
Valhalla, 786-87
Vanilla and the Villians, 789
Walker, Addison Mortimer (Mort; pseud. Addison), and, 796
Wash Tubbs, 220, 777, 799-800
Weary Willie and Tired Tim, 801
What a Guy!, 389
Where I'm Coming From, 806
Will Bragg, 364
Wizard of Id, The, 371, 597, 814
World of Lily Wong, The, 296-97
See also Parody strips; Satire
Humour Magazine (France), 134
Humpty Dumpty (U.S.) (magazine), 440
Hung-Chia Publishers (China), 824
Hustler (U.S.) (magazine), 809
Hwarang (Korea) (magazine), 444

I

Iger-Eisner Studios. See S.M. Iger Studios
Illustrated Chips (G.B.), 125, 157, 188, 205, 801, 823
Illustrated Sunday Herald (G.B.) (newspaper), 625
Illustré du Dimanche (France), 99
Ima (France) (magazine), 829
Image Comics (U.S.), 472, 476, 500, 749
India Book House (India), 595
Inside Comics (U.S.) (magazine), 701
Integrated strips
   Dateline: Danger!, 234-35, 502, 677
   Madam and Eve, 503
   Quincy, 635
   Sgt. Fury, 689
   Wee Pals, 635, 777, 803
   See also African-American strips; Ethnic strips
Intellectual strips
   Barnaby, 112-13, 446, 474
   Calvin and Hobbes, 173-74, 446, 556, 593
   Fabulas Panicas, 289

Fuku-chan, 325, 825
Jimpy, 418
King Aroo, 440, 445-46
Krazy Kat, 381, 457
Little Nemo in Slumberland, 446, 486-87
Peanuts, 446
Pogo, 446
Todano Bonji, 766
Tom Poes, 768
Inter Art (Sweden) (publisher), 348, 557
Intercontinental Features (Australia), 311, 713
International comics, 40-42
   Air Hawk and the Flying Doctors, 81-82, 255
   Alack Sinner, 85
   Blasco, Jesus, and, 138
   Blondie, 138-39
   Boucq, François, and, 149
   Bringing Up Father, 154-55
   Bristow, 155-56
   Bronc Peeler, 156
   Buffalo Bill, 161-62
   Ernie, 284
   exhibition of, 215
   Falk, Lee, and, 291
   Felix, 297-99
   Ferd'nand, 300-301
   Giardino, Vittorio, and, 338
   Gimenez, Carlos, and, 341
   Gim Toro, 342
   Globi, 346
   Hägar the Horrible, 365-66
   International Comics Festival (Switzerland), 436
   Kapitein Rob, 461
   Khalid, Mohamed Nor (pseud. Lat), and, 442
   König, Ralf, and, 453
   Legends Along the Silk Road, 734
   Mattotti, Lorenzo, and, 520-21
   Max, 523-24
   Melouah, Sid Ali, and, 525
   Mercenary, The, 688
   Miller, Sydney Leon, and, 535
   Modesty Blaise, 543
   Moomin, 412
   Mordillo, Guillermo, and, 548
   Nick Knatterton, 571
   Out of the Silence, 592
   Peanuts, 602
   Pepito, 606-7
   Potts, The, 626
   Radilović, Julio, and, 637
   Ranxerox, 476
   Rasmus Klump, 639
   Rod Craig, 535, 658
   Saturna Contro la Terra in, 677
   Si Yeoo Ki, 706
   Snake Tales, 713
   Suburban Cowgirls, 732
   Tiffany Jones, 760

Torpedo 1936, 771
Vater und Sohn, 581
Internationale Presse (France), 647
International Museum of Cartoon Art, 796
Internet web sites, 469, 551
Interpublik (Yugoslavia) (animation studio), 566
Intervalo (Argentina) (magazine), 239
Intransigeant, L' (France) (newspaper), 604
Intrepido, L' (Italy) (magazine)
   Battaglia, Dino, and, 118
   Billy Bis in, 132
   Bufalo Bill in, 161
   Buffolente, Lina, and, 162
   Caesar, Kurt (pseud. Avai, Cesare; Away, Caesar), and, 173
   Cossio, Carlo, and, 216
   Forza John in, 314
   Molino, Walter, and, 543
   Principe Azzurro in, 629
   Roland Eagle in, 659
I.P.C. (G.B.) (publisher), 119, 123, 574, 648, 714
Izvestia (Russia), 95

J

J. Walter Thompson Agency (Australia), 535
Jack and Jill (G.B.), 125, 147
Jack and Jill (G.B.) (magazine), 761
Jack Binder Shop, 223, 678, 691
Jack High (U.S.) (fanzines), 496
Jademan (Yuk Long) (Hong Kong comics company), 817-18
Ja Ja (Mexico), 99
James Henderson & Son Publishing (G.B.), 146, 157
Japan Comic Artists Association, 588
Japan Punch (Japan) (magazine), 451
J.B. Allen (G.B.) (publisher), 110, 393
Jewish Daily Forward (U.S.), 341
Jewish Weekly (U.S.), 218
Jež (Yugoslavia) (weekly), 256
Jianwan Bao (China) (newspaper), 270
Jidaimono artists, 452
Jiji Shinpou (Japan) (newspaper), 448
Johannesburg Star (South Africa) (newspaper), 503
John F. Dille Co., 173, 708
John F. Dille Co. (U.S.), 159
Johnny (Belgium) (magazine), 339
John Stone and Cushing Agency (U.S.), 267, 454, 725
Jornal do Cuto (Portugal) (magazine), 230
Jour, Le (Canada) (newspaper), 398
Journal de Francette et Riquet, Le (Belgium) (magazine), 830

Journal de Toto (France) (magazine), 790
Judge (U.S.) (magazine)
  Anderson, Carl Thomas, and, 91
  Cole, Jack (pseud. Johns, Ralph), and, 206
  Dirks, Rudolph, and, 252
  Ewer, Raymond, and, 709
  Fuller, Ralph Briggs, and, 325
  Godwin, Francis, and, 347
  Herriman, George, and, 381
  Holman, Bill, and, 392
  Howarth, F. M., and, 395
  Inwood, G. Burr, and, 647
  O'Neill, Rose Cecil, and, 584
  Outcault, Richard Felton, and, 589, 590
  Pete the Tramp in, 611
  Prince Errant in, 628
  Russell, Clarence D., and, 666
  Turner, Leslie, and, 776
  Van Buren, Raeburn, and, 788
Judy (G.B.) (weekly), 88-89
Jugoslovenče (Yugoslavia) (magazine), 512
Jumbo (Italy) (magazine), 143, 603
Jumbo (U.S.) (comic book), 693
Jungle strips
  Akim, 84-85, 759-60
  Animal Land, 749
  Anna della Jungla, 627
  Booma, 773
  Buntala, 462
  Caça aos Tubaroes, 215
  Conquista di Mompracem, La, 549
  Devlin, 462
  Diwani, 462
  Dumagit, 462
  Džungla Ved, 411
  Gruaga, 462
  Hagibis, 462
  Herr des Dschungels, 759
  Jakun of the Jungle, 631
  Jann of the Jungle, 693
  Jungle Jim, 427, 576, 641
  Junglemen, 627
  Jungle Tatei, 427-28, 754
  Korak, 462
  Kulafu, 462
  Kuma, 462
  Loana, 511
  Marabini, 462
  Mga Matang Naglilivab, 462, 563
  Misteri della Giungla Nera, I, 549
  Nizar, 799
  Nyoka, 693
  Og, 462
  Pantera Bionda, 596-97
  Rima, 462
  Robina, 462, 773
  Roy Tiger, 663
  Sadhú, 669
  Sargon, 462

  Sheena, Queen of the Jungle, 526, 693-94
  Shōnen Oja, 698
  Tad of the Tanbark, 262, 352, 611
  Tani, 462
  Tarzan, 315, 462, 510, 524, 573, 747-48
  Tarzan van de apen, 457
  Ted Towers, 749
  Tibor, 759-60, 799
  Tsannga Rannga, 462
Junior (France) (weekly), 174, 189, 396
Junior Mirror (G.B.) (supplement), 619
Junior Press (G.B.) (publisher), 628
Junior Star (G.B.) (supplement), 347
  See also *Star, The*
Justice League/Justice Society of America
  Atom, The in, 104
  Dr. Mid-Nite in, 259
  Fox, Gardner, and, 316
  Green Lantern in, 357, 358
  Hawkman in, 374
  Johnny Thunder in, 422
  Mr. Terrific in, 542
  Sandman, The, 673
  Starman in, 725

K

Kage (Japan) (publisher), 670
Kalayaan International (Philippines), 506
Kamishibai (comic strips for public narration), 580
Kangaroo (G.B.) (publisher), 500
Kansas City Star (U.S.) (newspaper), 787
Kapatid (Philippines) (magazine), 646
Kapoentje, 't (Belgium) (magazine), 564
Kashibon Manga Kage (Japan) (rental comics), 542
Kashibonya yō manga (rental comics), 387, 452, 542, 572-73, 670, 696
Kauka Comic Akademie (Germany), 437
Kauka Verlag (Germany) (publisher), 437-38
  allegations of nationalistic tendencies against, 494
  Andrax, 94
  Capitan Terror, 177
  Fix und Foxi, 305, 437-38
  Kuma, 462
  Lupo, 493-94
  Neugebauer, Walter, and, 566
  Pepito, 606
  Radilović, Julio, and, 638
  Roscher, Franz, and, 661
Kaw (Poland) (magazine), 436

Kay Features (U.S.), 354
Kenkoy Komics (Philippines) (comic book), 659
Kerempuh (Yugoslavia) (newspaper), 238-39, 566
Kidlat (Philippines) (comic book), 350
Kid strips, 20
  Akage no Hitotsu, 520
  Always Belittlin', 708
  Belinda Blue Eyes, 123
  Buster Brown, 168-69, 591
  Carter, Augustus Daniels, and, 187
  Compagnia dei Sette, La, 603
  Crimebuster, 222
  Dennis the Menace, 441
  Dennis the Menace (G.B.), 241-42
  Dennis the Menace (U.S.), 242
  Dondi, 262, 275-76, 373
  Dwiggins, Clare Victor, and, 272-73
  Elmer, 281-82, 554, 740, 813
  Fatty Finn, 293-94, 569
  Felix, 297-99
  Flenheimer Kids, The, 450
  4 As, Les, 217
  Freckles and His Friends, 320
  Gamin and Patches, 796
  Ginger Meggs, 343-44
  Gumdrop, 685
  Jerry on the Job, 388, 414-15
  Just Kids, 429
  Katzenjammer Kids, The, 436-37, 450
  Kelly Kids, The, 826
  Kid Sister, The, 826
  Kin-der-Kids, The, 297, 444-45
  Knerr, Harold H., and, 450
  Lazarus, Mel (pseud. Fulton; Mell), and, 470
  L'il One, 470
  Little Annie Rooney, 481-83
  Little Iodine, 483
  Little Lulu, 486, 724
  Little Orphan Annie, 487-88, 725
  Lord Snooty and His Pals, 491-92
  Mafalda, 503
  Marriner, William, and, 514
  Miss Peach, 470, 537-38
  Mitou et Toti, 670
  Mitsubahi no Bōken, 520
  Moustique, 604
  Muggs and Skeeter, 552
  Nancy, 560-61, 685
  Nicodemus O'Malley, 187
  Nipper, 574, 807
  Orvie, 539-40
  Pansy Potter, 595
  Peanuts, 601-2, 683
  Perishers, The, 608
  Pom et Teddy, 217
  Poor Li'l Mose, 591
  Professor Doodle's, 672
  Quincy, 635
  Reg'lar Fellers, 646-47

Riri, Gogo et Lolo, 604
Scary William, 450, 600
School Days, 272
Skippy, 222-23, 707-8
Tabibito-Kun, 559
Tatave, 467
Tiger, 760
Trac et Boum, 670
Vanilla and the Villains, 482, 499, 789
Wee Pals, 635, 777, 803
Wee Women, 470
Wide Awake Willie, 646
Yellow Kid, The, 589-90
Zig et Puce, 545, 647, 670, 829, 831
See also Children's strips
Kid superheroes
  Boy Commandos, 149, 447, 705
  Newsboy Legion, 447, 568, 705
  Star Spangled Kid, 725
  Young Allies, 827
Kids (U.S.) (magazine), 229
Kiebitz (Austria) (magazine), 731
Kindercompas (Netherlands), 157
King Comics, 308, 818
King Features Syndicate
  Ace Drummond, 451
  Agatha Crumm, 389
  Ahern, Gene, and, 80-81
  Aizen, Adolfo, and, 83
  Apartment 3-G, 97
  Archie, 100
  Baby Blues, 685
  Bald, Kenneth (pseud. Bruce, K.), and, 108
  Barney Baxter, 113, 563
  Barry, Daniel, and, 115, 474
  Barry, Seymour (Sy), and, 116
  Beetle Bailey, 122, 796, 809
  Betty Boop, 129, 309
  Big Ben Bolt, 130, 554
  Blondie, 138, 809
  Boner's Ark, 143
  Bonzo, 145
  Bozo Blimp, 404
  Brick Bradford, 152, 576
  Bringing Up Father, 356
  Bunky, 165
  Buz Sawyer, 169-70, 220, 777, 800
  Caplin, Elliot, and, 179
  Cap Stubbs and Tippie, 272
  Carr, Eugene, and, 186
  Carter, Augustus Daniels, and, 187
  Celardo, John (pseud. Lardo, John C.), and, 192
  Charlton Comics and, 809
  Cisco Kid, The, 203, 672
  continuity *vs.* gag strips, 469
  Cory, Fanny Young, and, 216
  Count Screwloose of Tooloose in, 217
  Curley Harper, 228
  Curtis, 379
  Danny Dingle, 233
  Dave's Delicatessen, 235

Dickenson, Fred, and, 246
Dick's Adventures in Dreamland, 247
Dr. Kildare, 257
Dumb Dora, 271, 826
Edson, Gus, and, 275
Elmer, 282, 813
Ernie, 284
Etta Kett, 286
Falk, Lee, and, 291
Felix the Cat, 299-300, 617
Flanders, Charles, and, 306-7
Flash Gordon, 115, 308, 637, 641, 809
Fletcher, Frank, and, 309
Godwin, Francis, and, 348
Goodwin, Archie (pseud. Franklin, Robert), and, 351
Gould, Chester, and, 354
Greene, Vernon van Atta, and, 356
Gross, Milton, and, 109
Half-Hitch, 367, 441
Hawkshaw the Detective, 375
Heart of Juliet Jones, The, 267, 376
Henry, 92
Henry in, 378
Hi and Lois, 383
Hoest, Bill, and, 389
Hopalong Cassidy, 720
Hubert, 395-96
on humor strips, 532
humor strips of, 548
Inspector Wade, 92, 402, 581-82
Jerry on the Job, 388, 414-15, 563
Johnny Hazard, 420, 653
Johnny-Round-the-World, 422
Judge Parker, 424
Jungle Jim, 427, 576, 641
Just Kids, 429
Kewpies, The, 441-42, 584
Kid Sister, The, 826
King of the Royal Mounted, 446
Knight, Clayton, and, 451
Lasswell, Fred, and, 469
Little Annie Rooney, 481-83
Little King, The, 485, 714
Lockhorns, The, 389
Lone Ranger, The, 307, 490
Lubbers, Robert (pseud. Lewis, Bob), and, 492
McClure, Darrell, and, 499
Mallard Fillmore, 507
Mama's Boyz, 218
Mandrake the Magician, 238, 291, 509
Mark Trail, 513
Marsh, Norman and, 232
Mary Worth, 519
Mickey Mouse, 353, 531-32, 593
Miller, Frank (1898-1949), and, 534
Ming Foo, 535
Mr. Abernathy, 538
Mr. Breger, 538-39
Moose Miller, 547-48

Murphy, James Edward, and, 553-54
Musial, Joseph, and, 554
Mutts, 556
Naylor, Robert, and, 563-64
Norris, Paul, and, 576
O'Keefe, Neil, 581-82
Outtaluck Club, The, 809
Ozark Ike, 594
Pa's Son-in-Law, 804
Pete the Tramp, 611, 666
Phantom, The, 116, 291, 611, 809
Popeye, 309, 687, 809
Prince Valiant, 628
Private Breger, 150-51
Quincy, 635
Raboy, Emanuel (Mac), and, 637
Radio Patrol, 638
Raymond, Alex, and, 641
Red Barry, 642
Redeye, 128, 643
Rip Kirby, 627, 641, 651
Room and Board, 589, 660
Russell, Clarence D., and, 666
Rusty Riley, 348, 666
Salinas, Alberto, and, 672
Sally Forth, 672-73
Sarge Snorkle, 809
Secret Agent X-9, 354, 641, 685-86
Skeets, 707
Skippy, 223, 707
Slylock Fox and Comics for Kids, 709
Ted Towers, 749
They'll Do It Everytime, 373, 755
Thimble Theater, 687
Thorne, Frank, and, 757
Tiger, 760
Tillie the Toiler, 761, 805
Tim Tyler's Luck, 763-64, 826
Tommy of the Big Top, 474
Toots and Casper, 553, 554, 769
Tumbleweeds, 667, 776
Turner, Leslie, and, 776
Van Buren, Raeburn, and, 788
Vanilla and the Villians, 482, 789
Way Out West, 420
What a Guy!, 389
When I Was Short, 593
Wildman, George, and, 809
Winner, Charles H. (Doc), 813
Young, Murat (Chic), and, 826-27
Zippy the Pinhead, 359
King-Ganteaume (G.B.) (comic book packager), 209, 517
King Kong (Italy) (magazine), 521
Kitchen Sink Enterprises (U.S.), 449-50, 721
Kjeine Zondasvriend, De (Netherlands), 458
Klein Blatt, Das (Austria) (newspaper), 765
Klein Zondagsvriend, De (Netherlands) (weekly), 767
Kodansha (Japan) (monthly), 676

Kodansha Publishing (Japan), 366, 542
Kolo (Yugoslavia) (magazine), 489
Kostyor (Russia) (magazine), 489
Kuifje (Belgium) (magazine), 738
Kuluttajain (Finland) (magazine), 604

L

L. Miller & Son (U.S.), 96
L.A. Free Press (U.S.) (newspaper), 289-90
L.A. Free-Press (U.S.) (newspaper), 694
Laatste Nieuws, Het (Netherlands) (newspaper), 283, 458
Ladies Home Journal, 388, 441, 584, 776
Lancashire Evening Post (G.B.), 118, 155-56
Lancet, The (G.B.) (magazine), 693
Lancio Story (Italy) (weekly), 278, 818
Larousse (France) (publisher), 508
Lasso-Sonderheft (Germany) (comic book), 161
Laughing Stock (South Africa) (magazine), 503
Leader, The (G.B.) (magazine), 631
Leatherneck Magazine (U.S.), 101, 468
Ledger Syndicate
  Babe Bunting, 348
  Connie, 212, 347
  Cory, Fanny Young, and, 216
  Godwin, Francis, and, 347-48
  Greene, Vernon van Atta, and, 356
  Hairbreadth Harry, 366
  Polly and Her Pals, 356
  Shadow, The, 356, 692
  War on Crime, 348
Leeds Features (U.S.), 389
Lefvande Livet (Sweden) (newspaper), 572
Lego (Denmark) (toy company), 535
Lehning Verlag (Germany) (publisher), 569-70, 702, 798
Lektyr (Sweden) (magazine), 282, 314
Leonard Miller (G.B.) (publisher), 517
Leoplan (Argentina) (magazine), 399
Leslie's Magazine (U.S.), 586
Leveller, The (G.B.), 124
Lev Gleason Publications
  Bald, Kenneth (pseud. Bruce, K.), and, 108
  Barry, Daniel, and, 115
  Barry, Seymour (Sy), and, 116
  Biro, Charles, and, 134-35
  Craig, John, and, 219
  Crimebuster, 222
  Crowley, Wendell, and, 223
  Giordano, Richard, and, 344
  Godwin, Francis, and, 348
  Guardineer, Frederic, and, 360

Heath, Russell, and, 377
McWilliams, Alden, and, 502
Meskin, Morton (pseud. Morton, Mort, Jr.), and, 526
Overgard, William Thomas, and, 593
Toth, Alexander, and, 773
Wildey, Doug, and, 808
Wolverton, Basil, and, 816
See also Lev Gleason Comics
Lew Little Syndicate, 327, 667, 777, 803
Leyendas Infantiles (Spain) (magazine), 302
Leyte Express (Philippines) (newspaper), 506
Liangyou Morning (China) (newspaper), 798
Libération (France) (newspaper), 816
Liberty Times (Taiwan), 201
Liberty (U.S.) (magazine), 325, 347, 497, 500, 554, 818
Libre Belgique, La (Belgium) (newspaper), 128, 217, 396, 781
Libro e Moschetto (Italy) (magazine), 543
Life in Hell Cartoon Company (U.S.), 478
Life (U.S.) (magazine)
  Anderson, Carl Thomas, and, 91
  Carey, Ed, and, 185
  Cory, Fanny Young, and, 216
  Crosby, Percy Leo, and, 222
  Dirks, Rudolph, and, 252
  Dumm, Frances Edwina, and, 272
  Fuller, Ralph Briggs, and, 325
  Godwin, Francis, and, 347
  Held, John, Jr. (pseud. Held, Myrtle), 378
  Herriman, George, and, 381
  Holman, Bill, and, 392
  Howarth, F. M., and, 395
  Outcault, Richard Felton, and, 589
  Van Buren, Raeburn, and, 788
lifte (Germany) (magazine), 664
"ligne claire" school, 739
Lincoln Newspaper Syndicate, 447-48
Link Studios (G.B.), 686
Linus (Italy) (magazine), 79, 118, 170, 221, 521, 781, 785
Lion and Eagle (G.B.) (comic book), 232
Lion Comic (G.B.), 209
Literary adaptations
  Akai Kageböshi, 452
  Battaglia, Dino, and, 118
  Bellamy, Frank, and, 125
  Botchan, 542
  Briefer, Richard, and, 152
  Buffolente, Lina, and, 162
  Caprioli, Franco, and, 180
  Carmen, 614
  Chōhen Dai Roman, 452
  Classics Illustrated, 204

Crepax, Guido, and, 221
Cruikshank, George, and, 224
Del Castillo, Arturo, and, 239
DeLuca, Gianni, and, 241
Doctor Niebla, 259, 384
Dottor Faust, Il, 266
Emil und die Detektive, 451
Evans, George, and, 287
Faust, 623
Feng Zikai and, 300
Frankenstein, 317-18
Gimenez, Carlos, and, 341
Haiiroguma no Denki, 696
Huckleberry Finn, 521
Iliad, 204
Inspector Wade, 408
Ishikawa, Kyūta, and, 443
Jacovitti, Benito, and, 408
James Bond, 408-10
Jusei, 588
Kama-Sutra, 614
Kibaō, 442-43
King of the Royal Mounted, 446
Kojima, Goseki, and, 452
Kuznjecov, Konstantin, and, 464
Lobacev, Jurij (Djordje) (pseud. Strip, George), and, 489
Lo Scimiotto, 508
Magic Flute, The, 623
Marcello, Raffaelo Carlo (pseud. Marc, Ralph), and, 511
Matena, Dick, and, 520
Memoirs of a Don Juan, 614
Meng Jiang Nu, 797
Michel Strogoff, 671
Mohican Zokuno Saigo, 733
Moroni-Celsi, Guido (pseud. Sterny), and, 549
Neugebauer, Walter, and, 566
Nizzi, Claudio, and, 575
Odyssey, 614
Peter Rabbit, 611
Pichard, Georges, and, 614
Poïvet, Raymond, and, 623
Prince and the Pauper, The, 529
Put oko sveta, 411
Red Detachment of Women, The, 642-43
Robin Hood, 125, 174, 175, 307, 575, 716, 812
Robin Hood and Company, 655
Salinas, José Luis, and, 671
Schultheiss, Matthias, and, 682
Seton Dōbutsuki, 696
Solovjev, Sergej (pseud. Gey, Moum; Solo, S.), and, 715-16
Tarzan, 315, 462, 510, 524, 573, 747-48
Terror Keep, 544
Three Musketeers, The, 671
Ulysse, 781-82
Ulysses, 614
Wang Shuhui, and, 797
Xi Xiang Ji, 797

Litigation
  Bancks *vs.* Associated Newspapers
    Ltd., 110
  Disney *vs.* O'Neill, Dan, 584
  Fisher, Hammond Edward *vs.*
    Capp, Al, 304
  Howard the Duck and, 395
  Inspector Wade vs. Terror Keep, 110,
    544
  Katzenjammer Kids and, 182, 253
  Kauka comic books and, 305-6,
    437-38
  Kriminal, and, 459
  Liefeld, Rob, and, 476
  Mager, Gus *vs.* Doyle's, A. Conan
    agents, 374, 375, 505
  Mutt and Jeff and, 305
  National *vs.* Fawcett (Captain
    Marvel), 121, 183, 517, 541
  *New York World vs. New York
    Journal* (Yellow Kid), 590, 825
  over *Eisele und Beisele*
    merchandising, 277
  Pantera Bionda and, 597
  Siegel *vs.* National (Superman),
    700, 701
Little Friends (China) (magazine), 827
Liverpool Daily Post (G.B.), 693
Liway Publications (Philippines), 438
Liwayway (Philippines) (magazine),
  462, 505, 659, 675
Lloyd Jacquet Comic Shop (U.S.), 287
Lodpot (India) (magazine), 626
London Daily Express (G.B.)
  (newspaper), 409
London Evening News (G.B.)
  (newspaper), 370, 412, 546, 750
London Evening Standard (G.B.)
  (newspaper), 155, 210, 391, 807
London Evening Star (G.B.)
  (newspaper), 609
London Features Syndicate (G.B.),
  413-14
London Opinion (G.B.) (magazine), 302
Longacre Press/Odhams (G.B.)
  (publisher), 232
Look and Learn (G.B.) (magazine), 282
Looney Tunes (U.S.) (comic book),
  162, 231
Los Angeles Daily News (U.S.)
  (newspaper), 218
Los Angeles Herald (U.S.) (newspaper),
  381
Los Angeles Mirror Syndicate (U.S.),
  720
Los Angeles Reader (U.S.), 478
Los Angeles Times Syndicate, 87,
  510, 726
Los Angeles Times (U.S.) (newspaper),
  497
Lucca Comics Convention (Italy), 170
Lucky Productions (Belgium), 129,
  493
Lui (France) (magazine), 548

LUPO modern (Germany) (magazine),
  494
Lutfisken (Sweden) (newspaper), 408
Lutin (Belgium) (magazine), 407

M

Maas en Roerbode (Netherlands)
  (newspaper), 156-57
Macaco (Spain) (magazine), 497
Macaquete (Spain) (magazine), 497
MacCall's (U.S.) (magazine), 788
Macchia Nera (Italy) (publisher), 494
McDougall's Magazine (U.S.), 499
Ma Chié (Italy) (magazine), 548
Machi (Japan) (publisher), 670
Mad (U.S.) (magazine)
  Aragonés, Sergio, and, 99
  Berg, David, and, 126
  Davis, Jack, and, 237
  Elder, William W., and, 278
  Feldstein, Al, and, 297
  Gaines, William M., and, 331-32
  Goscinny, René, and, 352
  Jaffee, Allan, and, 408
  Kurtzman, Harvey, and, 463
  Mad Fold-In, 408
  Orlando, Joe, and, 587
  Severin, John Powers, and, 690
  Wolverton, Basil, and, 816
  Wood, Wallace, and, 818
  Wood, Wally, and, 723
Magazine Enterprises (U.S.), 337
Magic strips
  Abu Fakir, 408
  Akumakun, 542
  Ali and His Baba, 424
  Dr. Merling, 258, 468
  Guardineer, Frederic, and, 360-61
  Jimpy, 418
  Mandrake the Magician, 238, 291,
    321, 508-9
  Merlin, 360, 361
  Renkin Jutsu, 542
  Tor, 360, 361, 460
  Zatara, 360, 361, 460
  See also Fantasy strips
Mago, Il (Italy) (magazine), 191, 338
Magyar Vasarnap (Hungary)
  (magazine), 830
Maharlika (Philippines) (magazine),
  418
Mainichi (Japan) (newspaper), 325,
  436
Mainichi Shogakusei Shinbun (Japan)
  (daily), 520, 716, 754
Mainline Comics (U.S.), 705
Majallah Filem (Malaysia), 442
Major Magazines (U.S.), 690
Male, Il (Italy) (magazine), 476, 600
Malibu Comics (U.S.), 748
Mali Jež (Yugoslavia) (magazine), 256

Mali zabavnik (Yugoslavi) (magazine),
  473
Mañana (Mexico), 99
Manchar, El (Algeria) (magazine), 525
Manchester Evening News (G.B.)
  (newspaper), 648
manga, 448
Manga Action (Japan) (weekly), 454
Manga Gekijo (Japan) (magazine), 576
Manga Kourakukai (Japan)
  (cartoonist association), 448
Manga Ō, 84
Mangaō (Japan) (monthly), 669
Manga Shōnen (Japan) (magazine),
  405, 427, 520
Manga Shudan (Japan) (cartoonists'
  group), 825, 826
Manga Shūden (Japan) (magazine),
  436
Manga Sunday (Japan) (weekly), 452
Manila Chronicle (Philippines)
  (newspaper), 675
Man's World Publications (U.S.), 391,
  414
Marc'Aurelio (Italy) (magazine), 86
March of Comics (U.S.), 162
"Marcinelle school," 319
Margaret (Japan) (magazine), 588
Marten Toonder Studios
  Argonautjes, De, 100
  Arman en Ilva, 101
  De Zwann, Mr., and, 630
  Hartog van Banda, Lo, and, 372
  Kappie, 435-36
  Koning Hollewijn, 453-54
  Kresse, Hans G., and, 283, 457
  Matena, Dick, and, 519
  Toonder, Marten, and, 768
Martial arts strips
  Dragon and Tiger Heroes, 817
  Igaguri-kun, 399
  Master of Kung Fu, 519
  Siulauman, 817
Martin & Reid Comics (G.B.), 96,
  246, 536, 544
Maru (Japan) (magazine), 576
Marvel/Timely/Atlas group
  Adams, Neal, and, 77
  Alcala, Alfredo P., and, 87
  Anderson, Murphy, and, 92
  Angel, The, 95
  Avengers, The, 104
  Ayers, Richard, and, 104-5
  Bald, Kenneth (pseud. Bruce, K.),
    and, 108
  Barry, Daniel, and, 115
  Barry, Seymour (Sy), and, 116
  Berg, David, and, 126
  Big Boy and, 131
  Binder, Jack, and, 133
  Binder, Otto O. (pseud. Binder,
    Eando), and, 133-34
  Boring, Wayne (pseud. Harmon,
    Jack), and, 148

Briefer, Richard, and, 152
Brigman, June, and, 154
Bulanadi, Danny, and, 163
Burgos, Carl, and, 166
Buscema, John, and, 166-67
Byrne, John, and, 171
Cadence Industries and, 449
Captain America, 180, 705
Captain Marvel, 183
Carreño, Albert, and, 187
Chaykin, Howard, and, 197
Colan, Eugene (pseud. Austin, Adam), and, 206
Conan, 212
Craft, Jerry, and, 218
Craig, John, and, 219
Daredevil, 234
Davis, Jack, and, 237
Ditko, Steve, and, 254
Doc Savage, 257
Dr. Strange, 259
Elfquest, 280
Elias, Leopold, and, 280
Everett, Bill, and, 287
Fantastic Four, 292
Finger, Bill, and, 303
Frankenstein, 318
Fredericks, Harold, and, 321
Ghost Rider, 337-38
Giordano, Richard, and, 344
Goodwin, Archie (pseud. Franklin, Robert), and, 351
Guardineer, Frederic, and, 360
Gustafson, Bob, and, 364
Heath, Russell, and, 377
Heckle and Jeckle, 378
Hercules, 379-80
Herron, France Edward, and, 381
Hildebrandt, Greg and Tim, and, 384
Howard the Duck, 394-95
Hulk, The, 396-97
Human Torch, The, 397-98
Infantino, Carmine, and, 400, 401
Iron Man, 403-4
in Italy, 685
Jaffee, Allan, and, 408
Jodloman, Jess M., and, 419
Kaluta, Michael Wm., and, 432
Kane, Gil, and, 433
Kanigher, Robert, and, 435
Kida, Fred, and, 444
kid superheroes and, 568
Kirby, Jack, and, 447-48
Krigstein, Bernard, and, 458, 459
Kubert, Joe, and, 460
Kurtzman, Harvey, 462
Leav, Mort, and, 471
Lee, Jim, 471-72
Lee, Stan, and, 472
Liefeld, Rob, and, 476
Lieutenant Blueberry, 477
McFarlane, Todd, and, 500
Magsino, Frank, and, 505

Master of Kung Fu, 519
Meskin, Morton (pseud. Morton, Mort, Jr.), and, 526-27
Mighty Mouse, 532-33
Miller, Frank (1957-   ), 534
'Nam, 560
New Mutants, 568
Niño, Alex N., and, 573
Orlando, Joe, and, 587
Pfeufer, Carl, and, 611
Powerhouse Pepper, 626
Rawhide Kid, 641
Red Sonja, 646
Robbins, Frank, and, 653
Robbins, Trina, and, 653-54
Robinson, Jerry, and, 656
Romita, John, and, 660
Schaffenberger, Kurt (pseud. Wahl, Lou), and, 678
Sgt. Fury, 689
Severin, John Powers, and, 690
Silver Surfer, The, 704
Sinnott, Joe, 705
Spider-Man, 718
Springer, Frank, and, 722
Steranko, James, and, 726
Sub-Mariner, The, 731-32
Tarzan, 748
Thomas, Roy, and, 756
Thor, 756-57
Thorne, Frank, and, 757
Western titles and, 424
Wildey, Doug, and, 808
Williamson, Al, and, 811
Wilshire, Mary, and, 812
Wolverton, Basil, and, 816
Wood, Wallace, and, 818
Woolfolk, William, and, 819
X-Men, 821
Young Allies, 827
Matin, Le (France), 149
Max Bunker Press, 685
Maximum Press (U.S.), 476
Mazō (Japan) (rental library book), 387
McClure Syndicate
Anderson, Carl Thomas, and, 91
Bobby Thatcher, 141-42, 614
Carey, Ed, and, 185-86
Carr, Eugene, and, 186
Hairbreadth Harry, 366
King Aroo, 440
King Aroo in, 445
Lariat Pete, 381
Marriner, William, and, 514
Mayer, Sheldon, and, 524-25
Pa's Son-in-Law, 804
Simon Simple, 185
Superman, 700, 737
Van Buren, Raeburn, and, 788
Wags, the Dog that Adopted a Man, 795
McFadden Publications, 611

McNaught Syndicate
Bo, 121
Bungle Family, 779
Bungle Family, The in, 164
Charlie Chan, 95, 195
Craig, Chase, and, 218
Dixie Dugan, 255, 304
Fisher, Hammond Edward, and, 304
Gould, Chester, and, 354
Hogarth, Burne, and, 389
Joe Palooka, 304
McBride, Clifford, and, 497
Mickey Finn, 474, 531
Muggs and Skeeter, 552
Toonerville Folks, 316
M.E. Comics
Ayers, Richard, and, 104
Craig, John, and, 219
Fox, Gardner, and, 316
Frazetta, Frank, and, 319
Guardineer, Frederic, and, 360
Ingels, Graham (pseud. Ghastly), and, 401
Meccano Magazine (G.B.), 368
Mediascene (U.S.) (magazine), 727
Medical strips
Docteur Justice, 511
Dr. Guy Bennett, 757
Dr. Kildare, 257
Doctor Merengue, El, 257-58
Rex Morgan, M.D., 649-50, 722
Megaton (U.S.) (comic book), 476
Melbourne Age (Australia), 383
Melbourne Argus (Australia), 383, 592
Melbourne Herald (Australia) (newspaper), 223, 364, 535, 658, 666, 797
Melbourne Morning Post (Australia) (newspaper), 364
Melbourne Punch (Australia) (magazine), 364
Melbourne Sun (Australia), 110, 364
Melbourne Sun-Pictorial (Australia), 110
Memphis News-Scimitar (U.S.) (newspaper), 804
Menelik (Italy), 170
Menomenee Falls Gazette (U.S.) (newspaper), 82
Merchandising
of *Ally Sloper*, 89
of *Archie*, 100
of *Barnaby*, 113
of *Beep Beep the Road Runner*, 122
of *Beetle Bailey*, 123
of *Bonzo*, 145
Bottaro, Luciano, and, 149
of *Buster Brown*, 169, 591
of *Capitan Trueno, El*, 178-79
of *Captain America*, 182
of *Carpanta*, 186
of *Dilbert*, 249
of *Dingbats, The*, 693

of *Eisele und Beisele*, 277
of *Elfquest*, 280
of *Familia Ulises, La*, 291
of *Far Side, The*, 468
of *Fix und Foxi*, 305
of *Fudge the Elf*, 648
of *Gasoline Alley*, 335-37
of *Ginger Meggs*, 110
of *Globi*, 346
of *Gumps, The*, 362
of *Jim Boum*, 416
of *Kewpies, The*, 584
Khalid, Mohamed Nor (pseud. Lat), and, 442
of *Life in Hell*, 478
of *Li'l Abner*, 479
of *Little Lulu*, 486
of *Little Nemo in Slumberland*, 487
of *Lurchis Abenteuer*, 495
McFarlane, Todd, and, 500
of *Mazinger Z* in, 559
of *Mecki*, 525
of *Mr. Kiasu*, 540
of *Mr. Natural*, 541
Mordillo, Guillermo, and, 548
of *Mortadelo y Filemon*, 549
of *Mother Goose and Grimm*, 551
of *Nick Knatterton*, 571
of *Nipper*, 574, 807
of *Nonkina Tousan*, 576
of *Sad Sack, The*, 107, 670
of *Schtroumpes, Les*, 680
of *Spider-Man*, 718
of *Superman*, 736
of *Tintin*, 764
of *Toonerville Folks*, 768
of *Tripje en Liezenbertha*, 774
of *Werner*, 805
of *Yellow Kid, The*, 825
of *Zig et Puce*, 829
Messaggero, Il (Italy) (daily), 338
Messaggero dei Piccoli, Il (Italy) (magazine), 548
Messaggero dei Ragazzi, Il (Italy) (magazine), 118, 173, 191, 770
Métal Hurlant (France) (magazine), 194, 345, 680
Metropolitan Newspaper Service (U.S.), 280, 747
Meyer-Both Syndicate (U.S.), 730
M.G.M. Studios (U.S.), 766
Miami Daily News (U.S.) (newspaper), 175
Mickey Mouse Weekly (G.B.), 125, 187, 333, 609, 650, 808
Mickey (Spain), 137
Mickeystrip (Yugoslavia) (magazine), 566
Micky Maus (Germany) (magazine), 324-25, 437, 566-67
Midweek Pictorial (U.S.) (supplement), 179
Mika Miš (Yugoslavia) (magazine), 464-65, 715, 829

Mikijevo carstvo (Yugoslavia) (magazine), 473, 829-30
Milap (India) (newspaper), 626
Millenium Publications (U.S.), 257
Millyet (Turkey) (newspaper), 571
Milson Publications (U.S.), 121
Milwaukee Bulgle-American (U.S.) (newspaper), 449
Minneapolis Star (U.S.) (newspaper), 672
Minneapolis Times (U.S.) (newspaper), 445
Mirabella (U.S.) (magazine), 392
Mireille (France) (magazine), 271
Miroir des Sports (France) (magazine), 604
Mis Chicas (Spain), 96, 137
Misterix (Argentina) (magazine), 239, 539, 549
Precinto 56 in, 552
Mister X (Argentina) (magazine), 627
MLJ. *See* Archie-Radio Group/MLJ
Modern Fiction (U.S.), 544
Modern Mag (G.B.) (magazine), 544
Mondadori (Italy) (publisher)
Albertarelli, Rino, and, 86
Bonelli, Giovanni Luigi, and, 143
Caesar, Kurt (pseud. Avai, Cesare; Away, Caesar), and, 173
Capitan l'Audace, 176
Caprioli, Franco, and, 180
Inspector Wade, 401-2
Moroni-Celsi, Guido (pseud. Sterny), and, 549
Pecos Bill, 602
Pedrocchi, Federico, and, 603
Rubino, Antonio, and, 664
Mondial-Presse (Italy) (publisher), 511
Monello, Il (Italy) (magazine)
Billy Bis in, 132
Forza John in, 314
Molino, Walter, and, 543
Narciso Putiferio in, 562
Pedrito El Drito in, 603
Pier Cloruro De'Lambicchi in, 616
Rocky Rider in, 658
Superbone, 734
Montreal Standard (Canada) (newspaper), 323
Montreal Star (Canada), 197
Mosquito, O (Brazil) (weekly), 215
Mosquito (Spain) (comic book collection), 177
Mother Jones (U.S.) (magazine), 392
Motor City Comics (U.S.), 224
Motorcycling (U.S.), 140
Motor World (G.B.) (magazine), 166
Moudjahid, El (Algeria) (newspaper), 525
Moustique, Le (Belgium), 129, 396
Movieland (Philippines) (magazine), 772
Movie News (Malaysia), 442

Movie strips
Fillum Fables, 353, 806
Midget Movies, 414, 537, 687, 755, 806
Minute Movies, 536-37, 789, 806
Thimble Theater, 22, 196, 554, 755-56, 806, 809, 813
Mowgli (Belgium), 228
MPG Newspapers, 732
M'Quidech (Algeria) (magazine), 525
Mujeres y Deportes (Mexico), 169
Mulo, Il (Italy) (magazine), 548
Münchener Bilderbogen (Germany) (magazine), 167, 276, 524
Mundo, El (Argentina) (newspaper), 503, 597
Mundo Joven (Spain) (magazine), 79, 512
Murphy Anderson Visual Concepts (U.S.), 92
Mushi Productions (Japan), 754
Mushi Productions Studio (Japan) (animation studio), 559
Muskete (Austria) (magazine), 765
Musse Pigg-Tidningen (Sweden), 127
Mystery Digest (comic book), 675
Mystery strips
Black Orchid, 525
Bomben, 348
Commissario Spada, Il, 211
Doctor Niebla, 259, 384
Dödens fågel, 348
Domu, 588
Don Winslow of the Navy, 263-64
Fantomette, 218
Guy Lebleu, 623
Judge Wright, 426
Kraaienhove, 455-57
Martin Mystere, 516-17
Mayer, Sheldon, and, 525
Mystiska 2:an, 557-58
Nazo, 775
Nus, 577
Orient Express, 464
Silent Three, The, 704
See also Detective strips

N

Nacional, El (Mexico) (newspaper), 631
Nakayoshi (Japan) (magazine), 366
Nanjing Morning News (China) (newspaper), 798
Nano Nanette (France) (magazine), 271
National Edition (G.B.), 95
National Enquirer (U.S.), 389
National Lampoon (U.S.) (magazine), 654, 723, 812
National Magazines (G.B.), 368
National News Company, 623
National News Syndicate, 727

National Periodical Publications/DC
    Comics (U.S.)
    Adams, Neal, and, 77
    Adam Strange, 78
    Alcala, Alfredo P., and, 87
    Anderson, Murphy, and, 92
    Aquaman, 98
    Aragonés, Sergio, and, 99
    Atom, The, 104
    Barry, Daniel, and, 115
    Barry, Seymour (Sy), and, 116
    Batman, 117
    Beck, Charles Clarence, and, 121
    Blackhawk, 136
    Blue Beetle, 140
    Boring, Wayne (pseud. Harmon,
        Jack), and, 147
    Boy Commandos, 149, 447
    Brigman, June, and, 154
    Bulanadi, Danny, and, 163
    Byrne, John, and, 171
    Captain Marvel, 183
    Captain Marvel Jr., 184
    Carreño, Albert, and, 187
    Charlie Chan, 196
    Chaykin, Howard, and, 198
    Christman, Bert, and, 200
    Craig, John, and, 219
    Davis, Jim, and, 315-16
    Ditko, Steve, and, 254
    Doc Savage, 257
    Dr. Fate, 257
    Dr. Mid-Nite, 258
    Elias, Leopold, and, 280
    Ernst, Kenneth, and, 286
    Evans, George, and, 287
    Finger, Bill, and, 303
    Flash, The, 307
    Fox, Gardner, and, 316
    Fox and the Crow, The, 315
    Frankenstein, 318
    Frazetta, Frank, and, 319
    Giordano, Richard, and, 344, 583
    Godwin, Francis, and, 348
    Goodwin, Archie (pseud. Franklin,
        Robert), and, 351
    Green Arrow, 355-56
    Green Lantern, 357, 358-59
    Guardineer, Frederic, and, 360
    Hasen, Irwin, and, 373
    Hawkman, 374
    Heath, Russell, and, 377-78
    Herron, France Edward, and, 381
    Infantino, Carmine, and, 400-401
    Jimmy Olsen, 417-18
    Jodloman, Jess M., and, 419
    Johnny Thunder, 422
    Jonah Hex, 424
    Judge Dredd, 424
    Justice League of America, 429
    Justice Society of America, 430
    Kaluta, Michael Wm., and, 432
    Kane, Gil, and, 433
    Kane, Robert, and, 434

    Kanigher, Robert, and, 435
    kid superheroes, 568
    Kirby, Jack, and, 447, 448
    Korak, 462
    Kotzky, Alex, and, 454
    Krigstein, Bernard, and, 458
    Kubert, Joe, and, 460, 461
    Lee, Stan, and, 472
    Liefeld, Rob, and, 476
    Lois Lane, 489-90
    McFarlane, Todd, and, 500
    Maroto, Esteban, and, 514
    Mary Marvel, 518
    Mayer, Sheldon, and, 524-25
    Meskin, Morton (pseud. Morton,
        Mort, Jr.), and, 526-27
    Miller, Frank (1957-), and, 534
    Mr. Terrific, 541-42
    Moore, Alan (pseud. Vile, Curt),
        and, 547
    Newman, Paul S., and, 567
    Newsboy Legion, 568
    Niño, Alex N., and, 573-74
    Norris, Paul, and, 576
    Ocampo, Abe, and, 773
    O'Neil, Dennis (pseud.
        O'Shaugnessey, Sergius), 583
    Orlando, Joe, and, 587
    Pitt, Stanley John, and, 621
    Plastic Man, 622
    Prentice, John, and, 627
    Redondo, Nestor, and, 645
    Rima, 462
    Robbins, Frank, and, 653
    Robbins, Trina, and, 653-54
    Robinson, Jerry, and, 656
    Romita, John, and, 660
    Sandman, The, 673-74
    Schaffenberger, Kurt (pseud. Wahl,
        Lou), and, 678
    Schwartz, Julius, and, 683
    Sgt. Rock, 689-90
    Severin, John Powers, and, 690
    Shadow, The, 692
    Shuster, Joe, and, 699-700
    Siegel, Jerome, and, 701
    Simon, Joseph, 705
    Spectre, The, 718
    Sprang, Richard, and, 722
    Springer, Frank, and, 722
    Starman, 724
    Star Spangled Kid, 725
    Supergirl, 734-35
    Superman, 515, 541, 699-700, 700,
        701, 735-37
    Swamp Thing, 738
    Talbot, Bryan, and, 744
    Tarzan, 748
    Tarzan of the Apes, 462
    Thomas, Roy, and, 756
    Thorne, Frank, and, 757
    Tor, 460
    Toth, Alexander, and, 773
    Watchmen, 800

    Weisinger, Mort, and, 804
    Wildey, Doug, and, 808, 809
    Wolverton, Basil, and, 816
    Wonder Woman, 816-17
    Wonderwoman, 515
    Wood, Wallace, and, 818
Nature strips
    Back Home Again, 260, 512-13
    Feng Zikai and, 300
    Foxy Grandpa, 317
    Games and Gimmicks, 504
    Larson, Gary, and, 468
    Mark Trail, 260, 512-13
    Schultze, Carl Edward, and, 682
Nedor Group, 526
    See also Better Group; Standard
        Group
Nedor group, 302, 656, 690
Nemo in blue (Italy) (magazine), 521
Népszava (Hungary) (newspaper), 294
Neue Blatt, Das (Germany) (weekly),
    451
Neue Post (Germany), 459
Neue Revue (Germany) (newspaper),
    580
New Babelonia (Belgium) (publisher),
    350
New Friday Comics, 133, 134, 360
New Fun Comics (Detective Comics),
    699, 701
New Idea, The (Australia), 384
New Juvenile Journal (China), 693
New Kent (Italy) (magazine), 221
Newnes-Pearson (G.B.) (publisher),
    125, 798
News Chronicle (G.B.) (newspaper),
    208, 803
News-Chronicle (G.B.) (newspaper),
    412-13
Newsday (U.S.) (newspaper), 461
New Society, 124
News of the World (G.B.) (newspaper),
    302
Newspaper Enterprise Association
    (U.S.)
    Adams, Neal, and, 77
    Affairs of Jane, The, 826
    Ahern, Gene, and, 80-81
    Alley Oop, 88, 367
    Billville Birds, 392
    Blosser, Merrill, and, 140
    Boots and Her Buddies, 147
    Born Loser, The, 148
    Bugs Bunny, 162-63, 625
    Captain Easy, 220
    Craig, Chase, and, 218
    Crane, Roy, and, 169, 220
    Eek and Meek, 276
    Freckles and His Friends, 140, 320
    Freyse, Bill, and, 322
    Harman, Fred, and, 370
    Kevin the Bold, 441

Little People, The, 488
Lubbers, Robert (pseud. Lewis, Bob), and, 492
Mitzi McCoy, 441
Myra North, 557
Our Boarding House, 322, 589-90
Out Our Way, 592, 810
Red Ryder, 370, 645
Robin Malone, 492
Short Ribs, 583, 698
Snake Tales, 713
Vic Flint, 791
Wash Tubbs, 220, 799
Winterbotham, Russ (pseud. Bond, J. Harvey), 814
Young, Murat (Chic), 826
Newspaper Feature Service, 317
Newspaper strips, 16-18, 32, 34
New Statesman (G.B.), 124
New Strait Times (Malaysia), 442
New Two-Fisted Tales (U.S.) (comic book), 690
New York American (U.S.) (newspaper)
  Buster Brown in, 168
  De Beck, Billy, and, 238
  Eisner, Will, and, 278
  Foxy Grandpa, 682
  Foxy Grandpa in, 317, 682
  Gross, Milton, and, 360
  Iger, Samuel Maxwell ("Jerry"), and, 400
  McDougall, Walter Hugh, and, 499
  Mager, Charles Augustus (Gus), and, 504
  Midget Movies, 806
  Mutt and Jeff in, 304
  Polly and Her Pals in, 727
  Sappo in, 675, 687
  Segar, Elzie Crisler, and, 687
  Toots and Casper, 553
  Toots and Casper in, 769
New York Daily News (U.S.) (newspaper)
  Caniff, Milton, and, 175
  Edson, Gus, and, 275
  Flubs and Fluffs, 656
  Gasoline Alley in, 445
  Gasoling Alley in, 445
  Gumps, The, 275
  Harold Teen in, 275, 370
  Hodgins, Dick, Jr., and, 367
  Little Joe in, 484
  Little Orphan Annie in, 355, 487
  Moon Mullins in, 809
  Spooky in, 722
  Springer, Frank, and, 722
  White Boy in, 808
New Yorker (U.S.) (magazine), 270, 325, 485, 713-14, 719, 724, 788
New York Evening Journal (U.S.) (newspaper), 186, 623
New York Evening Mail (U.S.) (newspaper)
  Boob McNutt in, 145

  Boob McNutt in, 348
  Bungle Family, The in, 164
  Goldberg, Reuben Lucius, and, 348
  Maxon, Rex, and, 524
  Russell, Clarence D., and, 666
  Tuthill, Harry J., 778
  Voight, Charles A., and, 792
  Wellington, Charles H., and, 804
New York Evening Post (U.S.) (newspaper), 275, 666
New York Evening Telegram (U.S.) (newspaper), 268-69, 497-98, 727
New York Globe (U.S.) (newspaper), 404, 524
New York Graphic (U.S.) (newspaper), 275, 474, 499
New York Herald (U.S.) (newspaper)
  Betty in, 128
  Buster Brown in, 168, 591
  Carr, Eugene, and, 186
  Foxy Grandpa, 682
  Little Nemo in Slumberland in, 486-87
  McDougall, Walter Hugh, and, 499
  Poor Li'l Mose in, 591, 825
  Prince Errant in, 628
  Sterrett, Cliff, and, 727
  Terrors of the Tiny Tads in, 750
  Upside Downs of Little Lady Lovekins and Old Man Muffaroo, The in, 782
  Verbeck (a.k.a Verbeek), Gustave, and, 751
  Westover, Russell, and, 805
New York Herald-Tribune Syndicate (U.S.), 656, 808
New York Herald-Tribune (U.S.) (newspaper)
  Bantam Prince in, 611
  Hershfield, Harry, and, 382
  Miss Peach in, 537
  Pa's Son-in-Law in, 804
  Peter Piltdown in, 610
  Reg'lar Fellers, 646-47
  Silver Linings in, 462
  Skeets in, 707
  Timid Soul, 802
  When a Feller Needs a Friend in, 806
New York Journal (U.S.) (newspaper)
  Abie the Agent in, 76, 382
  Berndt, Walter, and, 127
  Briggs, Clare, and, 153
  Browne, Dik, and, 157
  Buster Brown in, 591
  Desperate Desmond, 382
  Desperate Desmond in, 244
  Dingbat Family, The in, 251, 351, 457
  Dirks, Rudolph, and, 252
  Dorgan, Thomas Aloysius (Tad), and, 265
  Family Upstairs, The, 457
  Foxy Grandpa in, 682
  Gross, Milton, and, 360

  Haenigsen, Harry, and, 365
  Hershfield, Harry, and, 382
  Hoban, Walter C., and, 388
  Jerry on the Job in, 414-15
  Katzenjammer Kids, The in, 437
  Knocko the Monk in, 504
  Krazy Kat in, 457
  Mager, Charles Augustus (Gus), and, 504
  Mager's Monks in, 504-5
  Murphy, James Edward, and, 553
  Opper, Frederick Burr, 586
  Polly and Her Pals in, 727
  Sappo in, 687
  Segar, Elzie Crisler, and, 687
  Sherlocko the Monk in, 505
  Swinnerton, James Guilford, and, 740
  Thimble Theater in, 687, 755
  Toots and Casper, 553
  Yellow Kid, The, 589-90
  Yellow Kid in, 824
New York Mirror (U.S.) (newspaper), 356, 360, 388, 419, 420
New York Post Syndicate, 513
New York Post (U.S.) (newspaper), 267, 373, 438, 513, 622
New York Press (U.S.) (newspaper), 317, 682
New York Star (U.S.) (newspaper), 438, 622
New York Sunday Mirror (U.S.) (newspaper), 294, 531
New York Sunday News (U.S.) (newspaper), 294
New York Sun (U.S.) (newspaper), 150, 531
New York Telegram and Herald Co., 623
New York Telegram (U.S.) (newspaper), 171-72, 611, 646, 779
New York Times Book Review (U.S.) (supplement), 392
New York Times Syndicate, 160, 378, 490
New York Tribune (U.S.) (newspaper)
  Briggs, Clare, and, 153
  Heck, Frank Bem, and, 121
  Mr. and Ms. in, 538
  Pa's Son-in-Law, 804
  Pa's Son-in-Law in, 186
  Webster, Harold Tucker, and, 802
New York World (U.S.) (newspaper)
  Anderson, Carl Thomas, and, 91
  Banana Oil, 109, 360
  Captain and the Kids, The in, 182, 437
  Carr, Eugene, and, 186
  Count Screwloose of Tooloose in, 216
  Crane, Royston Campbell (Roy), and, 220
  Crosby, Percy Leo, and, 222
  Dirks, Rudolph, and, 253

Haenigsen, Harry, and, 365
Hawkshaw the Detective in, 374, 504
Help Wanted in, 360
Herriman, George, and, 381
Honeybunch's Hubby in, 600
Kahles, Charles William, and, 431
Krazy Kat in, 381
McDougall, Walter Hugh, and, 499
McManus, George, and, 501
Main Street in, 506
Man in the Brown Derby, The in, 802
Marriner, William, and, 514
Maxon, Rex, and, 524
Mike and Ike, 145
Newlyweds, The in, 567
Nibsy the Newsboy in, 568
Nize Baby in, 575
Outcault, Richard Felton, and, 589
Panhandle Pete in, 595
Sherlocko the Monk in, 374, 504, 505
S'Matter, Pop? in, 600
Smith, Al, and, 711
Timid Soul, The, 762, 802
Voight, Charles A., and, 792
Yellow Kid, The in, 168, 824
Nickle Comics (U.S.), 164
Nicolas (Spain) (magazine), 302
Nieuwe Gids, De (Belgium) (newspaper), 564, 566, 737, 789
See also Standaard, De
Niirokushinpo, 451
1984 (Spain), 301, 514
Ninja strips
  Kōga Bugeichō, 696
  Ninja Bugeichō, 572-73
  Shirato, Sanpei, and, 696-97
  Teenage Mutant Ninja Turtles, 749-50
  See also Samurai strips
Nora Aunor Superstar (Philippines) (weekly), 462
Norakura (Japan), 143
North America Syndicate (Field Enterprises), 326
Nous Deux (France) (magazine), 86
Nouvel Observateur, Le (France) (weekly), 192, 232
Novedades (Mexico), 169
Novelino, Il (Italy) (weekly), 548
Novelty Publications
  Barry, Daniel, and, 115
  Blue Bolt, 140-41
  Everett, Bill, and, 287
  Gustafson, Bob, and, 364
  Krigstein, Bernard, and, 458
  McWilliams, Alden, and, 502
  Montana, Bob, and, 545
  Simon, Joseph, and, 704-5
  Wolverton, Basil, and, 816
Novi List (Italy) (magazine), 554
Novosti (Yugoslavia) (newspaper), 566
Now Comics, 357

N.R.C. (Netherlands) (newspaper), 767
Nursery comics
  Bell, Walter, and, 125
  Booth, Walter, and, 146
  Foxwell, Herbert, and, 317
  Gunnis, Louis, and, 363
  Robinson, Fred, and, 656
  White, Hugh Stanley, and, 808
  Wilson, Roy, and, 812
Nuts! (U.S.) (magazine), 463

O

O. W. Comics, 819
Oakland Herald (U.S.) (newspaper), 805
Oberon (Netherlands) (publisher), 535, 647
Occhio, L' (Italy) (daily), 494
Odhams Press (G.B.), 118, 232, 368, 648
Oeuf, L' (Belgium) (magazine), 382
Offenstadt (France) (publisher), 313
Off-Side (Italy), 144
Ohio State Journal (U.S.) (college newspaper), 700
O.K. (France) (magazine), 781
Okki (Netherlands), 157
Oklahoma City Daily Oklahoman (U.S.) (newspaper), 353
Oko (Yugoslavia) (magazine), 522, 566
Omaha Bee (U.S.) (newspaper), 552
Omaha Examiner (U.S.) (newspaper), 552
Omaha Herald (U.S.) (newspaper), 584
Omashiro Book (Japan) (magazine), 463
O Mirim (Brazil) (comic book), 83
Omladina (Yugoslavia) (magazine), 716
Omoshira Book (Japan) (magazine), 698
Ons Volkske (Belgium) (magazine), 335
Ons Vrije Nederland (Netherlands) (newspaper), 767
Onze Krant (Netherlands) (newspaper), 156-57
00 Ongoy (Philipinnes), 462
Opera Mundi (syndicate), 511, 790
Opinion, La (Argentina) (newspaper), 263
Orbit group, 78, 166-67, 278, 819
Oregon Journal (U.S.) (newspaper), 553
Orient Express (Italy) (magazine), 150, 191, 278, 338, 439, 771
Oriflama (Spain) (monthly), 470
Oscar (Italy), 148

Ošišani Jež, 512
Osmoshiro Book (Japan) (monthly), 231
O Terror Negro (Brazil), 215
O Tico Tico (Brazil) (newspaper), 641
Otogi Pro (Japan) (animation studio), 825
Oui (France) (magazine), 548
Our Army at War (U.S.) (comic book), 689
Outcault Advertising Company (U.S.), 591
Outdoor Magazine (U.S.), 374-75
Overseas Weekly (U.S.) (newspaper), 673, 723
Oz (G.B.) (underground paper), 666

P

Pacific Comics (U.S.), 448
Pacific Search (U.S.) (magazine), 468
Paese Sera (Italy), 144, 731
Pageant (Philippines) (magazine), 675
Paget Publications, 110, 544
Paget Publications (U.S.), 96
Paginas de Columba (Argentina), 254, 671
Painted strips
  Wulf the Briton, 282
Paja Patak (Yugoslavia) (magazine), 473
Pajtas (Hungary) (magazine), 294
Panic (U.S.) (magazine), 297
Panorama (Netherlands) (newspaper), 616, 706
Panorama (Yugoslavia) (weekly), 489, 521
Pantomine strips
  Adamson, 77, 407-8
  Alfredo, 87
  Come On, Steve!, 210-11
  Ferd'nand, 300-301
  Henry, 378-79
  Little King, The, 484-85, 714
  Ljuba Truba, 255
  McBride, Clifford, and, 497
  Max, 382, 523-24
  Mr. Subito, 790
  Nipper, 574, 807
  Professeur Nimbus, Le, 630, 790
  Professor Pi, 630-31
  Tich, 267
Panzer Voran! (Germany) (newspaper), 678
Pa pa gei (Austria) (magazine), 731
Paperino (Italy) (weekly), 86, 176, 449
Paquin (Mexico) (magazine), 293
Parade (U.S.) (magazine), 389
Paraluman (Philippines) (magazine), 418, 675
Paramount Studios (U.S.), 189, 755

Pardon (Germany) (magazine), 169, 285, 647
Parent's (U.S.) (magazine), 179, 556
Paris-Match (France) (magazine), 604
Paris-Match (France) (weekly), 816
Parody strips
  Air Pirates, 584
  Beelzebub Jones, 498
  Billville Birds, 392
  Blook, 372
  Bunky, 165
  Cerebus, 192
  Chick Bill, 335
  Cocco Bill, 205, 408
  Crock, 597
  Don Antonio della Mancia, 543
  Ernsting, Volker, and, 285
  Extraordinaire Aventure de Monsieur Faust, L', 527
  Famille Fenouillard, La, 292
  Fearless Fosdick, 294-95
  Fighting American, 447
  Fillum Fables, 353
  Frank Fazakerly, Space Ace of the Future, 744
  Gionni Galassia, 408
  Gog, 773
  Herlock Sholmes, 695
  Howard the Duck, 394-95
  Jacovitti, Benito, and, 408
  Johnny Thunder, 422
  Klotjohan, 450
  Kraaienhove, 454-57
  Lucky Luke, 352, 492
  Mandrago il Mago, 408
  Mari Aguirre, 512
  Mickey Mouse meets the Airpirates, 584
  Nick Carter, 145
  Nick Knatterton, 571-72, 678
  Odd Bodkins, 583-84
  Og, 462
  Onorevole Tarzan, L', 408
  Parlor, Bedroom and Sink, 238
  Pedrito El Drito, 603
  Peter seltsame Reisen, 570, 813
  Philémon, 613
  Plastic Man, 621-22
  Powerhouse Pepper, 816
  Procopio, 630
  Rock Derby, 647
  Sherlock Lopez, 695
  Shifumai Yamana's Songokuku, 706
  Siopawman, 705-6
  Spare Ribs and Gravy, 501, 569, 596
  Submerman, 614
  Super Sam, 648
  Supersnipe, 737
  Teddy Sprin, 608
  Teenage Mutant Ninja Turtles, 749-50
  Telestrip, 750
  Tenebrax, 614
  Young Lust, 359
  Zorry Kid, 408

Parool, Het (Netherlands) (newspaper), 435, 456, 461, 630
Paseo Infantil (Spain) (magazine), 302
Passing Show (G.B.) (magazine), 302
Patoruzito (Argentina), 118, 140, 150, 380, 509, 598, 671
Patoruzú (Argentina) (magazine), 254, 380, 672
Patrie, La (Canada) (newspaper), 196, 598
Paul Terry Cartoon Studios (U.S.), 533
Pearson's Weekly (G.B.), 807
Pegaz (Yugoslavia) (magazine), 489, 716
Penthouse Comix (U.S.) (magazine), 214, 772
Penthouse (U.S.) (magazine), 282
People's Art Publications (China), 345, 393, 693, 733
People's Comics (U.S.) (magazine), 324
People's Daily (China) (newspaper), 527-28
People's Journal (G.B.), 693
Pepin (Mexico) (magazine), 291
Pep (Netherlands) (weekly), 100, 273, 457, 458, 491, 519, 792
Pep (U.S.), 136-37
Perry Rhodan (Germany), 103-4
Per Voi/For You (Italy) (magazine), 162
Pesti Izé (Hungary) (magazine), 830
Petit Echo de la Mode (France) (magazine), 605
Petit Français Illustré (France) (weekly), 290, 292, 399
Petit Illustré, Le (France), 130
Petit Journal, Le (Canada), 197
Petit Parisien, Le (France) (newspaper), 467
Petits Belges (Belgium) (weekly), 339
Petits Dessins, Les (Canada) (cooperative), 398
Phénix (France) (magazine), 781
Philadelphia Enquirer (U.S.) (newspaper), 514
Philadelphia Inquirer (U.S.) (newspaper), 450
Philadelphia Ledger (U.S.) (newspaper), 450
Philadelphia North American (U.S.) (newspaper), 82-83, 499
Philadelphia Press (U.S.) (newspaper), 268, 366, 431
Phillipp Marx Productions. *See* P.M. Productions
Philosophy strips
  Hi no Tori, 386-87
  Odd Bodkins, 583-84
  Question, The, 254, 344
Phoenix Features, 306
Phoenix Syndicate (U.S.), 400
P.I.B. (Denmark) (press service), 297, 382, 523
Pic Magazine (U.S.) (magazine), 356

Picto-Fiction (U.S.), 297, 459
Pictorial Review (U.S.) (supplement), 309
Picture News (Australia), 141, 364
Picture News (U.S.) (magazine), 474
Picture stories, 11-12
  Bécassine, 120, 617
  Billy Bunter, 132-33
  Busch, Wilhelm, and, 167-68, 524
  Facéties du Sapeur Camember, Les, 290
  Famille Amulette, La, 617
  Famille Fenouillard, La, 292
  Gunnis, Louis, and, 362-63
  Histoires en Estampes, 387-88, 770
  Idée Fixe du Savant, Cosinus, L', 399
  Max und Moritz, 524
  Nagagutsu no Sanjûshi, 559
  Patatras, 617
  Rowlandson, Thomas, and, 663
  Shōnen Oja, 698
  Töpffer, Rodolphe, and, 387-88, 770
  Vie des Grands Fauves, La, 617
  Vie des Hommes Illustres, La, 617
Pif (France) (weekly)
  Castelli, Alfredo, and, 190
  Cavazzano, Giorgio, and, 191
  Corto Maltese in, 215, 627
  Docteur Justice in, 511
  Milo Marat in, 145
  Rahan in, 638
  See also Vaillant (France)
Pilipino Development Associates Inc. (Philippines), 646
Pilipino Komiks (Philippines), 253, 350, 400, 418, 462, 573, 674, 772
Pilote (France) (magazine)
  Achille Talon in, 76-77, 647
  Astérix in, 103, 781
  Bevère, Maurice de (pseud. Morris), and, 129
  Bilal, Enki, and, 131
  Bob Morane in, 142, 788
  Boucq, François, and, 149
  Cellulite in, 192
  Charlier, Jean-Michel, and, 196
  Comés, Didiet, and, 211
  Démon des Caraïbes, Le in, 241, 396
  Druillet, Philippe, and, 269
  Extraordinaire Aventure de Monsieur Faust, L' in, 527
  Gillain, John (pseud. Jijé), and, 339
  Goscinny, René, and, 352-53
  Lieutenant Blueberry in, 345, 476
  Lucky Luke in, 493
  Mézières, Jean-Claude, and, 527
  Michel Tanguy in, 529, 781
  Mysterieuse Matin, Midi et Soir, 313
  Philémon in, 613
  Régnier, Michel (pseud. Greg; Albert, Louis), and, 647
  Scheuer, Chris, and, 678
  Schuiten, François, and, 680

Tardi, Jacques, and, 745
Valérian in, 527, 786
Yarzael ou la Fin des Temps in, 269
Pilot (Italy) (magazine), 508
Pines Company (U.S.)
　Anderson, Murphy, and, 92
　Bald, Kenneth (pseud. Bruce, K.), and, 108
　Barry, Daniel, and, 115
　Carreño, Albert, and, 187
　Elder, William W., and, 278
　Frazetta, Frank, and, 319
　Guardineer, Frederic, and, 360
　Heckle and Jeckle, 378
　Kanigher, Robert, and, 435
　Krigstein, Bernard, and, 458
　Mighty Mouse, 533
　Supermouse, 533
Pinoir (Yugoslavia), 123
Pinoy Komiks (Philippines), 439
Pioneer Komiks (Philippines) (comic book), 573
Pionere, Il (Italy) (weekly), 608
Pionir (Yugoslavia) (magazine), 566
Pippen (G.B.) (weekly), 665
Pirate strips
　Aroldo, 148
　Brammetje Bram, 149-50
　Brik, 193
　Capitan Caribe, 580
　Capitan Cormorand, 627
　Capitan Terror, 177-78
　Gert Jörg, 799
　Gigetto, Pirata Picoletto, 608
　Gusarsko Blago, 566
　Hawk of the Seas, 278
　Mladi Bartulo, 830
　Mouette, La, 396
　Penn and Chris, 720
　Pieces of Eight, 389
　Roland el Corsario, 580
　Tales of the Black Freighter, 800
　See also Sea-adventure strips
Pistolin (Belgium) (magazine), 396, 781
Pittsburgh Courier (U.S.) (newspaper), 587, 611
Pittsburgh Gazette-Times (U.S.) (newspaper), 238
Pittsburgh Post (U.S.) (newspaper), 600, 813
Planet (Philippines) (comic book), 350
Plavi Vjesnik (Yugoslavia) (magazine)
　African Adventures for Plavi Vjesnik in, 638
　Beker, Zarko, and, 123
　Delac, Vladimir, and, 239
　Dovniković, Borivoj, and, 266
　Furtinger, Zvonimir, and, 327
　Herlock Sholmes in, 380
　Kroz minula stoljeća in, 638
　Maurović, Andrija, and, 522
　Neugebauer, Walter, and, 566
　Povratak Starog Mačak in, 522

Playboy (U.S.) (magazine)
　Cole, Jack (pseud. Johns, Ralph), and, 206
　Cruse, Howard, and, 226
　Davis, Jack, and, 237
　Fabulous Furry Freak Brothers in, 290
　Hoest, Bill, and, 388
　Kent, Jack, and, 440
　Kurtzman, Harvey, and, 463
　Little Annie Fannie in, 237, 278, 378, 463, 481
　Moonshine McJuggs in, 757
　Robbins, Trina, and, 654
　Spiegelman, Arthur, and, 719
　Springer, Frank, and, 723
　Thorne, Frank, and, 757-58
Playmen (Italy) (magazine), 508
Playstories, 132
Plexus (France), 134
P.M. (Phillipp Marx) Productions, 125, 631
PM (U.S.) (newspaper)
　Barnaby in, 112, 474
　Hank in, 801
　Patoruzú in, 598
　Vic Jordan in, 576, 791
Pocholo (Spain), 137
Poetical Magazine (G.B.), 663
Point, Le (France), 149
Police strips
　Captain Zbik, 820
　Clarence the Cop, 431
　Collier's Cops, 404
　Detektive Schmidtchen, 244-45, 651
　Dick Tracy, 248-49, 353-54
　Evaristo, 714-15
　Fearless Fosdick, 294-95
　Gil Jourdan, 762
　Irving, Jay, and, 404
　Kerry Drake, 440
　Kosme the Cop, 675
　Mickey Finn, 474, 531
　Needlenose Noonan, 388, 415
　Nobby the Enchanted Bobby, 393
　Pottsy, 404
　Precinto 56, 552
　Radio Patrol, 638
　Red Barry, 354, 642
　Ric Hochet, 650-51
　Rip Kirby, 641, 651-53
　Risk, 820
　Secret Agent X-9, 351, 354, 641, 685-86, 811
　Willie Doodle, 404
Political strips
　Adèle Blanc-Sec, 746
　Adolf, 78-79, 754
　Adolf, Hermann and Musso, 666
　Agachados, Los, 79
　Bascule à Charlot, La, 746
　Bell, Steve, and, 123-24
　Bilal, Enki, and, 131
　Briggs, Raymond, and, 154
　Demonyo Made Me Do It, The, 646

Doonesbury, 775
Ernsting, Volker, and, 285
Feiffer, 295
Fils de Chine, 302-3
Gillray, James, 340
Girl from the People's Commune, The, 345
Griffu, 746
Grillo il Balillino, 549
Hit-Parades, 815
Ici Même, 746
Janne Ankkanen, 604
Je Ne Veux Pas Mourir Idiot, 815-16
Kitazawa, Rakuten, and, 448
Kobau, 444
Koning Hollewijn, 453-54
Lavado, Joaquin (pseud. Quino), and, 470
Lavinia 2.016, 470
Lefty Louie, 617
Liao Bingxiong, 475
Lo Scimiotto, 508
Madam and Eve, 503
Maggie's Farm, 123
Mallard Fillmore, 507
Maus, 522-23, 719
Michel, 528-29, 661
Molino, Walter, and, 543
Opper, Frederick Burr, and, 586
Pekka Puupää, 603-4
Peters, Mike, and, 551
Pinky Rankin, 617-18
Poo Yai Ma Kap Tung Ma Muen, 193-94
Prez, 705
Raymondo o Cangaceiro, 641
Red Detachment of Women, The, 642-43
Romano il Legionario, 659
Rumeurs sur le Rouergue, 745
Schmit der Sphy, 666
Supermachos, Los, 735
Tardi, Jacques, and, 746
Tobias Seicherl, 765-66
Uomo che uccise Ernesto "Che" Guevara, L', 640
Wang Xiansheng He Xiao Chen, 797-98
Wolinski, Georges, and, 814-16
World of Lily Wong, The, 296-97
Yue Xiaoying, and, 827
See also Satire; Social consciousness strips
Politiken (Denmark) (newspaper), 297, 491
Politiken Zabavnik (Yugoslavia) (magazine), 512
Pollystyle Publications (G.B.), 656
Populo d'Italia (Italy) (magazine), 543
Portland Oregonian (U.S.) (newspaper), 356
Post, The (G.B.) (magazine), 368
Post-Hall Syndicate, 513
PPP (Yugoslavia) (magazine), 554

Pran's Features (India) (syndicate), 627
Pre-historic strips
  Cro-Magnon, 382
  Dinoceras, 573
  Dzarto, Prehistoric Hero, 473
  Gyatoruzu, 716
  Peter Piltdown, 610
  Rahan, 638-39
  Siegfried, 534
  Tor, 460
  Turok, Son of Stone, 103, 524, 567-68, 778
Premier (G.B.), 96
Premier Syndicate, 271
Prensa, La (Argentina) (newspaper), 263
Presse, La (Canada) (newspaper), 607
Preview (U.S.) (magazine), 727
Primarosa (Italy), 143
Primera Plana (Argentina) (magazine), 503
primo (Germany), 94, 177, 462, 494
Princess (G.B.), 236
Prinses (Netherlands) (magazine), 519
Prize Publications
  Ayers, Richard, and, 104
  Bald, Kenneth (pseud. Bruce, K.), and, 108
  Carreño, Albert, and, 187
  Crowley, Wendell, and, 223
  Ditko, Steve, and, 254
  Elder, William W., and, 278
  Frazetta, Frank, and, 319
  Meskin, Morton (pseud. Morton, Mort, Jr.), and, 527
  Norris, Paul, and, 576
  Robinson, Jerry, and, 656
  Williamson, Al, and, 811
Prize Western (U.S.), 690
Provincial Comics, 386
Prusynski i S-ka publishing house (Poland), 200
PSG Publications (Philippines), 350, 573, 773
Psychological strips
  Numa, 775
Psycho (U.S.) (magazine), 318
Publishers-Hall Syndicate
  Apartment 3-G, 454
  B.C., 119
  Dateline: Danger!, 235, 502, 729
  Feiffer, 295, 296
  Funky Winkerbean, 326
  Saunders, Allen, and, 677
  Wizard of Id, The, 814
Publishers Syndicate
  Andy Capp, 547
  Apartment 3-G, 97
  Casson, Melvin, and, 189
  Dallis, Nicholas, and, 231
  Dan Dunn, 232
  Judge Parker, 424
  Kerry Drake, 95, 440

Mary Worth, 286, 518-19
  Overgard, William Thomas, and, 593
  Rex Morgan, M.D., 649
  Saunders, Allen, and, 677
  Sparky, 189
  Steve Roper, 593, 728
  Strange World of Mr. Mum, The, 730
  Tales from the Great Book, 474
Puck (G.B.) (weekly)
  Booth, Walter, and, 146
  Golden Arrow in, 609
  Rob the Rover, 146
  Rob the Rover in, 657
  Shaw, Ernest, and, 693
  Yeats, Jack B., and, 823
Puck (U.S.) (magazine)
  Anderson, Carl Thomas, and, 91
  Carter, Augustus Daniels, and, 187
  Ewer, Raymond, and, 709
  Fuller, Ralph Briggs, and, 325
  Hoban, Walter C., and, 388
  Howarth, F. M., and, 395
  Lulu and Leander in, 493
  McDougall, Walter Hugh, and, 499
  Marriner, William, and, 514
  O'Neill, Rose Cecil, and, 584
  Opper, Frederick Burr, and, 586
  Van Buren, Raeburn, and, 788
  Wags, the Dog that Adopted a Man in, 795
Pulgarcito (Spain) (weekly)
  Capitan Trueno, El in, 178, 407
  Carpanta in, 186
  Don Berrinche in, 261
  Inspector Dan, El in, 402
  Mortadelo y Filemon in, 549
  Silver Roy in, 703
Pum Pum Netherlands (weekly), 458
Punch (G.B.) (magazine), 116, 223, 302, 315, 333, 370, 581
PZ (Yugoslavia) (magazine), 465

Q

Quality Comics
  Berg, David, and, 125-26
  Binder, Otto O. (pseud. Binder, Eando), and, 134
  Black Condor, 135
  Blackhawk, 136
  Celardo, John (pseud. Lardo, John C.), and, 191-92
  Colan, Eugene (pseud. Austin, Adam), and, 206
  Cole, Jack (pseud. Johns, Ralph), and, 206
  Crandall, Reed, and, 219
  Doll Man, 260
  Feldstein, Al, and, 297
  Fine, Louis, and, 303
  Finger, Bill, and, 303

Guardineer, Frederic, and, 360, 361
  Gustafson, Bob, and, 364
  Heath, Russell, and, 377
  Hercules, 379
  Herron, France Edward, and, 381
  Jaffee, Allan, and, 408
  Kane, Gil, and, 433
  Kida, Fred, and, 443
  Kotzky, Alex, and, 454
  Kubert, Joe, and, 460
  Leav, Mort, and, 471
  McWilliams, Alden, and, 502
  Phantom Lady, 613
  Plastic Man, 621
  S. M. Iger Studios and, 400
  Spirit, The, 721
  Woolfolk, William, and, 819
Querschnitt (Germany) (newspaper), 580
Quick (Germany) (weekly), 571, 678, 679
Quick on the Draw (G.B.) (television program), 315, 545, 693

R

R. & L. Locker (U.S.), 544
Racing strips
  Charlie Sprint, 202
  Michel Vaillant, 529-30
  Muteki Dump Guy, 542
Radiocorriere (Italy) (weekly), 221
Raizon, La (Argentina) (newspaper), 263
Rakuta Puck (Japan) (magazine), 448
Rama Post (Austria) (magazine), 731
Rang Rekha Features, 595
Rasiska (Sri Lanka) (magazine), 607
Ration, The (G.B.) (magazine), 693
Raw (U.S.) (underground comic), 522, 719, 739
Rayo Rojo (Argentina) (magazine), 714
Razón, La (Argentina) (magazine), 480, 597-98, 639
Real Pulp (U.S.) (underground comic), 359, 719
Record (France), 605
Recycled Paper Greetings (U.S.), 327
Redbook (U.S.) (magazine), 351, 776, 788
Red Circle Comics (comic book), 675
Redondo Komiks (Philippines) (comic book), 462, 573, 743, 773
Referee (Australia) (magazine), 666
Register and Tribune Syndicate
  Bible Bee, 356
  Goldberg, Reuben Lucius, and, 349
  Red Knight, The, 644
  Spider-Man, 719
  Spirit, The, 720
  Tumbleweeds, 667, 776
  Wee Pals, 777, 803

Register and Tribune (U.S.)
  (newspaper), 367
Reich, Das (Germany) (magazine), 581
Relax (Poland) (magazine), 436, 662,
  820
rental comic books (Japan), 387, 452,
  542, 572-73, 670, 696
Reporter strips
  Arbre-Coeur, L', 211
  Brenda Starr, 151-52, 527
  Curley Harper, 228, 826
  Dateline: Danger!, 234-35, 502, 677
  Jane Arden, 411
  Lois Lane, 489-90
  Misterix, 539
  Scoop Smithy, 631
  Tom Ficcanaso, 408
Repubblica, La (Italy) (daily), 338
Reveille (G.B.) (weekly), 95, 282, 370
Revista Española, La (Spain)
  (supplement), 249
Revue (Netherlands) (weekly), 767
Revue Populaire, La (Canada)
  (magazine), 197
Rico Tipo (Argentina) (magazine), 213,
  254, 258, 291, 399
Rintintin (Italy), 143
Rip-Off Press (U.S.), 290, 350
  helton, Gilbert, and, 694
Rire, Le (France) (magazine), 614
Risata, La (Italy) (weekly), 173
Risquetout (France) (weekly), 781
Robert Hall Syndicate, 158, 389
Robinson (Italy), 143
Rocky Mountain News (U.S.)
  (newspaper), 534
Rocky Rider (Italy) (magazine), 603
Romance strips
  Albertarelli, Rino, and, 86
  Amanda, 818
  Brenda Starr, 151-52, 527
  Feldstein, Al, and, 297
  Fernandez, Fernando, and, 301
  Flamingo, 306
  Heart of Juliet Jones, The, 376-77
  Maison Ikkoku, 506
  Marcello, Raffaelo Carlo (pseud.
    Marc, Ralph), and, 511
  My Date, 447
  Mylene, 511
  Principe Azzurro, 629
  Robin Malone, 492
  Romita, John, and, 660
  Satonaka, Machiko, and, 676
  Star Ballerina, 511
  Torchy Brown, 587
  See also Soap opera strips
Roomsche Jeugd (Netherlands)
  (magazine), 156
Rotterdamsch Nieuwsblad (Netherlands)
  (weekly), 107, 773
Rydges (Australia), 384

S

Sächsische Sozialdemokratishche Presse
  (Germany) (newspaper), 580
Sadie Hawkins Day, 30
SAEV (Italy) (publisher), 143
SAGE Comic Books (France), 511
Sagédition (France) (publisher), 91,
  606
St. John Company
  Anderson, Murphy, and, 92
  Ayers, Richard, and, 104
  Berg, David, and, 126
  Colan, Eugene (pseud. Austin,
    Adam), and, 206
  Ditko, Steve, and, 254
  Foster, Harold, and, 315
  Heath, Russell, and, 377
  Heckle and Jeckle, 378
  Kubert, Joe, and, 460
  Mighty Mouse, 533
  Sinnott, Joe, 705
St. Louis Chronicle (U.S.) (newspaper),
  153
St. Louis Democrat (U.S.) (newspaper),
  153
St. Louis Post-Dispatch (U.S.)
  (newspaper), 237, 581, 778, 804
St. Louis Republic (U.S.) (newspaper),
  501, 804
St. Louis Star (U.S.) (newspaper), 778
St. Nicholas (U.S.) (magazine), 586
St. Paul Daily News (U.S.)
  (newspaper), 581
St. Paul Pioneer Press (newspaper),
  683
Salgari (Italy) (magazine), 86
Salt Lake Tribune (U.S.) (newspaper),
  378
Salvat Editores (Spain) (publisher),
  577
Samedi, Le (Canada) (magazine), 197
Samurai strips
  Akadō Suzunosuke in, 83-84
  Bugei Kikou, 671
  Hatanosuke Hinomaru, 373
  Hirata, Hiroshi, and, 387
  Kamui Den, 432-33
  Kojima, Goseki, and, 452
  Kozure Okami, 454
  Sasuke, 675-76
  Tenpei Tenma, 750
  See also Ninja strips
San Francisco Bulletin (U.S.)
  (newspaper), 264, 348, 805
San Francisco Call (U.S.) (newspaper),
  281, 373, 468, 553, 755
San Francisco Chronicle (U.S.)
  (newspaper)
  Bronc Peeler in, 156
  Casey Ruggles in, 776
  Dorgan, Thomas Aloysius (Tad),
    and, 264

Fisher, Harry Conway (Bud), and,
  304
Goldberg, Reuben Lucius, and, 348
Hershfield, Harry, and, 382
Mutt and Jeff in, 98, 555
Odd Bodkins in, 583-84
Westover, Russell, and, 805
San Francisco Comic Book (U.S.)
  (underground comic), 653
San Francisco Examiner (U.S.)
  (newspaper), 304, 483, 555, 740,
  806
Sathsiri (Sri Lanka) (magazine), 607
Sathuta (Sri Lanka) (magazine), 607
Satire
  Achille Talon, 76-77, 647
  Adolf, Hermann and Musso, 666
  Alan Ford, 85-86, 685
  Astronave Pirata, L', 221
  Ballerman, 285
  Barry McKenzie, 116
  Bloom County, 139
  Chaland, Yves, and, 194-95
  Demonyo Made Me Do It, The, 646
  Dilbert, 249-50
  Doonesbury, 264
  Ernest Ringard, 319
  Ernsting, Volker, and, 285
  Familia Ulises, La, 291
  Feiffer, 295
  Felix, 297-99
  Freddy Lombard, 194
  Gigi Bizz, 202
  Gyatoruzu, 716
  Jacovitti, Benito, and, 408
  Jaffee, Allan, and, 408
  Janne Ankkanen, 604
  Khalid, Mohamed Nor (pseud. Lat),
    and, 442
  Kitazawa, Rakuten, and, 448
  Kosme the Cop, 675
  Kriminal, 459
  Kurtzman, Harvey, and, 463
  Lavado, Joaquin (pseud. Quino),
    and, 470
  Life in Hell, 477-78
  Life with Robinson, 656
  Lone Spaceman, The, 776
  Looping The Loop in, 687
  Madam and Eve, 503
  Maggie's Farm, 123
  *Mannen som gör vad som faller honom
    in*, 510
  Marmittone, 513-14
  Mike Macke, 533
  Milton, Freddy, and, 535
  Minute Movies, 536-37
  Mr. Kiasu, 540
  Molino, Walter, and, 543
  Mother Goose and Grimm, 550-51
  Motley's Crew, 551-52
  Nero, 564
  Nick Knatterton, 571-72, 678
  Outland, 591-92

Over the Hedge, 593-94
Pekka Puupää, 603-4
Philémon, 613
Phoebe Zeit-Geist, 614, 722-23
Pieds-Nickelés, Les, 605, 615-16
Popol et Virginie ou Pays des Lapinos, 649
Robot Santōhei, 657
Sad Experiences of Big and Little Willie, The, 372
Sappo, 675, 687
Schmit der Sphy, 666
Shadow Troop, The, 734
Shoe, 697-98
StarStruck, 432
Sylvia, 391-92
Tank McNamara, 745
Telestrip, 750
Tobias Seicherl, 765-66
Tom Poes, 768
Toonerville Folks, 768-69
Trois Mousquetaires du Maquis, Les, 774
Zippy the Pinhead, 359
See also Humor strips; Parody strips; Political strips
Saturday Evening Post (U.S.)
 Anderson, Lyman, and, 92
 Casson, Melvin, and, 189
 Cole, Jack (pseud. Johns, Ralph), and, 206
 Cory, Fanny Young, and, 216
 Dirks, John, and, 252
 Hart, Johnny, and, 371
 Henry in, 91-92, 378
 Hoest, Bill, and, 388
 Holman, Bill, and, 392
 Kent, Jack, and, 440
 Little Lulu in, 485
 Mr. Breger in, 538
 O'Neal, Frank, and, 583
 Schulz, Charles Monroe, and, 683
 Superman in, 700
 Turner, Leslie, and, 776
 Van Buren, Raeburn, and, 788
 Walker, Addison Mortimer (Mort; also pseud. Addison), and, 796
Saturday Home (U.S.) (supplement), 309
Satyricon (Italy) (magazine), 521
School Friend (G.B.), 236, 309
Schwermetall (Austria) (magazine), 678
Science fiction strips
 Adam Strange, 78, 683
 Akira, 588-89
 American Flagg!, 197-98
 Andrax, 94
 Android Pini, 463
 Anibal 5, 96
 Arad en Maya, 372, 707
 Arman en Ilva, 100-101
 Astronave Pirata, L', 221
 Atlan, 103-4
 Atomas, 605

 in Australia, 592
 Barbarella, 110-11
 Barney Baxter, 114, 563
 Basura, 341
 Big X, 754
 Blade Runner, 811
 Blake et Mortimer, 137, 407
 Brick Bradford, 152, 354-55, 576, 653
 Buck Rogers, 159-60, 577
 Calkins, Dick, and, 173
 Captain Frank Hawks, 502
 Captain Ken, 351, 754
 Captain Power, 592, 620
 Century 21, 778
 Children of Doom, 583
 Cinco por Infinito, 203
 Cités Obscures, Les, 680
 Città, La, 771
 Cody Starbuck, 197
 Cyborg 009, 230, 405
 Dan Dare, 232, 778
 Delta 99, 239-40
 Denkō Ozma, 520
 Derickson Denie, 242-43
 Diego Valor, 249
 Don Dixon and the Hidden Empire, 262, 611
 Druillet, Philippe, and, 269
 Durga-Rāni, 605
 8-man, 276-77, 463
 Elder, William W., and, 278
 Electropolis, 604
 Elfquest, 279-80
 Elias, Leopold, and, 280
 Embleton, Ronald S., and, 282
 Empire Strikes Back, The, 726, 811
 Ergun L'Errant, 211
 Estrella Negra, La, 341
 Eternauta, El, 150, 286, 580, 714
 Fazekas, Attila, and, 294
 Feldstein, Al, and, 297
 Fernandez, Fernando, and, 301
 Fireball, 588
 Flash Gordon, 308-9, 637, 641, 811
 Fox, Gardner, and, 316
 Frank Fazakerly, Space Ace of the Future, 744
 Fushigina Kuni no Putchā, 328
 Futuropolis, 329, 604
 Gangbusters, 502
 Garage hermétique, La, 345
 Garth, 334-35
 Genma Taisen, 405
 Gesebel, 639
 Gionni Galassia, 408
 Gli ultimi della Terra, 240
 Gospodar sveta, 473
 Guerra de los Antartes, 580
 Guerre à la Terre, 361
 Hans, 663
 Infantino, Carmine, and, 400
 Jacht naar geluk, 491
 Jeff Hawke, 413-14

 Jet Scott, 656
 John Parade, 511
 Judge Dredd, 424, 778
 Jūichinin iru!, 366
 Kaiki Seidan, 463
 Kōsoku Esper, 520
 Kuwata, Jirō, and, 463-64
 Lavinia 2.016, 470
 Lone Sloane, 269
 Lost World, 754
 Lucky Starr, 301
 McLoughlin, Denis, and, 500-501
 McWilliams, Alden, and, 502
 Majin Garon, 754
 Manhuntress, 514
 Mannen från Claa, 348
 Marcello, Raffaelo Carlo (pseud. Marc, Ralph), and, 511
 Marc Reynes, 623
 Marginal, 366
 Mark Trent, 623
 Mazinger Z, 559
 Metropolis, 754
 Milady, 640
 Misterio de Susurro, El, 771
 Mort Cinder, 150, 549, 580
 Mystery Eve, 520
 Nathan Never, 562
 Naufragés du Temps, Les, 313
 Nausicaä of the Valley of Wind, 562-63
 Necron, 640
 Nelvana of the Northern Lights, 565
 Neznanac iz svemira, 327
 Nick, 799
 Nick der Weltraumfahrer, 569-70
 Nowlan, Philip, and, 577
 O-Man, 582-83, 754
 Orlando, Joe, and, 587
 Out of the Silence, 592
 Perramus, 150
 Perry, 609-10
 Philémon, 613
 Pionniers de l'Espérance, Les, 618, 623
 Planeta X, 773
 Ranxerox, 476
 Rayon U, Le, 407
 Return of the Jedi, 726, 811
 Rex Baxter, 649
 Robot Imperium, 657
 Robot Smith, 648
 Rocco Vargas, 771-72
 Rocket Man, 542
 Saga de Xam, 670
 Saturna Contro la Terra, 676-77
 Saxxon, 771
 Scarth, 677-78
 Segrelles, Vicente, and, 688
 Sexaroid, 520
 Sherlock Time, 150, 580
 Shōnen Dōmei, 405
 Silver Starr in the Flame World, 592, 620, 621, 703-4

S.K. 1, 549
Skymasters, 818
Slot-Barr, 714
Sorang, 717
Space Cadets, 502
Space Patrol, 383, 592
Space Patrolman, 511
Spare Ribs and Gravy, 501, 569, 596
Star Hawks, 433
StarStruck, 432
Star Wars, 725-26, 811
Stingray, 778
Stratosphere Jim, 502
Swift Morgan, 500
Tere Creuse, La, 680
Tetsujin 28gō, 752
Tetsuwan-Atom, 752-53, 754
Time², 198
Titanus, 570
Triton, 771
Twin Earths, 502, 592
Uchū Senkan Yamato, 520
Ulysse, 781-82
Valentina, 785
Valérian, 527, 786
V for Vendetta, 547
Virus, Il Mago della Foresta Morta,
543, 603, 792
W 3, 754
Wood, Wallace, and, 818
Yarzael ou la Fin des Temps, 269
Yureisen, 405
Scion Comics (G.B.), 147, 282, 391,
426
Scolaro, Lo (Italy), 148
Scottish Daily Express (G.B.)
(newspaper), 609, 650
Scourge, The (G.B.) (monthly), 224
Scribner's (U.S.) (magazine), 216, 586
Scripps-Howard newspapers, 80-81,
534, 791
See also Newspaper Enterprise
Association
Sea-adventure strips
Ballata del Mare Salato, Una, 108,
627
Bibor and Tribar, 790
Chanoc, 195
Corto Maltese, 215, 627
Davy Jones, 147, 502
Démon des Caraïbes, Le, 241, 396
Don Winslow of the Navy, 263-64
Hernàn el Corsario, 380, 671
Howard Flynn, 788
Kapitein Rob, 435, 436, 461-62
Kappie, 435-36
Kapten Groggs, 126-27
Mali moreplovac, 830
Middy Malone, 293, 569
Perils of Submarine Boating, The, 431
Pitch and Toss, 620
Ranger, The, 282
Robinson, 655-56

Squirt, 379
See also Pirate strips
Seac (South East Asia Command)
(newspaper), 96
Seattle Post-Intelligencer (U.S.)
(newspaper), 326
Seattle Times (U.S.) (newspaper), 468
Secondamano (Italy) (magazine), 521
Seduction of the Innocent (Wertham), 32
on *Black Cat*, 135
on Craig, John, 219
Gaines, William M., and, 331
on *Phantom Lady*, 613
on *Wonder Woman*, 816-17
on *Wonderwoman*, 515
SEI (Italy) (publisher), 221
Selecciones Illustradas (Spain) (comic
syndicate), 120, 514
Semaine de Suzette, La (France)
(magazine), 614, 617
Semaine de Suzette (France)
(magazine), 120
Semic Press (Sweden) (publisher),
348, 557
Semmel Verlach (Germany)
(publisher), 805
Sergio Bonelli (Italy) (publisher), 273,
301, 439, 562, 575, 771
Serial strips
Big Hit Swift, 501
Billy Bunter, 133
Booth, Walter, and, 146
Fury's Family, 501
Heath, George, and, 377
Holroyd, Bill, and, 393
Japhet and Happy, 412-13
Power the Danger Ranger, 501
Rob the Rover, 657
Saber, 209, 501
Terror in the Tall Tower, 501
Wulf the Briton, 282
Seriemagasinet (Sweden), 348
Serie-Pressen (Sweden) (comic book),
468
Settebello (Italy) (magazine), 86
Seventeen (U.S.) (magazine), 542
Shanghai Cartoons (China) (magazine)
elete, 798
Shanghai New Art Publishing House,
376
Sheffield Evening Post (G.B.)
(newspaper), 346
Shin Mangaha Shudan (Japan)
(cartoonists' group), 696, 825
Shinyūkan (Japan), 696, 826
Shogaken (Japan) (monthly), 676
Shōgaku Ichinensei (Japan) (magazine),
143
Shogakukan Publishing (Japan), 366
Shojo Club (Japan) (magazine), 542
Shojo (Japan), 97, 109
Shōjo (Japanese comics for girls), 676
Shōjo Kurabu (Japan) (monthly), 199
Shōjo manga (Japan), 366, 588

Shōnen Chambion (Japan) (weekly),
332
Shōnen Gahō (Japan) (magazine),
83-84, 463, 580, 750
Shōnen (Japan)
Ashita no Joe in, 101
Chikaino Makyū in, 199
8-man in, 276
Hakaba no Kitarō in, 366
Harisu no Kaze, 370
Kibaō in, 442
Kyojin no Hoshi in, 465
Saitō, Takao, and, 671
Sasuke, 675-76
Tetsujin 28gō in, 752
Tetsuwan-Atom in, 752
Shōnen Jump (Japan) (magazine), 559
Shōnen King (Japan) (weekly), 230,
580
Shōnen Kurabu (Japan) (magazine)
Bōken Dankichi in, 143
Fushigina Kuni no Putchā, 328
Gekkō Kamen in, 337
Hatanosuke Hinomaru in, 373
Norakuro in, 576
Robot Santōhei in, 657
Sugiura, Shigeru in, 733
Shōnen Magazine (Japan), 559
Shōnen Sunday (Japan) (weekly), 582,
588
Show Me (U.S.) (magazine), 796
Shueisha Publishing (Japan), 588
Shukan Bunshan (Japan) (magazine),
78
Simon & Kirby Shop, 527
Simplizissimus (Austria) (magazine),
765
Siné L'Enragé (France) (magazine), 815
Sittara (Sri Lanka) (magazine), 607
Sjors (Netherlands) (newspaper
supplement), 149, 157, 616
Skorpio (Argentina) (magazine), 239,
341, 714
Skull (U.S.) (comic book), 214
Skywald Comics, 376, 435, 690, 809
Sleazy Scandals of the Silver Screen
(U.S.) (underground comic), 719
S.M. Iger Shop
Celardo, John (pseud. Lardo, John
C.), and, 192
Classics Illustrated, and, 204
Crandall, Reed, and, 219
Eisner, Will, and, 278, 400
Feldstein, Al, and, 297
Fine, Louis, and, 303
Iger, Samuel Maxwell ("Jerry"),
and, 400
Kane, Robert, and, 434
Kida, Fred, and, 443
Kirby, Jack, and, 447
Leav, Mort, and, 470
Meskin, Morton (pseud. Morton,
Mort, Jr.), and, 526
Smith-Mann Syndicate, 587

Smith Service (U.S.), 711

Smith's Magazine (U.S.), 788

Smith's Weekly (Australia)
  armed services strips in, 797
  Cross, Stanley George, and, 223
  Gurney, Alexander George, and, 364
  Miller, Sydney Leon, and, 535
  Potts, The in, 625
  Russell, James Newton, and, 666

Snarf (U.S.) (underground comic), 90, 226, 449

Snatch (U.S.) (underground comic), 224

Soap opera strips, 32-33
  Doc Wright, 146, 349
  Grand Hotel, 543, 629
  Heart of Juliet Jones, The, 267, 376-77
  Jane, 410
  Liberty Kid, 476
  Mary Worth, 518-19, 677
  Principe Azzurro, 629
  Rex Morgan, M.D., 649-50
  Steve Canyon, 728
  Toots and Casper, 769-70
  Virtue of Vera Valiant, 722
  Winnie Winkle, 813-14

Social consciousness strips
  In Biblis ist die H'lle los, 648
  Children of Doom, 583
  Gimenez, Carlos, and, 341
  Kitazawa, Rakuten, and, 448
  Madam and Eve, 503
  Negro Raul, El, 564-65
  O'Neil, Dennis (pseud. O'Shaugnessey, Sergius), and, 583
  Pompeo, 601
  Satonaka, Machiko, and, 676
  Tanjo, 588
  Todano Bonji, 766
  Tokai, 766
  Torchy Brown, 587
  Villiams Verden, 535
  Watashi no Joni, 676
  Zanardi, 601
  Zankoku na kami ga shihai suru, 366
  See also Political strips

Soir, Le (France) (newspaper), 211

Soir Illustré, Le (France) (weekly), 217

Solar Sales Service (U.S.), 683

Soloway Publications (G.B.), 243, 246, 544, 631

Söndags-Nisse (Sweden) (weekly), 77, 93, 407, 510

Soujourn (U.S.) (magazine), 809

South China Morning Post (newspaper), 155, 296-97

South London Advertiser (G.B.) (newspaper), 544

South Wales Echo (G.B.) (newspaper), 609, 650, 808

1984 (Spain), 120

Spark Publications, 526, 637, 656

Special USA, 682

Spirou (Belgium/France) (magazine)
  Bibor and Tribar in, 790
  Blasco, Jesus, and, 138
  Boucq, François, and, 149
  Buck Danny in, 159, 396
  Culliford, Pierre (pseud. Peyo), and, 228
  Franquin, André, and, 318-19
  Gaston Lagaffe in, 319, 337
  Gil Jourdan in, 762
  Gillain, John (pseud. Jijé), and, 339
  Goscinny, René, and, 352
  Guerilleros, Les in, 361
  Hubinon, Victor, and, 396
  Jerry Spring in, 339, 415
  Lucky Luke in, 129, 492
  Max in, 382, 523
  Mézières, Jean-Claude, and, 527
  Natacha in, 562
  Poussy in, 228
  Rosinski, Grzegorz, and, 662
  Schtroumpes, Les in, 680
  Spirou in, 721
  Tillieux, Maurice, and, 762

Spokane Inland-Herald (U.S.) (newspaper), 553

Spokeswoman, The (U.S.) (magazine), 391-92

Sporting (France) (magazine), 605

Sporting News, The (G.B.) (magazine), 631

Sports Fun (G.B.), 693

Sports Illustrated for Kids (U.S.) (magazine), 722

Sports Mail (G.B.) (newspaper), 693

Sports Post, The (G.B.) (magazine), 631

Sports strips
  A. Piker Clerk, 97-98
  Asparagus Tipps, 354
  Barney Google, 114
  Bill Body, 472-73
  Bokutō kun, 399
  Bozo Blimp, 404
  Carson's Cubs, 393
  Cotton Woods, 594
  Daruma-kun, 399
  De Beck, Billy, and, 238
  Dorgan, Thomas Aloysius (Tad), and, 265
  Dovniković, Borivoj, and, 266
  Ed, Carl Frank Ludwig, and, 275
  Edson, Gus, and, 275
  Felix O'Fan, 354
  Fung, Paul, and, 326
  Gil Thorp, 127-28
  Goldberg, Reuben Lucius, and, 348
  Gould, Will, and, 354
  Greene, Vernon van Atta, and, 356
  Gross, Milton, and, 360
  Gunner, 672
  Harisu no Kaze, 370

  Hatlo, James, and, 373-74
  Hey Coach, 379
  Igaguri-kun, 399
  Inazuma-kun, 399
  Indoor Sports, 265
  As I Saw It, 581
  Jean-Jacques Ardent, 604
  Joe and Asbestos, 419
  Joe Jinks, 419-20
  Leonard, Frank (Lank), and, 531
  Michel Vaillant, 529-30
  Moon Mullins, 422, 423, 546-47, 809-10
  Murphy, John Cullen, and, 554
  Mutt and Jeff, 555-56
  Pellos, René, and, 604
  Petey Dink, 792
  Phool Phan Phables, 360
  Rista Sportista, 512
  Roy of the Rovers, 393
  Rusty Riley, 666-67
  Saturday Sammy, 424
  Smith, Sydney, and, 582
  Sporting Life, The, 551
  Super Fan, 237, 551
  Tank McNamara, 745
  Tenth Player, The, 379
  Wakefield, George William, and, 796
  Webster, Tom, and, 802
  Wilson the Wonder Man, 346
  See also Baseball strips; Boxing strips; Football strips; Martial arts strips; Racing strips

Sport y Trystika (Poland) (publisher), 436

Spotlight Comics, 378, 533

Springer Verlag (Germany) (publisher), 244, 305-6, 651

Spy strips
  Agent SS018, 639
  Billy Bis, 132
  Bruno Brazil, 159, 647, 788
  Giardino, Vittorio, and, 338
  Hot on the Trail, 393
  James Bond, 408-10
  K-51, 278
  Modesty Blaise, 543
  Mortadelo y Filemon, 549
  Nick Fury, Agent of SHIELD, 726-27
  Petra Chérie, 530
  Rapsodia ungherese, 338
  Sarutobi Sasuke, 733
  XIII, 788

Standaard, De (Belgium) (newspaper), 564, 566, 737, 789
  See also *Nieuwe Gids, De* (Belgium) (newspaper)

Standard (Canada) (weekly), 598

Standard Group, 319, 401, 533, 773
  See also Better Group; Nedor Group

Star, The (G.B.) (newspaper), 265, 333, 347, 803
  See also *Junior Star*

Star Company (U.S.), 145

Starlog (U.S.), 226

Stars and Stripes (U.S.), 90, 371, 395, 539, 782

Star Weekly (Canada) (supplement), 322-23

Sternchen (Germany) (supplement), 417, 451, 637, 746-47, 747

stern (Germany) (magazine), 121, 163-64, 169, 651

Stipple technique, 562

Stop (Belgium) (magazine), 407

Storia Illustrata (Italy) (magazine), 685

Story strips
  Apartment 3-G, 97, 454
  Dallis, Nicholas, and, 231
  decline of, 40, 179
  Gay Honor, 593
  Heart of Juliet Jones, The, 267, 376-77
  He Youzhi, and, 375-76
  Judge Parker, 424-26
  Mary Worth, 518-19, 677
  Minute Movies, 536-37
  Perry Mason, 757
  Rex Morgan, M.D., 649-50, 722
  On Stage, 584-85, 725
  Steve Roper, 593, 677, 728-29
  Tiffany Jones, 760

Strand (G.B.) (magazine), 363

Strasse, Die (Germany) (magazine), 163

Street and Smith (U.S.) (publishers), 108
  Binder, Jack, and, 133
  Celardo, John (pseud. Lardo, John C.), and, 191
  Doc Savage, 256
  Greene, Vernon van Atta, and, 356
  Kane, Gil, and, 433
  Lehti, John, and, 473
  Shadow, The, 691
  Supersnipe, 222, 737
  Van Buren, Raeburn, and, 788
  Wildey, Doug, and, 808

Street News (U.S.), 218

Strip Art Features (Yugoslavia), 256, 637

Strip Art (Yugoslavia) (magazine), 327

Strip books, 614

Stripschrift (Netherlands) (fanzine), 461

Strip (Yugoslavia) (magazine), 489

Studio Bierreci (Italy), 198

Studio Giolitti (Italy), 609

Studio Hachette (France), 345

Studiortega (Spain), 161

Studios Paget (Italy), 770

Studio Vandersteen, 564, 566, 813

Stuttgart live (Germany) (magazine), 664

Sun, The (G.B.) (newspaper), 704

Sunday Citizen (G.B.), 125, 686

Sunday Dispatch (G.B.) (newspaper), 210, 236

Sunday Express (G.B.) (newspaper), 166, 210, 236, 332
  See also *Daily Express*

Sunday Extra (G.B.), 125

Sunday Graphic (G.B.) (newspaper), 321
  See also *Daily Graphic*

Sunday Herald (Australia) (newspaper), 130, 569

Sunday Hochi (Japan) (newspaper), 575

Sunday Pictorial (G.B.), 95, 301, 302, 619, 627

Sunday Post (G.B.) (newspaper), 585

Sunday Sun (Australia) (newspaper), 130, 293

Sunday Sun-Herald (Australia) (newspaper), 293

Sunday Telegraph (Australia), 110

Sunday Times (Australia) (newspaper), 223, 364

Sunday Times (G.B.) (newspaper), 155

Sunday Times Magazine (G.B.), 125

Sun (G.B.) (newspaper), 390, 677

Sun-News Pictorial (Australia), 141, 364

Suomen Kuvalehti (Finland) (magazine), 604

Super Duper Comics (Canada), 565

Supergraphics Publishing Company, 727

Supergulp (Italy) (magazine), 516-17

Superheroes
  Adam Strange, 78, 683
  Airwave, 804
  Amazing Man, 90
  Amazing Mr. X, 346
  Amok, 91
  Anderson, Murphy, and, 92
  Angel, The, 95, 189, 364
  Aquaman, 98
  Arrow, The, 364, 492
  Asso di Picche, 102-3
  Atom, The, 104, 316, 434, 583, 773
  Atoman, 656
  Atomic Mouse, 533
  Avengers, The, 104, 756
  Batman, 117, 434-35, 534, 547, 583, 656, 683, 690, 722, 830
  Black Condor, 135-36
  Blackhawk, 819
  Black Hood, 136-37, 545, 819
  Black Marvel, 472
  Black Panther, The, 364
  Black Terror, 137, 526, 656
  Blue Beetle, 140
  Blue Bolt, 140-41, 704
  Brick Bradford, 152, 354-55, 576
  Bulletman, 164
  Buscema, John, and, 167
  Capitan Misterio, El, 177
  Captain America, 180-82, 705

  Captain Marvel, 182-84, 583, 683, 819
  Captain Marvel Jr., 184, 637
  Captain Midnight, 184-85
  Captain Wings, 185
  Cinco por Infinito, 203
  Citizen Smith, Son of the Unknown Soldier, 372
  Colan, Eugene (pseud. Austin, Adam), and, 206
  Conan, 211-12, 756
  Conquerer, 287
  Crimebuster, 222
  Daredevil, 233-34, 534
  Derickson Denie, 242-43
  Destroyer, 133, 472
  Diabolik, 245
  Ditko, Steve, and, 254
  Doc Savage, 256-57
  Dr. Fate, 257
  Dr. Mid-Nite, 258-59
  Dr. Strange, 259-60
  Doll Man, 260
  Eisner, Will, and, 278
  Elias, Leopold, and, 280
  Everett, Bill, and, 287
  Falcon, The, 377
  Fantastic Four, 292-93, 704, 705
  Fantomas, 293
  Fighting American, 447
  Fighting Yank, 302, 526, 656, 678
  Fin, The, 287
  Fine, Louis, and, 303
  Flash, The, 307-8
  Fly, The, 447, 705
  Fox, Gardner, and, 316-17
  Fox, The, 372, 545
  Frankenstein, 318
  Freccia d'Argente, La, 216
  Furio Almirante (x1), 216, 327
  Garth, 334-35
  Gekkō Kamen, 337
  Ghost Rider, 337-38
  Giordano, Richard, and, 344
  Goodwin, Archie (pseud. Franklin, Robert), and, 351
  Green Arrow, 355-56, 804
  Green Hornet, 356-57, 656
  Green Lama, The, 637
  Green Lantern, 357-59
  Gustafson, Bob, and, 364
  Hangman, The, 368
  Hasen, Irwin, and, 372-73
  Hawkman, 104, 134, 219, 316, 374, 460, 461, 583
  Heap, The, 376, 471
  Hercules, 379-80
  Herron, France Edward, and, 381
  Howard the Duck, 394-95
  Hulk, The, 396-97
  Human Bomb, The, 364
  Human Torch, The, 397-98
  Hydroman, 287
  Ibis the Invincible, 399

Infantino, Carmine, and, 400
Iron Man, 403-4
Jack Frost, 400, 472
Jester, The, 364
Jimmy Olsen, 417-18
Johnny Quick, 460, 526, 656
Johnny Thunder, 373, 400, 422
Justice League of America, 429-30
Kane, Gil, and, 433
Kirby, Jack, and, 447-48
Kriminal, 459
Lee, Stan, and, 472
Litening, 282
McFarlane, Todd, and, 500
Magirus, 123
Magno, 364, 462
Mandrake the Magician, 238, 291, 321, 508-9
Marvelman, 517-18
Master Man, 541
Master of Kung Fu, 519
Meskin, Morton (pseud. Morton, Mort, Jr.), and, 526
Midnight, 206, 364
Mighty Mouse, 532-33
Misterix, 539
Mr. Scarlet, 541
Mr. Terrific, 541-42
Montana, Bob, and, 545
Music Master, 287
Namora, 287
New Mutants, 568
Ogon Bat, 580
O'Neil, Dennis (pseud. O'Shaugnessey, Sergius), and, 583
Patriot, The, 287
Penguin, The, 606
Phantom, The, 611-12, 829
Plastic Man, 621-22
Powerhouse Pepper, 626, 816
Private Strong, 447, 705
Question, The, 254, 344
Quicksilver, 206, 303, 360
Ray, The, 303
Red Knight, The, 644
Red Ray, Space Raynger, 236
Sandman, The, 673
Schwartz, Julius, and, 683
Shadow, The, 583, 691-92, 692
Shield, The, 695-96
Sign of Freedom, The, 251
Silver Surfer, 704
Siopawman, 705-6
Spacehawk, 816
Spectre, The, 718
Spider-Man, 500, 660, 718-19
Spirit, The, 720-21
Spy Smasher, 723-24
Stainless Steel, 403
Starman, 316, 526, 724-25
Steel Sterling, 134, 435, 545, 726
Sub-Mariner, The, 287, 731-32
Submerman, 614

Superman, 541, 547, 583, 683, 699-700, 701, 735-37, 804, 830
Supermouse, 533
Super Sam, 648
Supersnipe, 737
Tank, 216
Tanku Tankurō, 745
Tenebrax, 614
Thor, 756-57
THUNDER Agents, 758-59, 818
Thunderbolt Jaxon, 502
Tiramolla, 764-65
Tornado, 544
Ultra-Man, 524
Vigilante, The, 526, 656
Watchmen, 800
Web, The, 801-2
Whizzer, 472
Wildcat, 434, 526
Witness, The, 472
Wonder Woman, 583
X-1 il Pugile Misterioso, 216, 327
X-Men, 821
Yak, 193
Zigomar, 829-30
Superheroines
Black Cat, 135
Darna, 645
Gabriel, 685
Invisible Scarlet O'Neil, 403
Isabella, 404-5
Lois Lane, 489-90, 678
Mary Marvel, 518
Nelvana of the Northern Lights, 565
Phantom Lady, 612-13
Red Sonja, 646, 757
Sheena, Queen of the Jungle, 526, 693-94
Supergirl, 734-35
Wonder Woman, 653, 816-17
Wonderwoman, 515
Suplemento Juvenil (Brazil) (children's supplement), 83
Surrealist strips
Rivolta dei Racchi, La, 170
Suspense strips
Dauntless Durham of the U.S.A., 382
Desperate Desmond, 244, 382
Feldstein, Al, and, 297
Hairbreadth Harry, 366, 431
Pauline McPeril, 470
Swan Features Syndicate, 630
Swiat Modlich (Poland), 200
Swimming World (U.S.) (magazine), 379
Sword-and-sorcery strips
Blackmark, 433
Corben, Richard Vance, and, 214
Falk, 799
Gin no hanbira, 542
Merlino, 818
Sabaku no Maō, 669
Segrelles, Vicente, and, 688
Sigfrid, 473

Sigurd, 702, 798-99
Thorgal, Fils des Etoiles, 436, 662
Ulf, 799
Viking Prince, 461
See also Fantasy strips
Sydney Evening News (Australia) (newspaper), 666
Sydney Morning Herald (Australia) (newspaper), 155, 384, 410
Sydney News (Australia) (newspaper), 569
Sydney Sunday Herald (Australia) (newspaper), 81, 255, 293, 343
Sydney Sunday News (Australia) (newspaper), 293, 339
Sydney Sunday Sun (Australia), 109, 383-84, 620, 703
Sydney Sun-Herald (Australia) (newspaper), 255
Sydney Sun News (Australia) (newspaper), 130
Szabad Szaj (Hungary) (magazine), 830
Szexi (Hungary) (magazine), 294

T

T. C. McClure Syndicate. *See* McClure Syndicate
Tagalog Klassiks (Philippines) (comic book), 86
Tagalog Komics (Philippines), 505, 516, 599-600
Tagalong Komics (Philippines), 462
Tampa Daily Times (U.S.) (newspaper), 469
Tanteiō (Japan), 463
Target Publications (U.S.), 246
Tasmanian Mail (Australia) (newspaper), 364
Tatler (G.B.) (magazine), 272
Taurinia Publications (Italy), 408
TBO (Spain) (weekly), 291
Teddy Bär (Austria) (magazine), 731
Teen strips
Archie, 99-100, 545-46
Date with Judy, A, 567
Ernie Pook's Comeek, 115-16
Etta Kett, 286
Fantomette, 218
Funky Winkerbean, 326-27
Harold Teen, 275, 370-71
Kenkoy, 438-39
Lupo Alberto, 494-95
Miss Mimi, 614
My Son John, 389
Our Bill, 365
Patti, 410
Thirteen, 724
See also Young adult strips
Teknophage (G.B.) (magazine), 744

Telegraaf, De (Netherlands) (newspaper), 107, 767

Telegraaf/Nieuws van de Dag, De, 453

Telegram (Oregon, US) (newspaper), 356

Tempo (Italy) (magazine), 603

Tennessean (U.S.) (newspaper), 804

Texas Ranger (U.S.), 694

Thai Rath (Thailand) (newspaper), 193

Thorpe & Porter (U.S.), 96

Thud (Sweden) (fanzines), 282

Tianjin's Daily (China) (newspaper), 269

Tia Vicenta (Argentina) (magazine), 232

Tid-Bits (U.S.) (magazine), 395

Tijd-Maasbode (Netherlands) (newspaper), 767

Tilt (Italy) (magazine), 189

Time Cartoons (China) (magazine), 798

Timely. *See* Marvel/Timely/Atlas group

Time Pictorial (China) (magazine), 798

Times, The (G.B.) (newspaper), 704

Time Traveller, The (U.S.) (fanzine), 683

Tinkle (India) (magazine), 595

Tintin (Belgium) (weekly)
  Alix l'Intrépide in, 87
  Arabelle la Sirène in, 99
  Bernard Prince in, 127, 398
  Blake et Mortimer in, 137, 407
  Bruno Brazil in, 159
  Chevalier Ardent in, 198
  Chick Bill in, 335
  Chlorophylle in, 199
  Comanche in, 209, 398
  Corentin in, 214
  Corto Maltese in, 215, 627
  Craenhals, François (pseud. Hals, F.), and, 217
  Cubitus in, 227
  Franquin, André, and, 318-19
  Gascard, Gilbert (pseud. Tibet), and, 335
  Goscinny, René, and, 352
  Herzog, Guy (pseud. Bara), and, 382
  Huppen, Hermann (pseud. Hermann), and, 398
  Jacobs, Edgar Pierre, and, 407
  Jugurtha in, 398
  Max in, 382, 523
  Michel Vaillant in, 529
  Modeste et Pompon in, 318
  Pratt, Hugo, and, 627
  Ric Hochet in, 335, 650-51
  Rock Derby in, 647
  Rosinski, Grzegorz, and, 662
  Vance, William, and, 788
  Zig et Puce in, 647, 829

Tip Top Comics (U.S.) (comic book), 233

TIP TOP (Germany) (magazine), 494

Titanic (Canada) (magazine), 647.398

Tit-Bits (G.B.) (adult comic), 778, 798

Toby Press (U.S.), 179, 299, 319

Todd McFarlane Publications, 500

Tokyo Puck (Japan) (magazine), 448

Toledo Blade (U.S.) (newspaper), 356

Toledo News-Bee (U.S.) (newspaper), 354, 677, 722

Tom Poes Weekblad (Netherlands) (weekly), 283, 767

Tongard Trading (U.S.), 544

Tony, El (Argentina) (magazine), 639, 671

Toonder Studios
  See also Marten Toonder Studios

Top (Argentina) (magazine), 284

Top (France) (magazine), 134

Topical Times (G.B.), 502

Top Komiks (Philippines), 418

Top-Magazine (France), 781

Top-Notch (U.S.)
  Black Hood in, 136-37

Topolino (Italy) (weekly)
  Albertarelli, Rino, and, 86
  Caesar, Kurt (pseud. Avai, Cesare; Away, Caesar), and, 173
  Canale, Antonio, and, 175
  Capitan l'Audace in, 176
  Caprioli, Franco, and, 180
  Cavazzano, Giorgio, and, 191
  Dottor Faust, Il in, 266
  Gino e Gianni in, 344
  Kit Carson in, 449
  Moroni-Celsi, Guido (pseud. Sterny), and, 549
  Rubino, Antonio, and, 664
  Saturna Contro la Terra in, 677
  Virus, Il Mago della Foresta Morta in, 792

Topps Comics
  Frankenstein, 318
  Kane, Gil, and, 433
  Maroto, Esteban, and, 514
  Spiegelman, Arthur, and, 719
  Thomas, Roy, and, 756

Top Sellers Comics (G.B.), 518

Top Star (Philippines), 163

Toronto Star (Canada) (newspaper), 322

Toronto Sun Syndicate (Canada), 392

Toronto Telegram (Canada) (newspaper), 655

Toronto Telegram News Service (Canada), 197

Toronto Telegraph (Canada) (newspaper), 499

Total Journal (France) (magazine), 527

Toutain (Spain) (publisher), 773

Tower Comics, 220, 254, 433, 758, 818

Tradotta, La (Italy) (magazine), 664

Tre Porcellini, I (Italy), 549, 676-77

Tribune Media Services
  Brenda Starr, 154
  Brigman, June, and, 154
  Collins, Max Allan, and, 489
  Dave, 235
  Herb & Jamaal, 379
  Mother Goose and Grimm, 551
  Motley's Crew, 551
  Pluggers, 697, 698
  Professor Doodle's, 672
  Shoe, 697
  Suburban Cowgirls, 732
  Terry and the Pirates, 384, 385-86, 752
  See also Chicago Tribune-New York News Syndicate

Trinca (Spain) (magazine), 94, 375, 511, 663, 695

Triumphant-Adventure (Canada) (comic book), 565

Triumph Comics, 251, 565

Triumph (G.B.) (weekly), 209, 243

Trouw (Netherlands) (newspaper), 457

Trump (U.S.) (magazine), 237, 278, 408, 463, 481

Truth (U.S.) (magazine), 395, 584

Tuffa Viktor (Sweden), 95

T.V. Comic (G.B.), 236

TV Century 21 (G.B.) (magazine), 125, 282

TV-Fernsehwod (Germany), 459

TV (Germany) (weekly), 417

TV Guide (U.S.) (weekly), 327

2000 A.D. (G.B.) (magazine), 424, 547, 744, 778

tz (Germany) (newspaper), 528, 661

U

Ukiyo-e artists, 390-91, 775-76, 783

Underground comix, 35-36
  American Splendor, 90-91
  Corben, Richard Vance, and, 213-14
  Crumb, Robert, and, 224-26
  Cruse, Howard, and, 226-27
  Dili Ako Mahadlok, 506
  Fabulous Furry Freak Brothers, 289, 694
  Fritz the Cat, 323-24
  Griffith, Bill, and, 359
  history of, 224
  Kitchen, Denis, and, 449-50
  Kurtzman, Harvey, and, 463
  Lynch, Jay, and, 496
  Malaya, and, 506
  Mr. Natural, 540-41
  Mom's Homemade Comics, 449
  Nard n' Pat, 496
  Odd Bodkins, 583-84

Shelton, Gilbert, and, 694
Spiegelman, Arthur, and, 719
Talbot, Bryan, and, 744
Torres, Daniel, and, 771
Werner, 805
Wet Satin #2, 812
Wonder Wart-Hog, 694
Zippy the Pinhead, 359
Undergrouond Press Syndicate,
583-84
Uneeda (U.S.) (underground comic),
224
Unicum (Netherlands) (weekly), 768
Union Jack (G.B.) (magazine), 512
Unita'L (Italy) (daily), 338
United Continental (Philippines) (comic
book), 350
United Features Syndicate
Abbie an' Slats, 75-76
Back Home Again, 260, 512-13
Bushmiller, Ernest, and, 168
Caplin, Elliot, and, 179
Captain and the Kids, The, 182
Casey Ruggles, 188, 467, 773, 776
Casson, Melvin, and, 189
Celardo, John (pseud. Lardo, John
C.), and, 192
Committed, 593
Crane, Royston Campbell (Roy),
and, 220
Davis, Jim, 237
Dilbert, 249
Dropouts, The, 269
Ella Cinders, 281
Ferd'nand, 301
Foster, Harold, and, 628
Fritzi Ritz, 168
Garfield, 333
Gordo, 101, 351
Hogarth, Burne, and, 389
Jim Hardy, 416
Judge Wright, 426
Jumpstart, 379, 427
L'il Abner, 179, 478
Long Sam, 490, 492
Lookin' Fine, 229
Lubbers, Robert (pseud. Lewis,
Bob), and, 492
Mamie, 599
Mauldin, Bill, and, 782
Miracle Jones, 389
Mixed Singles, 189
Mutt and Jeff, 556
Nancy, 685
Over the Hedge, 593-94
Peanuts, 601, 683
Peter Pat, 420
Rose is Rose, 661
Scott, Jerry (pseud. Kirkman, Rick),
and, 685
Skylark, 728
Tarzan, 389, 510, 573, 747-48
From 9 to 5, 711
Twin Earths, 502

Universal, El (Mexico) (newspaper),
201
Universal (Philippines) (comic book),
350
Universal Press Syndicate
For Better or For Worse, 312, 423
Calvin and Hobbes, 173
Cathy, 190, 672
Doonesbury, 264, 775
Far Side, The, 468
Feiffer, 295
Fusco Brothers, The, 327
Sylvia, 392
Tank McNamara, 745
Where I'm Coming From, 587, 806-7
Universo (Italy) (publisher), 132, 162,
734
Urania (Italy) (magazine), 173

V

Vaderland, Het (Netherlands)
(newspaper), 767
Vaillant (France) (weekly)
Arthur le Fantome in, 193
Fils de Chine in, 302-3
Forest, Jean-Claude (pseud.
Valherbe, Jean), and, 313
Gai Luron in, 331
Gire, Eugène, and, 606
Pif le Chien in, 617
Pionniers de l'Espérance, Les in, 618
Placid et Muzo in, 621
See also *Pif*
Valkyrie Press (U.S.), 744
Valvoline (Italy) (cartoonist's group),
521
Vampirella (U.S.) (magazine), 120,
301, 514
Vanity (Italy) (magazine), 522
Van (Japan) (magazine), 826
Vårt Hem (Sweden) (newspaper), 450,
572
Vault of Horror (U.S.) (comic book),
219
Ventura (Italy) (publisher), 162
Verkenner, De (Netherlands)
(magazine), 457
Veseli Vandrock's (Yugoslavia)
(magazine), 566
Viaggi e Avventure (Italy) (magazine),
86, 548-49
Vibora, El (Spain) (magazine), 771
Village life strips
Abbie an'Slats, 75-76, 788
Seidel og Tobran, 75
Village Voice (U.S.) (newspaper), 218,
226, 295
Vingtieme Siecle, Le (Belgium) (daily),
648, 764
Vi (Sweden) (newspaper), 408

Vittoriosio, Il (Italy) (weekly)
Battaglia, Dino, and, 118
Caesar, Kurt (pseud. Avai, Cesare;
Away, Caesar), and, 173
Canale, Antonio, and, 175
Caprioli, Franco, and, 180
Craveri, Sebastiano (pseud.
Pin-Tin), and, 221
DeLuca, Gianni, and, 240
Jacovitti, Benito, and, 408
Vittorioso, Il (Italy) (weekly), 575, 618,
630, 659
Vivre (Belgium) (weekly), 382
Viz Comics (U.S.), 506
V-Magazine (France), 110, 313
Voice of Comicdom (U.S.) (fanzine),
214
Volk, Het (Netherlands) (newspaper),
163, 564, 566
Volkskrant (Netherlands) (newspaper),
571, 767
Voorwarts (Netherlands) (newspaper),
107
Vorwärts (Germany) (newspaper), 580
Vrabac (Yugoslavia) (magazine), 411
Vrai (Belgium) (magazine), 217
Vreme (Yugoslavia) (newspaper), 411

W

Wahrer Jakob (Germany) (newspaper),
580
Wall Street Journal (U.S.) (newspaper),
496
Walt Disney Productions
Barks, Carl, and, 111-12
Chendi, Carlo, and, 198
Craig, Chase, and, 218-19
Donald Duck, 260-61, 535, 744
Gottfredson, Floyd, and, 353
in Italy, 148, 191, 198
Kelly, Walt, and, 438
Ketcham, Henry King, and, 441
in Latin America, 83
Mickey Mouse, 531-32, 744
Parker, Brant, and, 597
Rebuffi, Giorgio, and, 642
Silly Symphonies, 702, 744
Taliaferro, Charles Alfred, and, 744
Walter Lehning Verlag (Germany)
(publisher), 569-70, 702, 798
Warheit (U.S.) (newspaper), 341
Warner Brothers Studios, 625
Warner Publications, 401
WaRP (U.S.) (publisher), 279-80
Warren Publishing Company
Adams, Neal, and, 77
Bea, José-Maria, and, 120
Colan, Eugene (pseud. Austin,
Adam), and, 206
Corben, Richard Vance, and, 214
Craig, John, and, 219

Crandall, Reed, and, 220
Ditko, Steve, and, 254
Evans, George, and, 287
Frazetta, Frank, and, 320
Goodwin, Archie (pseud. Franklin,
   Robert), and, 351
Heath, Russell, and, 378
Kane, Gil, and, 433
Maroto, Esteban, and, 514
Severin, John Powers, and, 690
Vampirella, 787
Williamson, Al, and, 811
Wood, Wallace, and, 818
Warren Tufts Enterprises, 467, 776
Warrior (G.B.) (magazine), 547
War strips
   Adolf, 78-79, 754
   Airboy, 81
   Atlantic Patrol, 502
   Bab El Mandeb, 530
   Balloon Buster, 435
   Barney Baxter, 113-14, 563
   Bête Est Morte, La, 175
   Blackhawk, 136
   Blazing Combat, 351, 690
   Blue Sea and Red Heart, 141
   Bluey and Curley, 141, 364
   Boy Commandos, 149
   Buck Danny, 159, 396
   Buz Sawyer, 169-70, 220
   Caesar, Kurt (pseud. Avai, Cesare;
      Away, Caesar), and, 173
   Canale, Antonio, and, 175
   Captain America, 180
   Captain Flag, 502
   Capt. Storm, 435
   Captain Wings, 185
   Cato Zulu, 627
   C'était la Guerre des Tranchées, 746
   Charley's War, 209
   Colonel X, 623
   Cosacco, Il, 818
   Davis, Jack, and, 237
   Destroyer 171, 502
   Don Winslow of the Navy, 263-64
   Elder, William W., and, 278
   Enemy Ace, 460-61, 757
   *Episode Banal de la Guerre des
      Tranchées*, 745-46
   Ernie Pike, 284-85, 580, 627, 714
   Fernandez, Fernando, and, 301
   Four Aces, The, 744
   Frontline Combat, 377, 462
   Fuochi, 522
   Green Berets, 461
   Hashmark, 468
   Haunted Tank, The, 435, 690
   Jean-Jacques Ardent, 604
   Jeux pour Mourir, 746
   Johnny Cloud, 690
   Johnny Hazard, 420-22
   Kanigher, Robert, and, 435
   Knock-Out, 746
   Kubert, Joe, and, 460-61

Legija prokletib, 715
Marcel Labrume, 530
Maus, 522-23, 719
'Nam, 560
Paddy Payne, 209
Porta d'Oriente, La, 338
Qui la Legione, 818
Romano il Legionario, 659
Scorpions du Désert, Les, 627
Sgt. Fury, 689
Sgt. Rock, 435, 689-90
Spitfire, 502
Steve Canyon, 727-28
Stony Craig of the Marines, 729-30
Tardi, Jacques, and, 746
Ticonderoga, 286, 580
Trois Mousquetaires du Maquis, Les,
   774
Tueur de Cafards, 746
Two-Fisted Tales, 462
Underground Front, 820
Vic Jordan, 576, 791
Zero Pilot, 520
   See also Armed services strips
Washington Post Writers Group
   (U.S.), 139, 591, 593
Watkins Syndicate (U.S.), 611
Weekend (G.B.) (magazine), 166
Weekend Magazine (Canada), 197
Weekly Features Syndicate, 379
Weekly Forum (Bangladesh), 766
Weekly Mail and Guardian (South
   Africa) (newspaper), 503
Weekly News, The (G.B.), 166, 321
Weekly News (G.B.), 236, 424
Weekly Telegraph (G.B.) (newspaper),
   347
Weird Fantasies (U.S.) (comic book),
   214
Weirdo (U.S.) (underground comic),
   225-26
Wereldkroniek (Netherlands) (weekly),
   767
Weserkurier (Germany) (newspaper),
   651
Western Mail (G.B.) (newspaper), 223
Western Newspaper Syndicate, 499
Western strips
   Akakke ponii, 542
   American Eagle, 690
   Aventures de Franck et Jéremie, 345
   Bat Lash, 400
   Beelzebub Jones, 498
   Bessy, 128
   Big Chief Wahoo, 196, 593, 677, 728
   Black Bull, 462, 690
   Black Hawk, 282
   Blue Jacket, 745
   Boy's Ranch, 705
   Bronc Peeler, 156, 370
   Buffalo Bill (Italy), 161
   Buffalo Bill, 500
   Buffalo Bill (Germany), 161-62
   Bull's Eye Bill, 458

Cal McCord, 391
Capitan Miki, 176-77
Casey Ruggles, 188, 467, 773, 776
Chick Bill, 335
Cisco Kid, The, 203, 672
Cocco Bill, 205, 408
Comanche, 209, 398, 647
Coyote, El, 217
Daiheigenji, 231
Dan Dakota, 239
Daniel Boone, 321, 511
Daring Deeds of Buck Wilson, The,
   346
Davis, Jack, and, 237
Desperate Dan, 243-44
Diablo, The, 423, 435
Eleuteri Serpieri, Paolo, and, 278
En Los Dominios de los Sioux, 361
Feldstein, Al, and, 297
Ghost Rider, 337-38
Gohikino Yōjimnō, 520
Golden Arrow, 458, 609
Go West!, 647
Gringo, 359-60
Guerilleros, Les, 361
Gun Grontier, 520
Harman, Fred, 370
Hopalong Cassidy, 720
Hot Jerry, 570, 813
Infantino, Carmine, and, 400
Jane and Laredo, 411
Jeremiah, 398
Jerry Spring, 339, 415
Jim Boum, 270, 415-16
Jippi der Indianerboy, 730
Johnny Thunder, 435
Jonah Hex, 423-24
Kanigher, Robert, and, 435
Ken Parker, 439-40
King of the Royal Mounted, 370, 446
Kinowa, 446-47
Kit Carson, 449, 543, 603
Lance, 467-68, 776
Larrigan, 239
Latigo, 496
Lazo Kid, 690
Lemon Kid, 754
Lieutenant Blueberry, 345, 476-77
Little Joe, 355, 484
Lone Ranger, The, 307, 378, 490,
   567
Lucky Luke, 352, 492-93
Lynde, Stan, and, 496
McLoughlin, Denis, and, 500-501
Man from the Past, The, 631
Mani in Alto!, 509-10
Manos Kelly, 511
Marcello, Raffaelo Carlo (pseud.
   Marc, Ralph), and, 511
Matho Tonga, 458
Maxon, Rex, and, 524
Newman, Paul S., and, 567
Nyoka, 458
Oklahoma, 203

Old Mickey, 566
Outlaw, The, 435
Outlaw Kid, The, 808
Out Our Way, 592-93, 810
Pecos Bill, 602-3
Pedrito El Drito, 603
Piccolo Ranger, Il, 162
Piccolo Sceriffo, Il, 614
Pistol Jim, 619-20
Poncho Libertas, 624
Povratak Starog Mačak, 522
Randall, 161, 239, 462, 580
Rawhide Kid, 105, 641
Raymondo o Cangaceiro, 641
Ray Ringo, 788
Redeye, 128, 643-44
Red Rider, The, 609
Red Ryder, 370, 645
Reno Kid, 161
Rick O'Shay, 496, 651
Ringo, 239
Ringo Kid, 444
Rock Derby, 647
Rocky Rider, 658
Sargento Kirk, 579-80
Sgt. Kirk, 627
Severin, John Powers, and, 690
Shinigami Shōnen Kim, 696
Slim and Tubby, 411
Specialiste, Le, 339
Stari Mačak, 522
Teddy Sprin, 608
Teddy Ted, 384
Ted Strong, 187
Tex, 575
Texas Slim and Dirty Dalton, 422-23, 753
Tex Willer, 753-54
Tom Mix, 161, 162, 174, 175, 611
Tres Mosqueteros en el Oeste, Los, 239
Tumbleweeds, 667, 776
Ulceda, 549
Uomo di carta, L', 508
Valle del terrore, La, 640
Western Kid, 660
Western Willie the Cowboy Coughdrop, 386
West of Eden, 627
White Cloud, 609
Winnetou, 566, 813
Zorro, 170, 458, 567, 705, 773
Wet Satin #2 (underground comic), 812
Wet (U.S.) (magazine), 478
Wham (G.B.), 118
Wheeler Syndicate, 304-5, 316, 556, 768
Wheeling Register (U.S.) (newspaper), 140
Whitman Publishing (U.S.), 261
Wild Oats (U.S.) (magazine), 586
Wildstorm Productions (U.S.), 472
Wild (U.S.) (fanzine), 496

Wimmen's Comix (U.S.) (underground comic), 654
Windy City Features (U.S.), 708
Wochenend (Germany), 459
Woman's Day (G.B.) (magazine), 574
Woman's Home Companion (U.S.) (magazine), 584
Woman's Illustrated (G.B.), 693
Woman's Realm (G.B.), 236
Women cartoonists
  Becker, Franziska, 120-21
  Brandoli, Anna, 150
  Brandon, Barbara, 806-7
  Bretecher, Claire, 122, 192
  Brigman, June, 152, 154
  Buffolente, Lina, 161, 162, 202, 476, 684
  Carew, Kate, 271
  Connor, Dale, 677
  Corbett, Bertha, 271, 632
  Cory, Fanny Young, 215-16, 348, 632
  Drayton, Grace (pseud. Wiedersheim, Grace), 267-68, 271, 631-32
  Dumm, Frances Edwina, 180, 271-72
  Flinders, Evelyn, 309-10, 704
  Fradon, Ramona, 152, 154, 527
  Fuchs, Erika, 324-25
  Gibbs, Cecilia May, 130, 339
  Giussani, Angela and Luciana, 37, 245
  Guisewite, Cathy, 190, 423
  Hagio, Moto, 366
  Hasegawa, Machiko, 677
  Hollander, Nicole, 391-92
  Jansson, Tove, 412, 546
  Johnston, Lynn B., 312, 423
  King, Fay, 271
  Maki, Miyako, 521, 542
  Messick, Dale, 151-52, 154, 270, 527, 587
  Mills, Tarpe, 190, 537
  Mizuno, Hideko, 542, 755
  O'Neill, Rose Cecil, 441-42, 584, 632
  Ormes, Jackie, 587
  Orr, Martha, 518, 677
  Oshima, Yumiko, 366, 588
  Pini, Wendy, 289-90, 812
  Randall, Albertine, 271
  Robbins, Trina, 653-54, 787, 812
  Rogers, Barksdale, 271
  Rubichek, Dorothy, 820
  Satonaka, Machiko, 676
  Schmich, Maria, 152, 154
  Severin, Marie, 260, 397, 690, 732
  Shen Pei (Peijin), 694-95
  Simmonds, Posy, 704
  Takahashi, Rumiko, 41, 506
  Takemiya, Keiko, 366
  Tourtel, Mary, 22, 665-66
  Wang Shuhui, 797

Watanabe, Masako, 542
Wilshire, Mary, 646, 811-12
Yamagishi, Ryōko, 366
Women's World (Philippines) (magazine), 505
World, The (Australia) (newspaper), 364
World and His Wife, The (G.B.) (magazine), 761
World Color Printing Company (U.S.), 348, 381, 533, 709
World Color Syndicate (U.S.), 275
World's Press Publishing Company, 506
World War II, 27-28
  Adolf, 78-79
  Adolf, Hermann and Musso, 666
  Airboy, 81
  Barney Baxter, 113-14, 563
  Bête Est Morte, La, 175
  Blackhawk, 136
  Black Terror, 137
  Boy Commandos, 149
  Buck Danny, 159, 396
  Buz Sawyer, 169-70
  Captain America, 180
  Don Winslow of the Navy, 263-64
  Gasoline Alley, 336
  Green Hornet, 357
  Hubert, 395-96
  Kuznjecov, Konstantin, and, 465
  Little Joe and, 484
  Little Mary Mixup, 155
  Male Call, 507
  Maus, 522-23, 719
  Miss Fury, 537
  Pinky Rankin, 617-18
  Schmit der Sphy, 666
  Star Spangled Kid, 725
  Sturmtruppen, 731
  Terry and the Pirates and, 752
  Tim Tyler's Luck, 763-64
  Trois Mousquetaires du Maquis, Les, 774
  Up Front, 782
  Vic Jordan, 576, 791
  Yugoslavian comics during, 473
Wow, What a Magazine (U.S.), 278
Wow Comics (U.S.), 400
Writer's Forum (U.S.) (magazine), 354
Writers of comics
  Barbieri, Renzo, 111
  Binder, Otto O. (pseud. Binder, Eando), 133-34
  Biro, Charles, and, 134
  Bonelli, Giovanni Luigi, 143
  Calkins, Richard, 173
  Caplin, Elliot, 179
  Charlier, Jean-Michel, 196
  Chendi, Carlo, 198
  Crowley, Wendell, 223
  Dickenson, Fred, 246
  Dumas, Jacques (pseud. François, Jacques; Marijac), and, 270-71

Falk, Lee, 290-91
Finger, Bill, 303
Fox, Gardner, 316
Fuchs, Erika, 324-25
Gomez, Pablo S., 350
Goodwin, Archie (pseud. Franklin Robert), 351
Goscinny, René, 352
Guardineer, Frederic, 360-61
Herron, France Edward, 381
Hess, Sol, 382-83
Kanigher, Robert, 435
Kauka, Rolf, 437-38
Lee, Stan, 472
McEvoy, Joseph Patrick, 500
Nowlan, Philip, 577
O'Neil, Dennis (pseud. O'Shaugnessey, Sergius), 583
Pedrocchi, Federico, 603
Raab, Fritz, 637
Régnier, Michel (pseud. Greg, Albert, Louis), 647
Ritt, William, 653
Secchi, Luciano (pseud. Bunker, Max), 685
Severin, John Powers, 690
Simon, Joseph, 704-5
Thomas, Roy, 756
Töpffer, Rodolphe, 770
Weisinger, Mort, and, 804
Winterbotham, Russell (pseud. Bond, J. Harvey), 814
Woolfolk, William, 818-20

X

Xiao Peng You (China), 674
Xin Lei Publishing House (China), 269
Xinmin Evening News (China) (newspaper), 827

Y

Yale Daily News (U.S.) (newspaper), 775
Yamiuri-Shōnen Shinbun (Japan), 718
Yank (U.S.) (magazine), 107, 150-51, 539, 669, 782
Yarmak Comics (Australia), 621
Yarrowstalks (U.S.) (underground comic), 224, 540
Yellow Dog (U.S.) (underground comic), 226, 359, 653
Yomiuri Sunday Manga (Japan), 718
Yōnen Book (Japan), 143
Yōnen Kurabu (Japan) (magazine), 745
Yorkshire Evening News (G.B.) (newspaper), 609
Yorkshire Telegraph (G.B.) (newspaper), 347
Young adult strips
  Dropouts, The, 269
  Fire!, 542
  Fūten, 328-29
  Mixed Singles, 189
  See also Teen strips
Young Children Pictorial (China) (magazine), 605
Young Lust (U.S.) (underground comic), 719, 812
Young Magazine (Japan), 588-89
Young's Merchandising (Australia), 621
Youngston Telegram (U.S.) (newspaper), 238
Youthful Comics (U.S.), 587
Yow (U.S.) (underground comic), 359
Yuk Long (Jademan) (Hong Kong comics company), 817-18
Yurei Ikka (Japan) (comic book), 366

Z

Zack (Germany) (magazine), 178, 191, 382, 432, 437, 682
Zap (U.S.) (comic book), 224, 540
Ziff-Davis
  Anderson, Murphy, and, 92
  Berg, David, and, 126
  Carreño, Albert, and, 187
  Celardo, John (pseud. Lardo, John C.), and, 192
  Colan, Eugene (pseud. Austin, Adam), and, 206
  Leav, Mort, and, 471
  Orlando, Joe, and, 587
  Prentice, John, and, 627
  Siegel, Jerome, and, 701
  Wood, Wallace, 818
Zona 84 (Argentina) (magazine), 341
ZonaX (Italy) (magazine), 516
Zonneland (Netherlands) (magazine), 157
Zoom Komiks (Philippines), 418
Zorro (France) (magazine), 829